Shamanism,

Colonialism, and

the Wild Man

Shamanism,
A Study in
Colonialism, and
Terror and
the Wild Man
Healing

Michael Taussig

The University of Chicago Press   **Chicago and London**

MICHAEL TAUSSIG is professor of anthropology at
the University of Michigan, Ann Arbor. He is the
author of several books, including *The Devil and
Commodity Fetishism in South America.*

THE UNIVERSITY OF CHICAGO PRESS, CHICAGO 60637
THE UNIVERSITY OF CHICAGO PRESS, LTD., LONDON

94 93 92 91 90 89 88 87   54321

Maps by Tom Greensfelder

LIBRARY OF CONGRESS CATALOGING-IN-PUBLICATION DATA

Taussig, Michael T.
    Shamanism, colonialism, and the wild man.

    Bibliography: p.
    Includes index.
    1, Indians of South America—Colombia—Putumayo
(Indendency)—Medicine.   2. Shamanism—Colombia—
Putumayo (Indendency)   3. Colombia—Colonial
influence.   4. Rubber industry and trade—Colombia—
History.   5. Putumayo (Colombia : Indendency)—Social
conditions.   I. Title
F2269.1.P87T38   1986   986.1'6300498   86-11410
ISBN 0–226–79012–6

For Tico

CONTENTS

vii

    Topography of the Andes and Its
    Conquest   287
19 Even the Dogs Were Crying   336
20 The Old Soldier Remembers   337
21 Toughness and Tenderness in the Wild
    Man's Lair: The Everyday as
    Impenetrable, the Impenetrable as
    Everyday   342
22 Casemiro and the Tiger   358
23 Priests and Shamans   364
24 History as Sorcery   366
25 Envy and Implicit Social Knowledge   393
26 The Whirlpool   413
27 Montage   435
28 To Become a Healer   447
29 Marlene   468

    Notes   475
    Bibliography   495
    Index   503

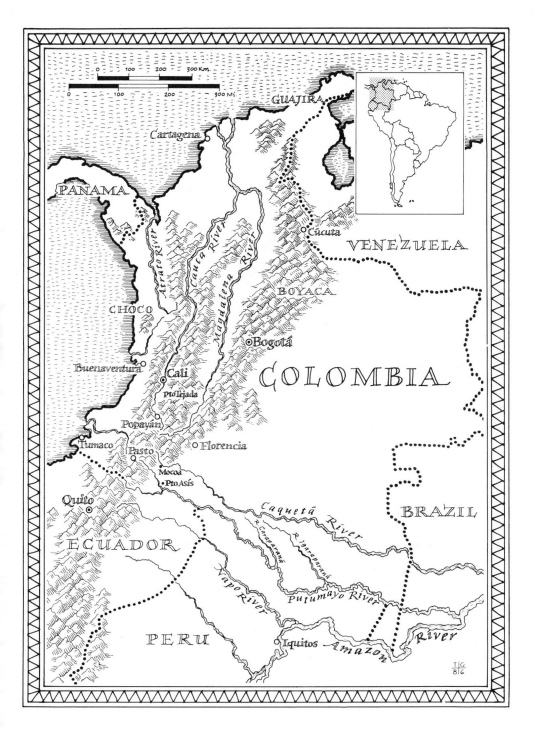

Colombia

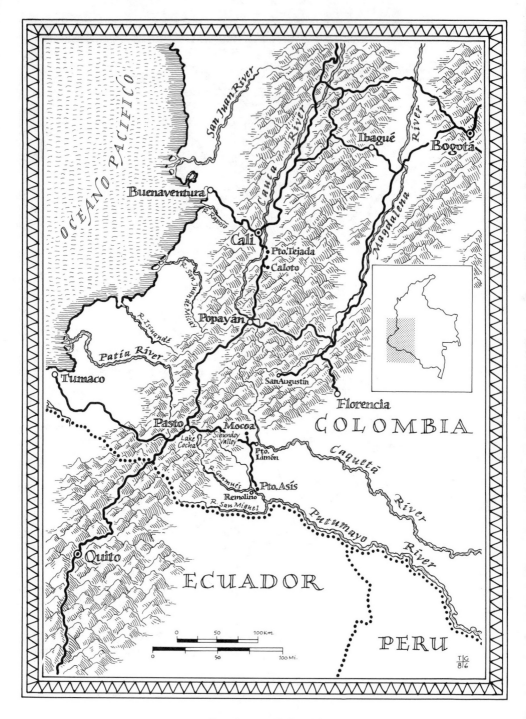

Southwest Colombia

Rubber Stations of the Putumayo

AUTHOR'S NOTE

This book of two parts, terror and healing, takes little for granted and leaves even less in its place. It derives from the almost five years I spent in the southwest of Colombia, South America, from 1969 to 1985, in periods varying from one month to two years. During those times my hand was tried at several things: history, anthropology, medicine, mythology, magic, to name but the nameable and leave the remainder where the subject matter of this book communicates itself—in the politics of epistemic murk and the fiction of the real, in the creation of Indians, in the role of myth and magic in colonial violence as much as in its healing, and in the way that healing can mobilize terror in order to subvert it, not through heavenly catharses but through the tripping up of power in its own disorderliness.

Killing and torture and sorcery are real as death is real. But why people do these things, and how the answers to that question affect the question—that is not answerable outside of the effects of the real carried through time by people in action. That is why my subject is not the truth of being but the social being of truth, not whether facts are real but what the politics of their interpretation and representation are. With

Walter Benjamin my aim is to release what he noted as the enormous energy of history that lies bonded in the "once upon a time" of classical historical narrative. The history that showed things "as they really were," he pointed out, was the strongest narcotic of our century.[1] And of course it still is.

To release this energy requires special modes of presentation whose aim is to disrupt the imagery of natural order through which, in the name of the real, power exercises its dominion. As against the magic of academic rituals of explanation which, with their alchemical promise of yielding system from chaos, do nothing to ruffle the placid surface of this natural order, I choose to work with a different conflation of modernism and the primitivism it conjures into life—namely the carrying over into history of the principle of montage, as I learned that principle not only from terror, but from Putumayo shamanism with its adroit, albeit unconscious, use of the magic of history and its healing power.

It should be noted that the names of a few people have been changed in order to preserve their anonymity, and that unless otherwise stated the speech recorded in this book was in Spanish.

ACKNOWLEDGMENTS

For this brief moment the onrushing tide of the text recedes to reveal, in its gathering eddies, the traces, otherwise barely discernible, of the people upon whom so much of this book depends: my comrades of the Sydney Push in the '60s, sustaining a climate, indeed a world, of oppositional practice (among whom I must single out Johnny Earls, who went to spend his life in the highlands of Peru and serendipitously studied with that great storyteller Jośe María Arguedas); Clare Hutchison and Chandra Jayawardena who made me curious about anthropology; Frank Atkins, one of the head nurses at Villa 21 of Shenley Mental Hospital in Hertsfordshire, England, with whom I worked in 1967 and who showed me, through his genius for such things, how psychiatry could be quite different, as soberly radical and responsible as it was fantastically shamanic, for which he paid a price; my comrades-in-arms at the London School of Economics, 1967–68, for initiating new directions of struggle, especially Lawrence Harris, Rod Burgess (who later came to Colombia, too), and Harry Pincus (now dead); Suzette Macedo for introducing me to the world of Spanish speech; Pam Cobb (now dead), for Spanish too; anti-imperialist activists in and around London in the late '60s, Robin Gollan, Lynne Roberts (now dead), John Roberts, Ian Parker (now dead), Daphne Skillen, Tony Skillen (through whose inordinately inquisitive imagination I have learned to appreciate what philosophy's task can be), Simon Watson-Taylor (whose translation of Aragon's *Le Paysan de Paris* I only recently discovered, excited about Benjamin'a excitement with that book), and Andrew Pearse, that lovable and somewhat mischievous man (now dead) who was in part responsible for my opting to go to work in Colombia (with romantic notions of lending my medical self to the guerrilla struggle), beginning in 1969; that painstaking student of Colombian rural economy, Sutti Ortiz, and that *gran historiador* of nineteenth-century Colombia, Malcolm Deas, for their good advice when I was starting out; Brian Moser (and his many films), Oscar Marulanda, and Humberto Rojas, for the same thing; María Cristina Salazar, cruelly victimized by the army, and Orlando Fals Borda, also for getting me going in Colombia and initiating the publication of my first book there, under the Puerto Tejada pseudonym of Mateo Mina (Mina being a common name given to or taken by African slaves who worked the placer mines in the southern Cauca Valley, and still a very common name, of the bandit Cenecio Mina, for instance); Eva Aldor, and Peter Aldor (now dead), of Bogotá, for an infinitude of kindness; Marlene Jiménez and Guillermo Llanos (both dead) of the little sugarcane town of Puerto Tejada in western Colombia for taking me in so generously and therewith initiating my absorption into the kindness as well as the violence of Cauca; their children, especially Dalila and Marcia, who will live in unison despite the violence that consumed their parents; those tireless radical laboring men, Luis Carlos Mina, and Alfredo Cortés (now dead), of Puerto Tejada and Santander de Quilichao, who incorporated me into the peasant syndicate of those heady days of the early '70s; those equally tireless but very old people, María Cruz Zappe, Tomás Zapata, Eusebio Cambindo, and Felipe Carbonero (all dead now), who in the slums of Puerto Tejada and in the adobe huts squeezed between the fields of the plantations, with wit and elegance and sometimes in epic verse, brought back the dead with their recollections of the slavery of their *antepasados* and the epoch of the *comuneros* and free peasants thereafter; a younger generation of peasant farmers and landless laborers, Aleida Uzuriaga, Robier Uzuriaga, and José Domingo Murillo, for their assistance with sociohistorical fieldwork and for the inspiration and wit which made of such work a theater of experience and not simply an instrument; Olivia Mostacilla and Regina Carabali, also of Puerto, for their high-spirited instruction and constant care; Orfir Hurtado and other budding anthropologists and historians who have recently sprung into existence in Puerto, working in ways unforeseen by their history on the traditions into which they were born; Diego Castrillón de Arboleda for his knowledgeable assistance in the Archivo Central del Cauca, that massive collection of colonial and nineteenth-century documents through which the views and strategies of the ruling elites would speak to me in the cool and quiet whiteness of Popayán's colonial buildings and streets, so amazingly different from the dusty heat and music, let alone oral histories, coming from the lower lands of the descendants of the slaves to the north in Puerto Tejada; Anna Rubbo, for joining in the work of those years of the '70s and making it worthwhile; Socorro Santacruz, Jacobo Naidorf, María Emilia Echeverri, Joe Broderick, María Teresa Salcedo, and Manuel Hernández, all of Bogotá, for their upbeat discussion and commentary, predicated on their inability to think in terms of academic conventions or without the wave's crest where imagining and wit boil; Augusto Corredor of the Colombian National Institute of Health who set me straight on the political economy of intestinal parasites, not to mention hammocks and Frantz Fanon; Father Gabriel Izquierdo, S. J. (and his colleagues at CINEP, Bogotá), for his unbridled curiosity concerning the anthropology of religion, insofar as it makes for a heaven on *this* earth, now; Bruno Mazzoldi for the genius of irregularity; Roberto Pineda Camacho and William Torres, anthropologists, in Bogotá, for telling me in detail about their recent experiences in hermeneutics with "Huitoto" Andoke people of what was once the northern frontier of Julio César Arana's rubber-forest kingdom; Teresa and Pedro Cortés for their bravery in the constant struggle over land and culture in the *cordillera central;* Larissa Lomnitz, anthropologist of Mexico City, for responding so aptly to my fabulations about the Putumayo, for she, too, had her life story to tell about wandering healers and herbalists from what Alfred Simson, in 1875, called "the mysterious province of the *oriente,*" in this case the valley of the Sibundoy; Victor Daniel Bonilla for his book *Servants of God, or Owners of Indians?,* drawing attention to the domination of that valley's Indian inhabitants by the Capuchin mission from the beginning of this century; Jean Langdon and Scott Robinson who as anthropologists lived in the lowlands and *montaña* of the Putumayo in the early '70s and were the first to tell me what it was like there, on the *other* side of the *cordillera;* Norman Whitten, whose books, extraordinary in detail and tone, concerned with society and thought on both sides of the northern Andes, have been for me a constant yardstick; Frank Salomon, for the reach of his writing and his raising the *yumbos;* Gratulina Moreno, and Salvador Moreno (now dead), of that tributary of the Putumayo called the Guaymuez, for taking me in, healing, and swapping stories about healing (which was of no small consequence, Salvador being widely considered the most powerful *curaca* of the region); Santiago and Ambrosia Mutumbajoy of the Mocoa river for doing the same and thereby making the mosaic of events, reminiscences, layers of meanings, and digressions on which this book largely rests (*"Its method is essentially representation. Method as a digression. Representation as digression. . . . The absence of an uninterrupted purposeful structure is its primary characteristic. Tirelessly the process of thinking makes new beginnings, returning in a roundabout way to its original object. This continual pausing for breath is the mode most proper to the process of contemplation. . . . Just as mosiacs preserve their majesty despite their fragmentation into capricious particles, so philosphical contemplation is not lacking in momentum. Both are made up of the distinct and the disparate; and nothing could bear more powerful testimony to the transcendent force of the sacred image and the truth itself. The value of the fragments of thought is all the greater the less direct their relationship to the underlying idea, and the brilliance of the representation depends as much on this value as the brilliance of the mosaic does on the quality of the glass paste.* [Benjamin, *The Orgin of German Tragic Drama*]); Silvia Natalia Rivera of La Paz, Bolivia (when not exiled) for understanding what this book was going to be about and thereby giving me the confidence to take it still further; Guillermo O'Donnell for getting me to focus down on my thoughts, let alone fear, about what he and his group called (after experiencing the rule of the military in Argentina after 1976) "the culture of fear"; Michael Geyer for discussing some of that too, but as it occurred in recent German history; Anna Davin, for sharing William Blake's type of empiricism and always seeing more than meets the eye, for the inspiration of the history workshop, and the singing too; the Marxist Literary Group (USA) for listening to and commenting upon some of the following chapters, especially John Beverly who helped me with countless points of criticism, Marxism, and things Latin American, Fred Jameson, who brought us all together and recast the possibilities for a social critique, and Susan Willis who more than anyone I know fulfills the Benjaminian aesthetico-political aspiration to not only dereify but to reenchant as well; Jean Franco for her book on Spanish-American literature (which I read in a canoe descending the Caquetá) and her opening my horizon not merely to the interweaving of fact and fiction but to politics and fiction; Juan Flores for encouraging me to develop my ideas about Brecht and (Latin American) magical realism as they together informed my understanding of the politics of disorder in neocolonial healing rites; Ross Chambers for help in thinking through the postmodern issue of the ways by which history and anthropology are kinds of writing; Joe Jorgensen and Eric Wolf for getting me started at Michigan; Marshall Sahlins for always asking the unsettling question; Barney Cohn, whose sense of the importance of the effects of the real has been absolutely crucial to my work here; Jim Clifford, because he has made it easier for all of us to draw upon the legacy of a critical modernism, and not simply expose ethnographic authoritarianism but to know what to do with such exposure; Tres Pyle for his Texan thesis on Walter Benjamin; Jeremy Beckett in Sydney for his constant interest and commentary, let alone comparisons with the colonial culture of the Torres Straits and mainland Australia; Martin Walsh for discussions about Brechtian tragedy, not to mention his direction of many Brecht epics; Bob McKinley for his wit and anthropological wisdom, particularly his observation regarding animism and Adam Smith's invisible hand; Janice Seidler for her translations from Konrad Preuss's German text on Huitoto religion; Charles Leslie for his being such a sane and steady voice in the vexed field of medical anthropologizing, his kindness, and the political convictions upon which such kindness rests; my fellow teachers at the University of Michigan, especially Christopher (Roberts) Davis for her sense of fantasy and refusal to compromise on what should be the social effects of our work; Elissa Miller, for keeping me informed about events in Guatemala, El Salvador, and death squads; Stanley Diamond for being so irascibly himself and refusing the great North American temptation to conventionalize the works of Marx in economism; Donovan Clarke in his Blue Mountains for the constant feedback and the irreverent finesse of his passion; Pat Aufderheide of *In These Times* for showing us what, in these lonely times, cultural critique can aspire to as a daily practice; and finally—Tico Taussig-Rubbo for his company to all the places mentioned and therewith making the necessary connection between the child's eye for symbol and the adult's eye for history; and Rachel Moore who so persistently provided the flash of insight for which this text is merely the thunder rolling long afterward.

For their advice and stimulus regarding illustrations I wish to give heartfelt thanks to Hugh Honour (not least on account of his book, *The New Golden Land: European Images of America from the Discoveries to the Present Time* [New York: Pantheon, 1975]), and to Charles Merewether. Acknowledgments are also due to Farrar, Strauss, and Giroux for the photograph of Roger Casement in the Congo, which appears in Frederick Karl's *Joseph Conrad: The Three Lives;* to the National Library of Ireland for the portrait of Casement in his thirties; to the Museu de Grao Vasco, Viseu, Portugal, for the copy of *The Adoration of the Magi* by the Master of Viseu; to the Museu de Arte Antiga, Lisbon, for a copy of the *Inferno,* by an anonymous artist; to the Metropolitan Museum of Art, New York City, for pictures of Alexander the Great and Wild Men that appear in the book *The Wild Man* by T. Husband and G. Gilmore-House; to the Cambridge University Museum of Archaeology and Anthropology for two photographs from their Whiffen collection; to Condé Nast of New York for the advertisement for *Gourmet Magazine* displaying an Indian woman in Quito; to Robert Isaacson of New York for permission to use a copy of de Waldeck's painting, hung in the Salon of 1870, *Being Carried Over the Chiapas;* and to Charles Merewether for the photograph captioned "The Sibundoy Indian Curing the Whiteman." Unless otherwise noted in captions, all other photographs are by the author.

PART ONE
Terror

ONE

Culture of Terror,
Space of Death

**Roger Casement's Putumayo Report and
the Explanation of Torture**

Most of us know and fear torture and the culture of terror only through the words of others. Hence my concern is with the mediation
of terror through narration, and with the
problem of writing effectively against terror.

Jacobo Timerman ends his recent book,
*Prisoner without a Name, Cell without a
Number*, with the imprint of the gaze of hope
in the space of death.

> Have any of you looked into the
> eyes of another person, on the floor
> of a cell, who knows that he's about
> to die though no one has told him
> so? He knows that he's about to die
> but clings to his biological desire to
> live, as a single hope, since no one
> has told him he's to be executed.
> I have many such gazes imprinted
> upon me . . .
> Those gazes which I encountered
> in the clandestine prisons of Argen-
> tina and which I've retained one by
> one, were the culminating point, the
> purest moment of my tragedy.
> They are here with me today. And
> although I might wish to do so, I
> could not and would not know how
> to share them with you.[1]

3

Ineffability is a striking feature of this death-space. In his not knowing how to share those gazes that pierce it, Timerman for an instant creates the illusion that we who follow him can be pierced by the emptiness of the hope that makes it real.

And how those gazes must have pierced the murk of death's coming! How they must have lit up its hollowness! For Timerman's burden was double. He was not just a victim: he was victim of what he had himself prescribed—military dictatorship as the solution to the disorder afflicting the nation.

And the result? A society shrouded in an order so orderly that its chaos was far more intense than anything that had preceded it—a death-space in the land of the living where torture's certain uncertainty fed the great machinery of the arbitrariness of power, power on the rampage—that great steaming morass of chaos that lies on the underside of order and without which order could not exist.

There is an old story in the Chilean countryside, Ariel Dorfman tells us, about what happens when a child is abducted by witches. In order to break the child's will, the witches break the child's bones and sew the body parts together in an abnormal way. The head is turned around so the child has to walk backwards, and the ears, eyes, and mouth are stitched up. This creature is called the *Imbunche*, and Dorfman feels that the military junta under Pinochet has done and continues to do everything in its power to make every Chilean and Chile itself into an *Imbunche*.

Writing in 1985, he insists that even if their bones are not actually broken or mouths sewn up, the Chileans are, "in a way, already like Imbunches. They are isolated from each other, their means of communicating suppressed, their connections cut off, their senses blocked by fear."

The control enforced by the dictatorship, he points out, "is as arbitrary as it tends to be at times absurd." A child's dictionary was removed from the newsstands because the censors did not agree with its definition of the word "soldier." Officialdom strives to create a magical reality. When 5,000 slum dwellers were rounded up and held in a stadium, a high official denied that the event had even happened. "What stadium? What slum-dwellers?"

What is endangered, concludes Dorfman, is the existence of the society's moral foundations. He has found many people, like the *Imbunche*, floating apart into fragments.[2]

The space of death is important in the creation of meaning and consciousness, nowhere more so than in societies where torture is endemic and where the culture of terror flourishes. We may think of the space of death as a threshold that allows for illumination as well as extinction. Sometimes a person goes through it and returns to us, to tell the tale, as did Timerman, who fell victim to the military force he at first supported and then criticized through his newspaper, *La Opinion*, fighting with words in and against the silence imposed by the arbiters of discourse who beat out a new reality in the cells where torturer and tortured came together. And on his return from there, he found: "We victims and victimizers, we're part of the same humanity, colleagues in the same endeavor to prove the existence of ideologies, feelings, heroic deeds, religions, obsessions. And the rest of humanity, the great majority, what are they engaged in?"[3]

The creation of colonial reality that occurred in the New World will remain a subject of immense curiosity and study—the New World where the Indian and African *irracionales* became compliant to the reason of a small number of white Christians. Whatever the conclusions we draw about how that hegemony was so speedily effected, we would be unwise to overlook the role of terror. And by this I mean us to think-through-terror, which as well as being a physiological state is also a social one whose special features allow it to serve as the mediator *par excellence* of colonial hegemony: the space of death where the Indian, African, and white gave birth to a New World.

Did the grim reaper ever take in a harvest larger than that caused by the Spanish conquest of the New World? And then the enormity of death of African slaves during the middle passage and on the plantations.

This space of death has a long and rich culture. It is where the social imagination has populated its metamorphizing images of evil and the underworld: in the Western tradition Homer, Virgil, the Bible, Dante, Hieronymus Bosch, the Inquisition, Rimbaud, Conrad's heart of darkness; in northwest Amazonian tradition, zones of visions, communication between terrestrial and supernatural beings, putrefaction, death, rebirth, and genesis, perhaps in the rivers and land of maternal milk bathed eternally in the subtle green light of coca leaves.[4] With European conquest and colonization, these spaces of death blend into a common pool of key signifiers binding the transforming culture of the conquerer with that of the conquered. But the signifiers are strategically out of joint with what they signify. "If confusion is the sign of the times," wrote Artaud, "I see at the root of this confusion a rupture between things and words, between things and the ideas and signs that are their representation." He wonders if it is that cleavage which is responsible for the revenge of *things*; "the poetry which is no longer within us and which we no longer succeed in finding in things suddenly appears on their wrong side."[5] Marx pointed to the same disarrangement and rearrangement between us and things in the fetishism of commodities, wherein poetry suddenly appeared on the wrong side of things now animated. In modern history the fetishism of commodities rejuvenates the mythic density of the space of death—with the death of the subject as much as with the new-found arbitrariness of the sign whereby a resurgent animism makes things human and humans things. It is in the terror of the space of death that we often find an elaborated exploration of what Artaud and Marx, in their different ways, see as the rupture and revenge of signification.

In Miguel Angel Asturias's depiction of the culture of terror of the Estrada Cabrera dictatorship in early twentieth-century Guatemala, it is unbearable to read how, as people become like things, their dreaming power passes into things that become not only like people but their persecutors. Things become agents of terror, conspiring with the president's need to sense the innermost thoughts of his subjects, who, once sensed, become not just objects but disjointed parts of objects. It is in the dictator's sensing of people's inner worlds that terror makes nature its ally; hence the forest surrounding the president's palace,

> a wood made up of trees with ears which responded to the slightest sound by whirling as if blown by a hurricane. Not the tiniest noise for miles around could avoid the avidity of those millions of membranes. The dogs went on barking. A network of invisible threads, more invisible than telegraph wires, connected every leaf with the President, enabling him to keep watch on the most secret thoughts of the townspeople.[6]

It is in the world of the beggars that the culture of terror finds perfection. They are misfits, cripples, blind, idiots, dwarves, twisted, and deformed. They can neither talk nor walk nor see straight, and they exist in two critically important zones: huddled on the steps of the cathedral in the main square opposite the presidential palace, or, like the idiot, splayed out on top of the city's garbage heap. Here indeed is the figure embodying the society as a whole: on account of his idiocy he has struck at a high-ranking army officer, and therefore at the president himself. Now the idiot is running away, half in a dream world like a man trying to escape from a prison of mist. He is exhausted, slobbering, panting and laughing. He is pursued by dogs and by fine spears of rain. Eventually he collapses—onto the garbage heap with its broken glass, sardine cans, brims of straw hats, bits of paper, leather, rags, broken china, pulped books, collars, eggshells, excrement, and nameless patches of darkness. The buzzards with their sharp beaks come closer and it is in the hop, hop, hopping of these ungainly birds of prey that feed upon offal that the dictator's *modus operandi* is expressed. They lunge for the soft flesh of the idiot's lips, here on the debris of the garbage heap where the city's strewn signs lay bare in their disjointedness the political function of their arbitrariness.

> Above the dunghill was a spiders-web of dead trees, covered with turkey-buzzards; when they saw the Zany lying there motionless the black birds of prey fixed him with their bluish eyes and settled on the ground beside him, hopping all around him— a hop this way, a hop that way—in a macabre dance. Ceaselessly looking about them, making ready for flight at the slightest movement of a leaf or the wind in the rubbish—a hop this way, a hop that way—they closed in upon him in a circle until he was within reach of their beaks. A savage croaking gave the

signal for the attack. The Zany got to his feet as he woke, prepared to defend himself. One of the boldest birds had fastened
its beak in his upper lip piercing it right through to the teeth
like a dart, while the other carnivores disputed as to which
should have his eyes and his heart.[7]

And the idiot Zany "escapes" by falling backwards deeper into the garbage.

Yet this space of death is preeminently a space of transformation: through
the experience of coming close to death there well may be a more vivid
sense of life; through fear there can come not only a growth in self-consciousness but also fragmentation, then loss of self conforming to authority;
or, as in the great journey of the *Divine Comedy* with its smoothly cadenced
harmonies and catharsis, through evil, good. Lost in the dark woods, then
journeying through the underworld with his pagan guide, Dante achieves
paradise, but only after he has reached the lowermost point of evil, mounting
the shaggy back of the wild man. Timerman can be a guide for us, analagous
to the ways Putumayo shamans I know are guides to those lost in the space
of death.

It was an old Ingano Indian from the Putumayo hot lands in the southwest
of Colombia who first told me of this space, in 1980:

> With the fever I was aware of everything. But after eight days I
> became unconscious. I knew not where I was. Like a madman
> I wandered, consumed with fever. They had to cover me up
> where I fell, mouth down. Thus after eight days I was aware of
> nothing. I was unconscious. Of what people were saying, I re-
> membered nothing. Of the pain of the fever, I remembered
> nothing; only the space of death—walking in the space of
> death. Thus, after the noises that spoke, I remained uncon-
> scious. Now the world remained behind. Now the world was
> removed. Well, then I understood. Now the pains were speak-
> ing. I knew that I would live no longer. Now I was dead. My
> sight had gone. Of the world I knew nothing, nor the sound of
> my ears. Of speech, nothing. Silence. And one knows the
> space of death, there . . . And this is death—the space that I
> saw. I was in its center, standing. Then I went to the heights.
> From the heights a starpoint seemed my due. I was standing.
> Then I came down. There I was searching for the five conti-
> nents of the world, to remain, to find me a place in the five
> continents of the world—in the space in which I was wander-
> ing. But I was not able.

But I was not able. Inconclusive. No cadenced harmonies. No cathartic
resolution here. Struggle and pieces of possible wholes. No more. We might
ask: In what place in the five continents of the world will the wanderer in
the space of death find himself? And, by extension, Where will a whole

society find itself? The old man fears sorcery, the stuggle for his soul. Between himself, the sorcerer, and the curing shaman, the five continents are sought and fought for. Yet here there is laughter too, puncturing the fear swelling the mystery, reminding us of Walter Benjamin's comment on the way in which romanticism may perniciously misunderstand the nature of intoxication. "Any serious exploration of occult, surrealistic, phantasmagoric gifts and phenomena," he wrote,

> presupposes a dialectical intertwinement to which a romantic
> turn of mind is impervious. For histrionic or fanatical stress on
> the mysterious side of the mysterious takes us no further; we
> penetrate the mystery only to the degree that we recognize it in
> the everyday world, by virtue of a dialectical optic that per-
> ceives the everyday as impenetrable, the impenetrable as
> everyday.[8]

In Timerman's chronicle and Miguel Angel Asturias's *El señor presidente* it is clear that cultures of terror are nourished by the intermingling of silence and myth in which the fanatical stress on the mysterious side of the mysterious flourishes by means of rumor woven finely into webs of magical realism. It is also clear that the victimizer needs the victim to create truth, objectifying fantasy in the discourse of the other. To be sure, the torturer's desire is prosaic: to acquire information, to act in concert with large-scale economic strategies elaborated by the masters of finance and exigencies of production. Yet there is also the need to control massive populations, entire social classes, and even nations through the cultural elaboration of fear.

That is why silence is imposed and why Timerman, with his newspaper, was important; why he knew when to publish and when to keep quiet in the torture chamber. "Such silence," he writes,

> begins in the channels of communication. Certain political lead-
> ers, institutions, and priests attempt to denounce what is hap-
> pening, but are unable to establish contact with the population.
> The silence begins with a strong odor. People sniff the suicides,
> but it eludes them. Then silence finds another ally: solitude.
> People fear suicides as they fear madmen. And the person who
> wants to fight senses his solitude and is frightened.[9]

Hence the need for us to fight that solitude, fear, and silence, to examine these conditions of truth-making and culture-making, to follow Michel Foucault in "seeing historically how effects of truth are produced within discourses which are in themselves neither true nor false."[10]

But surely at the same time, through "seeing historically," we strive to *see anew*—through the act of creating counter-discourse?

If effects of truth are power, then the question is raised not only concerning the power granted or denied by organizations to speak and write (anything), but also as to what form that counter-discourse should take. This issue of the politics of form has been lately of concern to some of us involved in writing and interpreting histories and ethnographies. Today, faced with the ubiquity of torture, terror, and the growth of armies, we in the New World are assailed with new urgency. There is the effort to understand terror, in order to make *others* understand. Yet the reality at stake here makes a mockery of understanding and derides rationality, as when the young boy Jacobo Timerman asked his mother, "Why do they hate us?" and she replied: "Because they do not understand." And after his ordeal, the old Timerman writes of the need for a hated object and the simultaneous fear of that object—the almost magical inevitability of hatred.

Hated and feared, objects to be despised yet also of awe with evil understood as the physical essence of their bodies, these are just as clearly objects of cultural creation, the leaden keel of evil and mystery stabilizing the ship and course that is Western history. With the cold war we add the communist. With the time bomb ticking inside the nuclear family, we add the feminists and the gays. The military and the New Right, like the conquerors of old, discover the evil they have imputed to these aliens, and mimic the savagery they have imputed.

What sort of understanding—what sort of speech, writing, and construction of meaning by any mode—can deal with and subvert that?

To counterpose the eros and catharses of violence with similarly mystical means is worse than counterproductive. Yet to offer the standardized rational explanations of torture in general or in this or that specific situation is equally pointless. For behind the conscious self-interest that motivates terror and torture, from the heavenly spheres of corporate search for profits and the need to control labor to the more strictly personal equations of self-interest, lie intricately construed, long-standing, unconscious cultural formations of meaning—modes of feeling—whose social network of tacit conventions and imagery lies in a symbolic world and not in that feeble "pre-Kantian" fiction of the world represented by rationalism or utilitarian rationalism. Perhaps there is here no explanation, no words forthcoming, and of that we have been uncomfortably aware. Understanding here moves too fast or too slow, absorbing itself in the facticity of the crudest of facts such as the electrodes and the mutilated body, or in the maddening maze of that least factitious of facts, the experience of going through torture.

Timerman's text provides a powerful counter-discourse because, like torture itself, it moves us through that space of death where reality is up for grabs. And here we but begin to see the magnitude of the task, which calls neither for demystification nor remystification but for a quite different poetics of destruction and revelation. In Timerman's case, the case of the prisoner without a name, the hallucinations of the military are confronted by the prisoner awkwardly patchworking the contradictions created in the dreams of socialism and Zionism yoked to the secular antiauthoritarianism of anarchism. The aspiration here was couched by another prisoner of fascism,

Antonio Gramsci, with his motto directed equally at the culture of capitalism as against the petrified dogmas of historical materialism: *optimism of the will, pessimism of the intellect.*

Through the text comes the figure of its producer and the producer can only figure in a preorganized gallery of positions taken and embodied long before with respect to the politics of representation. In his persistently critical yet optimistic position, the prisoner without a name stands in dramatic contradistinction to that other recent and much-hailed voice from the third world of V. S. Naipaul and the deeply pessimistic counterrevolutionary genealogy he extends from the Koestler of *Darkness at Noon* and *The God that Failed*, unraveling the ambiguous shroud of the master, Joseph Conrad.

Conrad's way of dealing with the terror of the rubber boom in the Congo was *Heart of Darkness*. There were three realities there, comments Frederick Karl: King Leopold's, made out of intricate disguises and deceptions, Roger Casement's studied realism, and Conrad's, which, to quote Karl, "fell midway between the other two, as he attempted to penetrate the veil and yet was anxious to retain its hallucinatory quality."[11]

The formulation is sharp and important: *to penetrate the veil while retaining its hallucinatory quality*. It evokes and combines a twofold movement of interpretation in a combined action of reduction *and* revelation—the hermeneutics of suspicion and of revelation in an act of mythic subversion inspired by the mythology of imperialism itself. Naturalism and realism as in the aesthetic form of much political as well as social science writing cannot engage with the great mythologies of politics in this nonreductive way, and yet it is the great mythologies that count precisely because they work best when not dressed up as such but in their guise and in the interstices of the real and the natural. To see the myth in the natural and the real in magic, to demythologize history and to reenchant its reified representation; that is a first step. To reproduce the natural and the real without this recognition may be to fasten ever more firmly the hold of the mythic.

Yet might not a mythic derealization of the real run the risk of being overpowered by the mythology it is using? Is there not the distinct desire in *Heart of Darkness* for Kurtz's greatness, horrible as it is? Is not horror made beautiful and primitivism exoticized throughout this book, which Ian Watt calls the enduring and most powerful literary indictment of imperialism?[12] Is not the entire thing overly misty?

But maybe that's the point: the mythic subversion of myth, in this case of the modern imperialist myth, requires leaving the ambiguities intact—the greatness of the horror that is Kurtz, the mistiness of terror, the aesthetics of violence, and the complex of desire and repression that primitivism constantly arouses. Here the myth is not "explained" so that it can be "explained away," as in the forlorn attempts of social science. Instead it is held out as something you have to try out for yourself, feeling your way deeper and deeper into the heart of darkness until you do *feel* what is at stake, the madness of the passion. This is very different from moralizing from the sidelines or setting forth the contradictions involved, as if the type of knowledge with which we are concerned were somehow not power and knowledge in one and hence immune to such procedures. The political artistry involved in the mythic subversion of myth has to involve a deep immersion in the mythic naturalism of the political unconscious of the epoch.

And here Roger Casement's reports offer startling contrast to Conrad's art, all the more vivid because of the ways these men's paths crossed in friendship and admiration in the Congo in 1890, because of the features common to their political backgrounds as exiles or quasi-exiles from imperialized European societies, Poland and Ireland, and because of a pretty well indefinable if only superficial similarity in their temperaments and love of literature. Yet it was Casement who resorted to militant action on behalf of his native land, organizing gun-running from Germany to the rebels at Dublin for Easter Sunday, 1916, and was hanged for treason, while Conrad resolutely stuck to his lonely task of writing, bathed in nostalgia for Poland, lending his name but otherwise unable to assist Casement and Morel in the Congo Reform Society, pleading with hyperbolic humility that he was but a "wretched novelist inventing wretched stories and not even up to that miserable game."

Yet he did pass on Casement's letters to his dearly beloved, wonderfully eccentric socialist friend, the Scottish aristocrat Don Roberto, otherwise known as R. B. Cunninghame Graham (whom Jorge Luis Borges has singled out together with that other great South American Romantic Englishman, W. H. Hudson, as providing the most accurate sketches and literary works of nineteenth-century pampa society). In the letter he wrote to Don Roberto, accompanying the Casement letters, Conrad fills the unknown space of Casement with a galaxy of colonial images whose differences and tensions articulate a triangular relationship between these three men of the front line of empire, each, in his own way, highly critical of it; each, in his own way having to come to terms with its romance and fascination.

Conrad begins with enthusiasm for Don Roberto's just-published book, (dedicated to W. H. Hudson) on the great Spanish conquistador, Hernando de Soto, emphasizing the sympathetic insight with which the souls of the conquistadors have been rendered. For in the mad medley of the romance and glamor and vanity of their monstrous achievements they were at least human—a great human force let loose—while the modern conquistadors such as King Leopold of the Congo are not human but gigantic obscene beasts whose aims are served by the pimps, bullies, and failures swept into the colonies from the pavements of Antwerp and Brussels.[13]

Having set the stage with these oppositions operating as much within the souls of the conquistadors as between them and their capitalist successors, Conrad launches a new figure into the molten stream of colonial imagery flowing between him and Don Roberto: "a man called Casement, premising

Roger Casement in the Congo. (From Frederick R. Karl, *Joseph Conrad: The Three Lives* [New York: Farrar, Strauss, and Giroux, 1979].)

that I knew him first in the Congo just 12 years ago. Perhaps you've heard or seen in print his name. He's a protestant Irishmen, pious too. But so was Pizarro.''

The connection made, the rhythmn accelerates:

> I can assure you that he is a limpid personality. There is a
> touch of the Conquistador in him too; for I've seen him start
> off into an unspeakable wilderness swinging a crook-handled

stick for all weapons, with two bulldogs, Paddy (white) and Biddy (brindle) at his heels, and a Loanda boy carrying a bundle for all company. A few months afterwards it so happened that I saw him come out again, a little leaner, a little browner, with his stick, dogs and Loanda boy, and quietly serene as though he had been for a stroll in a park.

Time embroidered Conrad's recollection, comments Brian Inglis, preferring Casement's more casual portrayal of the landscape in the letter he wrote to a young cousin describing it as grassy plains covered with scrub. "Inhospitable but hardly unspeakable," adds Inglis.[14]

The letter moves on. Conrad loses sight of Casement and in that disappearance a new Casement is born. The romance of the conquistadors dissipates to reveal in the mists rising from their ruins the heroic figure of their implacable opponent, the savior of Indians, Bartolomé de las Casas.

Then we lost sight of each other. He was I believe Bsh Consul
in Beira, and lately seems to have been sent to the Congo
again, on some sort of mission, by the Br Govt. I have always
thought that some particle of Las Casas' soul had found refuge
in his indefatigable body. The letters will tell you the rest. I
would help him but its not in me.

Four years later Casement underwent another metamorphosis in Conrad's writing, this time in a letter to the New York lawyer and Irish sympathizer, John Quinn. For Conrad, writing to Quinn was like being in a confessional, according to Zdzistaw Najder, and now Conrad re-presented his first acquaintance with Casement, categorizing him not as in his Congo diary as the man who "thinks, speaks well, most intelligent and very sympathetic," but as a *labor recruiter*. Even his espousal of the Irish cause was suspect. "A home-ruler accepting Lord Salisbury's patronage couldn't be taken very seriously."[15]

This letter to Quinn (with whom Casement had stayed while in New York in 1914) was written in the spring of 1916 while Casement was imprisoned, awaiting trial for treason. Although Conrad hoped Casement would not be given the death sentence (writes Zdzistaw Najder), he refused to sign the appeal for clemency signed by many prominent writers and editors.[16] But of course the appeal stood no chance with the king, the prime minister, and the attorney-general covertly showing influential people lurid pages from the diaries that the police had taken from Casement's lodgings[17]—diaries that some people still claim were forged by the police.

Including the time spent in the Putumayo, these diaries recorded in detail Casement's homosexual liaisons and dreams. Even before his case went to court in June, 1916, their nature was known to "many people who were strangers to the case," noted his (unenterprising) defense lawyer, and later, when the appeal process was under way in the two weeks set by the court for Casement's hanging, even the newspapers made open reference to the diaries. The day after the trial finished the *News of the World* claimed that nobody who saw them "would ever mention Casement's name again without loathing and contempt." Determined to head off an appeal based on insanity, the legal adviser to the Home Office, Sir Ernley Blackwell, told the prime minister's Cabinet—with whom decision for a reprieve largely lay—that Casement's diary showed "that for years he has been addicted to the grossest sodomitical practises." He continued:

> Of later years he seems to have completed the full cycle of sexual degeneracy and from a pervert has become an invert—a woman, or a pathic, who derives his satisfaction from attracting men and inducing them to use him. The point is worth noting, for the Attorney-General had given Sir E. Grey [foreign minister, Casement's boss, to whom his reports on the Congo and the Putumayo were written] the impression that Casement's own account of the frequency of his performances was incredible and of itself suggested he was laboring under hallucination in this respect. I think the idea may be dismissed.[18]

It appears it was Blackwell who was chiefly responsible for the dissemination of the diaries. His malignant hatred of Casement, a traitor not only to his country but to his "manhood," was further manifested in his suggestion to the Cabinet that discrete publication of the diaries after Casement was hanged would ensure that he would not become a martyr.

And this was certainly tried. "The English have been circulating reports on Casement's degeneracy," wrote Conrad's friend, the Irish sympathizer, John Quinn, from New York. "They come to me from all quarters." Alfred Noyes, professor of English at Princeton University and a propagandist in the employ of the British Government, wrote in an article published in a Philadelphia newspaper several months after the execution that the diaries, filthy beyond all description, touched the lowest depths of human degradation.

The potential for martyrdom was strong. Stemming from the sentiments attached to the Irish cause, it nevertheless owed much to the representation of his work in the Congo and the Putumayo, as expressed in this anonymous petition found among the effects of a former parliamentary private secretary.

> The fine character of his previous career, his great work for the world in the Congo and at Putumayo, should surely also weigh with the Government. The horrors he was brought in contact with combined with his twenty years' uninterrupted work in the unhealthy climates so told on his constitution that he had a complete break down in health, and by 1914 he was an utterly broken man.
>
> In this condition he faced the horrors, hardships and dangers of Putumayo with the same disinterested eagerness he had always shewn. He came back in a state of nervous collapse so

serious that he often wakened shrieking in the night, and there
were certain photographs and notes he brought back that he
could not look at without terribly intense mental agitation and
physical emotion.[19]

Conrad gave his reasons for his assessment of Casement's character—
assassination might be the more accurate word—but no reason was more
vivid than the roller-coastering flow of conflicting colonial imagery that writing about Casement stimulated in Conrad's brain. It was bigger than either
of their separate selves. It was their embodying the colonial adventure and
misadventure, Casement being not only the traitor imprisoned in the Tower
but the activist in whom was inscribed the attraction and repulsion of colonial
mythology. His was the elusive figure, passionate and political, embodying
the collapse of the daydreams that colonization had inspired in Conrad until
that rather late stage in his life when he set out for the tropics to work for
Leopold, king of the Belgians. It was as if what was soon to become the
maligned ghost of Casement would have in addition to bear the brunt of
what Conrad needed to kill in himself. It is this same death wish that can
come to haunt the anthropologist, still if not even more than ever before
society's embodiment of romance and science south of the equatorial line.
And Casement, by all accounts, would have made a marvellous ethnographer.

Perhaps the situation was even more intricate. Perhaps the dashing Don
Roberto, socialist heir to Scottish kings, fearsomely, eccentrically, aristo-
cratically of both the third and first worlds, with what Conrad saw as his
"good pen, keen, flexible and straight, and sure, like a good Toledo blade,"
tongue-in-cheek but all true too, came to present the more wholesome aspects of daring and colonial adventures for Conrad, leaving Casement as the
expression of all that was easily mocked and even dangerous in poetic men
ensnared by colonial dreams.

In one of his last essays, entitled "Geography and Some Explorers,"
Conrad made clear the ways in which, for him, the change in the mix of
magic and machine entailed in the shift from the fabulous geography of the
Dark Ages to the geography militant of the contemporary age was a change
in which accurate maps and scientific explorers made him dream about
journeys to the unknown. At least that was so for him as a boy, putting his
finger on the very center of the then white heart of Africa, exposing himself
to the taunts of his chums. "Yet it is a fact," he goes on to write, that
eighteen years later he was in command of a wretched stern-wheel steamboat
moored to the bank of an African river.

It was night and he was the only white man awake. The subdued thundering
of Stanley Falls hung in the air over the last reach of the upper Congo, and
there was a solitary light in the darkness glimmering across the water from
a little island. With awe he said to himself, "This is the very spot of my
boyish boast."[20]

Daydreams of the geography militant cascade into boyhood memories as the falls, *Stanley* Falls, pour their subdued thundering into the last reach of the river. It is the last reach of mythic hegemony, too. Only one white man is awake, conscious *and* mesmerized by this mutter in the dark under the stars and, because of this mesmerization, precariously sensing other meanings, discordant meanings, where the thunder mutters on the last reach of the river. Into the consciousness bringing itself into being, self-consciousness begins to flicker and glow—like the solitary light glimmering feebly in the foam of broken water. It is there and then that the arc of memory swings back to the boasts of boyhood and forward beyond the last reach of the river to engulf the daydreams of empire-making haunting the white man, leaving him very lonely.

> A great melancholy descended on me. Yes, this was the very spot. But there was no shadowy friend to stand by my side in the night of the enormous wilderness, no great haunting memory, but only the unholy recollection of a prosaic newspaper "stunt" and the distasteful knowledge of the vilest scramble for loot that ever transfigured the history of human conscience and geographical exploration. What an end to the idealized realities of a boy's daydreams! I wondered what I was doing there, for indeed it was only an unforseen episode, hard to believe in now, in my seaman's life. Still, the fact remains that I have smoked a pipe of peace at midnight in the very heart of the African continent, and felt very lonely there.

To the disillusionment was soon added illness severe enough to take him into the space of death, into what Ian Watt calls facing, alone, the fact of one's own mortality as he was borne down the Congo and back to Europe. "It may be said," suggests Monsieur Jean-Aubry, "that Africa killed Conrad the sailor and strengthened Conrad the Novelist."[21] And in this metamorphosis born of death it is important to register the hopelessness that served as the basis of his artistry, whose poetry of despair absorbed like a sponge the magic and romance secreted in the geography militant—surely not such a distant cousin of the science of anthropology? "It is not a pretty thing when you look into too much," he wrote. "What redeems it is the idea only. An idea at the back of it; not a sentimental pretence but an idea; and an unselfish belief in the idea—something you can set up, and bow down before, and offer a sacrifice to. . . ."[22] The snake curling to the heart of darkness in the center of the map of Africa had not so much lost its charm as turned on itself, feeding off the pain of disillusionment. The *Divine Comedy* is far behind in the insipid world of the geography fabulous, and in Conrad's case it is the divine tragedy, the bitterness and the gloom, that Jean-Aubry sees welling forth, like the twisting snake of the great river of dream that occasioned it all.

But though it did not actually fasten this deep gloom on his spirit, yet the Congo certainly caused it to rise up from the depths of his soul, and thus no doubt contributed to those deep currents of bitterness which seem to well out like a great river from the very heart of human darkness and carry to the confines of the land of dreams the strength of an unquiet spirit and of a generous mind.[23]

Conrad himself considered the Congo to be the turning point in his life: "Before the Congo I was just a mere animal," he told Edward Garnett. But Casement? "He was a good companion," Conrad confided to Quinn,

but already in Africa I judged that he was a man, properly speaking, of no mind at all. I don't mean stupid. I mean he was all emotion. By emotional force (Congo report, Putumayo—etc) he made his way, and sheer emotionalism has undone him. A creature of sheer temperament—a truly tragic personality: all but the greatness of which he had not a trace. Only vanity. But in the Congo it was not visible yet.[24]

One might well ask if this is not a case of the pot calling the kettle black, for is this not a rabidly emotional portrayal penned by a creature of sheer temperament? As for Casement's not being a man, "properly speaking," and the way that provides an opening for the investment of sheer emotionalism, the less said the better. Moreover, one could hardly refer to the Congo report, Putumayo—etc. as evidence of emotionalism. The reports themselves were texts not merely of the legal and sociological genres, but also exercises in the use of repressed emotionalism in order to convey all the more strikingly the incredibility of colonial terror. It remains a fact that it was reports like Casement's and not the wondrous art of the master that did much to stop the brutality in the Congo (and perhaps in the Putumayo) and, in Edmund Morel's words, innoculated the diplomacy of Britain with a moral toxin such that historians will cherish these occassions as the only two in which British diplomacy rose above the commonplace.[25]

In addition to the coincidences of imperialist history, what brings Casement and Conrad together is the problem they jointly create concerning the politics of social realism and magical realism. Between the emotional Consul-General who wrote effectively on the side of the colonized as a Realist and the great artist who did not, lie crucial problems concerning the domination of culture and cultures of domination.

The Putumayo Report

It is at this point instructive to work through Casement's Putumayo reports submitted to Sir Edward Grey, head of the British Foreign Service, and

Casement in his thirties. (Courtesy of the National Library of Ireland.)

published together with letters and memoranda as a "blue book" by the British House of Commons on 13 July, 1913 when Casement was forty-nine years old.

It should be noted at the outset that Casement's attachment to the cause of Irish home rule and his anger at British imperialism not only made his almost lifelong work as a British consul fraught with concealed conflict (as with his homosexuality), but that he felt that his experiences in Africa and South America influenced his understanding of colonialism in Ireland, which in turn stimulated his ethnographic and political sensibility south of the equator. He claimed it was his knowledge of Irish history which allowed him to understand the Congo atrocities, for example, when the Foreign Office would not because the evidence made no sense to them.

Making sense here meant a willingness and a developed instinctive capacity to identify not simply with a nation or with a people, but with the hunted and the marginal whose way of life and appreciation of life could not be understood through the soulless philosophy of commodities. In a letter to his close friend Alice Green he recalled:

> I knew the Foreign Office would not understand the thing, for I
> realized that I was looking at this tragedy with the eyes of an-
> other race of people once hunted themselves, whose hearts
> were based on affection as the root principle of contact with
> their fellow men, and whose estimate of life was not something
> to be appraised at its market price.[26]

In the article he wrote for the respected *Contemporary Review* in 1912, he argued that the Putumayo Indians were more highly developed, morally speaking, than their white oppressors. Not only did the Indian lack a competitive streak but he was, in Casement's assessment, "a socialist by temperament, habit, and possibly, age-long memory of Inca and pre-Inca precept." In conclusion, Casement asked, "Is it too late to hope that by means of the same humane and brotherly agency, something of the goodwill and kindness of Christian life may be imparted to the remote, friendless, and lost children of the forest?" Later he would refer to the peasants of Conemara in Ireland as "white Indians."[27]

In good part Casement's dilemma was not so much that of wooing himself from his Unionist and Protestant birthright under the Crown, or from what he increasingly came to see as hypocritical British culture "professing," as he wrote, "Christianity yet believing only in Mammon." His more acute dilemma lay in the way this very same hypocrisy insinuated itself into his life pattern of self-discovery through opposition in which nationalism and anticolonialism but not the covert life of the homosexual could be made manifest and be dignifying: "In these lonely Congo forests where I found Leopold [king of the Belgians, and owner of the Congo Free State], I found also myself, an incorrigible Irishman." In his diary covering his Putumayo journey, some ten years after portraying himself as an "incorrigible Irishman," Casement penned to himself a fragment that displayed the way his thought could work images of femaleness and maleness to represent the culture of imperialism. On the launch *Liberal* steaming up the Putumayo, on 17 September, 1910, he wrote:

> The man who gives up his family, his nation, his language, is
> worse than the woman who abandons her virtue. What chastity
> is to her, the essentials of self-respect and self-knowledge are
> to his manhood.

The *Liberal*. (From Eugenio Robuchon, *En el Putumayo y sus afluentes,* 1907.)

The young Quichua pilot on "Liberal" is named Simon Pis-
ango—a pure pure Indian name—but calls himself Simon Pizarro [to whom Conrad likened Casement in his letter to
Cunninghame Graham]—because he wants to be 'civilized.'
Just like the Irish O's and [undecipherable] dropping first their
names or prefixes to shew their respectability and then their
ancient tongue itself to be completely Anglicized. Simon Pis-
ango still talks Quichua, but another [undecipherable] of Pizarros will speak only Spanish! Men are conquered not by
invasion but by themselves and their own turpitude.[28]

Men are conquered not by invasion but by themselves. It is a strange
sentiment, is it not, when faced with so much brutal evidence of invasion
as one enters the rubber belt? As he wrote to Sir Edward Grey in 1912:

The number of Indians killed either by starvation—often purposely brought about by the destruction of crops over whole
districts or inflicted as a form of death penalty on individuals
who failed to bring in their quota of rubber—or by deliberate
murder by bullet, fire, beheading, or flogging to death, and accompanied by a variety of atrocious tortures, during the course
of these 12 years, in order to extort these 4,000 tons of rubber,
cannot have been less than 30,000, and possibly came to many
more.[29]

Hardenburg's Revelations: Truth, the Devil's Paradise, and the Meaning of Conquest

The British government felt obliged to send Casement—then stationed at Rio de Janiero—as its consular representative to the Putumayo on account of the public outcry aroused in 1909 by a series of articles in the London magazine, *Truth*, depicting the brutality of the Arana brothers' rubber company there, which since 1907 had been a consortium of Peruvian and British interests. Entitled "The Devil's Paradise: A British Owned Congo," these articles described the experience of a young U.S. "engineer"and adventurer named Walter Hardenburg who, with a fellow American, left his job on the Cali-Buenaventura railway in 1907 to descend into a remote corner of the Amazon basin from the Colombian Andes at Pasto via the precipitous trail that led down from the Sibundoy valley. Paddling down the Putumayo river,

Julio C. Arana

Jefe y socio principal de la firma J. C. Arana y hermanos

Julio C. Arana. (From Eugenio Robuchon, *En el Putumayo y sus afluentes*, 1907.)

these *gringos inocentes* fell into the hands of armed men, diabolically cruel, who had been terrorizing the Colombian traders who refused to submit to Julio César Arana—the soul and driving force, as a British parliamentarian later called him, of the Peruvian rubber company. Already there were reports in Iquitos newspapers about ugly things happening up river, and these reports were circulated beyond the river to the Peruvian capital itself. But it required the indignities heaped upon the outraged *gringo aventurero* for this ugliness to become a political issue in England and the United States. (Later on Hardenburg would write a pamphlet in favor of socialism in one of the western provinces of Canada, and after that a book on mosquito eradication.)

It was said that Arana began his spectacular rise to power by trading with the Colombian traders who had been the first to "conquer" (as the common phrase had it) the Indians of the Caraparaná and Igaraparaná tributaries of the Putumayo. These *conquistadores* had been establishing themselves along these rivers with their *derechos de conquistar*—their rights of conquest— since the 1880s in the wake of the quinine boom in the Andean foothills and (so Casement said) found it more convenient to trade their rubber down-stream with merchants like Arana than upstream into Colombia, through the forests to Tolima or over the Andes to Pasto. Just as they managed to get Indians to gather rubber by indebting them into a type of peonage, so these traders were themselves indebted to their suppliers, such as Arana—held fast in the same trapwork of obligations with which they held their Indians. But not quite. They could still, "on the side" so to speak, compete with Arana for Indians.

It was strange area where these Colombians settled and got the local Indians to gather rubber, a frontier prone to warfare and instability and whose sovereignty the nation-states of Peru and Colombia had never agreed on since the aftermath of the wars of independence from Spain in the early nineteenth century. Ground between the rival ambitions of states, it was in effect stateless, a sort of twilight zone whose propensity for violence was channeled by traders such as Arana into struggles for control over a dimin-ishing supply of Indian rubber gatherers. The *derechos de conquistar*, those tacitly agreed-upon conventions outside of any state law and supposedly guaranteeing to each "conqueror" his rights to the labor-product of "his" Indians, were *derechos* grounded as much in the likelihood of violence as in mutual accord—brittle conventions, it would seem, ever likely to self-destruct. The jungle and its Indians loomed large in the fears of the whites, it was said, but according to Joaquin Rocha, a Colombian who traveled through the region in 1903, the greatest threat to the life of rubber traders was that of assassination by a fellow trader.[30] With surprise he also noted how few children the traders fathered. They generally lived with Indian women but the unions were sterile. He surmised that this "extraordinary lack of mestizo children" was due to the Indian wives' drinking contraceptive plant medicine, perhaps "at the orders of the Indian chiefs as a political measure."

Seven years of rubber trading and ruthless elimination of the small traders in this frontier zone of sterility and assassination put Arana in total control and, in 1907, ready to expand on a massive scale with capital raised in London. Like Leopold, king of the Belgians and owner of the rubber-rich Congo Free State, Julio César Arana was, in the lower Putumayo, the state itself.

In 1903 he contracted blacks from Barbados to "conquer" and hunt down fugitive Indians. The notion, let alone the use, of "conquest" here seemed strange to many outsiders, causing the British House of Commons Select Committee on the Putumayo, for instance, much confusion. *Conquistar*, they were informed on more than one occasion, meant not what they thought, "but to distribute goods in exchange for rubber."

Confusion also beset the Committee's attempt to interpret the *Gastos de Conquestacion* (*sic*) item, translated as "expenses of conquest" in the Company's accounts for 1909. The manager in Iquitos, Pablo Zumaeta, wrote to his brother-in-law, Julio César Arana, contesting the prevailing view of the British accountant that £70,917 sterling should be written off as lost, "pointing out that this money represented really capital spent in conquering or more properly subjecting the Indians."[31] There was no need to diminish capital account because,

> as you are aware, in undertakings like ours the capital is ap-
> plied to and spent in conquering or more properly attracting to
> work and civilization the savage tribes, which, once this is at-
> tained . . . bring to us the property of the very soil they domi-
> nated, paying afterwards with the produce they supply, the
> value of any such advance. In undertakings like ours any
> amounts so applied are considered as capital.[32]

It seems to have been a situation in which rights to Indians were similar to rights to farm the forest. The Indians were there for the taking, but once taken, no other white man could trespass. The first white to get into one of the large communal houses with perhaps upwards of one hundred Indians and press trade goods upon them brought to fruition his "rights of conquest." In return the Indians paid with rubber, and before that, at least upriver, and to a much smaller extent, from the mid-nineteenth century onwards the payment had been in herbal medicines, poisons, lacquer, gums, resins, skins, and beeswax. In the 1860s there had been a flurry of activity radiating down from the Andes into the foothills of the *montaña* and to a very limited extent down the middle reaches of the Putumayo River, and that activity was caused by the demand for the famous febrifuge of cinchona bark. Misnamed after the wife of a Peruvian viceroy, this bark contained quinine needed by other *conquistadores* such as the British troops for fighting malaria in India.

I do not understand the power the traders had over the Indians. Most everything said on this topic is saturated with fantasy and wildly contradictory to boot. On the one hand is the strident emphasis on conquest as the ultimate sweaty *macho* affirmation of civilization unfurled on the frontier, penetrating the wild. On the other hand is a quite contrary picture, that of a sort of social contract between like-minded traders, Indians and whites, complementing each other's needs in the fastness of the forest, docile Indians and maternal, nurturing white men.

Certainly neither that paradox nor the docility seems to have been a part of talking and remembering in the first cycle of conquest in the sixteenth century. What little is known of Hernán Pérez de Quesada's mad sweep through the jungles of the Caquetá and Putumayo in 1541 in search of El Dorado is that the Spaniards claimed they generally met with ferocious resistance. Quesada's expedition is said to have consisted of 200 horses, 260 Spaniards, and some 6,000 Indian porters from the highlands of the western *cordillera* of the Andes. It is said that none of those Indian porters survived. Where the Putumayo and Caquetá rivers run close together, around Mocoa, Quesada encountered stiff opposition. Whenever his expedition passed into narrow spaces where horses could not maneuver, Indians attacked. If it was unconsummated rape on horseback, according to this historiography, then those narrow defiles were *vaginae dentatae*. At one place, notes John Hemming from his study of relevant chronicles, "a man-eating tribe managed to seize five men in view of the rest of the column and quartered them before anything could be done to save them."[33] Such are the histories handed down by conquest.

The fate of the missionaries who succeeded the men of the sword for the next two centuries was said to be not much different. Despite this continuity, however, it is nevertheless startling to rediscover the language and imagery of the conquest of the New World in the sixteenth century, reactivated not by gold or by the story of El Dorado, but by quinine and rubber in the late nineteenth. Those European and North American booms for the raw materials of the rain forests resurrected in even more exaggerated form the heroic mythology of the earlier epoch and embedded it in the culture of the trading relationship.

That always interesting commentator, Joaquin Rocha, who journeyed down the rivers Caquetá and Putumayo to Iquitos in 1903, found the notion of "conquest" no less odd than did the British House of Commons Select Committee. He felt it necessary to offer a definition:

> When a tribe of savages is encountered which nobody knew
> about or which has never had contact with whites, then it is
> said that they have been conquered by the person who man-
> ages to trade with them so that they will work rubber, will
> plant food, and will build a house for him to live in their midst.

> Thus entering into the great and common labor of the whites,
> these Indians are brought into civilization.[34]

This definition is not so much a deceit as a conceit, as necessary to conquest through trading as to trading through conquest. The astute *conquistador*, he goes on to note, would take steps to ensure reciprocity for his gift-giving and advances of trade goods—by holding Indian women and children hostages, for example.

But if brute force was advisable, why did they bother giving *gifts* and persist in the fiction of the "debt"? It is frequent, says Rocha, that the Indians fail to succumb to the art of verbal persuasion. Instead they attempt to run away, as in the story he retold about a rubber trader and his four peons returning with trade goods along remote and unexplored reaches of the Aguarico River a few years before. Discerning signs of Indians so far

A rubber trader and his interpreters. (From Eugenio Robuchon, *En el Putumayo y sus afluentes,* 1907.)

from any known tribe, the trader's heart leapt at the idea of conquering them, for through their work he could obtain vast quantities of rubber. At dawn by the light of a splendid moon the whites entered the Indians' communal house. Two of the whites blocked the door with their weapons while their *patrón*, the trader, told the panic-stricken Indians not to be afraid. The Indian men were asked to get food, which their women, who were not allowed to leave, would cook. Upon the men's return the whites presented them with gifts of trinkets and then gave them cloth, axes, and machetes, saying that they ought to bring them rubber in return while they, the whites, would maintain possession of the Indians' house with their women and children in the men's absence. Happy with their gifts and purchased goods, the men agreed, returning in a few days with the rubber they owed.

Needing more goods from the whites and having received such good treatment from those who were now their patrons, they agreed to build them a house and to prepare and cultivate fields for them. Thus was the conquest of this nation, Rocha tells us, consummated.[35]

It was in this way that in 1896 the Colombian Crisóstomo Hernández conquered the Huitotos of the Igaraparaná and Caraparaná rivers, affluents of the Putumayo forcibly appropriated by Arana a few years later. A mulatto from the remote mountain town of Descanse in the Andes, Don Crisóstomo was said to have been a runaway, fleeing from Colombian trading posts in

Huitotos in front of their house, 1908. (Courtesy of the Whiffen Collection, Cambridge Museum of Archaeology and Anthropology.)

the Caquetá on account of his crimes there. He had sought refuge in the deep woods of the Putumayo where he reigned over whites and Indians with great cruelty. Rebellion *and cannibalism*, so Rocha was told, he countered with death. The crime of one was paid for by all. On hearing of a group of Huitotos whose women and children as well as the men were said to be practicing cannibalism, Don Crisóstomo decided to kill them for this crime, decapitating them all, including babies sucking at the breast. The white man who told Rocha this baulked at killing little children but had to because Don Crisóstomo stood behind him with a machete.[36] It is a strange story, given how much stress is elsewhere put on the desperate need for Indian labor. Here we have the tale of a man killing off that labor down to children at the breast because of their alleged cannibalism—mirroring, at least in fiction, the spectacular show of carving up human bodies that, again through fiction, occasioned the white man's furious "reprisal."

A short time later Don Crisóstomo was himself killed, "accidentally" shot by one of his companions of conquest. Crawling along the floor in his own blood, Don Crisóstomo beckoned for his gun in the corner. But nobody would accede to his last request, for they well knew, says Rocha, that he would die killing, taking as many of his companions with him as he could.[37]

But perhaps it was neither the political economy of rubber nor that of labor that was paramount here in the horrific "excesses" of the rubber boom. Perhaps, as in the manner strenuously theorized by Michel Foucault in his work on discipline, what was paramount here was the inscription of a mythology in the Indian body, an engraving of civilization locked in struggle with wildness whose model was taken from the colonists' fantasies about Indian cannibalism. "In the 'excesses' of torture," Foucault gnomicaly writes, "a whole economy of power is invested." There is no excess.

Yet how common was the brutality as depicted in the story of Don Crisóstomo? Hardenburg, who was relentless in his condemnation of Arana's brutality, found other and earlier rubber camps, such as that of the Colombian David Serrano, with whom he stayed a few days on the banks of the Caraparaná, to be idylls of patriarchal benevolence. Serrano told him that the first settlers of the region, of whom he was one, had arrived ill and poverty-stricken to be welcomed warmly by the Huitotos, "plied with food, given women, and made far more comfortable than they had ever been in their own country." Hardenburg thought that the Indians around the camp were cheerful and willing. "They called Serrano their father, and indeed, treated him as such."[38]

"Far from inflicting bad treatment," wrote Joaquin Rocha about the Colombian rubber traders at Tres Esquinas on the Caquetá River, they "pampered the Indians like spoilt children, who for their part rendered implicit obedience to the whites" (except when the Indians were drunk during their "Bacchanalian orgies," which, according to Rocha, took up most of their time; then their esteemed *patrón*, despite his benevolent supremacy, had to lock himself in hiding until the fermented sugarcane juice wore off). These Tama and Coreguaje Indians were indebted to their white *patrón* (their *"jefe supremo,"* as Rocha called him) for cloth, trousers, mosquito nets, shotguns, machetes, and metal pots, which they paid for with rubber and with their service as canoeists. They were also given tobacco and rum, but these were classified, at least by Rocha, as "gifts" and not as advances (just as he made the distinction in the Aguarico story between "gifts" of "trinkets," on the one side, and things such as cloth and axes, for which rubber should be exchanged, on the other). When the Indians elected their chief, they submitted their choice to the *patrón,* who always complied, said Rocha.[39]

It might not therefore seem all that disingenuous of Julio César Arana to defend himself by claiming, under pressure of interrogation by the British House of Commons Select Committee, that "this word 'Conquistar,' from what I have been told in English, sounds very strong. We use it in Spanish to attract a person to conquer their sympathies." Presumably because words, exact meanings, and translation were so crucial here, the Committee felt it necessary to publish this response in Spanish too: "Porque esa palabra 'Conquistar,' que según me han dicho en inglés suena muy fuerte, nosotros la usamos en español para atraer a una persona, conquistar sus simpatias."[40] The object of a *conquista*, Arana went on to say, is distributing goods and fitting out expeditions with a view to converting the Indians to a system of barter—to give them goods in exchange for rubber. "Another term used for this is the word *correría.*[41]

But to Charles Reginald Enock, who had spent four years in the Peruvian Amazon and Andes as an engineer and author (*The Andes and the Amazon, Peru*), and was called to give evidence to the Select Committee toward the end of their hearings, to explain the meaning of words such as *conquistar*, *reducir*, and *rescatar*, the *correrías* were "nothing but pure slave raids."[42] As for the usage of the word *conquistar* in the Peruvian Amazon: "It has the same meaning as the English word 'conquest,' " he said, "undoubtedly— to obtain labor by force."[43]

Nevertheless, the question still remains as to the degree to which Arana was consciously trying to deceive and befuddle the Committee or was merely, as some sort of reflex, taking advantage of a way of speaking common among whites in the Putumayo rubber boom—"rubber boom common sense"— which made little or no sense to the Englishmen of the Committee. There would seem every reason for them to listen with more respect to their compatriot, Mr. Enock. Apart from his experience in the tropics, there was much to take pride in concerning the English as compared with the Peruvian respect for free labor, truth, and the unrivaled capacity of the English language to capture and convey facts. Mr. King of the Select Committee was questioning John Gubbins, chairman of the Board of Directors of the Peruvian Amazon Company and for thirty-eight years resident in Peru.

"Does your experience of that land lead you to say that in
the treatment of natives generally the Peruvian observes the
same standard as the Englishman?"

"I would not say it is up to as high a standard—No; but from
my personal experience they were well treated."

"But the Peruvian does not reach the same standard?"

"No."

"Could you also say there was the same respect for human
life in Peru when you lived there as in London? I will not press
you on that point. Would you say there is the same standard of
truth and public morality, and freedom from corruption in public life in Peru as there is in London?"

"It is axiomatic in all Spanish America," contested Mr. Gubbins, "that the word of an Englishman stands first. An Englishman's word is considered as good as almost any other
nationality's bond."[44]

It is also the case that without the esteem of the Englishman's word and
that without Englishmen like Mr. Gubbins there would have been no Peruvian
Amazon Company. In bringing together English capital with Arana's "know-
how" and rubber-boom common sense, Mr. Gubbins and his kind were party
to the terror of the rubber boom, whose mode of impressing Indians into
gathering rubber can likewise be seen by the way the English word and the
Peruvian were brought together elsewhere—as with Charles Reginald Enock
and Julio César Arana in the witness stand before the Select Committee.
For perhaps the upright Englishman was not much more correct than the
scoundrel Arana when he said that conquest meant obtaining labor by force
while the scoundrel said it meant to attract the sympathies of the Indians
with and in order to trade. Perhaps both were wrong and wrong in mutually
dependent ways, with neither statement alone expressing what was going
on in conquest and its associated debt-peonage, as if each man represented
but one of the outer poles defining the limits of the field within which conquest
and debt-peonage functioned. It was not even that this subordination of the
Indian was achieved by a *blending* of force and fraud, or of arms and persuasion, or of conquest through barter and of barter through conquest. All
that way of thinking is merely a truism that preserves the separateness of
the domains even while blending them; violence and ideology, power and
knowledge, force and discourse, economy and superstructure . . . Enock
badly overstates the case: "conquest means obtaining labor by force"—as
in English. Arana slyly dissimulates: "to attract the sympathies"—as in
Spanish. But when we put the two languages together it is not the blending
of force with what Rocha called the art of verbal persuasion that results,
but a quite different conception in which the body of the Indian, in the
process of its conquest, in its debt-peonage and in its being tortured, dissolves those domains so that violence and ideology, power and knowledge,
become one—as with terror itself.

The Good, the Bad, and the Ugly: The Place of the Grotesque and the Rituals of Melodrama in the War and Torture of Political Economy

As fate would have it, Hardenburg was canoeing downstream in 1907 when Arana's men were making their final attack along the Carparaná against the Colombian rubber traders who refused to sell out or join up. One of these, David Serrano, told Hardenburg how but a month before a "commission" of Arana's had chained him to a tree and then (in Hardenburg's words) "these model employees of the 'civilizing company,' as they called themselves, forcibly entering his wife's room, dragged the unhappy woman out on the porch, and there, before the tortured eyes of the helpless Serrano, the chief of the commission outraged his unhappy victim." They took all his rubber, together with his wife and son, and Serrano heard later that she "was being used as a concubine by the criminal Loayza while his tender son acted as a servant to the repugnant monster." Miguel Loayza was one of Arana's chief managers and what Hardenburg also found repugnant was that he was "a copper complexioned, shifty-eyed half-breed, who spoke a little pidgin English [and] seemed to spend most of his time taking Florida baths and fooling around with his different concubines."[45] Truly an objectionable type.

A few weeks later Serrano was again attacked. This time he ran into the woods leaving his little fiefdom of Indians and rubber to Arana. Elsewhere in this expedition 140 of Arana's men attacked twenty Colombians with a machine gun at the rubber station of La Union. Unfurling their nation's flag, the Colombians defended themselves for half an hour before abandoning their rubber and women to the Peruvians. Taken prisoner by Loayza, Hardenburg witnessed the fate of one of these women, who was many months pregnant and "allotted" to the captain of the marauding vessel: "this human monster, intent only on slaking his animal thirst of lasciviousness, and regardless of the grave state of the unhappy woman's health, dragged her to a place of privacy, and, in spite of the cries of agony of the unfortunate creature, violated her without compunction."[46]

Colombian state officials as well as rubber traders were brutalized in various ways, confined in tiny filthy cages where Hardenburg saw them spat upon, taunted, and, so he says, "abused daily by word and deed in a most cowardly manner." The Colombian trader Aquileo Torres was treated in this way, trussed in chains as a wild beast for over a year. So it was said. When released he became one of Arana's most sadistic station managers, with an especial proclivity for dismembering Indians' bodies while they were still alive.

Hardenburg evokes grotesque and melodramatic ritual as an organic part of the rubber boom warfare along this unhappy stretch of the Putumayo river. His form of expression matches the forms expressed. Organized as rites of degradation, these attacks were at one and the same time (as Casement told the British House of Commons)

> organized by the Arana brothers in order to dispossess the Colombians, who were not only competitors, but offered refuge to the Indians, who were flying from the persecution of the company; and as long as these independent establishments existed on the Caraparaná, Indians would fly there, and there was a means of exit from the region.[47]

What in Hardenburg's testimony came across as appalling and senseless brutality in a theater of sensual cruelty, in Casement's testimony was the logical outcome of the "competition for scarce resources"—in this case, those of "labor." Where Hardenburg fetishizes, Casement reifies; two sides of the one coin.

Casement's was a peculiar logic, to say the least, and one that in the final analysis could not be torn from the theatrical rituals of warfare and terror implied to be mere means to a more substantial end. Indeed, elsewhere Casement commented to the effect that the violent dispossession of the independent Colombian rubber traders made a mockery of the logic whose

"An incident of the Putumayo. Indian women condemned to death by hunger: on the upper Putumayo. (The Peruvians state that this was the work of the Colombian bandits.)" (From Walter E. Hardenburg, *The Putumayo: The Devil's Paradise*, 1912.)

aim it was to secure rubber through securing Indians. "Constant thefts of Indians by one *cauchero* [rubber trader] from another," he wrote in one of his reports to Sir Edward Grey, "led to reprisals more bloody and murderous than anything the Indian had ever wrought upon his fellow Indian. The primary aim of rubber-getting, which could only be obtained from the labour of the Indians, was often lost sight of in these desperate conflicts."[48] A few years later, watching drunken company officials dousing Indians in kerosene and burning them alive during a birthday party, Urcenio Bucelli gave voice to the same vicious paradox: "Estos indios traen tanto caucho y sin embargo se les mata—these Indians bring in so much rubber but still they are killed."[49]

It was a curious note that in 1915 the Peruvian judge Carlos Valcárcel appended in the margin of Bucelli's response to those burnings: "A few years ago a priest of the town of Bambamarca, in the *sierra* of northern Peru, burnt a woman alive because she was accused of being a witch." The history of criminality, the judge went on, "reveals to us that the most atrocious tortures, such as burning people alive, have been almost always applied for religious or political reasons."[50] The immortal Prescott in his *History of the Conquest of Peru* addressed this question of burning in his concern over the fate that befell Incan nobles. "Why this cruel mode of execution was so often adopted by the Spanish Conquerors is not obvious," he wrote, "unless it was that the Indian was an infidel, and fire, from ancient date, seems to have been considered the fitting doom of the infidel, as the type of that inextinguishable flame which awaited him in the regions of the damned."[51]

In a Way Fabricated

Much if not most of the power of Hardenburg's revelations came not from what he himself experienced or saw at first hand but from what he took from accounts published in two short-lived Iquitos "newspapers," *La Sanción* and *La Felpa*, created especially, so it appears, to attack Arana and his company's doings. The first number of *La Sanción* (The Sanction) announced it to be a biweekly commercial, political, and literary publication dedicated to the defense of the interests of the people. Prominently displayed in the center of the front page was a long poem, *El Socialismo*, exalting the socialist cause with hymnal passion.

The accounts in these papers seem to have been important to Hardenburg's mode of representing Putumayo horror because they were not merely local and hence "authentic" but also because they objectified word-of-mouth rumor in print. Furthermore, such accounts gave his limited and fragmented personal experience a wider, even overall view.

Some of his own observations were conveyed with dreamlike power, the same distanced death-space atmosphere as found in *Heart of Darkness*. For instance, he recalled walking around the rubber station of El Encanto, "The Enchantment," where he was prisoner:

> But what was still more pitiful was to see the sick and the dying lie about the house and out in the adjacent woods, unable to move and without anyone to aid them in their agony. These poor wretches, without remedies, without food, were exposed to the burning rays of the vertical sun and the cold rains and heavy dews of early morning until death released them from their sufferings. Then their companions carried their cold corpses—many of them in an almost complete state of putrefaction—to the river, and the yellow, turbid waters of the Carparaná closed silently over them.[52]

This should be compared with what he construed from conversations. Here the need to sensationalize is painfully obvious, moving from the surreal quality of the dream, distanced, inevitable, and maudlin, to the histrionic: "Armed with machetes, the Indians penetrate the depths of the forest, gashing frightfully every rubber-tree they can find, frequently cutting them so much and so deep, in their frantic efforts to extract the last drop of milk, that vast numbers of trees die annually."[53] Yet could not the histrionic be true?

For a few months from October of 1907 until they were forcibly suspended, the Iquitos newspapers *La Sanción* and *La Felpa* contained horrific stories of atrocities in Arana's rubber camps. Indeed, it was the courageous publication in late 1907 of Benjamin Saldana Roca's even more courageous sworn denunciation to the Criminal Court judge in Iquitos that provoked (at least the appearance of) national concern for sustained judicial inquiry, and also facilitated shifts in reality involved in the metamorphosis of gossip into fact and of story into truth.

In the social relation of the spoken to the published word, and of gossip to newsprint, there often comes a time when the latter not so much dignifies, frames, condenses, generalizes, and affirms the former as it thereby holds up a mirror to the community as a whole—a means for making and fixing collective self-consciousness. In the case of the Putumayo atrocities, this type of confirmation of reality through newsprint involved the barely conscious tension of fascination and disgust, binding the fantastic to the credible. Rarely do the two combine as they did so disturbingly in the Putumayo rubber boom where, to cite Peter Singleton-Gates's and Maurice Girodias's reaction to the denials of the Peruvian Legation in London alleging that *La Sanción* and *La Felpa* were dishonest and that their published stories were fantastic: "*Fantastic they were,*" contested Singleton-Gates and Girodias, "*their very authenticity made them fantastic.*"[54]

In the first article in *Truth*, and as the climax to the central chapter entitled "The Devil's Paradise" of his book, Hardenburg quotes "the following facts," which appear to be translated from *La Sanción*. Much of his further indictment, in its individual details as taken from sworn testimony and letters to the editor of that paper, as well as in its overall tone, can be seen as an elaboration of this sort of writing:

> They force the Pacific Indians of the Putumayo to work day and night at the extraction of rubber, without the slightest remuneration; that they give them nothing to eat; that they keep them in complete nakedness; that they rob them of their crops, their women, and their children to satisfy their voracity, lasciviousness and avarice of themselves and their employees, for they live on the Indian's food, keep harems and concubines, and sell these people at wholesale and retail in Iquitos; that they flog them inhumanly until their bones are visible; that they give them no medical treatment, but let them die, eaten up by maggots, or to serve as food for the chiefs' [i.e., rubber station managers'] dogs; that they castrate them, cut off their ears, fingers, arms, legs. . . .[55]

And they also tortured the Indians with fire, water, and upside-down crucifixion. Company employees cut the Indians to pieces with machetes and dashed out the brains of small children by hurling them against trees and walls. The elderly were killed when they could no longer work, and to amuse themselves company officials practiced their marksmanship using Indians as targets. On special occasions such as Easter Saturday, Saturday of Glory, they shot them down in groups or, in preference, doused them with kerosene and set them on fire to enjoy their agony.[56]

In a letter written to Hardenburg in 1909 by an employee of the company, and subsequently published in his book, we read how a "commission" was sent out by a rubber station manager to exterminate a group of Indians for not bringing in sufficient rubber. The commission returned in four days with fingers, ears, and several heads of Indians to prove that they had carried out their orders.[57] The writer thereafter witnessed Indian prisoners shot and burned, the smoldering pile of flesh remaining only 150 meters from the rubber station itself. It was on one of the days of Carnival, in 1903. The "higher employees" of the company, he noted, toasted in champagne the one who could count the greatest number of murders. On another occasion, at the rubber station of Ultimo Retiro, "The Last Retreat," the manager, Inocente Fonseca, called in hundreds of Indians. He grasped his carbine and machete and began the slaughter of these defenseless people, leaving the ground covered with over 150 corpses of men, women, and children—so wrote Hardenburg's correspondent (as translated in Hardenburg's book). Bathed in blood and appealing for mercy, continued the letter, the survivors were heaped with the dead and burned to death while the manager, Inocente, shouted, "I want to exterminate all the Indians who do not obey my orders about the rubber that I require them to bring in."[58]

The writer gives no reason as to why the Indians were "called in." Perhaps he did not know. Perhaps none existed. Maybe it was obvious.

The event—perhaps ritual is the correct term—most figurative of Putumayo terror, quoted as fact by both Hardenburg and Casement from testimony published in *La Felpa* in 1908, concerned the weighing-in of rubber brought by Indians from the forest. In his report to Sir Edward Grey, Casement declared that this description was repeated to him "again and again . . . by men who had been employed in this work."[59]

> The Indian is so humble, that as soon as he sees that the
> needle of the scale does not mark the ten kilos, he himself
> stretches out his hands and throws himself on the ground to re-
> ceive the punishment. Then the chief [of the rubber station] or
> a subordinate advances, bends down, takes the Indian by his
> hair, strikes him, raises his head, drops it face downwards on
> the ground, and, after the face is beaten and kicked and cov-
> ered with blood, the Indian is scourged. This is when they are
> treated best, for often they cut them to pieces with machetes.[60]

There is an uncanny, overblown tone to all of this, I think, which breeds skepticism no less than fear and revulsion. One can understand David Cazes, British vice-consul in Iquitos from 1902 to 1911 (whose trading business was dependent on Arana's rubber company), when in reply to questions put to him in 1912 by the British House of Commons Select Committee said,

> I started taking the first two numbers [of *La Felpa* and *La San-
> ción*], I think, but I thought they were rather fantastic in the
> horrors they depicted. Such a horrible state of affairs seemed
> to me incredible, and I did not have them brought up to the
> house anymore. My wife was with me, and they had a rather
> strong effect on her, I think . . . I suppose now that I know
> things better I think I should probably have given them much
> more credence, but I really thought at that time that they were
> in a way fabricated.[61]

Stories that seem to have a strong effect on Mrs. Cazes seem to her husband, the vice-consul, to be in a way fabricated, as if the marriage bond tightened the vexing relations binding horror to its depiction.

We may feel obliged to ask what truth these stories had, and where in the chain of language binding experience to its expression did the melodramatic tone enter: in the expressing or in the events depicted—or in both?

This chain of questioning assumes a world divisible into real facts and representations of real facts, as if the means of representation were a mere instrument and not a source of experience. "A whole mythology is deposited in our language," noted Wittgenstein, including, we might note, the mythology of the real and of language as transparent.

But to the vice-consul with his strongly affected wife on one side, and on the other his economic support, Julio César Arana, strongly contesting the representations of terror, this commonplace notion about the divisibility of facts from their representations must have started to appear simple-minded. To turn from the vice-consul, caught here between a wife and an Arana, to Consul-General Casement's evaluation, is to begin to appreciate the power of espistemic murk in the politics of representations.

TWO

Casement to Grey

Casement's report to Sir Edward Grey is staid and sober, like a lawyer arguing a case, in marked contrast to his diary covering the same experience. According to Casement's biographer, Brian Inglis, however, the manuscript that Casement forwarded to the Foreign Office had to be changed because its "tone" in "some places" lacked the "studiously moderate" language deemed fitting. The Foreign Office removed what Inglis terms "indignant asides" so as to create a report that would (again in Inglis's words) "seem more objective than it really had been"[1]—a pointed illustration not only of the problems involved in the depiction of terror but also of what we could call the "objectivist fiction," namely, the contrived manner by which objectivity is created, and its profound dependence on the magic of style to make this trick of truth work.

Much of the report—can we still call it Casement's report?—relied on the testimony of thirty blacks from Barbados, "that ghastly little island," Casement elsewhere wrote, "of princes and paupers."[2] They had been contracted by the rubber company in 1903 and 1904 together with 166 others to act as overseers in the Putumayo. By the time of Casement's arrival, many of them could speak an Indian language.

The power of the report is overwhelmingly indebted to their testimony as summarized by Casement, who rarely used their own words and was at pains to forestall criticism of his informants' veracity. After all, it had been said in the Foreign Office concerning these very men that "all West Indian negroes were liars."[3] Casement took pains to argue that by cross-checking testimony he could overcome the weakness of memory and inarticulateness to which, he said, illiterate men such as these Barbadians were prone, despite their obvious sincerity. Most of the testimony was delivered in hostile conditions on company territory with company officials in attendance, offering bribes as well as threats. Yet against these forces and despite their fear, the Barbadians seemed by and large to have had an almost physical need to talk to their consul-general.

The Barbadian Stanley Lewis told what happened to him when he refused to kill an Indian who was being held hostage in the "black hole" under the main house in Ultimo Retiro, because the people attached to this Indian had run away from working rubber. The station manager threatened to kill Lewis for his refusal and had him put down in the black hole and contained in the stocks for two days and nights without water or food. The entire house would often smell foul, Lewis said, because the bodies of the Indians who were flogged, staked out naked on the ground, would fester and fill with maggots. Each lash of the whip opened flesh. He was but fifteen years old when he arrived in these fearsome forests from Barbados, and the consul-

The rubber station "The Last Retreat." (From Eugenio Robuchon, *En el Putumayo y sus afluentes,* 1907.)

general had no doubts about his truthfulness, "in so far as his recollection held good." Since leaving the rubber camps four years before giving evidence, Lewis had sought, wrote Casement (on his behalf) "to forget as much as he could or wipe out from his mind the recollection of the many crimes he had witnessed"—not to mention the ones he had committed.[4]

The unreal atmosphere of ordinariness evoked in the reports—of the ordinariness of the extraordinary—makes the atrocities less startling than uncanny, like watching a sunken world underwater. To get to this world, Casement's launch had to pass through the mouth of the Putumayo. His diary records at that moment of transition mosquitoes, his being ill with fever, long delays, a few miserable Indians and, holding them in the river's mouth from 4:00 A.M., a prolonged white mist. Then, in the report,

> the employees at all the stations passed the time when not hunting Indians either lying in their hammocks or gambling. [p. 17]

> At some of the stations the principal flogger was the station cook—two such men were directly named to me, and I ate the food they prepared, while many of their victims carried my baggage from station to station, and showed often terrible scars on their limbs inflicted at the hands of these men.[p. 34]

From the evidence of scarring, Casement found that the "great majority," perhaps up to ninety percent, of the large number of Indians he saw had been flogged. (The reports are a little inconsistent about the surprisingly large number of Indians he saw; in one instance the figure given is 1,500, in another 1,600. But what is missing in consistency is made up in roundness.) Some of those affected were small boys aged ten to twelve, and deaths due to floggings were frequent, either under the lash or, more frequently, a few days later when the wounds became infested with maggots. Indians were flogged when they brought in insufficient rubber and, with the most severe brutality, for daring to flee. Flogging supplemented other tortures, such as near drowning and choking, designed, as Casement points out, to create a space of death, in his words: "to just stop short of taking life while inspiring the acute mental fear and inflicting much of the physical agony of death."[5] People were flogged suspended above the ground by chains around their necks, according to the Barbadian Frederick Bishop, but the "general method," wrote Casement, was to whip the bare buttocks "while the victim, male or female, was forcibly extended on the ground, sometimes pegged out." "Needless to say," added Casement, "I did not witness any of the executions."

He was informed by a "British subject" who had himself flogged Indians that he had seen mothers flogged because their little sons had not brought enough rubber and were held to be too small to chastise. While the little boy stood terrified and crying at the sight, his mother would be beaten "just a few strokes" to make him a better worker.[6]

Confirming allegations in *Truth,* Westerman Leavine stated that children were often burned alive to make them reveal where their parents were hidden. Children who were too small to whip, according to one testimony, were not too small to burn alive, according to another.[7]

Deliberate starvation was resorted to repeatedly, declared Casement, sometimes to frighten, more often to kill, and prisoners were kept in the stocks until they died of hunger. One Barbadian related how he had seen Indians in this situation "scrapping up the dirt with their fingertips and eating it." Another stated he had seen Indians eating the maggots in their wounds.[8]

The stocks were the instrument central to what was in effect a massive staging of punishment in a theater of cruelty, a spectacular on the proscenium of the open space cleared in the forest. Sometimes, as in the Ultimo Retiro rubber station, the stocks were placed on the veranda of the second story of the main dwelling so that those confined would be under the direct gaze of the chief and his subordinates and close to the cellar or what the Barbadians called the "black hole" (in which some of them, themselves, had been held).

In other rubber stations the stocks were placed in the large space below the raised living quarters of the main house. These houses were similar to stockades, and this military character had stirred the suspicions of the

The rubber station "The Enchanted." (From Carlos Rey de Castro, *Los pobladores del Putumayo,* 1914.)

members of Parliament who sat on the Select Committee on Putumayo when they looked at photographs from the book purported to be the work of the French explorer Eugenio Robuchon, who mysteriously disappeared in the Putumayo.

Children, women, and men could be confined in the stocks for months, said Casement, and some of the Barbadians told him that they had seen women raped while in them.[9] Casement felt it necessary to emphasize that such usage of the stocks was abnormal. He drew upon Lieutenant Herndon's report of his travels in 1851 through the *montaña,* south of the Putumayo. The lieutenant dwelled on the importance of the stocks for the missionaries in their attempts to civilize Indians, but *nowhere,* stressed Casement, did he speak of cruel abuses. It was important to Casement to isolate the means of terror in the rubber boom from their history and wider cultural context.

He related a story he had been told about the use of stocks with a Punchana Indian close to Iquitos at the time of his visit. The man had been drunk and had hit his wife. The local schoolmistress ordered him placed in the stocks by his fellow villagers. As the sun rose, his wife had built for him a shelter of palm fronds and she "sat with him throughout the day to console with him and receive his apologies."

"The story was told to me," Casement went on "in illustration of the friendly and affectionate character of the Indians, and stocks as thus employed, merely to reprove, are not objectionable instruments of correction."[10]

Edouard André's reaction to the use of stocks by the Church was not quite so sanguine. He was a botanist collecting plant specimens for the French government and in 1876 he traveled down the Andes, from Pasto to Mocoa. Near Lake Cocha in what he described as the "Indian village" of La Laguna, he was shocked at coming across stocks—"an instrument of torture," he later wrote, "which I believed relegated to the dawn of Spanish history, but which is still employed in La Laguna." He supplied a drawing of these stocks. They were notable for their size, serving for more than one victim at a time, and for the crucifixes suspended above, giving them the appearance of a sort of altar.[11]

In the foothill town of Mocoa, to the east and over the mountains, he found that not only the legs but also the head of the prisoner was clamped between the beams of the stocks. Sometimes flogging accompanied this punishment as well. Poor André. He lost his appetite for lunch.

Yet the enormous increase of this form of torture during the rubber boom down the Putumayo river thirty years later, with or without crucifixes, made such usage as had offended André's stomach appear routine and unobjectionable, soaked in custom if not eternal wisdom. At least that is what Casement implied.

The Colombian explorer, Miguel Triana, a member of the country's aristocracy, was also impressed by the traditional character of this form of punishment in Putumayo Indian life when he passed through Mocoa around

The punishment of the stocks, applied in Laguna. (From Edouard André, "América Equinoccial," 1884.)

1905 and at the invitation of a Capuchin monk stayed to watch an Indian festival.

The Indians wound their way from the site of their dancing to the church for the mass, and then back again. They had been dancing all night, and drinking. One man "forgot," in Triana's words, "the composure that the situation required." "I'm going to give that Indian a fright," said the monk, and he ordered that the Indian be caught by other Indians and jailed—where three whip strokes would be applied, *segun costumbre*. Everything is prohibited here, noted Triana, by using the phrase "no es costumbre"—"it's not custom."

Whether or not this phrase let alone the very notion of "custom" were present before colonization we will never know. What seems certain is the viewpoint of the colonists that Indians have "custom," that custom is the primitive equivalent of law, and that to rule Indians it is advisable to transmit colonial law not merely in the language of custom but by affixing to it the title and concept of *custom*.

Contrariwise, Indians under colonial rule could deploy the colonized sense of custom to defend themselves. The Capuchin monk cited examples of this for Triana. Indians would say they couldn't do this or they couldn't do that because it was not *costumbre*.

"Surely the punishment of whipping is not a custom that the Indians would wish to conserve?" asked Triana.

"Don't you believe it," threw back the priest, continuing:

> The punishment of whipping is probably the most difficult of all their customs to uproot. You've got to understand that the pain has a mysterious efficacy making people want it. I myself have

The church in Laguna. (From Edouard André, "América Equinoccial," 1884.)

> noted that the Indians become very tranquil, even joyful and
> festive, after a whipping. It is obligatory that after the whipping
> the person whipped says *"Dios le pague"* (God pays you/God
> be praised). If that is not said then the Governor [who is an
> Indian, agreeable to the Capuchins] orders three lashes more,
> and so on, until the punished person loses anger and displays
> gratitude. Flogging thus maintains the principle of authority,
> docility, and the purity of custom. Flogging is the basis of
> custom.[12]

The terrible irony of the Barbadians, themselves descendants of slaves,
being used to enslave others and in the process being virtually enslaved
themselves, is pathetically evoked in the testimony Casement collected. The
Barbadians were in effect indebted peons who were not only used to torture
and hunt down Indians but were themselves subject to torture.

From their testimony it seems that life in the rubber camps for *all* ranks
of employees most of the time was exceedingly mean and sordid with little
trace of companionship. What is conveyed is a Hobbesian world, brutish
and short, in which rites such as torturing the wild but defenseless Indians
were what held the camp personnel together. Otherwise they fought over
food, women, and Indians.

Clifford Quintin, for example, had been twice severely flogged during his
first two years of service. On the first occasion all the employees in the camp
were, as was frequent, short of food and forced to steal it from the Indians
or from their plantings in the forest. In his testimony he is alleged to have
said that when he tried to buy some cassava bread from an Indian girl, a
Colombian employee interfered and a fight ensued, whereupon the station
manager had Quintin's wrists tied behind his back and had him hung from

a pole by his arms, which had been lashed behind his body. He was given fifty lashes with a twisted thong of tapir hide wielded by the station manager and by Armando Normand, a Bolivian English-speaking interpreter (educated in England) who accompanied the group of blacks. The scars were clearly visible to Casement five years later.

He was flogged again eighteen months later on a charge of immoral dealings with Indian women, brought against him by a white Colombian employee name Bucelli. He and Quintin had been sent with a small group to round up Indians who had fled from working rubber. They captured eight of the Indians, four women, two men, and two children, put the men in chains, and started back. In the night the two Indian men under guard of another Colombian escaped. Not wishing to tell his station chief that this was due to the negligence of another Colombian, Bucelli accused Quintin and said he had been with the Indian women instead of performing his guard duties. There was, said Casement, truth in this. Quintin was flogged by Bucelli and the station manager, Sr. Normand, and became so ill that he had to be kept at the main rubber-gathering depot of La Chorrera for three months before he could work again. When Casement came across him four years later he was a sick and malnourished man with a limp caused by a wound sustained from a (probably poisoned) splinter laid by Indians to guard their homes. He had had to walk barefoot because he could not afford the company store shoes at their price of five *soles,* worth in Casement's estimation no more than half a *sol* in England. Most blacks received a salary of fifty *soles* a month.[13]

Joshua Dyall was accused by the station manager of the Ultimo Retiro section with having improper relations with the Indian concubine of one of the white employees. He was hung by the neck, beaten with machetes, and then placed in the stocks. The legholes were so small that two men had to sit on the upper beam to force it onto his legs. Although three years had passed by the time the consul-general saw him, he was deeply scarred where the wood had cut into the sinews of his ankles, which had been affixed three to four feet apart. Suffering terrible pain, he had been left all night. Freed the next day, he could not move other than by crawling on his belly. After six years of employment he had no savings and owed the company store 440 *soles.* He had had nine Indian women given to him as "wives" by the station managers from the supply kept by the company.[14]

These young men had barely arrived from Barbados when they were sent on "commissions," generally into the territories of the Bora and Andoke Indians on the northern extremity of the company's operation, where the Indians were said to be very fierce. According to Captain Thomas Whiffen, a British soldier who was on sick leave because of wounds received in the Boer War and who spent a year traveling through the lower Putumayo area in 1908, these northern Indians were of lighter complexion than the nations to the south along the Putumayo River, and despised the darker people as inferior and as savages.[15] Among the latter, Captain Whiffen included not only Huitotos but also Macú—of whom Irving Goldman reminds us of Theodor Koch-Grunberg's observation, also made at the turn of the century, that in their being defined as inferior in this way, as "not people," and as tame animals and slaves, these dark people were also held by the other Indians, the lighter ones, to be gifted sorcerers.[16]

Captain Whiffen had the good luck to procure as his personal servant a Barbadian, John Brown, who had worked for the rubber company and married a Huitoto, an attachment, the captain said, from which he was able to derive valuable information. A year after escorting the British captain through the forests, John Brown was giving evidence to the British consul-general. He had gone on many commissions and his first had been in 1905 to catch Bora Indians to make them work rubber. The Boras were the wildest and fiercest of the Indians, many of whom had not been conquered, according to Frederick Bishop, another Barbadian witness.[17] Brown's commission caught six women, three men, and three children. In so doing, they killed six other Indians: a little boy shot through the bowels while trying to escape, the captain, whom they shot, and three men and women whom they decapitated—held by their hair while their heads were hacked off with machetes. This hacking was done by the *muchachos,* the armed Indians working for the company and there at the orders of Señor Aguero.[18]

The prisoners were brought in and placed in the stocks. One was later shot dead by Aguero. The rest escaped, some when working in the fields around the house, one other while in Brown's charge, carrying rice up from the port on a two-day journey. Brown thought the women escaped too. During his stay at this rubber station of Abisinia, Brown was mainly engaged in commissions after Indians. He saw hundreds killed.

> They were shot, they were beheaded; there were men, women,
> and children killed. He has seen a woman suckling a small
> baby at her breast have her head cut off and the baby killed,
> cut to pieces. This was done by a man called Esteban Angulo,
> chief of the actual commission on which this crime occurred.[19]

During the two years he spent in Andoke territory, Clifford Quintin's work was to hunt Indians. He saw plenty of them killed. They were killed by the station manager, Ramón Sánchez, and by Normand too. In Casement's words, summarizing Quintin's,

> They were tied up and chains put around their necks; and they
> were hung up, and he, Sanchez, would take a 'sword,' or
> machete, and stick it right through them. He saw Ramon San-
> chez do this to plenty of Indians—men, not women. One day
> Sanchez killed twenty-five men—he shot some, others he cut
> their heads off—and some he hanged slowly with a chain

around their necks till their tongues came out, and they died
like that. Altogether he saw Sanchez kill with his own hands
some thirty Indians, and this in two months.[20]

And this in a political economy supposedly defined by labor scarcity.

Toward the end of 1904 Edward Crichlow was with thirty-six Barbadians
dispatched to Matanzas, "The Massacres," under the command of two company officials, Ramón Sánchez and Armando Normand. They found nothing
but a rude hut in the forest. They cleared ground and built a house. "Then
we had to make expeditions with guns to hunt Indians, like hunting wild
beasts. They came in quietly at first but then Sánchez tied them up."

> "Did the Indians not resist?" asked the Consul-General.
> "They were tied up and killed."
> "You saw them killed?"
> "Yes! I saw several shot, chiefly those that had run away.
> They burnt down their own house and ran away as far as they
> could go. We had to go out on expeditions and catch them. We
> got a few at that time and brought them in chained up. . . .
> There were about twenty-five of them chained like this. They
> worked during the day with the chains round them. There were
> women, and men and children—little children at the breast."[21]

The consul-general asked him what he meant by "calling Indians," while
engaged in an "ordinary" commission.

> "You go to the [Indian] 'capitan's' house with your 'mu-
> chachos.' We all sit in the 'capitan's' house and send out the
> 'muchachos' who are armed to call Indians. The 'capitan' is
> kept guarded, because if all the Indians do not come in he will
> be flogged."
> "Have you ever seen the 'capitan' flogged thus?"
> "Oh yes, often. The 'capitan' would be flogged out in the
> forest-house, and he would be flogged in the section-house too;
> tied out on all fours and flogged. Señor Velarde himself would
> flog Indians sometimes with his own hands. All would obey
> him because they had to. They ordered us to flog the Indians
> and we had to obey."[22]

Next year Crichlow worked as a carpenter and Aurelio Rodríguez, the
section manager, had him construct special stocks that would hold the neck
and arms as well as clamping the legs. Designed so that the two parts were
movable, people of very different heights could be placed face down and
flogged in it, small children as well as adults. In May of 1908 Crichlow had
a quarrel with another employee, a white Peruvian, who appealed to the
station manager, also a white Peruvian. The manager struck Crichlow over
the head with his loaded revolver and called other white employees to seize

him. Crichlow defended himself with a stick but was overpowered, beaten, and put into stocks, presumably the ones he himself had built, being released when he needed to urinate and defecate. Next day he was led to the Occidente station and again put in the stocks overnight with his legs wide apart. The day following he was sent downstream to the La Chorrera station and again confined in the stocks. At the time of his giving testimony, he owed the company 150 *soles,* mainly for food for himself and his Indian wife.

Every company employee had what the consul-general called "a large staff of unfortunate Indian women for immoral purposes—termed by a euphemism their 'wives.' "[23] They were nearly always unmarried girls when first acquired because men whose wives were taken would, according to the testimony of more than one Barbadian, die before gathering rubber for the abductors.

These women were considered company property, to be alloted and withdrawn at the whim of the station manager. Casement expressed more contempt than sorrow at their plight; they were generally fat and sleek, he noted more than once, while their kinsmen toiled on the edge of starvation. He also discerned a connection between sexual license with such women and what he called "the murderous instinct which led these men to torture and kill the very parents and kinsmen of those they cohabited with."[24]

This instinct could be turned onto the concubines, too. Westerman Leavine said that the station manager at Matanzas, "The Massacres," Armando Normand, set fire to an Indian woman because she refused to live with one of his men. They shrouded her in a Peruvian flag soaked in kerosene and ignited her. There were days then in Matanzas, in 1907, said Leavine, when you couldn't eat your food because of the dead Indians lying around the house. And he remembered often seeing dogs eating these Indians and dragging their limbs around.[25]

Frederick Bishop was witness to the anger of the station manager at Atenas, Elias Martinengui. After sleeping with one of his Indian girls, Don Elias discovered, so he said, that she was infected with a venereal disease. In the morning he had her tied up and flogged and then made one of the *muchachos,* the Indian guards, insert burning firebrands into her vagina.

It was Frederick Bishop who told the consul-general this. He had seen much. He had done terrible things. Yet with what coyness he alluded to the woman. He did not like to say where, wrote the consul-general, the firebrands were put, but indicated with his hand. As for the *muchacho* who was ordered to do this? He ran away. We never saw him again, said Bishop.[26]

These Indian guards were referred to as "the boys," the *muchachos* or *muchachos de confianza.* Armed with the weapon of greatest repute, the infamous Winchester rifle, they were recruited and trained by the company at an early age to bully other Indians into gathering rubber—usually Indians

Muchachos, 1908. (Courtesy of the Whiffen Collection, Cambridge University Museum of Archaeology and Anthropology.)

"from tribes hostile to which the boys belonged,"[27] according to Thomas Whiffen of the British army, who procured eight as personal carriers from the rubber company.

For every armed supervisor, there were between sixteen and fifty wild Indians of the forest gathering rubber. Of these supervisors, the *muchachos* (whom Captain Whiffen typed as "semi-civilized") outnumbered the "whites," that is the civilized, by two to one.[28] Casement thought the *muchachos* every bit as evil as their civilized masters.

Indian men could be the target of overtly sexual sadism as well as the women. James Chase testified to the consul-general that Fonseca put an Indian man in the stocks "saying 'I am going to kill you.' The man protested and said he had done no harm. He had not killed a White, he had not injured anyone or killed anyone and could not be killed for running away. Fonseca laughed at him and had him hung by the neck first with a chain drawn tight." He was then lowered and put in the stocks, one leg only, and Fonseca came at him with a club, placed his own leg against the Indian's free leg, pulled off his loincloth of beaten bark, and proceeded to smash his genitals. In a short time the man died.[29]

With a thick stick James Chase beat an Indian to death in the same way, while the station manager, Armando Normand, held the man's legs apart.

"You did that?" asked the consul-general (one imagines with some emotion).

> "Wait, Sir, you do not know how we do things here. If we do not do what the chief tells us he beats us. He puts us in the *cepo* [stocks] and then he sends us down with a letter to Senor Macedo, and he say: 'You have failed—you have not done your work,' and sends us back again where we are flogged. This Indian we beat to death—Normand tell me to do it, and he, too, helped. He said, 'Take a stick and beat him to death,' and I refuse at first, and then I say, 'All right; up here you can do it,' and we smashed him all up, as I have said, and killed him."
> "What had this Indian done?"
> "He would not walk. He did not want to go along with us and carry the *tula* [clothes sack]."[30]

James Mapp told the consul-general that, although he himself had never seen it, he had heard several of the Barbadian men speak of competitions between two station managers, Aguero and Jiménez, the aim and prize of the competition being the shooting off of an Indian prisoner's "——."[31]

When Barbadian men were present they were frequently assigned the task of flogging, but, Casement emphasizes, "no monopoly of flogging was enjoyed by any employee as a right. The chief of the section himself frequently took the lash, which in turn might be wielded by every member of the civilized or 'rational' staff."[32] "Such men," wrote the consul-general, "had lost all sight or sense of rubber gathering—they were simply beasts of prey who lived upon the Indians and delighted in shedding their blood." Moreover, with only one exception, the station managers were in debt. Despite their handsome rates of commission on rubber, they were running their operations at a loss to the company, in some stations amounting to many thousands of pounds sterling.[33]

As for the Indians? He became convinced that those remaining would soon die. "A Peruvian who spoke good English, having spent some years in England, confessed as much to me days before I left La Chorrera. I said to this man that under the actual regime I feared the entire Indian population would be gone in ten years, and he answered 'I give it six years—not ten.' "[34]

(Writing in the mid-1920s, some fifteen years later, the Capuchin father Gaspar de Pinell thought that there was probably *nobody* left in the core area of Arana's operation between the Igaraparaná and Caraparaná rivers.)[35]

It was at first sight a strange and even confusing observation that Casement had made with respect to one of the rubber station managers, Andreas O'Donnell, but perhaps now we can see how its very strangeness and confusion summed up the situation: he was the best of a bad lot, the consul-general had written, because he killed for rubber rather than for sport.

And the others?

THREE

The Economy of Terror

He was the best of a bad lot because he killed for rubber rather than for sport. We recall Urcenio Bucelli's exclamation on seeing company officials burning Indians alive to celebrate a birthday: "They bring in so much rubber and still they are killed!" Where was the sense in *that?*

One way of finding it was to make it with the cleaver of reason, splitting the morass of viciousness into two distinct parts, dividing the rational from the irrational, the economically sensible from the frivolous, as if by this ordering procedure the analyst and commentator was still, so to speak, on top of things, understanding, taming, coping if not dealing with the horror. Thus Charles Reginal Enock, F.R.G.S., in his introduction to Hardenburg's book could write:

> There is yet a further trait of the Latin American which to the Anglo-Saxon mind is almost inexplicable. This is the pleasure in the torture of the Indian as a *diversion,* not merely as a vengeance or "punishment." As has been shown on the Putumayo, and as happened on other occasions elsewhere, the Indians have been abused, tortured, and killed *por motivos frivolos*—that is to say, for merely frivolous reasons, or for di-

version. Thus Indians are shot at in sport to make them run or
as exercise in *tirar al blanco* or target practice, and burnt by
pouring petroleum over them and setting it on fire in order to
watch their agonies. This love of inflicting agony for sport is a
curious psychic attribute of the Spanish race.[1]

"In Matanzas," notes the anonymous letter writer published by *La Felpa*
and quoted by Hardenburg, "I have seen Indians tied to a tree, their feet
about half a yard above the ground. Fuel is then placed below, and they are
burnt alive. This is done to pass the time."[2]

Casement recorded the Barbadian Stanley Lewis as saying:

> I have seen Indians killed for sport, tied up to trees and shot at
> by Fonseca [the station manager] and others. After they were
> drinking they would sometimes do this. They would take a man
> out of the "cepo" [stocks] and tie him to a tree, and shoot at
> him for a target. I have often seen Indians killed thus, and also
> shot after they had been flogged and their flesh was rotten
> through with maggots. . . .[3]

Aquileo Torres was one of Arana's station managers. Before working for
the company he had been an independent Colombian rubber trader. He had
been captured by the company and placed in a cage, tortured for over a
year, some said. A Peruvian employee of the company told Casement that
Torres "had from sheer brutality or sport, according to Pinedo, killed this
man. He had put his rifle to the Indian's face, and had told him 'as a joke'
to blow down the barrel. The Indian obeyed; then Torres pulled the trigger
and blew his head off."[4]

Earlier Torres "for wanton sport" had shot an Indian woman. The Barbadian overseer told Casement that Torres had taken his knife to cut off the
ears of living Indians for sport. Chase saw him do this several times. "Once
he cut of a man's ears and then burnt his wife alive before his eyes." Chase
also described how Fonseca used his long rifle, a Mannlicher, from the
veranda to shoot Indians in the stocks. The last time Chase saw this was
when a young girl had her mouth, ears, and eyes covered over by Fonseca
and was then made to walk away, blindfolded, while Fonseca shot her "as
sport for his friends."[5]

But in the wantonness of the sport and in the *sheerness* of the brutality
lies an excess of meaning that undermines the very separation of reasonable
torture from the unreasonable—which poses a block to explanation.

Yet the consul-general had his job to do and that was to write a report
that made sense to Sir Edward Grey and, through him, Parliament and public
opinion. On the surface it seemed straightforward: the creation of a searing
indictment of a searingly awful situation, just like his earlier report on the
Congo atrocities. But there he had already felt the problem, as he had put

it to his friend Alice Green, that he was struggling with opposed ways of making sense of the situation. There was the way with which the Foreign Office felt familiar, the market-price way of understanding social events, political economy as official common sense, and then the other way, which was Casement's way, seeing with "the eyes of another race of people once hunted themselves, whose heart was based on affection as the root principle of contact with their fellow men, and whose estimate of life was not something eternally to be appraised at its market price."[6] The eyes of the hunted were many; the Congolese mutilated for rubber, the Irish and Putumayan Indians, and the homosexual, too.

But it was into the official common sense of political economy that the author, willy-nilly, had to squeeze reality. It was this that created the contradictions in the official report where so much sense-making was made dependent on market rationality to produce the following type of argument: It was not rubber but labor that was scarce in the Putumayo. This scarcity was the basic cause of the terror. Putumayo rubber was of the lowest quality, its remoteness made its transport expensive relative to most other rubber zones, and wages on the open market were very high. Hence the company coerced labor by means of debt-peonage and terror.

It was, then, a mode of interpretation that created capitalist sense from the raw material of the terrible cruelty meted out to the Indians. Unlike the *Capital* of Karl Marx, for instance, subtitled *A Critique of Political Economy,* this cost-accounting way of building sense presupposed and hence reinforced as eternal verities the notions of market pressure, the capital-logic of commodities, and the rationality of business. Thus even in blaming the market, its mode of appropriating reality and creating intelligibility was upheld.

Yet there was neither a commodity form of labor nor a market for it; only Indians with their quite different modes of exchange and evaluation, coexisting with various forms of colonial domination; patronage, concubinage, slavery, and debt-peonage. Indeed, this was the initiating point of Casement's analysis—that free labor barely existed on the Putumayo. There was no labor market. As for the rationality of the business in the Putumayo, surely that was what most needed explanation?

Casement argued that terror was efficacious for the needs of the labor system, and this heightens the most significant contradiction to emerge from this report, namely, that the slaughter of this previous labor was vast beyond belief and that, as Casement himself stated, not only were the station managers costing the company large sums of money but that "such men had lost all sight of rubber-gathering—they were beasts of prey who lived upon the Indians and delighted in shedding their blood." To claim the rationality of business for this is unwittingly to claim and sustain an illusory rationality, obscuring our understanding of the way business can transform terror from a means to an end in itself. This sort of rationality is hallucinatory, like the veil that Conrad and Casement faced earlier in the Congo, where, as Frederick Karl points out, Conrad abandoned the realism practiced by Casement for a technique that worked through the veil while retaining its hallucinatory quality.

As for the labor scarcity belabored by Casement, it needs to be pointed out that this "scarcity" can hardly have meant a scarcity of local Indians, who were to all accounts in surprising abundance, but rather that they would scarcely labor. They would not work *appropriately,* and this is a sociopolitical and cultural issue, not a demographic one. Casement avoided this feature, now often referred to as the "backward-sloping supply curve of labor" (even though he had himself complained in the Congo that the problem there was that the natives would not work), and confidently stated that if paid with more goods, the Indians would work to the level required by the company without force or torture.

There is in this confident assumption that curious and fundamental optimism of liberal decency that, when confronted by the brutality of labor exploitation in the tropics, proposes higher wages as a substitute for coercion. Higher wages would also prevent the short-sighted creoles from destroying tropical labor supplies—supplies that were then considered by some people as important if not vital to the future of the world economy. Viscount Bryce wrote in 1915, for instance, in his "Foreword on the Latin American Indian" (for Joseph Woodroffe's book, *The Rubber Industry of the Amazon*) that an effort should be made to protect the tribes of the Amazon forest and preserve their labor. "Some of them are docile and industrious in their own way and capable of being educated," he went on, and

> it is the unjust oppression practised by so many of the whites
> which has turned these tribes against us, the European races,
> kept them at a low level, and made their work of no benefit
> except when given under compulsion, and of much less value
> even then that it would be under conditions of freedom. Owing
> to this I am glad to see that you pointed out nearly three years
> ago, just after the publication of [Casement's] Putumayo Re-
> port, that, however uncertain and unsatisfactory the Brazilian
> native labourer may be, if Latin America is to be of permanent
> value as a producer of foodstuffs and raw materials to herself,
> to ourselves, and to others, steps must be taken at once, not
> only to stop the atrocious policy of cruelty and decimation
> which went on in the Putumayo region, but also to enable the
> number of natives to increase [and] if this is not done, trouble
> of a serious character will befall the regions mentioned, as well
> as Europe, as far as it depends on Latin America for supplies
> and a return on money invested out there.[7]

The Putumayo terror was like an omen of an impending disaster. Bryce was British ambassador in Washington and played an effective part in bringing Casement and his report to the attention of the U.S. government and to President Taft himself. Bryce concluded his foreword by quoting from his own editor's article:

> When our investments in Latin America suffer by their rail-
> ways being still and their docks are deserted and idle for want
> of freight and traffic through the absence of labour; when many
> of our factories have almost ceased work for want of orders
> from overseas, or through lack of tropical products at home,
> then perhaps John Bull and Uncle Sam will wake up to a sense
> that all is not well—wake up, that is, to cure the disease only
> to find the patient already dead.[8]

There was thus a high value attached to aboriginal labor supplies. The horror occasioned by the Putumayo atrocities was in part due to the strange but pervasive fantasy current at that time that the tropics would breed forth an endless supply of wealth-creating colored labor, provided it was not choked off in its infancy by the unbusinesslike predilections of creole entrepeneurs. That was long before all the talk about overpopulation in the third world that we hear today.

Harold Hamel Smith warned in his introduction to Woodroffe's book on rubber in the Amazon that

> if something is not achieved very soon in this way the "white"
> continents will soon be calling out for supplies of foodstuffs for
> their homes, and raw materials for their factories, and they will
> call in vain, for being totally unfitted to stand the life of toil
> under the tropical sun that is the lot of the dark-skinned peo-
> ple, we have no one to take the place of the latter, who will
> soon practically disappear off the face of the earth if steps are
> not taken to conserve what we have and then to increase their
> numbers. The marvel is that such wanton destruction of this,
> the most valuable of all the tropical "products," has been toler-
> ated so long. If Formosa were to burn out her camphor forests,
> India or Java their bark trees, or Ecuador, Malaya, and other
> centres their cacao, rubber, and coco-nut plantations, we
> should indeed think that they were bereft of their senses, and
> perhaps (needing the produce) take concerted action to stop
> such wanton destruction. To destroy these crops, however, in
> such a fashion, stupid as it would be, cannot be compared, so
> far as the welfare of the universe is concerned, for sheer crimi-
> nal wantonness to the mania that has always existed with the
> whites, and the colored half-breeds under them, to work or
> otherwise ill-use out of existence the darker-skinned people
> with whom they have come into contact. Such conduct, slowly
> but surely, removes for all time that which we can never re-
> place. To replant the forests may be costly, but it is compara-

tively easily done, but to replace an exterminated race is
beyond our powers, at any rate up to the present. Synthetic labour has still to come; its arrival, I fear will not be just yet.[9]

While Hamel Smith singled out the mania of the whites and the colored
halfbreeds serving under them as the basic cause of the extermination of the
human life of the tropics, Casement's report was ordered by the concept of
the businesslike rationality behind the slaughter. What was grossly irrational
from the business point of view of one man, was rational from the business
point of view of the other. In his official report, at least.

People with longer and more practical day-to-day experience in the Putumayo than Casement denied his naive opinion that Indians would gather
rubber without force, and did so from various points of view. The Barbadian
Joseph Labadie thought that if "Indians were not flogged they would not
bring in rubber; some might if they were well paid, but many would not."[10]
A month later the consul-general asked another Barbadian overseer, Edward
Crichlow, "Would the Indians come in voluntarily to work rubber in exchange for goods if simply invited—if they were promised bartered goods
in return for their rubber and were not flogged?" Crichlow replied that "he
did not think that any would so come in, for they would not come near the
section for anything the White man offered them if they were not forced—
that they would stay away because they were terrified."[11]

Jules Crévaux explored the Putumayo river in 1879 and had this to say
about Indian consumerism there:

> Sometimes these children of nature enter into relationship with
> somebody searching for sarsaparilla or for cacao, but this does
> not last long. As soon as they have exchanged their stone axe
> for a knife or for a machete, they find the connection with the
> Whiteman insupportable and they isolate themselves in the for-
> est. The problem in civilizing the Indians of South America is
> that they lack ambition. The Indian that has one knife will give
> nothing, absolutely nothing, to possess another.[12]

In his compilation of statements on Indian economies (published in 1924,
based on field research begun in 1907), the unsurpassable Walter Roth referred to another observation of Crévaux's: "When I give a knife," he says,
"they always ask me, 'What do you want?' "

The converse is equally true, Roth went on to point out, citing Coudreau's
as well as his own perplexity about what seemed to be the Indian's confusion
between gifts and commodities, between presents and business. If the Vaupés
Indians show one hospitality in the way of cassava and smoked fish, wrote
the Frenchman in 1887, they expect something in exchange, and often show
themselves very exacting in this respect. At the Patamona village of Kari-
kaparu, relates Roth, referring to his own experiences in Guiana, the chief's

brother, seeing Roth arrive lame and weak, gave him a stick to help sustain himself, saying it was a present and rejecting Roth's attempts to pay for it. A week later when Roth opened up his "trade" (sic), this man saw an item that he liked and asked for it, reminding Roth of his present.[13] "In trade and barter," Roth claimed, "the value of an article to an Indian depends upon his temporary want of it and not upon its intrinsic worth."

Leaving aside the puzzling question of how we, in a capitalist economy, distinguish between "temporary want" and "intrinsic worth," let alone the unsolved mysteries of intrinsic worth, it is worth our while to follow Roth's examples because they bear on the problem of trading that must have faced the rubber traders and their political economy of frontier capitalism up the Putumayo.

There were some amazing stories to whet the appetites of the traders. Hadn't the Indians of Santo Domingo (according to Diego Alvarez Chanca's letter of 1494 relating to Columbus's second voyage) bartered gold for tags, nails, broken pieces of darning needles, beads, pins, laces, and broken saucers? But on the other hand, this very same Indian profligacy, if that's the word, could frustrate the white man. Edward Bancroft observed from his stay in Guiana in the mid-eighteenth century that an Indian would at one time require an axe in exchange for that which at another time a mere fishhook would be demanded, "without regarding any disproportion between their value." And not only at different times, but at the same time with different Indians; thus Richard Schomburgk (from his travels in Guiana in the mid-nineteenth century): "For what one Indian would want a gun or an axe, another for the same thing, would want a couple of fishhooks, some beads, or a comb."

But, as usual, Roth's stories were the best: "One Makusi woman offered me a cow for two 'flash' finger rings, of a value under 16 cents, whereas at Samarang, on the Brazilian side of the border, I had to part with my trousers for two hindquarters of fresh beef."[14] And he began his chapter on trade and barter by quoting approvingly from George Pinckard's *Notes on the West Indies* (1816), to the effect that the Indians, those of Guiana in general as well as the Arawaks,

> have no interest in the accumulation of property, and therefore
> do not labour to obtain wealth. They live under the most per-
> fect equality, and hence are not impelled to industry by that
> spirit of emulation which, in society, leads to great and unwear-
> ied exertion. Content with their simple means, they evince no
> desire to emulate the habits or the occupations of the colonists;
> but on the contrary, seem to regard their toils and customs with
> a sense of pity or contempt.[15]

To Joaquin Rocha, who journeyed through the area just before Arana's company attained total control, it was a straightforward fact that the Indians

there were "naturally loafers" and that because they postponed paying off
the advances they received from the rubber traders the latter were compelled
to use violence.[16] (Rocha also pointed out, incidentally, that although the
rubber in the Igaraparaná-Caraparaná region of the Putumayo was of poor
quality, profits could be high because in that region "there are abundant and
cheap 'arms'—those of the Huitotos—whereas in the Caquetá, where only
white wage laborers can be obtained, brought from far-away and paid very
high wages, it is useless to think of working that sort of rubber.")[17]

While terror seemed to some people to be the logical response to the
political economy of "scarcity," to others a quite contrary solution seemed
logical and natural. Charles C. Eberhardt, who was the U.S. consul in Iquitos
in 1906 (and envoy extraordinary and minister plenipotentiary in Nicaragua
from 1925 to 1930, the years that saw the rise of the Sandinista resistance
to the U.S. marines), reported to his government that the Indian enters the
employ of some rubber gatherer "often unwillingly" though not infrequently
by force and immediately becomes indebted to him for food, and so on.
However,

> the scarcity of labor and the ease with which the Indians can
> usually escape and live on the natural products of the forest
> oblige the owners to treat them with some consideration. The
> Indians realize this and their work is not at all satisfactory,
> judging from our standards. This was particularly noticeable
> during a recent visit I made to a mill where "cachasa" or
> aguardiente is extracted from cane. The men seemed to work
> when and how they chose, requiring a liberal amount of the liq-
> uor each day (of which they are particularly fond), and if this is
> not forthcoming or they are treated harshly in any way they
> run to the forests. The employer has the law on his side, and if
> he can find the runaway he is at liberty to bring him back; but
> the time lost and the almost useless task of trying to track the
> Indian through the dense forests and small streams makes it far
> more practical that the servant be treated with consideration in
> the first place.[18]

Hence, while the British consul-general, against the evidence of his labor-
supervising Barbadian informants, stated that the Indians would work sat-
isfactorily without flogging and with better pay, and that the cruelty of the
Putumayo rubber boom was due to scarcity of labor, the U.S. consul drew
the opposite conclusion; namely, that "scarcity" made it wiser *not* to treat
Indians harshly, but with consideration. (Twenty years later, in Nicaragua,
with the marines installed, the U.S. consul's liberal sentiments may not have
been so forthcoming.)

It should also be observed that there is plenty to suggest that, because of
terrorization, Indians *did* run away from Arana's control. I have already

cited, for instance, John Brown's testimony regarding the commission in which he participated in Boras country. They got twelve Indians. They killed six of them. No reason given, except in the case of a little boy trying to escape. The Indians were brought in, put in stocks, and one more was killed. The rest, says Brown, escaped while working.[19] When James Mapp was out hunting Andokes for two months with Sánchez and Normand, they brought in 180 Indians to work. They were often flogged. It says in the report that owing to the treatment they got they ran away.[20]

The laborers on the company's plantation close to Iquitos were normally placed under lock and key in rooms beneath the house after six o'clock in the evening. They were Indians from the surroundings and two Huitoto women. "I had seen the whip used on several occasions on these unfortunates," wrote Joseph Woodroffe, an Englishman employed by the company in 1908.

> They had made several attempts to run away, owing to their
> treatment at the hands of the manager, who, when under the
> influence of drink was one of the most intolerant and inhuman
> men I have ever known.
>   The last occasion on which I saw the whip used was upon
> the girl who attended to the domestic duties, and she, for some
> slight misdemeanour, was cruelly flogged. This must have irri-
> tated the Indians to the utmost degree, for, although they were
> locked up as usual that evening, the next morning they had all
> disappeared. . . . They did however leave one small canoe, suf-
> ficient for two persons, knowing that two men dare not attempt
> to follow them. I may say that not one of them was ever
> caught again, and, as they numbered more than forty, they
> ought to have been able to do well in their new condition. At
> least, it has always been my hope that they would.[21]

A few days later Mr. Woodroffe was called to the river by blasts from a steam whistle. There he found an English army officer in pursuit of a canoe that had been stolen by two young Indians under his "care," it being his desire to carry them to England.

Indians could run away. Indians could be stolen from somebody else's "care." And they could be caught if they ran away.

The *muchachos* at El Encanto rubber station were armed with shotguns and rifles, noted Mr. Woodroffe, "owing to the confidence shown in them as fairly reliable instruments in the pursuit of Indians running away from the district, a duty in which these men rarely failed, and the reader can readily imagine what happens when any runaway shows resistance."[22]

In any event, however, with or without terror, it seems that the productivity of Indian labor fell far short of what employers wanted.

Casement himself provided a picture of the Indian as averse to work. In an article on the Putumayo Indians for *The Contemporary Review* he wrote:

While he abstained from providing himself with a stronghold,
or abiding place, or even cultivating beyond his most immedi-
ate needs, he was always ready for a dance, a game, or a hunting expedition. His dances, his songs, were a more important
part of his life than the satisfaction of his material wants. These
might have been much better provided for had he bent all his
energies in that direction. . . . Everything but his music, his
dance, and songs was temporary.[23]

And these were the people the rubber company tried to harness as diligent
laborers, the same people Casement stated in his report would bring in rubber
if paid higher wages.

Debt-Peonage: Is It Slavery? Can a Man Be a Debt?

Things make even less sense when we pause to look at the debt-peonage
"system," which Casement regarded as slavery. It was a pretext, he said,
that the Indian in such a relation was in debt, because the Indian was bound
by physical force to work for the company and could not escape. But then
one has to ask why the company persisted with this pretext, especially given
the whips, stocks, Winchester rifles—and slaving customs—at its disposal.
For in a variety of forms slavery was well known in the Putumayo and clearly
distinguishable from the institution of debt-peonage, with which it could fuse
and with which foreign critics, like Casement, confused it.

The Putmayo rubber boom rested on and stimulated the further development of three quite different forms of control over the human body: the
forced labor associated with the debt-peonage system of Indian men working
rubber; the concubinage of young and usually unmarried Indian women, of
whom many if not most of Arana's employees were said to have between
five and fifteen at a time; and the acquisition through force or barter of Indian
children for sale as servants in Iquitos at prices ranging between 200 and
800 Peruvian *soles* (£20 to £80) each. These three forms of domination clearly
differ in the ways that they dovetail degrees of freedom with degrees of
slavery.

To some early European observers, the institution of slavery among the
Indians themselves was a notable gentle affair—so much so that one cannot
but wonder why it was called slavery and how the power that entered it
came to function. Father Cristobal de Acuña wrote from Quito in 1639, for
instance, after his historic voyage down the Amazon, that the Omaguas or
Aguas supplied the slaves that they captured in battle with all they wanted,
becoming so fond of them that they ate with them out of a common plate.
While the Omaguas would trade many things with Acuña's companions, they
would not part with their slaves. "Here was the point of disagreement,"
wrote the good Father, "here was the subject which made them sorrowful;
then appeared arrangements for concealing them." And that was not—most

definitely not, he stressed—because they ate their slaves. While it was true
that there were other Indians who practiced cannibalism and did fatten up
their captives before eating them, this practice, he said, had been greatly
exaggerated by the Portuguese in order to legitimate their taking Indians as
slaves.[24]

The Jesuit missionary Samuel Fritz spent thirty-seven self-abnegating years
indoctrinating Indians along the upper reaches of the Amazon in the late
seventeenth century and has left us this vivid description of slavery among
the Omaguas:

> Everyone has ordinarily in his house one or two slaves or ser-
> vants of some tribe of the main-land that he acquired in the
> course of war, or bartered in exchange for iron implements or
> clothing, or some other like way. The Omagua haughtily
> stretched in a hammock in a lordly fashion dispatches his ser-
> vant or serving-maid, his slave or slave-girl, to provide his
> food, bring his drink and other similar things. In other respects
> they regard their servants with much affection, as if they were
> their own children, provide them with clothing, eat from the
> same dish, and sleep with them beneath the same awning, with-
> out causing them the slightest annoyance. In their heathen days
> they were accustomed to make raids into the interior of the for-
> ests in quest of these slaves, to assault the houses with armed
> hand, to kill cruelly the old men and women, and to carry off
> as captives the young people for their service. Such is the un-
> just custom that they have always practiced, and that many
> Portuguese practice even today among the Indians that are sub-
> ject to their sovereignty, offering them iron implements or other
> commodities, and compelling them with threats to carry on war
> with savage tribes so as to obtain slaves to give them.[25]

Almost two centuries later Jules Crévaux asked how it was that the Huitotos he was among in 1879 had more trade goods than the savages who
lived two hundred leagues away on the banks of the Amazon itself? The
Carijona chief he was staying with, for example, had at least ten rifles and
a similar number of cutlasses, together with four boxes of Western goods.

The answer was the trading in slaves whom the chiefs sold to itinerant
Portuguese. For an infant they paid an "American" knife. For a girl of six
years, a cutlass or at times an axe. And for an adult, female or male, a rifle
or a shotgun:

> Thus armed the Indians raid neighbouring rivers, attacking peo-
> ple armed only with arrows, kill those who resist, make pris-
> oners of the others, and go downstream to the buyers of human
> flesh. This trade, however, is not without risk. Often they dis-
> like the prices offered by the trader and seeing that they are
> stronger than he, they then rob and kill him.[26]

Thirty years later, in 1908, that veteran of African campaigns, Captain Whiffen of the Fourteenth Hussars, on sick leave and, as he put it, "wearying not only of enforced inactivity but also perhaps of civilization," spent a year traveling through the lower Putumayo area, through what he called "the rubber belt." In his opinion, slavery

> among the Indians themselves is little more than a name for a
> slave belongs to a chief, and soon becomes identified with his
> family. Though slaves frequently have a chance to run away
> they seldom do so, for they are usually treated with kindness,
> and probably are nearly as well off in the house of their victors
> as in their own.[27]

Yet if such slavery among the Indians was frequent, so was that to which the whites subjected the Indians. It was a common source of amusement on the Amazon River, wrote Captain Whiffen, how whites lured and stole slaves *from one another,* although "stealing" was not at all difficult given the curious character of the Indian: "He will always leave one white man to go to another. He is always on the alert to run, to go elsewhere. . . . The matter is hard to explain. It is simply in their blood. It is *Pia,* as Brown remarked. It is their custom."[28]

Indeed, enslavement of Indians by whites was so routine that even progressive antislavery-minded foreigners from the civilized shores and social classes of Great Britain could quite unself-consciously take advantage of it—or be taken advantage of. Alfred Simson, whose journey in 1875 to what he called the "almost mystical" Provincia del Oriente of Ecuador ended with his skippering the first steam launch up the Putumayo, was shocked by the many signs of Indian enslavement he encountered, such as those Coto Indians who hid themselves to prevent their children from being taken away by whites, "whose shameless kidnapping," he wrote, "is not only condoned by the authorities, but is also taken part in by them."[29] Ascending the Putumayo he noted that the Indians there were "undergoing practical slavery under unscrupulous masters." Descending the same river on his homeward journey he interpolates into his chronicle the fact that he himself somewhere along the way acquired two Indian boys:

> Before leaving. . . I gave two boys I had become possessed of
> to Fernando. . . I know these two boys would be better off
> with him than with anyone else, and that he would treat them
> kindly. One of them was the boy I had taken from Firmin
> whilst the other was obtained from the Orejones [Indians] and
> was given to me as a present. He belonged to a tribe of Indians
> called Monrois who dwelt somewhere far away from the river,
> and with whom the Orejones have some transactions of
> barter. The boy was very small, probably about seven years
> old, and the language he spoke was not known to any of us,

Whites or Indians. He was christened by the *corregidor* as
Yasotoaró Ponio Pilato [Pontius Pilate].[30]

And this was some fifteen to twenty years before the rubber boom.

Six weeks after passing into the misty mouth of the Putumayo, Casement
noted in his diary:

> I sent to the store for a case of salmon and distributed galore
> to men, women, boys and mites. I picked one dear little chap
> out and asked if he would come with me. He clasped both of
> my hands and backed up to me, and cuddled between my legs
> and said, Yes. . . . After much conversation and crowding
> round of Indians it is fully agreed on—he will go home with
> me. The Indian Capitan asked for a present on the agreement,
> virtually the sale of this child for a shirt and pair of trousers
> which I gave him and Macedo [the station superintendent] with
> great unction made me a present of the boy. The child's name
> is Omarion. . . .[31]

And Casement took him, with another boy, back to London.

With Casement, as with Alfred Simson, Putumayo realities made a mockery of principles, suggesting that there was a good deal more to understand
about slavery and debt-peonage than what at first met and offended the liberal
eye. The debt-peonage system was deceptively transparent, and the casually
authoritative way that it was and is still today referred to by outsiders,
whether "mere" travelers or sociologically astute historians and anthropologists, helped mystify even more the network of histories, moral obligations,and coercions ensuring that, just as indebtedness ensured peonage,
so peonage ensured advances of credit.

As with the word *conquest,* the House of Commons Select Committee on
the Putumayo found it difficult to understand what was meant by debt-
peonage, although no doubt, as Mr. Charles Enock did, clear definitions
could be attempted. "It is mainly what one might call debt-bondage," he
told the Committee in response to their appeal for a definite idea of the
system of peonage in the Peruvian *montaña*—"the system of employing
natives to do work and purposely getting them into your debt by advancing
them goods so that you can retain their labour by that means." *Correrías,*
on the other hand, were "nothing but pure slave raids for the purpose of
capturing and making use of Indians—men and women."

"And when they had them subjected, or whatever the word is," broke in
the chairman of the Committee, "then they were under the system of peonage, which is a much milder system and a system legalized in Peru?"[32]

"Yes," replied Mr. Enock who was then asked to comment on a letter
read by the chairman from Consul Mitchell in Iquitos, Peru, advising the
Foreign Office as to the true meaning of those words causing it and the Select

Consul Mitchell eyeing Huitoto drums. (From Carlos Rey de Castro, *Los pobladores del Putumayo,* 1914.)

Committee so much bother: *conquistar, reducir, rescatar.* In those gracious yet stern gothic buildings overlooking the Thames (this had also been one of the dark places of the earth) the chairman read: "It must be remembered that Peru was originally 'conquered' by the Spaniards in exactly the way in which Britain was conquered by Julius Caesar, and 'reduced' by the followers of Pizarro in exactly the way the British were reduced by the Romans." That certainly sounded like Julio César Arana. But is was only a prelude, might eventually giving way to right. Continued Mr. Mitchell: "The complete subjection and the docility of the Indians has made the process of conquest and reduction more a matter of moral domination and force by forms of law, more or less strained, in places where Indians have already been subdued."[33] It was a story accounting for debt-peonage whose plot moved, in Gramscian terms, from *dominio* and *egemonia,* from the opening blast of brute force (the *correría* or slave hunt) to the succeeding phase of debt-peonage and the subculture of mutually respected obligations it assumed. Perhaps the testimony of the Barbadian Westerman Leavine (as presented by the consul-general) was useful in illustrating this process, as he had himself participated in *correrías,* as had Edward Crichlow, some of whose testimony on this matter has been cited above. Leavine had been stationed in the district of Matanzas, from where his group would go out and catch Indians, tying them up to prevent flight. Other Indians, as we have already heard from Brown and Crichlow, were shot dead, while still others died from flogging.

> When the Indians agreed to work rubber, after being caught,
> they would get things given to them, i.e., cloth etc., a shirt, a
> pair of pantaloons, a cutlass, axe, powder and shot, and per-
> haps trade guns. When the Indians had finished paying for
> these things and carried the rubber to La Chorrera, they would
> get more goods given to them.[34]

Yet the consul-general presented a quite different story about the genesis
of debt-peonage than that implied in the official dialogue going on by the
Thames about laboring conditions along the Putumayo. Casement's story
flows in a direction opposite to theirs, like a melodramatic seduction, from
a magically and instantly achieved *egemonia,* a trance of conquest, to a
succeeding stage of *dominio*—social control by brute force at the end of a
trail of betrayal. At first the rubber traders are generous and kind, and the
Indian, whom Casement advises the reader to regard as a "grown-up child,"
delights in the new goods, accepts the trader's terms of exchange and brings
him "india-rubber." But having thus swallowed the bait, the Indian to his
dismay finds the relation hardening into one of a slave to a master. In his
own (or the Foreign Office's?) words, in the introduction to the main report,
Casement states:

> The Indian, who may correctly be termed "a grown-up child,"
> was at first delighted to have a white man with attractive arti-
> cles to give away settling in his neighbourhood, and to bring in
> exchange india-rubber for these tempting trifles seemed easy.
> Moreover the Amazonian Indian is by nature docile and obedi-
> ent. His weakness of character and docility of temperament are
> no match for the dominating ability of those with European
> blood in their veins. Yielding himself, first, perhaps voluntarily,
> to the domination of these uninvited guests, he soon finds he
> has entered into relations which can only be described as those
> of a slave to a master. . . .[35]

But the Indian is not a child, grown-up or otherwise, and it is worse than
mindless to invoke such an assumption. Moreover, if it was a slave "system,"
then why did the slavemasters persist in going through the motions, ritual
or otherwise, of paying something, no matter how little or unfairly? By the
same token, doesn't it appear strange in Leavine's account how the Indians
are lured, not into slavery, but trading!

Everything in this "system" depends upon the *appearance* of trade in
which the debtor is neither slave nor wagelaborer but a trader with an iron-
clad obligation to pay back the advance. Why this fiction of trade should
exercise so much power is one of the great oddities of political economy
and to this day there has been no way of disentangling the paradox that the
rubber traders, although they strove tirelessly to create and maintain this
fictional reality, were just as ready to claim the flesh of a debtor's body. And

as often as the relation came into focus as one between traders, only to blur into enslavement, so its terminology was peculiarly prone to somersaulting. In this topsy-turvy semiosis, who was to say who was creditor and who was debtor, let alone what made a man a debtor and a debt a man?

On the Propriety of Terms and the Deforming of Good Speech

Even an Englishman could be bound by debt-peonage and become a living debt. That disturbingly simple and straightforward author, Joseph Wood-roffe, who spent, he said, eight years trying his hand at making money from rubber in the Amazon, had a deeply ironic relationship with the strange institution of debt-peonage.

In 1906 in the little settlement of Nauta, seventy miles upstream from Iquitos, he ran a store and was on good terms with the local officials. Through the kind offices of the local governor he acquired many Indians, buying them as "debts."

> In time I was enabled to strike out as an employer of labour. It came about in the following manner: The Governor, with whom I was very friendly, visited my store and inquired if I could do with two or three or even more native labourers, and upon my acquiescing, suggested a plan which would entail the sinking of all the capital at my command. It was arranged that I should give employment to any labourers who cared to work for me, in which case I would assume responsibility for their debts. When their accounts were presented to me for payment, and as is the rule with an insignificant amount placed to the credit of the labourer, I arranged that the man's account was to be submitted to the Governor for registration. The Governor ordered the man to be questioned in his presence respecting the length of time he had been working, the amount paid by him in any ordinary store for articles of clothing, provisions, etc., which composed the greater part of his debt. He was able in every case to cancel the man's debt owing to shortage of credit for work performed, and the excessive debit for purchases made by him.[36]

Obviously the "economic" was highly manipulable and dependent upon "the political."

Gathering together in this way a troop of Indians, Woodroffe left Nauta to collect rubber up the sparsely inhabited Rio Tigre. He took some fifty-eight men and fourteen women, leaving the remaining women and children to care for his store and fields. After close to a year gathering rubber by the technique standard for the *montaña* region and for these expeditions—felling each tree and extracting its sap in the one operation, thus destroying the rubber forests—he returned to find that the price of rubber on the world markets had fallen dramatically and that nobody would, even at the reduced price, pay in cash. Furthermore, the man in charge of his store had run away with all the money and goods.

Now Woodroffe was himself in debt. He had to refuse advances to his Indians. Several ran away even though their indebtedness to him was over £200. But who was in debt to who?

He found the run-away Indians months later working an isolated river for rubber with a new *patron*. They told Woodroffe that now they only recognized this *patron* as their master and creditor "and that, in so far as their indebtedness to me was concerned, I must look to my partner for payment; as they would deliver their *caucho* [rubber] to him to cover his disbursements on their account."

The total amount of their indebtedness to Woodroffe, was about £900, and the Peruvian gave him a bill of exchange to draw against on the Inquitos houses. But the bill was scorned when he presented it there. Forlorn and beaten, Woodroffe paid off those Indians who had returned with him from the Tigre and had "credit balances."

> This done, I told all those who remained in debt that they could look for a new patron to guarantee for them, and that same evening they all had arranged with a very decent young Peruvian named Rengifo to accompany him to work caucho in the higher reaches of the Purus. He came the following day to arrange with me the payment of the debt, and, having checked the statements, he made me the offer of an immediate liquidation in cash if I would agree to allow him a discount of 20 per cent on the total of each account, to which I agreed.[37]

A year later Woodroffe was again in debt. But this time he was not just in debt but in debt-peonage—to none other than Arana's Peruvian Amazon Company. He had gone to work for them as some sort of accountant in the El Encanto ("The Enchantment") station. While there he received news that his rubber from the Tigre river expedition had been finally cashed in, but at a price even lower than the lowest he had expected.

> This had the effect of placing me heavily in debt, to the extent of several hundreds of pounds sterling, and my creditors, knowing of my presence in the Putumayo with the firm of Arana, applied to the Iquitos branch for payment of my debt, a demand which was acceded to without any reference to myself, though no money changed hands, as the Iquitos traders were debtors to Arana, and the amounts were simply placed to my debit and their credit. Consequently, I personally became heavily in debt to my patrons, for an amount which would require months of patience and self-denial.
>   I was now a victim of peonage; from this day on my life was a living hell. . . .[38]

"Cleared ground and compounds at El Encanto." (From Joseph Froude Woodroffe, *The Upper Reaches of the Amazon*, 1914.)

One gets the feeling that it was not the rivers that bound the Amazon basin into a unit but these countless bonds of credit and debit wound round people like the vines of the forest around the great rubber trees themselves. But while the vines were things you could see, even when overgrown with mosses and fungi and obscured by the dark hollows of shade in the forest, the bonds of credit and debit were not all that visible. Their effects were certainly clear. You could see the scars on the bodies. But the bonds of debt-peonage? Listening to Woodroffe after a while it becomes very difficult, even impossible, to follow who is the debtor and who is the creditor.

He underwent amazing adventures one after the other as if there were nothing strange about an Englishman walking barefoot through the Amazonian forests, one moment indebting Indians to his year-long rubber expedition, another moment being an indebted peon himself, then escaping, becoming shipwrecked and then being picked up by the S.S. *Hilda* steaming upriver with Sir Roger Casement on board with a pretty and affectionate blue macaw perched on his shoulder, returning to Iquitos after writing his report in Dublin for the Foreign Office. Woodroffe presented the unfamilar as no more remarkable than a stroll through a London park, and this applied no less to his rendering of the institution of debt-peonage.

But what he was talking about was no less deceptive than the simplicity with which he rendered it. He was the speaking subject determined by signifiers, no longer the transcendental producer of them, no longer able to alienate them as strangely normal.

"Power-knowledge relations" are to be analyzed, writes Michel Foucault,

> not on the basis of a subject of knowledge who is or is not free in relation to the power system, but, on the contrary, the subject who knows, the objects to be known and the modalities of knowledge must be regarded as so many effects of these fundamental implications of power-knowledge and their historical transformations. In short, it is not the activity of the subject of knowledge that produces a corpus of knowledge, useful or resistant to power, but power-knowledge, the processes and struggles that traverse it and of which it is made up, that determines the forms and possible domains of knowledge.[39]

In contrast to the debt-peoned English rubber trader, the Colombian traveler Joaquin Rocha did dwell on the switch-about in meanings and on the rampant confusion constituting debt-peonage. Something like amazement guided his pen. He thought the lists of Indian "debtors" sold between rubber traders gave a far more reliable figure of the Huitoto population than what he called "the wild estimates of geographers," but, he went on in perplexity,

> we have spoken here incidentally of the selling of debts of the Indians, and in expressing ourselves thereby we thus respect the propriety of the terms. But in the language of the Caquetá this propriety is not observed. There they talk of the selling of Indians or, if talking of white workers, of the selling of peons, as if they were slaves.[40]

To his perplexity was added horror, he said, when he heard that the manager of the Guepi rubber agency had gone downriver to the Caraparaná to *sell* his peons, and that a young friend of his, who had gone to Iquitos as an employee of a rubber firm, had been sold by this firm to another. "It was neither the peons nor my friend that were sold, but the value of their debts; it is sad how they thus err in the Caquetá and in this deplorable manner deform good speech."[41]

Was it perhaps the historic occasion for a new language, another manifestation of Amazonian multilingualism but this time created by the transposition of nonmarket principles of economics into the discourse of creditors and debtors within the capitalist system of signifying?

It was with savage irony that Karl Marx derided the language of the capitalist market, where value and the generation of profit were encased not only in the shrine of the free wage-labor contract with capital, but also in the discourse of "commodity fetishism," a discourse that, as it drained life from human beings, engaged in the production and exchange of commodities, so it endowed those commodities with a spiritual life force, mystifying, if not dominating their creators. It was a diabolically mischievous language, in which signifiers became signifieds. In the debt-peonage system, as befits a system built around the fiction of traders and not commodities, it is the debt and not the commodity that is fetishized—so that in answer to the question, What makes a man a man?, the answer lying closest to hand is his debt. And if one asks, What is a debt? in a situation in which goods called advances or even gifts are forced onto unwilling recipients, the answer is a man, or, failing that, an Indian or a peon. As commodity fetishism was to the discourse of the political economists of Marx's England and France and to the folklore of capitalism there in the heartlands of empires, so we might say "debt fetishism" was to the discourse of the colonizers and the colonized of the Putumayo rubber boom.

The deformation of good speech is further evident in Casement's report, where the terms "payment" and "advance" not so much lose as compromise their propriety, so that "payments" are called "advances," and the Indians had no option but to accept a "payment," meaning an "advance."

> Payments for rubber were not made at a 'puesta' but only on completion of a 'fabrico' [usually every three or four months] and these payments were termed advances, i.e., advances for the next 'fabrico.' The principle here is that the Indian having accepted an advance must work it off. He is a 'debtor'; on the Putumayo a compulsory debtor, for he could not evade the next 'fabrico' by rejecting the advance.[42]

Accounts were meant to be kept for each Indian debtor (i.e., "debtor") and of the payment (i.e., advance) made to that Indian. At one point while it was wading through the morass of confusing "facts," the House of Commons Select Committee calculated that in 1910 each Indian rubber gatherer got goods the equivalent of five British pence for every pound of rubber which then fetched nine times as much on the London market. (In West Africa, so the Committee was informed by Edmund Morel, natives were being paid five to six times as much as the Huitotos per pound of "Ibi Red Niggers" rubber, a type equal in quality to the "india-rubber" of the Putumayo.) But Casement saw no sign of accounts during his visit to the Putumayo, although the pathetic-sounding Henry Parr, who worked as a bookkeeper in the outlying rubber stations for three years (1910–12), informed the Committee that each Indian had a separate account, although there was no fixed rate of payment (meaning advancement).[43]

Casement found that the storehouses meant to contain the goods constituting "advances" were generally empty of "almost all save of very few things the white employees might need for their personal wants." Sometimes a station manager would give ("advance" or "pay") a very inferior type of shotgun for thirty-five kilograms of rubber, other times for seventy-five kilos. The Barbadian Frederick Bishop said he had seen payments where a single coin, the Peruvian *sol* (meaning "sun") or a British florin, was exchanged for seventy or eighty kilos of rubber. Casement met numbers of Indian women wearing necklaces of these coins. Joaquin Rocha wrote that the Indians of the Tres Esquinas rubber station valued coins not as a means of exchange but as precious objects-in-themselves—or *almost*-so-in-themselves, because first they had to work them over, not being content with their form in the white economy. They would beat the coins into smooth, shiny triangles to wear as nose rings or as ear pendants.

Yet who could assert that the Indians lacked interest in the terms of trade or that their vision was not enlarged by what the whites got for rubber in the outside world? "You buy these with the rubber we produce," said an Indian chief, like one entranced, while looking through Casement's binoculars.[44]

"Of course, you cannot tell us how the cost of goods to the Indians would appear in the company's accounts—you did not happen to see that?" the chairman of the Select Committee was asking Sir Roger Casement.

"I could not tell you that," he replied. "The so-called payment to the Indians never, so far as I could see, took place openly. I could not definitely at any time find what an Indian got. I asked when I was up in the sections in the forest, and I was told that was a question that could only be answered in La Chorrera, at the headquarters; and if I asked in La Chorrera, I was told that the payment was always made in the sections. . . ."

Then Mr. Swift MacNeill spoke up: "I take it the general system was by hook or by crook to get the Indians into debt and keep them there?"

"Yes," replied Casement. He then showed the Committee some of the things he had bought in the company store at La Chorrera, a gun, for example, for which he paid forty-five shillings, allegedly cost the company twenty-nine, and for which an Indian would be charged around about 100 kilos of rubber, worth roughly (because the price of rubber fluctuated so much) £16 or £17. Going back and forth over the factors affecting trade equivalents and prices, in reply to a question put by Lord Alexander Thynne, Casement concluded: "It was that system I declined to accept as commerce apart altogether from questions of ill-treatment, because the Indian was not a free agent, and I do not think he would voluntarily and willingly have worked for this trash except under compulsion."

"The hold on him was, was it, that he was supposed to be in debt to the company?" asked the chairman.

"No," replied Casement. "That would relate to the more civilized regions. The hold on the Indian in the Putumayo was that he could not escape. It was a pretext altogether that he was in debt."[45]

As regards this pretext, Father Gridilla related an episode of interest when he traveled up the Caraparaná in 1912, two years after Casement had first been there and at a time when Arana's power was well consolidated. It was the occasion when thousands of Indians came to the rubber station of La

Pith-helmeted Consul Mitchell surrounded by dancing Indians (Occidente rubber station). (From Carlos Rey de Castro, *Los pobladores del Putumayo*, 1914.)

Occidente to deliver rubber. First there was a great dance lasting five days (the sort of event Joaquin Rocha a decade earlier likened to a harvest festival, when he, at a time before Arana had consolidated his dominion, witnessed the ceremonial delivery of rubber by Indians to their Colombian *patrón*). Then the rubber was handed over and goods were advanced, Father Gridilla commenting that "the savages don't know money, their needs are very limited, and they ask only for shotguns, ammunition, axes, machetes, mirrors, and occasionally hammocks." An Indian he described as a corpulent and ugly savage declined to accept anything. On being pressed he replied, "I don't want anything. I've got everything."

The whites insisted again that he must ask for something. Finally he retorted, "I want a black dog!"

"And where am I going to find a black dog or even a white one if there aren't any in all of Putumayo?" asked the rubber station manager.

"You ask me for rubber," replied the savage, "and I bring rubber. If I ask for a black dog you have to give me one."[46]

"The Indian took his advance and made off—glad to escape," Casement had written two years earlier,[47] while Hardenburg wrote that the Indians received their advances with great pleasure, because if they did not, they were flogged to death[48]—all of which casts light on Captain Whiffen's finding that in 1908 there were tribes of Indians on the northern margins of Arana's territory who hated and mistrusted whites and would not receive presents from them.[49]

Pretext as it was, the "debt" that ensured peonage was nonetheless real, and as a pretense its magical realism was essential not only to the labor organization of the Putumayo rubber boom, but to its terror as well. To understand how these fictional realities killed and maimed so many thousands of Indians we need now to turn to some of their more obviously mythic features, enclosed as they are in the synergistic relation of savagery and business, cannibalism and capitalism. Interrogated by the British parliamentary Select Committee on Putumayo in 1913, Julio César Arana, said to be the "soul and creator" of the rubber company, was asked to clarify what he meant when he stated that the Indians had resisted the establishment of civilization in their districts, that they had been resisting for many years, and had practiced cannibalism.

"What I meant by that," he replied, "is that they did not admit of exchange, or anybody to do business with them—whites, for example."[50]

FOUR

Jungle and Savagery

Asked by the Select Committee on Putumayo what he himself saw of actual cruelties to Indians, Walter Hardenburg replied: "Of actual crimes being committed I did not see anything, practically; all I saw was that the Indians in [the rubber station of] El Encanto were nearly naked and very thin and cadaverous-looking; I saw several scores of them, and I saw what they were being fed on.[1]

His information consisted generally of an incident as related by another person. "In fact, I think I might say that most of the people came through others. They would say, 'I know another man who could state this and that,' and they would bring them."

"In addition to the sworn statements in your book," asked the Committee, "did you question the people in detail about a good many of their statements?"

"I cannot say I did much of that," replied Hardenburg. It was, he said, "common knowledge" and "common talk" in the streets of Iquitos that terrible things were going on up there along the Putumayo.[2]

Faced with the unbelievable nature of this common talk and common knowledge, it might have been wise for Hardenburg to question the people in detail about a good

74

many of their statements. But Hardenburg was no fool; perhaps there were reasons why he didn't. In any event what we are given are stories, vignettes, depictions, rumors—in sum, webworks and fragments of narratives woven around, permeated by, and chiseled into mythic ones. Casement's stories were far more numerous than Hardenburg's and seemed better substantiated. Certainly they were put down on paper in a steady dripping of fact after chilling fact, unlike the melodramatic mode frantically worked by Hardenburg. But despite *and* because of its studied facticity, Casement's Foreign Office report served not so much to puncture the mythic character of the situation as to render its terrific reality.

The meticulous historian might seize upon the stories and fragments of stories, such as they are, to winnow out truth from distortion, reality from illusion, fact from myth. A whole field opens out here for tabulating, typologizing, and cross-checking, but what "truth" is it that is assumed and reproduced by such procedures? Surely it is a truth that begs the question raised by history, in this case the history of terror and atrocity in the Putumayo rubber boom wherein the intimate codependence of truth on illusion and myth on reality was what the metabolism of power, let alone "truth," was all about. To cross-check truth in this field is necessary and necessarily Sisyphean, ratifying an illusory objectivity, a power-prone objectivity which in authorizing the split between truth and fiction secures power's fabulous reach. Alternatively we can listen to these stories neither as fiction nor as disguised signs of truth, but as real.

Two interlacing motifs stand out in these stories: horror of the jungle and horror of savagery. Truth here lay as if contrived in accord with Conrad's theory of art (as formulated in *The Nigger of the Narcissus*) with the appeal to the imagination aroused by the sense impressions evoked by the story-teller. Here the image of stark opposition and of otherness in the primeval jungle comes forth as the colonially intensified metaphor for the great space of terror and cruelty, and we think here of Europe of the late nineteenth century, working its way in the ancient forests of the tropics. Carlos Fuentes says that Latin American literature is woven between the poles formed by Nature and the Dictator, such that the brutal destructiveness imputed to the natural world serves to embody even more destructive relations in human society. A renowned Colombian author, José Eustasio Rivera, illustrated this embodiment when he wrote in the 1920s as a debt-trapped white peon in the Putumayo:

> I have been a *cauchero* [rubber gatherer] and I will always be a *cauchero*. I live in the slimy mire in the solitude of the forests with my gang of malarial men, piercing the bark of trees whose blood runs white, like that of gods. . . . I have been and always will be a *cauchero*. And what my hand inflicts on the trees, it can also inflict on men.[3]

Some twenty years earlier the same sadomasochistic appeal to a violent struggle between good and evil in the dark despair of the jungle was made by another Colombian, Joaquin Rocha, when he descended the Andes to the hotlands of the Caquetá and the Putumayo. He was carried on the back of a man, a white man named Miguel Velasco who had come to the region with the quinine boom and been stranded when the price of quinine fell, leaving him a sort of lordship over the Indians through his being appointed magistrate of the mountain villages of Santa Rosa and Descanse. He shuffled slowly forward at the pace of a bullock, wrote Rocha, who was carried astride Velasco's back as the two descended the mountains. It was his steed's "amiable obsequiousness" that caught Rocha's attention; a man elevated by race and state authority above the local populace, and Rocha elevated by him.

Poised on the brink of the mountains overlooking the jungle below, Rocha's thoughts fixed on gold, the washing of rubies, and then to the way that, in the breast of this craggy solitude (the figures of speech come from his pen), the fates had secreted unfathomable treasure. From the imagining of treasure hidden in the bosom of the wilderness he was led ineluctably to the image of treasure buried in hell—and of the lonely descent a man makes into the underworld for it. And we who come after him see this as figurative speech, this moralized, sexualized Dantean topography of going down and into the bosom of solitude, treasure, and wildness. We can see the self-satisfied male buttressing in this mock-surreal colonial picture, one man astride another, wending their way down into the murk. "The silence hangs heavy," he wrote,

> broken only by the clanging clamor of the torrents, the growl-
> ing of tigers, and the swarming of infinite vipers and venomous
> insects. In [the mountain village of] Descanse begins the plague
> of vampire bats that extends until Brazil, treacherously sucking
> in the hours of dreams the blood of men and animals. There
> also, by the side of the *Brossymum galactodendron* whose
> trunk when incised yields milk as delicious and nutritive as the
> cow's, grows the *Rhus juglande folia* whose mere shade puffs
> up and scars the careless wanderer. There one begins to suffer
> the privations and calamities of the wilderness, that in the Ca-
> quetá and the Putumayo grow so as to at times make of life
> there scenes whose horror could figure in the Dantean pages of
> Purgatory and Hell.[4]

The savagery of the forest is contagious.

> The wilderness of the Territory of the Caquetá, similar to the
> goddess Kali of the Hindus, displays at one and the same time
> the grandeur of its beauty and its murderous treacherous po-
> tency. There the person in perpetual contact with this savage
> wilderness becomes just as savage. Far from moral and social

sanctions, humanity succumbs to the empire of the passions
which in their overflowing are no less formidable than those of
death and extermination.[5]

Like a sponge the succulent jungle absorbs and magnifies human passion.
"And what my hand inflicts on the trees," Rivera came to write, "it can
also inflict on man." But between the world of man and that of the steaming
jungle there is a powerful mediator—the jaguar that was also a man, an
Indian man and a witch. Not only the Indians but many of the whites hold
this to be true, noted Joaquin Rocha, and these are not just the ignorant
whites but also those who have traveled, have come to know the world and
have some education. The soul of the Indian witch passes into the body of
a jaguar. They call that jaguar a *tigre mojano.* This jaguar differs from the
real animal in that the real one, as is well known, emphasizes Rocha, "only
attacks weak and unarmed people when the odds are in its favor, when it
can use treachery, or when it is persecuted and harrassed by hunters."[6] The
tigre mojano, the jaguar that is possessed by the spirit of the Indian witch,
however, is very different, for this will attack humans without provocation,
against all odds.

It can be a startling thing, this *tigre mogano,* and just as it mediates
between the domain of the forest and that of wild humanity so as to magnify
the mystery of both, so it emphasizes the doubleness and quintessentially
hybrid nature of the forest people, their treachery and timidity on one side
and their boundlessly open aggressiveness, mystically empowered, on the
other. Some colonists have told me that this jaguar can be identified because
it has the testicles of a man. It cannot be killed.

Yet it was not as an Indian but as a *white* peon, working for Arana, that
Rivera's narrator in *The Vortex* warned: "What my hand inflicts on the trees,
it can also inflict on man." And it was Joaquin Rocha's opinion, in 1903,
just before Arana's thugs cleaned out the small-scale independent Colombian
rubber traders along the Igaraparaná and Caraparaná, that although localized
Indian rebellions against one or the other rubber trader were a frightening
possibility, the greatest threat to the lives of the whites lay with themselves.

He described several such assassinations triggered by disputes over money
and rubber. It seemed to him that the basic cause was the atmosphere of
brooding suspicion that hung as heavily over human affairs as did the jungle
itself.[7] In Rivera's *Vortex,* the monstrous fears and uncanniness evoked by
the jungle are as nothing compared to the reality of Arana's rubber camps.
Yet it is always the colonial view of the jungle that provides the means for
representing and trying to make sense of the colonial situation. Emptiness
and absence become assailing presences. The nebulous becomes corporeal
and tangible. And in this dreadful object-making, as shadows of things acquire substance, a veil of lifelessness, if not of death, is drawn apart to reveal
the forest not merely as animated but as human.

"The air," wrote Captain Whiffen, "is heavy with the fumes of fallen vegetation slowly steaming to decay." The silence and stillness made one feel
that nothing lived there, that silence and stillness were themselves objects,
and that the very bush was not merely human but "a horrible, a most evil-
disposed enemy." These "High Woods" were "innately malevolent"—"in
truth there is nothing in nature more cruel than the unconquered vegetation
of a tropical South American forest. The Amazonian forest brings no con-
solation. It is silent, inhospitable, cynical." It was a simple but eventful feat,
he wrote, to pass from one's canoe to part the bushes and pass beyond,
"into the obscurity of barbarism."[8]

But it was not just cruelty. It was something more specifically vague, a
miasmic subspecies of terror, the pressing in of somethingness in the nothingness. Whiffen goes on:

> The eternal sludge, sludge of travel without a stone or honest
> yard of solid ground makes one long for the lesser strain of
> more definite dangers or of more obtrusive horrors. The horror
> of Amazonian travel is the horror of the unseen. It is not the
> presence of unfriendly natives that wears one down, it is the
> absence of all signs of human life. One happens upon an Indian
> house or settlement, but it is deserted, empty, in ruins. The na-
> tives have vanished, and it is only the silent message of a poi-
> soned arrow or a leaf-roofed pitfall that tells of their existence
> somewhere in the tangled undergrowth of the neighbourhood.[9]

It is not the presence of unfriendly natives that wears one down. It is the
presence of their absence, their presence in their absence.

But something else is absent, too: Arana's rubber company. Perhaps the
decenteredness of the sludge without an honest yard of solid ground and
this miasmic cruelty slowly steaming to decay, emptiness, absence, ruin . . .
this positively absent presence is the absence of the rubber company, their
presence in their absence? In which case not only the jungle but the Indians
themselves would bear the burden of being the figures that represented the
rubber company, barely a glimpse of which appears in the entirety of Whiffen's lengthy description of the Putumayo at a time when the company was
extremely active in the region. And when he does on a few occasions mention
the existence of the company, it is in a measuredly neutral tone, as if the
company were a fact of nature beyond all anthropomorphism, tropes, and
imaginative figuration, a thing-in-itself, gray, shut off from fancy, yet really
very big. It was from the company that the captain got his armed bodyguards.
It is into nature, on the other hand, that fancy pours; into the forest and
into the Indians—not things-in-themselves but things-for-us. And who can
say even now, eighty years after Whiffen's studies, that anthropology has
been able to cease creating such things-for-us so that other things can stay
in the grayness of in-themselves? But then the captain was not really a trained
anthropologist—just an amateur and a military man.

And he went on to recommend that the number of persons making up a party pushing through the forest be no more than twenty-five because of the way that the forest impeded movement. "On this principle," he noted, "it will be seen that the smaller the quantity of baggage carried the greater will be the number of rifles available for the security of the expedition."[10]

"It's an unfinished country. It's still prehistorical," intones the voice of the German filmmaker Werner Herzog in *Burden of Dreams,* the film of his filming *Fitzcarraldo* in the *montaña* west of Iquitos. There is a curse on the landscape and he feels cursed with what he is doing there. It is a land that God, if he exists, created in anger and where creation is unfinished and therefore tensed in untoward patterns of opposites, harmony and chaos, hate and love.

> There is some kind of harmony. It is the harmony of over-whelming and collective murder. And we in comparison to the articulate vileness and baseness and obscenity of all this jungle. . . . We in comparison to that enormous articulation, we only sound and look like badly pronounced and half-finished sentences out of a stupid suburban novel, a cheap novel. . . .
>
> And we have to become humble in front of this overwhelming misery and overwhelming fornication, overwhelming growth and overwhelming lack of order. Even the . . . stars up here in the sky look like a mess. There is no harmony in the universe. We have to get acquainted to this idea that there is no real harmony as we have conceived it. But when I say this, I say this all full of admiration for the jungle. It is not that I hate it. I love it. I love it very much. But I love it against my better judgment.[11]

Earlier Herzog speaks of what he saw in the jungle: "fornication and asphyxiation and choking and fighting for survival and growing and just rotting away. . . ." Misery everywhere. "The trees here are in misery and the birds are in misery. I don't think they sing, they just screech in pain. . . ."[12] A symphony of birds known as *wistwinchis,* insects, and frogs fills the screaming screen around what in the script are called "images of nature" consisting of a dead parrot, an ant carrying a feather, colorful insects, a red flower, and a green treefrog. It is a nature conceived as pitting extremes of meaning, a deconstructing tropicality that implodes oppositions in the profusion of their rank decay and proliferating disordered growth. The center is man and the center ceases to exist. What takes its place is dread, from which the word no less than the image arises and to which each returns.

Eighty years before Herzog, the Englishman Captain Whiffen wrote at some length about dread in its aspect of being abandoned and lost in the jungle. Desertion by one's Indian carriers was common, even when they forsook their pay and probably, he added, their lives as well. "In a watch of the night they depart," he said, "and although the country be swarming

with their blood-enemies, they vanish into the forest and are no more seen."
But even if they didn't desert there came a time when one wished they
would—"nauseated by their bestiality." One wanders away. One is lost. And
being lost from oneself, it would appear, is the worst of all. Then one panics.
The silence, he says, casts one back on oneself. Perhaps, however, there is
no such self. "He recovers his perspective, replaces the comrades of his
bush-life in their proper places—the glass-fronted cupboards of an anthropological museum. His self-respect regained, he pauses to admire his new-
found horizon."[13]

But to Casement the crucially important aesthetic-political principle was
the sensation of alienated memory clinging to the Indians, separating them
decisively as creatures of beauty and capable of great artistry from the dark
despair of the forest. They were creatures in the wild, not of it: "While
Nature in her garb of lofty trees was gloomy, overclothed and silent, the
Indian was laughing, naked, and ready to sing and dance on the slightest
provocation."[14] They were like the spirit in W. H. Hudson's *Green Man-
sions*. They were wild, but unlike the forest their wildness was ethereal. The
violent harshness of the materiality of the jungle provided the contrasting
backdrop to the spritelike delicacy with which they played with the bars of
their forest prison:

> While there was no way out of the forest for the body, turn his
> eyes where he might, he found a way out for his mind. While
> he lived in shadow mostly, he delighted in brightness, and even
> in beautiful things. His naked limbs he stained with vivid hues,
> and he rejoiced in the gloriously beautiful feathers of the forest
> birds, and decorated himself with these. To his dances he
> brought a graceful frond of some plant plucked by the track as
> he came to the meeting-place, and in the movements of the
> dance these varied staves of delicate leaves were waved in obe-
> dience to the movement of his limbs that themselves obeyed
> some carefully-remembered cult of motion he had not picked
> up by the wayside.[15]

Another Englishman by the name of Marlow, a sailor and ex-captain of a
Congolese river steamer, sits back introducing his yarn of pushing that boat
into the land of wild men. And behind him swirling in the tide's race runs
not merely the Thames, once one of the dark places of the earth, too, but
the narrator's narrator, like a Putumayo shaman in some respects, drawing
out the hallucinatory reality of the colonial vision, now fascinated by its
fascination, trying to exorcize its spell with the play of oppositions, fascination and abomination. He finds this in the image of the soldier (like Captain
Whiffen) of imperial Rome wading through the marshes of the Thames (the
eternal sludge without a stone or honest yard of solid ground) marching into
the high woods

and in some inland post feel the savagery, had closed around
him—all that mysterious life of the wilderness that stirs in the
forest, in the jungles, in the hearts of wild men. There's no initiation either into such mysteries. He has to live in the midst of
the incomprehensible, which is also detestable. And it has a
fascination, too, that goes to work upon him. The fascination
of the abomination—you know, imagine the growing regrets,
the longing to escape, the powerless disgust, the surrender, the
hate.[16]

And there in the obscurity of the pitch darkness of the vast communal
house of the Indians rushed the frenzied figure of the medicine man. Never
had Captain Whiffen seen a person so excited. Stuffing coca leaves into his
mouth he stooped over the woman stricken with fever. Placing his lips to
hers he sucked, exorcizing the evil spirit, dispelling it into the forest. Next
morning she was well. Fascinated by the abomination, the captain went on
to write, almost as an afterthought, perhaps in belated self-consciousness,
that "faith in the healing power of the medicine-man is not confined to the
tribesman."[17]

And when Father Gaspar de Pinell made the first of his glorious apostolic
excursions in the 1920s down the Andes from Sibundoy into the forests of
the Putumayo, exorcizing with the spells of Pope Leo XII the demon who
had for so long dwelt there, he too found that even among his band there
was alive a faith in the healing power of the Indian medicine man. It was
his guide, no less—a white by the name of Plinio Montenegro, well accustomed to those torrid forests, who when he sickened spurned the expedition's
pharmacy and sought out an Indian healer. Such healers have different names.
Anthropologists often call them shamans. Father Gaspar said it was a witch,
an act of naming that a little later must have seemed inspired when the guide
died, providing Father Gaspar with an opportunity to expound upon the
moral dilemma of colonization. "This shows," he wrote, as if chiseling an
epitaph,

it is more likely that the civilized man will become a savage on
mixing with the Indians than the Indians are likely to be civilized through the actions of the civilized.[18]

It was the Baroque stage all over again, like the conquest. Twentieth-
century *La vida es sueño*. Play and replay of the savagery within civilization
wherein everything was allegorical, each falling leaf a token to dark passions,
the Fall, the Resurrection, alone in those infernal crypts of the lugubrious
forest with its rotting undergrowth.

That's how Father Pinell portrayed it, a godsend ceaselessly reproducing
the malevolence necessitated by Christianity. But it was touch and go which
aspect would finally triumph. It had to be, otherwise it would be unreal.
The jungle had a magical attraction. It was a vortex, he wrote, that consumed

the person not born in it. There was sorcery at work by which the senses
of the body and the powers of the soul are so affected by the sadness and
the beauty of the forest that the pain it causes is soon forgotten. Suffering
is transcended by its own beauty and strength. The jungle is the sorcerer.
"It is here that death comes smiling and people die without realizing that
they are dying," concluded the good Father.[19]

On a more mundane level, he noted something of this very sorcery penetrating his own self, working its way in through the chink in his Christian
armor opened by disease. Because he had been drenched on the trail leading
to a camp of runaway Huitotos, savages all, rheumatism flared acutely in
his left arm. The Indians advised him to apply the claw of an iguana and
gave him one to try out. It was spectacularly successful.[20]

Joaquin Rocha had his story to tell of civilization seduced by the sorcery
of savagery, too. Not only had the Huitotos persisted with cannibalism despite the presence of the rubber traders, but there were whites, Christian
and civilized, who had partaken of human flesh also. He cited the story of
such a man, "syndicated with Huitoto cannibalism," who hailed from the
province of Tolima and had been arrested by the prefect in Mocoa in 1882.
But as he had not actually killed anyone, only eaten human flesh when invited
by the Huitotos, and as cannibalism was not a crime according to Colombian
statutes, the prefect set the Christian cannibal free.[21]

With a torrent of phenomenological virtuosity, Father Gaspar's Capuchin
colleague, Francisco de Vilanova, addressed the same vexing problem. In
a book devoted to Capuchin endeavors with the Huitotos from the 1920s
on, he wrote:

> It is almost unbelievable to those who are unacquainted with
> it, yet the jungle is an irrational fact, enslaving those who go
> into it—a whirlwind of savage passions conquering the civilized
> person possessed with too much self-confidence. The jungle is
> a degeneration of the human spirit in a swoon of improbable
> but real circumstances. The rational civilized man loses self-
> respect and respect for his home. He throws his heritage into
> the mire from where who knows when it will be retrieved.
> One's heart becomes morbid, filling with the sentiment of sav-
> agery, insensible to the pure and great things of humanity.
> Even cultivated spirits, finely formed and well-educated, have
> succumbed.[22]

But of course it is not the jungle but the sentiments colonizing men project
onto it that are decisive in filling their hearts with savagery. And what the
jungle can accomplish, so much more can its native inhabitants, the wild
Indians who had been tortured and scared into gathering rubber. It must not
be overlooked that the colonially construed image of the wild Indian was a
powerfully ambiguous image, a seesawing, bifocalized and hazy composite
of the animal and the human—like Nietzche's satyr in *The Birth of Tragedy*.

In their human or humanlike form, the wild Indians could all the better reflect back to the colonists vast and baroque projections of *human* wildness. And it was only because the wild Indians were human that they were able to serve as labor—*and* as subjects of torture; for it is not the victim as animal that gratifies the torturer, but the fact that the victim is human, thus enabling the torturer to become the savage.

Which raises a question.

How Savage Are the Huitotos?

> The Indian had been travelling with two others along the Arara river when the Huitotos surprised them and took them prisoner. One of his companions was tied hand and foot to a tree and then killed with a poisoned dart. During the torture the poor man cried like a child. "Why are you killing me?" he asked. "We want to eat you because yours have eaten ours," came the reply. They passed a stake through the tied hands and feet and carried the body to the beach as if it were a peccary. The chief then distributed the meat and sent some chunks to neighbouring tribes. The spectator to the horrible scene managed to escape during the night and floated downstream on a tree he had felled with a stone axe. The third prisoner was the young man whom the Huitotos wanted to sell. What would be his fate? It's more than likely that they split his skull. [Dr. Jules Crévaux writing about his journey to the Putumayo region in 1879. This was published in Paris in 1880–81 in *Le Tour du Monde*. One year later Crévaux was killed by Toba Indians of the Gran Chaco plain, south of the Amazon basin.]

The savagery of the wild Indians was important to the propaganda of the rubber company. The Huitotos "are hospitable to a marked degree," wrote Hardenburg, and while the Church improves their morals, since the time that the company has monopolized the region, priests have been carefully excluded. "Indeed," he continued, "in order to frighten people and thus prevent them from entering the region, the company has circulated the most blood curdling reports of the ferocity and cannibalism of these helpless Indians, whom other travellers as well as Perkins and myself have found to be timid, peaceful, mild, industrious, and humble.[23]

Father Pinnell published a document from Peru describing a film commissioned by Arana's company in 1917. Shown in the cinemas in Lima, it portrayed the civilizing effects of the company "on these savage regions that as recent as 25 years ago were peopled entirely by cannibals. Owing to the energy of this tireless struggler [Arana] they have been converted into useful elements of labor."[24]

One wonders why, if the company "monopolized the region," it had to bother waging war on the propaganda front; why this zeal to label the savages as savage? Casement found that "from the first to last I met no authority of the Peruvian government, and could appeal for no assistance in my mission save to the agents of the Peruvian Amazon Company, who were in absolute control not only of the persons and lives of the surrounding Indians, but of all means of transport and, it might be said, of ingress to or egress from that region." Every manager of a section, he wrote, was a law unto himself.[25] Again the question asserts itself. Given such absoluteness of control, why the need for propaganda?

Hardenburg derided as propaganda the notion that the Indians were cannibals. Yet the U.S. consul in Iquitos, Charles Eberhardt, had informed his government that "cannibalism is practised among certain tribes of the Putumayo River district, who not only enjoy the flavor of human flesh well prepared, but also believe that they assume the strength both physical and intellectual of their victims." This was read to Hardenburg by Raymond Asquith as part of the inquiry of the Select Committee.

"You yourself came across, I think, some instances of belief in cannibalism, did you not?"

"I do not recall it now," answered Hardenburg.

"I was looking at your book," went on Mr. Asquith, "and I see on page 73 you refer to a youth whom you tried to employ and who refused to go with you because people had told him stories about cannibalism?"

"That is correct."

"So there were stories of that kind going about?"

"Yes."

"And they were believed?"

"Yes, but at the same time we were told by better informed people that there was no such thing or we would not have gone down there. It seems to have occurred only among the ignorant people."

"Still, Consul Eberhardt was not an ignorant person?"

"Oh, no."

And Asquith went on to ask him about the rifle he carried in the Putumayo. He was glad he had the weapon, Hardenburg agreed, but looking back he thought he would have got on all right without one.

"But you felt much more comfortable with it, did you not?" pressed Asquith.

"Well, I suppose I might say so," replied Hardenburg.

Mr. Malcolm saw a connection and broke in (for rather than cannibals, might there not have been a more real wildness against which the gun provided comfort?). "Because of wild animals, or what?" he shot at Hardenburg.

"No, I wanted it more to shoot game with."

Mr. Asquith resumed his questioning.

"I see on page 113 of your book you say this: 'While I busied myself preparing dinner Perkins went to work cleaning up our rifles . . . for we had heard the most bloodcurdling tales of the ferocity of the jaguars and tigers, so common in this region?' ''

"That is true," answered Hardenburg.

"You had heard these tales?"

"We had heard that from similar sources as we had heard about the cannibals."

A few more words were passed and Asquith asked, "At the same time you believed the stories sufficiently well to be glad of having a rifle?"

"Yes, I think I might say that" said Hardenburg.[26]

Propaganda flowers where the soil has been well prepared, and surely Arana's was no exception. The profuse mythology concerning Indian savagery dated from epochs long before his (and is likely to continue for many more), and insofar as the rubber company, in Hardenburg's words, circulated "the most blood curdling reports of the ferocity and cannibalism of these [to Hardenburg] helpless Indians," those reports fell on ears finely tuned by the style and imagination with which colonizing folklore had long depicted the forest.

Who was immune? And is it not the case that people can hold alternative views simultaneously as well as being skeptical and credulous in quick succession? The interchange between Asquith and Hardenburg shows that no matter how much Hardenburg strove to establish a single reality, straight, simple, monochrome, and flat, what emerged was equivocation, possibility, shadow, and murk—like the light filtering through the forest itself, dappled on thorn and mud. And even though Hardenburg fumed that the rumors of savagery were baseless and emanated from Arana's churning propaganda mill, he was not averse to lending his ear to the grains of truth that possibly, just possibly, lay therein. But the use to which he put his pen lay elsewhere: in the task of simply inverting the propaganda of savagery with its counter-imagery of the Indian as helpless, timid, and generous.

Grown-up Children

This was of course no less a time-honored and patronizing mythology than the view it contested. Indeed, the two views were tenaciously linked and covertly complicit, the one feeding off the other. Mr. Enock put his finger on the mediating principle; it was the child in the savage. In the introduction he wrote for Hardenburg's book, with the weight of an authority earned by many years' residence as an engineer in Peru, he informed the reader that the "Indians of South America are in reality grown-up children with the qualities of such, but the Spaniards and the Portuguese have recognized in these traits nothing more than what they term 'animal' qualities."[27]

The children come naked and unadorned, as befits the bare fact, while the "animal" comes with little fig leaves of quotations marks, as befits a fiction masquerading as a fact.

But it was Casement who most fully developed the grown-up child. Time and again he declared that the Huitoto and all upper-Amazon Indians were gentle and docile. He brushed aside allegations about cannibalism, stated that the Indians were not so much cruel as thoughtless, and regarded what he termed their docility to be a natural and remarkable characteristic. This helped him explain the ease with which the Indians were conquered and forced to gather rubber. It helped him explain that otherwise magical-seeming moment of seduction of Indians by whites creating that instantly achieved *egemonia,* that fleeting moment of a Golden Age of trusting children at a first meeting before things go wrong and the allure of white commodities pales.

> An Indian would promise anything for a gun, or for some of the other tempting things offered as inducements to help him work rubber. Many Indians submitted to the alluring offer only to find that once in the conquistadores' books they had lost all liberty, and were reduced to unending demands for more rubber and varied tasks. A cacique or 'capitan' might be bought over to dispose of the labour of his clan, and as the cacique's influence was very great and the natural docility of the Indian a remarkable characteristic of Upper Amazon tribes, the work of conquering a primitive people and reducing them to a continual strain of rubber-finding was less difficult than might at first be supposed.[28]

Yet does not such natural docility make the violence of the whites even harder to understand?

Many other points can be questioned in Casement's account here, especially the deceptive simplicity he evokes in evaluating toughness and tenderness in a society so foreign to his own. It was in areas such as these, evaluating intangible qualities of character for people whose distinctive "otherness" lay every bit as much in colonial make-believe as "in-themselves," that the mythic quality of Casement's ethnographic realism was most apparent—the story of innocent and gentle children brutalized by colonialism. In addition, he displayed a tendency to equate the sufferings of the Irish with those of these Indians, seeing in both of their pre-imperialist histories a culture more humane than that of their civilizing overlords. There was also Casement's innate tenderness and his ability to draw that quality out of others, as testified by numerous people. It is this aspect of his homosexuality and not sexual lust that should be considered here, as shown, for example, in the fragmented impressionism of his diary entry written upriver at the rubber station of La Occidente:

> SEPTEMBER 30th. Another long talk with Tizon, he admits practically everything, the dance stopped only at 5 a.m. I was up in night from 2.30 to a glorious sunrise. Bishop told me that Fran-

cisco, the 'Capitan' of one of the 'Racion' and another had
come to him in the night complaining of recent grave ill-treatment here. One of them having been drowned by Acosta in the
river, the new method of torture being to hold them under
water while they wash the rubber, to terrify them! Also floggings and putting in guns and flogging with machetes across the
back. Told Barnes and Bell and they interrogated Francisco
and then I told Tizon at 1.30 when he came to talk to me. I
sent him and he went to B. and B. and then sent for Francisco
and will interrogate later tonight. I bathed in river, delightful,
and Andokes came down and caught butterflies for Barnes and
I. Then a Capitan embraced us laying his head against our
breasts, I never saw so touching a thing, poor soul, he felt we
were their friends. Gielgud must be told to stop calling me
Casement, it is infernal cheek. Not well. No dinner.[29]

Catching butterflies for the bathers, embracing, feelings of friendship—
Casement's Indians were beautiful and mysterious, never to be understood
outside of their lostness in the forest and some remote antiquity. Adept in
the ways of the forest, they were nevertheless strangers: their heart and true
home lay elsewhere. They longed for another life because of the mysterious
displacement of their true selves. That was why they succumbed with ease
to the white man, Casement explained in the ethnographic essay he wrote
for *The Contemporary Review* in 1912.

First he notes the mysteriousness of their alienation—in dance, mask, and
song:

> The drum and the flute pipes and the masked men were a nec-
> essary part of each performance, and the dancers always sepa-
> rated into diverging and irregular circles, while the song that
> accompanied this motion was rendered in words that none of
> the Peruvian and Colombian white men, who often spoke the
> native language of the tribe with extraordinary fluency, could
> understand anything of. They all answered my inquiry that
> when the Indians danced they sang "old, old songs" that no
> one knew the origin of, and the very words of which were
> meaningless outside the dance. No explanation was forthcom-
> ing—the songs were "very old," and referred to some dim, far-
> off events that none of the whites could learn anything about;
> the Indians only said they came down from their remote past.
> That that remote past was something wholly different from
> their present-day environment I became more and more con-
> vinced as I studied these friendly, child-like human beings.[30]

They went practically naked through the forest. Their bodies were stained
with colored dyes. For the dances they stuck down and fluff to their calves
and sometimes to their thighs. Their minds were quick. They were perceptive

but probably not receptive. They were cheerful. They had almost no possessions,

> and their surroundings depressing in the extreme—a morbid,
> dense, and gloomy forest inhabited by wild beasts, serpents,
> and insects, and subject to one of the heaviest rainfalls in the
> world, accompanied often by the most tremendous storms of
> thunder and lightning to appal the stoutest heart. . . . Such sur-
> roundings as these neither offered a future nor held a past.[31]

They were not of the forest.

> The stars and the heavenly bodies played no part in the lives of
> those sunk in this gloom of an eternal underworld of trees. To
> all intents and purposes their bodily existence was on a par
> with that of the wild animals around them, and if the wild
> beasts were at home in the forest the wild men, it might be
> thought, were equally its natural denizens. Yet nothing became
> more clear the more these Indians were studied than that they
> were not children of the forest, but children of elsewhere lost
> in the forest—babes in the wood, grown up, it is true, and find-
> ing the forest their only heritage and shelter, but remembering
> always that it was not their home.[32]

They "were strangers come by chance amid surroundings they did not love."
This meant that they were in a way playing at living. Their life was a pretense
and they infinitely preferred gamboling to laboring, dancing and singing to
the satisfaction of material wants. It also meant that they were intrinsically
capricious, that they were more appearance than essence, and in their appearance they were like chameleons, collages, now this, now that, inconstant
ephemera flitting through the woods that were not theirs, children of always
another nature "whose lives were spent in an hereditary picnic rather than
in a settled occupation."

Casement felt that if he could have conveyed them away from the forest,
whole tribes would have fled with him with shouts of joy.

> While naked in body, slim, beautifully shaped and propor-
> tioned, colored like the very tree-trunks they flitted among like
> spirits of the woods—their minds were the minds of civilized
> men and women. They longed for another life—they hoped
> ever for another world. And this longing was, and is, at the
> bottom of much of that ease with which the first white man to
> come among them was able to "conquer" them.[33]

Yet to Captain Whiffen, who stayed twelve months with Putumayo Indians
but one year before Casement arrived, "the gentle Indian, peaceful and
loving, is a fiction of perfervid imaginations only. The Indians are innately
cruel."[34] Just as they hated white men and were surly to them, so internecine

strife between Indian groups was unending. The Indians have been called docile and gentle, he observes with coarse irony, "he may be, if to fear an enemy as much as he is hated be docility."[35] How much more complicated is the dialectic of toughness and tenderness made when Whiffen goes on to point out that, in addition to their "innate cruelty," "inter-tribal hospitality is without end. I have given a single biscuit to a boy and seen him religiously divide it into twenty microscopic pieces for all and sundry."[36]

To all of which has to be added the problem of interpreting the meaning of emotional display and techniques of the body. To Whiffen, for example, "the Indian has an extremely nervous manner, is extraordinarily negative, never expresses violent joy or fear and will submit to much, bear greatly but laugh easily—invariably at another Indian's discomfort." But what the English mariner Alfred Simson found worthy of mention among the "Piojes" along the Putumayo river in 1875 was that they were, "like most Indians, usually taciturn and laconic with strangers, expecially white men, but amongst themselves often chatty and merry." He found much to admire in their endurance (under his jocular command) for hard labor, such as their cutting firewood for his steam launch, and wistfully remarked that "I have often thought since how desirable it would be if one could always meet with such happy, diligent, and untiring laborers.[37]

Steam Launches Required for the Marañon

Ten years after Simson steamed the first launch up the Putumayo, the following requirement was laid out by Señor Larrera, commander of the Peruvian Naval Station, dated Iquitos, 31 March 1885:

> What is required for this department are two steam launches, from thirty five to forty tons—one with a screw and the other built after the stern-wheel system, made appropriate for expeditions, and whose speed should be fifteen miles an hour. The hull should be after the model of the exploring ships *Napo* and *Putumayo,* should be constructed of steel plates, and have a draught of water of from three and a half to four feet maximum, with all its fuel of wood and provisions for victualling fifteen men. The hull should be divided into three sections—the first for seamen's quarters and naval stores, the second for machinery and fuel, and the after-part for provisions. A teak deck, with a small house on the poop; a wooden roof from stem to stern, seven feet high, on iron columns, with a gunwale three feet high, to serve to protect the crew from the arrows of the natives and from gunshots, and should also be provided with engines of high and low pressure, horizontal boilers, and furnaces for green wood four feet long, and twin screws, for improved speed, would also be required.[38]

"River Itaya, near Iquitos." (From Walter E. Hardenburg, *The Putumayo: The Devil's Paradise,* 1912.)

Betraying All the Opposite Traits of Character

Simson went into the mouth of the Putumayo thirty-five years before Casement and spent about the same amount of time there as Casement did. His assessment of Indians conflicts in many ways with that "natural docility" emphasized by Casement as "a remarkable characteristic of Upper Amazon tribes," and which supposedly made the work of conquering them "less difficult than might at first be supposed." Take Simson's characterization of the Zaparos who, like the Huitotos, Boras, and Andokes of the rubber belt, were categorized by the whites as wild Indians. Noting that they raid other groups whose children they abduct for sale to white traders, Simson went on:

> When unprovoked they are, like really wild Indians, very shy
> and retiring, but are perfectly fearless, and will suffer no one,
> either Whites or others, to employ force with them. They can
> only be managed by tact, good treatment, and sometimes sim-
> ple reasoning; otherwise resenting ill-treatment or an attempt to
> resort to blows, with the worst of violence. . . . At all times
> they are changeable and unreliable, betraying under different
> circumstances, and often apparently under the same, in com-

mon with so many of their class, all the opposite traits of character, excepting perhaps servility—a true characteristic of the
old world—and stinginess, which I have never observed in
them. The absence of servility is typical of all the independent
Indians of Ecuador.[39]

"They also gain great enjoyment," he added, "from the destruction of life.
They are always ready to kill animals or people, and they delight in it."[40]

And the truth of the matter, the savagery of the Indians? Each person's
opinion contradicts the next and each opinion contradicts itself in a surfeit
of ambiguous images—a montage of bits and pieces of possibility colliding
into one another, no less chaotic than a page from Casement's diary and no
less indebted to the surreality of the colonial unconscious with its phantoms
of various shapes and guises stalking each other in the thicket of their differences. Indeed, to Alfred Simson, the defining quality of the forest Indian
was precisely the imprecise in a wild medley of difference. "At all times
they are unchangeable and unreliable, betraying under different circumstances, and often apparently under the same, in common with so many of
their class, all the opposite traits of character." Except stinginess and, perhaps, servility.

Simson comes across as a perceptive and level-headed man (although we
know that any European out there, especially in the "mysterious *oriente*,"
must have been a little peculiar), yet he was a creature of his time and, more
importantly, he wrote for that time—indeed, writing scientific monographs
about savages was a way of defining and even empowering that time. There
was little point generalizing about savages, he declared, "for apart from the
fickleness of the completely untutored mind, which has no faith, no abstract
reason by which to govern its apprehensions and waverings, the low savage
is essentially independent; restrained from his infancy upwards by no law,
no guiding hand, and even frequently barely by custom . . . then again, the
social bond is so weak. . . ."[41] It was this anarchy of the savage episteme
that, in his opinion, made different travelers' accounts as different as they
were partial, a wild episteme so raw, so nakedly empiricist, untheoretical,
unabstract, and noncultured that it amounted to no more than the trembling
phenomenology of being, each head a world, each world alone and wavering.
Colonial terror could gather all that up and more, and men would strike out
at it, killing and torturing the phantoms of wild disorder they had realized.

There was also a quite different possibility buried in this colonial montage
of Indianness, and that was the possibility of magical healing, of whites going
to Indian healers, "witches," as did Father Gaspar de Pinell's guide and the
good father himself. In any event the transforming properties of the reality
constituting the savage were not made up by colonial artwork in harness
with the violence and politics of rubber gathering alone. Indian artwork
contributed to the colonial fantastic. The frontier united as much as it di-

vided. Rocha caught it nicely with the *tigre mojano,* which he was told about by the whites and in which, he said, many of them believed as much as the Indians were said to—that magically empowered tiger that metamorphosed back and forth from stealth and death-dealing into the quintessence of Indian ephemerality, the shaman. It was the same colonial artistry that went into the figure of the *auca.*

FIVE

The Image of the *Auca:*
Ur-Mythology and
Colonial Modernism

Poised between science and adventure,
Alfred Simson's *Travels in the Wilds of
Ecuador* had the trappings of an epic; a journey to the unknown and wild sources of
civilization, if not of the self, too, the epic
journey into the heart of darkness, fascinating because so far away, feasible because
of its advancing proximity. Marlow would
shortly go, as would Casement, and before
them went Charles Darwin. Like Darwin,
Simson would write learned papers—for the
Royal Anthropological Society and for the
Royal Geographical Society, papers about
Indian tribes and the navigability of rivers
running through forests rich with quinine
and rubber. Like Marlow, Simson took the
helm of a river steamer, one of the three
that were the first such craft to thread their
way up the Putumayo. That was in 1875.
The expedition was launched by a Colombian company anxious to ascertain the
possibilities of exploiting india rubber, sar-
saparilla, and cinchona bark. One of its
members was Rafael Reyes, a leading figure
in the cinchona trade. Later he became
president of Colombia.

The forests and their inhabitants were
falling to the axe of Western business and
to the branches of Western science, its ge-

ography, its anthropology, and of course its industrial sciences. From the Congo to the Putumayo the most backward was being dragged into the maw of the modern. With Goodyear's discovery of vulcanization, adding hot sulfur to hot rubber to make it more elastic and resistant, the sap oozing from old tropical forests could be used as rubbery belts and tires to further propel the machines of the north. There are calculations of the number of Congolese and Putumayo bodies that went into each ton of that rubber. Vulcan was in Roman mythology the god of fire. Both the name "volcano" and the name of rubber processing come from him. Walter Benjamin suggested that the volcanic bursting forth of commodity production in the industrialized societies, from the nineteenth century onwards, was a bursting forth that entailed the reactivation of latent mythic powers now charged, so to speak, in the fetishization of commodities appearing as self-powered dream images, the never-to-be realized realizations of desire built out of the misery of the exploited labor of the newly industrialized workforce. Vulcan was a blacksmith who forged weapons for gods and heroes. But in the colonies, from where the raw materials of vulcanization came, what there?

In the colonies labor was rarely detachable from the being of the worker. Labor was not turned into a commodity as in the industrial heartlands of the imperial powers. Instead of a proletariat "free" to offer its services on a labor market there existed a wide range of servitudes from slavery to debt-peonage and refinements on feudal-like paternalism. Vulcan, too, had his laborers attached to him and unfree; one-eyed giants, they were, tending his furnace and wielding his hammers. The question to be raised, then, is, Under such conditions, might not the laborer as much as the commodity be fetishized by mythic allusion to an imagined antiquity? And if so, would it not for the main part be a locally derived mythology, created at the frontier where Indian and colonist came together in their reciprocating fabulation—as with the *tigre mojano* and the *auca?*

"No one with the spirit of roaming within him can live long in Ecuador," began Simson's book, "without cherishing a growing desire to explore its unknown parts." It was mysterious and romantic. Even the hard-bitten anarchist B. Traven fell for the way it combined the real with the unreal, the empirical sensed facticity with the tone that made it, the mystery it pointed to and was illuminated by. Writing fifty years after Simson, he explained to his editors about Mexico: "I must travel. I must see things, landscapes, and people before I bring them to life in my work. I must travel to jungles and primeval forests, to visit Indians, distant ranchos, and to unknown, secret, mysterious lakes and rivers."[1] For Simson it was the grandeur of the mountains, the terribleness of the volcanoes, the fertility of the soil and the endless variety of its products that made the desire for closer acquaintance irresistible. And what most stimulated this desire was, in his own words, the "almost mystical 'Provincia del Oriente,' the wild easterly province of Ecuador of the northern headwaters of the Amazons." To journey there was to undertake the journey from civilization to hell itself: "In the civilized portion of the country," he observed, "the Oriente and the Napo are looked upon as neither more nor less than an '*inferno*,' wherein 'he who enters leaves hope behind.' " The man who went there was not normal, "almost mad" is what people said, what with the "wild and murderous tribes," snakes, jaguars, and diseases brought on by fatigue, bad nourishment, and constant exposure to the damp and insect-plagued climate. It was, furthermore, a descent through the circles of race down the rungs of civilization.[2]

It was a strange but typically exotic note that the French explorer Dr. Jules Crévaux inserted into the account of his journey up the Putumayo and down the Caquetá in 1879. His canoe approached two canoes with Indians in them, and one of the canoes, with a naked woman and a baby in a tiny

Crévaux's guide in the Putumayo, Santa Cruz, the pirate of the Andes. (From Jules Crévaux, "Exploración del Inzá y del Yapura," 1884.)

"Indians of the Peruvian Amazon Region: River Ucayali." (From Walter E. Hardenburg, *The Putumayo: The Devil's Paradise*, 1912.)

hammock, paddled away. Crévaux's Indian canoemen informed the strangers that remained that they were *calina*, a term that Crévaux understood to be *compañero*, that is, "all individuals of the Indian race." But why had the other canoe fled away? Because, came the answer, the woman had just given birth. If the newborn had seen a white it would have fallen ill and died no matter what remedies were applied. All the Indians of Guiana think the same, his black Guianan guide told him, and they emphatically refuse to show their babies to either blacks or whites.[3]

Thirty years later the Colombian traveler Joaquin Rocha said that there were but two classes of people in the Putumayo: whites and savage Indians. Curiously, whites were referred to not only as Christian or rational or civilized in everyday parlance but the term *blanco*, meaning white, also included people who were in no way phenotypically white—people such as *negros*, *mestizos*, *mulatos*, *zambos*, and Indians "of those groups incorporated into civilization since the time of the Spanish conquest and who have lost even the memory of their ancient customs and language."[4]

Simson expands part of this classification. He tells us that those whom he called pure Indians of the forest were divided by local whites and Spanish-speaking Indians into *indios* and *infieles*—Indians and infidels. While the *indios* are Quechua-speaking, salt-eating, semi-Christians, the *infieles*, also known as *aucas*, speak other languages, rarely eat salt, and know nothing of baptism or of the Catholic Church. The term *auca*, "as commonly used now in the Oriente," he (foot-) noted, "seems to bear the full meaning it did anciently in Peru under the Incas. It includes the sense of infidel, traitor, barbarian, and is often applied in a malignant sense. In Peru it was used to designate those who rebelled against their king, and incarnation of their deity, the inca."[5] Several modern Ecuadorian Quechua dictionaries clearly bring the various meanings together—savage, seditious, rebel, enemy—and in the Colombian Putumayo today *auca* also connotes, to my friends at least and with varying intensities, the unrepentantly "other" world of savagery down there in the jungles of the *oriente*, a world quintessentially pagan, without Christ, Spanish words, or salt, inhabited by naked, incestuous, violent, magical, and monstrous people, even wilder, perhaps, than the *tigre mojano*—animal, but also human, and unreal.

Even in Simson's studied realism it is obvious that wild Indians are conceived to be so like animals that their animality partakes of the occult, thus inspiring a paranoid vision of evil lurking in the wilderness, encircling society. Traven gets this across in his depiction of an overseer marching Indian peons early in the twentieth century through the mahogany forests of Chiapas, Mexico:

> However, the peons, agile as cats, and from childhood accustomed to march and wander over similar ground, took short cuts wherever feasible. In spite of their heavy packs they slid down rocks, jumped lightly over gigantic fallen trees. El Camarón [the overseer], on horseback, had to follow the entire length of the trail. There were periods when he found himself completely alone on the trail. It was then that he felt afraid.[6]

And about the so-called Zaparo Indians of the Ecuadorian *montaña* Simson wrote that their preceptions of eye and ear are perfectly marvelous and surpass the non-*auca* Indians considerably. Their knowledge of the forest is so perfect, he assures us, that they travel at night in unknown parts. They are great fighters, detecting sounds and footprints where white men discern nothing. On the trail of their prey they out-shadow the shadows of its passage, suddenly swerving, and then again, as if following its very scent—like the hunted animal itself. Indeed, their motions are the same as Traven's peons, "cat-like," and they move unscathed through the underwood and thorns. To communicate with each other they generally imitate the whistle of the toucan or partridge—and all this is in marked contrast to the non-*aucas*, the civilized Indians, "*who stand in fear and respect of them, but despise or affect to despise them as infidels behind their backs* [emphasis added]."[7]

Today high in the Colombian Andes overlooking the Putumayo forests, the highland shaman with whom I have worked talks of the lowland shamans

"Spirit of the wild"—making medicine.

as *aucas* or as *auca*-like: ethereal interminglings of animal and human—presences potent with the magic of the hot forests below. With them he makes his spiritual pact because, inferior and subhuman as they are, they provide the power he needs to defy fate, to do battle with evil, and to cure his patients. Farther down the mountain, in the foothills, my Ingano shaman friend Santiago Mutumbajoy calls his curing fan of leaves *waira sacha,* "spirit of the forest" or "brush of the wind." With this fan beating into the night throughout the whole night, he sings. The hallucinogen *yagé* brings the visions. With this fan of leaves imparting motion to the forest of envy and wildness that constitutes society and its troubled relationships, those relations are healed. It is by singing with this rustling fan that he makes his medicines and wipes the sick body clean of the sorcery or spirits that assailed it. One form of wildness, that of the wilderness, contends with another, usually that of envy, sometimes that of baneful spirits. In the body the battle wages, one form of wildness circling another, disorder tripping up disorder in its own disorderliness. Around and around darts the song, wordless, crying, full of the pain of human hearts, of frogs croaking in the slime of the forest. *Sacha,* says the son of the shaman ("as in *sacha gente*—people of the forest"), and he pauses, "like *aucas,*" as if the wild *auca*-presence in the leaves of the forest in the fan of the curer provided the magical force required to expel the *auca*-like demons lodged in the innards of the white folk who come to these Indian healers for cure—white folk who regard these Indian healers in the same way that Alfred Simson one hundred years ago said that *aucas* were regarded by civilized Indians "who stand in fear and respect of them, but despise or affect to despise them as infidels behind their backs."

It is crucial to grasp the dialectic of sentiments contained within the appellation *auca,* a dialectic enshrouded in magic composed of both fear and contempt—similar if not identical to the mysticism, hate, and awe that Timerman discerns as projected onto him in the torture chamber. In the case of *aucas,* this projection, conscious or unconscious, is inseparable from the imputation of rebellion against sacred imperial authority and the further imputation of magical power possessed by lowland forest dwellers as a class and by their oracles, seers, and healers—their shamans—in particular. Moreover, this indigenous (and in all likelihood pre-Hispanic) construction of wildness blends with the late medieval European figure of the magically savage and animal-like "wild man" brought to the Andes and the Amazon by the Spaniards and the Portuguese. Today, in the upper reaches of the Putumayo with which I am acquainted, this colonially combined mythology of the magic of the *auca* and of the wild man underlies the resort to Indian shamans by white colonists seeking cure from sorcery and hard times, while these very same colonists despise Indians as savages. During the rubber boom, with its need for "wild" Indians to gather rubber and with its equally desperate atmosphere of wild distrust and suspicion among the "civilized," this same ur-mythology and magic of colonial practices of signification nourished paranoia and great cruelty. Going to the Indians for their healing power and killing them for their wildness are not so far apart. Indeed, these actions are not only intertwined but are codependent—and it is this codependence that looms in so startling a fashion when we consider how fine the line is that separates the use of Indians as laborers, on the one hand, and their use as mythic objects of torture on the other.

Putumayo terror was the terror of the fineness of that line as international capitalism converted the "excesses" of torture into rituals of production no less important than the rubber gathering itself. Torture and terror were not simply utilitarian means of production; they were a form of life, a mode of production, and in many ways, for many people, not least of whom were the Indians themselves, its main and consuming product.

Fear of Indian Rebellion

> Deponent often went on expeditions with Normand—always after Indians—and very many Indians were killed by him (Normand) then. One day they came to an Indian house in the Andokes country and caught all the Indians in the house—there were women, and men, and young children, some about a month old, quite small. All were killed except the little children—they were left alive in the house to die there—but their mothers were killed. He cut off the heads of all these Indians, Senor Normand himself did it. Deponent will swear it—he saw him do it. He cut off their heads with a machete; he said, *Those were to pay for the white people they had killed.* The Andokes had killed some Colombians before this. [Casement, *Putumayo Report,* 128; emphasis added.]

In addition to explaining Putumayo terror as caused by the profit motive, Casement considered the possibility that fear of Indian attack or rebellion prompted the whites to commit atrocities. But in keeping with the picture he wanted to paint, of Indian docility and innocence, he vigorously presented reasons why Indian rebellion was unlikely. The problem, however, is that whether or not something is likely or unlikely often has little to do with its effects on consciousness and history, in this case that of the overseers and company officials living in the rubber stations.

Casement said that Indian rebellion was unlikely because Indian communities were disunited, from times dating long before the rubber boom, he said, and whereas the company employees were armed and well deployed, the Indians were poorly armed and their blowpipes, bows, and lances had been confiscated. Most important, in his opinion, was that the elders had been murdered for the crime of giving "bad advice." What that euphemism meant was that the elders, had, in Casement's words, gone so far as to "warn the more credulous or less experienced against the white enslaver and to exhort the Indian to flee or to resist rather than to work rubber for the new-comers." It was this that brought their doom. "I met no old Indian" Casement continued, "man or woman, and few had got beyond middle age."[8] In this regard it is worth noting that, according to the Capuchins, who went down from the Sibundoy Valley into the Putumayo forests fifteen years after Casement was there, the company removed the shamans (*desterraba a los brujos*) and sent them, as prisoners, to Iquitos.[9]

As regards the threat of rebellion, the Barbadian overseer Frederick Bishop provided a different perspective. "He is sure," summarized Casement in the latter part of his report reserved for the testimony of the Barbadians, "that many of the Indians hate and dread the 'whites,' and would kill them if they could, but they are too timid and cowed and have no arms. Sometimes some Indian will try to do that, to get others to come and attack the whites, so as to stop the rubber drives. That was how Bartolomé Zumaeta was killed 'a few months before.' "[10]

Bartolomé Zumaeta was no less than Arana's brother-in-law, a syphilitic and repugnant wretch according to some of Hardenburg's witnesses,[11] and one of the men alleged to have led the attack on David Serrano's rubber camp when the company was driving the Colombian traders away from the Igaraparaná. In reply to questioning by the Select Committee two years after submitting his report to the Foreign Office, Casement said that, in addition to Bartolomé, yet another brother was shot by Indians, on a separate occasion.

Thus, after his six weeks in the area, the consul-general gives us in his report a string of logically connected cause-and-effect, sociological and rational-sounding reasons why Indian rebellion was unlikely. Yet we know that two of Arana's brothers-in-law were shot by Indians, and that at least one of those shootings was fatal. Moreoever, Bishop, who was there as an overseer for some six years, intimated that he was not at all sure about that propensity to rebel; he felt that the Indians hated and dreaded their masters and would kill them if they could. To the overseer none of this was too clear, and while he could be reasonably sure about the state of arms, he could not be sure about the state of mind, and it is in that space of wondering between arms and mind where doubt locks horns with fantasy—the next attack, hidden things, the ambiguous multiplicity of signs.

A few days after Casement was hanged in London the Indians in the Atenas rubber station rebelled and killed, so it is said, thirteen of the company's white employees.[12] Father Pinell was told of a large uprising along the Igaraparaná in 1917 that required the use of Peruvian troops to put it down.[13] The threat of revolt was real.

There were other types of Indian revolt to consider as well. Bucelli and three other whites had all been killed by Indians for instance, and not just by Indians but by *muchachos,* the armed guards of Indians that the company trained and depended on. It was a sordid story. They had been raiding for Indians into Colombian territory, chasing runaways:

> Bucelli's Indian 'wife,' who accompanied him, and who was the mother of three children by him—two of whom I met—had had so much sympathy with the object of the 'muchachos' that she had not warned her husband of the plot against his life, although, as I was assured, aware of it. The four 'muchachos' had subsequently fought among themselves, and two had been killed in this way. The two survivors had after some months given themselves up to the station of Entre Rios. They had been flogged repeatedly and just before my visit had been confined in chairs in the neighbouring station of Matanzas. Not long before my visit to that station in October 1910 they had escaped from the house in which they were confined, and had got off into the forest with the chains still on them. As they were Huitotos, and their escape had occurred in the Andokes country, it was likely that they would meet their fate in the end at the hands of those Indians whom they had so often been engaged in maltreating.[14]

If we turn to Joaquin Rocha, who traveled through the area seven years before Casement when the independent Colombian traders were still there, the issue of Indian revolt is no clearer. On the one hand he interprets the situation by logically deriving consequences from what he takes to be a self-evident maxim to which the Putumayo Indians form no exception: that conquered people hate their masters. The Indians were constantly conspiring against their white masters, he says, until the tyrannical Crisóstomo Hernández, with savagery even greater than theirs, taught them the futility of revolt. Still, the jungle was awfully big. Don Crisóstomo's power must have been really something if it could not only force the Indians to gather rubber but could also prevent them from running away. Perhaps the stories about his oratory need consideration too. It was said that he joined in with the Indian men around the tobacco pot at night and that such was the power of his stories, in the native language, that he could bid the Indians do his will.

But on the other hand there was never that much to fear because the Indians, says Rocha, are like children and cannot keep a secret, thus condemning in advance any large-scale uprising through the loose tongues of Indian servants and concubines. When the rubber traders—meaning, at that time, the Colombian rubber traders—get wind of such a plan it is their custom to arm and gather together at a suitable place of defense, at which point the Indians retire because of their incapacity for direct and open fighting. When the Indians made such an attempt on the eve of Rocha's arrival it was defused by the smooth-talking Colombian Gregorio Calderón, head of the rubber trading firm of Calderón & Brothers, whom the Huitotos called "Capitán General of the Rationals." He explained to the Indians that the whites were not trying to take their land and that what little they used for their food crops they would return to the Indians as soon as they left the territory.[15]

Seven years later, at Entre Ríos, Casement heard about an Indian chief named Chingamui who in 1903, the year Rocha was traveling through the area, was said to have exercised a wide influence over all the Huitotos in that district. "He had fallen into the hands of a Colombian named Calderón," wrote Casement, "but not before he had shot at and wounded his murderer."[16]

Rocha tried to distinguish between *general* uprisings and *partial* uprisings. While the former had failed ("up till now," he wrote), there was no doubt that there had been "partial" revolts which had been fatal for the Whites who dominated the specific area which became the theater of revolt."[17]

To the dead whites and their families it must have mattered little whether the revolt was partial or general. To those who were not killed, this distinction between general and partial must have offered but small relief to their worries about what was going on in the minds of their peons and in the limitless forest surrounding them. No matter how partial, the effect of Indian revolts on the consciousness of the overseers in the camps in the jungle was not an effect that could be gauged by facts clear and simple. The effects on consciousness of this atmosphere of uncertainty obeyed forces other than statistical ones of general or partial.

It was an effect that depended on the circulation of stories. Traven understood this from his travels through the mahogany forests of Chiapas.

> Throughout the twenty years during which, up to that time, the exploitation of hardwoods in those regions had been carried on, only one serious mutiny had occurred. This mutiny was the basis for many terrifying narrations with which traders and agents passed their time during the long evenings when, in their travels through villages and fincas, they sat with finqueros and rancheros, after supper, on the porches, smoking, swinging in rocking chairs or lounging in hammocks.[18]

"Life for the Whites in the land of the Huitotos hangs by a thread," wrote Joaquin Rocha but one page after he had virtually dismissed the threat of rebellion, and he went on to describe just what he meant.

"Not so long ago" Emilio Gutiérrez navigated up the Caquetá from Brazil searching for Indians to establish a rubber station. Reaching the area he wished to conquer, he sent the greater part of his men back to carry merchandise, and while asleep he and his three companions were killed by wild Indians. Upon hearing this, other whites prepared to retaliate when news reached them that thirty of Gutiérrez's Indian workforce had also been killed, all at the same time yet in different parts of the jungle. Indians working for whites were sent in pursuit of the rebels, some of whom were killed outright, some taken as prisoners for the whites, while the majority escaped. Some were captured and eaten by these Indian mercenaries.[19]

Seven years later, in 1910, Casement heard of the same episode from a Peruvian, who introduced his tale by saying that the methods used by the Colombian conquerors "were very bad." He told Casement that the rebel Indians decapitated Gutiérrez together with an unstated number of other whites and exposed their skulls on the walls of their drum sheds, cutting off their arms and legs and keeping the limbless bodies in water for as long as possible so as to show them off to other Indians. Casement's informant said he had found the bodies of twelve others tied to stakes, assuring Casement that (in contrast to Rocha's account) the Indians had *not* eaten them because they "had a repugnance to eating white men, whom they hated too much." Terrible reprisals subsequently fell upon the Indians, noted Casement.[20]

Whether considered on its own or in comparison with Rocha's account, this story retold by Casement emphasizes the point that the uncertainty surrounding the possibility of Indian "treachery" fed a colonially paranoid mythology in which dismemberment, cannibalism, and the exposure of body parts and skulls grinned wickedly.

Fear of Cannibalism

> Three enormous Indians painted in red, their mouths full of
> coca bulging their cheeks, advanced to greet us, hitting us on
> the back as a form of welcome. Above us hung suspended from
> the roof four human skulls. They were trophies from a recent
> battle between Nonuyas and their neighbours the Ekireas. Each
> skull corresponded to a victim of the cannibals. I couldn't but
> feel a swift emotion, to see us, so few in number, surrounded
> by those Indians, strong and muscley, who could split us into
> pieces in the twinkling of an eye from the moment we
> arrived. . . .
> Sometimes you see dissected arms from which the meat has
> been stripped but the tendons left in place with the hands
> slightly bent. Tied to a wooden handle they serve as cooking
> spoons for the *cahuana*. In spite of all my attempts to obtain
> one of these kitchen utensils, I was not able. It is with great
> suspicion that the Huitotos guard their ornaments, their neck-
> laces of teeth, of feathers, and so forth. The reason they hide
> them is to evade the desires of the whites who often seize them
> against the will of their owners, giving nothing in return. [Eu-
> genio Robuchon, supposedly, *En El Putumayo y sus afluentes,*
> "edición oficial," (Lima, 1907).]

Whatever it meant to Indians, cannibalism for colonial culture functioned as the supple sign for construing reality, the caption point without which

otherwise free-floating signifiers wandered off into space as so many disas-
sembled limbs and organs of a corpus. Cannibalism summed up all that was
perceived as grotesquely different about the Indian as well as providing for
the colonists the allegory of colonization itself. In condemning cannibalism,
the colonists were in deep complicity with it. Otherness was not dealt with
here by simple negation, a quick finishing off.

On the contrary, everything hinged on a drawn-out, ritualized death in
which every body part took its place embellished in a memory-theater of
vengeances paid and repaid, honors upheld and denigrated, territories distinguished in a feast of difference. In eating the transgressor of those differences, the consumption of otherness was not so much an event as a
process, from the void erupting at the moment of death to the reconstituting
of oneself, the consumer, with still-warm otherness. In this manner colonization was itself effected.

Ascribed to Indians, cannibalism was taken from them as a cherished
dream image of the fears of being consumed by difference, as we see in the
case of Joaquin Rocha, who depicts the jungle and the Indians as devouring
forces. Just as important was the erotic passion this gave to the countermove
of devouring the devourer. Allegations of cannibalism served not only to
justify enslavement of Indians by the Spanish and the Portuguese from the
sixteenth century onwards; such allegations also served to flesh out the
repertoire of violence in the colonial imagination.

The interest the whites display is obsessive; again and again Rocha scents
cannibalism in the murk around him. He is frightened in the forest, not of
animals but of Indians, and it is always with what becomes in effect the
insufferably comic image of the person-eating Indian that he chooses to
represent that fear of being consumed by a wild, unknown, half-sensed
uncertainty. Among the whites, to stamp out cannibalism is an article of
faith like a crusade, he says. Cannibalism is an addictive drug; whenever
the Huitotos think they can deceive the whites, "they succumb to their
beastly appetites." The whites have therefore to be more like beasts, as in
the story retold by Rocha concerning Crisóstomo Hernández killing all the
Indians of a communal house down to the children at the breast for succumbing to that addiction.

The prisoner was bound between two stakes with his arms stretched out.
His legs were stretched apart and his feet were anchored to the ground by
sharp sticks hammered into the soles of his feet. He was in a half-crouching,
half-standing position and thus was he killed with a spear or a dagger—so
Konrad Preuss, a German ethnographer, wrote on the basis of having spent
an unstated length of time with Huitotos in 1914.[21]

He published two scholarly volumes on Huitoto religion and myths in
1921, including a somewhat ambiguous account of the *bai* or cannibal festival,
ambiguous in the sense that he never clearly distinguished between what he

himself witnessed and what he was told about at a remove from the event itself. (There was barely a mention of the rubber boom in his work.)

Only the men ate the victim, according to Preuss—they ate the heart, kidneys, liver, and the marrow of the bones after it had been partially cooked so it was still bloody. Before eating everyone took a cheekful of tobacco juice; otherwise they would be unable to eat. After eating they went to the river and vomited everything out. He who had eaten human flesh became a bold and clever warrior, understood how to make war magic and could, for instance, jump across the river or off the top of the house. Emptied of its brain and washed in the river, the skull was hung from the roof beams and the teeth worn as a necklace. The Muinane downstream were supposed to have smoked and eaten the whole body.

After they had eaten the flesh of the victim the festival was held. During the nights before it, so Preuss tells us, many stories were told—of the eating of whole tribes by the snake, the bat, the tapir, the Rigai, the fight with the Rigai, stories of the *bai* festival, and the destruction of the people by the dyaroka tree. Only two of the myths did not mention cannibalism, and they told of the destruction of the man in the moon. On the evening before the festival a speech was given in which it was related how the moon, father Buneima, the ancestor, ate members of many tribes. This story was also told when a member of one tribe visited another tribe. Father Buneima also ate stars, plants, and animals.

These are some of the songs that Preuss says were sung at the cannibal festival:

> *Husiniamui the sun god's song:* Down there behind the children of men before my bloody place where the sun rises, in the middle of the blood-covered scene at the foot of my blood tree are my Rigai sons. There they are at work full of rage. They crush the skull of the prisoner and singe off (?) the bird (?). [The question marks are Preuss's.] Near heaven in the river of blood are the rocks of my passion for fighting (i.e. enemies). Down there on the village square of the first people they are at work full of rage and they crush the prisoners. There they seethe.
>
> *Song of the toad:* It smells of blood! How shall I (the toad) speak to Egaide, the son of the Caimito tribe as his widow! When day breaks the toads go for this reason into the lake that is red with blood.
>
> *Song of the woodpecker:* "How shall I (the woodpecker) henceforth speak as his widow to Hifaidyagido, the son of the tribe of the Diuene!" All woodpeckers although they are not human will go on this account into the wood when day breaks.
>
> *Song of the great blue butterfly:* It flutters, bringing harm. "How shall I, as his widow, speak to Kuraveko, the son, etc."

> All the butterflies that are not human, will go to the Aguacate
> tree up by the old huts, at daybreak.
>   *Song of the Dyaroka people:* . . . Down river in the under-
> world the headman Hitidi Muinama sleeps and looks downward
> on account of Bogeiko's face. When it is up above, he turns
> himself down river to the underworld on account of the face of
> the tree. Only the people of the tree of decay in the underworld
> who made Bogeiko's face can look upwards freely. (The
> painted wood is war-magic which when looked at causes things
> to happen, including blindness.)

To the extent that this filtered through the woods, what would the colonists and the employees of the Peruvian Amazon Company have made of it? And as we dwell on this world dedicated to the sun god, naming the names, the places, the actions, the animals, and the spirits, in short this affirmation of a world, do we not also have to consider that the company's rites of torture also affirmed a world and did so in ways dependent on the colonist's understanding of Indian understandings of rites of cannibalism—of that fluttering forth in its heavy-winged adroitness of the great blue butterfly of sorcery into a world of bloody fire? In their mutilating, dismembering, and burning of Indians, and the burning of them alive in the Peruvian flag soaked in kerosene, for instance, were not the company employees engaged in the ritual enactment of their own colonial world? Were they not thus constantly reproducing their world over and over again against the savagery on which their world depended and with which, therefore, it was complicit? Were they not thereby affirming their place as conquerors, their function in civilizing, and their aura as whites with a magic even greater, perhaps, than the sun god's?

Something crucial about such complicity and the magical power of the company employees emerges from what has been said in recent times about Andoke Indians who claim that the rubber company had a stronger story than the Indians' story and this is why, for example, the armed uprising of the Andoke Yarocamena against the company failed and failed so disastrously.

By story (*rafue*) is here meant something like tradition and the telling of tradition such that (in the words of Benjamin Ypes and Roberto Pineda) the ideological and ritual conditions guaranteeing the efficacity of work are set in place.[22] The telling of the story is a sort of necessary mediation between concept and practice that ensures the reproduction of the everyday world. Not just stories then but (in the Spanish phrase used by the aforementioned authors) *Historias para Nosotros*—histories not of, but *for* us.

Yet if the story of the company employees was stronger than that of the Indians, one wonders why, as these same Andokes told Ypes and Pineda, that one of the tortures inflicted by the company on Yarocamena's followers was to cut out their tongues—and then make them talk.

From another direction one is reminded of the colonist's story about Crisóstomo Hernández, one of the first rubber traders to push his way into the Igaraparaná, slaughtering Indians only to be slaughtered by one of his own men. It was said by the colonists that Don Crisóstomo would spend nights orating with Indian men in their communal houses around the tobacco pot, seducing them into doing his bidding with the power of *his* storytelling.

It is the turn-of-the-century Colombian traveler, Joaquin Rocha, who tells us this—or rather retells and therewith adds his part to what, I presume, the Indians would call the colonists' "History for Us." What is important here is how Rocha strains both to blend and to distinguish the use of violence and the use of oratory. On the one hand he says that Don Crisóstomo used first oratory and later force, while on the other hand this distinction can only be maintained by deploying rhetorical measures ensuring that not only are violence and oratory codependent as a type of power/knowledge but that both are in some way dependent upon magic as well. Indeed, it is in their codependent difference that magic resides; Jacques Derrida's "deconstruction" here applies with telling force.

Rocha tells us, after establishing that Don Crisóstomo spoke with such power of seduction that assemblies of Huitoto captains would unanimously adopt his proposals, that

> this was before obtaining the omnipotence occassioned by terror and victories, such that he imposed his Dominion as much by force of arms as by force of words, becoming not only for the Indians the seductive orator and the invincible man of arms, but also by these means something greater—because for the Huitotos he was their king and God.[23]

And one should also study the epigraph to Gonzalo París Lozano's book, *Guerrilleros del Tolima,* about the War of One Thousand Days (1899–1901) in southern Colombia, an event that produced many of the first rubber traders in the Putumayo: "Those were other men, more men than those of today, wilder in action and more seasoned in the word" ("Aquellos eran otros hombres, más hombres que los de tiempos presentes, más bravos en la acción y más sazonados en la palabra").[24] Here it is not so much magic but nostalgia that both unites and distinguishes violence and oratory.

It was a life plagued by illness, heat, hunger, and insects and there was at least one colonial bard who set this sad litany to verse as Rocha's canoe drifted downstream ever deeper into the forest. It was like Purgatory, where the seven plagues afflicting Egypt existed a thousandfold, and death took many forms: drowning in the river, death from the sting-ray, lunch for the boa or the tiger . . . or for the Huitoto dinner. And no sooner had Rocha copied this down with the last line ringing when the Coreguaje Indians manning his canoe cried out "Charucangui!" "We had arrived for the second stage of our great trip, to the singular land of the cannibals, Huitoto-land, conquered by twelve valiant Colombians, heroic progeny of their conquistador forefathers."[25]

They were hardened foresters whose livelihood depended on outwitting competitors and maintaining hold of Indians in a Hobbesian world, stateless and cutthroat, where the literalization of man eating man made the otherwise proverbial jungle of unrestrained competition a grim reality. In cannibalism they and those who chose to represent them to the outside world found a "way station," so to speak, a point of strategic convergence in the rubber station where the assumed forms of life of the savage met the savagery assumed by the trade.

There were several such way stations where Indian and white society folded into the assumed otherness of each other, where what was taken to be an Indian practice met with what was taken to be a white one, where assumed meanings met with assumed meanings to form strange codependencies and culture itself—the culture of colonization. There were the rubber traders living with Indian "wives" (who bore strangely few children, according to Rocha); missionaries "baptizing" Huitotos with Christian names while Huitotos carried out lavish rites "baptizing" whites with Huitoto names (and let's not forget titles, a doubly circulated process in which Indians applied to whites' titles that whites applied to them, with changes where appropriate, of course—as with the informal leader of the Colombian rubber traders, Gregorio Calderón, "Captain General of the Rationals"); whites going to Indian medicine men; whites (so the tale goes) like Crisóstomo Hernández out-orating the Huitoto orators and thereby bending them to the whites' will; the great Indian festivals where the "advances" of trade goods were exchanged for rubber; and, of course, the host of interwoven Indian and colonist assumptions about the rights and duties built into the debt-peonage relationship itself.

These were vitally important practical affairs.

They were also ritual events.

As such they were in effect new rituals, rites of conquest and colony formation, mystiques of race and power, little dramas of civilization tailoring savagery which did not mix or homogenize ingredients from the two sides of the colonial divide but instead bound Indian understandings of white understandings of Indians to white understandings of Indian understandings of whites.

The colonists' appropriation of Indian cannibalism was one such metaritual, no less than was their fascination with the Indians' tobacco pot.

Into this pot of thick black juice many male fingers were stuck, then licked. From what we read it was an exciting as well as a reverential experience, male bonding through the intoxication of polyphonic discourse and nicotine and maybe coca as well in the dark fastness of jungle enclaves, women and children beyond the circle, the pot with its thick juice in the center. Its revelation demanded a curious blend of brash scientific/ethnographic disclosure combined with the coyness of a voyeur strip-teasing the veil of time from primal secrets. Author after author was enchanted by the spectacle their texts reproduced; Indian men staying awake at night in a circle around the pot of tobacco juice debating the issues of the day in a strange mixture of male democracy, classical nobility, and primitive mysticism. Every now and again at some important juncture in the debate they would dip a finger into the tobacco and suck it—hence the name bestowed on this by the colonists, *chupe del tabaco,* the sucking of tobacco—until agreement was reached to the general satisfaction.

"This is the Huitotos' most solemn oath," wrote Hardenburg, as if he too, serious and pedantic, were under some sort of oath himself. And well he might have been, for what followed was astounding. "Whenever the whites wish to enter into any important agreement with the Indians," he added, "they always insist on this ceremony being performed."

It is doubtful if he himself ever witnessed such sucking. Without making it clear whether he had or not, he went on to depict it. The captain begins by inserting his finger into the pot, he explained, and starts a long speech that is interrupted from time to time by the rest with an emphatic yell of approval. The group then becomes more excited, until each one sticks his own finger into the pot and applies it to his tongue.[26] That's it. Hardenburg then went on to describe the Huitotos' houses—ethnographic snapshots.

Twenty years later Father Gaspar de Pinell did witness the *chupe del tabaco* when Huitoto Indians stayed up late to discuss the religious teachings that he, his fellow Capuchin Father Bartolomé, and their interpreter had laid before them by means of oil paintings. Father Gaspar wrote that the sucking of tobacco occurs whenever the Indians have important things to discuss, such as when the chief gives instructions to his people to gather rubber for the whites, do agricultural work, go hunting, or attack another tribe or the whites themselves. Squatting around the tobacco with the women and children swaying in hammocks out of sight but within earshot, the chiefs and the Indians of most prestige begin long discourses, as if reciting. Three or four men may do this at the same time and they repeat, he said, the same idea a thousand times but in different words. When a pause is reached all the men repeat the last few words with a prolonged "mmm," thus preserving, emphasized the good father, their beliefs and customs intact from generation to generation.[27]

·"It is said to be administered," wrote Casement, "when it is sought to bind them to a solemn engagement by an irrevocable promise." Yet there was something more, concealed and threatening, in the *chupe,* as if the very use of it by the traders for rubber caused some vengeful spirit to emerge from the tobacco pot itself when the suckers said "No more!"

It was from the book purported to be the work of the mysteriously disappeared French explorer, Eugenio Robuchon, that Casement retrieved that spirit of vengeance, lifting the veil on the primal scene to reveal to Sir Edward Grey and the British public unsuspected depths to Indian gullibility. It was a tense situation. Robuchon had landed among some Nonuya Indians and had seen the human skulls hanging from the roof. He didn't feel very good. They were strong men painted red with their cheeks puffed full of coca, slapping him on the back. He kept his Winchester close and wrote in his diary to keep his thoughts straight. They surrounded his hut. It was night and the shadows from the fires projected shapes of Indians against the walls moving in a macabre dance. It was diabolic, he said. The growling of Robuchon's great dane kept them at bay. Suddenly more Indians arrived. Now there were some thirty all together, milling around a pot placed on the ground. One of the Indians who seemed to be the chief stuck his finger in it and spoke rapidly.

"From the beginning the scene interested me intensely," began the passage in the *edición oficial* attributed to the disappeared Frenchman,

> and in order to follow it better I set my papers to one side. It was the very *chupe del tabaco,* the ceremony in which the Indians recall their lost liberty and formulate terrible vows of vengeance against the whites. The conversation became more and more animated under the influence of tobacco and coca. The Indians became overexcited, almost threatening.[28]

He had been hired by Arana in 1904 as an "explorer." It was a task calling for a geographer and an ethnologist, a sort of commercial spying of the land and its people dignified by the appeal to civilization and science. Rumor had it that a year or so later he was killed by the company when his sympathies turned against it. He had married a Huitoto woman who went to live with his family in France after he died. Captain Whiffen provided a moving elegy, as much to the morbid spirit of the forest as to Robuchon's disappearance, where he describes in his book passing through the forest with John Brown, the Barbadian overseer, and coming across derelict photographic plates and vestiges of a camp which they presumed to be the French explorer's last.

Robuchon had taken a lot of photographs and the book published posthumously under his name was filled with them, many depicting waterfalls and bends in the rivers, pretty places enthusiastically commented upon as such by the leading newspaper of Lima, aptly named *El Comercio,* when the book came out. In the photographs in which white men appeared they invariably bore Winchester rifles, a point that impressed members of the Select Committee of the British House of Commons and made them wonder why such an amount of hardware had to be carried or photographed so conspicuously. In José Eustacio Rivera's novel of forest and rubber-peons,

Robuchon's wife and the Huitota Indian María, after the shipwreck of the steam
launch *Ciryl* in which they lost all their belongings. (From Eugenio Robuchon, *En
el Putumayo y sus afluentes,* 1907.)

The Vortex, which is more than a novel since it has passed into living mythology (I myself have encountered persons who said they migrated to the
Putumayo on account of the mysterious excitement it conveyed about the
jungle), there is a French explorer who, moved by the suffering of the peons,
undergoes a sudden change of heart and begins in secret to photograph the
mutilations that the company has inflicted on them. The Kodak becomes
the eye that will pierce the veil of hallucination that Arana has cast over the
Putumayo. But a short time later company men march off to rebut his
denunciations. He will never leave the forest again.

   None of those sort of photos appear in the book published under Robuchon's name. All we know of them are what Whiffen kicks around in the
ashes of an old fire in the forest a couple of years later—while in the book
said to be Robuchon's there are many photographs of naked Indian women,
scientific-anthropological mugshots with an anterior view, a posterior view,

Robuchon's wife and his sister in Poitiers, France. (From Eugenio Robuchon, *En el Putumayo y sus afluentes,* 1907.)

and an accompanying dissecting text—e.g., "In general the Huitotos have thin and nervous members. It is rare to find among them a pronounced abdomen." So begins one chapter following the abdomens with a swerve to discuss hunting habits of the Indians. The eye here is indiscriminate: Indian tummies, Indian hunting . . . all grist for the mill of the all-consuming eye of scientific ethnography. Lest it be thought that this is not science but something between pseudo- and protoscience, the reader is advised to consult the six volumes of the authoritative *Handbook of South American Indians* published in the 1940s for the Smithsonian Institution's Bureau of American Ethnology and prepared in cooperation with that disinterested patron of the sciences, the U.S. Department of State. In volume 3, for example, one finds the same colonizing eye at work in the photographs of Huitoto people, the same display of the body as artifact to be scrutinized for the mystery of its meaning—i.e., its meaning to us. Which is the more poignant in this respect: Susan Sontag's notion that in *capturing* reality through photography, the thing thus represented is all the more irretrievably lost, or Michel Foucault's notion that the modern sciences of society and of the person depend upon a clinical way of seeing that comes close in order to distance itself in the orbit of control?[29] These are the same eyes that put Huitoto baskets and blowpipes in museums and are taught to look at them as data in locked glass cases.

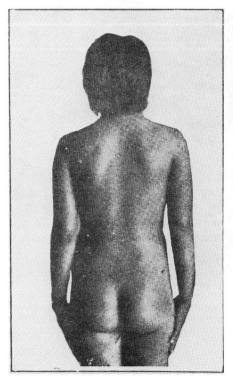 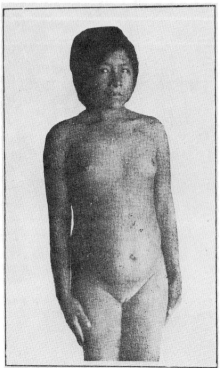

Cannibalism in another mode? (From Eugenio Robuchon, *En el Putumayo y sus afluentes,* 1907.)

There are no photographs of naked men. If the men are white they bear a hat and carry a gun. If they're Indian they sport a breechcloth. Are we being invited to participate in a colonial code of seduction and violence? While the women enchant, the men. . .

In the text of the Frenchman's book it is said that, unlike the Indian men, the women do not eat people (yet legend has it, in Rocha's account, that the fearsome Crisóstomo Hernández had killed an entire communal house full of people, down to the infants because the women as well as the children were cannibalizing), and the Lima newspaper *El Comercio* stated concerning Robuchon's Huitoto widow, on the occasion of the posthumous publication of the Frenchman's book, that it would not be all that unusual if tomorrow one of her Huitoto sisters were to encounter the same fate (referring, one imagines, to her marriage and not to her widowhood). "As you can see in one of our photographic reproductions," continued the newspaper article, "it seems that the employees of the zone are not indisposed to the enchantments of the Huitotas."[30] Mourning the disappearance of the French explorer, the newspaper appealed once again to a photograph. "Who knows

"Last Retreat. A group of Huitoto Aimene women. In what respect are these women weak? Mr. Mitchell referred to modesty? It should be noted that they disrobed themselves in the presence of the English consul in order to be photographed." (From Carlos Rey de Castro, *Los escándolos del Putumayo, 1913.*)

if one of his (Huitoto) companions of such placid demeanour that surround him in the photograph that today we reproduce did not figure among those who killed and ate him?"[31] Male companions to be sure, dwarfed by his pith helmet.

Another chapter of the book credited to Robuchon begins:

> The Huitotos have grey-copper colored skin whose tones correspond to numbers 29 and 30 of the chromatic scale of the Anthropological Society of Paris. Their hair is long, abundant, black, dark, and smooth. Both sexes let it grow without cutting. They cut or pull out their eyelashes, eyebrows, and the hairs from the other parts of the body. The men mutilate their noses and lips according to the tribe. Those of the Upper Igaraparaná perforate the nasal septum, where they place a tube of reed, the same thickness as the plume of a goose. Those of the Central Igaraparaná perforate the walls of the nose and affix colored feathers. They also go through the lower lip with a type of metal nail. Almost all have the ear lobe fitted out with a piece of hardwood, adorned with the shell of mother of pearl.
>
> The chest is broad. The breasts are elevated and flung back, giving an air of nobility. But the superior and inferior members, particularly the latter, are little developed.

"Indio huitoto caniane del Alto Igaraparaná." (From Eugenio Robuchon, *En el Putumayo y sus afluentes*, 1907.)

It is interesting to note their peculiar way of walking, especially that of the women. The habit of carrying their babies on their backs gives them an inclined position which they keep all their lives. The feet are turned inwards so that when they walk the muscles close against each other, giving the appearance of modesty.

On the contrary the men walk with their feet splayed outwards balancing their hips. But when they try to cross a log serving as a bridge over a river or a precipice, then they turn their feet inwards, thus acquiring more stability and avoiding slipping. The big toes of both feet are endowed with a great power of adhesion and serve to pick and gather up all sorts of objects from the ground. The genital organs of the men, covered by a belt of fiber which constrains them, never achieve their normal development. The member is small and with a ten-

Robuchon surrounded by Huitoto Fununas. (From Eugenio Robuchon, *En el Putumayo y sus afluentes,* 1907.)

dency to be always covered by the prepuce which is very large
and covers all the glans. In the women there is no anomaly.
The breasts are periform and stand out, even with the elderly,
in whose case they lose their volume but never hang.
    Among the weapons of the Huitotos figures the
blowpipe. . . .[32]

Where does the heart of darkness lie, in the fleshy body-tearing rites of
the cannibals or in the photographing eye of the beholder exposing them
naked and deformed piece by piece to the world? It is a clinical eye and one
never so lewd as in the closeness of the distance it maintains while dissecting
the body of the Indian—assessing skin color, functionalizing, measuring
breasts, observing toes, measuring penises. In his fear of the Indians, alone
and lost in the jungle, the calming thought came to Captain Whiffen of their
proper place: in glass cases in an Anthropological museum. It was this same
eye that through the Frenchman Robuchon (whether he was real or fictional)
could both measure skin color on a standardizing anthropologizing chromatic
scale *and* breathlessly portray the diabolic shadows of red and black reflecting the Indians moving at night around the glass case of his hut.

Speaking for the company, Arana assumed, *con fundamento,* that the
Frenchman had been the victim of the cannibal Indians that populate those

parts.[33] Cast as an ethnographic and geographical report, Robuchon's book had been compiled and edited by the able hand of one of Arana's closest associates, Carlos Rey de Castro, the Peruvian consul in Manaos, the foremost port during the Amazon rubber boom. His ingenuity was equal to the task. In his own work, *Los pobladores del Putumayo,* he set out to further Peruvian (and hence Arana's) claims to the disputed stretches of the Putumayo and its indigneous inhabitants by claiming the latter as descendants of the *orejones* of the sacred Incan capital of Cuzco, far away in the Andean mountains. (Casement argued a similar case in his beautiful and moving article for *The Contemporary Review* in which he depicted the Indians as in but not of the forest.) But that was not all. In 1909 Rey de Castro tried to wheedle maps and notes out of Captain Whiffen when they met in Manaos in the presence of Julio César Arana.

Whiffen was on his way back to England where reports were flying that the company was up to no good. "I showed him the notes and my draft maps," Whiffen informed the Select Committee on Putumayo. "He was very interested in it all. He informed me that he had edited Robuchon's book on the country in question, and that he would like to have my notes in hand, to treat in the same way as he had treated Robuchon's notes."[34]

A few months later Arana met with Whiffen in Paris at the Nouvelle Hôtel where they had lunch. Arana asked him his opinions about Hardenburg's revelations of atrocities in *Truth.* He was anxious to know if Whiffen had been approached by *Truth* in order to provide further condemnation. Two weeks later they dined at the Cafe Royal in London, on which occasion Whiffen informed Arana that he had to prepare a report for the Foreign Office. They drank champagne all evening. Arana suggested they stop off at the Motor Club. The next morning Whiffen's recollection was none too clear. It seemed that Arana had asked him how much money he would require to write a report for the Peruvian government. Whiffen told him his expenses had been £1,400 and started to copy down what Arana dictated to him. It was in Spanish and Whiffen's Spanish, he later admitted under cross-examination by the Select Committee, was very poor. When Arana asked for the paper Whiffen got suspicious and tore it up. "I thought he had laid some trap for me," he told the Select Committee. They were still drinking champagne.[35]

Later on in Arana's letter to the shareholders of the Peruvian Amazon Company this written statement of Whiffen's appeared in English. Someone had got hold of the pieces and stuck them together, a collage of the original. The words "one thousand pounds" were stuck in the wrong place. The Spanish pronoun *mis* was missing from one page and placed on another. It was grotesque. It was banal. Whiffen was supposed to have written that he was willing to write a report for the Peruvian government saying he had *not* seen any irregularities in the Putumayo.

Certainly his book, which came out a little later, contained no mention of ill-treatment of Indians by the rubber company—although there was a deep, brooding, malevolent tone throughout, the tone of the primal, the forest ill at ease. "My expenses were £1,400," ended his note, "but I am agreeable and will receive £1,000 as compensation—nothing else."[36] And the last two words appeared forged, presumably by Arana or at his bidding.

It was from such dexterous hands that Eugenio Robuchon's Putumayan notes and photographs emerged in book form—no less than 20,000 copies of which, so it was said, were printed by Arana in Lima in 1907.[37] And it was from this book that Casement extracted the notion of the *chupe del tabaco* as a ritual in which the Indians formulated terrible vows of vengeance against the whites—the same ritual that the whites were said to have used to bind Indians to debt-peonage and to the collection of rubber.

Doubtless many different fingers could be stuck into the tobacco pot and sucked. Many were the orations it facilitated. The one about itself, now that the white man has been added to the circle, is still going on.

It was Don Crisóstomo Hernández who wrought to perfection the colonial metaritual of the *chupe,* or rather, as in so many things about the Putumayo rubber boom, it was the story about Don Crisóstomo that was so perfect in this regard, the story about his stories—which were so compelling that, for the assemblies of Huitoto captains sitting with him, orating around the tobacco pot, there was nought else to do but unanimously agree to his proposals.[38]

Moreover, stories about the *chupe del tabaco* could be as mystically powerful as those related around it; in particular the story related by Rocha that brought the *chupe* into the very center of the charmed circle of cannibalism itself. Wildly extravagant and melodramatic, it certainly rings true, not necessarily regarding the cannibalism in question but regarding the poetics of fear and astonishment that I know from listening to colonists swapping yarns of the forest and its people. My mind goes back, for instance, to a night I spent in 1978 in a tiny store by the río San Miguel, an affluent of the Putumayo and maybe 150 miles upstream from where Rocha was absorbed in his tales of terror while the slow chit-chat of frogs croaking entranced the jungle night. Where I was, so many years later, the hardened men of the forest talked to each other for hours of stories they had heard about being lost in the forest, stories of its dangerous animals and its fearsome spirits such as the *espanta,* with her hair down to the ground and her long white breasts, a spirit so frightening that, on seeing her, all consciousness is lost. But never in all my nights with Indians in the foothills did I hear or overhear stories like these, spun with such fiendish and melodramatic aesthetic pleasure derived from fear and mystery.

Traven wrote in *The March to the Monteria* about a Chamula Indian from the highlands of Chiapas, Mexico, who went down into the jungle, the first step to enslavement as a lumberjack in debt-peonage in the mahogany industry. "All along the way the people he consulted told him the most terrifying stories about the jungle," wrote Traven.

> These people, however, had never been in the jungle themselves; they had not even approached the thicket at the outer edges. All of them recounted merely what others had seen or lived through.
>
> But the various stories related to Celso all contributed, without exception, to inspire in him a terrific fear of the vast jungle. Nobody really cared whether Celso perished in the jungle or not. The narrations were made mostly to enjoy the changing expressions of an interested listener, to pass the time away and to get excited over one's story. Ghost stories, tales of spooks, are not told at night to make someone desist from crossing the cemetery if that is his road home. They are told to spend a pleasant evening by watching with delight the terror-stricken faces of one's audience.
>
> Now a march through the jungle is by no means a holiday hike. The facts came very close to the terrifying narrations of its terrors. . . .[39]

Such is Traven's story. And he, too, went down into the mahogany forests. Joaquin Rocha tells us, presumably as he was told, that

> all the individuals of the nation that has captured the prisoner retire to an area of the bush to which women are absolutely prohibited, except for one who acts a special role. Children are also rigorously excluded. In the center, a pot of cooked tobacco juice is placed for the pleasure of the men, and in a corner seated on a little bench and firmly bound is the captive.
>
> Clasping each others' arms, the savages form a long line, and to the sound of drums advance dancing very close to the victim. They retreat and advance many times, with individuals separating to drink from the pot of tobacco. Then the drum stops for the dancing cannibals, and so that the unfortunate victim can see how much he is going to lose by dying, the most beautiful girl of the tribe enters, regally attired with the most varied and brilliant feathers of the birds of these woods. The drum starts again, and the beautiful girl dances alone in front of and almost touching him. She twists and advances, showering him with passionate looks and gestures of love, turning around and repeating this three or four times. She then leaves, terminating the second act of this solemn occasion. The third act follows with the same men's dance as before, except that each time the line of dancers approaches the prisoner, one of the men detaches himself and declaims something like this: "Remember when your people killed Jatijiko, man of our nation

whom you couldn't take prisoner because he knew how to die
before allowing himself to be dragged in front of your people?
We are going to take vengeance of his death in you, you cow-
ard, who doesn't know how to die in battle like he did." Or
else: "remember when you and your people surprised my sister
Jifisino bathing, captured her and while alive made a party of
her flesh and tormented her until her last breath? Do you remember? Now you god-cursed man we are going to devour you
alive and you won't die until all traces of your bloody flesh
have disappeared from our mouths."

Following this is the fourth and last act of the terrifying tragedy. One by one the dancers come forward and with his knife
each one cuts a slice of meat off the prisoner, which they eat
half roasted to the sound of his death rattle. When he eventually dies, they finish cutting him up and continue roasting and
cooking his flesh, eating him to the last little bit.[40]

Narrative Mediation: Epistemic Murk

It seems to me that stories like these were indispensable to the formation
and flowering of the colonial imagination during the Putumayo rubber boom.
"Their imagination was diseased," wrote the Peruvian judge Rómulo Paredes
in 1911, referring to the rubber station employees about and from whom he
obtained 3,000 handwritten pages of testimony after four months in the forest,
"and they saw everywhere attacks by Indians, conspiracies, uprisings,
treachery etc.; and in order to save themselves from these fancied perils . . .
they killed, and killed without compassion."[41]

Far from being trivial daydreams indulged in after work was over, these
stories and the imagination they sustained were a potent political force without which the work of conquest and of supervising rubber gathering could
not have been accomplished. What is crucial to understand is the way these
stories functioned to create through magical realism a culture of terror that
dominated both whites and Indians.

The importance of this colonial work of fabulation extends beyond the
nightmarish quality of its contents. Its truly crucial feature lies in the way
it creates an uncertain reality out of fiction, giving shape and voice to the
formless form of the reality in which an unstable interplay of truth and illusion becomes a phantasmic social force. All societies live by fictions taken
as real. What distinguishes cultures of terror is that the epistemological,
ontological, and otherwise philosophical problem of representation—reality
and illusion, certainty and doubt—becomes infinitely more than a "merely"
philosophical problem of epistemology, hermeneutics, and deconstruction.
It becomes a high-powered medium of domination, and during the Putumayo
rubber boom this mediium of epistemic and ontological murk was most
keenly figured and thrust into consciousness as the space of death.

The managers lived obsessed with death, Rómulo Paredes tells us. They saw danger everywhere. They thought solely of the fact that they live surrounded by vipers, tigers, and cannibals. It was these ideas of death, he wrote, that constantly struck their imagination, making them terrified and capable of any action. Like children they had nightmares of witches, evil spirits, death, treason, and blood. The only way they could live in such a terrifying world, he observed, was to inspire terror themselves.[42]

Sociological and Mythic Mediation: The Muchachos

If it was the telling of tales that mediated this inspiration of terror, then it behooves us to inquire a little into the group of people who mediated this mediation; namely, the corps of Indian guards trained by the company and known as the *muchachos de confianza,* the "trusted boys." For in Rómulo Paredes's words, they were "constantly devising executions and continually revealing meetings of Indians 'licking tobacco' [the *chupe*]—which meant an oath to kill white men—imaginary uprisings that never existed, and other similar crimes."[43] What is at stake here is in many ways the linchpin of the company's control, namely, the typical colonial ploy of using indigenous culture in order to exploit it. But, of course, things are never quite so simple. Even the manipulators have a culture and, moreover, culture is not so easily "used."

Mediating as semicivilized and semirational Indians between the savages of the forest and the whites of the rubber camps, the *muchachos* embodied the salient differences of the class and caste system in the rubber boom. Cut off from their own kind whom they persecuted and betrayed and in whom they often inspired envy and hatred, and now classified as semicivilized and dependent on the whites for food, arms, and goods, the *muchachos* typified all that was savage in the colonial mythology of savagery—because they were in the perfect social and mythic space to do so. Not only did they embellish fictions that stoked the fires of white paranoia, they also embodied the brutality that the whites feared, created, and tried to harness to their own ends. The *muchachos* traded their colonially created identity as savages for their new colonial status as civilized Indians and guards. As Paredes noted, they placed at the disposal of the whites "their special instincts, such as sense of direction, scent, their sobriety, and their knowledge of the forest."[44] Just as they bought rubber from the wild Indians of the forest, so the whites also bought the *auca*-like savage "instincts" of the Indian *muchachos*.

Yet, unlike rubber, these savage instincts were manufactured from the whites' imaginations. All the *muchachos* had to do to receive their rewards was to objectify and through stories give back to the whites the phantoms lying dormant in colonial culture. Given the centuries of Incan and Spanish colonial mythology concerning the *auca* and the wild man, and given the implosion of this mythology in the contradictory social being of the *mu-*

chachos, this was a simple task. The *muchachos'* stories were but fragments of a more encompassing one that constituted them as objects in a colonial discourse rather than its authors.

The debt-peonage established by the Putumayo rubber boom was more than a trade in white commodities for india rubber. It was also a trade in fictitious realities, pivoted on the *muchachos* whose storytelling bartered betrayal of Indian realities for the confirmation of colonial fantasies.

The "Illimitable Delirium"

Joaquin Rocha's man-eating tale ends not with the death of the prisoner but with his being eaten "to the last little bit," ingesting him so as to incorporate his strength and augment one's war magic, as Konrad Preuss wrote was the case with Huitoto cannibalism, or to degrade him, as Captain Whiffen was told.[45] If the torture practiced by modern states, as in Latin America today, is any guide, these motives by no means preclude one another. Nor does proof of these frequently disputed contentions necessarily lie in the eating. For now, as Captain Whiffen writes, "when the orgy of blood and gluttony is over, the warriors must *dance*"—and do so for eight days to what he describes as the gloomy rolling of drums, breaking off every now and again from the dance to stir great troughs of liquor with the forearms of dead enemies. With intoxication, the captain tells us, their songs become shrieks, demoniacal and hellish. "But the scene defies description,"[46] he notes with humility, and with wisdom, too. For tucked eighty pages away in the quiet eddy of a footnote he mentions that "I never was present at a cannibal feast. The information comes from Robuchon's account, checked by cross-questioning the Indians with whom I came in contact."[47]

"It is," he nevertheless goes on to write in the mainstream of his narrative, "a mad festival of savagery."

> The naked men are wildly excited; their eyes glare, their nos-
> trils quiver, but they are not drunk. The naked women abandon
> themselves to the movement of the dance; they scream their
> chorus to the tribal dance-song; but they are not lewd. There is
> about it an all-pervading illimitable delirium. The wild outburst
> affects even the stranger in their midst. Forgotten cells in his
> brain react to the stimulus of the scene. He is no longer apart,
> alien in speech and feeling. He locks arms in the line of canni-
> bals, sways in rhythm with them, stamps as solemnly, and
> sings the meaningless words as fervently as the best of them.
> He has bridged an age of civilization, and returned to barba-
> rism in the debased jetsam of the river banks. It is the strange
> fascination of the Amazons.[48]

And in that other rubber belt of King Leopold's Congo, toiling slowly up-stream "on the edge of a black and incomprehensible frenzy" a dozen years

before Captain Whiffen was locking arms swaying with cannibals, entering
the delirium returning to barbarism, another Englishman, Joseph Conrad's
storyteller, the sailor Marlow, also bridged an age, if not the very genesis,
of civilization: "They howled and leaped, and spun, and made horrid faces;
but what thrilled you was just the thought of their humanity—like yours—
the thought of your remote kinship with this wild and passionate uproar."

"And you say you saw the Indians burnt?" the consul-general asked Au-
gustus Walcott, who had been born in the Caribbean island of Antigua twenty-
three years before.

> "Yes."
> "Burnt alive?"
> "Alive."
> "How do you mean? Describe this?"
> "Only one I see burnt alive."
> "Well, tell me about that one?"
> "He had not work 'caucho,' he ran away and he kill a 'mu-
> chacho,' a boy, and they cut off his two arms and his legs by
> the knee and they burn his body . . . they drag the body and
> they put plenty of wood and set fire to it, and throw the man
> on it."
> "Are you sure he was still alive—not dead when they threw
> him on the fire?"
> "Yes, he did alive. I'm sure of it—I see him move—open his
> eyes, he screamed out."[49]

There was something else that the consul-general could not understand,
and he called Walcott back to explain what he meant by saying "because
he told the Indians that we was Indians too, and eat those—." What he
meant was that the rubber station manager, Señor Normand, "to frighten
the Indians told them that the negroes were cannibals, and a fierce tribe of
cannibals who eat people, and that if they did not bring in rubber these black
men would be sent to kill and eat them." "This is what he meant to say,"
added Casement. "Señor Normand had so described the Barbados men on
bringing them among the Andokes Indians, in order to terrify the Indians."[50]

James Mapp (who said that he, unlike other people, never saw or heard
of Señor Aguero killing Indians for food for his dogs) told the consul-general
he had seen Hilary Quales bite pieces out of four Indians. They were hanging
with their arms twisted behind their backs for about three hours and Quales
was playing with them, swinging them by the legs with Aguero, the station
manager, looking on. He bit the little toe off one man and spat it on the
floor. He bit the others in the calves and thighs. Aguero was laughing.[51]

"Have you seen Aguero kill Indians?" the consul-general asked Evelyn
Batson in the rubber collecting depot of La Chorrera.

> "No, Sir; I haven't seen him kill Indians—but I have seen
> him send *muchachos* to kill Indians. He has taken an Indian

man and given him to the *muchachos* to eat, and they have a
dance off it."

"Did you see that?"

"Yes, Sir; I seen that."

"You saw the man killed?"

"Yes, Sir. They tied him to a stake and they shot him, and
they cut off his head after he was shot and his feet and hands,
and they carried him about in the section—in the yard—and
they carries them up and down singing, and they carries them
to their houses and dances. . . . They carries off the pieces of
him, and they pass in front of the manager's house with
these—his feet and his arms and his head, and they took them
to their own house."

"How do you know they ate them?"

"I heard that they eat them. I have not witnessed it, Sir, but
I heard the manager Señor Aguero, tell that they ate this man."

"The manager said all this?"

"Yes, Sir, he did."[52]

Katenere was a famous rebel chief whose wife was kidnapped by the
rubber company. He tried to free her and was shot dead by *muchachos* sent
by Evelyn Batson.

"What did they do with the body of Katenere?" the consul-
general asked Batson. "Did they bury it?"

"Yes, Sir. Zellada [the acting manager] cut his head off, and
his feet and hands—they put these in the grave along with the
body."

"Did they show these members to everyone in the station?"

"Yes, Sir; the head they put in the river till the manager
come, that the manager could see it."[53]

Katenere had escaped from gathering rubber. He captured weapons and
shot dead Arana's brother-in-law. He was counted, says Casement, "a brave
man and a terror to the Peruvian rubber-workers." Imagined terror made
men do terrible things, as Judge Rómulo Paredes observed. In hunting down
Katenere, the display was spectacular and—as with the dismembering of his
body—it was focused on the head. James Chase was on one of these hunts,
and the consul-general summarized what he said about it.

At the next house they reached they caught four Indians, one
woman and three men. Vasquez, who was in charge, ordered
one of the *muchachos* to cut this woman's head off. He ordered this for no apparent reason that James Chase knows of,
simply because "he was in command, and could do what he
liked." The *muchacho* cut the woman's head off; he held her
by the hair of her head, and flinging her down, hacked her head
off with a machete. It took more than one blow to sever the
head—three or four blows.

Her remains were left on the path, as were the severed heads and truncated bodies of other people caught in this raid; Katenere's child, decapitated for crying, and a woman, an adolescent boy, and three adult men—all for walking too slowly. The company men were walking very fast because they were a bit frightened thinking of the Indians pursuing them.[54]

In assuming the character of the cannibals who pursued them, as much if not more in their fantasies than when they were pursuing Indians to gather rubber, the whites seemed oblivious to the tale that the Indians would *not* eat them. At least that's what Casement and Judge Paredes were separately informed. A rubber gatherer familiar for many years with the Huitotos and their language told the judge that the Indians felt repugnance toward the civilized, whom they called the *gemuy comuine,* kinsmen of the monkey, whose nauseating smell precluded their being eaten, dead or alive. "The only case of cannibalism I became acquainted with during my mission in the Putumayo," avowed the judge, "was that ordered by the civilized themselves."[55]

Perhaps it was their smell that made their orders to eat people that much more compelling? For in those stories recently heard by some anthropologists in the northernmost extremity of what was then Arana's territory, is said by Indians that the whites in the rubber company were immune to Indian sorcery. It could not enter them because they, the whites, smelled so bad. That was why the legendary revolt of Yarocamena failed. At least that's what some say. But the interpreting of such things is perhaps better left alone. For these Histories of Punishment and of Danger are for sorcerers only. Indeed, so I've been told, it's from the interpreting of such stories that sorcerers gain their evil power.[56]

SIX

The Colonial Mirror
of Production

The yarns of seamen have a direct simplicity, the whole meaning of which lies within the shell of a cracked nut. But Marlow was not typical (if his propensity to spin yarns be excepted), and to him the meaning of an episode was not inside like a kernel but outside, enveloping the tale which brought it out only as a glow brings out a haze, in the likeness of one of those misty halos that sometimes are made visible by the spectral illumination of moonshine.[1]

I hope by now it is obvious why I chose what may have seemed a strange point of departure—the mediation of terror through narration, and the problem that raises for effective counterrepresentations. I hope it will later also be obvious why I have to push on to work through the ways that shamanic healing in the *upper* reaches of the Putumayo, like the culture of terror, also develops its force from the colonially generated wildness of the epistemic murk of the space of death.

What began for me as a seaman's yarn aimed at cracking open the shell of other seamen's yarns to reveal their meaning—the tales of Rocha, Whiffen, Hardenburg, Casement, and so on, and the yarns their yarns were based upon—ended up like Marlow's, whose meaning lay outside, enveloping the tale that brought it out as a glow brings out a haze. Meaning was elusive. Doubt played havoc with certainty. Perspectives were as varied as they were destructive of one another. The real was fictional and the fictional was real and the haziness brought out by the glow could be as powerful a force for terror as it could be for resistance. In such a world of control, clarity itself was deceptive, and attempts to explain the terror could barely be distinguished from the stories contained in those explanations—as if terror provided only inexplicable explanations of itself and thrived by so doing.

For me the problem of interpretation grew ever larger until I realized that this problem of interpretation is decisive for terror, not only making effective counterdiscourse so difficult but also making the terribleness of death squads, disappearances, and torture all the more effective in crippling of peoples' capacity to resist. The problem of interpretation turned out to be an essential component of what had to be interpreted, just as resistance was necessary for control. Deeply dependent on sense and interpretation, terror nourished itself by destroying sense. This the Putumayo texts about terror faithfully reproduced.

Particularly wanting in this regard was the hard-bitten appeal to the logic of business, to the rationality of market logic, viewing the terror as a means chosen for cost-effectiveness. In making sense this view heightened the situation's hallucinatory quality. Cost-effectiveness and "scarcity" could be computed any which way, and if rationality suggested killing off the labor supply within a few years it was no less a sport to kill and torture Indians as to work them. Ostensibly a means of increasing production, the torture of Indians was also an end in itself and the region's most enduring product. In these outposts of progress the commodity fetishism portrayed by Karl Marx acquired a form that was both fantastic and brutal. Here, where labor was not free or capable of being turned into a commodity, it was not merely rubber and European trade goods that were subject to fetishization. More important still was the fetishization of the debt of debt-peonage that these commodities constellated and in which the entire imaginative force, the ritualization and viciousness, of colonial society was concentrated. A gigantic piece of make-believe, the debt was where the gift economy of the Indian meshed with the capitalist economy of the colonist. It was here in this strategically indeterminate zone of exchange where the line between war and peace is always so fine that the conditions were laid for an enormity of effort no less imaginative than it was cruel and deadly. Indeed, it was in the cultural elaboration of death and the death-space that the fine line between peace and war was maintained. They see death everywhere, wrote the Peruvian judge Rómulo Paredes, in speaking of the rubber company employees. They think solely of the fact that they live surrounded by vipers, tigers, and cannibals. Their imaginations are constantly struck by the idea of death as figured by these images of the wild and the only way they could live in such a world, he thought, after his tour through the area, was by themselves imspiring terror.

> The shrill voices of those who give orders
> Are full of fear like the squeaking of
> Piglets awaiting the butcher's knife, as their fat arses

> Sweat with anxiety in their office chairs. . . .
> Fear rules not only those who are ruled, but
> The rulers too.[2]

Thus wrote Brecht in exile in 1937, pondering a companion's response after a visit to the Third Reich, who, when asked what really ruled there, answered, Fear. Given the immense power of the regime, its camps and torture cellars, its well-fed policemen, Brecht asked, why do they fear the open word?

In modern times this culture of terror depends upon primitivism, and the revolutionary poet will appeal to the magic of primitiveness to undermine it too.

> But their Third Reich recalls
> The house of Tar, the Assyrian, that mighty fortress
> Which, according to the legend, could not be taken by an army,
> but
> When one single, distinct word was spoken inside it
> Fell to dust.[3]

And if there was anything to that notion of Benjamin's and T. W. Adorno's concerning the resurgence of primitivism along with the fetishism of commodities (think for a moment of Adam Smith's invisible hand as the modern version of animism), then it was in the theater of racist cruelty on the frontier uniting wildness with civilization that the fetish force of the commodity was fused with the phantoms of the space of death, to the dazzling benefit of both. I am thinking here not of steady incremental steps toward progress but of sudden eruptions of whitening the dark zones at the margins of the developing nations where the commodity met the Indian and appropriated through death the fetish power of the savagery created by and spellbinding the European. Here the Putumayo is but a figure for a global stage of development of the commodity fetish; think also of the Congo with its rubber and ivory, of the enslavement of the Yaquis for the sisal plantations of the Yucatan in Mexico, of the genocidal bloodletting in tragic Patagonia—all around the same time.

The new science of anthropology was no less a manifestation of the modernist fascination with the primitive, and in this it was in tandem with the new artistry: Flaubert's realism and the sensual exoticism of his Egypt/Cartharge, Rimbaud's season in hell where the pagan blood returns and the disordered mind becomes sacred, Yeats's sixteenth-century Moorish antiself ("this is our modern hope"), Conrad's modernizing heart of darkness, Richard Huelsenbeck beating "negro rhythms" for Dada evenings in the Cabaret Voltaire in Zurich at the time of World War I (we were like birds in a cage surrounded by lions, said Hugo Ball), Apollinaire's Paris evening turning to dawn:

You walk toward Auteuil you walk home on foot
To sleep among your fetishes from Oceania and Guinea
They are all Christ in another form and of another faith . . .[4]

And if Casement slept with his fetishes "colored like the very tree-trunks they flitted among like spirits of the woods" in a dreamy world that pictured Huitotos and all upper Amazonian Indians as naturally gentle and docile, Captain Whiffen could write an entire book under the spell of a nature that displayed its human inhabitants as well as its animal and plant life as innately wild and vengeful, nasty and thrillingly so. Against these views the inland mariner Alfred Simson portrayed the primitive as that plenitude of flitting shadowiness of possible anything betraying all the opposite traits of character (except, perhaps, servility) that not only constituted the wild Indian but also constituted the misty essence of wildness on which terror seized. If the commodity fetishism of Marx meant a wild oscillation between thing and phantom, then these figures of wildness caught that relationship with a precision no less binding than the stocks with which the terror pinned down its object, only to watch it writhe and die.

Of course there was some safety in numbers, even though they were diminishing. Rocha quoted anonymous authority in putting the number of Huitotos at a quarter a million. Others gave other figures and there was a magical number of thirty thousand Huitotos dead or fled between 1900 and 1910—numbers that were wild guesses but unacknowledged as such. Proffered the reader as implicit signs of control and order, gestures of expertise in tricky terrain, these numbers oozed epistemic tranquility as the measure of horror and provided a stolid ambience of reality, a back-stiffening jolt of certainty, awful as it might be, before steaming into the hermeneutic swamp of Putumayo terror and its explanation.

Casement said that if offered decent terms of trade the Indians would work rubber without torture, while Barbadian overseers, Rocha, and the U.S. consul in Iquitos were not all that sure. They doubted you could get an Indian to work intensively for long in any "system," just as Casement himself had said earlier when he was responsible for getting work done by indigenous people in the Congo. It was an intangible, teasing, and even deadly issue— work motivation and the evaluation of the worth and meaning of trade goods for forest people. It was the central problem involved in the industrialization of Europe, too; a compacted nugget of the history of civilization that lay at the very heart of the debt-peonage relationship and the meaning of its torture. It is not the sort of thing that is going to run away with an explanation, either then or now.

An unacknowledged uncertainty also constituted the morass of ideas, images, hunches, and feelings about the likelihood of Indian uprisings. Against the views of some of the overseers, Casement confidently and lucidly asserted that revolt was unlikely for this, that, and the other socio-logical reason. Yet in other places in his report he provided ample signs of its occurrence. Joaquin Rocha's book likewise created an unacknowledged medley of possibilities, at one point asserting that the whites had nothing to fear while at another saying their lives hung by a thread. Reasoning confounded itself in this situation. The search for law and order led to unacknowledged disorder. The blithe confidence of tone in the reports totally belied the uncertainty of their contents wherein the politically crucial feature of the situation was the way the standoff between terror and uncertainty created more of the same.

"The Phraseology of Conquest" was one of the subheadings in the introduction to the published account of the hearings held by the British Parliamentary Select Committee on Putumayo. The Committee members were perplexed as they sifted the sands of contrary meanings and plots associated with the words *conquistar* and *reducir,* conquer and reduce. In addition to the effort to bring an Englishman's words to bear on a sly Latin like Julio César Arana, who equated conquest with doing business and cannibalism with a distaste for trading, the Select Committee had before it wildly different versions of the history of conquest—a notably mythological subject in its authority and appeal as was nicely brought out when a letter from the British consul of Iquitos, read to the baffled Committee, explained that the conquest of the Indians of Peru was like the conquest of Britain by the Romans. On the one hand the Committee was presented with a picture of the conquest of the Putumayo as opening with death and destruction and closing with meek submission and trading. On the other hand was Casement's history of smooth-talking, seductive traders who used Western commodities to woo the Indians, "grown-up children," into an act of colonial pederasty and then into the bonds of slavery—for some reason not called slavery but dissimulated as "debt-peonage."

The source of the Committee's perplexity with "The Phraseology of Conquest" did not simply lie in habits of legal nitpicking or the inevitable methodological problem for anthropology of translating one culture's forms into another's. Beyond those considerations was the active social role played by the same sort of perplexity over what was called debt-peonage, that perplexity with which Joaquin Rocha observed the "deforming of good speech" and the failure to observe "the propriety" of terms. Yet on it went, day in and day out, a deformation of this, a failure of that, disorder writ large in the elusive opacity of social institutions that juggled floggings with ritualized displays of double-entry bookkeeping, and gift-giving rituals of exchange with no less ritualized practices of business—parodies of capitalist theatricality on the equatorial line. Were the rubber gatherers traders or slaves or debts? Could a person be a debt? Why were the "payments"—or were they "advances"?—forced onto Indians ("I want a black dog!")?—Why was there so much cruelty?

There is an image swimming into focus here, an image of the Indian in the stocks. The stocks hold the body tight, at least its head and its arms. Perhaps the rubber station manager and his employees are watching from the veranda. They are, so it has been said, the jaguars and the thunder of commodities.[5] Perhaps some of them are wondering when their turn will come to be fixed in the stocks. But for the moment the jaguar and the thunder are free. It is the Indian who is fixed tight. Yet all around in the forest nothing is fixed. The rain is beating. The water drips off the shining leaves in the dark forest. Rivulets form into streams and rivers gather force to form the muddy Amazon swirling past the Italian marble and Polish prostitutes of rubber-rich Manaos where Arana and Rey de Castro tried to bribe Whiffen for his ethnological notes and photographs. He accepts. He doesn't accept. Onward swirls the river to the sea close by where Columbus's boats met the heaving chop of the currents of the Orinoco, one of the four rivers of Paradise, onward to New York and to Europe where Whiffen gets drunk on champagne, signs a note declaring the Putumayo a paradise and then tears it to pieces. But the note is pieced together, disjointedly as it turns out, like the collages mocking representation with presentation that the Cubists were inventing to replace visual illusion by mental illusion, not far from the hotel where Arana and Whiffen were lunching, after which Whiffen wrote his book without a mention of the torture and killing of the Indians he studied. He may as well not have ripped the note into pieces, over in Europe where everything is fixed and nothing is fixed and where a British Parliamentary Select Committee is trying to get to the bottom of "The Phraseology of Conquest." Little makes sense. Little can be pinned down. Only the Indian in the stocks, being watched. And we are watching the watchers so that with our explanation we can pin them down and then pin down the real meaning of terror, putting it in the stocks of explanation. Yet in watching in this way we are made blind to the way that terror makes mockery of sense-making, how it requires sense in order to mock it, and how in that mockery it heightens both sense and sensation.

If terror thrives on the production of epistemic murk and metamorphosis, it nevertheless requires the hermeneutic violence that creates feeble fictions in the guise of realism, objectivity, and the like, flattening contradiction and systematizing chaos. The image of the Putumayo here is not so much the smoothly vicious horror of the vortex, which is the title of Eustacio Rivera's novel of Putumayo rubber and savagery, but rather the world frozen in death-dealing, as (in the story) when Don Crisóstomo, who held savages spellbound with the magic of his oratory, grasped for his gun in the frenzy of his death throes so as to die killing—the ultimate *tableau vivant*.

Here time stood still in an endless movement between banality and melodrama reproducing the terror represented. In Casement's rendition the Barbadian overseers' testimony comes across as emotionless and unamazing—zombies adrift in a dream world, we did this, then we did that—so different in its distanced remoteness from the histrionic testimony published by Hardenburg which included much material from Iquitos newspapers.

In both modes of representation, the banal and the melodramatic, there is the straining to express the inexpressible, what at one stage in the struggle on the stage of Putumayan truth was dismissed as "fantastic credibility." Fantastic it was; its very credibility made it so, went the retort—pointing to both magical (fantastic) realism (credibility) and to Brecht's *Verfremdungseffekt,* his "alienation effect" aimed at alienating alienation, making the everyday strange and the credible fantastic. Perhaps either of these modes of representation, the magically real or the Brechtian, would have succeeded better in transmitting and transforming the hallucinatory reality of Putumayo terror than Casement's Foreign Office's authoritarian realism or Hardenburg's lavish melodrama. But it was the latter two forms that were selected out by the political culture for the task at hand; they were deemed truth, factual, reportage, nonfictional, and as such they may have achieved much. We will never really know.

But the question remains whether the banality and the melodrama were only part of the act of representing or whether they were in the events represented. We shake ourselves clear. We insist on the distinction between reality and depictions of it. But the disturbing thing is that the reality seeped through the pores of the depiction and by means of such seepage continued what such depictions were meant only to be about.

So it was with the stories circulating during the Putumayo rubber boom in which the colonists and rubber company employees not only feared but themselves created through narration fearful and confusing images of savagery, images that bound colonial society together through the epistemic murk of the space of death. The terror and tortures they devised mirrored the horror of the savagery they both feared and fictionalized.

Moreover, when we turn to the task of creating counterrepresentations and counterdiscourses—deflectional, oppositional modes of arresting and diverting the flow of fear—we need to pause and take stock of the ways that the accounts reproduced by Hardenburg and by Casement, accounts that were critical in intention, were similarly fictionalized and aestheticized, drawing upon and fortifying the very same rituals of the colonizing imagination to which men succumbed when torturing Indians. In their imaginative heart these critiques were complicit with what they opposed.

From the accounts of Casement and Timerman it is also obvious that torture and terror are ritualized art forms and that, far from being spontaneous, sui generis, and an abandonment of what are often called the values of civilization, such rites of terror have a deep history deriving power and meaning from those very values.

In Whiffen's case the sensuous interpenetration of opposites is orgiastically enshrined, as when he writes of succumbing to the illimitable delirium of savagery in the cannibal dance, against which he defines civilization.

Father Gaspar, the Capuchin missionary, likewise finds holiness vividly wrought where it confronts the signs of the underworld as in the lugubrious crypts formed by the rotting treetrunks closing off the rivers and in the inhabitants of those crypts. On encountering what he called new and savage tribes in the forest his first act was to exorcize the demon who had held sway there for so long. The words of his exorcizing spell came from the pope. But where did his power come from? From God, or from the evil exorcized? His was a faith no less dependent on the antiself than that of the most brutal *conquistador.*

What stands out here is the mimesis between the savagery attributed to the Indians by the colonists and the savagery perpetrated by the colonists in the name of what Julio César Arana called civilization, meaning business.

The magic of mimesis lies in the transformation wrought on reality by rendering its image. In a postmodern age we are increasingly familiar with this "magic" and no longer think of it as only "primitive." In the notion of the changes effected in the world by carving and dancing with the spirit's mask, in the naming and the singing of one's enemy, in weaving into the magical cloth the image of the wildness as *auca* so as to tease and gain control over it—in all of this we see clearly how the word "magic" magically contains both the art and the politics involved in representation, in the rendering of objecthood. In the colonial mode of production of reality, as in the Putumayo, such mimesis occurs by a colonial mirroring of otherness that reflects back onto the colonists the barbarity of their own social relations, but as imputed to the savagery they yearn to colonize. The power of this colonial mirror is ensured by the way it is dialogically constructed through storytelling, as in the colonial lore retold by Captain Whiffen, Joaquin Rocha, and Robuchon's ever-active ghost, among others, concerning cannibalism and the inevitability with which the wild strives to consume as well as to distinguish difference. And what is put into discourse through the artful storytelling of the colonists is the same as what they practiced on the bodies of Indians.

Tenaciously embedded in this artful practice is a vast and vastly mysterious Western history and iconography of evil exemplified by the imagery of the inferno and the savage, which in turn is indissolubly welded to images of paradise and the good. We hear the voice of Timerman, we see the torturer and the victim coming together, "We victims and victimisers," he writes, "we're part of the same humanity, colleagues in the same endeavor to prove the existence of ideologies, feelings, heroic deeds, religions, obsessions. And the rest of humanity. What are they engaged in?"

Post-Enlightenment European culture makes it difficult if not impossible to draw apart the veil of the heart of darkness without either succumbing to its hallucinatory quality or losing that quality. Fascist poetics succeed where liberal rationalism self-destructs. But what might point a way out of this impasse is precisely what is so painfully absent from the Putumayo accounts, namely the narrative mode of the Indians themselves. It is the ultimate anthropological conceit, anthropology in its highest, indeed redemptive, moment, rescuing the "voice" of the Indian from the obscurity of pain and time. From the represented shall come that which overturns the representation.

But this very same anthropology tells us that we cannot take our place in the charmed circle of men orating through the night around the tobacco pot, chewing coca. It is said that the stories about the rubber boom are dangerous, "histories of punishment" meant only for sorcerers who, in interpreting such histories, gain evil power.[6] There is no place for us here, and anthropology, the science of man, confounds itself in its very moment of understanding the natives' point of view.

The lesson? Before there can be a science of man there has to be the long-awaited demythification and reenchantment of Western man in a quite different confluence of self and otherness. Our way lies upstream, against the current, upriver near the foothills of the Andes where Indian healers are busy healing colonists of the phantoms assailing them. There in the jointness of their construction across the colonial divide the healer desensationalizes terror so that the mysterious side of the mysterious (to adopt Benjamin's formula) is indeed denied by an optic that perceives the everyday as impenetrable, the impenetrable as everyday. This is another history, not only of terror, but of healing as well. (It is not meant for sorcerers, as far as I know.)

PART TWO
Healing

SEVEN
A Case of Fortune
and Misfortune

I first met José García in December 1975
when he joined a group of us waiting to
drink *yagé* with Santiago Mutumbajoy, an
Indian shaman of repute in the Putumayo
foothills where the eastern slopes of the Andes blend with the rain forest of the upper
Amazon basin in Colombia. He was the last
to join our group of poor white colonists
and local Indians watching the dusk sharpen
the silhouette of the mountains, and he was
pointed out to me as a close friend and pupil
of the shaman's. What struck me was that
José García was a white who had undertaken to study with an Indian healer.

I remembered how a few months earlier,
while I was staying with another shaman,
two white men had approached the house
at night, one screaming: "Thanks to God,
I *know*! Kill me now, with all *you* know—
great shithead, son of a whore! Shithole sorcerer, son of a whore! They can't do anything! Goddamn! But I know . . . I'm
standing here. . . . They don't know shit.
Ugly sons of whores. They can't do anything to me." And when I had first traveled
through the town near where Santiago lived,
a drunk technician attached to the government's special health service had bellowed:
"We of INPES combat the *curacas* [sha-

mans]. We are the vanguard of progress. Our job is to get rid of all that quackery.'' The white storeowners around the plaza assured me that the shamans were useless—or dangerous. Only later did I learn that these very same storeowners would approach shamans to cure their small businesses.

Years before, Santiago's brother Alvaro, also a shaman, had been waylaid in a ravine and hacked to death by whites who claimed he was a sorcerer. Santiago's other brother fled to live along the remote banks of the Caquetá. Santiago stayed put: "They'll kill me wherever I go if they want to."

I should also point out that *yagé* grows only in the rain forest of the lowlands and foothills, and that the Indians I know in the Putumayo foothills sometimes say it is a special gift from God for Indians and for Indians only. "*Yagé* is *our* school," "*yagé* is *our* study," they may say, and *yagé* is conceived as something akin to the origin of knowledge and their society. It was *yagé* that taught Indians good and evil, the properties of animals, medicines, and food plants. Some Cofán Indians just south of the Putumayo river once told me a story about the origin of *yagé* that illustrates the tensions as well as the mediations between Indian and Christian traditions: When God created the world he plucked a hair from the crown of his head with his left hand and planted it in the ground for the Indians only. He blessed this with his left hand. The Indians discovered its properties and developed the *yagé* rites and the entire shamanic complex. Seeing this, God was incredulous. He said they were lying. He asked and was given some *yagé* brew. He trembled, vomited, defecated, and cried profusely, overcome by the many wonderful things he saw. In the morning he declared, "It is true what these Indians say. The person who takes this suffers. But that person is distinguished. That is how one learns, through suffering."

Although they may drink *yagé* with an Indian shaman to rid themselves of evil, it would be exceptionally rare for a white seriously to consider assuming all the dangers that accrue to the person who takes responsibility for its preparation and ritual. José García is one of the few.

Night fell and we moved inside the two-room house perched on the hill. A candle flickered across the roof beams and swinging hammocks. Grimy Catholic icons gazed into the wavering darkness and San Miguel, the patron saint of the nearby town and whom Santiago Mutumbajoy claims is the Indians' saint who warned them of the coming of the Spanish, started to free himself from Satan locked in combat, sinking into the fires of hell. Quiet talk about each other's hard times gave way to expectancy and fear, somewhat dissipated by the healer, who was clowning and teasing. Copal incense filled the room and the night sounds of the river and wind blended with the croaking of the forest to fill our silence. A young man helped the healer fill a pot with *yagé*, which the healer then crouched over and began to sing in rhythm to the beat of his curing fan, *waira sacha*—spirit of the forest, brush of the wind.

He was curing the *yagé* of the evil it brings from the jungle, singing *yagé* sounds, not words, asking that it be strong and bring good *pinta,* painting, visions. After ten minutes or so he drank, spitting and hawking, and then served us all, in turn, singing over the cupful before each person drank. We sat and waited. After half an hour someone stumbled out into the dark to vomit, and the shaman began singing again, barely stopping until the dawn. He called for good visions, and his voice and beating resonated with the trembling in our bodies. Extracts from my notes on that night read:

> Then the *feo* (ugly). My body is distorting and I'm very frightened, limbs stretch out and become detached, my body no longer belongs to me, then it does. I am an octopus, I condense into smallness. The candlelight creates shapes of a new world, animal forms and menacing. The lower half of my body disappears. I learn to use dissociation as an advantage as a way of escaping from the horror. I am not the person being got at; rather I am the disembodied face-presence calmly peering in and watching this other and unimportant me. I watch my other self, safely now. But then this second me, this objective and detached observer, succumbs too, and I have to dissociate into a third and then a fourth as the relation between my-selves breaks, creating an almost infinite series of fluttering mirrors of watching selves and feeling others. Self-hate and paranoia is stimulated by horrible animals—pigs with queer snouts, slithering snakes gliding across one another, rodents with fish-fin wings. I am outside trying to vomit; the stars and the wind above, and the corral for support. It's full of animals; moving. My life history rolls out before me in a torrent of fear and self-deprecation. I go back inside, and as I enter I see the shaman, Santiago; he has become a tiger! sitting in his hammock with José García kneeling before him. The room is transformed and I feel vomit rising. I throw up outside and shit. I feel the hateful situations of the past and the fear being expelled. I rejoin the group, calm, now floating on colors and wonderful sights. I realize that Santiago has put on his necklace of tiger's teeth. His head is nestled in its bed of tiger's teeth creating an image of his upper body like a tiger's. He is softly caressing José García, asking him if he wants more *yagé.* They open a cloth and crouch down on the floor, aglow with excitement, and ask for a knife to open a pearl. Later José García asks about his cattle; he wants them cured that night and he wants Santiago to come to his farm and check it out. Later on I realize that he means checking for sorcery. In the morning Santiago told me he could barely function all night because he kept bumping into cattle; beautiful cattle. Oh! Such beautiful cattle of all colors, mooing, licking him, and very fat. The World Bank has financed a cattle-raising project in these rain-forest areas since the early 1970s.

> Santiago's son-in-law tells me that José García wants to be a
> shaman, that he knows a lot, and that he is having a streak of
> misfortune.

Much later it became clear to me that José García was learning to be a healer
as part of his being cured from a deeply disturbing affliction. In so doing he
was going through a cycle of affliction, salvation, and transformation that
seems as eternal as humanity. Yet the power of this cycle stems not from
eternity, but from the active engagement with history that affliction depends
upon for its cure. José García is not to be historicized, for the past upon
which both his affliction and cure depend is an active construction of the
past original to every new present. And that applies to shamanism as well.

These Putumayo foothills of the Andes were first traversed by Europeans
in 1541, searching for the city of El Dorado—the Golden King. The jungle-
dwelling Indians around the Mocoa river (described by contemporaries as
cannibals who ferociously fought off the Spanish) assured Hernán Pérez de
Quesada and his 260 companions of conquest that the Golden Land lay close
by in the mountains rising to the west in a fabled land called Achibichi,
where the Spaniards found the tillers of the Sibundoy valley but no gold,
and beyond that the new Spanish town of Pasto. Following this vicious
expedition a few Spanish slavers and Franciscan missionaries came, a handful of embittered men who suffered mightily from the climate, and from the
hostility of the Indians of the foothills, who were said to have rebelled at
the instigation of their shamans.

Nevertheless, Christianity assumed importance in the culture of conquest.
The distinction between Christian and heathen Indian became ideologically
decisive because of its importance in facilitating the legalities of enslavement
and the use of military force. In his instruction manual for missionaries, first
published in 1668, the head of the Franciscan mission stationed at Quito,
Bishop Peña Montenegro, provided an example of Christian rationalization
for the use of force against the Indians in the Putumayo. Conquest by means
of armed force, he wrote, was justified "to reduce those who, although not
one's vassals, gravely injured those who were—like the heathen Indians who
in these parts being neighbors of Catholic Indians, enter their lands and their
lives and haciendas, making prisoners of the women and children, as commonly occurs and occurred this year of 1663 in the foothills of Mocoa."[1]
Other Franciscan reports state that Christianized Indians from the Sibundoy
valley (probably the "Catholic Indians" referred to by the bishop) were
being used to enslave pagans (such as those in Mocoa) in the lowlands to
work in gold mining.

With Christianity, so it seems to me, the missionaries also introduced
magic—or *magia* as it is called in the Putumayo today in reference to power
that stems from a pact with the devil. The missionaries believed firmly in
the efficacy of sorcery, which they supposed Indians to be especially prone

to practice on account of their having been seduced by the devil. Bishop Peña Montenegro asserted that in their being so brutish and ignorant, the Indians had been conquered by the devil to the extent that he made flesh and blood with them and his characteristics became an hereditary trait. Through their rites and superstitions, Indians maintained the memory of idolatry and sorcery, and when they were sick and went to shamans they thereby furthered its hold. The bishop was further concerned about Indians having an heretical influence on whites, because whites were also going to Indian healers.[2]

The bishop instructed his priests to take care in removing the "instruments" from the Indian sorcerers and in prohibiting their dances and songs, "because in these they have the memory of idolatry and sorcery." To that end it was necessary to "destroy their drums, deerheads, and feathers, because these are the instruments of their evil and bring on the memory of paganism."[3]

Yet was not the diabolic memory here at issue that of the Spanish and not of the Indians? The momentous irony was that in struggling to erase these "memories," the Church was in fact creating and strengthening them as a new social force, thereby ensuring the transmission of myth into reality and memory into the future.

Expelled from mission work in 1767, the Franciscans left the Putumayo, which became even more of a backwater and virtually free from white contact for a century with the exception of a few traders seeking *barniz* lacquer and medicines for highland cities. Following the *cinchona* (quinine) bark boom of the 1860s and 1870s, the rubber boom ripped through the Putumayo lowlands at the very end of the nineteenth century, causing for some twenty years what Walter Hardenburg described as the "Devil's Paradise" of Indian enslavement and death some 200 miles southeast of where José García began to colonize half a century later. Capuchins from Spain were granted almost total control of the Colombian Amazon in 1900, establishing their first and major base in the highlands of the Sibundoy valley. Their schools and clinics succeeded where the Franciscans had failed, and their rather forlorn attempt to colonize the area with poor white peasants was greatly boosted by the Texaco Oil Company, which built roads in the early 1950s down which poor white and black peasants came in droves. One of these poor whites was José García.

Born in the Andean highlands of Nariño in 1925, José García had come down to the foothills of the Putumayo river drainage in 1950, together with his mother and brother, after the death of their father. They had heard of the beauty of Santa Marta, which they hoped would make them wealthy, and spent arduous years clearing the land for cattle. He told me that he first took *yagé* with a local Indian curer named Andrés Hinchoa. His sister had fallen seriously ill following her spurning tne man to whom she was betrothed. She and José García feared that she had been ensorcelled in revenge, and finally they approached Andrés Hinchoa to see what he could do. José García remembers this:

> Andrés Hinchoa was a *compadre* of mine. He was the first to teach me to take *yagé*. He gave me the first *pinta* so that I experienced things that I had never seen before. He told me, "Good. I am going to give you a cup of *yagé* for your good fortune so that you will remember me. But you will have to be tough, *compadre!*" So he gave me the first cup and then came the *chuma* [drunkenness and visions]. But Ave María! . . . I was dying. I saw another world. I was in another life. I was on a rather narrow path, long, endlessly long. And I was in agony, in agony. I had left for eternity. I was on this path, walking and walking along this path, and then I came to an immense plain, a beautiful plain like a savanna. The fields were green. And then there was a painting of the Virgin of Carmen and I said to myself, "Now I am going there, to the Virgin of Carmen." Then I saw a tiny bridge with a hole in the middle of it; nothing more than this tiny bridge no thicker than a finger, and I thought to myself, "I'm afraid to cross; most Holy Virgin don't let me fall here! Don't let anything bad happen here!" In the name of God and of the Virgin I crossed and blessed myself and started to traverse the bridge. But then I started to fall off. Suddenly I was scared. Right there and then I called on the most Holy Virgin of Carmen to help me pass. Then I reached the most Holy Virgin of Carmen and said, "I've come so that all my sins shall be pardoned!" Because I was dead, no? And then she said, "I'm not going to pardon anything!" Then I began to cry ever so bitterly, yelping, looking for that salvation that the most Holy Virgin was denying me, crying and crying, imploring her for salvation. Then she told me that "Yes, I was pardoned. Yes! I was saved!" Then I was happy and I returned to this world, sitting here, my face bathed in tears.

Then, as far as I can make out—for José García was certainly rather oblique on the matter—he himself became entangled in love and war, the end of the affair being nasty and acrimonious. Indeed, the scars, or what he considers to be the scars, are present to this day, and the young woman and her mother, owners of the adjoining farm, are never far from his mind when something goes wrong.

It was by taking *yagé,* so Santiago Mutumbajoy told me, that José García was able to choose between three women, and that was Rosario, whom he married in 1962. Born in 1935, she had come down from the Nariño highlands about the same time as José García and lived on a nearby farm. She was sixteen years old when the man she loved and wished to marry was killed in a truck accident, and she was heartbroken, and cried and dreamed of him for months.

Eight years after their marriage they came out of the forest to live in the foothill town of Mocoa, renting rooms from the aunt of the young woman to whom José García had been first betrothed. This aunt became the godmother of their first child, yet made life impossible for them, José García told me, by saying they were too proud of their daughter's beauty and she would soon die; thus would their pride be smashed.

Moving across the road their life assumed a downhill course of illness and poverty. Strange sounds would frighten them at night and Rosario was haunted by a spirit, which often sat just above her right shoulder. It would follow her around the house, especially when José García was away, she told me. It was not clear who the spirit was. (In 1977 she told me that it was a young man, deeply desirous of her with the appearance of a gringo, tall and handsome.) Her right side became heavy and unresponsive. Then it became partially paralyzed. In despair José García sought a powerful healer.

> I went to take *yagé* in one part and then another, and then another; but nothing! I saw nothing! I went to the shaman Flavio Peña. He knew! He knew how to cure! But not even he was able to do anything! "No!," he said, "this is really tough." He went over me well. He prepared good *yagé*. He cured me like they are meant to do. But nothing! I had no visions. The *yagé* was like sugarcane juice. Nothing! Nothing!
>
> We went to another shaman in Umbría. "This is a *maleficio* [sorcery] with *magia*," he said. "Not just anyone can cure this. We can cure *maleficio*, but *magia* we can't."
>
> When Andrés Hinchoa died, all my visions finished. Something terrible had happened to me. I went to six shamans, but with none did I gain success.
>
> Then a friend asked if I knew of Santiago Mutumbajoy. "Go there," he said. "He's a good person and one who knows, really knows, how to take *yagé*." So one day I got some presents and visited him. He was very attentive and after chatting a little he said: "Don José, according to what you have told me, you want to take *yagé* in order to see. But I can't promise anything! If God and the Virgin help me, then I can help. Come, but only on this condition."
>
> The appointed day came and we took *yagé*. And yes! This was what I wished! Yes! This was a clear vision of my household and I was seeing it all just like when Andrés Hinchoa used to give me *yagé*. We drank *yagé* all night. Six cups! Finally he said: "I like, I really like this José García. He is made to take *yagé*. He is a good person. You are going to be rich." And I was in a stupor, lying on the floor, but listening. I didn't ask him how or why, and stayed full of confidence in his words. But next day doubts entered my mind. I lacked faith, no!

In the light of day Santiago told him someone else would have to cure him. This was a terribly difficult *maleficio*, made with *magia*, and he didn't want to take his money for nothing.

Later on José García's wife, Rosario, explained to me: "There are Indians who do sorcery. Don Santiago doesn't, only the sorcery that goes on between Indians. Sorcery made with *magia*—very little! The Indians can't cure that because for *magia,* only the person who works with *magia.* . . . The Indians don't know *magia.* They can't cure it. The people who know it are the *compactados,* those who have studied the book of *magia,* those who have made a pact with Satan. They're the ones who know *magia!*"

"All that the Indians know," she went on, "is *yagé* and the plants with which they cure and carry out their own sorcery. The sorcerers place *ca-pachos*—that's what they call it. It's very special. And the white person makes crosses with soil from the cemetery with the soil of the dead. What else will there be? No?"

So José García continued his search for a healer powerful enough to combat *magia.* He consulted an old acquaintance, Luis Alegría, a mulatto spirit medium who cured with the spirits of the saints and the dead and who had previously given José García advice concerning his sick brother, Antonio, now a spirit medium with a successful practice, so I was told, up in the Sibundoy valley. Antonio had begun his career apprenticed to an Indian shaman and José García related his brother's story:

> Antonio was a *yagecero;* he knew how to serve out *yagé.* He
> had a lot of knowledge of *yagé,* but he was duped by the friend
> that was teaching him to cure. He was ensorcelled [*dañado*] by
> his teacher—an old Indian shaman living in Sibundoy. Well,
> there he was and all he could say was that *yagé* was terrible.
> He was in an awful way, fighting all the time, saying that *yagé*
> was dreadfully dangerous. That's what he would say. Later on
> he took up as a spirit medium, with a man from Sibundoy
> called Don Pedro. But then Don Pedro saw that he was pro-
> gressing tremendously with spiritism and he also ensorcelled
> Antonio. Thus he thrashed in his bed at night, unable to sleep,
> struggling with Satan, struggling with spirits. They would am-
> bush him in the forest with their traps, no?
>   No sooner did I tell Luis Alegría about this than he said:
> "Look! *Magia* is very good. For example *magia* contains a se-
> cret that involves the flower of *alhecho.* Look! With this flower
> you can cure anything! Anything! You can cure whomever,
> grant good fortune, and everything. Yes! It's a marvel." That's
> what he said.
>   "Go and buy the *magia,*" he told me, "and in such-and-such
> a page look for the secret. With this we too can make the se-
> cret, so as to ensorcel the sorcerer with the same *magia* he
> himself used!"

Luis Alegría set to work to cure José García, demanding a high price. Becoming suspicious, José García returned to Santiago Mutumbajoy to take *yagé* and divine whether or not Luis Alegría was swindling him. He had a vision that showed that was indeed the case, and on returning home confronted Luis Alegría. "You are swindling us; nobody will ever believe in you again."

"That's just a story, *compadre,*" he said. "Come again to my place and I'll *really* cure you." José García told him that he was expecting a white woman who divined with cards. Her name was Lydia. "All right," he said, "bring her along too. She can do the examination, and I will do the cure!"

So it came about. Lydia first made an examination of Luis Alegría and then of José García. "Aiee!" she cried, "but Ave María it's really hit you. You are a complete fool! If you really want to drown why don't you jump into the river? Tomorrow I'll come to your house and arrange a cure."

"But Luis Alegría was listening and implored us to stay and feast. I refused but Lydia ate and became ill. His last act was to try to get her too."

Lydia organized their cure. She took the family up the Andes to the city of Pasto, first to a hospital for a checkup and then to a spirit medium's house. But that house was closed and they went to another—the thriving center of "Sister" Carmela, a white woman who divined and cured by invoking the spirit of José Gregorio Hernández, now a tremendously popular folk saint in Venezuela and Colombia. José Gregorio died in Caracas in 1919 where he had been, so I'm told, the first man to introduce the microscope. He was exceedingly pious and charitable, a great surgeon, and was killed by a car

San José Gregorio Hernández, the Servant of God.

when he rushed across the road to get remedies for a poor patient. Pictures of him, little icons, really, such as the one depicted here, are easily obtainable in different sizes in Colombia and Venezuela. There's no doubt about José Gregorio bringing myth and legend into the modern age, albeit a legend rendered thoroughly bourgeois, what with him replete in his three-piece suit and tie, a tip of white kerchief protruding from his breast pocket, and him so smugly serene and quietly confident while in the background mountains stretch to the snowy skies above turrets and a grassy plain on which, snipped out of the purest surrealism, a figure in a white surgical gown, with mask and cap, crouches over a near-naked and emaciated figure lying unconscious on a pallet of straw that is also serving as a surgical operating table. "The servant of God," reads the caption.

Placing her hands over the patient, up there in her room in Pasto, a city on a grassy plain amid towering mountains, Sister Carmela calls on the spirit of José Gregorio and begins to tremble. His spirit is possessing her. Her voice becomes raspy and masculine as she names the diseased part and necessary treatment, which often includes major surgery, of the psychic kind. "She's a very good friend of the bishop of Pasto," José García told me. "He comes to her Spirit Center to say mass." She treats up to 150 patients a day.

"While there, at five o'clock in the morning," José García informed me, "we were lying in bed, awake but with our eyes closed, when I saw as clear as anything along the banks of the river a priest with a huge book making a conjuration. And it seemed as though I was seeing my own farm in Santa Marta. I was seeing it. I was seeing the conjuration of my own cattle, and it was with that huge book twenty centimeters thick."

This priest was the spirit of Francisco Montebello, a mulatto folk saint, so he said. He began to pray. "We were in a terrible situation. Someone had placed a *maleficio* against us. The children were sick, very very sick, and I and my wife also. All we had were our merits; nothing more."

That was in 1973. Around that time the World Bank initiated its cattle-raising project. In 1974 José García bought his first farm (for around the equivalent of 2,000 U.S. dollars), in 1975 a second, for an equal sum, and in 1978 yet another. By 1979 he possessed around ninety hectares and slightly more than 100 head of cattle. Adding to the children born in 1965 and 1971 were two more, born in 1973 and 1977.

Rosario was told by an Indian shaman that she was suffering from *mal aires,* spirit attack, and took *yagé* three times. The spirit stopped haunting her, her paralysis seemed cured, and in her visions she saw a wild confusion of unknown persons, a church, and the Virgin. The only person she recognized, she told me, was a niece, being married. During these years José García continued to take *yagé* with Santiago every week or two and occasionally visited Sister Carmela in the highland city of Pasto as well. In 1977 he persuaded Sister Carmela to come down from the mountains and cure his household, and then took her to drink *yagé* with Santiago who was feeling unwell. She conducted curing rites in Santiago's home and Santiago was impressed with the fervor of her praying. But he told me he understood nothing about spirits and spirit mediums, and remained, if not dubious, perplexed.

Thus José García prospered. His children flourished, Rosario was well, and he assiduously developed his healing powers.

He attracted patients, for some of whom he acted as an intermediary, sending them to Santiago or to Sister Carmela. His healing techniques and the mysteries on which they were based represented, so it seems to me, not so much the syncretism or unification of Santiago's and Carmela's healing as the fact that neither of these two healers existed in isolation of each other.

Each one in an important way presupposed the other, and figures like José García made this presupposition manifest.

His notions of what brought misfortune, or of what names to put to such things, were similar, so it seems to me, to those of the Indian shamans I knew: serious affliction was likely to be the result of sorcery substance penetrating the body or, alternatively, of capricious spirits—of the dead or of nature—apparently acting independently of human malice. Perhaps José García did differ significantly from Indian shamans in that he would give a weightier role to the spirits of the dead. But in any case, and like the shamans, the aim of his ritual was exorcism following divination attained through a hallucinatory or hallucinatory-like state of being. He used a curing fan like the shamans', and sang somewhat like them too. The crucial opening phase was when he consecrated his medicines with the power to transform evil into a life-bestowing power. It is here where we see more clearly the character of the oppositions he embodied and was empowered by, particularly when taking *yagé* with Santiago.

After Santiago had sung over the *yagé* and served it out, José García would begin to sing quietly. Calling on God and the Virgin, he would evoke the spirits of Catholic folk saints as well as those of the dead Indian shamans who had helped him in his earlier quest for cure. Thus with regard to Andrés Hinchoa, the Indian shaman who first taught him to take *yagé* and was now dead: "His spirit is entering into the spirit center run by Sister Carmela. He is now making perfect cures. He is entering into her spirit center. Tomás Becerra [another dead Indian shaman] is also entering the center. So is Salvador from Umbría. All with Sister Carmela. They are concentrating there. They speak in Indian languages." By entering her spirit center they are becoming purified . . . . as he sits in the candlelight at Santiago's on the edge of the forest. José García begins to see these things—how Sister Carmela up in Pasto is concentrating this power of the spirits of the Indian shamans, articulating them with the spirit of Catholic folk saints such as José Gregorio, the dead Venezuelan surgeon, merging them all with the Virgin of Lajas. Evoking this pantheon, articulating Indian and white, forest with city, Indian male shaman with the white woman spirit medium, José García would sing the Magnificat, purifying and empowering the *yagé* that will purify and empower him.

Thus he could see into the bodies and secret intentions of others. And just like an Indian shaman, when he took *yagé,* José García became delicate and open to attack, so that when he drank his way into the *yagé* world he had to be able to defend himself. He described this in the context of explaining how he combined *yagé* with what Carmela had taught him.

> *Yagé* gives me the power to work, no? I'm going to tell you a
> story. Once with *yagé* I saw a neighbor of our new farm trying
> to climb a very thick tree, but unable. [This woman turned out

to be the mother of the young woman he jilted in the early 1960s.] "Poor woman . . . poor woman, she can't climb up," I said to myself. But I couldn't work out what it meant. "That tree is very thick; she can't climb up," I said. "Poor old woman." That was in the vision of *yagé*, no?

I took *yagé* another night after that. It was very strong. I was with the friend Santiago. The *chuma* [intoxication] of *yagé* really caught me. It was very pretty. I was really under, when I saw that old woman again. I had my back to her and she came in and sprinkled a little water on my back. It was clear water. A terribly strong *chuma* caught me up. *Virgen Santísima!* I felt I was dying . . . what exhaustion, what terror! So much that I had no idea what to do.

Then, as I had my own medicines, I said to myself; "I know that woman, I know who she is behind me." I was on my farm. I knew who was doing this evil to me. At that moment I grabbed alcohol and my medicines and massaged myself with them. I wafted incense. I lit a tobacco. I caught the incense. Its fragrance made me cough. I conjured it in the name of God. Thus one cures.

Then I asked the friend Santiago for a branch of *ortiga* [the nettles with which the healer beats the body of the patient] and I went over my body very thoroughly striking myself with *ortiga*. The *chuma* left me, no? In other words, the evil had dissipated.

And it was a pretty *pinta* [vision] curing myself, no? At that time I saw they were doing evil to me that night. They tried to kill all my cattle. That was the first thing I saw and so I pleaded for help for my cattle. I saw the old woman that did me evil so that one day we would all be dead. So I asked God and the *Virgen Santísima* to help me, and I concentrated and settled into curing myself. I gained force, but I couldn't penetrate into her house so as to cure my farm.

I prayed and prayed until I could concentrate in her house. Then I was able to carry out the cleansings of all those evil things she had hurled at my cattle. She was empowered. She knew all that stuff. Well, God assisted me and I performed the curing right there in Santiago's house; spiritual curing. I gathered up the evil things, entered into her place, went back and did it again. Thus in the curing I saw that I was not ensorcelling her; I offended nobody, just made sure that nothing was left and it was all put back with her so there it would stay, leaving her tied up with it.

Upon returning home he told Rosario what had happened. "You know that woman?" he said. "Yes," replied Rosario, "I know her. To do bad, yes! She knows!" But Rosario was skeptical so José García told her he would go to Lydia, the diviner with cards, who indeed confirmed all that he had seen with the Indian.

A few days later, so he told me, Rosario became alarmed at the wildness of the cattle, which made milking difficult. José García said he would cure them. In the pasture he came across signs of sorcery. Stunned, he immediately got to work with his medicines and incense. In the afternoon he hurried to Santiago's but in such haste that he forgot to take his own medicines. They took *yagé* that night.

> When the *chuma* arrived—what a *chuma! Virgen Santísima!* I
> thought I was dying! What exhaustion. Vomiting and vomiting,
> and I could do nothing to stop it. I felt overwhelmed by the
> sorcery substances. I could do nothing. I was about to die. So
> I asked the friend Santiago, "Do you have any incense? For
> God's sake give me some." But he said there was none, not
> even a grain. Then I felt as though I would choke to death. I
> had none of my medicines; it was the end. I worked and
> worked in the *chuma* of the *yagé,* but to no avail. I had lost my
> power to the sorcery.
>
> I asked Santiago for some *ortiga.* "Take whatever you want"
> he said. I caught hold of a good branch and I blew over it,
> oosh, and cured it. I cured that *ortiga* really well. Then I puri-
> fied myself, curing myself, singing, singing, and cleansing my-
> self and praying, hitting myself with the *ortiga* but strongly!
> Really strong!
>
> And then I was being made clear. Things were lifting. Once
> again the ugliest of visions was passing away—the force of the
> sorcery. And I was seeing, most beautiful, my farm.
>
> I had been caught in a beautiful vision. I was looking at my-
> self and there was sorcery substance in three places. And that
> was a force; a force to crush me, to make me abandon hope
> that my farm was not worth the effort and I would do best to
> give it away. That was what it was all about. But I was able to
> cure. God helped me. The old woman was unable to get me.
> She is a sorcerer. Soon she will kill me. But she can't.

A year or so later, in 1978, Santiago fell ill. He lost the sight in one eye while fishing at night, and became dizzy, unable to stand without vomiting. His legs swelled. Death seemed imminent. He sat by himself singing curing songs in a soft whisper but when he took *yagé* he either saw nothing or had visions of porcupine quills by the hundreds, erect and sprung as when the animal is defending itself, coming into his mouth, choking him, and into his eyes blinding him.

> And this under the influence of *yagé!* What exhaustion this
> makes! And the snakes, frogs, lizards, alligators . . . inside my
> body. . . . And nobody who could take them out! And when-

ever I took *yagé* this is all that I saw. Only that.

But when one is not sick one sees beautiful things; birds of all colors, beautiful colors like when one sees a beautiful cloth and says, "Oh! I like this cloth. It has wonderful colors!" Then one is truly seeing, and one hardly feels drunk.

His house was full of people, mainly Indians, drinking corn beer and manioc beer and occasionally speculating—who had ensorcelled him and why? Was it another shaman using *yagé* and *yagé* only? Or was it sorcery that included *magia,* and hence likely to be beyond the powers of *yagé?*

José García went up the mountain to Pasto to consult with Sister Carmela, taking a candle that he had wiped over Santiago's body. She confirmed the suspicions circulating in the foothills that Esteban, a highland Indian (Ingano) shaman from the Sibundoy valley, had ensorcelled Santiago, using *yagé* and *magia* together.

The enmity between Santiago and Esteban seemed to me to focus and magnify many of the tensions wrought by the expansion of the national economy into the frontier, and to do so in an unusual sphere—namely, the commoditization of magical power and of the magical aura of "Indianness." For many decades, highland Indian shamans from the Sibundoy valley, Inganos such as Esteban, have been recorded as making a living by wandering through the cities and hamlets of Colombia where they sell to whites and blacks medicinal herbs, charms, pictures of Catholic saints, books of magical spells, and their services as folk healers. Now Sibundoy Indian shamans travel as far as Venezuela, where money is more plentiful than in Colombia, and some, by local peasant standards, have become wealthy. Rosario compared them with the Indians of the foothills and lowlands who, she said, are ignorant of *magia* and know only their plant medicines, their *yagé,* and their own types of sorcery.

"But the highland Indians," she said, referring to curers like Esteban from the Sibundoy valley, "they know another system—that gets one more money, no? They go and traverse the nations and wander here and there with their berries and nuts and things saying that they can cure when really they are swindling. They are the most cunning! With this they maintain themselves with good money. They go to Venezuela, to Peru. . . . Their system is different because they get money easier and because their curing is a lie and but a way to get rich with filth!"

"And the Indians of the lowlands don't do that?" I asked.

"Ha! No! No! The people from here? No! From here? No! Those others are so given to traveling. They love traveling. They are so cunning. They wander here and they wander there—saying they can cure. And they cure nothing! What they do is swindle and ensorcel!"

It is likely that Ingano Indians from the Sibundoy valley have been itinerant medicine men for centuries. Frank Salomon has described a trial held by

Spanish officials in 1727 concerning a highland Indian from a village close to Pasto charged with ensorcelling six kinsmen and a Spanish official. Witnesses attributed their survival to a curer from the Sibundoy who used a vision-inducing plant, probably *yagé*.[4] In performing this role it is probable that the Sibundoy medicine men were acting as mediators of an old, pan-Andean system of curing and magical belief that credited the jungle Indians of the eastern foothills and lowlands with unique shamanic powers that could be tapped by highlanders either directly or through the mediation of Indians living between the highlands and the lowlands, such as the Sibundoy.

Today in all the places they pass through and gain clients from, it is their mythic image as Indians possessing occult powers that assures them success. But not all Indians in Colombia do what the Sibundoy curers do. They have confidence and an overweening pride because they are closed off from magical counterattack because of their skill and knowledge of *yagé* and *yagé*-induced visions—or, more likely, because they merely intimate that this is so. And for this they rely on the existence of the shamans of the foothills or lowlands, not just for *yagé*, which only grows below the valley, but for the allegedly superior power of the shamans otherwise beneath them, literally and figuratively. The seeds of discord between shamans like Esteban, up in the Sibundoy valley, and Santiago, down below in the foothills, are planted in this peculiar yet firmly secured contradiction which has probably gathered intensity as growing market opportunities favor the Sibundoy shamans' capacity to gain more money and fame than the lowlanders. In the course of their healing journeys, the Sibundoy shamans and herbalists encounter head-on the full spectrum of prevailing healing techniques and demonological fantasies secreted in the anxieties of people more directly integrated into the national society than themselves. They become more cosmopolitan than the lowland shamans isolated in a far-removed pocket of the nation; they perfect the discourse of *magia* based on a pact with Satan, and they perfect the use of their image as mystically empowered *Indians*.

Trapped by their image as pagans with inherent links to the occult, they wrest a livelihood from that image, ensuring its vitality in the popular imagination of the nation, and beyond. But to fully appropriate and profit from that image, the itinerant Sibundoy shamans, such as Esteban, not only require the *yagé* (and perhaps the ritual services) of the lowland shamans such as Santiago; they also require the lowland shamans as mythic objects to fulfill the colonially inspired mythology that grants the pagan power.

Needless to say, the lowland shamans are not happy with this. By and large they distrust and even despise the highland shamans, whom they regard as swindlers and as inferior—except for their ability to do evil with *magia* and with sorcery bundles (*capachos*). This all comes to a head over the issue of supplying what is said to be increasingly scarce *yagé* to highland shamans. Lowlanders such as Santiago are reluctant to sell them *yagé*, and he had been adamant in his refusal of Esteban's request. The lowlanders with whom

I have spoken fear that with the *yagé* the highlanders will mix *magia* and dominate them, ensuring, among other things, an assured source of *yagé*. On the other hand, to refuse their request could mean being killed by their *magia*—supposedly the fate now befalling Santiago.

As Santiago's health deteriorated to the point of death, José García became involved in unprecedented ways. Up till now he had been a patient and a sort of pupil, struggling all the time to free himself from sorcery. Now he was called upon to cure his mentor.

> I went up to his place one afternoon and he was terribly drunk and his wife implored me to cure him saying that he was fearfully bad-tempered with her and with everyone else. So we sat around talking and drinking and when night came Santiago said we would take *yagé*—he, his nephew, his son-in-law, and I. "Good, we're all here," he said.
>
> He poured out the *yagé* and sang over it and gave each person a cupful, but forgot about me. Then he remembered and gave me the largest cupful I had ever taken. "Ah!" I said, "in the name of the Holy Virgin this will do something." And I consecrated the *yagé* and called on God and the spirits of the Indian shamans, Tomás Becerra and Andrés Hinchoa, to come and help me, to cure this *yagé* in the name of Tomás Becerra and so on because they were *yagé*-takers and of the best. Then Santiago said, "But who is going to sing? Nobody? Well, *you* sing Don José! Aren't you always singing to yourself under your poncho? All these times you've been taking *yagé* up here you've been singing and curing hidden under your poncho, no? Well come out into the public so we can see if you really know or not!"
>
> "All right, señor," I replied, "that's what we'll do." And in that instant he fell to the floor, as if dead. We jumped up and laid him back in his hammock, but he stayed like he was dead, with only his hands moving, mute, speaking with nothing but his hands, mute. The others thought they were going to die. His son-in-law implored me to try to cure them. Now the *yagé* was catching me. I took up a curing fan and started to cure. The *chuma* was taking me. It was beautiful and I began to see what state the house was in. It was a cemetery. There was a burial. It was total annihilation going on. Okay! So I got busy with my medicines and then the *chuma* caught everyone and it was terrible! His son-in-law was crying, "Don José please please come and cure me because I am dying!" I bent over him and exorcised, cleaning and sweeping and sucking. Then his nephew, the same thing. It was awful. I went from one to the other, and back again. Those too soon got better and then I attended to the friend Santiago. I worked on him till three in the

morning and then he began to revive, to speak again. "Ya, ha ha ha." And he would whistle and scream. "We're not just anybody, Don José," he said. "For we *know,* isn't that right, Don José?" And then he would fall unconscious again. "We *know*. They can't get us! Isn't that right, Don José?" He also saw the cemetery, all of it. "Ave María," he said, "dead people putrefying everywhere," he said. Others in agony about to die. The whole house a graveyard. Ave María!

So we kept on taking *yagé*. And finally he said, "Good! Come again on Tuesday. If they're going to kill us, then they too will die!"

On Tuesday we took *yagé* again and he was beginning to sing when he cried out that he had an illness deep within and that he was going into the other room to see if he could cure it. He took his curing fan and we could hear him singing. Suddenly the candle went out and it was completely dark. I stayed there, jittering with the *yagé,* frightened, sure I was about to die. And the friend Santiago became silent. He stopped singing. I cured myself with my medicines, over my body, blowing incense, and eventually I got better after an hour or so. When my force returned I began to sing and cure the others, singing and curing, singing and curing. "Ah, Don José," said Santiago, "looks like they are trying to kill us, no? But they can't! So, let's take some more and see if they can kill us. Take more *yagé!*"

So we took another cup and when the *chuma* came, "pow"—he fell to the floor again. This time it only lasted for half an hour. He got up and started singing and said, "On Friday we'll take some more." So on Friday I went again and the *chuma* was good. I went to Pasto and came back with holy water and incense. I cured cattle and went a second time to Pasto and got medicines for Santiago from Sister Carmela. So we finished.

Santiago's illness abated but little, until a month later the most esteemed shaman of the Putumayo foothills came and cured him. That was Salvador, whose mother was a Cofán Indian and father a whiteman, a *cauchero* (small-time rubber trader) from the highlands of Nariño who had left the little boy with the Indians. We had been waiting quite a while for Salvador to show up. He had a long way to come and had to harvest some rice quickly because of the coming rains. That was the word that came back to us as we waited day after day with Santiago humming his curing song to himself and everyone else drunk most of the time. But the real reason that Salvador didn't show, according to Santiago, was that his wife was frightened—frightened for Salvador's delicate voice and delicate health, what with all those Ingano Indians up around Mocoa boozing away like they always do, while the Cofáns barely even drink *chicha*. "She knows that if he comes here he'll get drunk, and then he'll get sick," that's the problem, sighed Santiago.

But eventually he did come, with his wife and her mother, the *mama señora*, widow of a Siona shaman. She is very old, the *mama señora*, drinks *yagé* with impunity and sings beautifully, Santiago told me. It is she and only she who prepares the very special *chicha* of pineapple, corn, and manioc that Salvador offers to the animals whom he calls for the hunters with his *yagé* song. Many other people came, for three nights of *yagé* curing, so I was told later, and most of them took *yagé*. The *mama señora* sang too; my betrothed, *mi novia*, is how Santiago referred to her, with a giggle. And Don Apolinar sang, too. He was an old Coreguaje shaman, father-in-law of one of Santiago's daughters, and he came from the province of Caquetá, a hard and even dangerous trip because of the campaign being waged there by the Colombian army against the guerillas.

Santiago improved dramatically, except for his eye. But it was never clear what had really happened to him or what Salvador had said about the cause of his illness. Was it *yagé* mixed with *magia*, as José García said that Sister Carmela had said? Was it really Esteban? Everyone said something different. And as time passed so everyone would change what they said anyway.

When I returned a year later at the beginning of 1979, I found a lot had changed. Santiago was fairly well and active, but Salvador had died and José García's wife, Rosario, was terribly ill. Salvador's nephew said he had died as a result of losing his power through curing too many outsiders, especially whites and blacks, thus becoming polluted and unable to withstand the sorcery attacks of the Indian shamans along the Napo river in Ecuador. Rosario was virtually paralyzed in her right arm and leg. Her right arm shook. Her speech was slurred. She looked gaunt and sad. In a deadpan way she said that the spirit of the man to whom she had been engaged at the age of sixteen, who had died in the truck accident, had come to haunt her. He would sit on her right shoulder.

This bout of illness started in 1978, she told me, when there were problems with one of their farms. Cattle had been robbed and she had to work hard milking while José García and their son were looking for them. She caught pneumonia in a rainstorm and was treated with antibiotics by one of the local (university-trained) doctors. She felt a little relieved but then began to feel heavy and developed a headache followed by the gradual onset of paralysis. She was further treated by the same doctor with tranquilizers until their old friend, the card diviner, Lydia, persuaded them to go for medical treatment to the capital city, Bogotá, where she was diagnosed and treated as suffering from a stroke. She came home, unable to stop crying, her daughter said, and returned to Bogotá where she visited many doctors—and a spirit medium who told her that her illness was partially due to God (a natural cause) and partially due to sorcery acting in concert with the "natural" cause.

Then Lydia, the card diviner who had been responsible for introducing them to Sister Carmela in Pasto in 1973, thereby setting them on the path to riches, set to work once more with her cards and divined that Rosario's illness was due to no one else than Sister Carmela! Carmela had evoked the spirit of Rosario's long-deceased fiancé to act as a malevolent power.

Now Rosario and José García remembered how Carmela had always insisted that José García's powers, as developed in association with her, were to be for the good of mankind; that he was buying too many cattle and too many farms and that he should give his cattle and lands to the poor, keeping only a little for himself. Carmela had turned against them because he was denying this, they told me with calm detachment. At the same time, José García added, Carmela was envious of his success and was acting out of spite.

José García himself understood his healing powers in terms paralleling Carmela's denunciation of his material success. A year or so earlier, for example, he had delivered this *pronunciamiento:*

> Yes! I have seen the greatness of this world, and one remembers, takes account of it, and manages one's life accordingly. That is why God helps me. God has specially chosen me to succeed in anything I want, but not too much; to do great things, to perform great cures . . . according to my faith and how I conduct myself. But do you know that it is not mine? I am only the administrator of the goods of this world. Of pride, I have none, not like those rich people to whom you say hello and they don't answer back. I am only an administrator. The day that my Father esteems me, he calls me to account for all; "Come *mayordomo!* Give me your account!"

This Christian anticapitalist sentiment leveled against the private accumulation and ownership of wealth is amply reinforced by other aspects of his healing philosophy as well:

• The picture of the world evoked by this text refers us to a feudal hacienda with God as the master and José García as a *mayordomo*—a steward caring for God's domain and not as a private property owner of the goods of this world. An important impulse behind the credibility of this picture or cosmology lies in José García's having "seen the greatness of this world" and remembering and taking account of it. This has come about in the especially potent way it has because of his taking *yagé*—an Indian medicine and an Indian rite. The organic interconnectedness of this world picture presupposes a hierarchy of reciprocities ascending to the godhead.

• In this hierarchy, a healer like José García sees himself as standing in a gift relationship to God, the Virgin, Catholic folk saints, and the spirits of dead Indian shamans. His power comes from this chain of reciprocating exchanges, a chain that evokes the myth-rendered past through the generations of saints and Indian shamans. This is the power that can cure illness and combat sorcery, as we see when José García describes his type of singing:

> I don't sing like the shamans, but another song that comes with *yagé;* for example, with a music that I hear. The very *yagé* teaches you what to sing . . . low or high, or whatever. You *see* prayers, but *sung* . . . prayers with the song of *yagé*. Thus you do your curing with this; singing . . . for example, the Magnificat. You are singing the Magnificat under the influence of *yagé,* curing the sick, or under the influence of one who is curing. The Magnificat says, "My soul is full of grace from our Lord and my spirit is lifted to God, my Saviour. In the light of his eyes, now all the generations call me, 'Welcome!' since in me great things have been made and here in me is the power almighty whose mercy extends from generation to generation to those who fear it, and his arms from my heart extend to those exposed. Get rid of the powerful; raise the humble. Fill the hungry with goods and farewell the rich with nothing. In memory of your compassion, your taking Israel for your servant, according to your promises, that made our fathers, Abraham and all his descendants, for the centuries of the centuries. . . . Amen."
>
> This is what I sing, drunk with *yagé,* singing the Magnificat, curing and cleansing. With this you cure sorcery, no matter how serious. With this you are singing, developing the Magnificat, with this, calming illness.

(Among the vulgar classes throughout Peru, wrote Hermillio Valdizán and Angel Maldonado in their opus *La medicina popular peruana,* printed in 1922, there is a great series of beliefs, more common among the whites and mestizos than the Indians, related to the restless spirits of Purgatory. When all else fails to drive these spirits away, when, therefore, they are the truly condemned and possibly of the devil himself, then one should sing the Magnificat, and they quote the closing lines: "Dispossess the powerful; Raise up the humble. Fill the needy with goods, leave the rich with nothing. . . . *Gloria al Padre y al Hijo.*"[5])

- The Christian emphasis upon the virtue of charity and denial of worldly goods engages with the healer's necessity to attend the poor. A man like Santiago would never be hypocrite enough to bother with the discourse of denial of worldly goods. He loves worldly goods. His appetite is Rabelaisian. The more the better, and none of this cringing sort of stuff that José García, the pious white spiritist, comes out with. Yet Santiago would consider himself no less a Christian and no less prone to the Envious Other.

  The subtext to this attending to the poor is the subconscious cosmic battlefield of vices and virtues in which the healer gains power through the struggle with evil. The healer's power is incumbent upon a dialectical relationship with disease and misfortune. Evil empowers, and that is why a healer by necessity attends the "poor," meaning the economically poor and those struck by misfortune. It is possible to understand the relation between God and the devil in this way, for they can stand not merely in opposition, but as a mutually empowering synergism. Dante's realization of paradise is only achieved by and after he has journeyed through the inferno and encountered Satan (and for our purposes it is apposite to note that Dante made this journey accompanied by a pagan guide—read "healer" or "shaman"—from the pre-Christian past).

But this necessity to descend and immerse oneself in the struggle with evil can be self-destructive. A healer's life is poised on the edge of this dialectic, and that is why a healer always requires an alliance with a more powerful healer—whom José García's found in Sister Carmela in the mountain city and in the Indian shaman, Santiago, on the edge of the lowland jungles. The more powerful healer, however, might kill you.

• Of all the reciprocities involved in this organic picture of the world with its hierarchy of forms and dialectical mesh of good and evil, the outstanding one is that between Christianity and paganism, equivalent to that between God and the devil. José García's powers derive from this reciprocation of contraries—an antiphony established in its concrete particularity as well as its harmoniously cadenced abstractions by the European conquest of the New World centuries before, as we witness, for example, in the writings of the Franciscans blazing the trail for Christ in the jungles east of Quito and Pasto. This antiphony, moreover, probably existed in trans-Andean society prior to the arrival of the Spanish, as in the relation between the highlanders of the Incan empire and the jungle Indians of the lowlands.

It is in what we might hesitantly call the "logic" of José García's curing and life story (as he tells it) that we see this patterning of oppositions, this billowing out of apocalyptic splendor fanned by oppositions. But with other colonists to the jungle, as with an old acquaintance of mine of the Guaymuez River, Manuel Gómez, this patterning may take a more vividly explicit expression as in Manuel's *yagé* vision, in which the Indian shaman, dispensing the *yagé,* was seen as changing into a tiger and then the devil. Then the viewer died and in the ascent to heaven, as in Dante's *Paradiso,* achieved the glory of evil transcended, gained God's blessing, and was cured—and something more than just cured.

In assailing the sorcery of *magia* leveled against him many years ago, José García had become not only a healer, thereby transforming this evil, he had also become a rich man in the eyes of his neighbors. In a society where the pressures for individual capital accumulation are resisted by the counter-hegemonic force of envy, his entrepreneurial career demanded at an ever-increasingly furious pace the development of his spiritual healing power so as to resist the barbs of that envy. But finally, as he had said on an earlier occasion, the day had come when his Father called him: "Come here *mayordomo!* Give me your account."

Since the beginning of Rosario's illness, José García had stopped taking *yagé* and visiting Santiago. Rosario had always been skeptical and even perhaps a little frightened of his mixing with Indians and especially of his taking *yagé*. Carmela and other mediums had often warned him of overindulging in *yagé* as well. Now he seemed frightened too.

Lydia told him to stop or take it very infrequently, because when one is *bien chumado* the other *yagé* takers "throw" sorcery at one. "Once I fell to the floor," he told me. "Don Santiago whipped me with *ortiga* nettles. I took another cupful and I saw some Indians from way down the Putumayo, their faces painted with *achiote*. It was they that had done it to me!" "Another time," he told me, "a fierce wind came up from nowhere. It blew out the candle. Strange. I sang the Magnificat. I defended myself. We continued curing."

Rosario got to hear of a famous physician in Popayán, a highland town north of Pasto, and she and José García went to him several times. His treatment was painful. He injected her tongue many times, she said. He was also outrageously expensive. A university-qualified physician, he had learned his specialty in Russia and many other foreign countries, so Rosario would reiterate. Then she became involved with a spirit medium new to the Putumayo, a white woman from Brazil, who would not allow face-to-face dealings so that Rosario carried out all transactions with her through an intermediary, a friend of both women. The *brazilera* was able to quit Rosario of the spirit floating on her right shoulder. She affirmed that Carmela had caused Rosario's illness, using *magia,* and went on to say that Carmela was also to blame for Santiago's brush with death. That was why he still suffered from fatigue, giddiness, and a bad eye. I should also add here that Carmela (a great friend of the bishop, as José García said) had but a few months earlier been driven out of Pasto by the combined efforts of medical doctors, police, and the Church, and was struggling to maintain herself in a small village a few miles from the city. Truly her star had fallen, at least for the moment.

I tried to persuade José García to come with me and visit Santiago, but he declined and so his son, Pedro, accompanied me along the trail and into the forest as night was falling. He was fourteen, and had taken *yagé* since the age of eight. We passed his father's farm. He told me how their cattle, as well as plantains and other crops, were always at risk of being stolen. His father had been attacked recently by a laborer demanding higher wages, and fought back with his machete. The laborer went away, then stole their favorite dog, castrated it, and cut off its ears. Pedro feared sorcery constantly, so it seemed. Why did he take *yagé?* He said that one took it to see who was ensorcelling you, to clarify one's situation, and at the same time to clean oneself of the evil (the *males* or bad things) that have been inflicted. He was afraid to walk along this road at night. We branched off to take the trail into the jungle. It was dusk. We reached the river and crossed the bridge made of bamboo and wire slung thirty feet over a cataract of rushing water and rocks. It was about ten inches wide and swayed above the glistening water. I asked him what he saw when he took *yagé.*

"I saw a man making what we call *brujerias* [sorcery] in our farm," he replied.

> He wanted to see all our cattle dead and us begging alms. He wanted to see us like I was seeing. Later I saw my father, and his bad friends wanted to see him as a sorcerer like them. Then I saw my father in his underpants with a tail [like the devil] like a chain, and his body naked. I saw that. The others said that was how they wanted to see him. And they laughed when they saw that I saw. They wanted to take him away. They said they wanted me to see it like that, like them, doing evil.
>
> Later on Sister Carmela also said that the man I saw doing sorcery was the sorcerer. She hears that from the spirits, and with them she can cure. She calls the spirits . . . like Tomás Becerra [the Indian shaman who first gave Pedro's father *yagé*, now dead].
>
> Later on, taking *yagé*, I saw my father curing the farm. The *chuma* caught me and took me there. I thought I was going to suffer too. Then I saw my father converting himself into a dove, and in the *yagé* I saw Sister Carmela and my uncle Antonio all dressed in white, cleaning the farm.
>
> Once I saw the Virgin. I passed to the other side and found her, mounted, like a statue. I prayed and I cried. Then after a little while the *chuma* changed and I saw her as a person like any other. Then I called my father and said "Look! Look! The Virgin of Carmen!" And he said, "Where is she?" And he also wanted to cry. But he said to me, "Don't cry. Why are you crying? Don't you see the Virgin of Carmen?" And she was there blessing me with the rosary in her hands. And from then the *chuma* changed and I saw no more.
>
> I was crying because I was asking her pardon . . . for all of us. Thus she gave me her blessing. . . . My father told me that the same happened to him, except that he passed over a chasm with a tiny staff and he couldn't see the bottom and that he was about to fall but she got him over safely.

Pedro made two drawings of these visions and later commented on them:

The Virgin.

The Virgin
This is the river where I was walking and which I had to pass.
This is the bamboo bridge I had to cross. I wanted to turn
around halfway across. This is the sun which lights everything
up—which illuminates where we were. The face of the sun was
in front of the Virgin. In front is the soil, yellow soil. There is
the rock-face [*peña*]—on which the Virgin is standing. All that
is *peña*. And that's where I met the Virgin . . . like a statue of
the saints in plaster. And then she converted, thus, like a
woman, alive, and then she gave me the blessing.

[The wire in the front of the drawing is a fence of a farm. It
seemed to him, on questioning, that she was in the farm, in the
fields where the cattle go.]

The Sorcerer.

The Sorcerer

This drawing consists of three parts; (1) top left, (2) top right, and (3) bottom.

1. This is the face of one of those evil Indians. I saw three, all with the same face, like those Indians from the highlands, from the Sibundoy valley.

2. Then I turned to the farm—and saw a neighbor placing sorcery stuff (a *capacho,* or sorcery bundle) into a black, rotting tree trunk.

3. This man is dressed in his underpants only, and has the tail of the devil and a broom in his left hand, and the *capacho* in his right. The *capacho* contains powdered human bones from the cemetery, soil from the cemetery, human hair, and so on. . . . This is the man, Sánchez [a neighbor], who wanted to see my father doing sorcery; thus he wanted to see it like he saw it.

A year later at the same place on the road and also at dusk I reminded him of our earlier discussion. He turned, pulling a pistol from under his shirt. "Yes," he said, "and now I have this."

I asked his mother, Rosario, whether she had thought of seeking treatment from an Indian shaman such as Santiago. She snorted with contempt. "The Indian is a brute," she said, "the Indian understands nothing. When they get drunk, reason stops falling on them; wherever they want to puke, they puke, and there they fall and sleep. Not like educated people! The Indian! Ha! . . . That's why I want nothing to do with them. I stay away. Apart. . . ."

"But what about José, your husband?" I asked.

"Ha! Well! He's happy with Santiago. He's caught their ideas. And that chokes me. That really chokes me because I'm not for that. He's carrying the idea. They are old friends. It's the *yagé*."

"What idea?"

"It's that he's caught their customs, no? The feeling, the *genio,* that's what." (*Genio* can mean temperament, brilliance, genius.)

"Up in Sibundoy," she went on, "there's an Indian who speaks fourteen languages. I forget his name. He's very expert. But when Carnival comes he's the piggiest of all the Indians. He piggifies himself, falls into mud and becomes filth or dances on the mud, singing. He puts on one of those Indian masks because normally he wears the cloths of a white, no? And then comes the time of Carnival and the Indians put on masks of Indians and they dance, they drink *chicha,* they fight, they wallow in mud like pigs. That's why I say education is wasted on Indians. What else! Fourteen languages. That's not a little!"

Rosario's brother came in and started talking about her recent visit to the shrine of the Lord of Miracles in the town of Buga, many hundreds of miles to the northwest in the agribusiness valley of the Cauca river. It is a popular shrine and, according to Rosario and her brother, its origin lies in its discovery by an Indian washerwoman many thousands of years ago who was saving money to buy an image of Christ. She was working by the river at Buga when police came by taking a man to prison for defaulting on a debt. Overcome with pity, the Indian woman gave the prisoner the money necessary for his freedom and, on returning to her washing, came across a piece of wood floating downstream bearing ingrained within it the rough figure of Christ on the cross. She fished it out of the water and every day it assumed a more and more perfect likeness. The bishop of Popayán condemned it as heresy and sent people to burn it, yet, sweating, it resisted the flames, assuming an ever more perfect likeness until the Church recognized it to be truly a miraculous image—one discovered for the redemption of colonial society by an Indian many thousands of years ago in mythic time.

EIGHT
Magical Realism

The power of the imagery brought to life by misfortune and its healing in the sickness of Rosario and José García is a power that springs into being where the life story is fitted as allegory to myths of conquest, savagery, and redemption. It should be clear by now that the magic and religious faith involved in this are neither mystical nor pragmatic, and certainly not blind adherence to blinding doctrine. Instead, they constitute an imageric epistemology splicing certainty with doubt, and despair with hope, in which dreaming—in this case of poor country people—reworks the significance of imagery that ruling-class institutions such as the Church have appropriated for the task of colonizing utopian fantasies.

In objectifying this reality as *lo real maravilloso* or *realismo mágico,* modern Latin American literature builds a (one-way) bridge with oral literature, yet still, so it seems to me, finds it hard to evade the heavy-handedness that Alejo Carpentier reacted against in Parisian surrealism—the effort to create magic where only a metaphorized form could exist. Surrealism froze time and denarrativized the predictable compositions of bourgeois reality with forms taken from dreams and from decontextualized (hence all the more surreal) artifacts from the primitive world as it was imaginatively glimpsed through African masks and such in the Trocadero. Well, Carpentier found he didn't need the artifacts because there in the streets and the fields and the history of Haiti the marvelously real was staring him in the face. There it was lived. There it was culture, marvelous yet ordinary.

His discovery of *lo real maravilloso* in 1943 bears all the marks of the marvelous itself. Describing how, after his return from Paris, he stumbled into the ordinariness of the extraordinary, he writes:

> This was made particularly evident to me during my stay in Haiti, on finding myself in daily contact with what we could call the marvelously real. . . . I realized, moreover, that this presence and force of the marvelously real was not unique to Haiti, but patrimony of all America whose inventory of cosmog-onies has yet to be terminated. The marvelously real is found at every step in the lives of those who inscribed dates in the history of the Continent and left names still borne by it: from the explorers of the Fountain of Eternal Youth. . . . And be-cause of the virginity of its landscape, its formation and ontol-ogy, the fantastic presence of the Indian and the Negro, the revelation that its discovery constituted and the fecund syntheses it favored, America is far from having exhausted its wealth of mythologies.[1]

But why is it that *lo real maravilloso* becomes such an important category in the consciousness of literary schools from the 1940s onward after 400 years of myth making and magic in Latin American culture? This awakened sensitivity to the magical quality of reality and to the role of myth in history is perhaps an indication of what Ernst Bloch called "nonsynchronous con-tradictions" and is ready-made soil for the sprouting of "dialectial images," in the terminology of Walter Benjamin, for whom (and I quote from Susan Buck-Morss's essay on his notes for his *Passagenwerk*)

> the dreaming collective of the recent past appeared as a sleep-ing giant ready to be awakened by the present generation, and the mythic power of both [the recent and the present genera-tions'] dream states were affirmed, the world re-enchanted, but only in order to break out of history's mythic spell, in fact by reappropriating the power bestowed on the objects of mass cul-ture as utopian dream symbols.[2]

The nonsynchronous contradiction comes to life where qualitative changes in a society's mode of production animate images of the past in the hope of a better future. Fascism in Germany channeled these images and hopes and, according to Bloch, the impoverishment of the Left in regard to revolutionary fantasy made it an accomplice in its own defeat. Benjamin similarly berated his companions on the Left; historical materialism could become the victor in ideological struggle "if it enlists the services of theology, which today, as we know, is wizened and has to be kept out of sight."[3] He argued that to the persistence of earlier forms of production in the development of capitalism there correspond images that intermingle the old and the new as ideals transfiguring the promise offered yet blocked by the present. These utopic images, although stimulated by the present, refer to the past in a radical way—to what he called "prehistory," that is, of classless society.[4] The fascists were willing and able to exploit these dreams, but that did not mean that myth and fantasy were necessarily reactionary. On the contrary, the images involved contained revolutionary seeds that the soil ploughed by materialist dialectics could nourish and germinate.[5]

In Latin America it has been, by and large, the political function of the Church to harness these images and collective dreams to reactionary social purposes. It is here where Carpentier's sensitivity to myth as the experience of history in the configuration of a changing present is so appropriate and necessary to the development of revolutionary culture and literature. This development stands in relation to the magical realism of popular culture as the only counter-hegemonic force capable of confronting the reactionary usage to which the Church puts that same magical realism in order to mystify it.

Yet those who attempt to use such forces run the risk of being used by them. When Carpentier lists reasons why "America is far from having exhausted its wealth of mythologies," we must ask how it is possible to evade their spell, most notably that woven by "the fantastic presence of the Indian and the Negro"—the very fantasia through which class domination permeates the political unconscious. In the painfully romanticized encounter between the Indian shaman and the European hero of Carpentier's 1953 novel *Los pasos perdidos* (*The Lost Steps*), we find both the promise and the pathos of the revolutionary dream's attempt to orchestrate the magic of realism with the reality of magic. This is one reason why I thought it useful to relate a history of fortune and misfortune in which José García, a poor white colonist, a storyteller, perhaps, but not a novelist, tried to tap the powers of a real shaman whose dilemma—that of freeing himself from an oppressive colonial mythology while remaining essential to it—is no less grave than our own.

But it is the colonist's wife, Rosario, who bears the sickness, and she does not frequent shamans. Indians are brutes! With their masks they dance drunk, wallowing in mud. Fourteen languages!

But she did go far away over the mountain to Buga to visit the shrine of the Lord of Miracles, our Lord who was delivered to this nation by a poor Indian woman many thousands of years ago.

In siding with the Indian-discovered Lord rather than with her husband-discovered Indian, however, did she not also endorse the colonial mythology of primitiveness that sees in it not only the sign of the pagan, but also the sign of power—in this case redemptive power? In the Lord of Miracles hanging on the cross in the gloom of the church in Buga do we not see this colonial configuration ritualized and adored as healing power? For it is not just that Indians and blacks have been identified with evil in the depths of a class structure mediated by whites ascending to the godhead, but that from those depths springs power.

As with their manual labor, skills, and land, this power of the primitive can be appropriated, in this case by grafting it onto the mythology of conquest so that illness can be healed, the future divined, farms exorcized, wealth gained, wealth maintained, and, above all, envious neighbors held at bay. But unlike land and labor, this power did not lie in the hands of Indians or blacks. Instead it was projected onto them and into their being, nowhere more so than in the image of the shaman. In attempting to appropriate this power, we see how the colonists reified their mythology of the pagan savage, became subject to its power, and in so doing sought salvation from the civilization that tormented them as much as the primitive onto whom they projected their antiselves.

And here we are not so much dealing with ideas as with the body, mediated by the image-realm. In the saga as it is represented by Rosario's and José García's endless search for peace, if not redemption, we see something more than how a construction of personal history intersects with this colonial fetishization and reification of savagery. We see something more than peasant colonists desirous of wealth in a political economy that uses the fear of envy to counter the accumulation of capital. What we also see is that an illness of the body is a bodily attempt at inscribing a history of otherness within the body that is the self, a tentative yet life-saving historiography that finds the dead hand of the past never so terribly alive as in the attacks by the spirits of the restless dead, such as Rosario's fiancé, or as in the sorcery of the envious. Through misfortune and its changing definition with attempts at healing, this picturing of the bodily self as the locus of otherness ineluctably enters into the exchange of magical powers established between Indian shamans and the Church, an exchange that operates with the powerful medium of visual images. Hallucinogens and points of rupture in everyday life—illness, accident, coincidence, dusk—can make this image-realm manifest and manifestly empowering, and it was Rosario's task to tie the power of the pagan to the power of the Church, ensuring in this circulation of images their dialectical solidarity. It was she who mediated the social circulation of meanings essential to the vitality of such images, from the shaman through José García to herself and the Lord of Miracles in the official temple of God.

In sanctifying an image such as the Lord of Miracles, the Church sanctifies itself. The aura of hypnotic mystery now assumed by the image in the artificial darkness of the church both reveals and conceals this exchange, so common in societies like Colombia's where the epiphanic discovery of saints and virgins is a frequent occurrence and a primary source for the regeneration of priestly power that sustains ideological reproduction and class oppression. But precisely because of this appropriation by the Church of a popular image as a cultural treasure adorning the altar, the image spreads through space and time as a member of the universal nation of saints awaiting the day of judgment when the class struggle over the means of production and exchange shall include the means of image production and interpretation. Official sanctification distorts and represses the political message latent in the image, but ensures the image a long life in its material form as a sculpture in which the afterglow of its popular creation keeps flickering with hope.

Copies find their way into the homes of wageworkers and peasants, weaving a finely laced web of connections to the original. At times of crisis these images absorb the shock, to release it later on in household memories that reconstruct the history of the original to every new present. Folk healing respectfully takes Church doctrine from the priests, and icons from the walls of the church, reappropriating for its own use what the Church has appropriated from popular mythology drawn from the dreams of the oppressed. Then the images otherwise petrified in paint and sculpture come to life from the opaque mystery in which the Church has enshrouded and preserved them in collective memory. They become live beings. They enter into the vibrant and contradictory texture of social life. The plaster figure of the Virgin of Carmen is transformed into a real woman, giving Rosario's son the blessing he so desperately needs to resolve the contradictions that force peasants to exploit each other. In achieving the blessing of the Virgin, through the magic of Indians, his father can continue to invest World Bank–derived capital and extract surplus value for the bankers as well as for himself from the labor of poor neighbors whose envy is magically held in check. Yet there are limits to the capacity of Church icons to mediate capitalist contradictions. Sister Carmela's prophetic warning registers such limits: José García has accumulated too many farms and too many cattle; they should be shared with the poor.

Confronted with this it is his wife, Rosario, who has to mediate the conflict, in the paralysis and virtual speechlessness of her being, whose history seeks to animate and give voice to a mute and sanctified statue from the colonized and mythic past. When I saw her in Decembeer 1980, several months after her visit to the Lord of Miracles, she told me she was being healed by a middle-aged white woman spirit medium up in Pasto.

"Does she work with the spirit of José Gregorio?" I asked.

"No," she replied. "She invokes the spirit of Tomás Huamanga, a Venezuelan who died 350 years ago." She was very precise. She showed me a photograph of this spirit. It was a touched-up photograph of a local Indian!

Rosario's photograph.

(Whether from the highlands of the Sibundoy Valley or from the lowland foothills, we will never know.) She went on to say that he spoke no Spanish, only Inga, and that he was in his lifetime a famous sorcerer.

When Santiago Mutumbajoy, the Indian shaman who had for so long attended her husband, José García, heard of this he sighed. "Didn't I tell you that the Indian is more Christian than the white?"

NINE

Las Tres Potencias:
The Magic of the Races

The mythic and magical space fixed by the image of the New World Indian is one studded with political irony. In a country like Colombia where all the people classified by government censuses as Indian would fit into a few city blocks, the enormity of the magic attributed to those Indians is striking, an attribution as forceful among the lower classes, black, white, and mestizo, as it is among the middle and upper classes and intellectuals—including archeologists and anthropologists.

The irony is not restricted to the fact that so-called Indians form a tiny fraction of the population. Indians are also among the poorest, most oppressed, and marginalized classes, and have furthermore a reputation for malice if not downright evil as well as ignorance and brutishness. Everyone knows that the *indio es malicioso*. Why they should also be credited with magical power is therefore an intriguing question and, moreover, an important political one since the magic of the Indian is intrinsic not only to their oppression, but also to the web of popular religion and magical curing of misfortune throughout the society as a whole, not to mention to the anthropologists (such as myself) who study it. This magical attraction

171

of the Indian is not only a cunningly wrought colonial *objet d'art;* it is also a refurbished and revitalized one. It is not just primitivism but third-world modernism, a neocolonial reworking of primitivism.

When a baby is born in the Cauca valley, at least of poor parents (and poor parents form the vast majority), its mother usually hastens to acquire a *coralito,* a bracelet of colored beads, once of coral, now of plastic, to ward off the evil eye, *ojo,* or *mal de ojo.* These beads should be "cured," which is to say consecrated with magical power—by an Indian, a Putumayo Indian. It is Putumayo Indians who sell these wrist bands and from whom it is best to buy them. Thus from birth a large if not preponderant number of people throughout this immense valley, if not elsewhere in the republic, are, so to speak, "baptized" into the realm of the magic of the *indio.* (I have been told the same in the Atlantic coast of Colombia, only there the bracelet, the *pepita,* is purchased from the Guajira Indians of the peninsula of that name.)

The baby is unaware of this pact in which it features between its mother and the Indian. Yet just as happened to its mother, this baby will, if and when it grows to maternity, do the same. The lack of awareness all the more firmly secures the potency of the practice and the mythology sustaining it. Such is the character of the implicit social knowledge at issue here.

The cause and to some extent the cure of this disease of the evil eye are also unconscious. The person whose eyes are evil and whose look causes the often fatal gastroenteritic illness is unaware of the power of that look. It is an unconscious power and an unpremeditated act, perhaps the quintessence of envy—*envidia* taking on a life of its own, over and beyond intentionality. And just as the cause is innocent in this way, what can we say of the cure when we realize that the evil eye is *not* a disease category among the Putumayo Indians, highland or lowland? They are in effect being asked by the rest of society to cure something that for them doesn't exist. Of course the wandering medicine men soon learn about it and go through the motions required for diagnosis and treatment, but the motions are those prescribed by the rest of society, not their own. They stand outside the charmed circle of believers necessary to the disease's existence. Down in the rain forest from where so many of these wandering medicine men (so they say) gain much of their magical power, I once asked a Cofán shaman and his wife about *mal de ojo,* the evil eye. They thought I meant something quite literal like a bad eye, conjunctivitis. As for *sal* and *capacho,* "salt" and the sorcery bundle, the predominant types of sorcery one hears about up in the Sibundoy valley or in the interior, they say that these are foolish things, *tonterías* of the whites which the Indians from the Sibundoy valley who wander through the Republic exploit in order to make money. One day the shaman told me he cured jewelry that white people brought him.

"I don't understand," I said.

"Neither do I," he replied.

"Why do you do it?"

"So as to make them content," he said, smiling not with malice or superiority, I thought, but rather coyly and with some embarrassment as he went on to tell of Doña Teofila, whose talisman he cured so she could win at cards. There was also that curious white man Gabriel Camacho, who wandered sick and solitary for two years from shaman to shaman through the Putumayo some fifteen years ago learning about *yagé* and trying to become a great healer himself. The shaman's wife found him weeping on a rock along the river and took him in, clothed and fed him for months at a time. He wanted to learn *yagé* very fast, too fast it turned out, because he fell into the hands of that other Cofán shaman, Pacho Quintero, who as everyone else warned him, was a witch, a *brujo fino,* as the other shamans said. Gabriel Camacho would have died there at Pacho's place along the Tiger River, desolate and starving, but for his *paisanos,* his countrymen, flying by in their oil company helicopter and dragging him out to Bogotá. From the shamans Don Gabriel learned to predict the winning horses every Saturday in the races far away in the nation's capital. He would see their numbers while taking *yagé* and would say, "Let's go up to Pasto to place bets on the *Cinco y Seis.*" But lying on his back drunk with *yagé* way down in the forest, how could he get up there?

Santiago Mutumbajoy never tired of laughing and retelling a story about Gabriel Camacho. The first time I heard it we had been cutting wood and cooking *yagé* all day long in a secluded grove by the river, beating the vine soft with rocks until our wrists ached. "Gabriel Camacho was taking *yagé* one night with a shaman down the Putumayo," Santiago told us. "The cook got no money but Don Gabriel paid the shaman sixty pesos. He asked for his gourd to be full. '*Lleno! Lleno!* Full! Full!' he ordered the shaman. Then the cook, out of envy burst out, '*Yo pobre indio del Putumayo, aguantando frio y hambre y ese Bogotano pidiendo lleno, lleno.* I, poor Indian of the Putumayo, suffering cold and hunger while that man from Bogotá asks full! full!'"

In the Putumayo even colonists openly scornful of Indian magic will take their children, sick with "fright" or *susto,* to an Indian healer to be cured. Rosario's brother, for example, who rarely let by a chance to ridicule Indian healing, had his child cured of *susto* by an Indian. There is much to ponder in the use of Indians as magical beings to thwart the things that frighten children and the "evil eyes" that frighten their parents. Perhaps the Indian is thought of as even more fearsome and even more evil, yet just as they were domesticated by Christian conquest, so can these illnesses be tamed.

In calming fright, the Indian's role is restricted neither to children nor to poor country people. A long way from the Putumayo in the old colonial city of Popayán in western Colombia, a woman named Emilia told me how much better she felt since last we met. She certainly seemed calmer and more animated. Now she said she wanted to separate from her lawyer husband, who had walked out two years before. She showed me a bottle of herbs mixed with *aguardiente*. It's a remedy that she got from an *indio,* she said, an *indio* from the Putumayo. Now she no longer would suddenly wake up in the dark with *susto*. Now she no longer had that terrible insomnia she had suffered since Elías left. Now she no longer suffered from pains throughout her body. She picked on the *indio* quite spontaneously. It just came to her to go up to him one day when she was walking through the market. Nobody recommended him. *Ellos saben.* They know.

María Sol, an eighteen-year-old black acquaintance of mine who works as a maid in the southern Cauca valley, assures me that Indians make the most powerful magic. When she lived in Cartago at the north of the valley, her sister fell in love with a young man, but he remained aloof and indifferent. A friend advised her to go to one of the Indian healers who came out of the rain forests of the Pacific coast of the province of the Chocó. He sold her a green bottle of medicine, telling her to put a few drops in her palm and then shake hands with the man for whose love she was aflame. She did. And indeed he fell madly in love with her, but her mother disapproved.

Wilma Murillo, another black friend of mine from the remote province of the Chocó who buys and sells its gold jewelry and is now married to a clerk with a good position running a computer in the nation's capital, once told me of an Indian in the Chocó being fooled by a black conjurer with the game of the *pepita*. Accused by the angry Indian, he denied engaging in trickery, making the Indian even more furious. Within a few days the body of the black conjurer was crawling with worms pustulating his skin, and soon he died.

Wilma's sister-in-law Juana told me about Don Miro, who lived close to her clothes shop in Puerto Tejada in the southern Cauca Valley. "He is famous," she said. "People come from Cali in taxis to consult with him." Juana was a skilled seamstress and had spent several years smuggling women's clothes into Colombia from Caribbean free ports, so she knew quite a bit about magic useful in thwarting officials. She was friends with a hairdresser in Cali, she said, who now owned a beauty parlor and owed all her good fortune to Don Miro, whom I never got to know. He was too surly. Yet he did tell me that he learned most from an Indian, a Cholo in Quibdó, the capital of the Chocó. He told me that this Indian was a Colorado from Ecuador. Seven years later I was told in the highland Indian village of Ilumán, famous throughout Ecuador on account of its sorcerers and healers, that much magical power passes back and forth between it and those same Colorados of the Pacific lowlands of whom Don Miro spoke to me in Colombia. In his book published in 1972 concerning the so-called Jívaro Indians of the Ecuadorian Amazon, Michael Harner mentions that Jívaro shamans were going over the mountains to visit the Colorados and deal in magic. The Ilumán healer with whom I spoke that rainy afternoon while he was drunkenly curing a married couple by moving smooth little odd-shaped stones and blowing lightning over their almost naked bodies, told me that his uncle had been to visit Don Salvador, the Cofán shaman who had saved Santiago's life and whose house (and now grave) was far, far, away in another country, down the Andes and north past Lago Agrio, past the río San Miguel until you got to the banks of the Guamuez before it ran into the Putumayo. This mountain healer of Ilumán had signs of power from those lowland forests: tiger skins on the wall, chonta-palm staves that he used in his curing, and those green and blue feathers of jungle birds formed into the same sort of luxuriant necklace that the Cofán shamans of the lowland forests use. "But they're only from the wings," pointed out Don Santiago, who was with me trying his best not to look scornful. "The good ones are from the tail. You only get a few feathers from the tail. To make a necklace from the tail you need a lot of birds."

Alejandro Casarán, a surveyor with many years of experience in the track-less forests of the Colombian Pacific coast, stems from a prominent black family in the sugarcane town where I lived for some years in the Cauca valley. He also told me that the Indian *brujo* or witch is the strongest there is. One night he told me how, in the mid-1960s during his journeys surveying for the Land Reform Institute, he stumbled across a curious incident along the Saija river, in the middle of nowhere, mangroves, swamps, mud, and mosquitoes—that terrible coast that so depressed the Pizarros when they were forced to halt their conquering expedition south to the unknown lands of the Inca, 450 years ago. The black descendants of the African slaves brought to work alluvial placer mines for gold in those parts were complaining bitterly of a terrible plague. They asked the local Embera Indians—"Cho-los"—to exorcize it. The Indian shamans agreed, and this (so Alejandro told me, for he was there) turned into a mammoth Indian festival, with Indians coming from as far away as Panama and Ecuador, paddling along the coast and threading through the *esteras* in their canoes. More than 300 Indians came, he told me, and any migrant black sugarcane laborer or maid in the Cauca valley, raised along the rivers of the coast, will tell you just how powerful those *brujos* of the Cholos are.

Yet perhaps as they become more civilized they become more palpably real and hence less magical. I remember early one morning seeing two small canoes stationed by the landing to the all-black town of Santa Barbara. In the canoes as still as statues with their hands on the paddles sat two Cholo women, naked from the waist up. In the store by the landing were two Cholo men waiting to sell plantains. "Go ahead!" the black storeowner told me, "they're Cholos. They're half-civilized now. You can touch them."

Far away from the Pacific coast and the scene of Alejandro's story of blacks asking Indians to exorcize plague, to the east of the vast bulk of the Andes dividing the coast from the Amazon basin, the Cofán Indian shamans I know in the Putumayo say that they can do nothing against such plagues. To deal with them they appeal to black wizards from the Pacific coast! "They are the ones who know how to deal with plagues," Gratulina Moreno insisted. She had heard of truly extraordinary cures of plagues by blacks from the Chocó region of the Pacific coast, using prayers from special books. "They come with their orations and *secreto,* they make the sign of the cross, spit over their shoulder. . . . Yes! They know!" There was the man with the uncontrollable nosebleed. They called in a black healer, a poor colonist from the Pacific coast, and he got one of those old five-cent copper coins, broke an egg over it, stuck the sticky coin on the patient's forehead and made the sign of the cross over it. He then dug up the blood that was on the ground, turned it over, made a cross of dirt where it had been—and the bleeding stopped! "All the blacks know those orations," she said.

"It's useful for us to have these remedies," her shaman husband Salvador told me that day along the bank of the Guamuez, a tributary of the Putumayo, as he was reminiscing about the time the bull sickened and became infected and inflamed after being castrated. They got a black healer who had migrated years before from the Pacific coast. That was only a couple of years before Salvador was killed by the sorcery darts of envious shamans on the Napo river in Ecuador. He was widely esteemed in the *montaña,* as far as the Napo, so it turned out. We knew it was going to happen, Gratulina said, because his voice was like a thready reed when he sang his curing songs.

Santiago Mutumbajoy told me that these black colonists from all the way across the other side of the *cordillera* know a lot of powerful magic to hurt and kill and that they got this magic from books. Manuel Gómez, who had come as a colonist to the Putumayo twenty-five years ago, told me the same thing. "In the Pacific coast there are people who are very strong in this, out of envy or to do harm to someone. Very bad. Bad. Bad." He told me: "They study books of magic and learn orations and they don't like to take *yagé.*" "There are *maestros* in Tumaco [the main port along the southern part of the coast]" Santiago told me, "and they come over the mountains down into the Putumayo to teach their pupils, who are sorcerers in Orito and San Roque."

There is supposed to be a lot of money in Orito, for it is the center of the Texaco Oil Company's operations in the eastern forests. It's the prototypical colonial tropical high-energy town, surrounded by forest with a constant flame of burning natural gas shooting skywards. Thick cables hang from the light poles. There are giant lights like searchlights along the crumbling edges of the open sewers that line its streets and the streets themselves are smeared thick with tar as with a giant trowel and it melts like ice cream in this cruel sun, doing God knows what to the horses' hooves. The Andean range is clearly visible far in the distance over the trees, topped with fluffy curls of clouds. The heat is oppressive and mixes with the smell of gasoline and melting streets. Women walk past in high-soled platform shoes, squelching and tripping in the sticky tar. Everywhere there are piles of soft-drink bottles.

The ingenuity and money that go into the distribution of Coca-Cola to reach the farthest-flung pocket of this land! The treeless streets are lined with corrugated iron shacks with television aerials poking out at odd angles on bamboo poles. Jungle Oil Town.

"It's an ugly hole, Orito," I say.

"But money isn't ugly," responds Santiago, who has often been called there to heal people with sorcery. The place is rife with envy. We were chatting about Doña Leila, a white woman who had come from Orito to have her truck and house cured of sorcery. She had been brought by a poor black colonist who was working for her. "Yes," said Santiago, "his name was Luis . . . Luis . . . Quiñones. He came here to beg me, he came from Tumaco, to find work there in Orito. He would find work and whenever he was about to start, the work would be given to someone else. Well! He decided to look for contract work. The same thing. Again and again. He couldn't find work. Then he . . . one of them from Tumaco came here and asked me to cure him, and it went well. He was a jeweler. No?"

"Yes."

"Then he asked me to give him a cure so that he could have luck selling things. To make money for his family. I did that and his life picked up and people came to him asking that he make them rings and earrings . . . and so on. And he told his *paisano,* his countryman, and said to him 'Go ahead! Go to the house of the friend Santiago. He will cure you.' He arrived. I cured him. But not with drinking *yagé!* With the *aguardiente* he brought, just like that, in passing, nothing more, I cured him with a plant. I said, 'Look! With this go back to Orito and when you want to make a deal break off a piece from this plant and place it in your hand and in your mouth and then make the deal. Nobody will ever take the job away from you. Make this experience!' . . . And that's how it was. He immediately found a job with Doña Leila."

We were sitting on the veranda of his house with his nephew Esaís, passing around *chicha*. It was early afternoon and the rain was clearing. Clouds scudded along the jagged silhouette of the *cordillera*. The flowers in the patio blended in free-floating movement with other clouds, tufted white, bobbing up the bright green slopes. The sun made spear points of glinting greens and yellows dart from the hills into our eyes. Sipping *chicha* with the tearing wind and the river roaring over its rocky bed, Esaís spoke. "The sorcerers learn from books," he piped into the wind's ear. "They use orations that they get out of books that they buy in the market. That all works through Satan. You either work with him or with *yagé,* one or the other; you can't work with both."

"That black guy we called 'eldest son' who came from the coast to take *yagé,* he turned out to be a sorcerer," Santiago said.

"That *morocho,* he worked with Satan," Esaís explained to me. "He was injured in a sorcery duel. He had terrible pains and was involved in all sorts

"It was early afternoon and the rain was clearing."

of sorcery. He was attacked one night, he said, out on the coast. Bullets hit his chest. He dived or fell into the river and escaped. When he came here he was deep in sorcery. My uncle Santiago took *yagé* with him and saw all that and scolded him, telling him to change his ways."

I had met this *morocho* in November of 1976. He had come out of the forest over the hill one hot afternoon looking for Don Santiago so he could take *yagé* and be cured of something. I was alone in the house and he told me while waiting that his luck was all out. His house had been burned down, his canoe had been stolen (on the coast at Puerto Merizalde) and he badly needed to be cured. He changed his clothes, took off his trousers, and (I could barely believe my eyes) put on an Indian *cusma*, the tunic that only Indians wear. He had been here before and loved *yagé* and all that went with it. He badly wanted to become an Indian *curaca* himself.

When I told Santiago that he had a patient waiting up at the house with a sad tale, he muttered and went on working with his machete. "That means he doesn't want to pay. He wants everything free!"

The "eldest son's" name was Félix. Sitting in his Indian *cusma*, he told me that he lived mainly off what he caught fishing in the muddy estuary of the Naya. Many years ago the blacks along his part of the river used to take *pildé*, the coastal name for *yagé* or a *yagé*-like vine that grows there. They used to take quite a bit, he told me. But the young people today say it's of the devil and steer clear. A little further up the Naya river he had had an experience with Indian healing, with Cholos from the Saija river.

"They make up an altar, a *mesa* with six little glasses of *aguardiente,* six with white wine, and six with soft drink, together with cigars and cigarettes. This is for the spirits," he told me as were waiting for Don Santiago to return. "The sick person is then laid down near the *mesa.* The *médico* has a lance which is really a toy canoe paddle, a special little seat, and a doll. Sometimes a *tonguera,* usually a woman, is given *pildé* to drink. She lies down, closes her eyes, and in a few minutes has the answer. The curer and the other Indians sing all night long and in the morning one should be better. But you don't see *anything,* Don Felix stressed, "not like here with *yagé;* neither shadow nor movement . . . and in the morning when they lifted the cover off the *mesa,* all the drink was still there!" He sounded dubious.

He first came here some ten years ago suffering from sorcery that nobody could cure. It began with bloody diarrhea and intense abdominal colic followed by pains in his peripheral joints advancing to the center of his body to become a chronic pain in his stomach as if there were something solid in there trying to pass upward and be vomited out. He told me that he was treated by doctors in Buenaventura, Cali, Bogotá, and other cities for amoebas, but to no effect. He sought cure from sorcerers in Buenaventura and Cali, but again without effect. Then a friend in Buenaventura, the foremost port of the Pacific, told him that there were very good *brujos* way away in the Putumayo.

Santiago came in from his work in the fields and they took *yagé* that night, the Indian from the Putumayo and the black man from over the mountains, both in their Indian tunics, their *cusmas.* Félix started to sing late at night, like a shaman. I liked his singing but it was not the same. After midnight Santiago swung out of his hammock and unsteadily stumped out to turn on a radio. He rarely listens to the radio and gets angry if it is on while *yagé* is being taken.

"Why did you turn the radio on last night?" I asked next morning.

"That *morocho* sings very ugly," he sighed.

Such are the dialectics of magic, healing, and race.

As my good friend Orfir says, heaving with laughter, wherever you go, the great *brujos* are elsewhere. In our town of Puerto Tejada it is said that the *brujos* of the Chocó are astounding. If you go to the Chocó they say the great ones are in Puerto Tejada. And so it goes, the far away rubbed against the familiar, the primitive against the modern, the forest against the city, race rubbed against race in a magic-creating friction. These imputations of magic in Otherness enchant the medley of difference in a poetics of place and race that is no less political and economic than it is aesthetic. Take servitude, for instance, as some friends were telling me in a village close to

In the canefields of Puerto Tejada, 1972.

In the canefields of Puerto Tejada, 1972.

Puerto Tejada, daughters of peasant farmers, now mothers themselves, some working in the canefields, others as peddlers, and many as servants in the cities, close by or far away. Walter Benjamin saw in the reunion of the returned traveler with those who stayed at home, no less than in the artisan's shop, the charmed occassion for spinning magical stories.[1] In today's third world there are far more servants than artisans, yet still the stories flow. "Some mistresses use magic to tie [*ligar*] their servants to the house and make them loyal and hard-working," my friend Elbia was saying. "Some servants enter into plots with their mistresses to practice sorcery on the mistress's husband and 'tie' him down!" And sometimes you hear of a servant who puts a *liga* on her mistress! The servants from the Pacific coast are the ones prone to this. Yes! They can come and go just as they please. Some even hit their mistress!

"The mistresses do so little," sighed a listener. "They play Bingo, wander the streets or talk on the telephone—mainly about how good or bad we are."

Here in this village only women witches could fly. "A man and a woman were learning witchcraft, learning to fly. They had to repeat '*sin Dios, sin ley, y sin Santa María*' [without God, without law, and without the Virgin Mary]. The woman said it okay and was thus able to fly. But the man, he said *con Dios, con ley, y con Santa María* [with God, with the law, and with the Virgin Mary] and was therefore unable to fly. Men never fly!"

Reciprocity.

But they do worry about being thought above others, of stirring the envious into action for perceived failures to reciprocate. That was why the husband of my friend Elbia had his small shop with its two rented billiard tables cured on three successive nights with baths of magical liquids, bottles of herbs dug into the threshold, and medicines to drink that made him fall into a deep sleep. "We did it in order to prevent envy from entering the shop and killing us," he told me. The healer was a mulatto, and was expensive (charging 2,000 pesos at a time when the daily wage was around 150 pesos a day). Where he came from, nobody knew. All they could remember was his saying he had learned his art from the *indios*—of the Putumayo. Nobody knew where he went to, either.

The Three Potencies

A new healing spirit was to be found in the capital of the nation. His name was El Negro Felipe and I was told that he came from Venezuela. People who until recently placed their faith in that other Venezuelan spirit, the pious medical doctor José Gregorio, were said now to be seeking cure with El Negro Felipe instead. I went to a spirit center in a working-class area of the city where white women spirit mediums served his cult. He was pictured and sculptured as a black man wearing a Hindu turban and a fancy soldier's coat with gold-laced collar and epaulettes. He was undeniably negroid, yet the white woman spirit medium told a group of around thirty-five of us who came to consult that he was an Indian—born to a tribe in Venezuela a long time ago and blessed by God with charisma.

A few days later down in the hot country I bought a postcard-sized and framed picture of *Las Tres Potencias,* the Three Potencies, in the market-place of Puerto Tejada from a man selling scores of pictures of different saints. My eye was caught by a familiar image, none other than El Negro Felipe, who now featured as one of the three *potencias,* and I asked the vendor, a white man from the city of Cali, who these three figures were. The face on our left, he said, is that of the wanderer Huefia, a black. The woman in the center is Teresa Yataque. That on the right is Francisco Chasoy—all three from the Putumayo!

I asked by friend María Sol. She stepped back in alarm, saying it was a picture used in sorcery; the person on the left is a black sorcerer, the *brujo* Mayombé; in the center is the queen of the sorcerers; and on the right is an Indian sorcerer.

With great authority an Indian woman selling medicinal herbs and magical amulets in the bustling streets of Cali told me that these were three Pana-manian Indians. An old white man selling lemonade passed by and became very excited. "This is a picture of three Putumayo Indians," he exclaimed. A young man from Bogotá selling pictures of the saints on the pavement outside the church of San Francisco in Cali told me that this was a picture

The Three Potencies.

of Venezuelan saints: the Negro Felipe on our left, María Lionsa in the center, and the *indio* Guaicaipuro on the right. At the stall next to his a black woman threw a glance at the three *potencias* and without hesitating announced that these were three Indians from Quito, Ecuador. "Each person has their own story" commented my fourteen-year-friend Dalila with a smile, and therein lies another story about how society plays with a storehouse of images and relations between images concerning the magic of the races, the Three Potencies.

The magical effluvium of the primordial Indian can also be found in the dreams of redemption of slumdwellers in the city of Cali, a settlement devoid of Indians since the first century of Spanish conquest began in 1536. Chris Birkbeck has published the following dream, an extract from his field notes of 1977.

> Don Colo owns a small shop in one of Cali's poorest neighbourhoods. One day, not too long ago, he was walking on the outskirts of the city and felt the call of nature, so he went into a banana plantation at the side of the road. Having no paper, he used the leaves of a nearby plant, and, on returning home, realised that his ring was missing. In bed that night, he dreamt that the loss of the ring was related to the plant, the leaves of which he had used that day. The following day he returned to the plantation, gathering some of these leaves and brought them home. He rubbed the leaves over his daughter's gold ring

and it became rubbery and malleable. He realised that he had found the long-lost lengendary plant the Indians had used to work their gold with such delicacy. He could in turn become a legend. Yet he has not, due to his fear of divulging his secret, his fear that someone else will take advantage of it, and make the fortune that should be his.[2]

This story has been taken as evidence of the miracle-mongering desperation of the poor and as an illustration of the "petty-bourgeois individualism" of those making a living in the "informal sector" of the economy. Yet there is more to be said (and not only about Don Colo rubbing his daughter's gold ring). To focus exclusively on the conscious economic interests of the individual is to lose sight of colonial mythopoeisis working through the political unconscious. The contents of the dream as much as the dreamlike story as a whole refer us not only to the miracle-mongering of the individual, but also to the popular conceptions of the miraculous and redemptive secrets of alchemical knowledge lost to manifest history yet accessible through coincidence and misfortune in the form of the dream, wherein history (and not only a gold ring) is made malleable through Indian magic.

The world-renowned Gold Museum in the headquarters of the Banco de la Republica in Bogotá must surely qualify as a national totem. Stuffed with Indian goldwork dating from the time of the European conquest and long before, its small but brilliant artifacts shine like stars in the artificial darkness, making of the museum a church whose daily rites of magic, planned and supervised by the scientific staff of ethnologists and archeologists in back rooms for the streams of pilgrims, recreate the dreams of slumdwellers like Don Colo in Cali. The peak experience defined by the museum is in its innermost sanctum, guarded by armed men and thick metal doors through which the crowd is shunted every few minutes. It is pitch black inside. We wait. The crowd moves uneasily. Then this *communitas* phase of what is in effect a sort of initiation rite is abruptly broken as a golden haze fills the room and all our senses. We find ourselves in a room jammed with Indian gold objects piled on top of each other, nose rings, breastplates, bracelets, pots, golden frogs, golden jaguars, golden bats, golden alligators, golden Indians . . . heaped on each other like junk in a yard with gold proliferating like old tin cans. The crowd gasps.

It caused Santiago Mutumbajoy much mirth, I remembered, that one of the first things the white women in Cúcuta asked him was not only if he was baptized and a true Christian, but whether he could give them the *secreto* to find gold.

A few blocks away from the Gold Museum by the street that runs past the Central Cemetery there gathers every Monday a large crowd devoted to the cult of the dead or, more precisely, to the cult of the souls—the lost and lonely souls—of Purgatory. Some people go to the tombs of the famous and there make magical rites asking for success, health, money. Others go to the empty black holes where bodies once laid but are no more and there light their candle in the space of death. Outside on the street beyond the women selling flowers and candles, magical perfumes and soaps, amulets and pictures of the saints, including now the *Tres Potencias,* and beyond the crowd—some stock-still erect, some rocking back and forth chanting magical orations over the sputtering crackle of generations of flaming candlewax—beyond all this there stretches up Twenty-sixth Street a carnival of the grotesque, the freaks, the most miserable of the miserable. The tiny tent-shaped bundle of a limbless dwarf. A pair of alabaster white eyesockets with bright red seams glistens from a man's head. An old thin man in black is seated very straight in a homemade wheelchair holding a black umbrella open over his head. In his lap he pats a small furry dog, obscenely normal and endearing in this land of the deformed and the unnameable. He is perfectly still. His elbow rests on a cumbersome wheeled platform upon which lies a totally paralyzed young girl, her face a frenzy of speechless vacuity. Beyond them are some Indian women, all the way from the Sibundoy valley at the country's southernmost extremity. They are selling *coralitos* and amulets—and something else as well, bottles of medicine out of sight under their trays.

The crowd is thick and milling there on Twenty-sixth Street, the day of the lost souls of Purgatory. The crowd is swarming like bees. What is going on? On top of a stepladder is perched a square wooden box, each side about three feet long. For 100 pesos the man on the street with the megaphone will open the doors of the box. Inside, expressionless, is a bodiless boy. Sweet—sweet as an angel. In his mouth he holds the corner of an airmail letter. It contains a prophecy. It's yours for 100 pesos. The doors close on the bodiless face. We want to see more. So sweet. Doors to the future revealed by the cut-off child.

Yes, Carlos Pinzón told me. There was a more or less identical thing a few months back, only instead of a sweet boy they used a brain in a plastic bag—an *Indian* brain. And that's what it was called, this oracle of the street: the brain of the *indio.*

Away from the noise and dirt of the slums, in the bookstores frequented by the middle classes, the rich, and tourists from what are called the developed countries, there are many books on Indians. Often these books are ones that display Indians, exotic wild animals, and plants, all together as if they all belonged to and constituted a single category. Such books are virtual fetish objects, icons resplendent in their glossy colored photography and handsome prices. Even the history texts used in the schools throughout the republic have between one-quarter to one-third of their chapters devoted to Indians, especially to pre-Conquest societies and custom (yet barely a mention, let alone one chapter, on African slavery or black history—in a society whose economy has rested to a far greater extent on the backs of blacks and their descendants than on Indians). Whether it is in the authoritative language of history, anthropology, or archeology, or in the dreams of the poor, the image of the Indian casts its spell—a spell that is no less binding in the magic of the Church and the epiphanic discovery of its miraculous saints and virgins, as we shall next see.

TEN

The Wild Woman of
the Forest Becomes
Our Lady of Remedies

The Lord of Miracles at Buga creates a deep irony in Transito's history of misfortune. Emphatically stating that she despises Indians, she made an arduous pilgrimage for many hundreds of miles over the mountains to visit a Christ whom, as she says, was discovered many thousands of years ago by an Indian. There are many miracle-yielding saints in Latin America who were discovered by or first manifested themselves to Indians, and each saint has some special twist to his or her discovery. These Indian-manifested saints and the particular twist in their story of discovery constitute a map of redemption drawn across the land. Each twist is like a signifier, dependent on the map as a whole to make its meaning. Each pilgrim with each pilgrimage is like an act of speech, bringing that meaning to concrete actuality.

Moving a few score miles south from the Lord of Miracles at Buga along the valley plain, we come to the largest city of the Colombian southwest, Cali, whose patron saint is Our Lady of Remedies in the chapel of the Church of La Merced. According to the booklet issued by the church fathers that I was given there in 1982, the first white to see her was a missionary advancing the faith in the Andes just north of Cali in 1560, only twenty-four years after the initiation of the Spanish conquest in that area. An Indian told him that deep in the jungle there was a statue identical to the one he venerated in his room. The Indians called her the "Wild Woman of the Forest," *La Montañerita Cimarrona*, and to her they made offerings from their gardens and the forest so that their harvests and their hunting would be bounteous. They played their flutes and danced to her "with the flexibility of bodies free of oppression of European clothing." In the seventeenth century notarized testimony cited in the church's booklet, the Indians are constantly referred to as *indios barbaros*.

The missionary, Miguel de Soto, was lame and he made the Indians carry him on their backs to their "Wild Lady" to see if what they said was true. He was lifted through jungles marked by the footprints of savage beasts. The sun filtered softly through the green lace of the jungle leaving sprays of gold on the fallen leaves that covered the edges of the trail. Far off he heard the hiss of cobras. Vines knitted together forming capricious monograms, while the nights were not only the darkest there ever were, but were filled by the jungle with infinite rumors. So we read.

There in those aromatic, rumor-filled jungles but a few leagues from Balboa's sea, Father Miguel de Soto came face to face with the most perfect image of womanhood he had ever seen—cut into the heights of a rockface in a niche adorned with vines and ferns. Her eyes were of mystic sweetness, her smile divine, and in her arms the Christ child clutched at a tropical fruit.

He ordered her cut down and carried to the convent of La Merced in the new city of Cali. One night she disappeared, to be found again in the jungle. She was carried back to her post in Cali but twice more managed to escape back to her niche in the forest but a few leagues from Balboa's sea, until a special chapel was built for her. As a consequence of the many attested miracles she worked for the white and civilized people of Cali, her name was changed from the Wild Woman of the Forest to Our Lady of Remedies. Conquered and tamed, wildness yields its healing power. Today figures of seminaked Indians surround her image.

As with the Lord of Miracles at Buga, that beacon of Rosario's pilgrimage, it is the Indian who is chosen by history to provide the civilized and conquering race with a miraculous icon. As a slave attends the needs of the master, so the conquered redeem their conquerors. In the case of the Wild Lady of the Forest transformed into Our Lady of Remedies, her Church-writ mythology is strikingly clear as regards the contradiction constituting what Jean Barstow calls "the unsuspected power of the powerless"; the ambivalent moral status of Indians as pagan-Christians, *indios barbaros* of the wilderness blessed with an aboriginal spiritual kinship with the mother of the god of the conquering Christians.

Although the Indians here are clearly wild and as such are clearly contrasted to the Old World of Europe, there is no hint of their being evil or combative. But the jungle enclosing the Indians and their miraculous icon is altogether different. It is truly malevolent, baroque in its lacelike foliage, speaking to man through capricious monograms in the night smells and rumors filtering the dark of the night through which, as into the circles of hell, the lame priest is carried by his pagan guides to find his Beatrice chiseled into the heights of the rock face—and as such his wondrous journey should be compared with Captain Cochrane's later on in this book, Captain Cochrane of the British Navy who was also carried on the backs of Indians, in the mid-nineteenth century, in this very same jungle "but a few leagues from Balboa's sea.''

The Niña María of Caloto: The Official History

The peculiar paradox that endows the figure of the powerless Indian with power to create miraculously empowered Christian saints and virgins is further manifested by a famous Virgin in the foothills of the central chain of the Andes some eighty kilometers south of Cali, the Virgin of Caloto, known as the Niña María. In her case, however, there is an inversion of the relationships manifested by the Wild Woman of the Forest cum Our Lady of Remedies. In the official Church history of the Niña María the Indians are most emphatically *not* portrayed as angelic and innocent but, to the contrary, as savage and rebellious pagan cannibals—stark antiselves of all that a Christian should be. Together with the wildly differing testimonies provided not by official but by oral history, this feature opens fresh paths for understanding the magical reality here at issue; namely, that the reality of this miraculous Virgin as much as the miraculous nature of the reality is in curious ways dependent on contradictory histories circulating around her in living speech. It is this effervescent and contradictory listening and talking surrounding the icon that need to be first considered, if ever we are to grasp the ways by which the miraculous is everyday and the icon serves as a means for the experiential appropriation of history.

The Niña María is a small wooden doll, sixty-seven centimeters high. Until the end of the eighteenth century she was known as the Virgin de Rosario and had a Christ child in her arms, but now she stands childless as the central figure behind the altar of the town's one church, a simple and striking colonial building forming the side of the main square. Her annual fiesta on the eighth of September is lavish, drawing thousands of devotees, principally people whom the townsfolk call *indios,* from the steep slopes of the Andes rising dramatically from town's eastern limits. While the town is inhabited mainly by whites, the hot valley plain stretching out west and north below the town with its cattle and waving sugarcane is mainly populated by poor black peasants and day laborers. I do not know what the Indians think about this little town tucked into the foothills. They rarely descend the

The annual festival of the Niña María.

mountains into it. But the blacks whom I know are quick to portray it as a white town—solitary, quiet, dull, and a Conservative Party stronghold.

According to the pamphlet published by the archdiocese of Popayán, the effigy of the Niña María was brought by the first Spaniards who founded the settlement of Caloto in the mid-sixteenth century, then a town of gold "miners" (usually meaning whites who forced Indian or African slaves to pan gold). This town had to be relocated several times over the next half-century because of raids by Pijao Indians. In 1585, according to this official history, these Indians attacked the town while mass was being said on Easter Thursday in order to take the Niña María. They killed the priest and took the effigy away. In Father Lozano's version, interpolated into the main narrative, it is said that the Indians killed the majority of the whites. As it was the Indians' custom after a successful raid to celebrate with intoxicating liquor for three days and then sleep for several more, the immortal Calambas, chief of the Christian Indians, set off in pursuit. Certain the Niña María would be horribly profaned, imagine their surprise, writes Father Lozano, when they found that the savages had instead raised her onto a beautiful throne of flowers. Following twenty-four hours of bloody combat, the Spaniards were able to overcome the cannibals and repossess her.

The Pijaos attacked twice more and on the third occasion, in 1592, again took the sacred image. Once more the Spaniards were able to win her back and since then she has performed many miracles, not the least of which has been her coming to the defense of the frequently persecuted *pueblo* of Caloto— as in the Wars of Independence in 1810 and in the unremitting civil wars of that century of turmoil when Caloto proudly sustained the Conservative cause against the Liberal Party, in the Wars of 1851, 1860, 1879, and 1899.

As with the Wild Woman of the Forest who became Our Lady of Remedies, the miraculous nature of the Niña María depends heavily on the presence of the Indian. But in sharp contrast to Our Lady of Remedies, the Indians in the Church-published history of the Niña María are depicted as militant rebels and savage cannibals. Moreover, the icon is not aboriginal. It is the Spanish who brought her to the frontier of this gold-rich wilderness, and the twist providing what we might call the "political key" to the legend—the political key that lives actively in the present—is that, despite their savagery, the Indians are seduced by her. It is this "miracle" that signifies, unfolds, and develops the miraculous nature of the image whose magic will henceforth serve to defend the Christians from further raids by savages and protect the town during civil war.

In the woodcuts recently carved by a pilgrim with the intention of depicting the official history, and on display in the priest's residence, a clear distinction is made between two different groups or types of Indians, the Catholic Indians who help the Spanish, and the wild Indians who steal the Virgin, assassinate the priest, and carry off his head. This distinction is important in that it not only reappears in the Franciscan reports on the Putumayo district in the colonial era (being also the distinction between highland and lowland Indians), and it not only surfaces repeatedly to the present day all along the Andean *montaña* of Ecuador, Peru, and Bolivia, with *aucas, chunchos,* and so forth as the wild Indians, but it also represents the dualized character of "the Indian" as a social category and as a moral personage. For not only were there converted Indians and pagan Indians existing as actual social groups, but the colonially propounded and still effervescent image of the Indian depends precisely on this combination of opposites in which wildness and Christianity sustain and subvert one another.

This gnawing at the semantic vitals of one's dependency is manifested in a different register by the contrast between the official history of the Niña María and the official history of Our Lady of Remedies. The gnawing becomes positively ravenous, however, when we turn to the disparities between the official and unofficial accounts of miraculous Virgins ushered into the kingdom of this world by pagan discoveries. Take the Niña María for example.

The Niña María: Popular History and Histories

Of the thirty-two people whom I met for the first time in 1982 and with whom I briefly spoke in the town of Caloto and along the main road leading to it from the plains, six said they had no knowledge of the Niña María. In all I spoke with three Indians, sixteen whites, and thirteen blacks, all adults. Only five people gave accounts that coincided with official history.

"She's a Spanish image," said the priest's niece. "The Indians robbed her. With her they could raid the Spanish and the Indians venerated her. The Spaniards got her back and since then were able to resist the Indians."

"The Indians worshiped her" stressed the priest to me. "They esteemed her and that is why they took her. They hated the whites but not the religion."

Contrary to this, fourteen people surprised me by saying she was an *Indian* Virgin who appeared first to the Indians, not the whites, and that it was the whites who stole her from Indians! Six blacks, six whites, and the two Indians told me that. A black man, owner of a tiny shop one kilometer outside of town, said, "The Spanish stole her from the Indians." A black peasant of the plains said, "Some *indios* found her, but I don't know much more." A white woman selling coffee in a nearby village said. "The Virgin appeared to the Indian savages in the hills above Caloto—to make them believers."

"This is a saint of the Indians" exclaimed a middle-aged white woman selling peanuts in the town plaza. "This land was all theirs and she protected them. When the Spaniards came she made it seem as though there were immense numbers of Indian warriors and that frightened the Spaniards away."

A black woman selling plantains in the marketplace said, "She belonged to the indigenous people, to their *caciques* [chiefs]. They found her up in the mountains. She appeared as a real person. Then another group of Indians stole her. The *caciques* got her back and put her in church in Caloto. The group that stole her also wanted her gold crown. She performs miracles. But the Indians don't appreciate her properly. On the eighth of September [her annual fiesta] they get terribly drunk. But they have a lot of faith in her even though they may lie in the gutter like dogs. Last year a thief tried to steal her crown. She was guarded by a policeman. The thief opened the door, but by a miracle it appeared to him that there were more than one thousand police standing guard there. Many *pueblos* are envious of Caloto and have tried to destroy the town and take the Virgin away. They envy the Virgin as much as the *pueblo*. Why the envy? Nobody can explain envy; it's just that the world has evil-hearted people [*gente de mala corazón*]."

Four people made no mention at all of Indians or of colonial history and conquest. Instead they placed her appearance forward, into the nineteenth century. A black man in the bus entering town simply said she first appeared in the epoch of "the civil wars" to save the Conservative Party. A very old white man, a barber, sitting in front of the plaza overlooking the church, said she first appeared in "the wars"—the wars between the Liberals and the Conservatives. The Liberals were confidently attacking the town but fled in fear; the Niña María had created an illusion of noise and confusion that the town was defended by Conservatives vastly outnumbering their assailants. The young white man administering the billiard parlor next to the barber shop said that he didn't really know her history, but she appeared during the *Violencia*—the bloody strife between Liberals and Conservatives that tore much of rural Colombia to the marrow from 1948 to 1958.

In the nearby and predominantly black town of Puerto Tejada, I was told by a friend that the Niña María made her first appearance in the War of One Thousand Days that lasted from 1899 to 1901. A famous black general, the usually Conservative (but somewhat a chameleon) Juan Zappe, was with his guerrilla force locked in fierce combat with Liberal troops. His ammunition was almost exhausted. Defeat looked certain. Then the Niña María miraculously appeared, causing the enemy to hallucinate, creating the illusion that the Conservatives were far stronger than they actually were. And so General Zappe's men were victorious and today the Zappe family proudly participate each year in the Niña María fiesta in Caloto.

An elderly white woman, Ana Guambia, is part of Caloto's elite—a painter and the major if not the only stimulus behind the local folklore movement. She sees the miraculous Virgin as a magical weapon in racial and spiritual warfare. She says that the Spanish were very superstitious, as were the Indians, and that in their campaigns of conquest the Spaniards carried a Virgin, possibly made in Quito, to protect them. The Indians understood this. They understood the Virgin to be a magical weapon and they determined to take her and thereby sap the power of their oppressors. They stole the Virgin and began to destroy her. Today you see that while her face is still unblemished, under her clothes her body is disfigured. But then the Indians began to suffer plagues like smallpox and measles, their *cacique* died of a heart attack, and they started to realize that instead of destroying they should venerate her. It was then that the Spaniards found her, adored by Indians heaping her with flowers.

Finally, a black woman nurse attending a dying friend of mine out beyond the town, in a hut squeezed between the fields of the sugar plantations, drew a lyrical connection between the Niña María and the Lord of Miracles at Buga, some 200 kilometers to the north of Caloto.

"Some Indians found her in a bamboo thicket, and then she went away. She was barefoot. Then the Indians found her again and brought her to Caloto and started having fiestas for her. Haven't you seen it?" she asked me. "It's a fiesta of the Indians!" She paused. "People say that when she went away she went to Buga to be with the Lord of Miracles—as he was then a kid too."

Double-Visioning Dialogue

Hence six of the thirty-two people with whom I spoke said they had no knowledge of her genesis. Only five concur with the official history claiming that the image belonged to the Spanish, that it was brutally stolen by the Indian cannibals, and that its miraculous power was brought into the world by savages succumbing to its Christian spell.

In complete contradiction of the official history, the most common oral version, held by blacks, whites, and Indians alike, holds that the Spaniards robbed the image from the Indians and that it is a quintessentially Indian icon. This encompasses several different accounts with different political implications.

In the account of the black woman selling plantains in the marketplace, two themes of importance are brought out. Acknowledging that the miraculous Virgin belonged initially to the indigenous people and that they place great faith in her, the plantain seller notes that the Indians don't appreciate her properly. At her fiesta they get drunk; they lie in the gutter like dogs. While the bestiality of the Indian is necessary for bringing the Virgin and her miraculous powers into the world, conscious awareness, appreciation, subsequent care and development of that power require a quite different sensibility, namely that associated with the non-Indian. There is here a racial division of spiritual labor in the creation of her miraculous power in which the bestial Indian, pagan and wild, is necessary in the same way that a dog or a drunk can sense and attract influences to which a civilized, sober human is insensible.

A second theme in the plantain seller's account concerns the primordial importance of envy, reciprocity, and illusion. The Virgin stimulates envy on the part of other *pueblos,* just as she also protects Caloto from the aggression of the envious. In both stimulating and deflecting envy she presents the dilemma basic not only to sorcery and magical healing, but to interpersonal relationships in general, as vividly illustrated in the lives of Rosario and José García. And as with them, hallucination leaps from as much as it pierces the breast of envy, causing or resolving it or both. Moreover, the Virgin's mode of protecting her people from the envy she stimulates in others is to induce hallucination in the enemy in a confusing transformation of one reality into another. Hallucination is said to have figured in the wars of conquest, the wars of independence, the civil wars in the nineteenth century, the mid-twentieth century *Violencia,* and but a few months back when a thief tried to steal her crown. (We might note here that magic is used to prevent theft in Colombia, and in most cases that I know the aim of such magic is the same as here ascribed to the Virgin: to create fear if not confusion through an illusion of a protecting force such as a snake or a tiger.)

Now let us return to the woman selling peanuts in the plaza. This is a saint of the Indians, she said. This land was all theirs. She protected them. When the Spaniards came she made it seem as though there were immense numbers of Indian warriors and that frightened the Spaniards away. What seems intriguing to me here is that the magical power of the Virgin to create a frightening reality through illusion is first deployed against the Spaniards, sustaining their myths and fantasies of Indian powers. Moreover, the story acknowledges the illusory basis of this power imputed to the wild Indian. At one and the same time this story speaks from within and without the spell of magic, thereby registering not merely a dualized but an interacting doubleness of epistemology, two universes apart, each requiring the other, each demolishing the other. Such is the paradox, if you like, of the very notion of illusion—less real, equally real, more real than the really real and that which makes the real really real. Such is the faith composing the stories composing the Virgin and her miraculous powers.

Behind the illusionary powers of the Virgin, of course, lurks the illusion of the image of the Indian as composed and decomposed by the ebb and flow of colonial history. And in both instances, that of the Indian-dependent miraculous Virgin no less than that of the Virgin-dependent Indians, the principle of adhesion to the reality of history is not unlike the principle of collage—in which presentation coexists with representation, each order of reality estranging if not mocking the other.

In another register this collage is manifested by the white woman selling coffee who said that the Virgin belongs to the Indians and appeared in order to make of them Christian believers. This seems tantamount to saying that the historical function of the Virgin is the political one of accommodating the pagan to the conqueror's god and thereby, in this case, establishing the divine legitimacy of white rule. This is the familiar critique of magical Virgins: that they are creatures invented by astute churchmen to hoodwink credulous Indians. Yet, one is prompted to ask, why were they so credulous about *this* particular issue? And if they were so easily duped, why need the churchmen bother with such devious ways of getting them to believe in the Spaniard's god and his virginal mother? Moreover, it is not the Indians' belief that is here at issue, but the white's belief of the Indians' belief. The point is that the woman coffee seller who made the observation that the Virgin first appeared to the Indians, and did so in order to make them believers, is herself a believer in the miraculous power of the Virgin. The force and logic her statement possesses as a skeptical interpretation depend upon and assume that very faith.

And not only is faith in the Virgin's miracle-creating power created and reproduced through such interweaving doubleness of story-fixed envisioning, and not only do the stories contradict one another, but they generally contest the official voice of the Church itself. I think this points to something more than simple negation, multiplicity, or dialectics. Instead it seems as if the life of the icon and hence of the reality of the miracle depend upon the social reproduction of a constantly inconstant reality in which meaning both depends upon and destroys its opposite in a ceaseless confrontation with the formally institutionalized source of truth. To repulse the enemy and wrest victory from defeat, the image of the Virgin creates further images, said to be illusions.

Virginal Historiography

When we turn to the four accounts in which no mention whatsoever is made of the role of the pagan Indian in eliciting the Virgin's power of salvation, we are prodded into asking more pointedly what sort of historiography the image sustains and puts into speech. For while it is tempting to say that icons such as the Virgin of Caloto may preserve myths of the origin of colonial society, these accounts further indicate that the origin myth allows the originary point to slide or skip through time to represent different events. For in these four accounts her origin is brought forward in time and situated in other fields of battle: in nineteenth century wars of independence, the succeeding civil wars, and the mid-twentieth-century *Violencia*. Rooted in a particular landscape as mythical as it is physical, rooted in a particular political party, the Conservative, the Virgin is free to wander through chronological time and fix memorable events with the freshness of her recurring genesis.

In doing this she serves as a mnemonic of focal points in social history, points charged with the messianic time of persecution and salvation of the moral community. The mnemonic function replenishes the present with mythic themes and oppositions set into semiotic play in the theater of divine justice and redemption.

The magic of the Indian—pagan, militant, anti-Christ obstacle to the gold of the wilderness—sets the Virgin on her redemptive course. The divinely wrought irony, whereby in their defeat the Indians both discover and create the miraculous defender of their conquerors, establishes the complex of mythic and magical relations with which stories compose and decompose the history of the Virgin. Where the Indian no longer features, the more general figure of an ominous outsider and "Envious Other" emerges in the nineteenth-century royalists or in the Liberal partisans of the civil wars and *Violencia* eliciting the contrast recurrence of the miracle.

This is a politicized class- and race-sensitive hermeneutic process of semiotic play with the structure of signs established as images in social experience by the Spanish conquest. Encrusted in colonial icons such as the Niña María of Caloto, this structure is brought into everyday life not as an inert and fixed model, but, to the contrary, exists by means of spasmodic dialogical creativity as a range of interpretive possibilities—and in this regard it is noteworthy that the most common oral account of the Virgin's genesis subverts the official voice of the past, as propounded by the Church, while retaining allegiance to the form sanctified by Church authority.

I have spoken of the image and the stories that come from, circle around, and go back into that image as if they were one and the same thing; one order of reality existing in two distinct media—the wooden doll, on the one hand, and the stories that adorn and animate her virginal nudity, on the other. I have said "image" when I could just as well have said "the community of persons among whom the image exists, the community of persons doing the imagining and therewith bringing the image to life over and over again." It is of course fetishistic to endow the image per se with the active role in what is a reciprocating relation between viewer and viewed.

There will come occasion to examine this relationship of interconnected viewers and the image in greater detail. What I want to warn against here is a type of blindness of the sophisticated who may grasp this relationship as an analogue of the now fashionably familiar model of text and reader wherein the reader is credited a significantly active role in the construction of the text being read. This analogy is useful here only if understood as more brutally political *and* more finely nuanced than is commonly credited. We have but to think back to the dialogical construction of the imagery in torture and in the horrors of the Putumayo rubber boom to appreciate the brutal politics. As for the second feature, regarding subtlety, it can be indicated by referring to the image-making that occurs in the relationship between Putumayo shamans and their patients, a relationship that has much to teach us about the dialogical construction of soul-stirring and bodily effective image-making in general. For here the shaman is said to be the one who truly *sees,* and by virtue of this capacity provides the healing images—the *pinta* or painting—for the patient, the one who cannot see. Yet it is not so much the shaman as the patient who gives speech and narrative form to these images, images that not only perturb but may also change awareness, the record of a life, and social relationships as well. It is thus in the combined activity of the one who sees but does not talk of what is seen, together with the patient who talks but does not truly see, that we find the crucible of socially effective image-making—and this seems no less the case with mute icons such as the Virgin of Caloto who, like the shaman, provoke images (*pinta,* painting) that otherwise sightless persons redeem for speech and story. In so doing they also redeem the messianic faith in the miracle, in focal points retroactively condensing in collage form the epic of imperialistic conquest, independence struggles, civil wars, and *Violencia.*

Dialectical Imagery and the Task of the Critic

This type of image-making and image-dependent historiography is also the subject of a pointedly eccentric contribution to the twentieth-century Western European theory of social revolution, namely Walter Benjamin's concepts of redemptive criticism and dialectical images. In his youth, in 1914, Benjamin argued for just the kind of historiography as is exhibited in the image-making provoked by the Virgin of Caloto. Contrary to the view of history as a progressive continuum, the young Benjamin advanced the notion that "history rests collected in a focal point, as formerly in the utopian images of thinkers. The elements of the end condition are not present as formless tendencies of progress but instead are embedded in every present as endangered, condemned, and ridiculed creations and ideas." The historical task, he went on to say, "is to give absolute form in a genuine way to the immanent condition of fulfillment, to make it visible and predominant in the present."[1]

The task of the critic of works of art is therefore to join with this task of redemption, in rescuing, as Richard Wolin puts it, "the few unique visions of transcendence that grace the continuum of history." Surely it is precisely this that the peasants and townsfolk of Caloto embed in every present with their renditions of the Virgin's beginnings in the past? Only here the secular and theological fragments of that past stand in a sharper, more concrete, less lofty, and more Brechtian configuration than suggested by the grandiloquent tone of Benjamin's formulation. It is the Indians' *land,* for instance, as much as their elicitation of the messianic force of history, which the focal point of history here collects; it is the confusing din of battle, race wars and wars of civilizations, that hums through this vision of transcendance that graces the continuum of history.

Later on in life when he refashioned redemptive criticism in order to engage it with his idiosyncratic attachment to Marxism, Benjamin referred to this task as one involving the "dialectic at a standstill." The gallery of images of concern to the critic of high culture is now expanded to include imagery that fires the popular imagination. If by this expansion the history of art comes closer to a view of history as art, it should not be forgotten that for Benjamin this is a class-conflict view of art, as well as a messianic one, entailing the notion that while the power of ideas and ideology lay more in the realm of images than in concepts, and while there could be no intact

revolutionary will without exact pictorial representation, this capacity of
images was, except on rare occasions, blocked by ruling-class representations of the past that imagery evoked. "This leap into the past," he wrote
in reference to the imageric evocation of ancient Rome by the French Revolution, "takes place in an arena where the ruling class gives the commands."
However, the same leap "into the open air of history is the dialectical one,
which is how Marx understood the revolution."[2]

Inciting the critic to devise ways of freeing imagery from the deadening
hand of tradition and the stronghold of the ruling classes, Benjamin seems
to suggest that images—or at least some images—lend themselves to this
task. Hence the critic dedicated to the method of the "dialectic at a standstill" is enjoined not to force dialectics into images, but to work with and
nourish this destabilizing potential when and where it exists as a sign of a
messianic cessation of happening. In his own words, close to the end of his
life, where he more or less defined this task (in 1940, in the turbulent wake
of the Stalin-Hitler pact):

> Thinking involves not only the flow of thoughts but their arrest
> as well. Where thinking suddenly stops in a configuration preg-
> nant with tensions, it gives that configuration a shock, by
> which it crystallizes it into a monad. A historical materialist ap-
> proaches a historical subject only where he encounters it as a
> monad. In this structure he recognizes the sign of a messianic
> cessation of happening, or, put differently, a revolutionary
> chance in the fight for the oppressed past. He takes cognizance
> of it in order to blast a specific era out of the homogeneous
> course of history—blasting a specific life out of the era or a
> specific work out of the life work.[3]

Yet, despite his boldness, he hesitates. There is a failure of nerve in his
concept of the dialectical image; too much emphasis on the task of the critic
as activist and not enough confidence in the way that (at least some) images
behave this way in popular culture by themselves. To elicit the dialectics of
such images as these, in the third world, at least, the dialectic imagician's
wand need give but the faintest tap.

Take the Virgin of Caloto. Here there is no need to invoke the surrealist's
heavy-handed art, no need to invoke as metaphor the messianic cessation
of time, no need to go to any pains to contest the official view of the past
evoked by the image, and, above all, no need to stretch a point by arguing
that the image can function as a "monad" in the sense quoted above. All
this exists as an everyday occurrence in the marvelous reality continuously
evoked through the dialogical creation of the Virgin's life and life force.

Perhaps Benjamin's work on this strategem so central to his conception
of the revolutionary artist and critic would have benefited by a closer study
of some popular images like the Virgin of Caloto. But then again it is possible

that this is really Alejo Carpentier's point in the prologue to *The Kingdom of This World,* that while the European surrealists were condemned by *their* society and its traditions (including its traditions of revolution and rebellion) to clumsily manipulate and juxtapose incongruent imagery, laboriously constructing outsized realities, in the European colonies and ex-colonies something like surrealism was *inherent* as a deeply embedded social practice in everyday life. As for surrealism, so (I would like to suggest) for dialectical images—the crucial difference between their European and colonial expressions being that while in Europe they were largely ignored by the populace yet (for the surrealists) "at the service of the revolution," in the colonies and ex-colonies these expressions are intrinsic to the form of life and at the service of its magicians, priests, and sorcerers.

Rarely was Benjamin able to wean himself from his infatuation with melancholia—no easy task for a soul so firmly wedded to the redemptive promise of a past whose quintessential feature lay in its premonition of catastrophe. Surrealism did, however, evoke in him an appreciation for the ways by which laughter could crack open the world, exposing the raw nerve-endings of the politicized imagician's zone of struggle—where "the long-sought image sphere is opened . . . the sphere, in a word, in which political materialism and physical nature share the inner man." For if surrealisim tried to change that sorcery-bundle of mythical representations on which Western culture is based, and did so using images that levered wide contradictions opening the doorway to the marvelous, its own representing had to be both iconic and ironic— bringing to mind not only Freud's analysis of the unconscious imagery mined and subverted by jokes, but also Mikhail Bakhtin's and Georges Batailles's fascination with anarchist poetics blending the the grotesque and the humorous in carnival-like upheavals of de-gradation and renewal.

And here I think the Latin American "magical realism" of the novelists and their critics fares poorly. There is truth in Carpentier's claim that the Europeans were forcing open the door to the marvelous in their own society with brutish despair, whereas in the colonies those doors stood ajar if not fully open. But neither in his work nor in that of Arguedas, Asturias, or García Márquez, is, to my mind, the force of laughter and anarchy punctuating the misty realm of the marvelous to be heard. Too often the wonder that sustains their stories is represented in accord with a long-standing tradition of folklore, the exotic, and *indigenismo* that in oscillating between the cute and the romantic is little more than the standard ruling class appropriation of what is held to be the sensual vitality of the common people and their fantasy life. Yet to the surrealists, precisely because of the acute self-consciousness that went hand in hand with the aforementioned "brutish despair," there lay engraved as axiomatic the wonder and irritation expressed by the nose specialist in Berlin, Wilhelm Fliess, who, upon reading the page proofs of his good friend Dr. Freud's *Interpretation of Dreams* in the autumn of 1899, complained that the dreams were too full of jokes.

Which brings us back to the joke-work and semiotic play in the dreaming of popular iconography. I am thinking here not merely of the strumming of the string of defeat and salvation that creates multiplicity of versions concerning the Virgin, this juggling with the semiotic of the miracle. I am also thinking of the way the heavy tone and mystical authority of the official voice of the past is brought down to earth and familiarized with gentle and sometimes saucy wit. The evidence indicates that the profusion of variation that knits and unknits a diverse reality is the work of play that deflates systematicity—a stratagem of *paroles* teasing, with all their multiplicity and double epistemologies, the pretentions of a master *language* not merely manifested but claimed by ruling classes. "Some Indians found her in a bamboo thicket," went the account told me with a laugh by the nurse attending our friend dying by the sugarcane fields. "And then she went away . . . People say that when she went away she went to Buga to be with the Lord of Miracles—as he was a kid too."

In this afterthought of hers, wit creates another world and way of seeing. The mischief of the saints is not so much exposed as it is a delight, and with the same generous gust of emotion the north of the valley at Buga is connected to the valley's southern pole at Caloto. The majestically aloof Lord of Miracles at Buga is brought gently to earth, to materiality and to the people by the prepubertal tryst between him and that wanderlust, the Niña María.

Perhaps it goes like this. While her *appearances* are miraculous, her *disappearances* are what make her human, and there is something strongly anticlerical in this, too, as if the noting of the disappearances noted the people's rights over the Church, which locks her up at night. Sometimes this is very clear, as with the Virgin of the island of Lake Cocha east of Pasto, who, according to an old soldier who fought the war against Peru in the Putumayo in 1933, was discovered by Indians and would disappear whenever the priest came to her chapel to say mass. People said she went to visit the Niña María in far-off Caloto, the old soldier told me.

Perhaps there is a secret life and a hidden Society of Saints and Virgins of which the Church is ignorant. Perhaps this society includes not only saints and virgins of fame in western Colombia but also admits popular saints from other places as well, far-off places such as Venezuela, for example, from where El Negro Felipe and José Gregorio Hernández come. In this society the saints seem more like us, perhaps even like our children, a far cry from the impassive faces they stolidly present to the public when esconsed behind the altar or when posing for their portraits sold in the marketplace and streets. And if people like to fill the lives of the saints and the virgins with all too human passions, displacing thereby the monologue inscribed by the Church, those same saints and virgins fill landscape with meanings inscribed by the routes of their interrelations. Given that they are as human as they are sacred, it would not be correct to say they thus "sanctify" spatial patterns, unless we endorse a notion of sanctity that endorses the strength of human weakness. If we do that then we can describe a "sacred" contouring of land made from interconnected chips and fragments of place meanings. Pilgrimages, rites to cure misfortune, wandering herbalists and folk healers intermittently bring these contours and places to light, but in the main they are no more than implicit networks, smoky trails, manifested but indirectly in the cracks, dreams, and jokes of everyday life.

Sometimes the icons of the Church enter into play with the icons of the state. Cali, the largest city of the Colombian southwest, straddles the angle where the plains cut into the steep slopes of the Andes. Overlooking and protecting the city from afar, on the mountain's peak, stands an enormous statue of Christ, arms outstretched, crucified. Down in the city, so I am told by one of its young *vagabundos,* is a statue commemorating its founder, the great *conquistador* Sebastián Benalcázar. He stands tensed with his hand to his hip, not to his sword, in anger and disbelief that his wallet has just been stolen. (Cali, it should be noted, is notorious for its pickpockets.) With his other hand he points not to the dream of the sublime and future prospects of the town he has founded, but to another statue, that of the first mayor of Cali (so my young friend tells me), accusing him of the theft. The mayor, in his turn, defends himself by pointing to the statue of another of the city's dignitaries, who in his turn points up the mountain to none less than Christ himself—standing with arms outstretched as for a police search: "I didn't steal anything. Look and see!" The lot of the urban vagabond and that of Christ are thus brought together, both unjustly blamed by the city's founding fathers, *conquistadores* and good bourgeois alike.

The Virgin and the Archangel

Far to the south in the rock face of a deep ravine high in the Andes and close to the highway roller-coastering into Ecuador is the painting of the Virgin of Lajas. The intensity with which she irradiates popular fantasy can be gauged from her presence in the *yagé* visions of Rosario's son, Pedro, way down the eastern slopes where her power flows down further still along the streams and major rivers like the Putumayo and the Caquetá which eventually create the Amazon. Blacks, whites, Indians—even Indians from way down in the rain forest—will visit her.

Salvador, the great Cofán shaman who brought Santiago back from the abyss of death, went to visit the Virgin of Lajas when his eldest daughter was blinded. She had refused to give her hand in marriage to a black colonist, her mother told me many years later. He stuck a needle into a photograph of her, through the eye, and she became blind in that eye. He asked her again for her hand, and again she refused. Again he pierced her photograph, and blinded the other eye. Salvador tried to cure her with his singing, with *yagé,* and with his herbs, but to no avail. They then went along the river through the forest and up the mountain to the cities and the shrine of the Virgin, but the daughter was very sad. "It's better that I go with the Virgin than be blind," she told her mother, and shortly thereafter she died. It was only much later they found out about the colonist and the photograph, when he got drunk and showed its pierced eyes to Salvador's brother-in-law who was drinking with him. Salvador did nothing, saying God would punish the guilty.

As with the Lord of the Miracles at Buga, Our Lady of Remedies in Cali and the Niña María of Caloto, the Virgin of Lajas was also discovered by an Indian. According to the Catholic priest Augustín M. Coral in his book *Nuestra Señora del rosario de las Lajas* (published in Bogotá in 1954), the Virgin of the Lajas made her appearance in 1794 in the ravine of Lajas near Ipiales, a spectacular ravine feared by travelers as a mouth of hell where the devil claimed many a victim, toppling people into the Guáitara River below. A son of one of the prominent families of Pasto heard that his old wet nurse, an Indian, was living in misery in the countryside, and went to bring her back to live in the comfort of his home. As they were crossing the ravine she heard music. She climbed around some rocks and beheld the Virgin, whereupon she fell into a trance, calling her companion to bear witness. Upon seeing the Virgin he collapsed, to all appearances dead. Walking through the night to Pasto she raised the alarm. The priest and others hurried next day to the site of the apparition, and found him alive, kneeling before the Virgin, his face bathed in tears.

But as with the Niña María of Caloto, the official history is but one in a medley of voices giving life through their interconnecting differences to the miraculous powers of the Virgin.

Rosario and her husband virtually turned the official version inside-out, telling me that the Virgin of Lajas was found not by an Indian woman being led by a rich white man but by an Indian woman traveling on her own with a baby on her back. It was not to the woman that the Virgin appeared but to the baby. "Look," the baby said. And there she was.

Doña Emilia, a poor and old black woman being treated for her rheumatism by Santiago, told me that the Virgin is *milagrosa,* miraculous and miracle-making, and that she has visited her shrine four times. As for the Virgin's origin: "A long time ago an Indian woman was walking by there with her baby daughter looking for firewood. The daughter said 'Mama! Look! That *mestiza* is calling me.' " Doña Emilia explains that a *mestiza* is not merely the daughter of an Indian and a white, but is a *gringa,* a fair-complexioned foreigner. The racial appellation given voice by the baby, let alone its specific meaning as a *gringa,* became all the more significant when Santiago's grandson, young César, aged ten, visiting from the Caquetá, said on hearing our conversation that the baby daughter, until that epiphanal moment, had been mute! In that instant, upon seeing the *mestiza gringa* Virgin, the Indian baby acquired the power to speak (and to name racial categories).

César's mother, Natividad, has also visited the Virgin four times. On the last visit she was with her mother-in-law, who saw the Virgin not as a painting but as a statue. "Her look was alive," she told Natividad. Other people saw this transformation of the Virgin into a sculpture and this look too. Rosario's son saw the Virgin of Carmen change like this in his *yagé* vision, which occurred as a counterpoint to the frightening vision he had of his home being subject to sorcery. Explaining his drawing of his vision of the Virgin, he described the fearful crossing he had to make over a river to reach her and how the sun illuminated the Virgin encased in the rock of the ravine. Then, breaking free from the rock, she converted "like a woman, alive, and then gave me her blessing"—freeing him and his family from the rock encasement of sorcery and envy.

"To some people she just disappears!" said Natividad's mother, Ambrosia, joining us in the kitchen, her arms full of firewood. But her husband Santiago, the shaman and man of vision, has never seen her live look or looking alive. For him the Virgin stays in her painting, and I, who have never seen her, am told that in the face of the ravine opposite her stands my namesake, my *tocayo,* Saint Michael, stamping down hard on the serpent. Ambrosia, Natividad, Emilia, and I were fanning the smoke from our eyes. The conversation had a sharp edge. "The Virgin of Lajas can cure the sick, the blind, and the lame," Ambrosia declaimed. "She also exorcizes sinners."

"If you go with faith, you'll be cured. If you don't go with faith—nothing!" exclaimed Natividad, each statement bearing the authority of the sunlight piercing the smoke.

I raised the topic of Indians bringing miraculous saints and virgins to the society of Colombia as a whole. Natividad mentioned yet another such saint in Huila, paused, then said, "It's that we Indians are innocents, that's why.

"More religious," broke in Roberto, her husband.

"But that was before," said Natividad. "Now the Indians have degenerated," and her solemnity broke into a giggle. "But those ancient people," she continued, "they weren't just innocent. They were also very wild. They ate people. They killed people. They lived like animals. . . . Ask Don Santiago. There are still some like that."

In the Church's history of Our Lady of Remedies in Cali, the Indians involved in the finding of the Virgin are stunningly peaceful. In the Church's history of the Virgin of Caloto, the Niña María, the Indians are formidably wild. The power of the pagan Indian to reveal the miraculous signs and saints of God to their Christian conquerors is a power that depends on both innocence and savagery, intermeshed in such a way that when one characteristic, such as the innocence, is stressed, it is to make its repressed opposite, savagery, loom emotionally large thought its absence. Unlike this, Natividad, daughter of an Indian shaman, brings both the innocence and the savagery of the Indian simultaneously to our attention. She does this in a way that unites the present to the past as pathos to humor, mediated by the Fall from an "innocence" that harbors savagery—a fall that she refers to as degeneration.

In the room where for over twenty years her father has cured blacks and whites with this same imagery of innocence and savagery, represented for them in his very person, there hangs a dusty picture of Saint Michael the archangel beating the demon down into the smoke and flames of hell. In his left hand he holds the scales of justice close to the demon's head, while in his right he holds high his sword. His wings are tensed. Except for his halo, his adornment is that of a soldier, like an ancient Roman. I have often wondered about this picture, hanging in the center of this room where for so many years so many people have taken hallucinogenic medicine and with the Indian song put down the demon as Saint Michael does. He also stands in that far-off ravine opposite the Virgin of Lajas, and the way that Ambrosia, Natividad, and Emilia talk about this in the kitchen makes me wonder what it could be like for the pilgrim walking there through a field of power composed by the Virgin on one side of the ravine and the archangel on the other. She is a sort of mother to us all, this *mestiza* discovered by an Indian baby, and, as Ambrosia declares, she cures the sick and cleanses sin. And opposite her is that implacable warrior driving evil down into the underworld.

I have not seen this, but on many nights I have seen this old man, Ambrosia's husband, Don Santiago, down in the underworld of the hot country far below the Virgin's shrine seated in his hammock across from the cobwebbed picture of the archangel laughing with tears streaming down his face and singing and curing people burdened with misfortune. It seems obvious to me that healers like him contain the image of both the mother and the warrior, just as his daughter Natividad with pathos and laughter brings together Indian innocence and Indian savagery, otherwise divided between iconic histories of miraculous icons such as Our Lady of Remedies/the Wild Woman of the Forest and the Niña María.

Indeed, there is the weight of Old World traditions supporting such a view of Saint Michael the archangel as containing *within himself* the dual powers of healer and warrior. Donald Attwater says that the reference in the book of Revelation to the war in heaven contributed to Saint Michael's being honored in the West from the beginning of Christendom as captain of the heavenly host, protector of Christians in general and of soldiers in particular. In the East, however, as in Constantinople, it was not his status as warrior but his power to heal the sick that was important.[4]

This archangel also happens to be the patron saint of the small town of Mocoa. There is an enormous painting of him to the side of the altar but nobody in the town seems to know much about him. I don't think any of

Saint Michael.

the priests or nuns knows anything of his local origins. For acquaintance with these I am indebted to Don Santiago, who head of these things from his *papa señor,* his grandfather, who lived a remarkably long life, the later years of which he spent virtually doubled over on account of the weight of the priests and the other white men he had carried up the Andes. In turn the *papa señor* had heard of the coming of the whites from people older than himself.

It was from a *tomador*, a taker of *yagé*, that the Indians around Mocoa heard of the imminent arrival of whites, and there were in that vision intimations of evil and pain. Before fleeing, the Indians hid their most precious saint, Saint Michael, in the labyrinthine fastness of the roots of a *higuerón* tree by the river.

When the Spaniards arrived they set up the saints of the Indians in the Indian's church as chopping blocks to cut up meat. In their shock, some Indians ran away in such haste that they left their children behind. Others stayed but refused to do anything and slowly died. Others sold their land for a pittance, for a few machetes or for a bale of cloth. One night the hut in which the Spaniards slept caught fire. They were burned from their feet up to their knees and lost their legs. It was the punishment of God.

Indians from the hills and mountains, from Aponte, Descanse, Yunguillo, and Sibundoy, came down to the Mocoa river to fish. In those days the river was alive with fish. They gathered *barbasco* poison from the trees along the banks and in looking for firewood discovered the hidden statue of Saint Michael, which they placed in the church in the old town. The Spaniards forced them to build without pay a new church in the new town, downriver, where the statue of Saint Michael rests to this day.

"If you get permission from the priests you can see it in a locked room at the very back of the church. It is carved of wood and is small," said Santiago, holding his hand about thirty inches above the ground.

I went to the church. The priest who escorted me into that back room was as confused as I was. To be sure, as he pointed out, there was a splendid statue of Saint Michael the archangel, about five feet high and dressed in Roman armor with helmet, breastplate, and calf-length boots trampling the horned demon underfoot. But search as we might amid the debris of wings and arms and halos in that forest of well-preserved saints and ruins of others, we could not find any Saint Michael other than that one.

"It's there for sure!" insisted Don Santiago when I accosted him in the evening. "He has his arms lifted up, silver wings, and is small."

I went back to the church, to the storeroom of saints, and there indeed was the statue. The priest had no idea who or what it was, yet it was the only one that fitted Santiago's description. But what sort of St. Michael was this! There was neither sword nor demon. Instead he floated on outsized silver wings, a tiny cherub, arms and eyes uplifted, the sweetest angel ever made.

ELEVEN
Wildness

I am trying to reproduce a mode of perception—a way of seeing through a way of talking—figuring the world through dialogue that comes alive with sudden transformative force in the crannies of everyday life's pauses and juxtapositions, as in the kitchens of the Putumayo or in the streets around the church in the Niña María. It is also a way of representing the world in the roundabout "speech" of the collage of things—as in the *coralitos* (cured by *indios*) around the wrists of babies. It is a mode of perception that catches on the debris of history such as the limbless, halo-less saints and Virgins strewn in the back room of the church in Mocoa where dust covers bits of a chopped-up, butcher-blocked sacred world—a mode of perception that foregrounds these fragments strewn upon the order reigning on the altar in the artificial obscurity of the Church proper.

It is an irregular, quavering image of hope, this inscription on the edge of official history, the "true" and truly obscure Saint Michael, small and swordless, floating on outsized wings in the confines of the church's back room. In a gust of sentiment we may wish to mutter encouraging and brave things about "resistance" and so forth, emphasizing the fragility of such counterhegemonic voices and signifiers hugely winged and ready to fly. But that sort of response is more for us than for those voices. It is we who gain courage from their confluence of strength and fragility, the strength in their fragility given to the weak and the defeated, inscribed into miraculous icons, sometimes, and into Indian shamans too.

With the defeated lies redemptive power; with the savage there is sanctity, affirms Natividad, the shaman's daughter, with a giggle.

The Master of Viseu, *Adoration of the Magi*, ca. 1505. Courtesy of the Museu de Grão Vasco, Viseu, Portugal.

Similarly there was sanctity in savagery, but without, one feels, much laughter, in that Portuguese painting of the Adoration of the Magi, painted in the first decade of the sixteenth century, where the place usually occupied by the black magus has been taken by a Brazilian Indian with a feather headdress, gold earrings, bracelets, anklets, and a pearl necklace. In one hand he carries a bowl made of half a coconut filled with gold, and in the other a wooden club that Brazilians were said to use. Dressed in richly patterned breeches and shirt, "few savages could appear," writes Hugh Honour, "more gentle, courteous, and eminently human."[1]

Yet in another Portuguese painting done some fifty years later, an Indian with the same headdress and mantle of featherwork presides as the devil over the torments of the damned in an underworld similar to those painted by Hieronymus Bosch. They were gods or demons, notes Richard Comstock, "unfallen creatures possessing an original innocence or dev-

ils with a brutish evil beyond human ken. In the early encounters of European settlers with Native Americans we see both images operating in the white man's imagination."[2] Less mythic, perhaps, but with no less an appreciation for the duality in the image of the Indian, the North American Indian trader Henry Boller put it this way, in a letter to his brother in 1859:

Anonymous, *Inferno*, ca. 1550. Courtesy of the Museu Nacional de Arte Antigua, Lisbon.

> I could "paint" you were it not for constant interruptions
> . . . two pictures.
> The one would represent the bright side of Indian life, with
> its feathers, lances, gayly dressed and mounted "banneries,"
> fights, buffalo hunting, etc.
> The other side, the dark side, showing the filth, vermin, pov-
> erty, nakedness, suffering, superstition, etc. Both would be
> equally true—neither exaggerated, or distorted; both totally
> dissimilar![3]

When Manuel Gómez, a white colonist in the Putumayo foothills of the Andes, took *yagé* with an Indian shaman, he too saw things that way, dual- ized, light and dark, before he died. Years later he told me that after the chaos of shapes changing and moving, sounds buzzing and humming in stops and starts, and after the snakes swarmed into his mouth through his vomiting, a tiger approached, then disappeared. Where the shaman had been, by the fire, now sat the devil.

He was just as they paint him, Manuel said, heated and red, with horns and tail, and as Manuel kept watching him sitting there by the fire in the great forests of the Putumayo, the devil turned back into the shaman, smok- ing a cigar, asking him if he was afraid. Then again the Indian turned into the devil and Manuel knew he was dying. In fact he was already dead, he told me later, and started to ascend a gorgeous stairway till he met an old man at the edge of nothingness. This man blessed Manuel and told him to return to earth. Back down he went, step by step, down into the clear green light of the dawn breaking across the forest. It was the Indian as shaman and the shaman as devil who had enacted this passage for him through the space of death and redemption. The language is dramatic, no less than the experience recorded, and the experience is to be perceived not merely as a gloss on colonial power but as a way that that power provides a view of its inner constitution where fable and fantasy enter into the everydayness of race and class oppression—mundaneness made hyper-real where society abuts the wilderness at the frontier. Thus blessed, colonists like Manuel Gómez and José García stave off the sorcery of the envious: the colonizer reifies his myths about the savage, becomes subject to their power, and in so doing seeks salvation from the civilization that torments him as much as the savage on whom he has projected his antiself.

Looking at the mid-sixteenth-century Portuguese painting of the Indian as devil presiding over the torments of the damned, Hugh Honour comments that this image framed the Indian as a beast of the jungle. In contrast to the first painting, of the Adoration of the Magi with its links to the mythology of a Golden Age, the second painting links the Indian not merely with the devil, he says, but also with the cruel, lascivious, bestially hirsute and de- formed savages or wild men of medieval and Renaissance legend.

It was those legends that provided the imagery of the New World natives as monstrous, suggests John Friedman in his work on the monstrous races in the medieval art and thought.[4] He implies an iconographic development paralleling the development of European imperialism, beginning with that gallery of fabulous creatures and monsters, the marvels of the East, in India and Ethiopia at the edges of the (Old) World, becoming reduced to a single figure, the wild man, conflated with the people found in the New World. These marvels of the East included giants, pygmies, unicorns, gold-digging ants, people with heads of dogs, others with tails, some with their heads in their chest, cannibals, and amazons—half-human, half-spirit creatures populating the margins of society further marginated onto exotic lands. These creatures found their way into influential books, such as Pierre d'Ailly's *Imago Mundi*, Pope Pius II's *Historia Rerum*, and in Sir John Mandeville's travels—all of which, and especially the first two, are known to have attracted the attention of Christopher Columbus. In his esteemed biography of the admiral, Samuel Morrison states that the *Imago Mundi* and the *Historia Rerum* were Columbus's two main sources (as far as sources have been preserved) for intellectual arguments to sustain his plans. It was from the latter that he learned of the Anthropophagi (cannibals) of the Amazons, on both of whose trails he thought he was in 1492 and 1493.[5]

In his study of the marvels of the East, Rudolf Wittkower concluded that, through pictorial dissemination in popular as well as scholarly forms, these marvels impressed themselves on large numbers of people and were influential in many branches of medieval thought. Their meanings could change and whereas, for example, in the late medieval period they could figure in Christian iconography as fabulous races of humankind capable of redemption, awaiting Christ's apostles, in the early sixteenth century, the period of the conquest of the New World, this view seems to have been replaced by one that saw the monster as foreboding evil—a view associated with an upsurge of popular beliefs that had no place in the official medieval conception of the world. Yet such a sharp change in judgment, from the monster as potential Christian to the monster as the harbinger of evil, should come as no surprise. As Wittkower himself emphasized in the closing lines of his erudite essay, "the monster has been credited everywhere with the powers of a god or the diabolical forces of evil."[6]

This monstrous duality of the diabolical and the godly is sharply delineated in the portrait drawn by Richard Bernheimer of the wild man of the late Middle Ages, a figure that is indeed, as Hugh Honour suggests, useful for understanding the magical quality immanent in the European's imagery of savagery at the time of the conquest of the New World (if not to the present day).[7] Half-human, half-animal, bereft of speech and reason, this hairy creature of the woods is like a gigantic child, feared for his awful temper and magical power. Easily angered, he may tear trespassers to pieces, assault women, and abduct children, especially unbaptized children. He uproots trees, makes lakes disappear and cities sink into the ground. Preferring to live alone in hidden places such as caves, he is constantly fighting other wild men and the beasts and dragons of the forest. In his wrath he creates tempests and hail—the weather he likes most—conditions best suited to the return of the dead. Ignorant of God, he wields power over the forest's animals (as do shamans) and possesses occult knowledge of the magical powers of plants (as do shamans). Inferior to humans in the great chain of being, he is also superior to them.

The powers attributed to him make him no less dangerous than desirable. Bernheimer includes in his book a painting by Brueghel the Elder showing peasants capturing a wild man by force of arms in order to kill him—as happened to Santiago Mutumbajoy's brother, also a shaman, many years ago in the Putumayo. But Bernheimer also draws attention to the sculpture of a wild man on the portal of a thirteenth-century church in Provence, which shows his hand through the arm of a man counting money into a sack. This is meant to show, says Bernheimer, the profit man can reap from an intimate association with the wild man—an interpretation with which many a Putumayo colonist like José García would concur (but perhaps not his wife, Rosario).

And of course sometimes the wild man steps forth of his own good will to minister to the needy, perhaps to tend with magical herbs the wounds of that knight in Spenser's *Faerie Queene* who strayed into the woods of the wild man. Colonists today in the Putumayo may dream of obtaining plants like those. José García uses some in his bottle of remedies, and my now dear departed friend, Chu Chu, a mulatto healer who lived far from the Putumayo in the valley of the Cauca river, advised me with great care what plants I should get from the Indian herbalists of the Putumayo, for my well-being as much as for his. In the slums of Cali, Don Colo also dreamed of a magical secret Indian plant that could be his—the plant, lost to history, that softened gold. And perhaps something of Spenser's knight lost in the forest empire of the wild man is reproduced in the life as it is told of that white man from Bogotá, Gabriel Camacho, who for so long wandered lost and crazed in those Putumayo forests, cared for by shamans with their magical herb of *yagé*.

The startling inversions involved in the conqueror's attribution of magical powers to the primitive is displayed in Renaissance depictions of Alexander the Great's exploits with the marvelous races of India. In a French manuscript of the early fifteenth century, we see illuminations of Alexander and his soldiers in deadly combat with a wild man and a wild woman, throwing them into fire.

By sharp contrast (in an *Alexanderbuch* of the same century), we see this mightiest of kings, accompanied by his courtiers, beseeching the wild man, now described as a priest, to consult the oracle-trees of the sun and of the moon. Tall, black, and hairy, this priest/wild man has large fangs and a long tongue, like a dog's. He stands naked but for a gold earring and a bishop's

Alexander the Great ordering wild man and woman thrown into fire. (From T. Husband, *The Wild Man: Medieval Myth and Symbolism* [New York: Metropolitan Museum of Art, 1980], p. 52.)

Wild man as priest takes Alexander the Great to consult with the trees of the sun and the moon. (From T. Husband, *The Wild Man: Medieval Myth and Symbolism* [New York: The Metropolitan Museum of Art, 1980], p. 55.)

miter. In the Latin texts, notes Timothy Husband, Alexander, on hearing from the wild man the prophecy of his imminent death, acknowledges the might of the pagan, intoning *Jupiter omnipotens*.[8]

Of the many aspects here, I want to draw especial attention to what Bronislaw Malinowski called a "well-known truth" that a "higher race in contact with a lower one has a tendency to credit the members of the latter with mysterious demoniacal powers."[9] He was drawing upon his fund of experience with colonial discourse in the southwest Pacific around the time of World War I—a long time on from the late Renaissance depictions of Alexander and his exploits with the wild and marvelous races of India. And a long way away, too.

This imputation of mystery and the demonic by the more powerful class to the lower—by men to women, by the civilized to the primitive, by Christian to pagan, is breathtaking—such an old notion, so persistent, so paradoxical and ubiquitous. In our day it exists not only as racism but also as a vigorous cult of the primitive, and it is as primitivism that it provides the vitality of modernism. "This is our modern hope," intones the modern voice in W. B. Yeats's "Ego Dominus Tuus" (and I quote from a 1912 draft):

> By the help of images
> I could call up my anti-self, summon all
> That I have least handled, look upon them all
> Because I am most weary of myself

It is this draft that most clearly exhibits, according to Mary Cathleen Flannery, that Yeats was writing under the influence of a spirit who had visited him in a séance—the spirit of the Moorish writer and explorer Leo Africanus who had been held captive at the court of Pope Leo X and whose views on Africans were, in the mid-sixteenth century, accorded some weight. Yeats maintained a correspondence with this spirit in deliberately disguised handwriting.[10]

Whatever the role of this spirit in the formation of the modern antiself, our modern hope, by whose light "We have found the gentle, sensitive mind," it comes as somewhat of a shock to be informed by Margaret Hodgen in her *Early Anthropology in the Sixteenth and Seventeenth Centuries* that Leo Africanus declared that Negroes not only led a beastly life but "were utterly destitute of reason"—a declaration that she discerns as important in the tide of European ideas and sentiments separating pagans from the great chain of human being so that the pagan entered, with the utmost ambiguity, into a nether zone between the animal and the human.[11]

The dependence of the modern on primitivism is frighteningly clear in the voyage into the *Heart of Darkness*:

> The earth seemed unearthly. We are accustomed to look
> upon the shackled form of a conquered monster, but there—
> there you could look at a thing monstrous and free. It was

unearthly and the men were—No, they were not inhuman. Well you know, that was the worst of it—this suspicion of their not being inhuman. It would come slowly to one. They howled and leaped, and spun, and made horrid faces; but what thrilled you was just the thought of their humanity—like yours—the thought of your remote kinship with this wild and passionate uproar. Ugly. Yes, it was ugly enough. . . .[12]

To the magic of the primitive, colonialism fused its own magic, the magic of primitivism. That distinguished sire of anthropology, E. B. Tyler, noted in his book *Primitive Culture* (first published in 1871) that many a white man in Africa and the West Indies at the time of his writing dreaded the power of the Obi-man—startling confirmation of his thesis concerning the class structure of magic and the evolution of societies, were it not for the fact that these very same white men surely belonged to a nation whose education had, in Tyler's terms, advanced far enough to destroy the belief in magic.

His thesis was one that drew attention to the ubiquity with which a group of people deemed primitive were alleged by their self-proclaimed superiors to possess extraordinary powers:

> The modern educated world, rejecting occult science as a con-
> temptible superstition, has practically committed itself to the
> opinion that magic belongs to a lower level of civilization. It is
> very instructive to find the soundness of that judgment unde-
> signedly confirmed by nations whose education has not ad-
> vanced far enough to destroy the belief in magic itself. In any
> country an isolated or outlying race, the lingering survivor of
> an older nationality, is liable to the reputation of sorcery.[13]

He provided examples, such as the Hinduized Dravidians of southern India, who, in times past, he asserted, lived in fear of the demonic powers of the slave caste beneath them. From contemporary reports he culled a case in which it was not the class beneath so much as apart, in the wilds, that was the beneficiary of such an imputation. Certain Dravidian tribes, he noted, were in mortal fear of the Kurumbas, "wretched forest outcasts, but gifted, it is believed with powers of destroying men and animals and property by witchcraft."[14] But it is not only the power to do harm. He makes specific mention of healing magic being part of these attributions.

As regards the Obi-men of whom (Tyler said) many a white man in Africa and the West Indies stood in dread, we might also take stock of the fact that Obi-men can themselves stand in dread of persons even wilder than they—those medicine women and men of the Jamaican maroon communities, the descendants of runaway slaves, who, possessed in dance and theater with the spirits of their maroon ancestors and thus with an especially colonial and Jamaican history of "wildness" and wild magic, are able to lay to rest the harm caused by Obeah-men today.[15]

In the nearby island of Cuba, according to its highly esteemed anthropologist Fernando Ortiz, in his book *Hampa afro-cubana: los negros brujos* (first published in 1906), it was common for whites of *all* classes to avail themselves of black witches (*brujos*) who were also slaves. Furthermore, for health, love, and revenge, it was still common at the time of his writing for whites, including those of the upper class, to place faith in black healers and sorcerers, the result, in part, he asserts, of "a not very solid culture amongst the directing classes of Cuban society."

It is an interesting notion, is it not, that faith in the magic of the underclass is due to a "not very solid" culture among the ruling class? There is a curious synergism here between rulers and those who may sustain them magically as well as through more material labor. And beyond the division of labor into those who rule and those who supply them with magic there is a picture of society as a whole with very different sorts of places for rulers and ruled, cosmic spaces united vertiginously as in a dream of world history swooning. Despite the "advanced psychology" of the whites in Cuba, writes Ortiz, "the superstitions of the blacks attract them, producing a type of vertigo so that they fall into those beliefs from the height of their civilization; as if the superior planes of their psyches first drown and then become detached, returning to primitiveness, to the nakedness of their souls."[16]

In his study of voodoo in Haiti, published in 1959, the French anthropologist Alfred Métraux provides a suggestion concerning the history of the "vertigo" and primitive deluge of the ruling-class psyche of which Ortiz writes. In warning against the morbid and hallucinatory image that surrounds voodoo in Haiti, Métraux advises us that this image is but a legend associated with the sorcery used by slaves against their masters. Whether such sorcery existed or was only thought to exist is unimportant to the legend, which, as Métraux writes,

> belongs to the past. It belongs to the colonial period when it
> was the fruit of hatred and fear. Man is never cruel and unjust
> with impunity: the anxiety which grows in the minds of those
> who abuse power often takes the form of imaginary terrors and
> demented obsessions. The master maltreated his slave, but
> feared his hatred. He treated him like a beast of burden but
> dreaded the occult powers which he imputed to him. And the
> greater the subjugation of the black, the more he inspired fear;
> that ubiquitous fear which shows in the records of the period
> and which solidified in that obsession with poison which,
> through the eighteenth century, was the cause of so many
> atrocities. Perhaps certain slaves did revenge themselves on
> their tyrants in this way—such a thing is possible and even
> probable—but the fear which reigned in the plantations had its
> source in deeper recesses of the soul: it was the witchcraft of
> remote and mysterious Africa which troubled the sleep of the
> people in 'the big house.'[17]

A similar pattern of troubled sleep can be discerned in the description provided by Henry Charles Lea of the Inquisition in the Spanish colonial slave port of Cartagena, south across the Caribbean from Cuba and Haiti, on the coast of the colony of New Grenada, today called Colombia. It was a colony overrun by the sorcery of three continents, said Lea, writing but a few years before Ortiz:

> The slaves brought from the Guinea coast the mysteries of Obeah and dark practises of sorcery. The native Indians had ample store of superstitions, to cure or to injure, to provoke love or hatred; the colonists had their own credulous beliefs, to which they added implicit faith in those of the inferior races. The land was overrun with this combination of the occult arts of three continents, all of which was regarded by the inquisition, not as idle fantasies, but as the exercise of supernatural powers, involving express or implicit faith in the demon.[18]

Now that is a very Putumayan way of seeing things. It coincides with a view that folds the underworld of the conquering society into the culture of the conquered, the peon, and the slave. Moreover, it sees that folding as an active and more or less continuous stabbing at the eye of power—at the security system of Church doctrine and its rituals of power embodied in the Inquisition. And it is a view that implicitly understands that folding of the underworld of the conquering society into the culture of the conquered not as an organic synthesis or "syncretism" of the three great streams of New World history—African, Christian, and Indian—but as a chamber of mirrors reflecting each stream's perception of the other.

Together with other studies of early Cartagena, based on colonial documents prepared by inquisitors, priests, and government officials,[19] Lea's history of the Inquisition there suggests that this chamber of mirrors was, from the colonizer's point of view, a chamber conflating sorcery with sedition, if not in reality at least as a metaphor, as if the notion of an "underground" took on a wide range of connotations, from the inferno worshiped by the followers of Satan to the underground of conspiracy and defiance of the social order. It is striking how important race and gender are as signifiers of this underground threatening to erupt through the crust of white maleness incarnated in colonial authority.

The leaders of the *palenques* or runaway slave settlements were as likely as not to be wizards and witches, according to the official texts. The rebellion of the slaves in the gold mines of Zaragossa figured in the inquisitor's report to the Supreme Tribunal in 1622 as a massive effusion of sorcery aimed at consuming in fire and sterilizing by magic the mines as well as their owners as well. Black women, slave and freed, working as servants, were said to be adept sorcerers, serving their white mistresses in the arts of divination and preparation of love philtres. The Inquisition claimed to have uncovered covens of female witches worshiping the devil, and even in the covens of

Spanish women it was alleged that women from Africa played a crucial role. It was also said that beyond the town of the Christians, slave and free, pagan Indians were supplying those black women sorcerers with the herbs they required.

These official texts reproduce an inquisitorial vision of power, mystical and malevolent, surrounding and undermining the colonial terms of order. Fantastic as the vision is, if the Putumayan experience is any guide, it is a vision that becomes incorporated into the magic and sorcery of the subaltern classes. Such evil is not without allure. As Bernheimer goes to some length to illustrate, the wildness of the wild woman and the wild man is constituted by bringing together the extremes of destruction and healing.

In 1632 the Inquisition claimed to have discovered a great assembly of black witches in the port of Tolú some sixty-five miles south of Cartagena, to which the epidemic, no doubt fanned by the inquisitorial process, then spread. (Incidentally, in his celebrated *Natural and Moral History of the Indies*, first published in 1588, Father Acosta singled out the balsam of Tolú for its medical virtue.)[20] Two of the alleged leaders, both black women, were sentenced to burning, yet one of them, Paula de Eguiliz, was permitted to leave prison to work as a healer, including among her patients the inquisitors as well as the bishop of Cartagena, in whose house she spent twenty days as a guest. For these excursions she could discard the garb symbolic of her diabolic status, the *sanbenito*, and appear in public in a mantle bordered with gold, borne aloft in a sedan chair. From this medical practice as a prisoner of the Inquisition she was said to have gained much money, part of which she shared with the other women prisoners. After six years, years that included torture, her sentence was commuted to a mere 200 lashes and life-long imprisonment.[21]

In what does the healing power of wildness lie? It is true, as Wittkower says, that the monsters of the marvels of the East gave shape not only to the daydreams of beauty and harmony of Western man but also created symbols by which the horror of real dreams could be expressed. Yet is there not an issue here that extends beyond the shaping function of symbols and dreams?

Wildness also raises the specter of the death of the symbolic function itself. It is the spirit of the unknown and the disorderly, loose in the forest encircling the city and the sown land, disrupting the conventions upon which meaning and the shaping function of images rest. Wildness challenges the unity of the symbol, the transcendent totalization binding the image to that which it represents. Wildness pries open this unity and in its place creates slippage and a grinding articulation between signifier and signified. Wildness makes of these connections spaces of darkness and light in which objects stare out in their mottled nakedness while signifiers float by. Wildness is the death space of signification.

Bernheimer reminds us that wildness in the Middle Ages "implied every-thing that eluded Christian norms and the established framework of Christian society, referring to what was uncanny, unruly, raw, unpredictable, foreign, uncultivated."[22] Quite a list! Surely, we have to ask, the healing and not only the evil magic of the wild folk is not unconnected with just this raw unpredictability and eliding of frameworks?

Yet wildness is incessantly recruited by the needs of order (and indeed, this is one of anthropology's most enduring tasks and contributions to social order). But the fact remains that in trying to tame wildness this way, so that it can serve order as a counterimage, wildness must perforce retain its dif-ference. If wildness per se is not credited with its own force, reality, and autonomy, then it cannot function as a handmaiden to order. The full im-plications of this paradox are submerged in a violent act of domestication—witness the following prophetic claim by Paul Ricoeur used to introduce a recent anthropological study of exorcism: "If evil is coextensive with the origin of things, as primeval chaos and theogonic strife, then the elimination of evil and of the wicked must belong to the creative act as such."[23] Ifs aside, it is this insipid equation of evil with primeval chaos, and of their elimination with creativity, that the wildness of the wild women and men contests.

The wildness here at stake tears through the tired dichotomies of good and evil, order and chaos, the sanctity of order, and so forth. It does *not* mediate these oppositions. Instead, it comes down on the side of chaos and its healing creativity is inseparable from that taking of sides. Club in hand, battered by hail and tempest with lightning flashing the return of the dead, these creatures of the wild not only bear the burden of society's antiself, they also absorb with their wet, shaggy coats the best that binary opposition can deliver—order and chaos, civilized and barbaric, Christian and pagan, and emerge on the side of the grotesque and the destructive. "Their de-structive aspect is stronger than their salutary one," writes Bernheimer with regards to the wild men of the Middle Ages, "and it would seem that whatever benefits their appearance may hold for the human community are ultimately derived from their macabre traits."[24]

TWELVE
Indian Fat

I want to run wildness and its mediations together with topographies of magical zones, following the threads of what I found most general and interconnected in the life history of Rosario and José García, namely the attribution of wildness and magical healing power to the Indian by the colonist, and the way that this attribution made magic out of the eastern slopes and rain forests stretching from the base of the Andes into the immensity of the Amazon basin. It is with *aucas, chunchos,* and other fabulous creatures of the forest that I am concerned mainly, but I am also intrigued by the generality of this attribution of wildness to what one could call colonizable species, with wildness imputed to the other, objectified, then taken back as a magical substance, as it is said to be done with the fat from the bodies of Indians of the Peruvian highlands.

I had long been struck by the fact that in their place of residence, as well as in their journeys for medicines and patients, the Sibundoy medicine men mediated highlands and lowlands as iconic signs of civilization and wilderness. In wondering about this mediation as a source of magic, my eye was caught by those other Indian medicine men of repute in the highlands of Bolivia—the

Collahuayas. They seemed to me identical in some important formal way with the less well known practitioners of the Sibundoy valley far to the north in Colombia. Like them, the itinerant Collahuayas are set apart from the rest of society and are credited by many people, sometimes dogmatically, sometimes with doubt, with having considerable knowledge of occult matters in the great struggle of life. Most significantly, they are connected to the wildness concentrated in the dank forests below their mountain homes. To what degree the Collahuayas are truly connected is a matter of debate, but as with most things in the sphere of myth and magic, let alone in the politics of race and conquest in which the myth and magic intrude, it is the appearance that is often decisive. "We met them everywhere," wrote the archeologist from the United States, Adolph Bandelier, around 1900, while engaged in a dig in the islands of Titicaca and Koati.[1] "Between Puno and Sillustani we saw these quaint figures walking single file, wending their way in silence from Indian village to Indian village, from isolated dwelling to isolated dwelling, everywhere tolerated and everywhere received with undemonstrative hospitality." These were the famous Collahuaya medicine men, he explained, undertaking tours that lasted years and took them as far afield as Buenos Aires, or further still into Brazil and beyond. "On the island," wrote Bandelier from his vantage point on the great lake of Titicaca high on the massif of the Andes between Bolivia and Peru, "they are sometimes called *Chunchos,* but they have nothing in common with these forest Indians except inasmuch as they pretend (and it is probably true) that some of their medicinal herbs are gathered in the *montaña* or forests, where the wild tribes (often called *Chunchos collectively*) dwell and roam."

He bought some of the medicine man's wares: against melancholy, *yerba de amante;* against rheumatic cold, *uturuncu,* to be rubbed in; against headache, *yerba de Castilla* (as in Castille, the crowning glory in the mosiac that was mighty Spain); and another remedy, this time gringo, sternutative powder of hellbore. But the principal treasure of the itinerant Collahuaya medicine men seems to have been figurines of a mineral, said to be abundant in the Collahuayas' home region of Charasani: white alabaster shaped into things such as a clenched fist, to provide wealth, and also, though Bandelier was never allowed to see these, human figurines, in black, for sorcery.[2]

To carry out his archeological excavations, Bandelier's Indian laborers had had to perform rites to placate the spirits of the mountain peaks, to the "grandfathers" of those great peaks, the *achachilas,* as well as to the earth herself, rites that involved, among many preparations and magical substances fed to the spirits, shavings rasped with a knife from an alabaster figurine, in this case, says Bandelier, representing a bull or a cow. The magical figurines (or scrapings thereof) supplied by the itinerant Collahuaya medicine men thus entered into the sacrifices to the peaks and to the earth, offerings to the maleness and femaleness of the productive life-space to be eaten by the gods as part of rites associated with the harvest, the flocks, and the people—as a whole and individually, in their torments and in their hopes. It is with some insistence, therefore, that the question is raised as to the whys and wherefores of the power associated with these itinerant Indian medicine men whose figurines, stated Bandelier, *"are sold not only to the Indians (and perhaps less to these), but to mestizos, and even to whites occasionally, as faith in the cures and supernatural gifts of the Callahuayas is very common and deeply rooted in all classes of society, though seldom confessed* [emphasis added]."[3] That was around 1900.

"They are sometimes called *Chunchos*," Bandelier had written, "but they have nothing in common with these forest Indians except that they *pretend"—"and it is probably true,* [emphasis added]," he inserted parenthetically—"that some of the medicinal herbs are gathered in the *montaña* or forests, where the wild tribes (often called *Chunchos* collectively) dwell and roam." It is this equivocation that I have emphasized, aimed at a zone of reality where pretense and possibility combine to create through the poetics of uncertainty a zone of power "deeply rooted in all classes of society, though seldom confessed," where the identification with *and* the disassociation from the wildness of the jungle and its people run through ritual into the desires and misfortunes of civilized daily life, and back again.

Seven years after the publication of Bandelier's book, another gringo, G. M. Wrigley, published (in *The Geographical Review* in 1917) an article entitled "The Travelling Doctors of the Andes: The Callahuayas of Bolivia." Here the connections between the traveling doctors and the jungles stretching east of the Andes were made more explicit, or at least more sensuous and therefore more resistant to skepticism, than with Bandelier. You could smell the jungle of the *chunchos* up in the highlands as the traveling medicine men approached. Included in their wallets of drugs, wrote Wrigley, were aromatic gums, resins, barks, and herbs of the hot forest.[4] Pointing out that the Collahuaya's territory extends close to the foothills or *montaña* of the eastern Andes, Wrigley asserted without equivocation that it was the *montaña* that furnished the valuable medicinal plants, adding this note: "To the Indian inhabitants is commonly attributed an extensive empirical knowledge of their properties. Wiener speaks of the Piros of the Urubamba valley who annually ascend to Hillipani to exchange woven goods, pottery, live birds, and certain medicinal plants of which these "Chunchos" have more knowledge than the Quechua [highland] Indian."[5]

Prior to their long journeys, the Collahuaya medicine men would first make a trip, stated Wrigley, "to the *montaña* for outfitting their wallets. As this trip takes them into hot country they wear little clothing for it, a circumstance which has led some travellers to suppose the forest their actual home."[6] Or if not their actual home, then some other home more akin to a magically generative death-space from where, fortified with *chuncho* medicines, they would be resurrected with new power for journeying back into the highlands and across the republic. Exploring the "golden forest" of

Caravaya east of the Andes and below Collahuaya territory in 1860, the English explorer Clements Markham, engaged in surveying antimalarial, quinine-bearing cinchona forests for Her Majesty's Government, hesitated for a moment, preparing with his porters to enter "the dense entangled forest, where no European had been before." Half a dozen pale-faced men emerged from the thickets. "They looked wan and cadaverous," he observed, "like men risen from the dead, and worn out by long watching and fatigue."[7]

They turned out to be not forest dwellers but mountain people, Colla-huayas, "collectors of drugs and incense," he said, "who penetrate far into the forest to obtain their wares, and come forth, as we saw them, looking pale and haggard"—a most peculiar race, he thought, traversing the forests east of the Andes, then setting forth to practice the healing arts in all America. "They walk in a direct line from village to village," he wrote, "exercising their calling, and penetrating as far as Quito and Bogotá in one direction, and the extreme limits of the Argentine Republic in the other."[8] They are called *Chirihuanos* on the coast of Peru, he added, and Wrigley, citing a book published in 1860, stated the same.

Twenty years before Markham's survey of cinchona, the German traveler Johann Jakob von Tschudi noted that there was much trading between the Andean highlands and the forests stretching east, especially with regard to the precious vermifuge of cinchona bark, a legendary drug ever since it had cured the viceroy's wife, the countess of Chinchon, and been promoted with fervor by the Jesuits in Europe in the seventeenth century. Prior to the South American wars of independence, claimed von Tschudi, the Indian gatherers of this valuable remedy had supplied all the apothecaries of Europe. Aromatic gums and plants from the eastern forests also filled the churches of highlands and the cities. Priests bought them as incense.

There is a class of Indians, von Tschudi observed (committing exactly the error against which Wrigley later warned, confusing Collahuayas with forest Indians), who live deep in the jungles of southern Peru and Bolivia and employ themselves almost exclusively in gathering medicinal balsams and aromatic gums. They also collected magical medicines such as the claw of the jungle tapir to cure "falling sickness," and the teeth of powerful serpents to cure blindness and headache. They bring these to the highland markets, he said, and some of them even wander two or three hundred leagues from their native forests, traversing the greater part of Peru and even visiting Lima, carrying large gourds of balsams. With surprise, he remarked how these wandering "tribes" seek frequent contact with other nations. "They are not distrustful and reserved, but on the contrary, annoyingly com-municative."[9]

He was mistaken in confusing the itinerant medicine men with the Indians who lived deep in the jungle, but then his mistake was preordained, a social convention reproducing a myth entwining wild Indians and magical medicine in an empire of forested exotica. It was a mythology that feasted on the distinction between Christian and *chuncho*. From that it drew its strength. The Indians who gather and distribute the jungle medicines, von Tschudi emphasized, all profess to be Christians. As such they must be distinguished from the pagans of the forests of the eastern foothills of the Andes, like the *chunchos*, very dangerous and "one of the most formidable races of Wild Indians." They are most set against Christians. The derelict remains of haciendas and missions along the foothills provide testimony to their long history of defiance. They are cannibals who cruelly murder all the Christian Indians they meet. Any kind of friendly intercourse with them is impossible. In their marauding they go practically naked, and their hair, face, and breast are stained red with *achiote*. Their weapons are the bow of *chonta* palm and the great wooden sword, the *macana*. When a cross was erected in the forest, *chunchos* fastened to it a few days later a *macana* and two arrows "as symbols of their irreconcilable enmity to Christians." The great messianic rebellion of 1741 led by the prophet who took the name of Juan Santos Atahuallpa (a highland Indian who went to Spain and on his return to Peru created his base of support among these lowland Indians of the eastern forests) was said to have involved *chunchos* as well as Campa Indians. The churches of the foothills were laid waste, the sacred images and the priests were trussed together and cast into the swirling rivers, villages were burned, cultivated fields destroyed—and this history, intoned von Tschudi, is the history of the whole of the *montaña*.[10]

They had featured dramatically, these *chunchos*, as archetypal wild folk in renderings of Incan history. The Incan aristocrat, Garcilaso de la Vega, always one to promote the Christian cause through the image of the "good Indian" in a colonized world, relates in his famous work *The Royal Commentaries of the Inca* (the first part of which was first published in 1609) how when the good Incan king Yupanqui took possession of the empire, he undertook to tour his domain. It took him three years, at the end of which he decided to conquer the *chunchos* living in the jungles to the east of the sacred capital of Cuzco so as to purge them of their barbarous and inhuman customs. He made his entry down the great and hitherto hardly known River of the Snake. It was impossible to enter by land on account of the wild mountains and numerous lakes, swamps, and marshes abounding in those parts. Ten thousand Incan soldiers descended on rafts that took two years to prepare. After mighty skirmishes they subdued the *chunchos* who then served the Inca in further conquest of wild Indians—a point I wish to emphasize as it is this taming of wildness, so as to use it for civilizing, that lies at the heart of the magical imputation and appropriation of wild power.

This crusade down the River of the Snake to take possession of the wild people's wildness is narrated at length by the highland Indians, avowed Garcilaso. They boast of the prowess of their ancestors in these battles along the banks of the jungle rivers. "But," Garcilaso continued, "as some of these deeds seem to me incredible . . . and as the Spaniards have never so far possessed the area the Incas conquered in the Antis [lands of the *chunchos*], and one cannot point to it with one's finger as one can to all the rest of area we have previously mentioned, I thought that I should not mingle fabulous matter, or what appeared to be such, with true histories."[11]

Four years after his expedition to purge the *chunchos,* the Incan king Yupanqui mounted an unsuccessful expedition against the *Chirihuanos* in the lowland forests (east of Charcas in present-day Bolivia). Yupanqui's spies reported (and I quote Garcilaso) "that the land there was extremely bad, consisting of wild forests, swamps, lakes, and morasses, very little of which was of any use for cultivation. The natives were utterly savage and worse than wild beasts, for they had no religion and did not worship anything at all, living without laws or good customs, like animals on the hillsides, having no villages or houses." They were cannibals, eating their enemies as well as their own people when they were dying. They went naked and slept with their sisters, daughters, and mothers. On hearing this report, the Inca king assembled his kinfolk and announced: "Our obligation to conquer the *Chirihuanos* is now greater and more pressing, for we must deliver them from the beastly and vile state in which they live, and reduce them to the life of men, for which purpose our father the Sun sent us here." Ten thousand warriors were readied, but after two years they had to admit the impossibility of their mission. Now the *Chirihuanos* are not quite as savage as before, says Garcilaso, yet their beastlike way of living persists. Indeed, it would be a great wonder to be able to deliver them from it.[12]

In his late sixteenth-century account, *The Natural and Moral History of the Indies,* the Jesuit Father Acosta makes it clear that the *Chirihuanos* are indeed a paradigm of wildness. Father Acosta was part of Viceroy Toledo's ill-fated campaign against them, a campaign that surely added luster to their infamy, and he places them in the same category of savagery and resistance to the Spaniards as the *chunchos.* What shall we say of the *chunchos* and the *Chirihuanos* he asks, "Has not all the flower of Peru been there, bringing with them so great provision of arms and men, as we have seen? What did they? With what victories returned they? Surely they returned very happy in saving their lives, having lost their baggage and almost all their horses."[13] And not only are the *chunchos* and *Chirihuanos* an epitome of wildness; they are also the epitome of the first men in the New World, suggests Acosta, disregarding the Indians' own accounts of their beginning because such accounts are "more like unto dreams than to true Histories."

But it was hardly an issue of true history versus dreams. The dreams were not without history. Nor was the history without its fantasy. Wildness was a fantasy where pagan and Christian came together in the *montaña,* across which, back and forth, went the medicine men disassembling order and disorder, the wild in the civilized, thereby making magic out of a moralized topography. The *montaña* made it real. the *montaña* made it natural.

The geographer Wrigley is helpful here. Referring to the Collahuaya medicine men, she noted that the valuable medicinal plants come from the *montaña* and commented that "a people," meaning the Collahuaya, "with relatively easy access to sources of supply would *naturally be selected* to act as purveyors of the medicinal plants of the *montaña*" (emphasis added).[14] In effect recruiting the magic of the image of the Collahuaya medicine men for the cause of materialism in general and geographical determinism in particluar, in effect invoking a mystical agency as in the language of "would *naturally be selected*" (by whom? by what?) and providing a simple but elegant prototype for a later ecological determinism of "vertical archipelagoes," Wrigley leaves us at the end of her essay twitching at a whisker of a memory presumed deep within us all. "He reminds us," she writes in reference to these wandering Indian healers and sorcerers, "of the strength of the old geographical controls that rule in the Central Andes."[15]

Now it is of course this *strength,* these *controls,* and that *rule* which the wild and mythical figures of the dank forest are made to contest. That is their burden. They make the best of it they can.

It is as if we were faced with an hallucinatory image in the shaman's fabled art, the art of magic wherein mimesis and the power to transform run together, except that the image in question, the moralized topography of the Andes, is not the work of an individual artist but of popular culture itself, creating out of space and its distinctions one great difference separating wildness from civilization traversed by peripatetic medicine men prior to their traversing the woes of the nation. It is here that the earliest sociological studies of binary opposition, as in Robert Hertz's study of the preeminence of the right hand—published in 1909 midway between Emile Durkheim's and Marcel Mauss's essay on primitive classification and Durkheim's classic *The Elementary Forms of Religious Life*—come to mind, as in this dramatic passage from Hertz:

> All the oppositions presented by nature exhibit this fundamental dualism. Light and dark, day and night, east and south in opposition to west and north, represent in imagery and localise in space the two contrary classes of supernatural powers: on one side life shines forth and rises, on the other it descends and is extinguished. The same with the contrast between high and low, sky and earth: on high, the sacred residence of the gods and the stars which know no death; here below, the profane region of mortals whom the earth engulfs; and lower still, the dark places where lurk serpents and the host of demons.[16]

It is, of course, this stunning contrast between high and low, this allegory of the heights, that concerns the myth- and magic-making power of the Andes and the sea of rain and cloud forest from which they spring. Yet is not this sociological Kantianism too consumed by its own mythology of the fundamental categories? Might not the cherished order of the "fundamental dualism" itself be nourished by, if not dependent on, the allegory of the heights where order reigns supreme? Where can death and profanity, the sordid materiality of the below, the object in itself, gain an epistemological toehold in this towering organum of sublime knowledge? Perhaps the very magic of the shamans, or at least the magic attributed to the shamans, is generated by that question, and in the ruptures and breaks with experience it finds its toehold. In any event in the wildness attributed to the below there is this chance—of twisting out of reach of being nothing more than the height's other. In the mimesis of the magical art imputed by society to the lowland forest and its exotic powers, this chance glimmers, what Georges Bataille, some twenty years after Hertz and in the same city, would pit as the "old mole" of Marxist revolution against the imperialist eagle of *the idea,* soaring resplendent in holy alliance with the sun, castrating all that enters into conflict with it.[17]

The Star of the Snow

In his essay about the great Andean festival of the Star of the Snow, *Collur Riti,* published in 1982, Robert Randall specifies the images acquired by above and below east of Cuzco, ancient capital of the Incan empire, where the mountains plunge into the forest. He describes this annual festival as "problably the most impressive and dazzling spectacle in the Andes," in which (in the years around 1980) some 10,000 pilgrims ascend the mountains at the time of Corpus Christi to reach a sacred valley set in the peaks. Let me quote his very first lines, depicting this landscape.

> Rising straight out of the jungle, the snowpeaked Colquepunku
> mountains are brilliant white massifs which float above the
> clouded rainforest. The interior of this range cradles an isolated
> valley that is, for most of the year, home only to herds of llama
> and alpaca which graze at 4,500 metres beneath these glistening
> glaciers. During the week before Corpus Christi, however,
> more than 10,000 people, mostly Indians and *campesinos,* make
> a prilgrimage to the Sinakara Valley: music echoes off the val-
> ley walls and dancers in feathered costumes prance through the
> smoke of hundreds of cookfires.[18]

Later on, where I discuss Indians carrying whitemen on their backs up from the jungle and over the mountains in Colombia, we will have reason to return to these images and marvelous metaphors of brilliant white massifs rising straight out of the jungle, floating over the clouded rain forest. Now I want to be carried by the momentum of the passage cited, from the contrast of the jungle and the glacier, to the feathered dancers, *chunchos,* and their climactic dance at sunrise. This rite is interpreted by Randall as having several meanings, such as "a great celebration of the civilization process, of the transition from the last world to this one, of the regeneration and resurrection of Pachamama [the earth], of the curing of the sick, and the beginning of another year (marked by the return of the Pleiades)."[19] Following recent studies in the field of ethnoastronomy, especially those of T. Zuidema, Randall suggests that this annual pilgrimage not only marks the annual disappearance and reappearance of the Pleiades from the heavens, a lapse of some thirty-seven nights, but that it also marks what he calls "the transition from disorder to order (from chaos to cosmos),"[20] an interpretation that fits well with Zuidema's observation that for the Incas this thirty-seven-night period was calendrically one of what he calls chaos. Randall is careful to emphasize that the disorder of the dancing pilgrims ceases with the final dance at sunrise, which he says is perfectly ordered and synchronized. With their unremitting concern for order and for the formal analysis of what they call "the Andean mind," there is little interest on the part of this school of Andeanists in "chaos" other than to chart the ways by which it is recruited for the celebration of order. It is with equanimity that this festival is portrayed as a "great celebration of the civilization process," fed if not created by the mad dancing of the wild men from the jungle, the *chunchos,* and that this is seen as a rite of stellar if not cosmic transition, social renewal, and individual healing—all resulting from the transition from disorder to order.

As for the *chunchos,* Randall cites stories from the *campesinos* of the mountainsides saying that the *chunchos* are their ancestors. One story tells of how the old ones, the *naupa machu,* occupied the mountains in the epoch before this one when there was no sun and no light other than that of the moon. They were mighty beings, these ancestors, able to flatten mountains and move great rocks. The chief spirit of the local peaks asked them if they wished to have some of the power of those magic mountains, but in the pride of their strength the *naupa machu* scorned his offer, causing the peaks' chief to create the sun, which, rising over the jungle, turned the ancestors to stone—except for those few who fled into the dark chaos of the forests below. With this creation of the *chunchos* in the darkness below, the Incan order was created in the sunlit mountains above.

Entire epochs of time are buried below, too. Like the flight of the ancients into the forests below, so great cycles of history are said to be buried underground from where, through "flowerings" (the term comes from Randall's informants) into the present they may exert a powerful influence on contemporary life. Such flowerings whereby an anterior epoch exerts its usually baneful influence on the present occur with the full or new moon, at dawn or at dusk—and we shall have reason to remember this flowering of an underground of time when we later consider the ways by which history itself acts like a sorcerer in the creation of *la mala hora,* the evil hour, in the Sibundoy valley in Colombia. There, also, connections are made with what seems like an underground of pre-Spanish conquest "other" time, and while this buried epoch flowers in quasi-satanic form to bewitch the present, and even kill, this very same deposition of history can be appealed to for healing as well.

As with mythic time, so for the *chunchos* east of Cuzco, too: inferior, wild, and hostile, yet they are healers and bestowers of fertility. In what seems a significant contradiction to his overarching thesis that ordering is curative, Randall cites testimony to the effect that the people of these mountainsides send their shamans, responsible for healing the sick and caring for the fertility of the fields, down to the jungle to learn there for a year, "in order to bring that fertility back up to the sierra." The very wildness of the jungle (and presumably its inhabitants) is curing and fertilizing.

We may wish to qualify this notion and insist on some sort of "dialectical" coalescence between upper and lower, mountain and lowland forest, order and disorder, and so forth, but I do not think this substantially detracts from the unidirectional character of the attribution of magical power to the underclass by the elevated. Nor does it detract from the characterization of that underclass as a force whose health- and fertility-bestowing capacity, no less than its danger, spring from its wildness. Listen to Randall's evocation of the jungle, an evocation presumably resonant with views of the mountain people themselves:

> The jungle is also a place of darkness, chaos and disorder
> where, hidden from the sun, plants grow wildly, twining about
> each other in a riot of confusion. In this it represents, in Inca
> mythology, the benighted, disparate, and uncivilized tribes of
> the preceding era before the sunlit conquest by the civilized In-
> cas who brought order to the world.[21]

And he points out that Incan painted wooden beakers generally depict *all* Incan enemies as jungle savages (*chunchos*) (which brings to mind the use of the word *auca,* further north in present-day Ecuador, and along the Putumayo border with Colombia, too). Randall also observes that nowadays during the Festival of the Star of the Snow, the wild feathered figure of the *chuncho* assumes the function of representing Indianness per se; not just the mythic beings east of the Andes, but all "Indians." Contrariwise, the Colla group of Indians, regarded as rich traders and hailing from the highlands, are now portrayed not by Indians but by mestizos (people of Indian and white ancestry but in this context "white"). In the Star of the Snow the *chunchos* defeat the Collas in mock combat.

Wildness, fertility, magical healing, suppressed, repressed, contained *below* in the dark tangled forest— this wild underground of history can heave upwards in rebellions, messianic in tone, curing and fertilizing not just this or that person or this or that field but an entire society overlaid wrongly by another epoch. Such is the interpretation one can derive from the repeated assaults carried out during and against the Spanish colonial era by forest dwellers, peaking in the romance, the might and the splendor, of myth objectified in the movement headed by Juan Santos Atahuallpa in 1741, and Randall detects modern manifestations of this constellation of myth and social rupture in the politico-moral geography of the rebellion associated with Hugo Blanco in the 1960s. In both instances highland leaders or "prophets" went down from the high country into the forested lowlands of the east, with the serpents and the demons, to find not merely a social base of support but to reassert a mythico-historical one. The raw forces of wildness and disorder were recruited in the attempt to do away with the old order, and failed. Yet the mythology lives on. Randall himself recruits the nostalgia of the political failure to inspire a poignant identification with the demons of history and social renewal, while all the more securely consolidating the triumph of the will to order; yet without *chunchos* and jungle—"place of darkness, chaos, and disorder where, hidden from the sun, plants grow wildly, twining about each other in a riot of confusion"—there would be no basis for order itself. Indeed, it is from this dependence that magic and fertility "flower."

In this collective artwork drawn onto as much as from nature, it is said that the lowland forest stands in relation to the elevated zones not only as disorderly but as female—as in José María Arguedas's crypto-autobiographical novel *Los ríos profundos,* set in the Peruvian highland town of Abancay some fifty years ago. Here, in reaction to a usurpation of use-values by the market system, it is women who defy the injustices of the commercial system and the state. In so doing they create not only "disorder" in the form of rebellion (and here we would do well to pause and ask ourselves why it is always the rebellion that is termed disorderly and not the system against which it is aimed). They also provoke the animation of the landscape and of otherwise mute things. Central to this giving voice to things, in the heat of female-inspired disorder aimed at the disorder created by the market system of things triumphing over persons, is the descent of woman to the eastern forests and to the (female zone of the) *chunchos.*

Because of hoarding by merchants there is a severe shortage of salt. The local *chicheras* (women who make and sell corn beer) lead a rebellion aimed at securing this salt and distributing it, free, to the women of the town and to the Indian serfs on the surrounding haciendas. The army steps in to quell the insurrection, and the figurehead of the struggle, Doña Felipa, flees to the river and thence, so it is rumored, down to the jungle from where she promises to return with the *chunchos* and set fire to the haciendas. The authorities fear that if this happens the serfs will run away and join the *chicheras.* The *chunchos* are said to get awfully angry, and the boys in the college speculate that the Pachachaca River may take sides with the *chunchos* and with Doña Felipa, reverse his current, bring them up on the *chunchos'* rafts to burn the valley and sugarcane of the hacienda owners, and kill all the Christians and their animals. In the Abancay church, the rector of the college, who is also a priest, announces that a detachment of *guardias civiles* made up of police well trained to maintain order will be installed permanently in the barracks, and continues with the following sermon (in Spanish, rather than in Quechua):

> "The rabble is conjuring up a specter to frighten the Christians. And that is a ridiculous farce. The serfs on all the haciendas have innocent souls, they're better Christians than we are; and the chunchos are savages who will never leave the bounds of the jungle. And if, by the devil's handiwork, they should come, their arrows would prove powerless against cannons. We must remember Cajamarca . . . !" he explained, and turning his eyes toward the Virgin, he begged in his high metallic voice, for forgiveness for the fugitives, for those who had gone astray. "You, dearly beloved Mother, will know how to cast out the devil from their bodies," he said.[22]

Set in motion like this we see how the politicized ambiguities of "disorder" imputed to and transmitted through the doubleness of women, diabolic and virginal, bring life to the binary distinctions, otherwise static, staid, and intellectualist, unified by highland and lowland. We can sense how the escalating course of events set off by contradictions in the market system of exchange not merely sets off these latent yet powerful distinctions, but that the course of events owes much to chance and the unexpected conflation of oppositions. It is a sort of semiotic play wherein signs relinquish their precision to the political resonance now animating the landscape conspiring with the wildness of women redeeming use-value.

"Remember Cajarmarca . . . !" intones the priest, his eyes moving toward the Virgin—Cajarmarca being the plain where the Inca Atahuallpa and his mighty host fell to a handful of Spaniards, thus marking the end of one empire, the rise of another, and an acutely colonized doubleness of identity thereafter. It is this foregrounding and backgrounding of identity that Frank Salomon has recently pictured, a vast colonial history writ into the dancing and killing of the *yumbo* on the outskirts of the city of Quito in the highlands of Ecuador, whereby *yumbo* is pretty well meant *auca*, the northern Andean equivalent of *chuncho,* and where, as with the festival of the Star of the Snow so remarkably brought to our attention by Robert Randall, this annual ritual of *yumbo* dancing and killing is associated with Corpus Christi.[23] For the man who cares for the radio masts that guide airplanes in and out of Quito and who guides Salomon into the world of *yumbo* (as that world is created in the imagination of highlanders), the dancing brings out the polarities of an Indian versus a white America. With Corpus Christi, the "compass of existence" (an image of which his guide is fond) rotates 180 degrees and what Salomon calls the "effort of becoming" is turned away from the city of hierarchy and whiteness, "returning not to the ancestral world—it is lost beyond recall—but toward that contrary *alter,* the jungle into which the powers of persecuted America have withdrawn." In his guide, Salomon continues, "a sense of ethnic distinctiveness deprived of its original ground survives as an electric tension between two equally unrealizable potential selves."[24]

Those who take on the role of *yumbo* dancers become explicitly *auca*—unbaptized, unsocialized, akin to animals and the spirits of the mountains and springs, says Salomon. As such they cannot enter a church, and unlike their Christian counterparts in this New World version of Corpus Christi, their meal, while formally similar to the *santa mesa,* parodies its substance. Not beams but lances form its table; not fresh bread but scraps stolen or begged, a pig's skull, picked clean, a bag of potato chips spilled across the improvised "table" while the prayer to God is derided. "You'll have to pay, though!" screams the monkey to the *yumbos,* and there follows a deliberate paying of bills up the line of men, bills classified by denomination and tucked under the thong of the drum following which the *yumbo* music begins once again while money, as Salomon points out, is not mentioned or touched in a true (Christian) *mesa.* As in a disorderly Rabelaisian burlesque shot full with Brechtian grim humor and down-to-earthness, the *yumbo-aucas* mock the serene hierarchical order of the Christian officiants, and therewith the Christian state.

They live in the lap of their mountain mothers and fathers, these dancers from the forest below. "I have come to visit the *apu* to cure. I give good luck," they might say, and by *apu* they mean not merely mountain or lord but also the Christian officiants of Corpus Christi. The mountains love these lowlanders. When thunder is heard at dusk from Mount Guamani, it is said that Guamani is weeping because his Quijos shamans from the foothills are passing him by on the road to the city of Quito. They dance to the Christians' houses and sing "I've come, I've arrived with my Mountain Mother. What is it you desire? Do you want a cure, or do you want to kill?" And when they leave, days later, they say, "Now we must go to our home. Now our mountain is calling to us, now our mountain is playing. When our mountain plays, we go away, our mountain does not let us stay."

And the playing of the mountains? This is lightning flickering from the far side of the mountains, the side of the lowland forests, visible from Quito as a pale glow (in Salomon's words) backlighting the dark profiles of the crests. This flickering beyond the crests surrounding the city is a sign of the *yumbos'* power. They are acting as shamans from the Pacific and the eastern rain forests, decked out with brilliantly feathered birds, shamans who have come to the mountain-city to sell jungle animals and practice magical medicine. It is true that the *yumbos* are spoken of as dependents of these mountains that love and weep for them, these mountains that are their mothers, their *apus* or lords whose mothering lordship extends to denote the Christian officiants who the *yumbos,* now representing not just jungle people but their magical and wild quintessence in shamanhood, complement in point counterpoint in Corpus Christi. But it is a profoundly ambivalent dependence. The shamans come up from the jungle offering their superiors what their superiority denies them, namely the magical power of wildness to kill and to heal, and in front of the Christian officiants they act out their wildness on *themselves,* killing one of their own and then, with shamanic art, bringing the victim back from the space of death into life, into something perhaps bigger than life, an articulated, codependent difference of forest and mountain, "Indian" and Christian, acted out up here on the outskirts of the city. Hunting down the victim in a symbolized rain forest with the divinatory power of its hallucinogens the day after Corpus Christi, the killer shaman hails his fellow wildmen (and I quote Salomon): "And what news have you brother? Haven't you seen somebody come by here with his feet and toes twisted backward, with his whole ass and his balls all full of fleas, with maybe a short rope tied around his neck? Didn't you see somebody like that passing by?" The killer wants to eat the fugitive, yet is persuaded to resuscitate him if paid money. "Brother, where have you come from?" they ask the man brought back to life. "What did you see?" And in a voice too low for the public to hear he replies, "Brothers, I walked over the entire world; I saw all the animals and I saw all my brothers, and now I have brought back the sweet seeds. I went to another world and I brought back what was there: oranges, *colación,* and every fruit." And so the brothers *yumbos,* shamans, wild men all, sing farewell to the mountains, the Christians, their hosts:

> From year to year we drop by
> Like the bird *veranero.*
> Ah, now you see, Oh now you see
> Death now you see, life now you see
> Ay no, yes! That's so, yes![25]

There is this flickering of light in the shadow of death: "Death now you see, life now you see, Ay no, yes!"—the flickering of the lightning beyond the dark crests encircling the city of the mountains, an age-old play of difference manifested as much in trade as in ideological exchanges, perhaps made sharper right now because of the rapidity with which commoditization has created "the modern" and "the traditional." *Yumbo* dancing flourishes most, Salomon tells us, "where the headlong expansion of oil-rich Quito has brought a sudden and dramatic invasion of formerly rural communities."[26]

Which raises some points Benjamin essayed concerning the cultural effect of the leap forward in commoditization in Baudelaire's Paris: first, the confrontation of the city's discipline with its wildness ("James Ensor liked to put military groups in his carnival mobs, and both got along splendidly—as

FEEL.

Ah, to journey to a city of artistry. And spirit. A city that
has no longings for sophisticated civilization.
Gourmet takes you to Quito, the capital of Ecuador.
You can feel its soul in the exquisite ancient
churches. The voluptuous architecture. And the women,
still bent double carrying huge bundles and babies
contentedly on their backs. A Gourmet Holiday is so
much more than just a tourist's eyeview. It's a rich pilgrimage
into the heart of wherever it takes you.

Gourmet. The original lifestyle magazine. We're good
living at its peak. We're glorious food and drink. Glorious
people and places. We shop with imagination. We entertain with passion. We inform with warmth and wit. And we
always give a great deal of pleasure.
Gourmet sets the standards people live by. That's why
our hold on 2.5 million readers is so profound. Our copies
are treasured for years, referred to again and again as a
trusted, personal guide to life at its best.
Gourmet is more than a magazine. It is a way of life.
It is quality and style that endure.
Very quietly, over the last 43 years
Gourmet has become a classic.
Now a Condé Nast publication.

Gourmet
THE STANDARD OF LIVING.®

(Photograph by Mathias Oppersdorff. Copyright © 1984 by The Condé Nast Publi-
cations Inc.)

the prototype,'' observed Benjamin, "of totalitarian states in which the police make common cause with the looters");[27] second, how the quantum leap forward in technology and the sway of the market inscribed a pathos of denied promise in commodities, stimulating through them visions of utopia drawn from fantasies of the primal past—such as the jungle and its fabulous *yumbos, aucas,* and *chunchos.*

And in relation to the cities of the first world, the third world city itself approaches the status of the *auca.* Take the full-page advertisement in the *New York Times* (21 October 1984) centered on a color photograph of an highland Indian woman carrying a small sleeping child on her back. She wears a brilliant red cloak and sports a Panama hat with a multicolored band. Around her neck are gold and silver balls and from her ears hang golden pendants. Behind her lie empty cane baskets, their capacious insides dark and inviting, sexualized cavities awaiting goods to buy and sell. She is looking down and slightly away from the camera as if absorbed in a world other than the photographer's or ours. It is an advertisement for *Gourmet* ("the standard of living") magazine with a self-declared readership of two and a half million.

But the tropical birds from the foothills that the *yumbo* shamans brought to Quito died on the journey. Nevertheless the colors hold fast, and it is with these that the shamans are aided in the creation and transmission of their fantastic visions.

As to the antiquity of this vast distinction articulating the demonic magic of the forests below with the stately order of the highlands—all, of course, from the point of view of the latter—a case can be made for its stretching back to very remote times indeed. Henry Wassén summarizes a good deal of evidence on this subject in the monograph he edited on the contents of a Collahuaya medicine man's tomb with its lowland medicines carbon dated at around A.D. 350.[28] Salomon cites studies suggesting dates older by some 700 years for lowland trade of this sort with highlands, while he himself goes so far as to say that, for the sixteenth century at least, there is evidence strongly suggesing "some degree of lowland ideological sway over highlanders."[29] Yet such "sway" is likely to be as much self-induced as other-induced, a socially institutionalized highland fantasy about the eastern forests, whose unsurpassing romance, savagery, beauty, and mystery cannot fail to cast the ideological as natural, the fictional as really real. And who remains immune?

To the scienticity of the archeology and the carbon-dated antiquity, we add the heroic passion of the shaman-led revolts of the lowlanders against the Spanish and, so it is said, before that against the incursions of the Incan empire as well. To that we add the observation that highlanders, rich and poor, white and Indian, urban and not so urban, go down to the lowlands seeking out shamans there for magical power—and it is we, too, no less dependent on the elusive distinctions wrought by myth through historical events in landscapes, internal and external, that follow them down, observing, standing back, but ultimately, like those who descend, figuring the world ritualistically and no less beholden to the magic of the woods and the primitive, wild and first, as if myth inevitably reproduced itself in rituals that for some are healing and for others are called explanation.

And in closing, Salomon leaves us this powerful image: that wave after wave of foreign people have conquered and sanctified the mountain city of Quito. The ab-original powers are extruded toward the periphery out and over the brim of the mountains into the refuge of the outer forests. "Thus," he writes, "the forest becomes—is forever becoming—the refuge of the ancient, the aboriginal, the autochthonous. It is a reservoir for the kind of knowledge which the powers of the center wish only to expel and replace."[30]

But how autonomous is that knowledge which the center extrudes? Does not the otherness with which the extruded is marked also mark it as desired and necessary to the center? Is not the magic of the wild zone created as much by the center as by the shamans who are made to act as the shock-absorbers of history?

In the body this is actively inscribed. Take the history of Spanish wounds and Indian body fat.

Bernal Díaz fought with Cortés and won an empire for Spain. His field of battle was Mexico and he wrote what is surely the most widely read account of that conquest. It was a plump Indian, he noted in his description of the first confrontation with the Tlascalans, whose body was opened up to get fat to heal the wounds incurred in that battle. There was no oil, he said, but there were Indian puppies that provided a satisfying meal, and presumably they were not without grease that could have dressed wounds. And in the next engagement the fat of Indians was again applied to heal fifteen wounded Spaniards and their four wounded horses. That night there were hens and puppies to eat. It was curious, wrote Bernal Díaz, how the Indians in this battle and all others carried away their wounded and the Spaniards never saw the Indian dead.[31]

That great horseman Hernando de Soto was also reported to have used the fat of Indians slain in combat, as in his expedition against one of the Inca's captains holding out in the Sierra de Vilcaza in the Peruvian Andes.[32] How magical such a usage was I cannot say, but certainly the Frazerian principles of sympathetic and contagious magic are clear: with the fat of those who have wounded me I will heal that wound. And who knows what is here being said about fat as a benificent excess of vitality, of healthy living bodies, of the fatter as against the unfortunate thinner, and so forth. But if speculation is idle with respect to the Spaniards' views of the magical virtues of Indian fat, it is not quite so idle when we come to the Indians' views of the matter—which is to say, and as always must be said in this play of mirrors, is not so much the Indians' views as the Spaniards' views of the

Indians' views of the Spaniards' views of, in this case, Indian *untu* or body fat.

Drawing his little book on Incan rites and fables to a close, some forty years after de Soto's soldiers were healing their wounds with the fat of slain Indians, the Catholic priest Cristóbal de Molina thought it fit to dwell on the sanctity of mountains, the extraction of fat from the bodies of Indians, the Dance Sickness revolt against the Spanish, and the healing rites that flourished during and after this uprising—by far the largest Indian rebellion of the first two hundred years of colonial rule. Ten years before his writing, a revolt that the Indians called the Taqui Onqoy or Dance Sickness uprising had developed in the diocese of Cuzco, previously the Inca's capital, and was spreading rapidly. It had been put about, wrote Father Molina, that Spain had commanded that Indian body fat be amassed and exported for the curing of a certain illness there, and though nobody could say with certainty, it was probably the sorcerers of the Inca, secreted in the mysterious fastness of Vilcabamba where the Andes plunged into the Amazon forests, who were responsible for this tale designed to sow enmity between Indian and Spaniard. Now the Indians were loath to serve the Spanish, fearing that they would be killed and their body fat extracted as a remedy for the people of Spain.[33]

Almost four hundred years after the Dance Sickness uprising, the Peruvian Efraín Morote Best published in Cuzco an article on the Nakaq, a phantasm in the southern highlands of Peru, who people say attacks individuals under cover of darkness in public places in order to extract the fat from their bodies to sell either to the pharmacies where it is used in medicines or to people who use it to grease machines, cast church bells, or shine the faces of the statues of the saints.[34] Rarely was the Nakaq said to be an Indian. Nearly always it was said to be a white or a mestizo. In some versions the victim would immediately disappear. In others, the victims were first put to sleep or into a trancelike state by means of magic powders and after their fat was extracted they would awake without remembering what happened. There would be no sign of a wound. They would continue their journey and slowly die. Some people didn't die but became forever sick with sadness. Upon awakening some people did remember, as if it had all been a dream.

In his essay on the same phantasm, Anthony Oliver-Smith suggested it serves to confirm in grotesque fashion the Indian's everyday experiences of class and racist oppression, and as an aside noted that mestizos with whom he talked in Ancash, Peru, in 1966 told him with much hilarity that they would kill a dog or a pig and leave its entrails with blood-drenched clothing to make the Indians think that the fat-taking phantasm was close by and would murder them if they did not work harder or behave themselves.[35] Yet there is more than one joke in this simulacrum of reality wherein the mestizos laugh at what they think the Indians think the mestizos are thinking about the Indians.

In his field work in the highland province of Ayacucho, in the early and mid-1950s, the Peruvian ethnologist and novelist José María Arguedas came across a man, a *misti*, as the Indians called him (meaning a non-Indian and member of the "señorial" class), who could with great charm embellish on the fact—surely well known—that mestizos (as well as whites) of these societies may go to Indian diviners and healers when in sore straits, thus crediting these Indians with the power to stem the tide of fate—as if there were an implicit pact between Indianness and redemption. Arguedas was asking people of the little highland town of Puquio about the *wamanis*, the spirits of the surrounding mountains whose priests are referred to as *pongos*, the name given to servants and serfs throughout much of the Andes. His *misti* acquaintance told him what happened when he was serving as governor of an interior district of the province.[36]

There was a big to-do because people in the capital of the district as well as the outlying areas had heard that there was a *pongo* in a cave in a mountain who could perform miraculous cures and divine the future. Because of the disturbance, with people rushing off to consult with the *pongo,* the governor decided to put an end to what he called the farce of the Indian. He sent four men to take the *pongo* prisoner. They brought him tied up back to the town, where the governor treated him badly and made him sleep tied up in prison. But people of all social classes, the ignorant and the lettered, pleaded with the governor to set him free. The governor decided to put the *pongo* to the test. The *pongo* asked for ingredients and set up his *mesa* or altar to call the *wamanis*, the mountain spirits. He and the governor waited alone in a dark room. The *wamanis* flew in making a great noise and flapping their wings. The governor said he could see one of them because he had left a window open. It had the form of a small but imposing eagle. He also told us that the *wamanis* spoke with majestic fury and whipped the *pongo*. The most furious was the spirit of the largest mountain, Quarwarasu. The *wamanis* told the governor what would befall him in the course of his life and they gave him remedies for his illnesses. Thus was he convinced of the *pongo*'s power and was moved to initiate a close friendship with him, one day confiding that he too would like to be a *pongo*. But that was out of the question, the *pongo* told him. This was not a profession a *misti* could follow. They couldn't resist the punishment and tests to which the *wamanis* subjected their *pongos*. So the governor relinquished his ambition but maintained affectionate relations with the *pongo*. One day a friend of the (now ex-) governor's, in Nazca, far away down on the southern coast, asked him to bring the *pongo* to heal an illness that no doctor could diagnose. The former governor called the *pongo,* who lived three days from Puquio, and in an express taxi they traveled to the coast to Nazca where in a darkened room the *pongo* prepared his altar and called his *wamanis*, the spirits of the far-off Ayacucho mountains. As he was on the coast he also called the spirits of the mountains near by, especially White Mountain, but this proved his undoing because White Mountain, being in an area where there were few Indians, spoke Spanish, and that the *pongo* couldn't understand. The *wamanis* became angry.

Next day the former governor asked White Mountain if he could serve as an interpreter. White Mountain agreed and the *wamanis* proceeded. White Mountain reproached the sick woman for being a sorcerer. He said she was sick with sorcery herself, because one of her victims had retaliated against her with sorcery too. The chief *wamani* ordered his two smaller mountain spirits to go and gather up the sorcery substances and bring in the stuff the sick white woman had deployed against her victim, as well as the stuff her victim had used against her. In the twinkling of an eye the birds dropped the pestilent objects onto the altar, two packages of sorcery, and these were immediately put into the fire. The *pongo* and the former governor returned to the highlands, and the patient began to get better.

The ex-governor told Arguedas that the mountain spirits care for the Indians and that the secrets of these spirits can only be learned inside the mountains. It is said that the ex-governor's friend, the Indian *pongo,* stayed six months inside one of those mountains and that at the end of that time he reappeared, asleep, on a field. He is still alive, they told Arguedas.

He is the lowest of the low and the servant of all, the *pongo,* and he reappeared sleeping, the *misti* told Arguedas. He is also the servant of dreams and of the archeology of racist myth curving into the present from the concealed interior of the mountainous earth, emerging asleep as dreamtime to redeem the señorial class of its self-induced sorcery. And just as this *pongo* reappeared sleeping, so other *pongos* disappear sleeping, violated by *mistis* and whites in the form of *nakaqs* who sell their fat as medicine, as grease for machines, or to shine the faces of saints.

In the midst of the techniques constituting these rites, there is a figure who provides the substantiality necessary to bind the flashing ephemera of attributions and counterattributions into a redemptive force. It is an imaginary figure, one constituted by that flashing field of othernesses—whites' representations of Indians' representations of whites' representations of Indians. It is the figure of the wild woman and the wild man, pagan figures attributed with magic to kill and magic to heal socially caused illness and misfortune by their thus-defined civilized superiors. These are the great artifacts: fetishized antiselves made by civilizing histories—the wildly contradictory figure of the Primitive, less than human and more than human. This is the figure of the black woman slave in Cartagena with her love charms and magical medicines. This is Paula de Eguiliz, condemned by the Inquisition to burn at the stake for allegedly leading the black witches who were beleaguering Cartagena. Yet thus signified she would be solicited by the signifiers, the bishop and the head inquisitor, to come and heal them. Discarding the *sanbenito* robes of penitence that marked her as an ally of the devil, she would journey from prison in a mantle trimmed with gold, carried aloft in a sedan chair, not unlike the Wild Woman of the Forest, *La Montañerita Cimarrona*. This is the *pongo* in his cave in the mountain healing *mistis*. This is the *chuncho* in the wildness below the mountains. This is the shaman exorcizing José García of the sorcery that other whites envious of his good fortune have imploded into him. These are images of wildness imputed to these slaves, ex-slaves, and *pongos,* then extracted from them drenched in the otherness this imputation so heightens, as is the fat extracted by the *nakaq*—power slippery and magical that can exorcize from the colonizing self the evil of having more.

We are all *nakaqs*.

THIRTEEN
Surplus Value

1971 was a year of reawakened hopes for
many poor country people where I lived in
Colombia. Not since the thirties had there
been so much political activity by peasants
fighting landlords for control of land. One
day I accompanied two peasant union leaders up the mountains that fan out to the west
from the southern rim of the valley. They
were friends of mine, Luis Carlos Mina and
the late Alfredo Cortés, peasant farmers
from around Puerto Tejada with personal
experience of strike actions in the sugar
mills. They wished to enlist Indians in their
new union by asking them to contribute
lumber from the mountains for the construction of a *casa campesina,* a "peasant house,"
to be built in the main market town. It would
give people a place to stay overnight before
the market so they would not have to sleep
in the street; a place to get together, discuss
mutual concerns, and organize.

We rode all day up the western *cordillera*
on scrawny ponies and found the hacienda.
We needed permission from the owner to
speak with his workers. In effect they were
his serfs. In return for a tiny parcel of poor
land they worked three days on the hacienda. They were Paéz Indians from the
cordillera central, four or five little families

"We rode all day up the western *cordillera* on scrawny ponies."

Don Luis checking out the hacienda owner.

"They would close their homes up tight when we approached."

Don Alfredo, Don Luis, and the serfs.

living in huts scattered across the ridges. They would close their homes tight when we approached and look at the ground when we managed to get a conversation of sorts started, which wasn't often.

The owner was no less scrawny than out peasant ponies, wiry and tough, with sweat-stained clothes and a machete hanging from his belt, its leather case polished from constant wear. He was a *blanco,* a whiteman, as they would say in those parts, and had had a few years of secondary school. He lived on the farm, pretty well alone, and went down into the valley once a week or so for market. He was courteous and although not enthusiastic about what we were doing, probably felt it better not to antagonize the new and growing union. So he let us go and talk to his *obreros.*

When he heard I worked as a *médico* he started to tell me about his insomnia and stomach aches. When they got very bad he felt it was time to go, sometimes with his son who had served as a mechanic in the Colombian navy, down to the valley and take a bus south, almost to the frontier with Ecuador. There he'd stay the night and get another bus, this time east over the rim of the Andes down into the eastern forests to find himself an Indian shaman, a *curaca.* There he would stay and drink special medicines, he told me, until he was cured. Sometimes he would take soil from the farm to have it cured too, especially when the crops were doing poorly or the cattle were thin.

That's strange, I thought. It was the first I had ever heard of this sort of thing, and I knew next to nothing about *curacas, yagé,* the geography of which he was talking, or, truth to tell, about sorcery or *maleficio.* It was *maleficio* that was causing him the pain and the sleeplessness. It was *maleficio* that made the crops do poorly and the cattle thin.

A few weeks later down in the market town on the day of the market we bumped into some of the serfs. They were a little drunk, rolling along, smiling and playful in the crowd of peasants gathered in the quarters of the new union.

"The boss says he suffers from *maleficio,*" I said, trying to level with them. "Who could be doing it?"

"Why," the nearest contended, a smile breaking across his face, "*los mismos compadres!*"—meaning the very Indian serfs whose children the hacienda owner godparented! His smile lingered. We will never know whether the serfs did in fact ensorcell the owner and his farm. But the owner felt strongly enough about it to go a long way to buy magical protection from other Indians, lowland forest Indians, whose power would equal or dominate that to which his exploitation of highland Indian serfs exposed him. It was magic enlisted in the class struggle. And it enlisted me too.

Five years later I got to know a stocky mountain man living in the Andes close to the road that connected the eastern forests of the Amazon basin with the highland city of Pasto. He was an industrious and well-to-do peasant farmer, a *blanco* by local reckoning, and had been down on his luck for three years. He was a morose and graceless monument to social conformity, his beady eyes sunk into the ovoid innocence of his fat face. His farm stretched down swathes of bright green pasture and beautifully tilled fields of potatoes saturated with fungicides and fertilizer, coming to rest at the edge of an icy blue lake into which only the hardy ventured. It was said to be enchanted. There were small huts around belonging to day laborers, *blancos* like him. They were poor people and he worked his fields with some of them, side by side in his thick, rich, pesticided mud. His parents had brought him to farm this uncannily still lakeshore when he was a child. His name was Sexto. It was up behind his farm a few miles over the plateau of the *páramo* of the mountain tops and down into the Sibundoy valley where I had first met him, taking *yagé* one night with an Indian healer named Pedro, with whom I used to stay on my journeys to the lowlands.

It was toward the end of 1976 and the priests were making a great to-do with their plan to convert the church into a cathedral. No less a dignitary than the archbishop of Bogotá, with his entourage of bishops, was coming to consecrate the new cathedral, and in the meantime missionaries busied themselves scuttling around the valley in rather vain attempts to inspire their type of religious fervor.

The mother of Pedro, the Indian healer, was clearer than I was about the meaning of all this fuss. She told me that at long last Father Bartolomé's bones, hidden in the church, were to be exhumed and that the pope was going to make him a saint—the same Bartolomé who sixty years before with Father Gaspar de Pinell in a legendary apostolic excursion had descended the mountains into the dense forests of the Putumayo and Caquetá rivers to baptize Huitotos and other new and savage tribes (as the Church-published texts put it). His spirit is *milagroso* and Pedro carried a portrait of him in his wallet.

But the wind was emptying from the world's sails. Pedro's wife joined us in talking of Padre Bartolomé's bones and of his exploits with savages, both below the church in an underground of redemptive time. Her wit gave way to a drawn-out sigh. No longer were there the great shamans of the lowlands, she declared. Nor was there Padre Bartolomé, who died in 1966. "In earlier times there were great *curacas*," she said wistfully, meaning by *curacas*, shamans.

> They could become tigers and parrots. They could fly. Now
> they are finished. They ate one another. They fought each
> other. They were consumed with envy. They would turn into a
> tiger to eat the whole family of their enemy. Now there is no-
> body, now that Salvador is dead. He was like Padre Bartolomé.
> He knew how to heal. He was of quality. There was no doctor
> like him, and there are none today. Padre Bartolomé would
> even help women in childbirth. And it was all free. He'd go far
> into the countryside, even when it was raining. That's why he's
> a saint. He is in heaven. He was the father of us all. He

founded the cathedral, the convent of the Holy Sisters and of
the Fathers too. He was the founder of Sibundoy.

"Why did the Capuchins leave the valley?" I asked.

"Because Padre Bartolomé died," she answered. "He got a letter from
INCORA [the Colombian government's land reform agency which appropriated most of the Capuchin's land—land that the Capuchins had taken
from the Indians in the early twentieth century]. He opened the letter and
had a heart attack. The Capuchins sold nearly all their farms to INCORA.
Now the people have to pay INCORA. But this is no good. All you hear
now is people talking money and getting loans so as to work land, buy barbed
wire, and use tractors. It's better to be poor and be able to sleep without
those worries." Neither she nor Pedro had land other than a tiny parcel of
poor soil in the hills above the town whose meager yield they supplemented
with a trickle of income from his healing, divining, and carpentry.

That night the missionaries had selected their home as the venue for one
of the meetings designed to consolidate the faith prior to the arrival of the
archbishop. It so happened that it was also this night that Pedro had planned
to take *yagé* with his group of patients. Quite unshaken, he told me and the
others to wait quietly, without being seen, in the earth-floored main room,
while the priests' reunion would take place in the front room. Separated by
nothing more than the rough-edged planks of the wall, we sat in the dark,
our fears and expectancy concerning the *yagé* we were to take later on
punctuated by chinks of light and sound from the other room.

Some thirty neighbors, adults and children, had been gathered together
by a priest and a nun. They sat stiffly on benches under the glare of a naked
lightbulb. The priest began.

"We are here to discuss problems. I am here with the Sister and we should
call each other by our first names. We are all equal in the eyes of God."

Silence.

"We are to seek unity, the basis of everything," declared the priest, who
then went around the room asking each person's name. There was a lot of
giggling.

"We must be friends," asserted the Sister. "We must make friends because
our problems come from lack of communication." Then she made a speech
criticizing Protestants. Pedro butted in with a jest he had developed from
the priest in their exhortations against communism. He equated communists
with Prostestants, their worst feature being disregard for the Virgin, the
mother of the soil. The Sister berated the group for not being friendly enough
to each other. So far, except for Pedro, nobody had ventured to say anything.
She was clearly struggling.

"Let us sing a song about friends," she suggested, and handed out a song
sheet. "What! You can't read!" She wound up a gramaphone with a record
in place. The priest was standing. Everyone else was sitting. He stood over

The order of the church, its steps, and its homage (Sibundoy).

The bishop blessing the Indian (Sibundoy).

The Sibundoy Indian curing the white man.

Don Pedro divining.

Don Pedro's *mesa*

and lectured them, asking all manner of questions about conflicts between spouses.

"What is lacking?" he asked, and triumphantly supplied the answer. "Comprehension! Lack of comprehension!" He pleaded for fraternity. "We all come from God and we all return to God."

The Sister demanded: "Do you feel alone or accompanied?"

For the first time the group responded: "Accompanied!"

The Sister read from her song book and played her record. She forced a woman to read a song out loud. She and the priest talked about poverty.

"How do we get out of poverty?" they asked.

"With money," said someone.

"No! No!" exclaimed the priest, "everyone can get money. There is something more important than money. What is it?"

There was a long silence. "With the word of God," he said, "knowing the word of God!"

Some young people waled by outside and screamed, "Reunions are for shit!"

"It is difficult for neighbors to communicate," said the priest, "truly difficult." And so, after an hour the meeting came to an end.

Pedro came bustling into the main room saying, "Now for the real stuff." A fire was lit and we settled onto the ground around it, eight of us chatting animatedly as he prepared the pot of *yagé*. He did not call on us to give our

Don Pedro and the author in the healer's garden of delights, 1977.

names or to be friends, and although there would be much talk of poverty and conflict that night, it would not be resolved by an appeal for comprehension, communication, or the word of God.

Silence. Pedro began to chant to the *yagé*. Someone echoed the priest's word, "fraternity." Gentleness filled the room. Pedro was singing more vigorously and after we drank our first cup there was a long but splintered conversation about crop prices and profits. After half an hour Pedro was sitting with his head in his hands, suffering. Suddenly he looked up at Sexto, the man from the lake, and asked:

"Have you anyone in mind over there who could have put *sal*?" By *sal,* the world for salt, he means sorcery. Sexto said he did.

"Good," said Pedro, "we should keep thinking, concentrating, making a check." After a while he turned to Julio, a middle-aged black man who migrated here many years ago from the Pacific coast, and said he knew who caused him harm, the man who . . .

After what seemed like an hour or thereabouts a local Indian man moved over to Pedro's suffering side. Pedro had been vomiting. "It's violent, this remedy," he said between retches.

The man began his tale of woe. "My woman has escaped from me . . . my son is sick . . . the home is filled with evil . . . I don't know what to do. . . ."

"Damn!" exclaimed Pedro with empathy and pain as he pressed his face back into his hands.

This went on all night. People got up to shit and vomit and came back to the fire. It was cold away from it. They talked mostly of the prevention and cure of sorcery. There was much joking and teasing, and in stops and starts, in rivulets and in waves, the colors and patterns of *yagé* advanced and receded; the yellow waves of flowers around the lake, pink-white jelly-like fronds moving in slow motion as growths under the sea, blended with snakes and pigs. A shadow moved, the fire flickered, a sound rustled, an emotion sparked in the interstices of the slow, rambling discussion—these sudden eruptions raked over and pricked our being, patterning out consciousness like the healer's garden of delights at the back of the house, an interplanted higgledy-piggledy profusion of plants, vines, shrubs, and great bell-shaped datura flowers, white ones and orange ones, fluttering.

At dawn Pedro began to exorcise the evil from the sick people, one by one, with his curing fan of rustling leaves beating strongly to his chanting, viewing the interior of the body with his quartz crystal, his "lens" or *lente.* He got the sick person to breathe into the *lente,* and every so often asked him to look into it and see the shadowy form of the evil. He passed the fan of leaves over the body, in rhythm with the chant, rustling and quavering, gathering up the evil within. He sucked the bad stuff from patient's body and spat it into a corner of the room with a lot of noise. It took a long time—some two and half hours for four people.

Everyone seemed relaxed and open. The fire was stoked, *aguardiente* offered, and the talk kept coming back to the night's events to touch fleetingly but frequently on the sorcery brooding over everybody's life story while all the time but in a constantly interrupted way Pedro was chanting, beating time with his curing fan, sucking and spitting.

Normally tight-lipped and stoic, Sexto, the man from the lake, described his past three years of suffering. He paused.

"Evil wind, *mal aires,*" concluded a woman in a confident tone.

Sexto fixed her with a beady stare. "No! . . . Sorcery!" he said.

"Pure *sal,* pure sorcery," chimed a young man seated in the corner, "for sure!"

He was fifty-seven years old, Sexto. When he came to the lake with his parents there were few other people. Now there were many. Few had farms larger than one hectare. Sexto's measured close to sixty. To fatten cattle and produce potatoes now required capital and peons—the poor whites who lived in the tiny huts surrounding his fields.

When I went to visit him it was clear he feared their envy and the sorcery to which it could lead. "People here are consumed with envy," he said, "and they ensorcell the farm. They don't work hard like me. They see me prospering and they try to harm me, but," he went on, "if you take *yagé* every six months or so then you are secured against *maleficio*. Nothing can harm you. What happened to me was that I became careless. I stopped taking it for a while."

Three years ago he had been walking the streets of Pasto, as pleased as a man can be with a good sale at market, when he was waylaid and knifed. He fell heavily on his right leg and was taken to hospital. X-rays showed no fracture, he was told, and the doctors discharged him after a week but he could barely walk. For a year and a half he needed a crutch, and he still had a limp impeding his capacity for heavy labor—of which he still managed to do plenty, as I witnessed during those days by the lake. As if that weren't enough his daughter suffered attacks of paralysis for which there was no obvious cause. And at great financial loss he had to sell the little country bus he had bought because the hired chauffer was cheating him.

Out of curiosity he first took *yagé* when he was twenty-one. Since then he had taken it many times and had got to know most of the shamans in this highland valley. At the moment he seemed happy with Pedro and was supplying him with patients from around the lake, acting as a sort of inter-mediary. In fact, Sexto had a quiet ambition to become a shaman himself.

We passed the hut of a poor neighbor. Only the children were home and of these a little girl was ill. With pomp and mystery Sexto pulsed her and made passes with his hand, saying he would get her some herbs. At his home he had a carefully cultivated garden of medicinal plants, a plot of magical promise.

Later on, as we shivered in the night air whipping off the lake, coughing in the smoke of the fire over which potatoes were boiling, he talked of his dream to acquire divining quartz crystals and shaman's feathers—from the lowlands. But the singing lay beyond his reach. Until he received that gift he had to be patient. "When you take *yagé*," he explained, "you acquire the power of the shaman. The shaman gives you this gift and this is what cures people, cattle . . . everything, including sorcery of the soil and of the crops." He paused, bringing the magical exchanges together in the one enchanted landscape, "The *highland* shamans sing," he said, "and with that they call the spirit of the *lowland* shaman that taught them to come and help. They do this because he has given the gift to them."

It is Sexto's view, as I understand it, that the lowlands to the east are connected to the highlands by a chain of spiritual discourse stretching back through time grasped as a spatial image; landscape looping back into the present as we encountered earlier with our discussion of *chunchos* east of Cuzco, first people buried in an underground of time in the lowland jun-gles, seed endowed with magical force to flower into the present. What Sexto indicated was a temporal connection fixed in a moral topography consisting of successive empowerments through gift exchanges occurring between spirits and shaman, shaman and patient, patient and you, dear reader.

The gift of the past to the present, of lowland shamans to highland shamans, was here grasped by Sexto, the rich peasant, to thwart the sorcery he suspected was coming from his wage workers. The mantle of magical protection provided by Indian shamans and by *yagé* became for him a tool of labor control in a peasant economy where capital and wage labor are becoming defining features, sometimes supplanting, sometimes coexisting with a different and older agriculture of subsistence worked with neither pesticides nor fertilizers, neither with capital nor with wage labor. As with José García, the gift that a peasant entrepeneur like Sexto acquired from *yagé* and the shamans of the lowland forests was a gift easing the spread of the market economy into subsistence agriculture where inequality fertilized envy and envy bred sorcery.

In this situation it befalls the *highland* shaman, such as Pedro, to act as a medium not only for the spirits of the primal past buried in an underground of time in the fastness of the lowland forest. He also mediates the class struggle, as between Sexto and his peons. We also appreciate another set of mediations alongside that: his mediating the dominant cultural force of the region, the mysteries and the authority of the Catholic Church, with sorcery and everyday imponderabilia. When I asked him how the priest's reunions in his front room had worked out, he giggled. "I'm halfway to heaven," he said.

FOURTEEN
Hunting Magic

It was Pedro who had pictured for me when I came to the Putumayo a world in which he called on the spirits of the "first tribe" and on the Huitotos in the hot forests below. It was with them he created the power necessary to heal and divine, with those fantasy creatures from the beginnings of time and beyond the edge of the civilized world in that zone where sacred figures like the Fathers Bartolomé and Gaspar had penetrated with the cross decades before. You couldn't help but sense the presence of the lowlands in these highland shamans. It was there staring you in the face, of course, because of their dependence on *yagé,* which only grows in the hotter forests of the lowlands. Yet that dependence is not as straightforward as it might appear. It is not a "natural fact." There are plenty of shamans and healers the wide world over who do not require hallucinogenic drugs. What is more, there are plenty of hallucinogens in the highlands, beginning with the great abundance of datura festooning the Sibundoy valley and which the shamans there use a lot. The importance and magical power of *yagé* in the eyes of the highlanders, so it seems to me, is largely the result of its being invested with the mythic and metaphorical power of the lowland forests and their inhabitants, powers of primitiveness and wildness specified by colonization and the Catholic Church. To drink *yagé* is to take in all that with one nauseating hallucinatory gulp.

You can't help but see the imagery of the lowlands in the ritual adornments of the shamans too, all drawn from the hot forests—the feathers and the quartz crystals that Sexto yearns for, let alone the song he dreams of coming his way. "Why do you wear the tigers'-teeth necklace?" I remember asking an old man in the Sibundoy valley.

"Why? Because it has the same owner as *yagé*. It comes from the same place, from the *monte,* and that's the *yagé* we call *tigre ahayuasca.*"

"And the *cascabel?*" I asked, referring to the chirruping necklaces of seedpods.

"They are the sound of the forest, from where comes the *yagé.*"

"How do they help curing?"

"They show you . . . well, everything!"

And the feathers? They came from the birds of the forests of the lowlands. They helped make the *pinta,* the painting you create when you take *yagé.*

Yet despite this dependence on the lowlands, his daughter made it very clear to me that the shamans up here are better than those below; *más inteligente* (more intelligent) was the phrase when used. "God created us with different intelligences," she said, "and the Sibundoy shamans are esteemed by the shamans of the lowlands." As for the Indians who live at the western end of the valley, around the town of Santiago, "They have a different intelligence from us. They love to wander, to Palmira, Pereira, Bogotá, Venezuela. The sell odds and ends of things [*cacharro*] and learn a little medicine from books."

"We're too lazy to leave our town, Sibundoy," broke in her father.

Three years later I was discussing these things with my shaman friend, Santiago, down the mountainside, in the low country.

"Until now the lowland shamans have more wisdom than those above," he said. "Until now nobody has ever heard of a highland shaman turning himself into a tiger, or into a bird and able to fly. That's what Miguel Piranga could do. That's what Casemiro could do. That's what Patricio could do, when he was young." We talked about Patricio, with whom Santiago had taken *yagé* a few times when he was a young man.

"The others were asking him for luck to make money. But I asked him for luck for hunting. 'That's the good one,' he said. 'He who asks for hunting, that is good. That brings all.' Then a guy there said to me, 'You are refusing wealth?' And Patricio explained: 'By no means. Hunting is better than money. That is the good one. That brings everything, he who asks for hunting. Other people come and ask; I want to *chontear* [to kill people with magic blowpipe darts], and to kill *brujos* [witches, shamans]. But it's bad to learn that.' That's what Patricio explained. Magic for hunting is wisdom and it includes

money-making. Hunting magic is more powerful than magic for money because it brings everything, first animals and later money. Magic for money
is only good for money. The other *pinta* allows you to learn how to heal *and*
have luck in getting money." He paused. "Those guys who came down from
the Sibundoy valley, they were the ones there asking for magic to make
money. But I asked for the vision of hunting. Then the shaman said 'that is
the good one. From that comes all.'"

"How does that magic for making money work?" I asked.

"Those who drink *yagé* for that purpose, they're the ones who know that.
They try to damage people out of envy so they remain with nothing but
mal—badness, evil. Do you understand?"

Rosario had told me much the same in her home at the foot of the mountains. "The highlanders have another system," she said, "that gets more
money, no? They traverse the nations and wander here and there with their
berries and nuts saying they can cure when they are really swindling. Their
system is different because they get money easier, and because their curing
is a lie and but a way to get rich with filth!" And by filth she meant sorcery.

Salvador's son was just as scornful about the wandering Indian medicine
men from the highlands of the Sibundoy valley. "They know nothing of
plants," he told me down in the hot country of his home along a tributary
of the Putumayo. "They are illusionists. They go all over the country so as
to make money. Now they go to Venezuela. Some have been imprisoned
there for cheating."

Nevertheless there are some friendly ties between those below and those
above. How else could the latter get the *yagé* they value so highly? Salvador's
wife told me in 1975 how two brothers, healers from the town of Santiago
in the Sibundoy valley, used to come to her house every year just before
Carnival. They would come with their wives and children all the way from
Venezuela where they were practicing magical medicine, flying from Bogotá
down into the jungle, and from there upriver by canoe. They would stay
and drink a lot of *yagé* out in the forest with Salvador, she told me. They
said they did it to get luck and be able to cure. They brought many gifts—
food, clothes, and kitchen utensils like plastic buckets from Venezuela. They
gave us a lot of things, she went on, because they said they made a lot of
money in Venezuela and that they owed this to Salvador who is their *taita*
or father. Then after two weeks or so they would go up the mountain to
their hometown of Santiago, for Carnival, taking one thousand pesos' worth
of very thick *yagé* that Salvador had prepared for them to take to Venezuela.

On the other hand were relationships like Santiago's and Esteban's, in
which the highland healer becomes the implacably envious enemy of the
lowland shaman and may use not only the weapon of the sorcery bundle,
the *capacho,* for which the highland shamans are notorious, but may also
have access to *magia* as well, the noxious power that comes from making

a pact with the devil from books of magic. That was what was said to have happened to Santiago when he refused to sell *yagé* to Esteban, his long-standing enemy from the highlands.

It seemed like a case where a man who had asked for hunting magic was being attacked by a man empowered with the magic to make money. So far the man who had asked for hunting magic has been able to defend himself, although there had been a time when it looked as though he would go under. But what was that *magia* and those books of *magia* all about?

FIFTEEN
The Book of *Magia*

Like most if not all of what I liked to think of as fundamental concepts, nobody was terribly clear about *magia*. Florencio, an old Indian friend, said it had come with the whites and only with them. "They use it to take our land," he told me, adding that wherever he went he always tried to have a root of *chondur* in his pocket; *chondur blanco* because he needed strong magic against the *magia* of the *blancos*, the white people.

There seemed general agreement that *magia* required a pact with the devil *and* the use of magic books. It was unclear whether a powerful lowland shaman using *yagé* could be stronger than *magia*. Santiago had been saved by Salvador. True. But then neither Salvador nor anyone else, when pressed, had made it clear whether or not *magia* was present. Adding more confusion was the fact that whites flock to Indian shamans to be cured of sorcery cast by other whites, and although they don't call this sorcery *magia,* it would seem to amount to the same thing.

When José García's brother, Antonio, was struck ill, thrashing in his bed at night, unable to sleep, struggling with Satan, ambushed in the forest, José García's friend, Luis Alegría, a mulatto migrant to the re-

"He would sit down with the young girl. . . ."

gion, had given counsel. "Look!" he said. "*Magia* is very good. For example *magia* contains a secret that involves the flower of *alhecho*. With this flower you can cure anything! Anything! You can cure whomever, grant good fortune, and everything. Yes! It's a marvel!" That's what José García told me long afterwards.

Then Luis Alegría went on. "Go and buy the *magia*," he advised José García, "and in such-and-such a page look for the secret. With this we too can make the secret so as to ensorcell the sorcerer with the *magia* he himself used!"

Several years after José García told me about this an old Indian woman brought a sad girl to Santiago Mutumbajoy. Every now and again he would sit down with the sad girl and gently chant, sweeping her clean with his rustling fan of leaves. They would be very quiet, the two of them alone in the space of the gentle humming and the sound of the river in the distance breaking itself on boulders and slicing through whirlpools, like the whirring of thought made conscious of itself in the space between words. Someone told me that her father had died recently and kept calling on her mother, who then sickened and died too. Now there were just the young daughters, the healer chanting over them, slowly, quietly.

The father had gone fishing early one morning and had seen a strange person by the riverbank. When he got home he started to vomit and feel feverish. He died within a week.

Much later Santiago Mutumbajoy told me that the father had been studying *magia* from books but wasn't strong enough to engage with the evil spirit whom he had conjured up from the prayers and spells he had learned from the books. You have to be very brave and have strong blood to resist, he said, and as the father was a weak man, he began to die. He came to take *yagé* once or twice. But it was hopeless. He couldn't tolerate the *chuma*, that opening out of the world into dizzying sounds and fragments of smells and colors. With only a little *yagé* he would fall to the floor, screaming and crying out, "Give me the *contra!*"

After he died he kept on coming back to his house and *espantó a la mujer*— I guess we might say that his restless soul kept returning, as happens with the souls of those who die violently or in Satan's embrace, to pull his wife into the same unquiet grave—and she then died too.

With this in mind one would surely be rather foolhardy to follow the advice of José García's friend, Luis Alegría: "Go and buy the *magia*," he said, "and in such-and-such a page look for the secret. . . ."

It was as if *magia*, and more precisely the book of *magia*, were a mythic prefigurement of not only what might be called the commoditization of magic, but of the magic of commoditization too. What we are listening to in these accounts of tormented souls and the buying of magical books is the uneven inscription into the social body of the meaning of being able to buy on a market. The vividness of this meaning is brought about by making magic the commodity under discussion, and by magic it should be here plainly understood that we are talking about knowledge and words, words and their ability to effect things. In effect we are talking about the marketing of a theory of signification and of rhetoric, indeed, not just of knowledge but of what is in a deeply significant sense the knowledge of knowledge that has to remain inaccessible for that knowledge to exist.

As opposed, say, to buying *pinta* from a *yagé* healer as a way (so it is said) of becoming a *yagé* healer oneself, the buying of magic by way of buying a book is a quintessentially anonymous and individualist act, a market transaction in which cash is turned over for standardized knowledge. By contrast, *yagé* knowledge is acquired through immense privation and is quintessentially the accentuation or extension of the substance of the shaman, the donor. It is his *pinta* and part of him. Moreover, it is the antithesis of standardized knowledge and draws its power from the ineffable, from the feeling-tone of shadow and light, innuendo and sudden transformations. Its power is in its style, not in substance. Or, rather, its substance is its style.

Both powers are dangerous for their practitioners, whether in the acquiring or in the practice, but whereas in the case of *yagé* it is the envy of another shaman that is feared, with *magia* it is the personification of an abstraction, of evil itself in the emblem of Satan that is feared, in keeping with the abstract power of market forces themselves. The struggle here is with the ubiquitous and omniscient effluvium of evil, with the miasmic aura of the oppressive, not with this or that particular shaman for this or that concrete fear of envy.

What is fascinating and not just complex here is the way that this uneven inscription into the social body of the meaning of buying on a market entails a discussion from various perspectives, the most important of which is the perspective immanent in colonial discourse with the views of whites, on the one side, and Indians' views on the other—Luis Alegría's advice, if you will, and Santiago Mutumbajoy's story on the other. What is important here is not only the way that *magia* is identified by Indians as intrinsic to colonial culture, but also how what is in effect obtained through the purchase of magic books is the magic of the printed word as print has acquired this power in the exercise of colonial domination with its fetishization of print, as in the Bible and the law. *Magia,* so it seems to me, does not so much magicalize colonizing print as draw out the magic inherent in its rationality and monologic function in domination.

One of the first things told me by Indians in the days after mysterious guerrilla fighters took over the tiny Putumayo town of Villa Garzón in the late 1970s was that the *guerrilleros,* whom the Indians called *bandidos,* burned the papers in the judges' office and the police station. A few years later I sat for a long time watching a young Indian trying to prove to a priest up in Sibundoy that he was really who he said he was and needed his certificate of baptism. But the priest refused because the identity card issued by the state authorities didn't match with the entry in the church's registry, where the young man's grandmother's name appeared as one of his last names instead of his mother's. What's more, his mother was unmarried. It was amazing but it was an everyday occurrence: the young man didn't exist, but the books and papers did.

In B. Traven's book, *The Rebellion of the Hanged,* set in Chiapas, Mexico, the school teacher expounds on his revolutionary ideas:

> If you want us to win and stay winners we'll have to burn all the papers. Many revolutions have started and then failed simply because papers weren't burned as they should have been. The first thing we must do is attack the registry and burn the papers, all the papers with seals and signatures—deeds, birth and death and marriage certificates. . . . Then nobody will know who he is, what he's called, who was his father, and what his father had. We'll be the heirs because nobody will be able to prove the contrary. What do we want with birth certificates. . . . I've read a mountain of books. I've read all that's been written about revolutions, uprisings, and mutinies. I've read all that the people in other countries have done when they become fed up with their exploiters. But with regard to burning papers I have read nothing. That's not written in any book. I discovered that in my own head.[1]

In her ideal-typical account of Siona cosmology, Jean Langdon describes what these Putumayo lowland Indians have told her about the ultimate layers of the universe where a being called *diosu* (compare the Spanish for God, *Dios*) sits with a few "living God people" or angels flying around while he tends to his book (the Bible?) containing all the remedies. Above him in the highest heaven are doves writing on paper. This profusion of book, writing, and paper in the pure clouds above at the colonized godhead of this Indian cosmos then exhausts itself in the utmost nether zone where the cosmic layer of the writing doves gives way to absolute nothingness—except for a tree trunk from which hangs a solitary spirit.[2]

In the dream symbolism of the Sibundoy Indians, according to the priest-ethnographer Castellví, who spent close to half his life in the valley, to dream of papers is a sign that the dreamer is going to encounter a white man and that some misfortune such as a legal suit is going to occur.[3]

But the priests themselves are no less prone than the law to feature in the dream magic of books. When he was dying, passing through the space of death, as he put it, my Ingano Indian friend, Florencio, saw the priests consulting their books for remedies. In the *yagé* vision he told me about wherein he ascended to the Sibundoy valley and saw Indian shamans there dressed in feathers and mirrors, and then the Colombian army dressed in gold, dancing and singing, the next *pinta* that came was one of three bishops in a room full of books, golden books spewing gold—a waterfall of gold, he said.

The eastern end of the passway to the lowland forests formed by the Sibundoy valley is now occupied by a little town called San Francisco. It was founded by the Capuchins in the early twentieth century. In the introduction to Father Jacinto María de Quito's book about its history, published in 1952, we find these words of Father Damián de Odena's, testimony to the glittering *magia* of letters:

> Certainly all the works fashioned by the heralds of Christ remain indelibly written with letters of gold in the book of eternity . . . it is also to the glory of God to record and exalt the prowess of his saints, the works of those who announce "peace and well-being," the conquests achieved by those who sought souls, conquests more precious than gold. To a Father Superior who offered Pope Pius XI a large collection of books and journals published by his monks, the most Holy Father, upon examining them said, "This is worth as much as any mission."[4]

In literalizing these golden sentiments, in seeing the bishops' room of books spewing a waterfall of gold, Florencio redeems his vision with the power of fancy and innocence that the Church effaces. His unofficial vision renders the official one rhetorical. In so doing, the magic is squeezed out of officialdom like juice from ripe fruit.

The book of the Church, nature as the book of the Lord, the books of law, writing, paper atop official paper—these leak magic into the hands of the people they dominate. The symbol of all that is civilized, Christian, and the state itself, writing and books create their counterpoint in the magic books sold in the marketplaces by wandering Indian herbalists and healers from the Putumayo.

Don Benito told me of the mess he got into with one of these books of *magia*. He had left the town of Santiago in the Sibundoy valley when he was a young man, he said, after being cured of *maleficio* with *yagé* by a shaman in the lowlands near Mocoa. Benito's father had been an herbalist and Benito settled into the life typical of men from his town, that of a wandering herbalist and healer—now strengthened, *curado y cerrado,* thanks to his lowland healing. He learned more medicine working as a porter in the hospital of San Juan de Dios in the city of Cali, but was forced to leave, he told me, because of too close a liaison with the head doctor, who was gay. Somehow Benito got hold of a book of *magia* which he determined to put to some good use. It weighed close to thirty pounds and gained five more when the moon was full. In the seclusion of a bamboo grove in the Hacienda San Julián, near the sugarcane plantation town of Puerto Tejada at the south of the Cauca valley, he prepared a talisman according to this book. It involved the killing and cooking of a black cat, but the damned thing backfired creating nothing but trouble, terrible trouble. For over a year he was sick, his money left him, he was hungry, and he had no clients. He went back to the Putumayo, traveled past his mountain home of Santiago and continued down the mountains to the foothills at the rim of the Amazon basin where he once again undertook treatment with a shaman and once again was cured.

Yagé has a spirit. *Yagé* is king of the plants. *Yagé* is the owner of the plants, he would tell me, and he claimed to use it himself in his thriving practice where the plains of the agribusiness Cauca valley meet the foothills to the south. "It opens up a person's spirit," he would say, "and gives mental force." But in his day-to-day treatments he rarely used strong medicines, and when he did, as for a woman from the city of Cali who was crazy, it was with a highland hallucinogen that he called *Tunga Negra.* He used emetics and purgatives in his curing of sorcery, as with the man who had set up a tiny store next door to him, Don Juan, a grizzled old white from the region's capital city of Popayán. Don Juan was the all-too-typical enigma—full of hatred for Indians (and blacks), yet he came to an Indian to get cured. He told me that he used to own a flourishing stall in the marketplace of Popayán until he was attacked through sorcery, lost his money, friends, wife, goods, and, finally, his stall in the market. But Don Benito, the Indian, cured him, with *yagé,* said Don Juan, and he showed me not one but three bottles of *culebritas,* little snakes, he had vomited. Telltale signs of sorcery.

It was a curious situation, the down-at-heel and mean old white storekeeper now cured by the *indio* and, like a parasitic growth, establishing a store by the gateway to the curer's house, taking advantage of the trickle of patients that each day brought. It was a remote spot, close to a railway, just a couple of houses, a bridge over the river, and Don Juan with his wobbly adam's apple and bony elbows like a puppet visible only from the waist up above the counter of his store, sliding back and forth ready to tell the newcomers what to expect, proudly showing off his *culebritas.* At the end of the week hundreds of black peasants would cross the bridge, winding in an endless caravan of people, adults and children, mules, ponies, chickens, and tools, winding in a serpentine around Benito's house and Don Juan's tiny store. Occasionally one or two would drop off to consult with Don Benito, their *compadre.* At the beginning of the week they would return, hooves and feet drumming across the bridge then winding up and over the rim of the western *cordillera* to the thickly forested slopes descending to the Pacific ocean. They were colonizing those far-away slopes, but they still wanted to live in the communities where they had been born, barren red clay for the most part, and not even enough of that anymore. Now and again a small gang of women would work a stream, washing gold, a reminder of the slavery that had put them in those barren foothills centuries before.

There was a "proper" medical doctor who used to come to the nearby village once a week as part of a government service. He charged but half of what Benito did for a consultation. Benito's popularity was in no way due to his being cheaper than the official medical system. He took on illnesses that didn't appear in the official catalog of human distress, illnesses such as sorcery or *maleficio* afflicting adults to *mal de ojo* or "evil eye" killing infants and the newborn. Many mothers brought their tiny babies to him to be cured of *ojo*. Looking over my notebooks for September of 1975 I find, for instance, this entry:

> A white woman aged about 25 came in at 9:30 A.M. to the main room carrying a five-weeks-old baby, a girl, complaining of diarrhea since five days. Three hour journey on horseback. She lives up in the *loma* [foothills] to the east. Don Benito has been working clearing a field for planting *maíz* since 7 o'clock, is tired and dirty, does not wash his hands and he begins to cure the baby. Diagnosis: he puts his left hand over the baby's forehead for about 20 seconds. Takes it away and then places it palm uppermost on the table and stares intently at it for a minute. Asks, or rather asserts, "The diarrhea has been like water!?" "Yes," she replies. Asks another question I can't make out. Then he tells the mother to undress the baby. He puts it on his lap and strokes it around the head with both hands and massages its abdomen. The baby begins to fart loudly. Benito continues massaging for some two minutes, with GREAT CONCENTRATION, and finally says, "The baby is *ojeado!*" The mother nods, says nothing, watching intently all the time. She comes forward to comfort the baby. Benito tells her to desist. He returns the baby to her a minute later and begins, as he always does, to write out a long and minutely detailed list of treatment instructions in his notebook. He tears out the page, reads it to her (green alcohol, etc. etc.) then goes into the back room and comes back with an aguardiente bottle of yellow medicine, something with bismuth, and gives it to her, charging 50 pesos (around a day's wage in the fields of the valley at that time).
>
> Shortly after this comes another woman with a baby with the same complaint. He passes his hand over the baby's forehead and says it has *mal de ojo* but that he hasn't got any more *remedio!* He can only get it on Wednesday. Today is Monday. The mother gives him a 20 pesos advance but he knocks it back saying it he will wait until he gets the *remedio* from Cali. But she says to take the money as it will help him to buy the *remedio*.

What always struck me at Benito's was the informality and interruptedness, very much including the healing, constantly punctuated by domestic activity. All manner of people sat around the patient and Benito in the main room, listening and adding their comments, especially an ancient man who had fled from an old persons' home set up by the government near Cali. He would ramble aloud about his past, sparked off by the discussion between the curer and the sick. He was never told to shut up, an old white man, a penniless refugee, ensconced in the Indian healer's treatment room, plucking at the past as kids wandered in and out or peeked through the curtain behind which burned candles to the Virgin of Lajas and the Lord of Miracles at Buga. Above us all, in lazy ellipses, swung the skull of a great fish, from Venezuela, Benito told me.

Benito often seemed lost in thought, distant and taciturn. It was his wife Carmen who made the place jump. She remembered everyone and everything and always had a crowd around her in the kitchen organized into little tasks. She was a mulatta from the city of Cali where she had made a living selling seafood to restaurants. Years ago she had become terribly sick. It was a *maleficio* made by an envious competitor. She went from healer to healer without success until in desperation she was taken south to the Sibundoy valley and treated by an Indian there. Now she was married to Don Benito and had her own Indian right by her side all the time.

Many young people came to Benito. Their hearts had been broken by an indifferent lover and they had gone crazy. Someone had slipped something into their drink, and only a curer like Benito could make them better. He also made talismans, and now and again got involved in labor disputes in the sugar plantations. Indeed, this was how I first heard of him, when I was living in the sugarcane town of Puerto Tejada in the early 1970s and a black friend of mine working with a gang of ditch-diggers told me the following.

They were being paid by a labor contractor who had a contract with one of the plantations. The contractor and the gang tried to bribe the plantation's tallyman into recording more work than they had actually done. But the tallyman refused, so the gang decided to send my friend all the way, a whole day's trip, to the end of the Cauca Valley to consult with Benito to see if there wasn't a way they could get rid of the tallyman. Benito told my friend to return with mud casts of the hoofprints of the tallyman's horse. It was a considerable expense and bother for people like these who rarely had the bus fare for even a couple of miles. They supplied the casts, and waited. But instead of the tallyman, it was their very own contractor who was eliminated. He lost the contract and with it their jobs. "Maybe we got the wrong hoofprints," my friend remarked.

Some time later his full sister Juana got into a massive row with one of his half-sisters. She was using sorcery to win away her husband, said Juana. She had gone to Don Benito to do this.

Benito was not the only Indian from the Putumayo highlands who had traveled far and found a place in the health and sorcery of agribusiness towns like Puerto Tejada. I would often see two or three such men, sometimes

EL   *Dr. Papus*

EMBRUJAMIENTO

COMO SE PRACTICA EL EMBRUJAMIENTO. — CONTRAEMBRUJAMIENTO.—
QUE DEBE LLEVAR LA PERSONA EMBRUJADA O QUE CREA ESTARLO.—
CONTRA LOS HECHIZOS Y LA MALA INFLUENCIA. — PARA HACERSE AMAR
DE UNA PERSONA AUSENTE Y TENGA DESEOS DE VENIR A VERNOS.—
AMULETOS, TALISMANES, ETC.

with a woman, selling their wares spread out in the street alongside the
marketplace on market days twice a week. Despite the heat the men would
often wear a distinctive *ruana*. A few, generally the older, had their hair cut
in a distinctive "basin-cut" style. Usually their stalls were small and their
goods simply laid on the ground. But no matter how small, prominence was
always given to books of *magia* alongside the roots, barks, heaps of sulfur,
iron filings, and mirrors. They were small but expensive, those books, costing

the equivalent of two days' wages. It seemed to me that they were rarely sold. One I often saw was *The Sainted Cross of Caravaca,* subtitled

Treasury of Prayers
of Enormous Virtue and Efficacy
for Curing all Classes of Pains,
as Much as of Body as of Soul,
together with Countless Practices
to Free One of Sorcery and Enchantments: with Blessings and Exorcisms
Excetera

Another favorite was *The Book of Cipriano.*

The Complete Book of True Magic
or
Treasury of Sorcery
Written on Ancient Hebraic Parchment
Delivered by Spirits to the German Monk
Jonas Sufurino
contains:
The Clavicle of Solomon, Pacts of Exorcism, The Red Dragon
and the Infernal Goat, the Black Hen, School of Sorcery, The
Great Grimorio and the Pact of Blood, the Magic Candle for
the Discovery of Enchantments, Compendium of Chaldean and
Egyptian Magic, Filters, Enchantments,
and Magic Spells

When I walked down the main street of Puerto Tejada the last Sunday of November of 1976 past the market there were three men identifiable as Indians from the Putumayo highlands. Yes! one of them answered, he did have some *yagé.* He sold it to people in Cali so they could *asegurar* and *cerrar,* secure and close themselves off to sorcery and envious persons. He told me he was about to return to the Putumayo and go down into the lowlands to get more remedies and then head off to Venezuela. One of the other men told me that he was trained by a *cacique* (a term widespread in Colombia, meaning chief but not in use in the Putumayo) called Mauricio, near Mocoa in the hot country. On the other side of the street was a man dressed like a highland Putumayo Indian, but with a demeanor quite the opposite of these quietly confident, reserved, occasionally haughty herbal-ists. He was surrounded by a partly cynical, partly gawking crowd and was pacing up and down, gesticulating and berating the onlookers. A galaxy of Catholic medallions hung from his chest and he would break into sounds like Putumayo shamanic chants, interspersed with Christian prayers and songs. On the ground in front of him was paper currency. He was going to cure these bills so they would reproduce more of their kind, and to achieve that he was going to use sacred blood.

"Selling herbs and magical remedies in the different markets of the province."

Putumayo herbalist's stall set up in the Cauca Valley.

In the nearby town of Santander de Quilichao, about the same time, I made the acquaintance of a young woman and man from the Putumayo highlands, Andrea and Luis Miguel, who were selling herbs and magical remedies in the different markets of the province, Monday in Popayán, Tuesday in Silvia, Wednesday in Santander, and so on. They had three children. The one-year-old was carried by Andrea on her back all the time. The other two they left with a "nanny" in Popayán where they rented a wretched room. They spent the night of this market day on the floor of the corridor of one of the kiosks that lined the highway. They got up at 3:00 A.M. to catch the bus for the market in Corinto next day.

Luis Miguel told me he had been trained by Don Daniel, a *cacique* who lived along the Putumayo river below Puerto Asís and with whom he took *yagé* once a week. "You see snakes . . . even tigers!" he said. "It's the salvation of life," declared Andrea as she turned to discuss some medicine with a prospective client. "Because I'm purged with *yagé*," went on her husband, Luis Miguel, "I don't need injections." He paused. "I'm ahead!"

They would go back to their little village in the Putumayo mountains for Carnival, which was beautiful and special. There they would stock up with medicines. Young and inexperienced, they would hardly be thought of as in the major league of herbalists, but in their little bags and bundles spread out on the street there were at least sixty-five different remedies:

- *Linaza*—for fever, they said.
- *Yagé Zaragoza*
- *Yacuma Negra*
- *Misclillo* (a *caracol*) *tatolia*—these last three all used together for the treatment of fright, *susto* and *espanto*. Mix them together in *aguardiente* brandy and blow and spit the mixture over the patient (with *oraciones*).
- A rabbit's foot—for good luck.
- *Gualanday*—for the kidneys. Comes from the hot country.
- *Romero* (rosemary)—for insomnia and nightmares. Make incense with it.
- For diarrhea: *Japio, Granízo* from the *páramo,* and *Guavilla* of the *páramo.*
- *Quina*—for baldness, it comes from the Pacific coast.
- *Barbasco*—a purgative of wood shavings. They say it's from the *páramo* of the mountaintops, but in the Putumayo lowlands we use *Barbasco* as fish poison and it grows along the riverbank.
- *Raíz de China* (China root), looks like knucklejacks—for the kidneys, comes from the *páramo.*
- *Pionía*—for the gall bladder. Very small, polished-looking red and black seeds. Comes from the Pacific coast.
- *Guacia*—for fever and for the liver. Part of the trunk of a tree. Comes from the Pacific coast, they say.
- *Paradero*—to stimulate fertility. Comes from the *páramo,* tiny little knobs attached like bells to a thread of a vine.
- *Tuercemadre*—to inhibit fertility. Comes from the hot country of the lowlands, a twisting corkscrew-like nut with petal-shaped ends.
- For pains of the uterus: *Tamarindo,* from the hot country; *Balsamo Rosado* (pink balsam), from the hot country; *Balsamo Espingo,* from Ecuador.
- *Cedrón Chocuana*—for attacks of nervousness. Comes from the coast, a heavy seed with a nut inside. Scrape a little off.
- *Spingo*—for attacks of nervousness. Comes from Ecuador, from the hot country, a scallop-shaped seed.
- Bear fat—for rheumatism, sold in empty vials that used to contain antibiotic solution for injection. Comes from the Putumayo, "recommended."
- *Bilimento Chocuano*—smelling salts sold in small bottles for colds and headaches. Luis Miguel says he makes this up from seven plants.
- *Chondur de Castilla*—comes from the hot country. Chew it or grind it up in *aguardiente* brandy then spit and blow over the sick person to get rid of *espanto* or *susto* or whatever. (This root is indispensable for the lowland shamans I know. They chew it when divining and curing.)
- *Altamisa,* various sorts—for making baths for the curing of a *casa salada,* a bewitched or ensorcelled house.

- The skin of a snake (of the type known as a *cascabel*), the skin of a rabbit, and the paw of a tiger—serves for many things, possesses a secret, prevents theft.

There were many more plant remedies, and also:

- Rings, whistles, razor blades, mirrors, needles, cotton, hair clips, beads, combs, blocks of sulfur, and iron filings "from a mine in the Putumayo. You use them with other remedies to compose a person's good fortune."
- Little booklets of prayers, many for the spirit of the famous Venezuelan surgeon, José Gregorio Hernández.
- Pictures, colored and framed under glass, of various saints and Virgins.
- Twelve different booklets on magic—little offspring, perhaps, of Don Benito's, which weighed close to thirty pounds (and gained more when the moon was full)?

SIXTEEN
Filth and the
Magic of Modern

From the vantage point of his house by the river in the foothills beyond the sugar plantations and the great groaning mass of humanity sustaining them, Don Benito can afford to be a little snooty. "Nothing but pig stys," he says of the sugarcane towns, rural slums one and all, created by the new agribusiness systems. "Pure filth!" he exclaims. And by filth he means sorcery.

But he could just as well mean filth in the literal sense, because that pretty well summed up these densely packed, unsewered towns of day laborers with neither clean drinking water nor the food necessary to nourish their children, pot-bellied with ascites and roundworms, dying of diarrhea and bronchitis. "On the coast there is food but no money," wail the women migrants who have fled from the subsistence economy of the trackless forests of the Pacific coast. "Here there is money but no food."

There are many doctors and pharmacies in these agribusiness towns. In Puerto Tejada, for instance, there were in 1982 around 30,000 inhabitants, five pharmacies, three of them very large by any standards, and something like twelve doctors. People did not go to folk healers because of an absence or shortage of state-licensed, university-

"On the coast there is food but no money. . . . Here there is money but no food."

trained doctors. Nor were they sick because of a shortage of such doctors and their drugs. Those who went to these doctors would receive huge prescriptions for veritable cornucopiae of pills, capsules, and injectable substances, and return to the same dirty water and food shortage that created the preconditions of the health problem in the first place, preconditions that created a bonanza for the multinational drug companies, in effect carrion living from garbage and offal.

A friend of mine who secured a job as a permanently employed plantation hand, and was thus eligible for health benefits, was chopping firewood and got a splinter in his finger. He went to the doctor and I saw him on his way home. The finger was slightly swollen but hardly anything serious. The doctor had barely looked at his finger, he said, and prescribed steroid tablets (Phenylbutazone, twenty tablets), something called "narcotic 222," and very expensive Lasonil cream containing heparinoid and hyaluronidase to break up and absorb bruising! Even the worst folk healer would be no worse than this type of official medical treatment, and for most people, especially in the third world, this is the type of treatment to be expected, whether for a splinter, the birth of a baby, or a truly life-threatening situation.

My friend Juana had been advised to have her baby—her first—in the local hospital, unlike her mother, for example, who had delivered on the earth floor of a hut in the Chocó forests. Nobody was allowed to enter the hospital with Juana the night she went to deliver, in Puerto Tejada, and a guard saw to it that nobody set foot in that sacred precinct. When she actually gave birth, she told us much later, she was absolutely alone, just herself with this emerging life, nobody else, no nurse, no doctor, no friends, and no family other than that coming out of her. It was late at night. The staff found her in the early dawn with the baby that she and mother nature had delivered on their own. So much for the romance of the third world.

Yet everyone accorded the doctors great respect, and the faith, which indeed was a magical faith, in the medical wonders of modern science, was restrained only by the fact that few could afford it, or afford more than a nibble at it—like the young women who couldn't afford the full month's cycle so instead, with the encouragement of the pharmacist, bought just one oral contraceptive pill, for the night in question. At other times it was not just a question of settling for a part of the whole, one pill instead of twenty-one, but a question of making a cruel choice between who in this morass of sick people should be the one to go to the doctor. My friend Rejina pointed this out in her forthright way.

She made a living of a sort by selling drinks of cold porridge to plantation workers out in the fields on payday. She lived with her three children in one room of an earth-floored three-room house she had built in the town of Puerto Tejada with money won from half a lottery ticket a friend had given her. There was no toilet other than a shallow pit in the small back yard, and there was no water. Her situation was sort of average for that town. She rented the other room to a young woman named Maura who worked sometimes as an agribusiness field hand and other times as a servant in Cali. Maura lived with her little boy of one year, and was pregnant. She and Rejina shared the third room where they cooked on a wood fire on the floor.

I stopped by a few weeks after Maura's baby was born to find both Maura and her one-year-old son sick. She was coughing badly, talking of tuberculosis. The little boy, cast from the breast, ate nothing. He was in an advanced state of starvation, stupefied, as in a trance. Maura had practically no money, just enough for one person to have a consultation at the cheapest health clinic. The new baby's father refused to help, saying the baby was not his. Her mother and sisters across the way were dirt poor and not very concerned at her plight. It was common enough. That left Rejina and Maura discussing what to do.

"If you go to the doctor instead of the little boy going," said Rejina, "then he'll die but you'll survive and so will the baby. But if the little boy goes to the doctor instead of you, then you'll die, the baby will die, and the little boy will probably die too. So it's better you go to the doctor and not he."

As it happened we did find some money so that both mother and son could go to the doctor. He was young, experienced, and enthusiastic. He ordered X-rays. But Maura couldn't pay. He prescribed antibiotics and special protein foods for the little boy. But Maura couldn't pay. And if he took the boy

"We were surrounded by rich fields of agribusiness."

into the hospital for a week or two of intravenous feeding, what then? What would he be going back to?

We were surrounded by rich fields of waving sugarcane and rust-red sorghum set against the blue of the mountains. The soya was turning yellow as it hugged the warm soil. Yet it was planted within a social field that ensured that kids like Maura's were starving to death and that people like Maura, who worked those fields, couldn't buy enough food to live on. No doctor could cure that, not with all the X-rays and antibiotics in the world—not even the Rockefeller Foundation doctors from the United States in the nearby medical school of the University of Valle, who said the problem was that women like Maura were having too many babies.

Yet amazingly awful and absurd as they are, these services supplied by the official medical system and its university-trained doctors, backed by the multinational corporations of "science," agribusiness, and pharmaceuticals, are sought by many. This optimistically desperate search is testimony to a magical attraction, in this case to officialdom and to "science," no less and probably a good deal greater than that involved in the magic of so-called magical medicine.

Existing in the shadow of the economic and scientific might of the United States, this third-world cult of the modern illuminates the magical power inherent in that might and necessary to it. As in the relation between the

Day laborers (*iguazos*) congregated at the crossroads at dawn and were hauled to the fields if there was work (1972).

magic that glistens as gold in the books fashioned by the heralds of Christ
and the books of *magia* sold by Putumayo herbalists, so there exists in these
modern agribusiness towns of landless laborers this curious and deeply magical relation of power between ruling-class reason and the dominated classes
squeezing out the magic implicit in that reason, the magic that makes such
reason socially effective. This squeezing out the magic implicit in the discourse of ruling reason is an art. Even when straight-faced it may imply
burlesque.

Take Brother Walter's hospital in Puerto Tejada as I saw it in 1981, for
instance, when his two black women helpers from the Pacific coast showed
me through because the mother of a friend of mine had gone crazy, and said
it was here, at Walter's place, that she wanted to be treated. She herself
had come from the forests of the Pacific coast a good twenty-five years
before, and now lived precariously from casual day-laboring on the large
farms. Her husband had left her a few years back. She had the two youngest
children to care for, and every so often in the midst of this distress she went
crazy, tearing off her clothes and wandering in the streets, mouthing *pen-
dejadas,* foolish things.

There was no altar in Brother Walter's place, nor were there candles
burning for the miraculous saints and Virgins. But what there was in the
room they called the treatment room was a large blue bulb fixed to an
elaborate wooden shield at eye level against the wall. It was an important
therapeutic device. Draped along the walls, sensuously and beautifully, was
plastic tubing from I.V. sets. Hither and thither in great profusion were
absolutely stunning technicolored advertisements cut out of glossy professional medical journals of the sort to which doctors subscribe. Pictures of
chest X-rays and flesh-toned cross-sections of the human body glistened on
the worn and cracked adobe walls smoothed over with cow dung. A pair of
lime-green rubber gloves clenched two pink kidneys, squeezing golden urine
from their ureters. It was an advertisement for a diuretic: *Made in USA.*
"Don't look at the blue light," warned our guide, "it can cause cancer."

Rejina's aunt, Sebastiana, introduced me to another form of healing with
the magic of modern medicine. She was a cook for one of the sugar plantations and had the right to free consultation with the company's doctor.
She had a sudden attack of colic in her right loin, fever, and burning urine.
He treated her with three intravenous injections and oral ampicillin, a broad-
spectrum penicillin. Two days later she had not improved and her son took
her to a spirit healer in the city of Cali who told her she had a problem with
her kidney and gall bladder and prescribed 800 pesos' worth of drugs to be
bought at any pharmacy—this at a time when the highest rate of pay in the
fields was 50 pesos a day. She was told to return three days later, for her
operation, and was already feeling a lot better when she arrived.

"Why did you need an operation?" I asked.

"Who knows!" she answered. During the operation the spirit healer said,
"Oh! you've got stones in your kidney!" She doesn't know what he did to

Sugercane plantation, 1972.

Pulping coffee, peasant farm, 1971.

her but she had to stay in bed for six days and maintain a special diet. The operating room had many candles burning and an altar. The healer wore a white coat. All the patients were gathered together, praying. He would call and the patients would answer, she told me. Then the healer became possessed with the spirit of José Gregorio. He began to shake and sweat and his voice changed. Everyone was ordered out and one by one they were then called in for their operation. There were about twenty patients and her operation lasted some twenty minutes. The place was called 'El Centro Hospitalario de José Gregorio' after the famous Venezuelan surgeon whose spirit is now invoked by spirit healers all over Colombia.

In the Putumayo, José García and Rosario were very taken with Sister Carmela, and she was a medium for the spirit of the famous Venezuelan surgeon too. It was José Gregorio who had made Venezuelan medicine scientific and modern, so the newspaper cuttings declared to all and sundry from the walls of her spirit center in Pasto. He had introduced the microscope, that which magnifies the invisible, to Venezuela, yet it was modernity that killed him. He was run over by one of the first cars in Venezuela, in 1919, rushing across a street to procure remedies for a poor patient.

The magic of science and industry expressed by Brother Walter's hospital and in the cult of the Brother José Gregorio is a magic that holds out the promise of the power and wealth of the modern world, a promise as yet denied the vast majority of their patients without whose labor and talent there would be little wealth. On the other hand, the magic of practitioners like Don Benito and the Putumayo herbalists speaks to the beginnings of time, to primitiveness itself—as conceived by modernism.

Together these very different healers compose the spectrum of ritual effacement of misfortune afflicting agribusiness towns like Puerto Tejada; co-determining magics, the one cradled in the hope of the future offered and simultaneously denied by the modern world, the other in the dream mythology latent in that hope, drawn on the imagined origins of things.

In his incompleted manuscript on commodity fetishism and the modern European city, Walter Benjamin wrote that "in the dream which every epoch sees in images the epoch which is to succeed it, the latter appears coupled with elements of prehistory—that is to say of a classless society."[1] Certainly there was a passion for classlessness among one set of "prehistoric elements" in the modern agribusiness town of Puerto Tejada, and that was the large grouping of black migrants from the trackless jungles of the Pacific coast. They did most of the tough menial labor, as domestic servants in the cities or as cutters and loaders in the sugarcane plantations. They were fiercely egalitarian and decidedly stamped with primitiveness—quintessentially awkward face to face with civilization. Forming a sort of untouchable class, said to be like apes, contaminated with the smell of fish and unable to speak properly, there was also added to their collective portrait a reputation for sorcery and magical healing. They were alert to the slightest infraction of sharing and equality. Reciprocity was their code. "Here on the coast," went an expression, "one hand washes the other." And they feared and mustered the weapon of the *maleficio* if that code was denied. It was a coastal sensibility, intensified by their having migrated for wage labor.

From the rivers of the coast they brought many secrets. Some secrets came from the old colonial Church frozen in time when the whites left because the blacks would not work for them after the abolition of slavery in 1851. Other secrets came from the Indian shamans who lived along the coastal rivers, the "cholos," who used a *yagé*-like hallucinogen called *pildé*—for "long-distance" work as my friend Otazio, a black wizard from the coastal rivers of the Chocó, told me. The coastal migrants were famous for their poisons and spells with toads, their innumerable *oraciones,* their cures for snakebite, and their superlative art with *maleficios* making the victim's stomach swell to enormous girth, inflating and deflating with the movement of the tides up those far-away rivers. Yes! They were a notorious bunch. Didn't the women down the road in Villarica say that in Cali there were some servants who put a spell on their mistresses; that the servants from the Pacific coast were the ones prone to this? They came and went as they pleased. Some even struck their mistresses!

There were other stories about the way these "primitive" people from the forests over the mountains and by the sea used sorcery to strike at the propertied classes who took advantage of them. I remember the young son of the woman who went crazy every so often telling me how his mother reacted when she was evicted with her four children from the shack in which they lived in Puerto Tejada. They were way behind on the rent and the landlord took the tiles off the roof to force them out. This fragile, troubled woman from the coast then dug a shallow hole in front of the house, in full public view, and into it placed a mass of sorcery substance, soil and bones from the cemetery, and so forth. The house was thence *salada,* bewitched, and the landlord has been unable to rent it ever since, her young son told me with satisfaction.

On the coast the Indian shamans use wooden dolls in their magic. Fifty years ago some Swedish ethnologists said that they found dolls on the coast that were strikingly similar to "fetishes" in central Africa. Be that as it may, in Colombia the dolls are unique to the coast and its magical art, and it is certainly interesting to note that in the stories about the wage-workers on the sugar plantations around Puerto Tejada who allegedly make a pact with the devil to augment their productivity, and hence their wage, the pact is made with the assistance of a wooden doll. The "primitive" influence of the coast would seem decisive in this strange ritualization of the magic of large-scale capitalist production. With the pact with the devil the wage-worker increases his wage without increasing physical effort. But the cane field is rendered barren, as are the wages. They serve only to buy what are considered luxuries and not fertile goods such as land or livestock. Neither women nor peasant producers are said ever to make such a pact, and there is reason for such a denial. Why would the peasant want to render her or his little plot barren, no matter how much they needed money? Why would the women, peasant or landless, want such barren wages when it was her responsibility, so everyone says, to provide for her children, growing creatures? No! The demonic springs into being where the rapid making of a wage-working class exposes and draws out the magic implicit in the commodity fetishism of capitalist culture and its organization of persons as things through the market mechanism. And it is here that the "primitive" makes its strategic contribution—in the form of the black workers from the subsistence economy of the coast, ever sensitive to infractions of equality and to the fine calculus of growth and sterility embedded in the reciprocity economy: here on the coast (but not there on the plantation) one hand washes the other. On the coast there is food, but no money, wail the women. Here there is money but no food; hence "filth" and the magic of the modern, as Indian healers like Don Benito both fear and appreciate.

SEVENTEEN
Revolutionary Plants

Putumayo herbalists combine and distribute the healing plants of Colombia. They bring the rain forests of the Pacific coast to those of the upper Amazon basin, and the cold marshy *páramos* of the mountaintops into contact with the hot lands as well as the temperate zones between. Putumayo herbalists embody this ecology. Wandering from trouble spot to trouble spot, they write the language of magical signifiers across the face of tropical topography. Laid out in dusty streets, bespattered with the mud of passing trucks or mules, their plants are like signatures of a vivid if unconscious mythology about space and race. The magical power imputed to these herbalists as *Indian* and more specifically as *Putumayo* Indian herbalists is an imputation that frames and surrealizes the stranger traveling an enchanted landscape, a mosaic of place-meanings awkwardly correlated through the root, the plant, the piece of bark, with body parts and diseases of those body parts: China root, looks like knucklejacks, for the kidneys, from the *páramo; Pionía,* small shiny red and black seeds from the hot forests of the Pacific coast, for the gall bladder; *chondur* roots with the taste of peppermint, from the Putumayo lowlands and used to treat children with *susto* . . .

These herbalists may also act as healers, transmitting, acquiring, inte-
grating, patching together new words, new spells, new concepts, as they
move from city to city, hamlet to hamlet, coast to coast, charging the new
with Indianness. Like lightning conductors they absorb the envy and sorcery
assailing small communities and neighborhoods of large cities. My mulatto
healer friend Chu Chu was saved, he told me, by one such traveling Putumayo
medicine man.

Some stay in the one place, drawing plants from a large area into their
pharmacies. Antonio Benavides did that. Twice a week you could find him
in the market of Puerto Tejada managing a huge stall of plant remedies, a
heavy-set, middle-aged man who had left the Putumayo highlands twenty
years ago and now lived in Cali. A spectacular mixture of common sense
and make-believe, he would tell me how he regularly went to the Pacific
coast to get 300 different types of plants, including the *yagé*-like hallucinogen
of *pildé*. "Around the *pildé* there are a lot of snakes," he told me, "because
that plant has a lot of power." With a special plant from the coast he could
cure leprosy and cancer. He kept around 4,600 different plants, he said, and
sold 200 to 250 varieties in Puerto Tejada, he said.

Plants are not like the drugs one buys in the pharmacies. They come with
a mystery and one has to pray and concentrate before picking and using
them, he assured me. A well-traveled man by his own account, having sold
plants in Venezuela and Panama, he had studied from the books of magic
too. His parents were herbalists and his aunt, he said, was so famous that
she was taken to the United States from their village of San Francisco in
the Sibundoy valley to see if it was true that Indians could cure crazy people.

"My aunt showed them that she could," he told me as his little boy
wrapped up some leaves for an old black peasant who needed something for
rheumatism, "but she wouldn't show them the secret. She used *yagé* for
curing, as well as other plants. I used to go with her to the forest to gather
plants. But nobody really taught me other than God. It's a hereditary profession. My mother was a midwife, so was my aunt. My uncle was a fixer of
broken bones and a masseur."

"No," he replied to my question, "I did not study under a lowland *cacique*.
I only got to know them when I was a professional *naturalista*." He paused
to attend to a client. "In the first place you have to be alert, clean, and with
a soft heart so you can follow what God has in store for you. Those *caciques*
do know certain things, that's true, but not as well as a *naturalista*. A
naturalista has to keep a sharp watch-out. Why? Because in this world of
ours there is so much envy and greed. How can one be a good doctor when
the doctors from the university heap shit on you? To be a good doctor you
have to be almost a saint. Clean. I used to do a turn with snakes in the
marketplaces. For many years. I am a legitimate *cacique*."

We talked about *yagé*.

"It's got ninety-nine percent of the power of the plant kingdom!" he declaimed, "but you have to be very expert to work with it. I'm not," he confessed. "*Yagé* has its great power by virtue of the Divine Design to transport the spirit to any place in space . . ." and his voice trailed off, picking up again as the conversation turned to the city of Cali, where he had been living for so many years and that had been so good for him. It enabled him to study *la metafísica,* metaphysics, "and for this I don't need *yagé!*"

I guess it was the city that had taught him about astrology. And capitalism, too. When he tried to explain more about *yagé* he would talk about the way it opened up the body, made it awaken by coordinating the bodily forces with those of the stars and the minerals so that the person fused with the *globo,* the universe. But there was also the problem, he said, that capitalism is destroying the *globo* and that the leaders of the world are contaminating it. The people, he said, using the word *pueblo,* are in confusion and ruin. Now there are no more ties holding us together. "It all comes from the Great Powers when they constructed the weapons of war, the *armas bélicas.* They said this was for defense but in reality it was to destroy their very brothers and sisters who could serve later on. And not only in Vietnam," he added, "it's already closing in here." (That was in 1976.)

Up came a black peasant woman from Obando to buy something that would, she hesitated, "*asegurar la vida,* help secure one's life . . . *como la vida hoy en día es muy complicada.*" The sugarcane plantations are spreading rapidly through the peasant plots in Obando, uprooting the interplanted mixtures of peasant crops, cocoa trees, plantains, and coffee trees.

Antonio's reaction to the spread of agribusiness was pretty well the same as that other Putumayo highland medicine man, Don Benito, now perched in the foothills on the very rim of this vast and rich valley. "Good for the rich, bad for the poor," Antonio said. "The fumigation does terrible damage to the culture of coffee and cocoa so the people here have to sell their little farms and become slaves. Often they have to go to other parts to live. The productive plants are being destroyed—the yucca and the plantains. . . . They are becoming sterile."

Referring to his urban-inspired system of metaphysics, that wondrous mixture of *yagé,* astrology, and medieval organicism, he went on: "The human being has to implore the plants of the world to produce, and to produce for everyone. If they don't, then we're all shafted. Everything becomes infested, beginning with the roots. With the failure in the productive sphere there will be the failure of the creative one."

As if reading my thoughts he continued: "The problem with people at the university is that they study only two lines, the economic and the material—of the body and of the spirit, nothing! I am teaching," he added, "I have been teaching people revolution through my work with plants."

EIGHTEEN
On the Indian's Back: The Moral Topography of the Andes and Its Conquest

I want now to ask about history and land-scape, about the way men interpret history and recruit landscape to that task, and about the different but complementary ways that they gain power from these interpretations according to whether they are being carried or whether they are carrying other men over this landscape.[1]

The landscape I wish to depict is the oft-dramatized one of the Andean mountains soaring out of the rain forests in northern South America. It is also a *landscape* of the imagination, an image whose force as well as its form soar from the moral topography of power in society.

As I view this landscape created as much by social as by natural history I am forced to ask whether or not there is a poetics of imagery, sensous and passionate, that is active in binding ruled to ruler and colonized to colonizer. Can we understand the effects of truth in ruling ideologies without taking their poetics into account?

Perhaps in Antonio Gramsci's notion of hegemony we find a starting point. Gwyn Williams notes that this notion emphasizes that in any sociopolitical situation philosophy and practice fuse or are in equilibrium, *one sense of reality* crucial to the moral character of social relations is diffused throughout society, and while it is implied that this sense is directed by the ruling class, such direction is by no means necessarily conscious. Gramsci's concern is with the social basis of *conviction,* which can be reduced neither to interests (since conviction asks what is interesting about interests) nor to the forlorn attempt to separate truth from ideology, but which can be approached, as Michel Foucault envisions, by "seeing historically how effects of truth are produced within discourses which are in themselves neither true nor false."[2]

The phrasing is important. *"One sense of reality* crucial to the moral character of social relations is diffused throughout society." The stress here is away from the clearly focused idea, the hard-edged concept, the Platonic form. It may well include such worthies but the accent falls on a modernist concern for knowledge that is not so clear-cut, explicit, and conceptual—a sense of reality deliberately vague, implicit, and open-ended—sense as in sense impression, sense as in common-sensical implicit social knowledge.

It is this very diffuseness that allows not merely for the oneness of the "one sense of reality crucial to the moral character of social relations diffused throughout society," but for the interplay of multiple perspectives, of submission and of opposition, as well.

We have to push the notion of hegemony into the lived space of realities in social relationships, in the give and take of social life as in the sweaty warm space between the arse of him who rides and the back of him who carries. Even there—perhaps especially there on account of its closeness— one glimpses how the poetics of control operates with imagery and feeling located in the subconscious realm of fantasy (and no less social or historical for so being).

With his notion of a structure of feeling Raymond Williams points to something like the same political and historical force; a communal possession with all the firmness that structure suggests, yet operating in the most delicate and least tangible aspects of our activity and thereby eluding analysis couched only in terms of the well-scored categories of material life, social organization, and the dominant ideas of an epoch.[3]

I take it that a modernist view would stress the possibilities for disjunction, contradiction, and estrangement of structure from feeling, an estrangement in which the firm may yield to the soft but disruptive power of the "most delicate and least tangible aspects of our activity." Such a view would go a long way toward engaging the creative power of chaos underlying the healing artistry of the *yagé*-nights I know. But before we can appreciate that artistry we need first to work through the form it butts against, namely the romance, the ecstasy, and the catharses of the fantasy of order by which the conquest of the New World has been so constantly rendered.

I am of course thinking of Dante's great epic and behind him an age-old movement from despair to grace through the descent into the world of the dead and of evil, a structure of antiphonies in which ideas were generally subordinated to a simple, passionate framework of imagery projected into space and, as Northrop Frye so skillfully and persistently reminds us, confused and identified with it. Far from being restricted to poets and priests, as a vision experienced in trance and in deathlike states, it was frequent enough among the common people to constitute what E. J. Becker calls an epidemic with an enormous influence upon the mental life of the Middle Ages.[4] In this moral topography wherein the cosmos is divided into heaven, the human order, the natural order, and the depths of hell, a person's place is poised on a moral brink from which one either falls into the abyss or rises to the lost Garden of Eden.

Columbus's cartography owed much to the sway of what Frye calls this "stubborn structure." Of note is his letter to the sovereigns Ferdinand and Isabella relating his third voyage in which he identified the swirling mouth of the Orinoco with one of the four rivers flowing from the Garden of Eden, and suggested that what he perceived as his ascent from the mid-Atlantic to be further testimony to the proximity of the terrestrial paradise. Some fifty years later the area he thus indicated of the Amazon basin became the site for the frenzied search for El Dorado, and the angelic natives that Columbus espied suffered dearly. For just as landscape perforce reflected moral topogrphy, so did the races of mankind. The early identification of Indians with angels made by Columbus and the Franciscans was soon inverted into their assuming the status of the demon, both subhuman and superhuman. Their function in the larger scheme of descent and salvation remained, calling to mind that it is only when he meets the devil and mounts his back, that Dante is carried to the terrestrial paradise.

The Text of Conquest

No part of the Andes was more difficult of access to the conquistadors than that known today as Colombia. Such is the opinion of J. H. Parry, Gardiner Professor of Oceanic Affairs at Harvard University, in his work *The Discovery of South America*. The coasts and the jungles were bad enough, and the lowland Indians with their arrow poisons even worse, but it is for the mountains that Professor Parry holds most respect, and it is with them that he begins the story of the conquest of the Muisca kingdom lying far inland on the heights of the savanna of Bogotá. From the Caribbean coast around Santa Marta, he writes,

> the way inland is blocked by the Sierra Nevada de Santa
> Marta, an isolated bold mountain *massif* running up directly
> from the coast to 19,000 feet—a barbican, so to speak, of the
> ramparts of the Andes. Inland the country is extraordinarily
> broken, even by Andean standards. East-west travel is almost
> impossible; even today almost all roads run north and south. In

Pasto the great chain of the Andes fans out into three distinct
ranges . . . separated by rivers . . . flowing north to the Caribbean through deep-cut valleys choked with rain forest. The
central and eastern *cordilleras* are further sub-divided at their
northern ends, the central into several minor ridges which finally dip into the lowlands, the eastern into two well-defined
ranges . . . a huge pair of pincers almost enclosing the Gulf of
Maracaibo. Of the three major *cordilleras,* the central is the
most abrupt, containing many high peaks, though none as high
as the giants to the south.[5]

Lifting us into an animated landscape, this passage sets the scene for a
great tale. These bold mountain *massifs,* barbicans, ramparts, great chains
fanning out alongside deep-cut valleys choked with rain forest, mountains
dipping down, pincers enclosing the gulf—these are not inert lumps of dirt
and granite! They are living creatures and, unlike those "giants" further
south around Quito in the province of the mightly Incan empire which display, as befits imperial mountains, "a majestic symmetry," the Colombian
ones are *bold.*

We should also note how nature is here portrayed as blocking the author
and the people for whom he writes, and is also something that should be
not only whole, but harmoniously whole: the way inland is *blocked* by the
Sierra Nevada; this Sierra is a *barbican* of the *ramparts* of the Andes; the
deep valleys are *choked* with rain forest, and so forth. Nature is here like a
medieval castle that has been secured by one's foe. This portrayal coexists
with a powerful sense of a whole being sundered. Inland the country is
extraordinarly broken; the Andes *fan out;* the ranges are *separated* by rivers;
the valleys are *deeply cut;* the *cordilleras* are further *sub-divided;* ridges *dip
into* lowlands; ranges are a *huge pair of pincers.* And so on. Not only the
Spanish conquistadors but this form of writing itself strains to reconstitute
the totality thus sundered in countless ways.

The first and most significant conquest was that of Gonzalo Jiménez de
Quesada, who set out from the Caribbean coast with 800 Spaniards and 100
horses in 1536. By far the longest part of their arduous journey was through
the lowland jungles. Ten months later the 166 surviving Spaniards dragged
themselves and their remaining 60 horses up 2,700 meters to assume their
ascendancy over the Muisca kingdom, where they were held to be gods born
of the sun and the moon. The story has been often told, and Parry tells it
well by stringing together quotations from the colonial chroniclers to achieve
the desired effect. First comes the always reliable Oviedo (in Parry's mas-
terful translation):

I have been thirty-four years in the Indies and know whereof I
speak. I make bold to say that nowhere in the world have
Christians endured greater labours and worse discomforts than

did the Spaniards in the Indies; and certainly these soldier-sinners, fighting by land and water against savages, against sickness, against hunger and thirst, against heat and cold, often half naked, without shoes for their horses or themselves, through deserts and swamps, through thorny scrub and tangled forest, cutting their way with knives and axes, bruised and weary, suffered daily more hardships than I can adequately describe.

The Indians in that land travel mostly by water. On land, the forest is so thick and so tangled with underbrush and creepers, that at best one can make only about two leagues [7.2 miles] in a day; and each day of this arduous march, more men died or fell sick, without any possibility of remedy, having no beds and no shelter against the incessant rain. . . .

Besides these hardships they were constantly harrassed by the forest Indians; a number of Spaniards were killed in these skirmishes. The rivers they have to cross were infested with crocodiles, and the forests were full of jaguars. Three Spaniards were dragged down by the crocodiles, and another three carried off by jaguars.[6]

But, Parry warns, they still had to scale the mountain. Their relief when they topped the savanna to find what he calls the "promised land" is captured by their chant:

Great land; Great land
Land that will overcome our suffering
Land of gold, land of goods,
Land to make a home forever,
Land with overflowing food
Land of towns, flat and clear,
Land of clothed people . . . .[7]

Then comes the poet Castellanos:

The hungry saw themselves standing among ripening crops . . . the naked saw themselves surrounded by people dressed in gaily colored cottons, orderly settled people—how different from the savages of the swamps and forests they had left! Some, as I have heard, thought that with their weakened forces, . . . they could not hope to conquer so numerous a people . . . but our valiant man of law [Gonzalo Jiménez], with the weary people he had with him felt able to conquer the entire world.[8]

Castellanos is further cited to indicate the paradisal quality of the now conquered mountain kingdom:

> All the land within the confines of this hidden country is under
> a benign influence. It has gold and silver, copper, lead and pre-
> cious stones. Its climate is always temperate and pleasant . . .
> though much of the land is high and open, it easily grows
> wheat and corn, vegetables and fodder, and now also we have
> much cattle in abundance. . . .[9]

Nowhere in the world have Christians suffered as much as here. Not only have they suffered but they are sinners, soldier-sinners, locked in combat with jungles, savages, sickness, hunger, crocodiles, and jaguars. Many die, and as Pedro de Aguado informs us, many die because of the poisoned arrows of the savages which kill them, trembling, convulsing, raving, losing their reason and saying bold and terrible things of dubious faith. But their leader pushes on, feeling he can conquer the entire world. From the jungle they made their desperate ascent hauling the horses in cradles of creepers, and after this enormity of suffering are blessed as gods with a paradise, a kingdom, and an easy victory.

Of especial importance to this New World version of the theme of descent, ascent, and salvation is the way by which the tropical hell of jungle and jungle Indians is so clearly opposed to the terrestrial paradise of the highlands above. The imagery proper to each realm, as well as the cycle of death and rebirth connecting them, reappear persistently down through the ages—as we shall see in curing visions of poor white colonists, Indians, and Capuchin missionaries in the twentieth century in the Putumayo.

The Dazzling Beauty of Death That Was America

Parry's tale can be rounded out with that of a Colombian historian, Joaquín Tamayo, writing in 1938 in the official organ of the Colombian Historical Association. The first phase of Tamayo's narrative takes Quesada and his men through the swamps to the left bank of the Magdalena River where they halted for weeks "at the limits of the known universe," overcome by growing despair and entranced by the jungle, depicted by Tamayo as

> a symphony of twilight shades and dissonant chords, murmur-
> ing of the river, songs of birds, humming of insects, chattering
> of monkeys, deafening monotonous clamor of the jungle, soli-
> tude in the land, silence in the air, terror in the men, repugnant
> smell of stagnant creeks, impassable forest, rotting trunks, resi-
> dues of organic putrefying life, heat fierce as fire, the dazzling
> beauty of death, the pain of sun-scorched skin—that was
> America, so pondered by navigators and wily conquistadors.
> Fever came. . . .[10]

Seven months later on the banks of the Opón River they found manufactured cakes of salt, which, writes Tamayo,

similar to the grapes in the land of the Bible, opened their eyes
to new horizons, soon to be conquered. . . . This day of February 1537 saw the end of the most transcendental passage
through the jungles. In pursuit of their ambition for gold, Quesada's soldiers appearing like demons, sick and shameless,
clambered through the impassable forests in whose chinks of
light they nourished the fantasy of their oncoming victory. Only
one other ascencion of glory is remembered in Colombia equal
to this of Opón. . . . Cavalry and infantry overcame the last
few meters of the unnamed land separating the ancient from
the new world: they had finally conquered. Great Land! Land
of Blessings! Clear and serene; Land that will see the end of
our travail. . . .[11]

On his return to Spain Quesada suffered ignominy and a barrage of law
suits. "All he got from Charles the First," writes Tamayo, "was the right to
bear a coat of arms—lions, mountains, and emeralds in a field of gold—
heraldic insignias of no economic utility."

After years of struggle he regained royal favor and returned to the colony
where, as an old man in 1569, he orgainized the mightiest of all expeditions,
this time through the plains of eastern Colombia. He emerged after three
years with no gold, having lost most of his men and horses, planning yet
another expedition in search of El Dorado. But he was too old and sick. He
retired to a provincial town, alone but for the expeditions that shone in his
brain: "the luxury and pleasures of the fantastic city of Manao, the streets
and tiles of gold, palaces built of precious stones, purple clothing, spellbinding maidens, the sacred mountain on whose seven peaks giants guarded
the treasure of the Golden Man."[12]

Tamayo concludes his homage:

Eternally disillusioned, Don Gonzalo Jiménez de Quesada ap-
preciated the fate of his fortunes. He knew beforehand the destiny of human greatness—a bottomless abyss, in which, with
the passage of the centuries disappeared men and illusions—
and in his indifference to vainglory, in his disaffection towards
earthly existence, grieving his destiny, he had engraved on the
stone of his tomb these words:
I await the resurrection of the dead.

Horses and Porters

It was not Indians who carried the conquerors across the Andes, but horses.
Indeed, horses were so important that at least on one occasion, as during
Diego de Almagro's expedition in the southern Andes, instead of carrying
the Spanish, the Indians were forced to carry their horses on litters. It was
only later, when the conquest was consolidated, that they horse gave way

"Heraldic insignias of no economic utility. . . ."

to the more sure-footed mule and that in Colombia the mule gave way to the even more sure-footed Indian as the bearer of men.

The Spanish made much of the terror inspired by the horse, attributing to it the ease of their victories. Yet the Spanish themselves were enthralled by the horse, so aptly illustrated in the art of the times, by the medieval romance of the knight, and by the still prevailing use of the term *caballero* or horseman to indicate a gentleman of rank. The care with which artists seated their kings and noblemen in the saddle of power was no more considerate than the care Spanish captains lavished on their steeds. Moreover, colonial law largely forbade to Indians and blacks the use of the horse.

In the vast expanse of the Andes under the sway of the Inca, the Spanish found marvelous roads and bridges making it easy for their horses, which otherwise would have been next to useless. Yet they still required masses of Indian women and men to serve as porters. Sebastián de Benalcázar took thousands with him north to Quito and beyond, for example, and the great expeditions in search of El Dorado in 1541 took many more.

This fabled city was then held to lie somewhere in the jungles just east of the Andean cities of Quito and Pasto, in an area bounded by the Napo, Putumayo, and Caquetá rivers. Gonzalo Pizarro's disastrous venture involved his leading 4,000 Indians down the eastern slopes of the Andes to perish in the jungle-clad foothills. At the same time, Gonzalo Jiménez de Quesada's brother, Hernán Pérez, set out from Bogotá in search of El Dorado with 6,000 Indian porters (all of whom were said to die), 260 Spaniards, and almost 200 horses. Like Pizarro, he tortured lowland Indians he encountered on the way to the Caquetá and Putumayo drainage, plaguing them as to the whereabouts of the Golden Man and his city of gold. The jungle Indians around Mocoa at the base of the Andes, said to be cannibals who fiercely resisted the Spaniards, told him that the golden land lay close by and up in the mountains rising to the west in a land called Achibichi. When Quesada's tired and sick men ascended the Andes from Mocoa, they found themselves in the beautiful Sibundoy valley with its carefully tilled fields but no gold, and a little further to the west, to their chagrin, lay the town of Pasto, recently founded by Benalcázar, Quesada's archrival in the search for El Dorado.[13] The circle of fantasy and destruction had closed, but the legend of El Dorado survived in a curious space of jungle forays and mountainous ascents that would weigh heavily on the backs of future generations of Indians down to the present day.

Indian Carriers

As he struggled with his mules across the high pass of the *páramo* of Assuay in Peru in 1801, Alexander von Humboldt forlornly observed remains of the Inca road upwards of twenty feet wide and paved with well-hewn blocks of black-trap porphyry, which surpassed any of the Roman roads he had seen in Italy, the south of France, or in Spain. With vexation he noted that not only had the Spanish neglected to maintain these roads, but that they had wantonly destroyed them to gain stone for other purposes, leaving him to flounder through bogs and risk his manuscripts and dried plants fording the now bridgeless cascades.[14]

In Colombia there had been no such roads as the Incan ones. Yet the rugged terrain was crisscrossed by Indian trails sustaining a dense traffic in salt, slaves, gold, and cotton, prior to the Spanish conquest.[15] Spanish mercantilism dismembered the economic unity that had prevailed, and their roads there, considered the worst in the Indies, were testimony to this. "It is believed that not in the entire world are there worse roads than in this province," wrote a sixteenth-century official traveling in Popayán, and even the most frequented road, from Honda up to Bogotá, was described in the late eighteenth century as "a road the very sight of which will horrify your excellency[16]." Furthermore, upkeep of trails demanded much labor yet the Indian population was in sharp decline and owners of African slaves were loath to lend out their precious *piezas* for public works. Indian trails had not been meant for horses and mules who soon turned them into impassable quagmires so that by the late eighteenth century the Indian carrier reappeared in certain regions as a mode of terrestrial transport.[17] With the switch to laissez-faire policies and new types of exports such as tobacco and cinchona bark, which replaced gold after the War of Independence and abolition of slavery, the roads declined further as but a tiny number of privileged enclaves were bound by riverine transport to European ports, leaving the vast remainder of the country a mosaic of autarchic units. "If we advance further afield to the eastern and western ranges of the Andes," wrote an embittered and distinguished ex-slave owner from his seat in Popayán in 1857, "we will find ourselves in the midst of jungles overgrown and inhabited by reptiles, abandoned trails, mute but eloquent witness to the decadence of our internal commerce."[18]

The mountains loomed large in both the political economy and the imagination of this extensive republic. The early nineteenth-century British resident, Charles Empson, something of a romantic poet and given to quoting Byron, has left us a lively account of the song-duels between lowland and highland porters at their point of meeting and separation where the plains of the Magdalena meet the steep slopes of Andes.[19] "Nothing can equal the vast, the stupendous sublimity of the scene presented at this station," he wrote, "where the land of Parrots, Mockingbirds, Lizards, Monkeys, and Mackaws" gives way to the summit of the giant Andes, "those ribs of the world" whose changing colors "betray emotions that language could not reveal." The mountain porters begin (in Empson's rendering):

Farewell, farewell ye lowland steers
Ye never can be cavaliers
Like us the hardy mountaineers
     Adios! Adios! Adios!

The sluggish blood creeps through your veins
As turbid streams glide through the plains
Until a stagnant pool remains.
     Adios! Adios! Adios!

Like the pure breeze our thoughts are free:
Ye bear the stamp of slavery;
Respiring foul impurity.

To which the lowland porters responded,

Vagabonds, fly to the clefts of your mountains,
To monkeys and apes, who serve you for rations;
They're spoiling your homes, and polluting the fountains
Ye drink from, whilst eating your tender relations.
     Go! Go! Sinners!

All nature will, shuddering, your friendship disclaim:
Skulk back to your pestilent climate with shame!
     Go! Go! Sinners!

And when Captain Charles Cochrane of the British Navy visited the newly created House of Representatives in the fledgling republic, he found it to consist of two parties—the *Mountain* party and the *Valley* Party! The members of the former were mainly priests, while the Valley Party was of the Liberal persuasion. A priest of the Mountain Party had just caused the Valley Party a good deal of mirth when he solemnly declared that the highland city and capital of Bogotá should resume its ancient colonial title of Sante Fé, as "tending to evince its gratitude to Heaven for accorded mercies, and divine deliverance."[20]

Cochrane found the roads of Colombia very bad in his travels in 1823. There was not a single carriage road and there was no traveling in any sort of vehicle beyond a mile or two out of Bogotá. The viceroy had formerly had a carriage, but in 1823 the capital boasted but two gigs. In his survey of Colombia for the British Government in 1824, Colonel J. P. Hamiltion was also appalled at the state of the roads, which added further proof, if such was necessary, of the decadent corruption of Spanish rule. Observing that most roads were indebted to the earlier work of Indians, he concluded:

All improvements of the means of transportation were checked
by the old Spaniards, since it was evidently the policy and
great object of the court of Madrid, that the different provinces
of these extensive colonies in the New World should have as

little communication as possible with each other, in order to keep them in ignorance of their strength and resources. . . . I trust that the age of barbarism is ended at last, and that ere many years have elapsed, the traveler and merchant will be able to traverse this vast continent from the Atlantic to the Pacific with facility.[21]

The barbarism had yet to end, however, and the most distasteful reminder of it to the colonel's eyes was that of using Indian *silleros* to carry people on their backs across the Quindio pass, the principal east-west axis of the country. There were three to four hundred of such men stationed at Ibague, said to gain much money, dissipate their earnings in drunkenness, and seldom live beyond the age of forty, dying from the bursting of a blood vessel or from pulmonary complaints. "I have been told," wrote the colonel, "that the Spaniards and the natives mount these chairmen with as much sang froid as if they were getting on the backs of mules, and some brutal wretches have not hesitated to spur the flanks of these poor unfortunate men when they fancied they were not going fast enough."[22] Indeed, an oft-recounted story concerns an otiose official spurring on his *sillero,* who became so angry that he bent forward and hurled his tormentor into the abyss below.

The normal load for a porter was around 100 pounds, while some were known to have carried 200. Even with these weights they were said to climb the mountains with the greatest ease and seldom stop to rest. Captain Coch-

SILLEROS IN THE QUINDIO.

"It was best to ride asleep or read a book." (From Isaac Holton, *New Granada: Twenty Months in the Andes,* 1857.)

rane described the *silleros* as "never stumbling, and seldom halting, climbing up the mountains, and sometimes running, when the ground will permit. They are entirely naked except a handkerchief around the middle."[23] Of course, there were comments upon their good looks, fine build, and intelligent countenances. The Connecticut Yankee, Isaac Holton, who traversed the Quindio Pass on muleback and his own legs in 1852, noted that the rider had to keep absolutely still lest the *sillero* fall.[24] It was best to ride asleep or read a book.

Colonel Hamilton refused to mount Indians. Nevertheless he was weighed in at the beginning and was much amused by his appointed *silleros* eyeing him all over. When asked by the local official what they thought of their load, they said they had carried far heavier men, and from what the official had told them had expected to find the English "Consul-General" a much greater personage. He stubbornly walked the nine days over the pass. Captain Cochrane, who made the same journey a year earlier, found that when the government needed carriers it was custom to imprison the required number until the day of departure, when they were put under the charge of soldiers and torn from their families for five to six weeks at a time with scanty provisions and no pay. This reflected what Holton considered to be the most amazing problem of political economy he had ever tried to solve: "How to nerve a naked vagabond up to almost superhuman exertions, day after day, in a land where starvation is impossible."[25]

As they labored through the mud these nineteenth-century foreign travelers soon found one good reason why well-to-do Colombians preferred to ride Indians. The roads were so bad, even in the dry season, that the normally sure-footed mules were endangered and outstripped by human carriers. Hamilton soon had to abandon his mule and wade through the mud in which he got stuck and from which the peons hauled him. Several times he lost his footing while his companion, who stuck to his mule, was knocked off its back six or seven times by branches when passing through the narrow galleries. Through overusage the roadway had sunk up to thirty feet below its original level to form dark tunnels up to two miles in length and barely three to four feet wide with fierce vegetation crowding the sides. Captain Cochrane had to lay his legs along his mount's ears for fear of being crushed and peons had to hack the way so the mules could pass. With remorse he observed how his companion traveled safe and dry on the back of an Indian, and eventually he too had to dismount from his mule.

When he came to climb the western chain of the Andes to inspect the gold mines of the Chocó, he overcame what was left of his bourgeois principles and mounted a *sillero*. Even so, the discomfort was considerable. "How often, whilst I was scarcely able to keep my seat in the chair from the soreness of limb, and the rain falling in torrents, and drenching me to the skin, did I wish myself safe out of these mountains!—how often did I vow

E. Finden sculp.

VIEW OF THE PASS FROM QUINDIO,
IN THE PROVINCE OF POPAYAN, & CARGUEROS (OR CARRIERS) WHO TRAVEL IT.

Published March 1827 by John Murray, London.

"View of the pass from Quindio, in the province of Popayan & cargueros (or carriers) who travel it." (From John Potter Hamilton, *Travels through the Interior Provinces of Colombia*, 1827.)

"Precipitous Descent of a cordillera of the Andes in the Province of Choco." (From Charles Stuart Cochrane, *Journal of a Residence and Travels in Colombia during the Years of 1823 and 1824*, 1825.)

never to cross them again."[26] Extremely galling was his dependence on the *sillero* and porters, who held their masters at their mercy. They were notorious for deserting and would always loiter, complaining of strange fevers and rheumatism of the neck. From these heights of suffering the end to Cochrane's journey was dramatic. Around noon his *sillero* turned suddenly to climb down an almost perpendicular precipice backwards. While Cochrane faced a 2,000-foot drop his carrier descended, clinging to tree roots and calming his terrified passenger.

On reaching the lowlands our traveler saw nature in a new mode, confirming, as is not uncommonly nature's wont, heart-felt views of social philosophy. The beautiful jungle of evergreen creepers matted together the foliage of the trees to mount their tops and hang fantastically in elegant clusters and festoons agitated by every breeze—somewhat, may we suggest, like the rider of the *sillero* himself. "Such is the great luxuriance of nature," wrote Cochrane,

> that each shrub or tree weakens or destroys its neighbor, by its excess of produce, which is greater than the space will admit. One plant springs up to destroy its predecessor, and is doomed to the same fate itself by the growth of its successor. It appears as if a war existed amongst plants, similar to that which devastates the human world, and prevails even amongst brutes and insects. All strive for mastery, and the weak yields to the strong, who in his turn, is subdued by a stronger. It is a curious fact that all nature appears warring with itself; whether we contemplate the sea, the earth, or the air—rational or irrational beings, all is at war with its own species. Why it should be so—what good or great object is gained by it, we know not; we only perceive that all are under some irresistible influence, and impelled by some invisible power.[27]

What could be more natural? At the end of his dangerous descent on the back of an Indian, our captain of the British Navy finds himself standing on his own two feet amid a jungle animated by the invisible power and irresistible influence of none other than Thomas Hobbes—with the addition of a tropical yet malevolent beauty unknown to Mr. Hobbes but which a little later would inspire another famous Englishman by the name of Charles Darwin.

And to Isaac Holton descending into the Magdalena valley there was another sort of beauty to be found, not in the lowlands but on the mountain. "Once I caught a view, through a gap of trees, of the mountain beyond, and of the distant plain. I was in a deep shade of trees and clouds; the distant scene lay in bright sunshine, but covered with a mantle of that blue scarcely seen except upon mountains. No painter would have dared to color it as I saw it. It looked like heaven."[28]

The *sillero* caught the eye of the foreign painter elsewhere in Latin America, as in this work of Jean Frédéric Maximillien de Waldeck, *Being Carried over the Chiapas,* exhibited in the Salon of 1870. From the collection of Robert Isaacson, New York.

"It looked like heaven." Holton's table of altitudes, edible plants, and place names in the Colombian Andes (mid-nineteenth century).

The magic of mountains: von Humboldt's fantastic cross-section of Ecuadorian volcanoes relates growing zones to an interplay of altitude and temperature. A supreme
figure of the European Enlightenment, von Humboldt clearly displayed the dependence of the science of his era on Romanticism. The mountains depicted here are
similar in form to those that cross-cut Tumaco, Pasto, and Mocoa in Colombia.

The Putumayo: The Devil's Paradise

In the summer of 1913 an eminent Scotsman named A. C. Veatch crossed
the Quindio pass in but half the time it had taken Hamilton in 1824, yet
during the rainy season the trail was still a nightmare and "nothing but a
graveyard of animals and men." *Silleros* were not in use except by some
women and children, but, Veatch went on to note, Indian carriers were still
in use in less developed regions, some carrying incredible loads up to 350
pounds.[29]

To one of those regions we now turn, where Indians claim that their
grandfathers did indeed carry up the Andes from the Amazon basin to Pasto
loads of 200 pounds of rubber, not to mention the occasional Capuchin priest.
This was the Putumayo around the time of the rubber boom and the atrocities
recorded by Walter Hardenburg and Sir Roger Casement. The rubber-rich
forests in the lowlands there had long been a bone of contention between
the Peruvian and the Colombian governments. It was not merely a rivalry
over rubber, of course, but a passionate matter of patriotic pride, and it
erupted into war in 1932.

"This task was entrusted to Capuchin monks. . . ."

At the turn of the century and after some five decades in opposition and enfeebled by civil wars, the Colombian Conservative Party (descendant of the Mountain Party that caught Captain Cochrane's eye in 1823) was now in power following its decisive victory in 1901 over the Liberals in the War of One Thousand Days. Peace settled heavily over the land. Foreign investment soared. The shackles binding the Catholic Church were broken and Church and State arose triumphant from the liberal ashes of the nineteenth century as the hinterlands aswarm with the heathen were given over to the fishers of men to rule and to rule absolutely. Nowhere was this holy alliance more felicitous than in the Putumayo, where the potential wealth of rubber demanded a strong and visibly Christian presence to keep Arana's brutal rubber company esconsed in Peruvian territory south of the Napo river. This task was entrusted to Capuchin monks from Barcelona, invited to the region by the bishop of Pasto in 1893. The landscape that awaited them was far from a *tabula rasa* awaiting their inscription. But it did require their energetic presence to bring those inscriptions to life.

Already in 1855 there was an aura of the mysterious unknown shrouding the Putumayo. Already it was known as a source of medicines and savage tribes. The priest Manuel María Alvis had his impressions of his Putumayo explorations published in 1855 in Popayán (and in the journal of the American Ethnological Society in 1860):

At a time [1854] when the nation was seeking to revive on the field of battle its almost extinguished freedom, an unknown priest, faithful to the civilizing mission confided only to the Christian apostle, crossed desert mountains, defied death disguised under a thousand forms, and surprised the Indian in his hut, investigated his habits, studied his customs, learned his language and, not content with this, transferred to paper the knowledge he obtained.[30]

But before he could surprise the Indian in his hut and investigate him the scene had to be set, in a rite of activating passage:

Passing the craggy and extended cordillera that divides the province of Neiva from the vast wilds of Andaqui, the traveller is moved on finding himself separated from the civilized world, and in contemplation of an immense and unknown country, inhabited by barbarous tribes, of which a very small proportion have any intercourse with the inhabitants on the other side of the mountains.

We should pause for a moment. It is silent in those high hills separating civilization from the barbarous tribes. It is also the beginning of anthropology, and Alvis supplied an appendix entitled "Remedies Used by the Indian."

Aguayusa	is heating, and good for those who are poisoned. The burnt leaves are given with barley water and honey to women who suffer from amenorrea. Boiled and mixed with the grated bark of a vine called *yoco*, it is good for dysentery.
Aceite de Maria	mixed with balsam it is applied to ulcers.
Cobalongo	good for epilepsy[31]

Yet the good father made it clear that he was not to be duped by the quackery of these lowland Indians:

Every morning by daylight the Indians are out on the banks of the river taking *yoco*, and telling their dreams during the night—all these referring to their luck during the chase of the [coming] day. After breakfasting they go out armed to hunt the tapir, or the birds they have seen in their dreams, in which they have the greatest confidence. This belief is inherited from their forefathers, and they hold it as a treasure in their bosoms; but their dreams are never directed to any object other than that of gaining food. Their doctors are accustomed to taking an infusion of a vine called *yoge* [i.e. *yagé*?] which produces the same effect as the *tonga* or *borrachero,* and under the illusion produced by this intoxication they believe they see unknown

things and divine the future. The greater part of these quacks
pretend they have in the woods a tiger which tells them everything, and they devote themselves to their profession with as
much attention and minuteness as if it were a real science.
They believe that the tiger is the devil, pretending that it
speaks to them; and they are so absorbed with their chimeras
that they become themselves the earliest believers of their own
fictions.[32]

Yet their poisons were certain, be hastened to point out, and they killed
without scruple any person they hated.

Twenty years later the French botanist Edouard André presented the
articulation of the marvelous with the real in a different manner. He was
told that the trail was so bad from the city of Pasto across the Andes to
Lake Cocha and thence to the eastern slopes of the Andes and the Putumayo
lowlands that the Indians themselves called it "The Monkeys' Trail." Only
Indians were dexterous enough to use it, particularly the Mocoa Indians
from the eastern foothills of the other side of the craggy cordillera, who
were important, he was told, to the economy of the city of Pasto because
they carried up from the Amazon lowlands dyes essential for the making of
woolen and cotton ponchos, Pasto's main industry, and a special resin of
barniz used in what was Pasto's second most important industry, cabinet
making.

Thus these dreamers with their exotic remedies and poisons were crucial
providers for the city's industry. Perhaps it was there in that intersection of
work and the dream-work that further trails of association were established
linking the remote forests on the other side of the mountains to the city's
workshops and looms, ever more firmly, ever more transcendentally, binding
fantasy and storytelling into the one landscape of city and country, civilization and savagery.

"Finally we reached the Monkey's Trail," recorded André, along which
it was only possibe to proceed provided they did not detach themselves for
an instant from the footprints of the Mocoa Indians. Up and up they went,
often on all fours, scrambling in the mud, slipping between roots, sinking
into swamps. High up at 3,200 meters the trail became a canyon many meters
high covered by an interwoven fabric of branches and roots. It was a veritable
catacomb, André said, which the Indians call *el perro caruncho* and into
which they hurl themselves fearlessly.

At the entrance to this "capricious subteraneity" was a small niche with
crucifixes. "Now and again a greenish ray of light slipped into the dark
pathway whose walls, covered with hepatic lichens, mosses and hymeno-
phyllas, produced one of those fantastic effects impossible to describe."

Impossible to describe. That is where the work and the dream-work collide, where myth filters its greenish rays into dark pathways secured by
fearless Indians' footprints.

In the marshes of the Cocha. (From Edouard André, "América Equinoccial," 1884.)

Once through the catacomb they reached the top of *La Cruz,* the Cross, "the culminating point from which is glimpsed the magnificent panorama of Lake Cocha." It was close to religious ecstasy, to an overflowing orgasm, nature erect and spraying droplets dribbling down its hot flanks to form the mighty Putumayo River.

> What a striking spectacle! Around us vapor constantly condensed on the *páramo,* decondensing into a fine rain made iridescent by the sun's rays giving incomparable freshness and tints to the vegetation. To the left the volcano of Bordoncillo or Patascoy with its erect cone displayed its flanks covered with ignaceous material, still threatening, from which originate the springs that eventualy form the Putumayo or Isá, one of the most important affluents of the Amazon river.

The Indians held the dull roaring of the volcano in superstitious terror,
noted André, and his little group encountered on the trail right there in that
resplendent place two Mocoan Indians who stood stock still—perhaps amazed,
as André put it, that some white men had dared to penetrate their dominion.
They were two women, mother and daughter, carrying up to Pasto medicines,
resin, dyes, hammocks, and other things from the hot country.

> During the conversation I drew the type of that ugly creature
> and took down her characteristics: color, shiny carbonated;
> nose, flat, curved, and fine at its extremity; big mouth, well
> made and pretty teeth; oblique eyes; hair regular length,
> greasy, lank, black, and shiny falling in big strips behind the
> ears onto the shoulders; arms and legs thick and meaty, hands
> and feet fine and nervous and shoulders very broad.

Obviously the *naturales*—the natural people—did not inspire as did the
natural landscape. Yet surely there was something human about them too?
They were, after all, terrified by the volcano's roar and in answering the
questions put to them by the priest in André's party their voices were sweet
and full of respect. Upon leaving, they kissed his hand.[33]

After the expulsion of the Franciscans by royal decree in 1767 there had
been no missionary activity in the Putumayo region except for a brief in-

School for Indian girls and some whites in Mocoa around 1912. The Indians are
dressed in clothes donated by the "Dressers of Lourdes" in Bogotá.

terlude of seven years between 1842 and 1850. Still, there were a few parish priests, such as the one in André's group who was in fact the priest of Mocoa down in the eastern foothills on the other side of the cordillera. Yet what a multitude of good works remained to be done! When the Capuchin monks came, at the end of the nineteeth century, "with no obligation other than their desire to spiritually aid the Indians and whites dispersed in the immense and secular jungles," as Father Canet de Mar expressed the matter in 1924, they estimated there to be around 9,000 Catholics, of whom 3,000 were whites and the rest Indians, and about 40,000 *infieles* or infidels disseminated along the rivers and tributaries of the Caquetá, Putumayo, Aguarico, and the Napo.[34]

In 1899 there were only five Capuchins at work. In two and a half years they performed 1,010 baptisms and 263 marriages. By 1927 there were 62 missionaries, 29 churches, 61 schools, two hospitals, five dispensaries, and 29 cemeteries.[35] The missionaries strove to eliminate local languages with a zeal no less than that with which they encouraged the Indians to hide their nakedness in European clothing. A photograph in a 1912 Capuchin publi-

Mission-school Indian children around 1912 in Yungillo, Caquetá River, dressed in mission clothing. At this time Father Monclar, head of the mission, wrote in his appeal for support for the road to Mocoa: "The 762 children distributed in the various schools of the mission, and thus gathered together with such effort, do they have to return yet again to the barbarous customs of their parents, and thus sterilize the seeds of the eternal life that we with such love have deposited in their tender hearts? . . . Poor Indians, eternally savages."

cation proudly displays, as in a shop window, 1,300 articles of clothing presented by the Junta Auxiliadora of Madrid, Spain, to the indigenous people of the Caquetá and the Putumayo. Another photograph, however, shows the Indians in "traditional" costume in the Sibundoy valley during the festival of Carnival.[36] Indianness in outward display was recast into a thing that could be exhibited under controlled circumstances only. With regards to local administration over both Indians and poor white colonists entering the region, the authority of the Capuchin mission was well-nigh absolute—including the ability to raise corvee labor and get the Indians to use the stocks and the whip to enforce mission edicts.

Reminiscent of the extensive Jesuit empire in Paraguay in the seventeenth and eighteenth centuries, the Capuchin presence in the Putumayo in the twentieth constituted a colonial theocracy which was administered from the splendid heights of the Sibundoy valley—that very same valley up into which in 1541 the desperate Hernán Pérez de Quesada had climbed from the eastern jungles acting on information wrung from the Indians of the Mocoa river that that valley, their fabled Achibichi, was his fabled dreamland of the Golden One, *El Dorado.*

There in 1900 on the eastern rim of the Andes, perched over the immensity of the Amazon basin, the Capuchins established their base and yearned to win over the heathen in the jungles below, who could only be reached by an arduous descent *a lomo de indio*—on the back of an Indian carrier, a *sillero.* In his oration in the cathedral of Bogotá, the nation's capital, Father Carrasquilla described what this was like:

> In order to traverse the trail between the capital of Nariño [city
> of Pasto] and the residence of the missionaries of the Putumayo
> [in Mocoa] took me an entire week, carried on the back of an
> Indian crawling on hands and feet over terrifying cliffs along
> the edges of vertiginous abysses, descending precipices like
> those portrayed by Dante in the descent to hell.[37]

The Road to Redemption

To further their network of control, the Capuchins needed above all a road connecting the highland cities with the jungles below. Father Monclar, the head of the mission, persistently stressed the economic importance of his crusade, citing experts such as the one who proclaimed that the value of rubber extracted from the Amazon area was of the order of forty million dollars. The same authority declared that this sum indicated there to be many thousands of rubber tappers and gatherers involved, generally earning good salaries which they spent on costly provisions imported from Europe and the United States. Once the road from Pasto down to the Putumayo

From Edouard André, "América Equinoccial," 1884.

river at Puerto Asís was completed, however, Colombia would be able to capture the major part of that commerce of the Amazonian rivers.[38]

To inspire public enthusiasm (not to mention money) for the construction of the road, the head of the mission in 1906 published in Pasto a broadsheet entitled "The Savages of Caquetá, Putumayo, and the Road to Mocoa," centered on the question, "Why Have the Missionaries Shown Such Interest in Opening Up the Road to the Putumayo?"

> A few leagues from Pasto on the other side of the western cordillera one finds thousands of Indians who since four centuries have resisted the forces that Church and State have made to introduce civilization in their virgin jungles. One has to defend oneself from enormously high mountains crowned by icy páramos, deep valleys covered by muddy swamps, craggy rocks, profound precipices, and innumerable dangers in order to arrive at the vast solitudes where these our brothers live. On several occasions self-sacrificing missionaries conquering all types of barriers have been able through their heroic abnegation to haul these savages out of the woods and unite them in towns, imbuing them with the rudiments of our saintly religion, habits of work, and sociability. But when the most delightful hopes shone forth from the highest minister presaging that the light of the Evangelist was going to be diffused rapidly into these dens of savagery, unexpected events, civil wars, or political changes

obliged the missionaries to leave, destroying in a few days the
work of many years, leaving those wretches yet again enveloped in the darkness of infidelity. . . . Poor Indians, eternally
savages.[39]

How could this darkness be lifted? "By removing the insuperable barrier
which for so many centuries has kept them apart from their brothers—in a
word, by opening a road penetrating the jungles of the Caquetá and the
Putumayo."[40]

The sentiments materialized in the road as a work of redemption are
illustrated in a 1952 publication by Father Damián de Odena which looks
back over the missionaries' great achievement:

Conquering the unbreakable chain of the Andes by tenacious
and arduous boldness so as to consolidate the evangelization of
those exuberant lands and thus open them to civilization, a
double labor was required; on the one hand the stabilization of
its nomadic tribes, on the other the penetration by colonists of
those millenialist jungles stretching into the Amazon basin.
Only God knows at what cost so many sacrifices were carried
out in but half a century, resulting in this work of redemption
of the Colombian Southwest whose striking results our eyes
now admire.[41]

Among the documents he published in 1912, Father Monclar, the head of
the mission, included the following account by a journalist depicting the
laborers

organized in numerous guerrilla units spread out over ten kilometers, like a combat-hardened army forcing itself to conquer
the obstacles placed by the enemy. "It is civilization" says one
of my companions. "Led by the Church at the command of its
champions, the missionaries, it penetrates with conquering
steps these jungles so as to plant in its thickest parts populous
cities and repeat for the thousandth time the examples that
have been made in old Europe and in the pampas of young
America."[42]

Monclar also included a passage from a Pasto newspaper, *El Seminario
Comercial de Pasto* (no. 24, June 1911):

If the Caquetá is no longer asylum for wild beasts and half-animal people, . . . if the light of intelligence has penetrated into
these uncultured brains, and if the deadly bows and arrows
have disappeared from their hands, it is not the Indians who
are responsible. All this is owed to the fecund labor of the missionaries, with their assidious and constant abnegation."[43]

"Ilustrísimo y Reverendísimo Padre Fray Fidel de Montclar, Prefecto Apostólico de las Misiones del Caquetá y Putumayo."

He emphasized the symbiosis of Church and State, as with his publication of a letter written by General Benjmain Guerrero to the president of the republic.

> Whereas before they used to flee into the jungle like wild
> beasts on seeing someone civilized, there are now elements of
> science. To hear the little Indians of the woods intone the
> songs of the Creator and the National anthem is most moving.
> The missionaries raise their spirits to immortality. They teach
> them to know and adore God, just as they do the Fatherland.[44]

From *Misiones Católicas de Putumayo: documentos oficiales relativos a esta comisaría*, 1913.

In the missionaries' 1913 publication there is a fine photograph of a boat made in their new carpentry workshop in the Sibundoy Valley. Flags fly astern and in the bow. A strong bearded man stands in the boat grasping an oar. Behind him, seated, is a little boy, presumably an Indian boy. And the name of the boat, in bold letters on the bow, LA PATRIOTA, the Patriot.[45] More dramatic still was the newspaper *La Sociedad* of the nation's capital, Bogotá:

> In time Puerto Asís will be an emporium of wealth and a bulwark of Colombian integrity. When in that new city the sound of work is heard and the glorious tricolor unfurls to the wind, then proud of the name and condition of being Colombians, the reduced and civilized tribes will keep watch with their arms ready for the honor of the great father that is the nation.[46]

The missionaries labored mightily to construct this road from Pasto across the cold *páramo,* down the precipitous mountainsides to Mocoa, and from there through the jungles to Puerto Asís on the left bank of the Putumayo— gateway to the Amazon, western Europe, and the eastern seaboard of the United States. One imagines that the 1,600 men they daily employed labored just as hard. The missionaries represented the road in imagery entailing passions no less fabulous than those of salvation. In their own published words they envisioned the road as the tie between civilized Colombia and savage Colombia, as the Dantean descent into the mysterious world—the inferno of jungles enveloping the Indian in the darkness of infidelity (and in those forty-odd million dollars cited by Father Monclar). The road and the landscape it traversed configured an uncanny confluence of cathartically organized meaning, at once economic, religious, and nationalistic. In taking stock of this vision created by the Capuchins and materialized in the road we cannot but ask ourselves to what degree it may have blended with preexisting images of shamanic flight and salvation held by local Indians, forming, as it were, through the mediation of the poor white colonists, an unacknowledged pact about marvelous and even therapeutic realities in which both colonizer and colonized played a role as creators and created.

In descending those Dantean abysses and thrusting light into the dark jungles, was there not being perfected here in the road a magical concept fusing powerful elements of religous fervor with those of frontier capitalism from which each race and class would draw its quotient of redemption? The intensity of the fusion between mystery and reason, wildness and civilization, frontier capitalism and the Church, guaranteed that the forces of modernity here would perpetuate if not augment the "second nature" of the Putumayo as a therapeutic fetish whose driving force at the beginning of the century was rubber and the ferocity of its exploitation. Personified in the ambiguous figure of the semi-Christianized Indian shaman, this fetishization owed as much to ruling-class poetics as it did to the magic of the wild Indians enveloped by colonization in the darkness of infidelity.

Building the road was in itself a lesson in civilization for the Indians, assured the bishop of Pasto, Leonidas Medina, in an impassioned address delivered in the nation's capital in 1914. For the Indians did not understand that a trail leading straight up and down the mountains was unsatisfactory, forcing the priests to ride on their backs while they jumped like goats and traversed the terrain with the sure but free abandon of birds skimming crags and swamps. To be carried by an Indian, he pointed out, is thus to be starkly exposed to death and nature. The sun strikes one's face. Into one's eyes comes the intense living light illuminating those remote and strange lands. Death stalks the priest on the Indian's back every minute of the way. And it took five days to travel like this from Sibundoy to Mocoa. Now, thanks to the road, both nature and Indians have been tamed. The new steam engine brought to Puerto Asís with its "whistle and noise of machinery announces to the four winds that the wild beasts have gone and that the savage has now entered civilization. The cruel inhabitants have now exchanged their bloody theater for allegiance to the Apostles of Christ." There is now not one idolator in the entire territory and the schools have been particularly successful, though of course this was not easy to achieve.

ENTRADA TRIUNFAL DEL SR. GOBERNADOR Y PREFECTO
APOSTÓLICO AL PUEBLO DE SAN FRANCISCO
EN LA INAUGURACIÓN DEL CAMINO

Triumphant entry into San Francisco by the governor and the apostolic prefect at the inauguration of the road.

The parents tenaciously opposed the schools, fearing their children would lose their customs, or as they themselves say, that "they would become whites."

To participate in a mass with the newly converted Indians, with whom the bishop celebrated the Holy Sacrifice of the missionary fathers and the success of their apostolic labors, was to be seized, he wrote, by indescribable emotions. One's own soul—forever prone to spiritual drought—becomes "reanimated by the work of divine grace so that one can adore the hidden presence of God with a faith more alive and a charity more growing." It is, in effect, the metaritualization of the Indians' first steps toward the ritual of mass, together with the way that this ritual makes trascendent the "lessons of the road," that here catches the eye. It is the ritualization of savagery succumbing to the Lord that the bishop finds so uplifting. The crucial feature of the poetics no less than the politics hereby involved is the enormity of the emotional charge invested in the interplay and constant working back and forth of savagery into Christianity and Christianity into savagery. And just as the bishop succumbs to the indescribable emotions thereby aroused, what of the poor colonist who follows in his tracks down the Putumayan road of redemption to also join in Christianized Indian rites, not of mass but of *yagé*-nights?

The road today.

It was neither in a cathedral nor in a basilica, intoned the bishop, that these feelings overcame him, but in a tiny chapel of mud and thatch. The simple altar was adorned with wildflowers. Against the dark depths of the wall stood a life-size statue of Christ eaten by time and the baneful climate, yet nevertheless faithful testimony to the heroism of the first missionaries to penetrate the Putumayo and the Caquetá.

At the feet of this venerable image the priest began the tremendous sacrifice. At the feet of the priest knelt 300 or more Indians. Their clothing was shabby but their souls were white, clothed with the brilliance of divine grace. There was no silver incense burner. There was no organ. But there came a silver voice, breaking the silence. It was like a flute. It was the voice of the virgin, the wife of Christ who, abandoning homeland, family, and the enchantments of Europe, became buried in these jungles to redeem souls. At first weak and timid, this sweet voice became increasingly sonorous until, strengthened by two or three missionaries, it rose to heaven, Indian voices with missionaries', echoing in the mountains till, lost in space, they arrived at the throne of God with whose blessing they will return as beneficent rain of grace.[47]

The road became an object of Indian image-making too. Victor Daniel Bonilla has published this story told by Sibundoy Indians concerning the sacristan in charge of the statue of Christ known as Our Lord of Sibundoy:

The sacristan, noticing that the Lord's clothes were wet
through every morning, suspected him of going out at night,
and decided to find out. Under the pretext of renewing the candles, he went to the church late at night. . . .

The Lord had vanished. The sacristan told the governor,
who, in agreement with the other leading men, ordered that the
culprit [Our Lord of Sibundoy] be beaten with twelve strokes
of the whip. After this punishment had been carried out, the
Indians expected that the Lord would ask forgiveness and
promise not to do it again; but instead he stood up, turned his
back upon them, and went off on the road to Pasto. . . . They
tried to catch him but he became invisible, and all they could
do was go back to the village sadly and repent of having beaten
him. Their remorse became even more acute when they discovered [from the wax tears lying alongside the road] that the reason why the Lord had gone out each night was to take their
place working on the road from Pasto to Mocoa.[48]

Begun in 1909, the road was completed within a few years. With the
migration of poor white colonists from the highlands to the lowlands a society
formed which one missionary later on described as

two antagonistic races persecuting each other to the death. The
whites treated the Indians as slaves, and sometimes as beasts.
The Indians had to serve them with everything and just in the
ways that the whites wanted. . . . For their part, the Indians
upon seeing the tyrannical conduct of the whites, returned it
with interest and with all the force of their savage nature. As a
consequence there was constant and bloody struggle, requiring
only the smallest spark to light up a terrifying outburst that was
only extinguished with the blood of some of the combatants.[49]

With the outbreak of war between Peru and Colombia in 1932, the Putumayo lowlands were made much more accessible. In 1906 there had been
2,200 colonists. By 1938 there were an estimated 31,775.[50] In the 1950s the
Texaco Oil Company began pumping oil through a pipeline that straddled
the girth of the Andes and the roadway further improved. The population
of the port town at the end of the road, Puerto Asís doubled between 1957
and 1964. Peasants forced off their lands in the interior and fleeing the
virtually nationwide civil war of the *Violencia* came now in droves, raising
cash crops, cutting back the jungle and the Indians with it.

They were poor and often desperate people. Driven onto the frontier, it
was as if they found in the Indian the foil for their own lowly status. Yet
just as the Indian became that against which one defined oneself as superior
and civilized, so the Indian shaman could be a source of esoteric power, a
beacon of relief in a beleaguered world.

Manuel Gómez put it like this when I stayed the night at his small farm, hacked out of the forest along the Guamuez river, in 1976. He had come to the frontier as a boy twenty-five years before. "The colonists here say they take *yagé* with an Indian for distraction, or when they are sick," he told me.

They say they are *dañados* [ensorcelled]. I am sick. I go to the jungle to hunt. Then I shoot an animal. But it doesn't die. The gun doesn't go off, or whatever. Thus I don't kill it. Then I say, "No! I'm *dañado*. I can't kill anything!" Well after that, what next? . . . I'll go to the *curaca* to cure me . . . to the Indians because with *yagé* they can cure one, so that one can kill when hunting. This is the custom at times for people; they go and drink *yagé* with the Indians. They take *yagé* with the Indians to cure *maleficio*. . . . Many people take *yagé* for that. Many come from far away, from different places. They come to take *yagé* with Salvador.

Later on he told me what happened to him when he took *yagé* with *taita* Martín, a Cofán Indian shaman upriver at Santa Rosa. But before I recount what he told me I want first to lay out what Jean Langdon has presented as an ideal-typical *yagé* vision of shaman novices retold by some Siona people with whom she stayed in the early 1970s on the banks of the Putumayo river below Puerto Asís. There had been no *yagé* nights there for quite some time, as the shaman was frightened of drinking it. It was said that Salvador, the Cofán shaman living upstream along the Guamuez, had ensorcelled him, Salvador who had saved Santiago's life.

Siona Vision

After weeks or even months of preparation and isolation, the novices are ready to take *yagé* with the shaman. Night falls and they retire to the forest. Taking *yagé* with the shaman, listening to his chant, the novices feel drunk, drowsy, disoriented, and fearful. Vomiting and defecating, the body is cleansed for traveling. The visions begin and the shaman sings of the visions they will see and of those he sees. You are frightened and expect to die. The *yagé* people appear. They are like the shaman, only tiny and they are crying. They say you are going to die. Fire comes, followed by snakes wrapping themselves around you. If you have the courage to persist, then you meet the jaguar mother. She is large, big-breasted, and beautiful, dressed in white. She is the mother of the shamans and of *yagé* as well. She takes the novice to her breast and wraps him in the blanket in which the Siona wrap their babies. Then she throws you away, crying, "Why did you take *yagé?* Now you are going to die!" Hundreds of snakes appear (which Langdon was told are also the leaves of the *yagé* vine) and then they form into one enormous boa, which is the owner of *yagé*. He may wind himself around you. Death is imminent. Then the boa straightens out and carries you up into the heavens where the *yagé* people come to teach you about the heavens and introduce you to the spirits who live there. You have left your body. You are dead.

After many such trips, the novice may finally reach the penultimate heaven and meet with God (Diusu) who lives there with the "living God people," the angels, and with his book—the book of "remedies" (the Bible?). Above God in the highest heaven are doves who write on paper, a lonely tree branch from which a spirit hangs (Christ crucified?), and a door opening to nothingness. God says to the novice, "You have arrived. What were you thinking of?" The novice replies, "Only in god," and is given a beautiful staff (as the Spanish did in bestowing authority on Indian chiefs in colonial times and as the Capuchins did this century). God tells the novice to always drink *yagé* and care for his people, correct them in their wrongdoing and curing them when sick.[51]

And the Capuchin Father Francisco de Igualada cites the notes of a fellow Capuchin, prior to 1948, recording a description of heaven made to him by a Siona shaman; Diosu in his chair of gold, many good spirits, many groups of people singing and dancing in front of God, heaven is a great city whose streets are carpeted with wool and whose walls are of gold but transparent too.[52]

The Heavenly City and the Magical Healing Power of the Colombian Army: The Vision of an Old Ingano Indian Man

I once asked my old friend Florencio what was his most memorable *yagé* vision. This is what he told me, in Spanish, as we sat outside watching the stars emerge an hour after sunset. As far as I can make out, this vision occurred twenty years ago while he was accompanying a shaman from Puerto Limón on the Caquetá river who was curing a sick woman. It is perhaps relevant to know that in his youth Florencio served as a guide for the now legendary Father Bartolomé in his apostolic excursions downriver among the feared Huitoto Indians and that for several years thereafter Florencio was sacristan of the tiny church at Puerto Limón.

> First I saw angels, coming from the clouds, let us say. They come to place the crystals they carry onto my forehead. Good. These they bring. Each angel. They put them on my forehead to know what illnesses the sick have; to capture the experience so they can cure, no? And after that they place them here in the chest so that one will have good spirit with people, umm, without one even thinking of doing evil. And they also place them in one's hands, these crystals they carry. And to have clear consciousness of the future they place them here in one's

mouth so that . . . so that one can speak with anyone, so that one speaks well, umm? And this is what *yagé* makes you see.

And later, when the *yagé* makes you drunker still, then comes those *tentes,* forming a queue, and they keep on coming. *Paujiles* also come in. It looks like the room fills with birds, nothing but birds. . . . It looks real, doesn't it? But by the medium of its drunkenness it is the painting [of *yagé*] and nothing else that does this.

And after this, now it has passed, comes another class of painting. And this forms a street, like a city, no? It gets clearer and in this city each room has its own vision, while from still others comes music. First to come out is a person from the Sibundoy valley; thus. Others come with the plumage of shamans who take *yagé* . . . all like this they form up the street. They keep on forming themselves, some dancing with their music, others with other music. Over here they bear different feathers, dressed with mirrors—people, *yagé* people—with necklaces of tigers teeth and curing brooms and clothed in gold. That is beautiful. And they keep on coming and coming, singing the while.

Then, finally, emerges a batallion of the army. How wonderful! How it enchants me to see that! I'm not sure how the rich dress, no? But the soldiers of the batallion are *much* superior in their dress to anybody! They wear pants, and boots to the knee of pure gold, all in gold, everything. They are armed, and they form up. And I try to raise myself . . . so that I too can sing with them, and dance with them, me too. Then, the shaman . . . with the painting, he already knows that I am trying to get up to go there, to sing and to dance with them just as we are seeing. And then, he who gives the *yagé* [i.e., the shaman], he already knows, and he is quiet, knowing, no? Thus, those who know how to heal are given account. Seeing *this,* they are able to cure, no? And they pass this painting to the sick person. And he gets better! And I said to the shaman who was curing me, I said to him, "Seeing this, you know how to heal?" "Yes," he told me, "thus seeing, one can cure, no?"

And after the last of the batallion of the army passed, I went along, but without dancing at all. I went into a street of immense beauty with no garbage—no garbage at all, nothing, nothing. It was like the firmament, let us say. Midst all the people lining up I walked and walked until I reached the very end of the army, seeing all, no? Catching their breath, no? And then I entered a house that was opposite, thus, with its floor the color of the firmament. And the vision was pure crosses, no? There were two doors closed, but the middle one was open and this I entered, umm. There I entered. There were three men. And here there was a sort of store of books, nothing but

books, that were spewing forth gold, no? A waterfall of gold.
And these books are covered with crosses. And seated at the
table are three men, like we are here, all the same color and
each one identical to the other. They are the same. And they
hold forth a staff. Good! And so I went up to them, with the
drunkenness of the *yagé* . . . with the painting impelling me to
go there to understand. "Good!" they said to me, "You have
come to understand. But you don't have to. You already
know!" The man in the middle said to me, face to face: "All
that you have seen is what God allows to life; all for you. But
you have to look after and love everyone, and be respectful to
all. Take this staff!" It looked like a baton of gold, no? I received it, knelt, and was given his blessing. I left the room and
went out by the balcony below where I had seen all the people
forming up, and that was it. Nothing more. The drunkenness
had passed.

The White Colonist's Vision of the Indian Shaman and the Devil

Both the ideal-typical Siona vision and Florencio's should now be compared
with that of Manuel, the white colonist who came down from the highlands
around 1950 when still a boy. His attitude toward Indians along the river
could be summed up as one of scornful contempt. He talks of them as
malicious and lazy drunks, never to be trusted, and although he is fond of
repeating, with the gravity of the sage, that "He who walks with Indians,
walks alone," it is a fact that his two teenage sons attend the *yagé* nights
of a nearby Indian shaman every few months. Manuel himself had to be
persuaded by his uncle, so he says, to take *yagé,* and that was when he was
fifteen years old. He has never taken it again.

Despite his disparagement of things Indian, he employs Indian techniques
of curing evil spirits, *mal aires.* He learned this from his uncle who learned
it from Indians. I was once with Manuel when he blew *soplos* over his teenage
daughter for *mal aires,* in effect copying Indian shamanism. I asked him how
it was that *yagé* healed, and he replied:

Well, *yagé* itself never knows. It's with the spirit of *yagé.* One
takes *yagé* when one needs an explanation. We take *yagé* [with
a shaman] when we are sick, as when someone has performed
magic and when . . . bad spirits turn against one. Understand?
Thus the same thing occurs with *yagé.* Thus with the drunkenness that comes with *yagé,* they see the sicknesses. *Yagé*
shows them what the sickness is—that's to say, to the Indians.
They come and converse with each other, just as you and I are
talking right now. Thus it is said if it can be cured or not. *Yagé*
itself doesn't do the cure! *Yagé* is the medium allowing the doc-

tor to understand the sickness, and what remedy to use. . . .
Taking *yagé* is what we here call . . . the transformation, the
electricity, no? It's like an injection of electricity. The sick person drinks and the shaman drinks, together, and as the drunkenness enters into us, so the *yagé* converses.

As for his own "conversation" with *yagé* when he was fifteen,

I took my cupful and nothing much happened. The shaman
gave me a second, and still nothing much. Shortly after a third.
Then the drunkenness came; strong!
  Suddenly some Indians came in *guahuco* [loincloths] whis-
tling, rattling their curing brooms, whoosh, whoosh, whoosh—
which means "come come strongly the drunkenness." And
then they blew "oof, oof," like that, so that the drunkenness
comes strongly. Then I was asleep, my eyes closed. Then suddenly came a troop of *sainos* [wild pigs]. Then a hurricane,
lights and dark shades, like in a movie film. Darkness. Then
suddenly I saw the devil, Oh!
  I forgot to say that after I saw the pigs I saw tigers. They
went away, growling and chattering. They didn't come back.
But it was so awful, so ugly. Suddenly, some snakes came, you
know, out of my own mouth, coming out of my mouth . . . but
it was lies, nothing but drunkenness.
  Well, as I was saying, I was sitting, half asleep, when I heard
someone talking to me, singing rather, and I saw something
there, it was frightening, it was the devil himself. But how
could that be? Sitting there; right behind me. But then it wasn't
the devil; it was the shaman. It was he who had been the devil.
  Then I opened my eyes and saw all the Indians sitting there
with the shaman. He's put on his feathers, his crown too, sitting by the fire chewing tobacco. *Taita* Martín . . . the tiger, the
devil, it was *taita* Martín. The devil, he had horns and . . . *co-
lorada* [heated and red]—you should have seen him—with a
long tail down to his knees . . . like they paint him—with spurs
and everything . . . but *ugly!*
  Well, it was the drunkenness! I looked again and there was
the shaman dressed in his crown of feathers, beautiful, with his
necklace of tiger teeth and all the other things that they dress
themselves with. You know. So there I was seated and there I
stayed. Then the *taita* ["father," shaman] said: "What are you
thinking friend?" "Nothing," I said. "Is the drunkenness
hard?" he asked. "No," I answered, "a little, just a little."
"You're not scared?" "No. Just a little scared."
  So things went by and went by, and then, came these Indians
[*yagé* people] blowing and sucking. You know. Strongly. Singing their chants, their "heh, heh, heh . . . " and sucking and

blowing, and they did that to me . . . and then I knew I was going to die.

It was then clear to me that I was going to die. I was already dead. And after my death, who would see me? My uncle? He was already dead. Who was going to tell people that I had died? Dying, I left. My soul went up a staircase, up and up. Ooh. It was beautiful. The staircase was like that in a palace of the very rich, with gold. And beneath and around it was a beautiful landscape. I was seeing beauty, like when the night is full of stars. It was so beautiful. Up, up, up, always moving upwards, fast. And I thinking I was dead. But it was only the drunkenness.

I went up. I got to the top. There was a salon, sort of like a balcony, with a raised portion. I went up to the top part. I was then in the air. There was nowhere more to go to. I'd finished, and at the end I saw God. He was on that side, in the air, in his palace, alone, bearded and with a crown—like they paint him.

So I'd arrived. I'd finished. And then he gave me his blessing. And so I thought, what's this? Aren't I dead? And my God said to me "No! Nobody called you. You should go down." Well, I just turned around and went down backwards, step by step backwards descending until I was well down and when I got to the end of the steps I turned around and continued going down.

I went down and down and everything was beautiful. It was like when the day is dawning and the night is clearing. It was a beautiful plain of grass, still a long way off, but I knew it was the earth. It wasn't dark. There were shafts of light with the coming of dawn. The mist was rising. Further down I saw the green of the jungle. And so I reached earth and the drunkenness was over. Then I was happy. All was clear. Now we had arrived. I had spent the night . . . drunk.

When I told the shaman what had happened he said "Now you could become a shaman."

"Did God look anything like *taita* Martín?" I asked.

"No! God is God! What are you coming at! He's not a shaman but my blessed God! There was no shaman there! When the *devil* appeared, *then* there was the shaman. But I only saw that he was the shaman later. When I turned around at that change in the staircase, coming down and I turned around and everything changed—then everything was clear. I arrived. Then I saw it was the shaman."

Healing through the Hallucinogenic Creation of the Antiself: The Army of Gold and the Indian as Devil—A Colonial Dream Dialogue

In the lowland Indian's vision it is primarily the image of the splendor of the Colombian army in the highland city that provides the shaman with powers to heal—to exorcize destructive spirits, to undo sorcery, and ultimately to gain for Florencio the blessing of the Church. The image of the army is decisive. Its beauty, its gold, its arms, its music and dancing constitute a picture transforming evil. He tries to enter into this picture in order to sing and dance with the soldiers. It is the shaman who passes on this image.

> Seeing this they are able to cure, no? *And they pass this paint-*
> *ing to the sick person. And he gets better!* And I said to the
> shaman who was curing me, I said to him, "Seeing this, you
> know how to heal?" "Yes," he told me, "thus seeing, one can
> cure, no?"

By contrast the white colonist undergoes his transformative experience by means of the image of the shaman as devil. He dies at that point, ascending to the godhead of redemption. This process of death and rebirth swings on the pivot of wildness, as invested in the storming hurricane, light and shade, wild pigs, snakes coming into and out of oneself, and, finally, the metamorphosing trinity of tiger-shaman-devil.

Here colonization becomes a replenishing of grace through immersion in the wild evil apportioned to the people of the forest. That evil magic invested into colonized people and so useful in creating colonial hegemony is here pictured into the world to serve as the means by which the colonizer gains release from the civilization that so assails him.

On the other hand, in Florencio's vision, it is the splendid image of the army that creates magical power.

The two visions are uncannily complementary, each pivoting on the glory of the antiself as colonially contrived, each thereby drawing its fund of magical potency. So perfect is this complementarity that we could think of it as a dream dialogue, underlying colonial reality.

How often we have been told that rites enforce solidarity, bringing people together affirming their unity, their interdependence, the commonwealth of their sentiments and dispositions. But what are we to make of rites such as this wherein the Indian heals the souls of the colonist? Surely the healing here depends far more on the existence, the reproduction, and the artistry of difference as otherness and as oppression than it does on *solidarity?* And how the odds are tilted! The magnitude of the difference involved here— the magnitude necessary for the healing power to emerge and flow, the colonized turning back to the colonizer the underside of his hate and fear congealed in the imagery of savagery.

How often we have been told that ritual's function brings spirit and matter into a divine unity as with the Romantic understanding of the symbol (the understanding implicit in anthropological discourse). How often we have been told that rites, especially healing rites, recruit the passions in order to consolidate the cake of custom, sustaining the normality of the norm, the internalization of convention (and so on). But here with the shaman healing the pain in the souls of the civilized, where lies that divine unity? Surely it lies in the divine creation of evil? Both Manuel's vision and the published texts of the Putumayo Capuchins are committed to a poetics of racist exploitation in which racism and redemption work hand in hand.

No doubt this attempt to harness savagery to the divine task of redemption existed long before the Capuchins missionized the Putumayo. But no doubt they added something important—the magic of ruling-class authority and ruling rituals endorsing, explicitly, in print and in sermon, the fantasy of the redeeming savage. No less important was the transcendental meaning of the entire Amazonian adventure that these few self-effacing Capuchins undertook for Colombia, for world markets, and for God.

And no doubt the ease with which the Capuchins exploited and elaborated the image so central to this imperialist mission, the image of the inferno and the Indian as its denizen, was automatic. Deconstructing the mystery of grace in evil was for them second nature, their ritual art, their poetics of catharsis. At the edge of the jungle the poor white colonist Manuel reproduces this beautifully. In his shit and in his vomit his soul flows for us all.

But with the elderly Indian, Florencio, things don't flow so smoothly. With him the process of painting a tapestry of images creating healing power proceeds jerkily, like cards pulled out of a shuffled pack, one tableau put on top of the other or side by side. *Otra pinta.* Another painting. And here there is no obvious catharsis of rebirth through the colonial encounter with death and evil. Florencio's painting seems *epic* while the colonist's is *dramatic* as Bertolt Brecht defined and experimented with the differences in formal construction, differences that for him, one of the foremost innovators of theater in the twentieth century, were intimately connected with the overthrow of capitalism. The *dramatic* entailed

> strong centralization of the story, a momentum that drew the
> separate parts of the story into a common relationship. A par-
> ticular passion of utterance, a certain emphasis on the clash of
> forces are hallmarks of the *dramatic* [think of Manuel's theater:
> the lightning of the hurricane, the tiger, the shaman, the devil,
> death . . .]. The epic writer Döblin provided an excellent crite-
> rion when he said that with an epic work, as opposed to a dra-
> matic, one can, as it were take a pair of scissors and cut it into
> individual pieces, which remain fully capable of life.[53]

Epic theater aimed not at overcoming but at alienating alienation, twisting the relationship between the extraordinary and the ordinary such that the latter burns with a problematizing intensity in a world that can no longer be seen as seamless and whole. The fractured universe is worked into a fractured format that lobs ill-fitted and therefore likely-to-be-questioned juxtapositions of tableaux into a studied art of difference. One still-life follows the other in a jumbled collation of images butting against one another as in Florencio's and other Indians' representations of their *yagé* visions, the hallucinatory art of the real.

This modernist mode of representation comes from what we are often told is not only the oldest form of art, namely the shamanic séance, but something more, not just old but originary. "And in the vast jungle filling with night terrors," writes Alejo Carpentier, trying to depict the shaman's song in the Venezuelan forest in his novel *The Lost Steps,*

> there arose the Word. A word that was more than word . . .
> this was something far beyond language and yet still far from
> song. Something that had not yet discovered vocalization but
> was more than word . . . blinding me with the realization that I
> had just witnessed the Birth of Music.[54]

"Don't look at the good old times, but at the bad new ones," said Brecht, and that very wordlessness of words that are more than words, that gurgling of frogs in the millennial mud of the jungle of the throat of mankind that cures in Putumayo, that too was taken up as a weapon in the confrontation with the bad new times—as the German Dadaist poet Hugo Ball wrote in his diary on 5 March 1917, planning an event for the Cabaret Voltaire in Zurich:

> The human figure is progressively disappearing from pictorial
> art, and no object is present except in fragmentary form. This
> is one more proof that the human countenance has become
> ugly and outworn, and that the things which surround us have
> become objects of revulsion. The next step is for poetry to dis-
> card language as painting discarded the object, and for similar
> reasons. Nothing like this has existed before.[55]

Nothing like this has existed before? Certainly it is not the poetics aflame in the colonist's vision, that classical harmony of moral aesthetic as in Dante's uplifting adventure, the journey of the soul through sacred space and time that sustains the Christian Church—that, fleeing the chaos of Dada, not to mention the world of war-torn Europe, Ball joined in 1920.

Florencio's vision engages with this soulful journey and disengages it from its beautifully contrived scaffolding of orderly time and orderly space bound to great authorities, Church and State. He does this with respect.

It is a sacred disengagement. But he cannot find the yield in dying nor the profit in evil that belongs to the colonist. What he finds instead is the *pinta* that the shaman passes onto the sick, a passing on wherein Florencio becomes the voice for the shaman's wordless imagining and song without words, the Word that is more than words, poetry that had discarded language.

And Florencio has put this into words, for us, while the colonist's relation to the shaman is not to give voice to the *pinta* that the shaman passes on but to use the shaman himself as an image and, in a way that merges the literal with the metaphoric, climb to heaven on his back.

And if the poor colonist finds he did not really die, the old Indian finds he already understands. Their different dreams presuppose a common colonial history presupposing in so many ways the magic of each other's otherness in what is, in effect, a joint construction across the colonial divide. The very jointness of these visions takes us into what could be called the nether regions of racial class war where the struggle with sorcery locks horns with the search for redemption in virulent and fantastic forms. These visions plunge us into an oneiric underworld of colonialism whose passionate imagery makes no less a claim on the colonized than on the colonizer, and no less a claim on the seignorial class than on the poor colonist one.

The Blind Man and the Lame Man

It was with the sweeping authority of a Renaissance man that Miguel Triana depicted at the beginning of the twentieth century in his book *Por el sur de Colombia* his exploration of the Andean slopes cascading into the Mocoa region.[56] To the grace of the bellelettrist he added the hard-nosed practicality of the scientist in a blend that was no less romatic than it was positivist—and he too rode up those massive flanks astride the brawny back of an Indian.

His was a heart that was whole and whose vision was penetrating, wrote the elder stateman Santiago Pérez Triana in London in 1907 in the prologue. It was of the utmost importance for Colombia, went on the statesman, that an easy route be established between the Colombia of the mountains, where most of the people lived, and the Colombia of the immense lowlands stretching east from those mountains. It was for that purpose that Miguel Triana had been dispatched as an explorer by the Colombian government then headed by that veteran of the quinine boom in the Putumayo lowlands, that man who had given Alfred Simson his job skippering the first steam launch up the Putumayo, that unquenchably energetically stereotypically capitalist entrepeneur Rafael Reyes—to whom Miguel Triana respectfully dedicated his book.

To effect true ownership, noted Santiago Pérez, the lowlands had to be connected to the nation by the living ties of industry and commerce that would pump the blood of the nation through those remote parts. It was for Miguel Triana to locate the stream for that blood of the nation, and it was in terms no less full-blooded that Santiago Pérez prefaced his endeavor, concentrating on the descent

> down the rugged flanks of the Andes beneath the incessant rain
> and thunder of the countless torrents beginning their way to
> far-flung valleys. The treachery of the trail demands prodigious
> care. A false step may mean death. . . . The surrounding dan-
> gers are indicated by ominous signs—the vestiges of unfortun-
> ate travelers who succumbed to fatigue or abandonment. And
> yet none of this stopped him. Forward! Forward! Forward! Un-
> til at last he was able to free himself from that arid region
> where all is dangerous and threatening.[57]

And didn't Santiago Pérez have intimate knowledge? Hadn't he himself in escaping from one of those innumerable civil wars that shook the republic fled from Bogotá down those Andean flanks to the eastern plains—and go on to tell the tale in his book *De Bogotá al Atlantico,* which was translated and published in English as *Down the Orinoco in a Canoe* with a generous preface by Joseph Conrad's great friend Don Roberto—otherwise known as Cunninghame Graham? Indeed, Don Santiago Pérez had served history and art in other ways, too, as the partial model, for instance, for Don José Avellanos in Conrad's novel *Nostromo.* In the author's note of that book Conrad said that he had, for the history of that fictitious Central American republic of Costaguana, depended upon the *History of Fifty Years of Misrule* written by the late Don José Avellanos!—a fictitious creature modeled on a real one, Don Santiago Pérez, so as to provide a real picture of a fictitious country and its real history inscribed in a nonexistent book. It was, moreover, Don Santiago who offered to help a dispirited Conrad make real his dreams of journeying south to Spain, and his name was thereby invoked in that letter of 1903 that Conrad wrote to Cunninghame Graham about a man called Casement pleading help for the Congo Reform Society.

It was raining the night around 1905 when Miguel Triana arrived at Mocoa. A religious festival was in progress but only Indians were taking part, keeping the whites well away as they taunted the mock-bull with flaming horns, the *toro encandelillado,* dashing at the bystanders clustered at the foot of the convent. Then the drums pounded and rockets flashed and off into some house hidden down in the tree-line went the *indios* to dance the night through until mass was held the day following in the Mocoa church.

The nave was occupied by the whites, of whom there were many more men than women. At that time there were only about twenty houses in the settlement of Mocoa and about 200 whites, many of whom were political prisoners captured during the last of the civil wars. In the space left vacant in the center of the church were the *indios*. On the left side, looking at the altar, were slumped the Indian women with their legs stretched out and their heads bare, nursing their children and generally disheveled. The only one who crossed herself was an old woman who traced out a cross on her left cheek and then the right, noisily kissing her finger. On the other side sat the Indian men, more circumspect than their consorts but bearing unmistakable signs of the night's revelry.

When the mass was over the *naturales* stayed behind. A Capuchin then instructed them in Christian doctrine, which they repeated in Spanish word for word, like a chorus. They came across as a servile lot, these *naturales*, although not without charm, of course. Triana recorded an instant of dialogue with an alert young chap who caught his attention.

"What's your name my dear little friend?"

"Bautista Descanse, my Lord, one of your servants."

"Leaving the valley of Mocoa," wrote Triana,

> the arduous ascent of the mountains begins at Pueblo Viejo,
> from where the mounting of an Indian is imposed as the only
> possible means of transport. There where the ordinary walker
> has to go on all fours, digging fingernails into the slippery clay,
> the Indian places his foot firmly without the slightest hesitation;
> where it is impossible for the vulgar acrobat to find balance on
> a tortuous, sloping, and slippery root, the Indian walks with
> enviable grace; in the pinched rut where not even the sole of a
> boot can fit, nor even one's knee push a way through, the elas-
> tic foot and iron-hard knees of the Indian opens a pathway
> without any lesion and with frightening skill; when the giant
> nose of Rumpiña or of Carnicería [mountain bluffs] blocks the
> path, to scent the frantic waves of the deep river, there is no
> traveler capable of even imagining that on this wet precipitous
> path there is a place for the human foot. Yet, nevertheless,
> with short steps—sometimes forwards, sometimes sideways,
> and also backwards, making turns in all directions—according
> to the marvelous formula conjured by danger, the Indian passes
> along that defile of death. When a river rushes precipitously
> across the path, tumultuous and deep, the Indian saves the sit-
> uation by wading up to his armpit or by crossing a wobbly
> length of *chonta*-palm meant to serve as a bridge. From the
> height of the Indian's shoulders, the traveler views the spumy
> angry torrent running beneath his feet, walled in between two
> huge rocks, as if he was a man condemned for cursing and
> denying God. In Nature, one always hears a canticle of glory to
> the infinite beneficence that reigns over the world—but the
> river of the mountain chain, blackened with rage, smashes and
> bellows back against the walls of its prison, breaking the har-

mony of agreeable echoes and imitating the lugubrious wail of
the sinful. All the way across the slippery *chonta*-palm bridge,
the traveler shivers from the spray of these rivers—sustained
by the Indian carrier who thereby attains the stature of a beneficent mountain god to whose providence and custody the life of
the traveler is entrusted.[58]

So he becomes a mountain god, this humble Indian carrying the white
man up the mountain from Mocoa! It is the Indian shaman carrying the
colonist from hell to heaven with *yagé,* too, and in wondering about how
and why and what sort of connections are hereby involved in letting a text
speak for a sociohistorical reality we should not lose sight of the character
of the movement whereby this rite of passage from carrier to god is sustained—a fragmented, asymmetrical disjointedness of sidestepping and back-
stepping across the sliding surfaces that mark the defile of death. At the
same time there is the pumping of ethical substance into the screaming
ravines and mountainsides smashing and billowing, cursing and wailing as
a ritualized prelude to the metamorphosis of Indian carrier into shaman
walking the defile of death amid nature storming in its moral stance, as *mal
aires* or as sorcery, for instance. We cannot here rest easy with the notion
that opposites have been reconciled, contradictions assuaged; our Dante has
not found his Beatrice, nor has the sacred been redeemed by the profane.
On the contrary, this poetics of staggering frenzy speaks to the power that
conceals the dependence of the exploiter on the exploited, the same power
that issues forth in the hallucinogenic fantasies that Miguel Triana experiences so vividly lurching on the sweaty back of the Indian.

> The displacement of one's center of gravity together with the
> unconditional subjection to another's will soon produces a
> strange emotion transforming the initial and satisfying novelty.
> The rider of the Indian now begins to feel the humiliation of a
> healthy man who has been transformed into a cripple through
> his own inclination. . . . The elbows become numb and swollen
> on the sweaty back of the Indian. The knees stiffen as they are
> permanently doubled up. The feet itch and lose all feeling be-
> cause they are tightly bound up. And your guts are pressed up
> against the planks with the pressure of your hunched back
> causing fatigue. And what fatigue! It is the fatigue of the
> loafer—who now seeks frivolous distractions to kill time.
>   The breathing of the Indian becomes as familiar as the snort-
> ing of the mules on the Honda trail, and so as to make the voy-
> age more entertaining it occurred to us to try out a fantasy;
> between the Indian carrier and the person carried there is a
> pact similar to that between the blind man and the lame man.
> "You look out for me," said the blind man. "With the condi-
> tion," responded the lame man, "that you walk for me!"

And the pact was complied with so faithfully that the blind man and the lame man formed one single person, at first with two souls. And these two souls needed a language to harmonize their wills and to profit from their complementary organs so that each would mutually support the other. And so, after a time, the nervous currents established from the feet to the back and from the eyes to the stomach overcame the resistance of clothes and flashed from point to point like rapid telegrams so that the blind man walked without having to hesitantly feel his way, and the lame man felt as with his own feet, like a punishment for his carelessness, the stumbling endured by his companion.

Similarly, there are also nervous currents flowing between the rider and the horse so that the brute becomes sad or happy when the rider is overtaken by fatigue or becomes excited in combat, or smiles to see the end of the trail. To confirm these first intimations of our fantasy we should not forget that horse-breakers train their young steeds more by suggestion than through the mute movement of the reins.

So, with these thoughts we begin to effect our fantasy. But then we immediately discern how necessary it is to energetically develop a strategy to recuperate the dominance of our will which we have abdicated in favor of the barbarian. For just as we have made ourselves unable to walk through our cowardice, so we have made ourselves blindly unintelligent.

Between us two, who should rule? Clearly we should. For if the relation of the Indian to his human cargo is that of a horse to its rider, then it is obvious that in addition to sustaining the weight, the Indian has also to renounce his freedom and walk not as he wishes within the terms of the contract, but under our sovereignty. Thus worked out within our jurisdiction which allows no input from him, we derive the rationale for our moral right to govern without saying anything except by means of our thought and psychic powers[59]

The Colonization of Space

What we have glimpsed through these texts (or should we say *pintas?*) produced by Parry, Oviedo, Tamayo, Hamilton, Cochrane, the Capuchins, Florencio, Manuel, and Triana are eminently political images wherein myth and history collide to become accessible to magical art. Carried down through the millennia of Western tradition, the great moral epic of descent and salvation has obviously served as a major orgainizing force for that tradition. Pivoting on the demon, evil, and suffering as its point of dénouement, this epic came to rest in the New World on the back of the Indian. Nowhere, to my knowledge, was this more securely fabulated than where the Andes loom

above the rain forest, where the moral topography of highland Indian imperialism paralleled that of their Spanish colonizers.

Laminated by this confluence of historical streams, that stubborn structure
of imagery has remained engraved in the imagination and in the magic of
mountains to the present day. In both their actions and in the renderings of
those actions by chroniclers, the conquerors of the Andes such as Gonzalo
Jiménez de Quesada were in their turn conquered by this force and lost in
its magnificent appeal, their hands awash in the blood of its victims. Down
through the centuries, the historiography of the conquest has been beholden
to the same narrative, and the mythology of the conquest still awaits its
conquest.

To imbue a landscape with moral and even redemptive significance is for
most of us nothing more than romantic fantasy. But there are occasions when
to travel through a landscape is to become empowered by raising its meaning.
Carried along a line in space, the traveler travels a story, the line gathering
the momentum of the power of fiction as the arrow of time moves across a
motionless mosaic of space out of time, here primeval and divine. So it is
today that Indian medicine men of the Putumayo, those who stay at home
no less than those who wander, arouse the slumbering meaning of space long
colonized by the white man and carry him through it to uncover the hidden
presence not only of God but of the sorcerer.

NINETEEN
Even the Dogs Were Crying

I wonder a lot about the meanings of the army in Florencio's vision, that wonderfully golden beautiful singing dancing army taking the place of the dancing shamans dressed in feathers and mirrors like *yagé* spirits, that army which in a sense replaces those spirits—"Seeing them you cure?" Yes, replied the shaman. And Florencio tried to get up and sing and dance with them.

Only once he told me about the army. He saw the men rather than the institution, but the resplendent discourse of nationalism was well secured. It was in that brief flare-up of a war between Peru and Colombia when Indians were used to transport gasoline by canoe from Umbría down to Puerto Asís. Florencio was one of those Indians. All he told me was that "when the army came to Puerto Asís they didn't sleep. They played their trumpets, singing goodbye to Colombia and to their families. . . . But what sadness! Even the dogs were crying. The sickest of us got up to watch and listen. Never had we heard sound so sad, extracting tears, the sound of that music."

TWENTY
The Old Soldier Remembers

I met an old man, still lithe and hard-working, in the interior of the country, in Puerto Tejada to be exact, who had fought as a soldier in the war with Peru in the Putumayo in 1932. Eighteen months he had spent there. He was sick a lot and had to be cured of malaria in Bogotá. But all in all it was a worthwhile thing to have done, to defend the fatherland like that. But, he added, lifting an eyebrow, today the army is different.

I think I knew what he was getting at. In the very seat he was sitting in, a year before, there had been a robust young man who had just completed his military service, telling us how, during the presidency of Turbay Ayala, he had, as part of regular duties, helped torture civilians in Bogotá. He made it sound almost exciting. Applying electrodes to the nipples of pregnant women. His own wife sat expressionless beside him as he spoke. She was pregnant. Yes. I had an idea what the old man was getting at.

I picked him up at his house where he was watching an American movie on T.V., a lovely formal man, graceful and courteous. Two dwarf women were watching with him, smoking cigars.

Trucks could enter only as far as the great lake of La Cocha set into the mountains east

of Pasto, he told me. From there the soldiers had to march along the Capuchins' road and the mud was up to their thighs crossing the rainswept
páramo. Some road! The Indians left them piles of potatoes by the roadside.
They were very considerate. The ones who wander selling herbs and curing,
they're swindlers. But there! There exists the science!

As a young man in Puerto Tejada in the 1920s he had seen the Indians
selling herbs as well as the bracelets, *coralitos,* for babies against *mal de
ojo.* Its proper name is *susto* he said.

At that time, in 1933, Mocoa was no more than a *cáserio* with about fifty
houses and a church built by the Indians. There were tribes there. They
were the most religious of all the Indians and owners of lands. Further on,
at the end of the road on the banks of the Putumayo, Puerto Asís consisted
of little more than the school set up by the Capuchins. There was a kiln for
firing bricks that the Capuchins worked. They did almost everything themselves. Sure they stole the Indians' land, but they protected them and gave
them education. Why, now there are even lawyers from the Putumayo! By
the ton!

The soldiers were issued a gray blanket, an aluminum water bottle, a
cartridge belt, and a very heavy Mauser M-1 rifle. (Where did Florencio's
vision of them dancing with their uniforms and boots of gold come in?) As
for the *indios,* aha! They were our life!

What did he mean?

Because they were the boatmen. They were our dear friends. They brought
us food from their plantings. Yucca. Plantain. Game. No! I don't think the
army paid them a cent. And their shamans helped enormously. They attended
the wounded. They had things against seasickness. Patricio Patimocho, the
Siona shaman, he was 149 years old at that time. His head was covered with
sores. He was the colonel of the Indians, the strongman. He sallied forth to
the battlefront to cure the wounded. He had a huge canoe.

I wanted to learn to cure but they wouldn't teach me.

Later on he took *yagé* and saw all that was happening back in Puerto
Tejada. Someone was dying in his home. It was true. *Yagé* is accurate
(*positivo*).

A mile or so out of town I tracked down another old veteran. He looked
astonishingly like the first, as if that war or something associated with it had
molded a special type of man: alert, clean-cut, confident, infinitely gracious,
and worldly wise. He had been one of the famous *macheteros* of Cauca,
"men of the machete," peasants recruited to put an end to the Peruvians
by means of their long knives and long reputations, blacks mainly, from the
Cauca Valley.

The soldiers grew beards and wore gloves to protect themselves from the
mosquitoes. It was rough. Peru wanted to steal the Colombian town of
Leticia. That was the cause of the war. One night they camped with some
Huitotos at Piñuna Blanca. The chief of the tribe took a section of a vine,

"Do you want to hear something incredible?"

cut a cross into both ends, opened up his body and with the vine inserted ointment. It was magic. He could heal internal pains in whatever part of the body. Next day the soldiers marched on. They say the *indio es bruto,* that the Indian is a brute. *No! Bruto es uno!* No! We are the brutes!

Do want to hear something incredible?

The Putumayo River is born from a lake—Lake Cocha. In the center of the lake is an island where the ancient Indians discovered a Virgin. I can't remember her name. They carried her to Pasto but she secretly made her way back to the island. The Indians therefore had to make her a chapel. But whenever a priest came to celebrate mass, why, it was the most curious thing! She would disappear! People told us that she went to visit the Niña María of Caloto—whom you may remember, dear reader, not only has her residence but a few miles from where the old soldier came from, namely Puerto Tejada, but has her own startling histories of disappearances, to visit, some say, the Lord of Miracles at Buga.

And the other memories of this *machetero* from Cauca? Why, it was in the jungles of the Putumayo that he had the good fortune to come across a "Collins" machete. The Peruvians left it behind in their flight. He had never seen one before.

Now, fifty years after the war the Colombian veterans are still fighting for a pension in recognition of services rendered the fatherland. They won the war but to date have received nothing, while the Peruvians, who lost the

The postcard the soldier sent his mother, with his portrait inserted in the top corner.

war, won a pension. So much for the fatherland. So much for the Putumayo. And Florencio down in the hot country drinking *yagé,* envisioning the soldiers in gold dancing and singing. With them you cure, he asks the shaman. Yes. Seeing them you cure.

But, on the other hand, didn't the old soldier say that the Indians "were our life"? Wasn't it Patricio Patimocho, the famous Siona witch with his head covered with sores, who cured the soldiers?

TWENTY-ONE

Toughness and Tenderness in the Wild Man's Lair: The Everyday as Impenetrable, the Impenetrable as Everyday

To what extent can the Indian carrier's perspective provide a point of release from the power of conquest mythology? The carrier has of course little option but to act out the role enforced by colonization. True, there is the story of the exasperated *sillero* who, with a swift stoop, hurled his tyrannical rider into the abyss, and Cochrane and others complained bitterly of their *silleros'* taking advantage of their rider's dependence, just as the wandering Sibundoy Indian medicine men were said to take advantage of their patients. As a Capuchin Father complained more than four decades ago,

> The Santiagueños [Ingano Indians from the town of Santiago in the Sibundoy Valley] are addicted to the system of wandering through the cities of Colombia and other countries as well, selling leaves, roots, vines, herbs, and amulets, exploiting the ignorance of those who should be wiser than those same Indians. . . . Many of the civilized have lost their sense of morality. They ask for herbs and charms for indecent aims. . . . *This is proof of the perfect exploitation of the civilized by the Indians* in this area, selling valueless herbs at a high price or in picking leaves and

herbs from anywhere and then selling them as if they were
picked in the *most remote jungles* or from *the highest peak of
the Andes.* [Emphasis added.]

But if this allows the Indians, or at least their most salient and representative image, that of the medicine man, to exploit the civilized, is it not at
the cost of reinforcing the racist exploitation from which the Indians suffer
in the first place? The more shamanic, mystic, and wild the Indian becomes
as a way of exploiting the exploiters, the more tightly is the noose of ethnic
magic and racism drawn.

Yet there exists one feature to ponder that does perhaps disrupt this in-
terlocking structure, and that is the two senses of the *comic* represented in
the vision journeys by whites on the one side and by Indians on the other.

For Dante, as in his letter to Can Grande, the comic moves from a foul
and horrible beginning to a desirable and joyful end, and as with the Passion
of Christ himself, this is the mode of salvation at work in the visions of José
García and Manuel. José García seems to be able to turn this on with ease
and I cannot but think that this is closely connected with the quality of evil
with which he, like just about all colonists I know, white or black, paints
the underside of the world—in tones melodramatic and mysterious in depth.
It is this artistry of the uncanny and of the mysterious side of the mysterious
that distinguishes their evocations in story and gesture from those of the
Indians I know, wherein a rippling teasing sets the world on its oscillating
course. This quite different sense of the comic is doubtless bound to colonizing poetics too. Think back, if you will, to the complaint that makes the
bishop's mode of transport, on the Indian's back, a sacrifice: the Indians
not only go in too straight a line but in doing so they jump like goats and
soar with the free abandon of birds. It is to that colonial perception of an overly
straight poetics jumping and soaring that we should turn, so I suggest, in
searching for an alternative to the heavenly catharses of colonizing narrativity.

When I returned to Santiago's and Ambrosia's home on the twentieth of
December, 1977, I found that not only had he recovered from his illness,
which I had presumed fatal, but that he had gone off with his son to cure a
dancehall on the other side of the republic in far-off Cúcuta near the Co-
lombian-Venezuelan border. Among those awaiting his return was a young
white couple from the mountains near Pasto, Angela and her husband Juan,
who told me he was suffering from rheumatism and eye trouble which none
of the hospitals, folk healers, or pharmacies where he lived could cure. He
was first brought down to Santiago fifteen years ago by his mother and father.
He had just written a letter:

Señor Don Santiago:
I beg of you to cure my person of all these pains which prevent
me from walking and of the damage to my vision which pre-

> vents me from seeing. Also, I am doing badly in the selling of
> my agricultural harvests. Also, I want you to cure some soils
> from where I cultivate my crops. There are four plots, two are
> mine and two are my mother's. I would also like you to cure
> my wife.

Daily life set into a monotonous routine of small chores involving almost
everyone, patients and workers alike. Many were the spaces set up by such
an irregular work rhythm for talk and speculation, a rhythm every bit as
important to the shaman's healing power as are the spectacular flights into
the unknown with hallucinogens. For the patients it provides some distance
from their problems, just as it condenses the discourse of magic and sorcery
by having a group of afflicted people all together, gradually letting each other
know, in spurts and in starts, about their misfortunes. Every day or second
day a new patient arrived, from nearby or far away, and in discussing his
or her problems with the others, no matter how obliquely, so the world of
sorcery was empowered, and the shaman's house became a discursive fount
circulating this social knowledge.

The daily coexistence of the patients and the shaman's family in the shaman's house also demystifies and humanizes, so to speak, the authority of
the shaman. Unlike the situation of a priest or a university-trained modern
physician, for example, whose mystique is facilitated by his functionally
specific role defining his very being, together with the separation of his
workplace from his living quarters, the situation in the shaman's house is
one where patients and healer acquire a rather intimate knowledge and
understanding of each other's foibles, toilet habits, marital relations, and so
forth. By and large I think it fair to say that the therapeutic efficacy of the
shamanism with which I am acquainted owes as much to the rough-and-
tumble of this everyday public intimacy as to the hallucinogenic rites that
allow the shaman to weave together the mundane and the extraordinary.

A flashlight beam winked over the rise from the river. The dogs bark. Who
could it be? "It's the friend Santiago," shouted young Gabriel, a peon adopted
by the household since his father, an Indian from the Sibundoy Valley, had
left him here saying he would be back soon. That was years ago. Someone
said he had drowned. It was too dark to see anything. Then, sure enough,
in stomped Santiago, supporting his stocky bulk with a staff. People woke
from their dozing. Two sick patients lying down to sleep on the floor stumbled
out. *Aguardiente* flowed. The youngsters put a record onto an old battery-
powered record player and began to dance as Ambrosia stood next to the
exhausted Santiago on the veranda, receiving fold after fold of his *chaquira*—
kilos of colored beads hung around his neck. He told of his travels and
people hung on every hilarious and astonishing word. Then they drifted off.
Nothing stays the same for long.

He went to cure a discotheque—a block long! With twenty-two rooms,
each of which had to be cured! How fatiguing! And no *chicha,* only bottled

". . . receiving fold after fold of his *chaquira*. . . ."

beer! The discotheque belonged to a man called Alejandro who was suffering
from sorcery involving human bones and soil from the cemetery. No customers were coming to drink or dance. The parking lot was especially bad;
while chanting and blowing incense there, under the effect of *yagé*, Santiago
was startled to find a bat falling into the tin can holding the smoking incense.
People would drive into the lot and then drive away for no obvious reason.
It was close to Christmas, a peak time for dancehalls, and Alejandro was
losing money hand over fist. He had heard of Santiago way over on the other
side of the nation from a man who lived in Cúcuta but who used to have a
bar in Puerto Asís, which Santiago had cured of the same complaint years
before.

   He spent a week working in Cúcuta. And he cured it! All twenty-two
rooms. Customers started to come, and Alejandro, his family and friends,
implored him to stay. Alejandro's wife asked him if he was baptized: "I told
her I was baptized before those priests in the cities!" And he laughed and
laughed, repeating this again and again.

   They came to him with talismans to be cured. They came to him with
jewelry to be cured. And they asked if he could locate gold for them. They
implored him to stay but they were rich people said Santiago, with workers.
They needed no more, while he had his farm and home waiting. And if his
wife got sick? What then? Who would cure her? "She can't go to the hospital
because [he made a sign with his hand across his throat] they would kill
her."

Then, around midnight, late as it was, tired as he was, he started curing, the curer needing to cure no less than the patient needed the cure, taking Juan into the main room of the two-room house saying, "Now I'll make an examination. Tomorrow we'll cure." Juan stripped to the waist. Santiago took his right arm. Juan complained, saying it was not his arm but his leg that was sore. Santiago fixed him with a steely look: "Listen! When I make an examination it's with the head and the pulse. I've got to pulse!" He would chant for a few seconds, that wonderful Putumayo healer's chant, and every so often let off a gun-shot click with his tongue from the back of the throat. He slowly stroked Juan's arm. They talked of Juan's life.

"It's because of the envy they bear you . . . the evil," said Santiago.

"Yes, señor. We work hard. But, Don Santiago, we pay the workers well! And now the whole world has turned against us, beginning with my father dying . . . everything . . . everybody sick, my father, my mother, myself, and all that. Before my father died I was in hospital. But the doctors couldn't cure me. After that, my feet. . . . Everything is rotten."

A radio was pouring out music from the coastal lowlands and from the mountains, too, *vallenatos, cumbias,* and crying flutes, while people sat around chatting and drinking liquor with half an eye on the curing. Others settled down to sleep, some young Indian men giggling and playing in the dark corners of the room. Snatches of conversation wafted toward us in the shadow-play of candlelight.

"You've got lots of enemies," Santiago asserted.

"Yes! Lots of enemies."

Santiago chided him. "You haven't taken care of yourselves! You know you can't trust anybody!"

They are talking with a mighty passion, their dialogue dynamiting passageways through the spongy morass of envy. Santiago is pulsing Juan, stroking him into himself, interspersing his questions and sermonizing with short bursts of chanting.

Almost crying, Juan said, "When I first came here I could barely stand. I was at the point of death!" Santiago grasped his head, sucking at the crown. He turned to me and laughed with delight.

"See this, Don Miguel. The Indian knows! The Indian knows how to cure!" And he laughed uproariously.

He asked Juan about the medicines he had been taking and retold yet another incident from Cúcuta while blowing over Juan—"Whoosh fire, Whoosh,"—the magical breath of the curer, expelling.

"Will it leave me?" asked Juan. "Am I going to get better? Will we see who they are?"

"Tomorrow we'll take *yagé.* If you can't tolerate it then we'll go up to your place."

"That's exactly what we were hoping. My mother and I are in evil times. Things are marching horribly. We are out of control."

In the background people were laughing. The radio continued its dancing. Santiago continued his chanting, interrupted bursts, stopping to give instructions: "the curing fan . . . *cascabel,* all. . . ." It's Cúcuta again. He was in high spirits and pretty drunk. Someone asked, "In Cúcuta you have all?"

"Yes!" he replied, "the women!" He was teased about the young women in Cúcuta.

"Young girls!" he retorted. "Young girls nothing! It's the old one! In Cúcuta she asked me if I was baptized a Catholic! I told them that we Indians are more Catholic than they are! 'In what form were you baptized?' they asked me." He laughed with tears streaming: "I'm telling you the truth."

Juan broke in, "This is the truth."

"On the part of the Indian witch, speaking nothing but the truth in Cúcuta, just the facts," intoned Santiago.

"Just the facts," echoed Juan.

"Who is willing to dispute it," Santiago went on, "when the hour comes we all have to die." And Ambrosia took him aside.

One morning, freshly washed and combed, Santiago sat down to cure the little bags of soil that Juan had brought down from his mother's tiny farms in the mountains. With an opening gun-shot crack of the tongue he began to chant softly into the open neck of each bag, close to his mouth, singing into the soil, *yagé* sounds with barely any words. Now and again a Spanish phrase surfaced from the rasping chanting sounds of the night forest, phrases like "Don't let them molest anyone. . . ." This went on for what seemed a long time, maybe half an hour. Then he spat into the soil and turned the bags over and over again, molding and crunching up the soil.

"Now!" he exclaimed, "Now you've got the song of the *indio* of the Putumayo!" And he told Juan to take the soils back to the farms up in the mountains and sprinkle them over the accursed lands. He did not tell him whether or not the farms were "damaged"—*dañado,* that great euphemism for sorcery—at least not immediately, and Juan told me that he understood this chanting into the soils to be something that divines whether or not sorcery is at work in the farms and, if there is, then cures it. If there is no sorcery, then this singing acts as a *contra,* as a preventive measure for some months into the future.

Santiago talked about his chant. The gun-shot clicks of the tongue were so that the song of *yagé* would penetrate better. He did not learn this from anybody—he learned it from *yagé* itself. When you *chuma bien,* when you get really "high," then you fly into the sky and the spirits of *yagé* teach you all this. They have their faces and limbs painted. They have musical instruments and they dance. Seeing and hearing this, you too can learn the same. They teach it all. These "*yagé* people" or *yagé* spirits have beautifully painted tunics, *cusmas,* like Santiago's only better, feathers on their heads

Divining the soil for *maleficio*.

feather caps, and shoes that are pure blue. But not even Santiago sees them often.

To divine these soils with maximum accuracy he must wait until the early morning after a *yagé* night. Then with his chanting the *yagé* sounds and beating with his curing fan, *waira sacha,* he can see into the soil and see if it has bad things like snakes or scorpions, signs of sorcery.

Not only soils and livestock and not only farms are afflicted with sorcery following in the wake of envy. Small businesses are just as prone, and in this regard it is worth relating that Santiago, for at least a year, had a man patiently awaiting his services in a nearby town. He was a black man from the Pacific coast who had made some money and bought a bar. Now he wanted it cured.

I yearned to see the *yagé*-curing of a bar and would pointedly remind Santiago of his promise to the bar owner. But he was always lethargic. "Tomorrow!" he would say.

That day finally came but around lunchtime a nuggety little man came struggling out of the forest over the rise carrying a boy on his back. They were colonists from the highlands of Cauca. The hospital had done no good. The boy was very sick and could not walk. He had a mild fever and his knees, elbows, and ankles were swollen. He was listless and thin and sallow.

There was but half a bottle of *yagé* and without hesitation Santiago canceled the trip to cure the bar. He wanted to stay the night with the sick boy and drink the last of the *yagé* to see if he could be cured, what might be wrong with him, and what herbal medicines to use. *Yagé* can show you all that if things go well.

That night we drank *yagé* by the sick boy's bed, Santiago and I. The boy sipped a little, just a taste, and his father didn't want any, he said, in case he had to carry the boy outside. It was an uneventful night with soft chanting and talk of hunting in the Putumayo, what it was like in the forests for Santiago when he was a kid by his father's side, how he'd killed an anteater with a lance, but never a tiger, whether or not there was envy in the countries where I had lived, and so forth. He couldn't conceive the notion that envy as a maliciously wounding force capable of even killing people did not exist in the places I came from. Years later I began to see how right he was, especially with regard to academics.

In the morning he said the boy was suffering from *mal aires* (evil winds, spirits) and asked Ambrosia to help him prepare remedies for the boy to drink. Next day the boy walked a little and his pains had subsided. By the end of the week he could walk home.

"What's the meaning of the 'Whoosh fire, whoosh' that you put into the *yagé* song when you are curing?" I asked him.

"So that all those *mal aires* get out and away from this kid," he replied.

We talked about different types of *mal aires: sacha cuca waira* from the forest; *yaco cuca waira* from the river; *ánima waira* from the *ánimas* (which in other parts of Colombia can mean the spirits of the dead); and *yaco ánima waira* from the spirits of drowned people.

Waira is the Inga word for *espiritu*, spirit, Santiago said. *Yaco cuca waira*, the evil wind from the river, appears like a *duende*, he went on to say, and I knew from my friends in the plantation towns in the interior that a *duende* was a little mischief-making fairy with a large hat and his feet reversed who molested people in dreadful ways and stole children. I assumed he was a Spanish colonial import.

"Yes, the *Yaco cuca waira* looks like the *duende*," Santiago was saying in a matter-of-fact way. "Like a *cristiano* (a "Christian," meaning a civilized human being) dressed in pure ice, nothing but ice and water and spume, shoes of spume, and hair everywhere from his head all over the place. They are tiny, about one meter high. They'll do a lot of damage if you're not careful."

"Do they attack people?" I asked.

"Sure."

"Why?"

"Out of envy."

He paused and then took up a story. There was a man from Bolívar (on the other side of the Andes) who was afflicted by a *duende*.

> He was a student from a well-to-do family and one day he went fishing and disappeared. Everybody looked and looked but no-

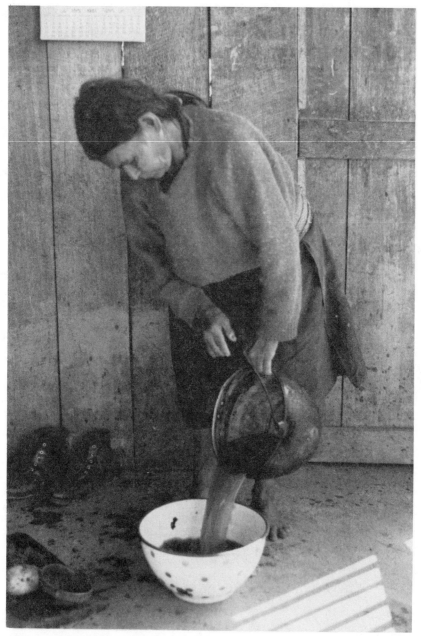

Ambrosia preparing remedies.

> body ever found him. Some five months passed and a fisher-
> man came across him by accident, deep in a cave by the river.
> He hadn't eaten a thing for five months and was all thinness,
> just pure thinness and hair everywhere—*enduendado.* They got
> him out of there but he disappeared. They found him in the
> same cave. He would let men feed him but not women. People
> would throw stones at him. He wanted to stay in the cave.

Santiago heard about him when he was taken to cure sorcery all the way
to Bolívar, now a more than usually envy-riddled town on account of the
coca boom there.

"He was like an animal," Santiago continued.

> There are a lot of people like that in the forests. A lot. Some of
> them become evil spirits. Before they were people like you and
> I. It's like a tribe. They have a captain too. They learn to do
> harm. Only men belong. You find them in the Putumayo also.
>   People in Bolívar told me I could cure him with *yagé.* But it
> would have required a *lot* of *yagé!* I heard about him when I
> was curing a madman who dressed in women's clothes and
> wandered all night talking funny things. He made himself a red
> dress and he would walk in the town and across the fields in
> that.
>   I cured him. That's why they all said I could cure the man in
> the cave who had been afflicted by the *duende.* The madman
> was also a victim of a *duende!"*

"What about the *ánima waira?"* I asked in reference to one of the other
types of evil wind.

"Ah! That's in the form of a skeleton," he replied, "rotting, pure bone."
There are female as well as male forms of this and they are very harmful.
They can attack any sort of person, good or bad, and they achieve their
harmful effects through *susto* or fear.

As for *sacha cuca waira,* the evil wind of the forest, he is naked and just
pure leaves, pure leaves and branches. They are very cold and almost the
size of a human. Like the *ánima waira* (the spirit of the dead) and the evil
wind of the rivers, these evil winds of the forest achieve their harmful effects
through fright. On seeing them one is so frightened that any sort of illness
can result.

Wondering about all of this and his curing of the boy suffering from evil
winds, I went on to think about the man who owned the bar and wanted it
cured. What could it be suffering from?

"Well," said Santiago, "he says the bar is suffering from a *maleficio;* that
somebody has subjected it to sorcery and that's why while the other bars
are full, his is empty."

He gazed over the forest stretching to the mountains.

"He had a small shop and he wanted more out of life so he sold it and

with the money bought a lot of booze and a few tables and chairs and made
a bar. He hired pretty girls with miniskirts to wait on the tables and things
went well. Then he started to flirt with the girls. His wife got furious and
grumpy and picked on the girls and on him too. Then the girls got grumpy
and picked on the customers, so the customers left and never came back."

Over the days that followed, Santiago, with Ambrosia's help, settled into
curing Juan, the farmer from the highlands assailed by the envy of his poorer
neighbors and laborers. Juan's vision cleared and the pains in his joints
subsided, yet he continued to complain. *Yagé* was taken several times. The
sorcery was sucked out. *Cabalongo* seeds bought from wandering Sibundoy
medicine men who got them from the far-off Chocó or the even farther plains
of Casanare were prepared. "Parchment of the Lion" made in Germany and
bought from the local pharmacy was applied to his joints. Santiago sang over
Juan's wallet. As the days passed more and more problems came to light
and more and more things had to be cured. Each solution to each problem
raised yet another. The ramifying threads of magic meshed with the ramifying
problems and questions constituting the patient, a luxuriant growth enlarging
with each passing day.

The Stranger's Strange Dream

One morning a white man aged about forty came to the farm and was shown
into the larger of its two rooms where people were sitting around in that
slightly dazed and euphoric state that exists after a *yagé* night. Santiago was
chanting softly, curing.

The stranger briskly announced that he had to be cured—cured from
maleficio. He sat down and in a loud voice told whomever was interested
that until recently he had lived in Cali on the other side of the Andes and
had come to the Putumayo three months ago looking for work with the oil
company in Orito. But he found none and now lived along the road in La
Hormiga working for peasant-colonists with farms where he suffered one
crisis after another. It was in La Hormiga that he had heard about a great
curer in this foothill region and, unable to cope any more, he had come here.

Santiago listened for ten minutes or so, then walked away. *Aguardiente*
was passed around and there was a quiet hum of talk. A boy came by carrying
a screaming pig. Some of the younger patients started to clean out and paint
an old oil drum. A baby crawling about the floor of the kitchen almost upset
the pot of milk but fell over and into its father's arms instead. *Chicha* and
fermenting sugarcane juice were passed around. Ambrosia and her granddaughter Delia were pouring boiling water over a neck-wrung duck prior to
plucking its feathers and, lying on one of the two plank beds, a sick girl lay
quietly, floating on the hubbub.

Thrown into the center of this the stranger from Cali was sat down shirtless
on a stool about two feet from the hammock in which Santiago placed himself

and started chanting, working over the stranger with his song and the curing fan. The singing was beautiful and lasted about twenty minutes. Then he stood and went around the stranger's seminaked body sucking out the bad stuff, sometimes putting it into his clenched fist and at other times going outside to blow and throw it away into the wind. After about ten minutes of this the old man, who had barely slept a wink all night, started to sing again, beating a powerful rhythm with the curing fan, crashing thunder and crackling fire into our drowsy midst. From outside came the sound of someone scraping the oil drum, and a young man from the Putumayo River bobbed in every now and again, offering sugarcane juice to the various bodies lying around the floor and to Santiago, interrupting his singing. Someone else stirred every so often to chase chickens from the room. Santiago seemed half asleep as he chanted. He stopped suddenly.

"You're very bad. You're going to need three curings!" he told the stranger.

"How many days?"

"You'll have to come back on Friday. Then we'll give you the purgative—yagé."

"Can't I take it now?"

"No! Because you're too weak." Santiago offered to prepare medicine for him to help in the meantime, explaining to him that he was sick because somebody had slipped something in his food.

"I eat a lot of crude sugar—panela—because it's the most economical," responded the stranger.

"Without taking yagé you won't get anywhere," said Santiago resignedly.

"And I want to know where I can find work! I want to know if it would be good in Puerto Asís!"

"Later on! After you've been cured. I have contras for the enemies and also to make friends. We have secrets."

"Yes Don Santiago. I need your counsel. I want to go forward. . . . I was with my brother in Cali and he was the one who told me to go to Orito. But no luck! In La Hormiga they told me about the great médicos like you."

"In your land aren't there good curanderos?" broke in Santiago.

"In Tolima?"

"Yes."

No. I don't think so. I left there young. My life was horrible. I went from place to place, an adventurer, getting to know new people and places. It was always hard. Finally I came to La Hormiga. People just won't help me. I need the curation—the liberation, as they say.

I had some dreams. I had to leave my brother's house in Cali. The house was full of people dressed in black. But there was nobody dead. My cousin came and blocked me. But I passed on and then I saw a long wide path stretching out before me.

To me this meant I had to leave the house. A witch from my
home town in Tolima, also living in Cali, told me I had been
dañado [ensorcelled].

The cousin who obstructed me was always tormenting me.
He attacked me and there was nothing I could do other than
trust in God. That really frightened me. In the year of '78 he
tried to kill everyone.

So I left that day and in the church, during mass, I realized
there could be a slaughter and that we had to do something.
Thanks to Holy Communion I saw that he was going to kill
everyone. This vision remained but my brother did not agree
with me. I went to a church for help, in San Nicolás in Cali.
There are women there who help people and they got me a job
in a grain store in Pasto but at the last moment the municipality
of Cali ran out of money and the woman who was helping me
had to leave.

I was very sick during all of this. Then I had an important
dream. A priest, perhaps from San Nicolás, said "Go and
search in such-and-such a place for the flower of the chalice!"
And in that instant there came another dream. There were two
figures in black, a decapitated man and woman. "We condemn
you to die in the house of your brother," they said to me, and I
was also dressed in black. What ugly figures they were! I was a
double person. One of me was a child. The other was a *monos-
abio* [the assistant to the picador in the bullfight; according to
this dreamer from Cali, the one who presents the ear as trophy
and is dressed in black].

In the first dream, the priest—I think he was a priest—told
me to look for the flower in such-and-such a place. But I
couldn't work out what place that might be. It took me two
years to work that out, until April of this year. Then I met a
young guy in Cali where I was working as a builder's laborer
and he told me that there was a lot of work in oil—*petroleo*.
Then I remembered! The name of the place that the priest had
told me was Puerto Asís! So I went! The witch in Cali told me
that my destiny was to walk under a river covered with logs
from which it would be difficult to emerge. He said it was possible. Perhaps.

We listened in silence to the poor man's tale. He asked Santiago how
much he would charge and Santiago said 10,000 pesos (at a time when the
day rate for laboring in the fields was fifty pesos). The poor man said he'd
better be moving along then. He would try his luck up in the Sibundoy valley.
Santiago said they didn't treat you as well up there and the fee would be
the same. And if you went to a *médico*—meaning a university-trained and
state-licensed doctor—they would charge you even more and would be certain to fail. "What's more," he added, "I charge by the gravity of the case!"

Don't Call Me *Taita,* Call Me *Indio!*

Santiago was waiting for Berenisa, a white woman healer from Pasto who had come down ten years ago to drink *yagé* and buy several liters. She used *yagé* in her healing practice—just a little, said Santiago, just to purge patients and see a little. She sent a letter saying she wanted to buy some more. But it costs more than she thought, said Santiago. It cost him 450 pesos (around twelve U.S. dollars) for a large sackful of *yagé* vine together with its female companion, *chagropanga,* without which no visions occurred. When scraped, mashed, and cooked some six hours in a vat of water down in a secluded grove by the river tabooed to women, this yielded close to three liters of *yagé* brew. If the *yagé* cook was to be paid for his day's labor, then another fifty pesos, the standard rate for a day laborer, had to be added to the cost. If Santiago charged a person for partaking in a *yagé* séance, he at that time generally asked around 100 pesos per cupful, a sum that often included divining and treatment. I had yet to see him ask money from another lowland Indian, and it was extremely rare for him to ask money from someone obviously rock-bottom poor—and there were plenty of colonists in that category. Yet he often charged by whim, sometimes outrageous prices and sometimes nothing.

He got to know Berenisa when she asked him to come to Pasto and help cure a restaurant. He was forced to leave before midnight, and the memory angered him. "Why did you have to leave?" I asked. "Because I am in my *cusma* [Indian tunic] and the neighbors there see that an Indian has been in the place and they say bad things." Juan, who knew of Berenisa by repute, added that if the neighbors had seen Santiago, they might say that the owner of the place was involved in evil magic. Someone else in the discussion ventured the opinion that the person who ensorcelled the restaurant would get to hear this and retaliate with stronger magic.

In mid-afternoon four whites stumbled out of the forest and clambered up the hill: Berenisa, her little granddaughter, her husband Luis, and the man who drove them down from Pasto. Luis, a thick-set, chain-smoking man, drew several bottles of brandy out of a sack. Soon everyone was pretty smashed and Berenisa was declaiming to all the world how the Indians of the Putumayo sure know how to cure.

"You are my *taita,* my shaman, lord, esteemed one, Don Santiago. You are my *taita.* He who knows, knows!"

"Don't call me *taita!*" bellowed Santiago. "Call me *indio!*"

"To me you are Santiago—whether negro, Indian, or white, it doesn't matter," retorted Berenisa.

Santiago got more and more angry. Berenisa kept shouting, calling on God and the most saintly Virgin that this house was sacred. She was furious with Santiago for claiming he had no *yagé.* She (rightly) suspected he was lying. To spite him she said she would go down the Caquetá River and get *yagé* from his brother Jacinto. "Jacinto doesn't *eat* Pasto women!" laughed Santiago (i.e., doesn't make love with them). He was angry on account of the humiliation he suffered years ago at their hands in Pasto, forcing him to leave early, saying he was an *indio* who came only to *eat*.

The situation eased a little and Santiago offered to cleanse Berenisa by means of ritual purification. She was prostrate on the floor, muttering bitterly, with her granddaughter rolling by her side. At her husband's insistence she dragged herself over, taking the crying child with her as Santiago half-heartedly began the cleansing. Ten minutes later she collapsed once more onto the floor.

It was now close to 11:00 P.M. Santiago and Berenisa's husband, Luis, kept on trying to get the better of each other through pointed chitchat, interrupted by Juan, the rheumatoid, complaining of a sore wrist and asking Santiago to heal it. Santiago peremptorily massaged and blew over his wrist, declaring it cured, as Luis rambled through a complicated story about how the last time when he came down here Santiago was mean, and now that Santiago was a rich man, with plantains in such abundance that they lay rotting, and cows supplying milk each day, he was even meaner, while he, Luis, was but a poor policeman for the municipality of Pasto, which had paid its employees only one month's salary during the past five months . . . and so forth.

The sleeping and half-sleeping bodies of peons, children, and patients crowded the room. The wind whistled from the thundering river and the last candle wavered and spat. Don Luis cleared his scratchy throat and with solemnity began a morbid tale about the time he almost died from the terrors in the highlands where he lived.

Only six months after he was married to Berenisa some forty years ago he was working on contract for the Jesuits of Pasto as a bullock driver hauling stone. Toward dusk, driving through a lonely part of the countryside, he heard the most awful cry: "Aiee, aiee. . . ." Chilled to the marrow he looked into the darkness wrapping its cloak around those windswept mountains. But there was nobody. Nothing but the wind and the dark. He felt sick. He started to vomit. Then he started to shit. He got hot and cold and started to sweat. He was dying.

They called the priest who hurried to his home. The priest contacted a nearby healer who told him to await his coming by preparing tobacco and *aguardiente*. That night the curer, a white man, came and diagnosed his illness as caused by the Old Lady of the Swamp, also known as Turu Mama, a hideous hag with long pendulous breasts swung up over her shoulders. Yes! It was she who had uttered those terrible cries that relentlessly echoed in Don Luis's memory as he let them loose in their blood-curdling intensity into the unsteady light of our deathly still midst: "Aiee, aieee. . . ."

Santiago was quietly smoking a cigar, sitting next to Juan, whom he would tap every now and again in order to look at the pattern being made by the ash—something many curers do as an aid to divination.

As for the Turu Mama, when her tale came to an end Santiago was incredulous, shaking with laughter. "What's she like to eat [eat and fuck]?" he demanded from Don Luis, who blanched with disgust and chagrin. But Santiago kept up this line of inquiry with the manic drive of an ethnographer determined to get to the bottom of peasant superstitions. Long after midnight he wiped the tears of laughter and lurched off to bed. Silence descended, broken by his telling the now awakened Ambrosia about Turu Mama.

Slowly the giggling and murmuring died away into the coolness of the blanketing night. Then a scream rent the darkness.

Aiee!

"Watch out for the Turu Mama!"

And peals of laughter vied with the wind in rocking the house to sleep.

TWENTY-TWO

Casemiro and the Tiger

This is a story told to a group of people, including myself, by Santiago one afternoon on the veranda of his home during a discussion of what I would count among his greatest interests and, indeed, an obsessive concern: namely, shaman-teachers envying a promising pupil, and the way in which envy between shamans can be channeled by one of them to kill or seriously impair the pupil of the other (a situation with which those in academia may have some understanding from personal experience). Santiago tirelessly reiterated his father's counsel that the only way to become a shaman was by learning directly from taking *yagé* alone and not by acquiring the *pinta* of a teacher-shaman. His father almost lost his life and was forced to forget his *yagé* knowledge when he got caught in the rivalry of two shaman-teachers, one of whom was his very grandfather, Casemiro, the man who turned into a tiger in the following tale. (Anthropologists and zoologists use the word jaguar rather than tiger. Locals say tiger and so will I.)

And this turning into a tiger? The shaman heals but he can also kill. Magical power is just that doubleness. Even when teaching, the shaman may kill the pupil. And think

358

back over the preceding days. Here was a man, a great healer, who instructed his patients, such as Juan from the highlands, not to trust in *anyone*. Much of his healing art lay in the evocation of a Hobbesian war of all against all. Yet at the same time both the man and his healing depended on a fine sense of the ridiculous and on the exudation of warm-hearted amity. It was this splicing together of the terribleness of the human war with the laughter of carnival that underlay the transformability of the shaman into the tiger.

The first night I took *yagé* with Santiago in 1975 he turned into a tiger, suspended in his necklaces of *cascabel* and tigers' teeth, seated in his hammock. Among the Siona people with whom Jean Langdon lived it was said that the jaguar-mother was also the mother of the shamans and of *yagé*. As recorded by some Capuchin monks, both live and dead shamans are prone to be transformed into the tiger. The dead ones come from their homes in the skies, acquire the form of a tiger, and harm or kill people. One monk reported a Siona informant as saying that this home of the dead shamans in the sky was the devil's house and that all dead shamans were devils. When Manuel, the white peasant colonist, took *yagé,* menacing tigers came which changed into the devil and then into the shaman, oscillating back and forth in a composite shaman-devil image.

It is well known in the Putumayo that shamans can turn into tigers. Rosario's brother, for instance, explained to me that the name for such a tiger is *tigre mojano* and that one of its distinctions is that it bears the testicles of a man. Rosario's daughter, aged fourteen, established the tiger transformation in a wider context of interregional imagery and proneness of Indians to practice evil magic.

Discussing the latter tendency she said:

> The Indians are evil because in times past all this was pure jungle and they worked with herbs. That is why it is said that the Putumayo is the land of witches—witches who are the Indians. In the Cauca valley [on the other side of the Andes] that is what they told my father. They told him that the Indians transform themselves into tigers, snakes, and . . . what do you call them . . . Ah! yes, alligators that pass in the rivers. They scrape and then drink that vine [*yagé*] which is called *tigre huasca* and they convert into tigers. The people in the Cauca valley asked him if it was true—if the Putumayo is very filth-ridden.

Santiago told me that the shaman turns into a tiger when he wants to be alone. This tiger is "pure spirit" and must not be attacked or killed. On another occasion when I asked why it was the tiger and not some other animal, he replied that it's because the tiger is the wildest of all the animals. "Why do shamans want to be the most wild?" I asked. "To ensorcell" was his answer. Later on he said that in this state the shaman thinks like a tiger. In discussing the ritual adornments of the shaman, a slightly different idea was expressed. The crown of feathers, he said, is to promote wisdom and a good *yagé* night—provided the feathers are cured and hence *consecrated*—then "one knows that with such feathers one will be helped in seeing all those birds, singing and warbling and thus helping you." By contrast, the consecrated necklace of tigers' teeth helps the shaman to see and mingle with wild beasts and with one's enemies.

Here is Santiago's story, the only framed story I ever heard in the Putumayo.

Don Apolinar wanted to buy *yagé* so he could learn to be a sorcerer and a healer and be able to shoot blowpipe darts for hunting. To kill *choruco* [monkey], no? Magic for hunting and for sorcery, to do evil to people, to send darts and all of that. He went to *taita* Casemiro who said, "Well, I will prepare *yagé*. Let us prepare *yagé*." They cooked enough for a whole month's drinking. Once it was ready Casemiro said, "Let's go hunting every day, there where it's full of monkeys and pigs and *dantas*," and for three days they hunted, coming back each day with their canisters full of meat. They began to drink *yagé* so that Apolinar would learn. They would drink at night, and in the morning they would drink *chicha*. It was very pure *yagé*; aggh, aggh . . . they would vomit.

Well, that went on like that till the end of the month and they drank the last of the *yagé* that Apolinar had paid for. All night they drank and around five or six o'clock, when the sun's rays came, Casemiro poured out an even bigger pot, full of *yagé*. This one was to teach how to *chontear* [ensorcell by means of magic blowpipe darts]. "You have to take *all* of this!" ordered Casemiro, "all at once!" And since it was paid for, Apolinar drank, then collapsed. He could only walk on all fours, and then fell over as if dead on his back with his hands and feet in the air, shitting and vomiting right where he was.

Then, so my father said, Casemiro began to sing and sing, and his singing became the growling of a tiger. He leapt to the roof beams. His hands still those of a Christian, and there he hung. Ah! My poor father who was then only about ten years old began to cry: "Look! now he's turned into a tiger and he's going to eat me!" He growled and growled and then leapt to the banks of the river where there was a fallen *yaracuma* tree bridging the water. He jumped onto it and clung to the trunk. Now his hands were those of a tiger, as were his legs. His face and clothes had not yet changed.

Growling, he left the beach and poor Apolinar remained like a man dead, immobile. Only his eyes moved, from side to side. He couldn't move his head. Spume frothed from his mouth and nose as he was lying in his own shit and vomit—the man who had brought *chonta* and paid to learn how to be a sorcerer and to cure. There he lay, dead. And it was all paid for.

"Oh!" exclaimed my father, "my cousin is going to die." And he worked on the fire so its smoke would drive the flies away. But Apolinar stayed dead and the little boy was scared. It was six o'clock in the afternoon, and still

Casemiro hadn't come back. My father ran to the house where Casemiro's wife was; "*Mama señora,* cousin Apolinar is dead. The *papa señor* gave him *yagé* and now he's going to die!" He cried and cried. The *mama señora* was very angry. "And where did that old man go?" she demanded. "Oh! He went to be a tiger" said the little boy. "Aieee" she screamed, "going off and making a nuisance of himself damaging the neighbors. Wait till I catch him!"

While the old lady was scolding and fuming, from the woods like a tired cat, walking very slowly and very deliberately, slowly, slowly, returned Casemiro, no longer in the form of a tiger but as a Christian. The *yagé* had passed.

"What do you think you're doing," screamed his wife, "giving this man *yagé* and then leaving him unattended in his shit—you shameless man you!" Casemiro protested; "What! What! He's not dead. He's watching the *pinta* [painting] so he will know how to be a sorcerer. He paid for this." And turning to the small boy he said, "Quick, go and get me the plant of freshness, the plant that revives!"

Straight away the boy raced to get the plant. He yanked it out and ran back to find the dead man now carrying a blowpipe to Casemiro to have it cured, with shit all over his behind. And was he pale! One month without eating, weak and dried out, suffering all that *yagé* and still asking for more! And now he was buying other darts—darts to *hunt* with, darts to *kill people,* and darts to *cure people.* Those were the three that he bought. And thus he learned to be a sorcerer, Apolinar Arida from Umbría.

Then my father seized his chance, and forgetting his fears approached Casemiro, "*Papa señor,* why did you become a tiger? Where did you go?" And Casemiro replied, "Be careful and I'm going to tell you—but nobody else. Don't tell the *mama señora,* okay? I didn't do any harm. I wasn't silly. No! I went to know far-off places. There I have a friend. He lives way over in the Caquetá. He also knows how to change into a tiger, and we know how to meet each other. He invited me to come and eat those *auca* Indians— he said he had hunted *aucas* and he said to me 'Come and let's catch some, they're delicious.' "[In an aside Santiago added, "Meat of Indians— wild Indians!" and he laughed.] But Casemiro said, "I don't want to. They'll kill us." "No," said the other tiger. "They'll do nothing. Nothing. Let's go!"

And so he lost his fear. They came to a path and the other tiger said "I'll stay here and you go over the other side, singing like a bird, like a *tente* or a *pajuil.*" Thus there they were, the two tigers. The other was a Coreguaje Indian, descendant of Miguel Paranga [a famous Coreguaje shaman]. They began to hunt. Casemiro knew how to kill, how to pounce right there on that point of the back of the neck—right there, *tas.* "That's how they die," he said, "let's make two attacks. You take one and I'll take another." But because the other tiger was no hunter he didn't know where to bite. Oh! He began to sing like a bird when, in that moment, they were surrounded by *aucas.* Surrounded. Everything went wrong. *Aucas* came at them from all sides and like lightning the two tigers leapt up a tree, up and up to the topmost and tiny branch onto which they clung. Right up to there came the blowpipe darts of the *aucas,* like rain. Then came harpoons of *chonta* palm, harpoons as thick as your wrist. *Chonta* darts were falling like rain. "See my earlobe? Look! See where it's torn? That's where the darts of the *aucas* went through. Here in my heel, too, this hole was made by their darts. They almost killed us!"

Then the other tiger said: "If only we had some thunder *chondur!*"

Casemiro didn't go around with that sort of stuff. But the tiger from the Caquetá did, oh yes! He was a tricky one. And he went on to say, "I've got some. Yes!" And from out of his ear he pulled some thunder *chondur.* "Help me to sing! Let us make tempests! Let us make thunder! Both of us sing!" He blew, "oosh, oosh . . . " and they sang and in a moment the world grew dark with clouds and blackness was everywhere and rain fell in torrents. Thunder crashed, lightning flashed—and those *aucas* were spattered on their backs. *Tran! Tran!* Rain everywhere. The tigers raced down and over the *aucas.* They escaped. Then the day became clear, just like it is now, clear with sunshine.

Then the Coreguaje said, "Let's go back!" But *taita* Casemiro said, "No! Now we've escaped and left them furious they will surely try to kill us. I'm not going back!"

The other said "No! They can't do anything. They will do nothing. Let's go back."

Casemiro stalked off alone and angry. He set off for his home through those thick forests. He was walking up a hill when he heard "*cua, cua, cua . . .*" like a child crying. He said to himself, "*Caramba!* In this thick forest, what could it be?"

Suddenly naked people emerged with long green hair down to their ankles and long breasts slung over their shoulders. The crying noise, *cua, cua . . .* was coming from those low breasts. It was those very breasts that had been crying.

These people were giants called *chupias.* They live in the forest in caves and in the trunks of huge trees like the *sumbo* trees. One of the things they do is confuse hunters so that they don't know where they are or what they are doing. They follow the hunter's trail in the forest and gradually the hunter feels sleepy. However, there is a cure for this. The hunter has to take some of his poison (*curare* for blowpipe darts), breathe into it, and then rub it over his face. *Chupias* kill people and then suck the blood from the cadaver which they puncture with the finely sharpened tooth of a *cerillo* or of a *puerco zaino.*

Casemiro climbed a tree. Psst! Ready to attack. But what happened? It was like a wind. So light and so fast. He was lifted up and carried away and fell, pong! Back by the bank of the Mocoa river.

Then he got frightened. "If there are a lot of them, they'll catch me with the force they possess." And in that instant he ran along the river and crossed over because he was scared of that other side.

Casemiro laughed as he finished his tale. But the little boy was frightened and asked, "Do you go there to become acquainted with animals?"

"Yes," said Casemiro, "I went first to escape from the *aucas,* because of my friend, and then I got involved with these *chupias* that are hair, pure hair, crying like monkeys or babies . . . . This is my story—but make sure you don't tell anyone. Nobody!"

After he got married my father told us kids this. Thus he told us what *taita* Casemiro told him; *taita* Casemiro who knew how to heal and how to do sorcery and all that.

TWENTY-THREE
Priests and Shamans

Don Apolinar learned to be a powerful sorcerer. He went back to live in Umbría on an affluent of the Putumayo. He killed many people; Indians, people from Pasto, people from Antioquia. He killed people of all races. He enlisted the aid of the best Indian witches he could find—Sionas, Huitotos, Inganos, Coreguajes, Macaguajes, and from the Sibundoy valley as well. He imbued black flies with poison so that whenever they bit a person that person fell sick with fever, vomited blood, and died. And he did the same with ants and whatever little insect that bites. He also ensorcelled the river so that people would have accidents in their canoes, tip over and drown. Those who didn't fall sick fled. Some went to Yunguillo, some to Condagua, others across to the Caquetá. Umbría became a deserted town.

Taita Hilberio was a famous shaman at Umbría. He went up the mountain to Sibundoy to plead with the Capuchin monks to come and exorcize the town. He did not tell them of the actions of Apolinar. Father Plácido came and made a conjuration. This saved Umbría. Later Father Plácido wrote:

> I am convinced that the Indians call us frequently to their side and receive the sacraments not because

they are frightened of death, but because they believe that
God's power is greater than that of their witches, or perhaps
because they see in us a power superior to that of their shamans, or, finally, because they conceive of the sacraments as a
type of exorcism or conjuration against the spirits.

But not all believe that God's power is greater than that of the witches,
or that in the priests there is power superior to shamans. Take the whites
like Juan, the rheumatoid peasant from the highlands, for instance, now
securely ensconsed in the Wild Man's lair. I remember him telling me, "Some
people have the gift of healing. But only a few. What would happen if we
all had it? One is born with the gift. Anyone can make sorcery. But with a
shaman! Yes! Then you can see."

TWENTY-FOUR
History as Sorcery

It is not with conscious ideology but with what I call implicit social knowledge that I am here concerned, with what moves people without their knowing quite why or quite how, with what makes the real real and the normal normal, and above all with what makes ethical distinctions politically powerful. And in stressing the implicitness of this knowledge, which is also part of its power in social life, I think we are directed away from *obvious* to what Roland Barthes called *obtuse* meaning in his analysis of images and their difference from signs. Whereas the obvious meaning in an image is taken from a common stock of symbols and is forced upon one like a code "held in a complete system of destination," the obtuse meaning seems to Barthes (as he contemplates a still from Eisenstein's *Ivan the Terrible*)

greater than the pure, upright, secant, legal perpendicular of the narrative, it seems to open the field of meaning totally, that is infinitely. I even accept for the obtuse meaning the word's pejorative connotation: the obtuse meaning appears to extend outside culture, knowledge, information; analytically it has

> something derisory about it: opening out into the infinity of lan-
> guage, it can come through as limited in the eyes of analytic
> reason; it belongs to the family of pun, buffoonery, useless ex-
> penditure. Indifferent to moral or aesthetic categories (the triv-
> ial, the futile, the false, the pastiche), it is on the side of
> carnival.[1]

It is with imagery in the constitution of power/knowledge that the Putumayo
world I am looking at is much concerned. And it is very much this obtuse
and not the obvious meanings of imagery that leap to the mind's eye—as in
the sliding stops and starts of the phantasmagoria of the *yagé* nights, no less
than in the social relations embedded in sorcery and in the trances that
wander through rulers' minds as they are being carried over mountains.

I take implicit social knowledge to be an essentially inarticulable and
imageric nondiscursive knowing of social relationality, and in trying to understand the way that history and memory interact in the constituting of this
knowledge, I wish to raise some questions about the way that certain historical events, notably political events of conquest and colonization, become
objectified in the contemporary shamanic repertoire as magically empowered
imagery capable of causing as well as relieving misfortune.

The connection between history and memory here invoked would seem
to have little in common with the historicist view of events unfolding pro-
gressively over time. On the contrary, we are startled by an image from the
past, a magically empowered image flashing forth in a moment of danger—
bringing to mind those lines of Walter Benjamin written in his moment of
danger facing the conflation of fascism and Stalin: "The true picture of the
past flits by. The past can be seized only as an image which flashes up at
the instant when it can be recognized and is never seen again . . . . Historical
materialism wishes to retain that image of the past which unexpectedly
appears to man singled out by history at a moment of danger."[2] In which
event, then, historical materialism bears an unexpected kinship not only with
shamanism, in its colonized form, but with history as sorcery.

History, Memory, and Dialectical Imagery

In her analysis of the resurfacing of witch mythology in contemporary European feminism, Silvia Bovenschen argues that the resurgence of this image
illustrates not so much the historian's knowledge of witches and their persecution, but instead a more direct "preconceptual" relationship between
the image of the witch and the personal experiences of today's women.[3] She
points out that this sort of experiential appropriation of the past differs from
the professional historian's assumed modus operandi in that it incorporates
historical and social fantasy sensitive to the underground existence of for-
bidden images. In turning to such images, people are reflecting on their
symbolic potential to fulfill hopes for release from suffering. Related to this

is the proposition that the blocking of experience by political oppression and psychic repression can entail a subsequent process whereby that experience becomes animated and conscious by means of myths. I wish to suggest that this process is also involved in the European conquest of "primitive" societies and in the colonial decomposing of their religions. However, the "bits and pieces" that remain of these religions are *not* testimony to the tenacity of tradition, as the historicist might argue. Instead they are mythic images reflecting and condensing the experiential appropriation of the history of conquest, as that history is seen to form analogies and structural correspondences with the hopes and tribulations of the present. In noting that this sort of appropriation of the past is anarchical and rebellious in its rejection of chronology and historical accuracy, Bovenschen stresses its redemptive function, citing Walter Benjamin: "The past carries with it a temporal index by which it is referred to redemption. There is a secret agreement between past generations and the present one."[4]

Yet surely this secret agreement, despite its messianic promise, is also subject to conflict. Indeed, Benjamin finds in such conflict favored terrain for revolutionary praxis because (as in his "Theses on the Philosophy of History") he believes that it is where history figures in memory, in an image that flashes forth unexpectedly in a moment of crisis, that contending political forces engage in battle.

> To articulate the past historically does not mean to recognize it 'the way it really was' (Ranke). It means to seize hold of a memory as it flashes up at a moment of danger. Historical materialism wishes to retain that image of the past which unexpectedly appears to man singled out by history at a moment of danger. The danger affects both the content of the tradition and its receivers. The same threat hangs over both: that of becoming a tool of the ruling classes. In every era the attempt must be made anew to wrest tradition away from a conformism that is about to overpower it. The Messiah comes not only as the redeemer, he comes as the subduer of Antichrist. Only that historian will have the gift of fanning the spark of hope in the past who is firmly convinced that *even the dead* will not be safe from the enemy if he wins. And this enemy has not ceased to be victorious.[5]

In provocatively probing into hitherto little-explored zones of political control, Benjamin was also urging fellow Marxists to ponder more deeply their own implicit faith in a messianic view of history, to face up to that faith in a conscious fashion, and to consider for their activism the power of social experience, imagery, and mood in constructing and deconstructing political consciousness and the will to act politically. Another way of putting this is to point out that he didn't place much faith in facts and information in winning arguments, let alone class struggle, and that it was in the less conscious image realm and in the dreamworld of the popular imagination that he saw it necessary to act. "To convince is to conquer without conception," he wrote in "One Way Street."[6] F. Gary Smith says that in place of concepts Benjamin presents us with images, "whose conceptual dimensions, however, are as clearly legible as the outline of the 'sails' in which the dialectician captures 'the wind of world history' by his manipulation of them."[7] He is thinking of that note of Benjamin's: "What matters for the dialectician is having the winds of world history in his sails. Thinking for him means: to set sail. It is the way they are set that matters. Words are his sails. The way they are set turns them into concepts."[8]

What Benjamin came to advocate was a sort of surrealist technique using what he called "dialectical images"—an obscure yet compelling notion better left to example than to exegesis: what his friend Theodore Adorno referred to as "picture puzzles which shock by way of their enigmatic form and thereby set thinking in motion."[9] Picture puzzles is of course how Freud referred to the manifest content of dream imagery, and if it was to the manifest and not to the latent level that Benjamin was drawn, that was because of the way such images defamiliarized the familiar, redeeming the past in the present in a medley of anarchical ploys. Unlike current modes of deconstruction, however, the intent here was to facilitate the construction of paradise from the glimpses provided of alternative futures when otherwise concealed or forgotten connections with the past were revealed by the juxtaposition of images, as in the technique of montage—a technique of great importance to Benjamin. Indeed, Stanley Mitchell tells us that "Benjamin came to regard montage, i.e., the ability to capture the infinite, sudden, or subterranean connections of dissimilars, as the major constitutive principle of the artistic imagination in the age of technology."[10] The understanding we are led to is that the "dialectical image" is *in itself a montage,* both capturing the aforementioned connections between dissimilars and also that which is thereby captured.

What was at stake then was the issue of *graphicness* in Marxist method, and with that the whole way not only of representing history but of changing it. As Benjamin wrote in another note:

> A central problem of historical materialism, which ought finally
> to be seen: must the Marxist understanding of history necessar-
> ily come at the cost of graphicness? Or: by what route is it
> possible to attain a heightened graphicness combined with a re-
> alization of the Marxist method? The first stage in this voyage
> will be to carry the montage principle over into history. That is
> to build up the large structures out of the smallest, precisely
> fashioned structural elements. Indeed, to detect the crystal of
> the total event in the analysis of the simple, individual moment.
> To break, then, with historical vulgar naturalism. To grasp the
> design of history as such. In the structure of commentary.[11]

From examples that Benjamin presents of this graphicness in action in the "dialectical image," as in his "One Way Street," we can see that such images are created by the author but are also already formed, or half-formed, so to speak, latent in the world of the popular imagination, awaiting the fine touch of the dialectical imagician's wand—not unlike Victor Turner's description of the central African herbalist and curer whose adze, in chopping bark off the chosen tree, arouses the slumbering power of material already there awaiting the copula of the magician's touch.

This notion of the activist acting on something ready to be activated is well conveyed where Benjamin writes that "opinions are to the vast apparatus of social existence what oil is to machines: one does not go up to a turbine and pour oil over it; one applies a little to hidden spindles and joints that one has to know."[12]

But how does one know?

It is with this question that I turn to consider the slumbering power of the imagery of the dead in their redemptive relation to the living in shamanic ritual.

The Magic of Precolonial Pagans

"Only that historian will have the gift of fanning the spark of hope in the past," wrote Benjamin, "who is firmly convinced that not even the dead shall be safe,"[13] and this certainly comes to mind when one views their fate in the principal town of the Sibundoy Valley, that valley which for centuries has probably served as a passageway for trade goods and magical power between the people of the Amazonian lowlands and those of the Andean valleys and plateaus of southwest Colombia. Here the whites are the superior caste: they bury their dead in the part of the cemetery nearer the church and memorialize them in brick and mortar, while the Indians make do with that section of the cemetery farthest from the church, marking their graves with small wooden crosses that time soon turns to dust.

Even farther from the church, however, in the countryside and *monte* surrounding the town, and especially in the mountains enclosing it but for the narrow trail uniting the *páramos* with the hot lowlands, lie, so it is said, the bones of the "ancient ones," *infieles* (pagans, heathens, infidels), who lived here in some vaguely detailed but definitely "other" time prior to European conquest and Christian time, and today are feared as causing illness and even death through "evil wind" (*mal aires*).

Now of all the ethnomedical distinctions here, none would seem as basic and all-encompassing as that between sorcery and evil wind, which in effect are moral and metaphysical principles dividing the causes of misfortune into two great domains. Sorcery (in the forms of *capacho, sal, maleficio,* and so forth) is preeminently the domain of active human agency, the result of the conscious intention of the *envious* other. Evil wind, however, is not. It "can be said to be an impersonal agent," as Haydée Seijas writes in her treatise on the medical system of the Sibundoy Indians.[14]

While sorcery is personal and moral and inheres in the constantly generated inequality and envy of social ties, evil wind by contrast is amoral and asocial, preponderantly affecting through fright and shock the very young, i.e., those who are not held to be morally or socially responsible. As its name suggests, evil wind appears like a force of nature, emanating beyond the tortured confines of the envious social relations of the living.

If we inquire further into its origin, we may receive an enigmatic shrug of the shoulders, mimicking the uncertainty that is true to its nature, or we may hear of its links to the dead, especially if the misfortune seemed to strike at the time of *la mala hora,* the "evil hour"—the time or times of the day that nobody is quite sure about or in agreement about with anyone else, when the dead wander in the streets and public spaces to haunt the living. It depends on whom you talk to. One person told Haydée Seijas that the evil hour is like fate, for sometimes it is not one's destiny and then nothing happens, but if it is one's destiny, then one catches evil wind. Another person told her that the evil hour is when evil wind passes by. "When the wind passes very strongly, at that time the evil hour is around. The wind that passes very strongly is like thunder; they say it is a damned woman, and when she moves and goes by, the wind sounds like that. That woman is very old; she is dressed like us but her clothes are very ragged. Her breasts can be seen."[15]

Some dead seem more dangerous than others, and the evil wind associated with them may kill. Such, for instance, are those who according to Catholic doctrine are damned—an indictment that claims those whose deaths offend doctrinal purity, such as those who died in accidents without the sacraments of Confession and Absolution, suicides, and so forth, as well as those whose lives, and not the circumstances of their deaths, offended Christian doctrine, condemning them to the domain of the devil himself. A middle-aged woman told Haydée Seijas that the evil wind appeared to her one night as she was walking through the fields. "It was a tall and slim man reaching to the skies, all wrapped in shrouds."[16]

Society itself dies a little with each individual's death, suggested Robert Hertz in his now classic essay, "The Collective Representation of Death," published in 1907: "Thus when a man dies, society loses in him much more than a unit," he wrote, "it is stricken in the faith it has in itself."[17] He saw funeral rites and mourning as society's way of restoring life and integrity to the social bond itself, to what we might call the very principle of being social and being constituted by the collectivity.

Nevertheless, Hertz noted, there were certain deaths that society could not contain: "Their unquiet and spiteful souls roam the earth for ever," he wrote in reference to those people who died a violent death or by an accident, women who died in childbirth, and deaths due to drowning, lightning, or suicide. The normal funeral rites are suspended for such deaths, he observed, and in scanning the customs surrounding death in many very different societies it seemed to him that what he called the "intermediary period" between death and the final abode of the soul (similar to what I call the "space of death") is a period that "extends indefinitely for these victims of a special malediction and that their death has no end."

It is as if, he speculated, these deaths were endowed with a sacred character of such strength that no rite will ever be able to efface them. As to the nature of this sacred character, he was both obscure and unsure. It seemed to him that its strength lay in the "sinister way" these people were torn from society and that this was engraved in an ineradicable image of the death itself, "as he was when death struck him down, which impressses itself most deeply on the memory of the living. This image, because of its uniqueness and emotional content, can never be completely erased."[18]

Is it possible that, as with the image so firmly impressed on memory of an individual struck down by violence, accident, drowning, childbirth, or suicide, so the ghost or the evil winds of a whole society, struck down by Spanish conquest, could exist as unquiet, spiteful souls roaming the earth forever? Indeed, we may be told in the Sibundoy Valley that evil wind issues forth not just from the dead, whether condemned or not, but quite specifically from the dead pagans of preconquest times—as if those "other" times, prior to the violent arrival and colonization by the Spanish, constitute an entire epoch of damnation in not so much a spatial as a temporal hell located in a fermenting, rotting, organic underground of time. "Where does evil wind come from?" echoed an Indian shaman friend of mine who lives and works in the town of Sibundoy,

> from the streams that flow with movements of the air, clouds
> all joined together like strands making a skein of wool, from
> the spirits of the *infieles*, the ancient people that lurk in the
> earth in certain special places around here that Christians can-
> not or should not enter.

Or, on another occasion:

> Evil wind is caused by the bones of these *infieles* buried around
> us in the countryside. In those times there were no churches
> with graveyards. As the corpses and bones pulverize in the
> earth, so heat and vapors ascend, as evil wind, to harm people,
> susceptible people with weak blood.

As we listen to this it surely dawns on us that there are grave difficulties in thinking of the evil of evil wind as impersonal and asocial in origin. Nor is its wind strictly physical. On the contrary, these preconquest pagan dead seem to act as "dialectical images," deconstructing the conscious categories of the living. Listen, again, to the pictures evoked by these evil winds: like the streams that move with the air and the clouds playing in the sky, like the corpses being pulverized in the earth, creating heat and ascending vapors, these winds pulverize and heat up the divisions of living existence. Above all, we are now invited to entertain as in carnival and in primary-process thinking a metamorphizing network of associations intertwined with a variety of coexisting possibilities, e.g.:

- That these pagan dead mediate the social relations of the living with nature's elements, with earth, wind, and water, and beyond that.

- That these dead mediate the social relations of the living with perceived relations in nature, with a nature seen relationally as a system or structure of relationships, primarily of contrasts—not merely earth, wind, and water, but with dialectically opposed contrasts of mountain and lowland forest, highland and lowland, until we exhaust the very categorical system on which this mediation is based, namely, that dividing society from nature, with the pagan preconquest dead as its intermediaries, and entertain the succeeding semantic horizon.

- That these preconquest pagan dead come back to make a mockery of the distinction between *sorcery* and *evil wind;* that these *categories themselves change* once the whiff of death and heresy passses through them and that nature is not only a biological entity, but is also something whose distinctions are used by the mythic imagination to think with— so that this nature is also an enchanted *and* echanting landscape in which the *history of the conquest itself acquires the role of the sorcerer.*

Evil wind can thus seem like a type of sorcery employed by history to bewitch the living and created by the sort of agreement obsessively bewitching Benjamin too; that "secret agreement" (of redemption) binding past generations to this one.

The Space of Death

In pondering the implications of this concept—that the history of conquest can itself acquire the character of the sorcerer—we must not lose sight of the fact that the space of death is of necessity a zone of colonization and also a colonizing zone. Just one example of this, inviting inquiry and speculation into one of the great unwritten histories of imperialism, is the way that the "ancient people," the *infieles* or pagans of that other (preconquest, pre-European) time, have been enfolded and iconicized into the bowels of the Christian cosmos as Antichrist figures—so that they live on forever rustling the leaves of memory in the colonially constructed space of death. It is here where the great signifiers of death and the underworld, drawn from Spanish, indigenous New World, and West African sources, blended in harmony and in conflict in the process of conquest and formation of the culture of conquest.

The colonized space of death has a colonizing function, maintaining the hegemony or cultural stability of norms and desires that facilitate the way the rulers rule the ruled in the land of the living. Yet the space of death is notoriously conflict-ridden and contradictory; a privileged domain of metamorphosis, the space par excellence for uncertainty and terror to stun permanently, yet also revive and empower with new life. In Western tradition we are well aware of how death and life, and evil and salvation, are therein conflated. So in northwest Amazonian indigenous tradition the space of death is a privileged zone of transformation and metamorphosis. Only here, of course, the terms of order are quite different.

And with what tenacity the dead call the living to join them in the space of death! Haydée Seijas presents us with the following magical song as the one commonly used to cure a person afflicted with evil wind. Imagine the patient's name as Miguel:

> Wind, wind, go away, go away
> Miguel, Miguel,
> come back, come back.

And she was invariably told that it was *because the patient was going to the other world* (that of the dead) that she or he had to be called back.[19]

Just as the winds from the dead (and, one is tempted to say, therefore from the past) are to be reversed by the curer in an elegantly contrapuntal movement drawing the patient back to the society of the living, so it would seem that the magnetically attractive power of the pagan has to be counterposed—as in the use of quintessentially Christian signs accompanying the song, the burning of palms blessed by the Catholic priest on Palm Sunday, and the sprinkling of holy water, brought preferably from the far-off shrine of the Virgin of Lajas. (Discovered by an Indian!)

For it is not history understood as the passage of time that here acquires the character of the sorcerer, but history as an opposition in meaning that the passage of time marks and about which the victors and the vanquished of history array their cosmos. Herein lies the magical attraction of the evil wind of history, in the tension between the prehistory of the New World pagan and the succeeding history of class and racial struggle between the conquering Christians and those whom, because of the success of their conquest, they were able to name in memory of a geographic fantasy as "Indians."

It is from this dualism as embedded in figures of savagery and in *memories of figures of savagery* that magical power is drawn; from the ancient people, the pagans of preconquest times fermenting in the earth, to the *aucas*, Huitotos, and other fantastic pagans and *chuncho*-like beings supposedly living in the lowland forests today.

Savage Memories

I say *memories* of figures of savagery advisedly, because not only is it as memory that the ancient ones, the preconquest pagans, evoke evil winds, but this sort of memory image played an important role in the politics and theory of the conquest itself—in the intertwining of the memories of the victors with those of the vanquished.

Oviedo—the famous and very early chronicler of the Spanish conquest of the New World, Gonzalo Fernández de Oviedo y Valdés seated on the island of Hispañiola—well sets the theme, reminding us of the interest, and apparently very strong interest, that these Spaniards of the late Middle Ages had in memory and the ways by which a society transmitted its history. In his chapter entitled "Images of the Devil Possessed by the Indians . . . and the Form by Which They Retain in Memory the Things They Desire to Be Remembered by Their Descendants and Their People," he pointedly displays this curiosity concerning memory:

> In all the ways possible since I have been in these Indies, I have made it a point, in these islands [of the Antilles] as much as in the Tierra Firme to find out how the Indians remember things from their beginnings and from their ancestors, and whether they have books or by what vestiges and signs they do not forget the past. In this island, as far as I can make out, it is their singing that is their book or memorial, which from person to person remains, from parents to children, and from those in the present to those to come, as here I will tell.
>
> And I have found nothing in this generation more anciently painted and sculpted, or more revered, than the abominable and wicked figure of the demon, painted and sculpted in various ways with many heads and tails, deformed and monstrous, with ferocious teeth. . . .[20]

And on the mainland, the *Tierra Firme,* the devil is also represented by being tattooed onto the Indian body—so that as with the impress of a seal, Oviedo suggests, he is stamped into their flesh so that he will never be forgotten.

These are the figures of the *cemi,* "which is the same as what we call the devil," notes Oviedo, and they are attended upon by special men who are diviners, great herbalists, and healers. The faculty of divination is given these men, insists Oviedo, by the *cemis,* and this art is of necessity blended with medicine and magic because medicine is a most saintly and excellent thing. With the hopes and promises it raises it becomes tied to the force of religion. That is why, in our parts of the Indies, he declares (with what could, with equal force, be applied to *montaña* region of the Andes, too), the principal healers are also priests and diviners and it is they who conduct the idolatrous and diabolic ceremonies.

In these ceremonies the form of singing, together with dancing and drumming, is the "effigy of the accord of things past [that] the Indians wish to be communicated to children and adults so that they will be well known and fixedly sculpted in memory."

It is this same moral and political function of memorizing that so concerned Bishop Peña Montenegro in his lofty station in Quito in charge of the Franciscan missions during the mid-seventeenth century. In his instruction manual for missionaries, first published in 1668, the bishop notes that Indian sorcerers and magicians are the principal obstacle to the spread of the Gospel: "They resist with diabolical fervor so that the light of truth shall not discredit their fabulous arts. Experience teaches us that to try to subdue them is like trying to soften bronze, subjugate tigers, or domesticate lions."[21] It is they who threaten the Christian Indians with drought, failure of harvests, and with sending tigers and serpents to eat them. Moreover, it is these sorcerers who stimulate uprisings against the Spanish—a charge reiterated time and again by the missionaries filing reports from the foothills east of Quito, who at times associated these shaman-inspired rebellions with the holding of mortuary rites and with the drinking of the ashes of the dead.

Bearing in mind this association, (by the missionaries) of shamanic-led uprisings against the Spanish with the drinking of the ashes of the dead, it is illuminating to hear the bishop further expound on the intertwining of memory and the flesh in the moral constitution of the Indian's soul. "It is normal," he wrote,

> for the Indians in their pagan state to be idolatrous and super-
> stitious. Utilizing his malign astuteness, it was easy for the
> devil to set up his tyrannical empire among them, for they are
> people, brutish and ignorant, whom it is easy to deceive. And
> thus when the Spanish first came to this land, they found that
> these barbarians since time immemorial had been worshiping
> the devil and other creatures through various superstitions and
> abominable rites, solicited by the devil and his ministers mak-
> ing them believe in an infinite number of errors.
> This evil seed planted such deep roots in the Indians that it
> appeared to become their very flesh and blood so that their de-
> scendants acquired the same being as their parents, inherited in
> their very blood and stamped in their souls. Hence today al-
> though they have had preachers, teachers, and priests, for 135
> years trying to erase their errors, they have not been able to
> erase them from their hearts.[22]

What seems crucial about this ancient pact with the devil is not just that it is inherited in the Indians' blood (and with their mothers' milk), but that the memory of the pact is also necessary to its transmission as a reality into the future. Hence the mnemonics of that pact—anything that keeps it alive in memory—must be extirpated.

"They venerate their memories constantly with great love," wrote the bishop in connection with the way the Indians treasure their ancestors in "the hidden depths of their hearts," and he repeatedly emphasizes the need to prohibit Indian dances and songs because "in these they have the memory of idolatry and sorcery." It is also necessary to destroy the drums, deer heads, *antares,* and feathers, because these are the instruments of their evil and bring on the memory of paganism.[23]

But while this seventeenth-century bishop has something to teach us today concerning the function of memory in politics and history, this very same ideological environment that made him thus sensitive also blinded him to the fact that the memories to be concerned about were not the Indians' but his! He did not or could not realize that since it was the Church that had taught the Indians about the devil and whatever else was important in Christian demonology, these "memories" were hegemonic fictions read into the past as an outcome of the ideological struggles of the present—an invented tradition, fictions held by both Christianized Indians, such as those of the Sibundoy Valley, and the Church, as well as by the colonists as a group. The momentous irony of this is that in struggling to extirpate all traces of these "memories," the Church and its culture of conquest were in fact strengthening them as a new social force, ensuring the transmission of myth into reality and of memory into the future. Yet while a mystique was thus built into the past to haunt the living as *mal aire,* this same invented past could be seized for magical power to thwart not only *mal aire* but the vast range of distressful conditions ascribable to sorcery.

Primer Tribu

When he sings into the *yagé* just prior to our drinking it, my Sibundoy Valley shaman friend, Don Pedro, frequently appeals to the *primer tribu* or first tribe. With this he invokes two streams of tradition, the ancient people and the *sacha gente,* the people of the forested lowlands. The two streams are blended into one; the ancient with the savage, the lowlands with the beginning of time. From this stream comes power to divine and to heal.

Yet they are less old than venerable, these first people whom he conjures up in his song high up in the cold night of the highlands singing deep into the *yagé* brew itself. There is Miguel Piranga, one of the mightiest shamans, a Coreguaje, who died but three or four decades ago. There is the famous Siona shaman, Patricio, to whom both Santiago and Salvador went on occassions to take *yagé.* They are neither all that ancient nor "first." But they are certainly of the lowland. *Yagé* only grows in the lowlands and it too is connected by Don Pedro, in his own way, with the ancient pagans of long ago. "They lived in the *monte* and there they wandered," he told me, "planting remedies, including *yagé.* You go there today and you hear someone singing. There is singing there. All the visions are there, singing. Singing his song, the song of *yagé,* no? And then you exclaim to yourself, 'There wanders a shaman!' "

Huitotos

Three years later we went over a divining and curing song for an Indian woman named Andrea who wanted to know what had happened to her husband, Domingo, who had left months before to travel to Venezuela as a healer. The shaman said that this song was to attract her husband who wouldn't come back, and that normally the song would be far longer with many elaborations. Here is his line-by-line exegesis, the numbering corresponding to each "line":

1. This is sensibility declaiming delicacy; to put all the world and life into clarity as a function of time illuminating itself.
2. Good path, pretty path.
3. Huitoto people, Huitoto people: making a pact with the people below.
4. Let the illness rest.
5. I desire that the Other or the Others think well of me; that there will be friendship.
6. With my science, all will be well.
7. Come Domingo! Come!
8. I am the one who will cure Andrea.
9. Wandering in Venezuela; wandering in Venezuela.
10. I have to concentrate, I have to think hard to see if they are going to separate or not.

We discussed the line "Huitoto people, Huitoto people: making a pact with the people from below." I had never heard the word "Huitoto" before. My shaman friend tried to explain to me:

> What this word "Huitoto" means is that I have to call on the people from below, for they are strong and have the strong remedy of *yagé.* But I also have to call on the masters from up here, to defend myself. Those of below are hot, very hot, and feel nothing, while those from here, from above, are also strong and have suffered cold, cold on the plateaus. Thus you have to make a compact with the ones above and those below.
>
> We are civilized. We have clothes and housing. We eat salt and we know about God and the devil. But the Huitotos don't know, and they are with the devil, just as they are not Christians. They are like dogs. They have no soul. But *sensibility*! *That* they have! Like animals. And as animals they can see the invisible. For instance, a bad spirit comes here. We don't see it, but the devil [and he corrects himself quickly], that is to say, the dog, the dog sees.

He continued:

> There is a story about a woman who had a white dog, no? And
> the dog howled and howled at midnight. It molested her aw-
> fully. "Scat! Get away!" But the dog kept howling, howling
> and howling. Finally the woman caught the dog and cleaned
> the muck out of its eyes, saying, "Why are you howling so
> much? Are you trying to see something?" Then the dog ran
> just like a Christian, as if to bite something. When the dog re-
> treated, she said, "What's going on here?" Then she saw a
> skeleton filling all the space, everywhere.

"Thus," he concluded, "the dog sees and knows the phantom, just as other
animals see evil spirits and evil phantoms. And the Huitotos too, they are
in league with the devil, they see and converse with each other. Because
the Huitotos have no soul, but just a spirit of air. They don't eat. What they
eat is wind, or flowers, nothing more than the fragrance of flowers" (like
those spirit creatures, freaks, and monsters in the medieval bestiaries depicting the "marvels of the East," the savages of India and Ethiopia). These
Huitotos are like snakes that even from a few meters away can suck out
your blood, he told me. They have long fingernails that they sink into your
flesh to extract blood. The distances over which they can leap and fly are
vast. In a flash they can bound from the forests to the tops of the Andes to
Sibundoy or even to the city of Pasto.

Tied to the devil as they are, the Huitotos have no moral sensibility. Like
animals they don't know the difference between right and wrong. But like
animals they are powerful and have sensibility and knowledge possessed by
no human.

The relationship between the highland shaman and the Huitotos, and scored
in the curing song, is like that of a master to a well-trained dog. As in the
story of the woman with the white dog howling at midnight, it is the highland
shaman's function to clean the eyes of these lowlanders and in so doing
appropriate their vision and sensibility, fusing it with the aid of the lowlanders' *yagé* to the power and reason of the Christian civilization that not only
defines but imputes such awesome power to otherwise inferior savages.

But Why Huitotos? The Story of an Apostolic Excursion

When Manuel Gómez, a white colonist from the highlands, first entered the
Putumayo lowlands and took *yagé* with a Kofán shaman some forty years
ago, he felt as though he had died. He was convinced, he told me years
later, that he had died that night upon drinking his third cup of *yagé*. And
in the prelude to that space of death, at death's door, so to speak, in the
rushing of a hurricane and darkness broken by flashing lights, snakes en-

veloped him and erupted from his vomiting mouth. Then came a tiger and the Indian shaman asked him if he was scared. "No, just a little," he replied. The tiger disappeared and by the fire Manuel saw, to his horror, the devil, just as he is painted, with horns and all, hot and red. And then the devil changed into the shaman, sitting by the fire, so relaxed, smoking tobacco. But then he changed back into the devil and Manuel died—only to ascend to heaven and receive God's blessing, and with it to feel the fresh mists rising off the green of the forest as he descended, a new man. It was this composite and alternating image of the tiger-Indian shaman-devil that swung him into the space of death, just as it was a white man who swung a Siona Indian boy of the Putumayo lowlands into the space of death when he took *yagé* with his shaman father, I presume approximately seventy years ago, at the time of the rubber-boom atrocities in the lowest reaches of the Putumayo.

> When I was given the third helping of *yagé* I saw snakes emerging from their homes, in incalculable numbers. Then I saw a white man, armed with a machete and a bayonet. That was another *pinta* [painting or vision]. It started off as a white man who wanted to kill me with his bayonet, and, what is more, throw me on a fire. I screamed in horror. This was another *pinta*. But then came a woman of advanced years to wrap me in a cloth and put me to suckle her breast, and then I flew far away, very far away. Suddenly I found myself in a place shot through with light. Everything was very clear, placid, and serene. This is where the *yagé* people live. They look like us only much better. That is where I arrived. I entered into a very pretty house. All the people came adorned with feathers and *cascabels*. They beseeched me to dress as they did. Their tunics had paintings of tigers and other things. This was another *pinta*. After that I saw God who has a large cross. He blessed me. This is another *pinta*.
>
> After that I saw a church, large and beautiful. I went in to see the ceremony and how the people ought to conduct themselves. They gave me a sort of wine of sugared water that represents the refreshing medicines that the shaman gives sick people. This is another *pinta*.
>
> They took me to where the sun is born, where there are two compartments, one transparent and one dark. To get there you see the night and the day. This is another *pinta*. . . .[24]

In 1926, a decade or so (I assume) after this Siona boy had this vision (as recorded by the Colombian anthropologist Milciades Chaves in the 1940s), two Capuchin priests from Spain, Gaspar de Pinell and Bartholomé de Igualada, began their famous and heroic "apostolic excursion" to discover and Christianize what they called "new and savage tribes" in the jungles of

the Putumayo downstream from the Siona. Following the international outcry aroused by Sir Roger Casement's report in 1912, validating with much
detail the charges of hideous atrocities in the rubber belt of the Putumayo,
there was subsequently a call to douse the violence there with Church influence. The estimated 30,000 to 40,000 Indians, mainly so-called Huitotos,
in and around the center of rubber extraction along the Igaraparaná and
Caraparaná affluents of the Putumayo in 1909, had by missionary calculation
dropped to a pitiful 8,500 by the early 1920s. Many had died from smallpox
brought by the whites. Many had fled. Others had been sold into the debt-
peonage networks in the forests and wound up in Bolivia or Brazil. But the
main causes of the massive decrease in population, thought Father Gaspar,
were the horrible tortures and massacres carried out by Julio César Arana's
Peruvian and British rubber company.

The preparations for the apostolic excursion were carried out in the highlands with great zeal. Masses were held in the schools and churches of Pasto
and the Sibundoy Valley to celebrate this crusade to save the savages of the
jungles below. Spiritual exercises with a large complement of the Capuchin
order were held, in which Father Gaspar and Father Bartolomé were declared
to be the patrons of this excursion of the Divine Shepherdess, the beloved
mother and patron saint of the Capuchins. Trade goods, gifts, and medicines
sufficient for six months' to a year's travel were amassed, but by far the
most important item, as far as Father Gaspar was concerned, was the painting
of the Divine Shepherdess, approximately four feet high and three feet wide,
that he had specially commissioned in Pasto "so that our Divine Mother
would not only accompany us with her invisible protection," but also that
"the love toward her would penetrate into the souls of the savages and the
civilized of those regions, *not merely by means of our evangelical word, but
also through the eyes of all*" (emphasis added).[25]

The effect of such soul-penetrating colonial imagery was no less intense
when provided not by artifice but by nature. While waiting for the Huitotos
to prepare a great dance at the junction of the Caguán and Caguetá rivers,
Father Gaspar observed how "rarely such a savage picture presented itself."
The site was virtually hidden from the rivers but when entered proved to
be large and, to his mind, like a celestial crypt. "Its waters are dark," he
wrote, "old logs rot in the riverbed, its banks are lugubrious, and the tall
trees covered with growths and funereal mosses create a crypt so saddening
that to the traveler it appears like walking through a tunnel leading to ghosts
and witches." The four or five huts built by the Indians (adopting a form of
housing favored by whites) somewhat diminished "the note of terror, to
augment that of savagery." He was "surrounded by a circle of secular jungle
filled with the roaring of wild beasts and the strident tones of birds and
insects, which, far from making the situation happier, filled it with melancholy." This "celestial crypt" so narrowed the sky that during the day the

"Grupo de indios salvajes del Caquetá." (From Gaspar de Pinell, *Excursión apos-tólica por los ríos Putumayo, San Miguel de Sucumbios, Cuyabeno, Caquetá, y Caguán*, 1929.)

sun focused its burning rays, while at night, the spectral light of the moon and stars lit up romantic fantasies. The final touch was the plague of insects that bit night and day.

> There, far from civilization and surrounded by Indians who, ac-
> cording to their customs, could at any moment kill and serve
> us up as tender morsels in one of their macabre feasts, we
> spent spiritually blissful days—as we shall see when I give ac-
> count of the results obtained from our apostolic labors.[26]

White colonists immersed in this jungle claimed the Capuchins' attention too. One day Father Gaspar came across a family of colonists in great distress. A six-year-old boy had disappeared in "a manner extraordinarily strange and mysterious." The parents had gone off to Puerto Asís to celebrate Easter, leaving their seven children in the care of the eldest. The six-year-old went off fishing with two of his brothers and disappeared without anyone realizing how. They said a *duende* had taken him, and when Father Gaspar pressed for details they said a small shadow had passed by; their little brother was caught in its tow. They called and searched, but the boy was never found.

A similar thing occurred to a peasant family in Florencia when a father and his young son of seven or eight years were walking in the jungle. The son disappeared and was never found. Another instance concerned an Indian family gathering rubber for their *patrón*. The parents left for a day's work, leaving the children behind. The *patrón* (a white man) heard a voice from the forest calling the children. It sounded like their mother, and the children ran off. When their parents came home their children were nowhere to be found and they accused their *patrón* of murdering them. Three days later the son was found at the foot of a tree, fresh and happy as if nothing had happened. Two weeks later the daughter was located in the center of a bamboo thicket, again as if nothing had happened. When asked what she had eaten during that time, she replied that a little *señor* had taken good care of her.

In the neighborhood of the Angels in the subdistrict of Bethlehem of Andaqui, four or five years before Father Gaspar's apostolic excursion, a two-year-old girl was lost in the forest. She was eventually found on top of cliffs so steep that adults could barely climb them. It had been raining heavily, yet the tiny girl was dry and happy. When asked how she had got there and who had given her food, she said it was her father who had done that. "What on earth does this mean?" asked Father Gaspar.

Even more miraculous things happen in these jungles, he went on to note. One day he was called to a house that people said was plagued by a *duende* that was biting and molesting a woman. At first incredulous, Father Gaspar had cause to reconsider his skepticism when, in front of his very own eyes, bites of various sizes together with saliva began to appear on the woman's arms. "I blessed the house, exorcized the site, and exhorted the woman to leave. It seams that the affair thus finished with no more consequences."[27]

Through such encounters is faith fortified and the Church assured its role in society. Yet the ironies and even subversions are not to be underestimated. It was not a priest but an *Indian*, albeit a shaman, that the whites in Bolívar, Cauca, on the other side of the cordillera, called upon to deal with a *duende* a few years ago. That's what Santiago Mutumbajoy said. Father Gaspar came long-gowned and rosary-beaded from the city to the jungle, exciting the Indians' attention and spreading the light like sun into the dappled forest; the Indian went feathered and tiger-toothed from the jungle to civilization, spreading hallucinogens into the envy-riddled lives of coca growers and traders.

To mobilize Indians for Christian conversion, Father Gaspar found it convenient to enlist the aid of Colombian rubber traders. Indeed, by the time of his apostolic excursion, in 1926, Father Gaspar indicates that there was a type of concordat operating in the Colombian Putumayo whereby rubber traders asked permission from the Capuchins to *conquer* (as the expression went) Indians and use them as rubber gatherers. The traders coached the missionaries how to track down hidden Indians, while for their part the traders appear (so unlike Arana) to have found it beneficial to have their debt-peoned Indians influenced by missionaries.

Although at first skeptical about the *duende,* Father Gaspar was never in doubt that the nameless dread in those forests demanded religious warfare. "Great is the faith I hold in the exorcisms of Pope Leo XII against Satan and his angels," he declared, and

> because of this, at all the places we arrived to exercise the
> ministry during our excursion, my first act was to perform this
> exorcism, with the aim of banishing the influence of the demon
> from those jungles whose length and breadth had for so long
> been occupied by him because of the lack of ministers of God
> to dispute his reign.[28]

And when he did finally meet with Huitotos, rachitic runaways from Arana's rubber camps, Father Gaspar's first action was indeed as he declared, the exorcising of the demon according to Pope Leo's rites.

There was much about the missionaries to arouse the Indians' curiosity— their beards, spectacles, long gowns, and their rosaries. "They commented with animation," noted Father Gaspar, "and made jokes about everything, creating great guffaws." Twice a day with an interpreter the fathers expounded on the mysteries of the faith with the aid of their large oil paintings. With satisfaction Father Gaspar observed with what care the Indians inquired into the smallest detail of these icons, and "how into our explanations they intercalated long commentaries connected with their own traditions."[29] During these three weeks of preparation, the Huitotos would of their own accord pass periods contemplating the paintings, after the priests' explanations, and they never tired of asking questions, says Father Gaspar, about the most insignificant details. As events drew to their climax, the night before the baptisms, the Indian men stayed awake, orating in a large circle, sucking now and again from their fingers dipped into the tobacco pot—the famous *chupe de tabaco,* performed, Father Gaspar informs us, whenever the Indians have important matters to discuss, as when the chief gives instructions to his people to gather rubber for the whites, do agricultural work, go hunting, attack another tribe, or attack Whites. Three or four men may orate at the same time, and they repeat the same idea a thousand times but in different words. When a pause is reached, all the men repeat the last few words with a prolonged "mmmm," thus preserving, noted the good father, "their beliefs and customs intact from generation to generation, without the necessity of books or newspapers." From generation to generation, from Oviedo to Father Gaspar, the same fascination with memorizing, tradition-binding and tradition-making, with songs, mmms, and collective rites, all without books (or newspapers). All this takes place, observed Father Gaspar, in the lugubrious obscurity of the night, in a form supremely monotonous.[30]

The mortification caused the missionaries by this interruption of their sleep was more than mitigated by their learning what it was that the Indians were discussing, "recapitulating all the things learned in these days about the

". . . they never tired of asking questions. . . ." (From Gaspar de Pinell, *Excursión apostólica por los ríos Putumayo, San Miguel de Sucumbios, Cuyabeno, Caquetá, y Caguán*, 1929.)

mysteries of our saintly religion, focusing most especially on the impression caused by the paintings of the death of the sinner, the judgment, heaven, and hell."[31]

It had been Father Gaspar's explicit intention to use paintings to ensure that the souls of the savages would be penetrated not merely by the evangelical word but by visual imagery. Yet for that imagery to take hold of the savages' souls and become part of their imagining, the savages had to put that imagery into words, their own words, through the medium of communal ritual and narcotic stimulation. And if beneath and permeating and commutating their words there now lay the power of this colonizing imagery, there was also their "own" history, the rubber-boom history of terror and diaspora ready to be shaped into the space of death—the death of the sinner, the Last Judgment, heaven and hell.

The advantages savage rites offered the missionaries were not lost on Father Gaspar. Following his first experience of the tobacco ceremony he noted: "Blessed be the God that permitted a medium employed so many times by Indians to do damage to their brothers, to serve this time for the good of their souls and for divine glory."[32] He saw that when the Indians did this, they added to their stream of traditions the teachings of the missionaries. More than just an advantage, the (male) rites of discoursing and tobacco-taking "could be the best means for inculcating the tribes, even the most ignorant, with the true ideas of religion and with Christian customs, provided that beforehand a chief of prestige and eloquence has been instructed." Perhaps he would have had the same opinion of the *yagé* rituals, carried out not by Huitotos but by Cofáns, Sionas, Coreguajes, and Inganos, much farther up the river. In this regard it is worth noting the story I have heard from upriver Indians, that Father Bartolomé, Gaspar's companion, championed their taking of *yagé* and advised the Church not to harass them for it.

But the irony is obvious enough. Poor old Gaspar! Could he have envisioned that now, many decades later, it would be the white colonists, not the Indians, who would be inculcating into their traditions what they held to be Indian magic and religion?

In any event, does he not overstate his case? Inculcating the Indians with his religion by means of their rites could create new and strange forms. For instance, Father Jacinto de Quito, who traveled through those forbidding Huitoto forests in 1906, fifteen years before Father Gaspar, found the Indian men absorbed in a ball game. With amazing skill they would pass a ball of rubber—the very substance Arana's men were killing them for—to each other, from knee to knee. They called this ball the "heart of Jesus" and regarded it with reverence. Father Jacinto said it would not be an exaggeration to say they venerated it in the same way that we venerate the reliquaries of our saints. Asking "one of the most intelligent *indios* why they held such an insignificant object in esteem he was told that in remote times some whites

The performance of the sacraments. (From Gaspar de Pinell, *Excursión apostólica por los ríos Putumayo, San Miguel de Sucumbios, Cuyabeno, Caquetá, y Caguán,* 1929.)

came there. They were good people and brought images of the Virgin. The Child in her arms was carrying something round, the heart of Jesus, and that is why our playing ball is like playing with the heart of God.[33]

My Ingano Indian friend, Florencio, was at the age of around fifteen years chosen to accompany Father Bartolomé on an apostolic excursion down the Caquetá River, to the land of the *auca* Huitotos, as Florencia calls them. I do not know if this was the same excursion as Father Gaspar records, but it well could have been, and I think it important to contrast his memory of this event with that of Father Gaspar's chronicle.

Like the good Fathers, Florencio partook in a farewell ceremony, but one that was probably a good deal less splendid. A Siona shaman invited him to drink *yagé* before setting forth, to protect him from the Huitotos. When Florencio eventually got to meet them he was very impressed. He calls them not simply Huitotos but *auca* Huitotos, meaning something like "wild men" Huitotos. "You wouldn't believe how those people can cure," he told me. "What remedies they must have!"

On his first encountering Huitotos,

Father Bartolomé said they would kill us. We had to camp elsewhere. Then a large canoe full of *aucas* went by full of pots,
bows, and arrows. We found a huge house, but empty of peo-

ple. Nobody! They'd gone! Someone was tied up in there, even
the feet. There was blood on the earth, and heaps of skulls,
broken bows, corpses, murder. They'd done it to rob, and then
fled. That was the day of San Francisco, and Father Bartolomé
said mass to ask for faith and the fatherland to locate those *aucas*. The interpreter knew where they were. "Padre, we're getting close!" Father Bartolomé said, "You go first. I'll wait."
The interpreter said, "I'll go and talk to the captain." He was
chewing coca. Poom . . . poom, . . . and spitting. We watched
from afar. The interpreter said, "I'll signal if you can come."
They had a huge rounded house with many people and full of
hammocks. The priest talked to the interpreter and the interpreter talked with the *aucas*. The priests brought mirrors, perfumes, cloth, lights . . . little presents. It was good. We spent
months there, five months! The priest . . . living in the one
house. And it was a good time. The people learned "Padre
Nuestra," "Ave María," . . . all the prayers. If they wanted to
be baptized, they were baptized. What was the meaning of the
cross, of an image, of a saint, what it all meant—they learned it
all. And when the priest left, how the people cried! He said to
me, "It grieves me and makes me lament to leave."

When the day came for Father Gaspar and Father Bartolomé to celebrate
the holy rite of baptism and of marriage the Indians adorned themselves in
the new clothes given them by the missionaries, together with their necklaces
of animal teeth, feathers, and seeds. The missionaries had problems controlling the hilarity of the Indians, yet were pleased with the performance
of the sacraments, following which they distributed more gifts to commem-
orate the day: pictures of Christ and religious medals "which the Indians
received with gratitude and devotion, putting them immediately to their
chests as trophies of the triumph obtained against Satan and his angels."[34]
The most dramatic conversion was that of Rigache, the fearsome killer
who had been one of the brutal guards maintained by the rubber company,
and who was now precariously maintaining his chieftaincy over this motley
band of local and refugee Huitotos. As a killer for the rubber company, he
wore necklaces made from the teeth of his victims. As a neophyte of the
missionaries he now instead hung medals of Christ and of the Virgin of Lajas
from his neck, demanding that his name be hispanicized to Antonio. He was
presented with a large painting of the Trinity intended for the main house
of the group.
The bones of Father Gaspar's steadfast companion, Father Bartolomé,
now lie, so my Sibundoy Indian friends tell me, in the cathedral of Sibundoy,
where they are as revered as deeply as they are concealed from sight. After
more than a decade of discovering and Christianizing new and savage souls
in the forests below, he came back to live in these mountains where his fame
as a medicine man conversant with both Western and Indian medical systems,

with both God and with sorcery, ensured his posthumous popular sanctification. It is said that Huitotos taught him to drink *yagé*, and that he thought highly of it.

As for the Huitotos, we have at least one sign of how their history has been rendered by the present, and that is in their being called by the Sibundoy shaman as a way of gaining magical power to discern the future and overturn evil. While Father Bartolomé's memory is cherished, that of the Huitotos is used—and who could say why?

From Sign to Image: The Obvious and the Obtuse and the Tripping Up of the Disorder of Power in Its Own Disorderliness

The apostolic excursion to discover and Christianize the heathen in the jungles below had occasioned much splendor and ceremony in the missionaries' home base of Sibundoy in the mountains overlooking those jungles. Other crusades followed and the Indians and whites of Sibundoy seem to have been constantly informed of, if not aroused by, their progress and successes, especially with regard to the savage Huitotos. These crusades were also commercial and nationalistic in their stated purpose, and the missionaries' texts display pride to the point of religious ecstasy that they had opened up for the Colombian state this enormous fraction of the Amazon basin to commodity extraction and to colonists.

Could it have been from these crusades that the magically empowering image of the Huitotos fell into the repertoire of my highland shaman friend? Perhaps the magic lies in good part with an identification with the fate of the Huitotos, with the sadness and romance of their history. Could it be that, as with the misfortune brought by the patient to the shaman for remission, so the Huitotos represent not only misfortune but its healing as well? In the use of the image of the Huitoto for the purpose of making a compact with them, might there not lie a profound empathy not merely with the victims of history but with their subsequent "salvation" at the hands of the Church fathers as well (notwithstanding and in fact precisely because this salvation was largely ceremonial)?

Thus we could suggest a magically empowering analogy of this sort: a set of narratively organized structured isomorphisms connecting a history of savage Huitotos, colonial terror, and Christian salvation, on one side, and the fate of the misfortunate brought for the highland shaman to relieve fifty years later in the mountains far away, overlooking those hot Huitoto forests.

Such an analysis spreads its healing currents of magic farther still, to spill into the lives and work of many of us involved in historical analysis and textual commentary today, for it arouses not only a deeply cherished love of creating order from disorder, but also evokes one of the cherished chartering texts of structuralism, namely Claude Lévi-Strauss's essay "The Effectiveness of Symbols," wherein he explains the use and the efficacy of a

Cuna Indian shaman's healing song for a woman in obstructed labor (in the region of northwest Colombia and southern Panama).[35] In a self-enclosing view of the song as a text ripped out of any world but its own internal referentiality (and in ignorance or defiance of the strong likelihood that the patient did not understand that text), the analysis proceeded in just those terms of analogy and of narrative ordering climaxing in an isomorphically established catharsis that could, perhaps, be imputed to the therapeutic role of the Huitoto image in the Sibundoy shaman's song, too.

Many readers found it a pleasing picture: the pregnant woman lying in her hammock with the smoke from the cacao beans swirling around her as she passively absorbed the meaning and the order—above all, the order—that the man sang into her as a prerequisite for the settling of chaos and the birth off new life.

But now as the smoke clears do we not discover this very analysis to be a magical rite too—albeit one adorned in the garb of science? Is it not the case that the very analysis of the magic of the shaman was no less magical than its subject matter? The controlling figure here is that of the anthropologist or critic ordering meaning into the disordered, passive, and forever female vehicle of the text—so as to "permit" the release of a new meaning rescued from the blockage of disorder.

But what would happen if instead of this we allow the old meaning to remain in the disorder, first of the ritual, and second of the history of the wider society of which it is part? My experience with Putumayo shamans suggests that this is what they do, and that the magical power of an image like the Huitoto lies in its insistently questioning and undermining the search for order. To the extent that the Huitoto image in the highland shaman's song might embody a narrative of redemption from colonial terror, it functions as an allegory tripping up the disorder of misfortune in its very disorderliness—bringing to mind the techniques implied in Benjamin's "dialectical images" as well as these shamanic rituals' artistry with montage, and laughter. So much laughter. "It belongs to the family of pun," wrote Barthes with reference to the obtuse meaning of images. "It is on the side of carnival."[36]

There is a curious way by which the shamanic technique of tripping up disorder in its own disorderliness is boosted by the terms of order inhering in the civilizing process and in the daily execution of colonial authority. The point could be briefly summarized by understanding the image of the Huitoto in the shaman's song as an image of *tamable savagery*—suggesting the paradox, the contradiction, and the magnitude of the deconstructing strain in the Putumayo history of civilization and the terms by which first the rubber company (with its terrible violence) and then the Church (with its extraordinary use of magic) represented civilizing history and savagery. It is not just that a morass of contradiction and paradox is thus generated by the necessary semantic interdependence of civilization and savagery, as that dependence is made concrete and particular by the materiality of Putumayo history, but that for the creation of magical power in healing rites what is important is that the Huitoto image makes it virtually impossible to ignore the dependence of meaning on politics—in this case colonial, racist, and class oppression. The eruption of the dialectical image of the Huitotos in the highland shaman's song is aimed with surreal precision at the conceit of modern world history taming savagery. It is an image that arrests the flow of thought not with order but with a question: Whose order, whose savagery? In making his compact with the Huitotos, as with a hunting dog, the shaman tames savagery—not to eliminate but to acquire it.

After all, this was how the rubber company in the forests below had viewed and used the *muchachos,* the Huitoto men trained from youth to serve as company guards, torturers, and killers. In thus using them, the company objectified its fantasies concerning the people of the forest, creating very real savages from its mythology of savagery in order to coerce the people of the forest into gathering rubber.

Behind this apparent resonance set up between the highland shaman's invocation in the mountains and the rubber company's use of the Huitotos in the far-off jungles below, lie centuries of similar imputation of magical powers by higland Indians to lowland ones. To the determination by memory of the imagery of the Huitoto condensing the structure of feeling of the twentieth-century history of what Walter Hardenburg called "the devil's paradise" of the Putumayo rubber boom, with its suffering and salvation and taming of savagery, so there is also this overdetermining arc of memorization rendering a sweep of time further back than even the Spanish conquest of the Andes.

As these two arcs of memorizing coalesce in the imagery of the magically savage Huitoto invoked in the song that the highland shaman pours into the maw of uncertainty widened by misfortune, so there is a coalescing of the two opposed ways by which memory, supposedly the Indians' memory, was used to ensure their conquest. Bishop Peña Montenegro in the seventeenth century urged that Indian rites be extirpated root and branch because these rites brought into consciousness what he called "the memory of paganism." But working with the same premise, that ritual embodied and reawakened memory, the twentieth-century Capuchins, such as Father Gaspar working with the Huitotos, developed as if by accident quite the opposite conclusion and strategy: namely that to erase the pagan-stimulating function of memory, the rituals should be maintained so that with the memories they embodied could be intertwined the images—the oil paintings—of Christian suffering and redemption: the death of the sinner, the Last Judgment, and heaven and hell.

Is it possible that these opposed modes, whereby history has put memory at the service of colonization, are themselves registered in contemporary healing magic and are necessary to its power? Is it possible that the evil winds buffeting the living with the memories of the preconquest pagans correspond to the bishop's and the early colonial politics of memory, while the resurrection of the Huitotos corresponds to a modern mode of trying to use memory to change and dominate people? Is it possible that these winds and savages stand as mnemonic images of distinct historical modes of memory production and reproduction, whose most finely wrought expression is to be found in shamanic imagery where it is precisely the task to rework, and if possible undo, the history of sorcery with its memory?

TWENTY-FIVE
Envy and Implicit
Social Knowledge

Quite often in the Putumayo, listening to people in a healer's home talking about life and problems, I get the feeling that the sensitivity to envy is as ever-present and as necessary as the air we breathe. This sensitivity is not merely a foundation of what we might call shamanic discourse, organizing a sense of the real and of personhood; it can also be thought of as a sort of sixth-sense or antenna of what I call "implicit social knowledge" slipping in and out of consciousness as a constantly charged scanner of the obtuse as well as the obvious features of social relatedness. Acquired through practices rather than through conscious learning, like one's native tongue, implicit social knowledge can be thought of as one of the dominant faculties of what it takes to be a social being.

We can think of this knowledge as a set of techniques for interpreting not so much the seemingly direct as the various shades of meaning of social situations—the "situation," as Henry James depicts the intertwining multiplicity of possibility in group affairs, the splitting and the further splitting of meanings and suggestions in such a profusion of gatherings and precisions that not only society but life itself is turned about for reflection.

And the interpreting enters into the situation interpreted. Implicit social knowledge is not simply a passive, reflecting, absorbing faculty of social being; it should also be thought of as an experimental activity, essaying this or that possibility, imagining this or that situation, this or that motivation, postulating another dimension to a personality—in short trying out in verbal and visual image the range of possibilities and near-impossibilities of social intercourse, self and other.

Above all it is envy—discussing its manifestations and ramifications—that provides, as it were, a theater of possibilities in social life. It is on this stage that implicit social knowledge roams and scavenges, sharpening its sensitivity, its capacity to illuminate, its capacity to wound.

It is not the least extraordinary accomplishment of *yagé* nights to make this implicit social knowledge explicit, in both its discursive and nondiscursive or imagistic dimensions. *Yagé* nights can be thought of as epic theater addressing and redressing the discourse of envy, the outstanding feature of which is the failure to reciprocate and treason in friendship. The larger issue to which this epic theater responds is one's spurning of the social bond itself, in a violent enactment of the mythology of the self-nourishing asocial individual who thereby motivates society's counterblow of sorcery.

After partaking of many *yagé* nights you can see this epic theater at work in a person's face or in a fragment of a situation. it is hard to forget Rosario and José Garcia matter-of-factly telling their tale of envy with their tightened faces, or of being with their son at dusk walking past poorer neighbors in the deepening shadows of his fears of their envy and readiness to deploy sorcery.

Envy is not so much the cause of sorcery and misfortune as it is the immanent discursive force for raking over the coals of events in search of the sense (and senselessness) of their sociability.

As the organizing "principle" for delineating misfortune, as the sociopsychological "theory" of the evil inevitably flowing from (perceived) inequality, and as the dominant signifier of perturbation in the social bond, the presence of envy is not so much analyzed as talked around in its concrete particulars and ratified as immanence—with a hint or a gesture as that ominous, tiresome, and unpleasant fact of nature, framing and staining the human condition. Perhaps here the notion of a "discourse" is powerfully appropriate, envy being a theory of social relations that functions not by setting up a hierophany of causes, but as a presence immanent in the coloring of dialogue, setting its tones, feelings, and stock of imagery.

In which case it would be mistaken to think of envy as a theory that can be excavated out from under the welter of its surface manifestations, fragments in a drunken spree of wild empirical cavorting surrounding as a nimbus the maidenhead beyond which lies the pleasure of orderly Truth to be "taken" by the social scientist. But what if there is no more truth than what meets the mind's eye on the surface in the fragments and nowhere else? Then the inquiry gives way to depiction—in precisely the way that anybody in the Putumayo caught in the coils of envy strikes out into the bubbling stream of implicit social knowledge in order to interpret those fragments and their feelings, which have neither beginning nor end but a plethora of effects.

Vomiting the Envy of the Other

Sometimes envy is represented in iconic, stage-filling, monumental ways, as when Borbonzay, a young Indian man from the mountains who lived and worked on Santiago's farm for several years, owning little more than the shirt on his back, could not stop vomiting that night in October of 1976 when a group of us were taking *yagé*. He asked Santiago for a drink of the calming "fresh water" of special plants and asked him to cleanse him well—to sing over his body, to breathe into him, to wipe down his legs, chest, and back, down his arms to the end of his fingers, his face, and all round his head to suck the evil out from the crown of his head, and then to beat his almost naked body with stinging nettles of *ortiga* which, lime green and fleshy-red, hangs limp and forlorn after it has beaten and opened up the body to let the evil of others' envy out. But Borbonzay kept on vomiting. After midnight he sat down again on a stool in the candlelight in front of Santiago and started to talk softly as the rest of us stirred, confiding in him, confessing, so it first seemed to me, as if to a Catholic priest. But what he talked of was neither confession nor his sins, but, on the contrary, of what scared him and what his vomiting meant, namely the *envidia* that someone or ones had for him. It was their envy that was in him and making him heave out the slime of his insides into the frog-quavering night.

The healer's voice quavered too. I do not know if he was frightened but he was, at this instant at least, very serious, drinking in Borbonzay's words. For in a way his stake was even greater than Borbonzay's. His was a more constant battle with envy leveled at him, on occasions by people no less powerful in the magic arts than he. Perhaps this involvement in the coils of *envidia* was not only a dangerous byproduct of his healing task but was also necessary to it. In any event it was clear and important that the sick person and the healer suffer this fear of envy jointly entwined as I remember them in the shadows of that night.

Envy is nearly always spoken of as producing its evil effects by lodging inside the bodies of the people envied, in their stomach, head, chest, and lower back. Curing exorcizes it from those bodily zones through the shaman's sucking and stroking, and by the purgative effects of *yagé*. Purgation is stressed by peasant colonists in the Putumayo as one of the great virtues of *yagé,* and here the physical and the metaphysical are unfathomably intertwined in the poetics of vomiting and shitting, evacuating envy from the inner recesses of one's being.

Talking Envy: What the Blind Woman Saw

Thus there is this powerful imagery of *far away* and *inside* the body, explosive reversals in shitting and vomiting the bad stuff out, purgation—not confession but the making physical of a sense about a social relationship, envisioning it as the putrid substance of envy imploded into the fastness of one's body—then the magic of curing, strange plants, strange people (Indians, blacks, wizards, magicians, possesed people) hallucination, "purgation."

And then as counterpoint to this graphic and too-direct way of imagining the twisting of social bonds, there is another plane of discourse in which envy glistens but for an instant as a hint in a conversational crack, inviting speculation as much as ratifying the way of the world—like a note I jotted down one afternoon on a day-long journey to the Putumayo river in December 1982: "Santiagueña women in green dress weeping by her stall in the quiet little marketplace of Villa Garzón; telling another market woman about the death of her husband one month ago. '*Malhecho, envidia,*' she cries, tears streaming, 'nobody to joke with anymore.'"

That night we took *yagé* with Santiago's sister and her household in their raised house by the banks of the Putumayo. His sister had been part of the flight of Ingano Indians from the Mocoa region, relinquishing those fertile lands to the incoming white colonists. Now old, she lived with her aged husband and some of their adult children in the still-forested margins of the Putumayo, a hut here, a hut there, making a small Ingano community of sorts, beleagured by the wave of incoming colonist peasant farmers. One of these, a man reputed to be using sorcery, whas saying her husband was a witch, an Indian witch, and that the way to deal with him was to set fire to their house.

As we settled into our hammocks waiting for the night to settle in, Santiago reminded me of how I had left him a present of the hammock he was now using. After years of use the strings had worn through and he was about to throw it to one side when a young girl staying at his house had said, "Don't do that! My mother makes hammocks for a living. She'll fix it for you." They had come all the way from Venezuela. The mother had become blind a few years earlier and she picked up the hammock, disentangled the strings, measured out the lengths on her thigh, and indeed repaired it beautifully; a marvel! She had been told by people in Venezuela that her blindness was due to sorcery, *maleficio,* and she wanted very much to know if that was true.

A wandering Indian herbalist from the Sibundoy Valley had been selling his wares in Venezuela and had fallen in love with her daughter. "In my land," he said, "there is nobody who can really help you, but *below,* he stressed, in the hot country, there is someone that knows. His name is Don Santiago."

So the three of them, the blind Venezuelan, her daughter, and the Indian herbalist from the Sibundoy Valley, traipsed all the way across the great ups and downs of Colombia to its very border with Ecuador where they rested in the herbalist's home. But it was the time of the fiesta of Todos Santos when the Indians go from house to house drinking *chicha*. The Venezuelans lost their guide. They became solitary and bored. "What else would you expect with all that cold up there in Sibundoy and no manioc to eat. Only corn!" But then they found a woman who said she'd help them find that man called Santiago in the *tierra caliente* below.

They came to his place and he had some uncooked *yagé,* good and thick, "like we are going to take tonight," and he gave her a gourdful.

She saw who did the *maleficio*. It was her sister. She screamed at her invisible presence for hours.

"Why did you do it? Why did you do it? Why did you become envious? After all the food and clothes I'd given you! Why did you do it?"

And she stopped and demanded: "Give me a knife! Now!"

The daughter cried and cried to hear this. "Oh Mama! Oh Mama!"

"Next day," continued Santiago, "I gave her a cure and asked her if she was sure."

"Of course I'm sure," she contested, "I saw it as clear as day. I saw her doing it to me, every little bit."

"She told me I should go to Venezuela," said Santiago. "I would make a lot of money."

One Can't Be Sure of Anything

People can be envious of just about anything, so it seems. And the envious person is dangerous, so aroused by envy that she or he will try to kill through magical means—*chonta* (blowpipe darts in the case of the lowland Indians); *magia* and *capacho* (in the case of the highland Sibundoy Indians); *magia* and *sal* and *maleficio* (in the case of the civilized castes and classes—the blacks and the whites).

It is by no means only the rich who are the targets of the envious. I remember being with a lanky sixty-year-old fever-stricken white man named Alquimedes. He was a wage-laboring migrant from the moutains. His gauntness typified the rock-bottom poverty of that barely nourished class who cut the cane, tend the mills, weed the cattle pastures, and plant the corn and manioc of their better-off neighbors.

"It's *envidia!*" he told me, referring to the fever that shook his wretched frame.

Years before his wife had died, five months pregnant, in the mountains where they had lived all their lives. "One suffers much up there in Las Mesas," he told me. "The *journales* [days of wage labor] are very scarce

and goods are very dear." That's why he came to live here. With his son
and two daughters he rented a room and built a hut by the side of the road.
The only land he could now afford to buy for farming was a long way
downriver and in the forest—"*bien adentro*," he sighed—deep in the hot
country whose climate and illnesses he feared. It was nine years ago that
day when he left his home in the mountains at Las Mesas to look for work
with his daughter Miriam way in the north, in the sugarcane plantations
around the town of Palmira in the great agribusiness valley of the Cauca
river.

"And the day that we left, Miriam and I, that night my wife had an attack.
And that attack went on till she died. Before reaching Palmira I received a
telegram saying I should return because she was in the agony of death. So
I went back and when we arrived already, already the house was lit with
candles. She was dead." It was only ten or eleven months later that he heard
she had been killed out of envy. It was a *maleficio,* he told me.

His son offered us a glass of brandy, but the old man declined and we
joked about Miriam now working in the province's official brandy distillery
and the opportunities that offered. Alquimedes returned to his story.

"It was at a gathering of roadworkers, right there by the road, a man told
me he had been paid to give a medicine to my *señora* . . . to kill her."

"What?"

"A *señora* paid him to give a medicine. That medicine took her to the
tomb. She was five months pregnant, and failing twenty minutes to her death
she expelled the child, and twenty minutes later she died. There were two
deaths in one. . . . That was tremendous, *Don,* let me tell you!

"We buried the two cadavers in the same coffin. Later my father-in-law
asked me to place a denuciation with the police to try to prove who had
done this. But the sorrow involved in digging out the cadavers, and the
problems with the Registry . . . so it remains with my God to punish them."

In the mountains there are no powerful curers like the Indians down here,
he said. But people who know how to harm? Yes. There are those!

"They said that she had been given soil of the dead, taken from the
cemetery and put into her coffee. These were things against which there
was nobody capable of fighting. The *médicos* said it was a heart attack and
a cerebral hemorrhage. But whatever it was she has left us. And she never
harmed anybody. We were always correct."

One night years after his wife died, Alquimedes went over to Santiago's
place. It was a special occasion. It was the second of those three nights I'd
only heard about that it took Salvador the Cofán shaman, to cure Santiago
of the deadly illness inflicted, it was said, by Esteban, the highland Indian
shaman who was using *magia.*

"I only went one night," laughed Alquimedes. "How could I take more
than one night of drinking *yagé*? Don Salvador was too drunk with *yagé* to

cure anybody, but he certainly did have a curious and rare understanding of things. Rare was the understanding of that man.''

"Like what?"

"He could tell what you were suffering."

"Just from looking at you?"

"Yes! What ailed you. What had happened to you in your life. He was very drunk and he said to me, 'You're the person that Don Santiago recommended?' 'At your orders,' I replied. And he said 'A long time ago something very strange happened to you.' And I said 'What could it be?' 'Aieee . . .' he exclaimed. 'Your *señora* didn't die because my God called her but because she was killed! Listen! . . .' Then we began to talk and Don Santiago came over and told me, 'This is a man in whom I have great confidence. Talk with him. I'm going to reserve a gourdful of *yagé* so that you can see how your *señora* was killed.'''

"I saw something" said Alquimedes, "But . . . who knows? One can't be sure of anything."

The poorest of the poor, like Alquimedes, can feel they are victims of envy. For what a poor man has may not be measurable in coin of the republic or so visible. I remember being taken by surprise cooking *yagé* one afternoon in the woods by the river. I was helping a young Ingano man and the hours passed in excitement and monotony as we talked of this and that. He told me his household had all come to be cured because someone had damaged them so they would fight all the time. Everything they touched, so to speak, turned into a neighborly quarrel, sometimes bloody. His mother's arm had been in a machete fight. People attacked them all the time, he told me, envious that the sons stayed home with the parents and helped them.

The Envy of Cattle

Now and again people come to have their animals, espeically their cattle, cured of sorcery. Spurred on by a World Bank cattle-rearing program, which introduced Zebu and later dairy cattle, some peasant farmers have acquired herds. Before 1980, when illegal coca cultivation was many a poor farmer's *el dorado,* it was cattle and only cattle that put cash into one's hands. At the same time there was the feeling that cattle created more inequality and more visible grounds for envy, as grimly illustrated in Rosario's and José García's life history.

One heard a lot about cattle stealing, yet worrisome as that was, it was really the least troublesome problem with cattle, José García assured me, because it could be prevented, as were his farm and Santiago's, with magical potions prepared from tiger's fat. But it could cost 4,000 pesos (at a time when the daily rate for field labor was around 100).

How did the beauty and tail-swishing silence of cattle emerge in *yagé* visions? In the squatness of their four-hoofed solidity, spreadeagled knee-high in mud or soaring grasses, unaware of the hot passions they so dangerously evoked in the human breast, how did they figure in the hallucinatory pastures roamed over by the mind's imagining? I used to wonder about Santiago's visions of velvety soft, moist, mooing cattle jostling him all night that first time we took *yagé* together in 1975. It was his imagining that caught mine: the stocky yet infinitely graceful man in the candle's chiaroscuro, floating in his diadem of tigers' teeth between the heaps of people lying in misery and exaltation, cleaving and calming his way through their tears and laughter just as he was doing with those beautiful cows at the very same time.

Later, as I tried to stand outside the situation's self-portraiture and explain it, there were other images to contend with, such as a World Bank utopia of a tropical forest cow heaven. Was Santiago's image making a response to his new and consuming anxieties about cattle, whether his own or his patients'? Was this furry bovine world displacing that of the angels? Certainly in what might hesitantly be called an Indian "cosmology," changes were observable. It was a far cry from the plains of a Texas cattle ranch for the Cofán shaman Don Salvador and his sons searching two whole days in the Putumayo rain forest for their one cow. They found it stuck fast in the mud to its shoulders and it took them another day to lever it out with thick saplings.

"Each class of animal has its owner," Salvador told me, "and the shaman has to negotiate with that owner when you want to hunt that animal. The shaman pays the owner with beer or with *yagé*. He talks with the owner when he takes *yagé:* 'I want one *danta*,' he says. And it comes. Easy and tame it comes; and fat, too."

I wondered, however, about these bovine newcomers to the forest and its muddy environs, especially because, unlike other animals, it appeared they did not have spirit-owners.

"Yes, all animals have their owner," reaffirmed Salvador. "Our owner is God. We are the owners of the cattle because we kill them just as God decides when we have to die."

But it does not seem that this concept of property rights vested in killing rights does much to dignify the rather different concept of property and capital (Old English: cattle) promoted by the World Bankers. On the contrary, *envidia* aimed at making cattle ill so that they fail to thrive or even die is rampant, and after the human body I'd say the body of the cow or the bull is the most sensitive sign of envy. Many's the time that Santiago has been asked to consecrate during a *yagé* night a mixture of cornmeal, salt, and *ganado chondur* for cattle to eat to cure or protect them from sorcery motivated by envy.

Still, it was only at the very end that he was asked to intervene when his son's beautiful bull (worth about 18,000 pesos, so he boasted) became terribly ill. It stood under a tree motionless, without eating, white foam bubbling slowly from its blue-membraned mouth. "It's a *maleficio*," Santiago's son told me, "it's common. *Envidia!*" And he was pretty sure from whom the *envidia* had come. To cure cattle thus suffering is far harder than to cure human beings because cattle can't take *yagé* and be purged, he added.

He tried everything but the bull slowly sank to the ground as the days passed. On Christmas Eve Santiago contrived to have a small party at his house because (he told me) he feared that when the young men went into town that festive night they would drink hard and brawl. He borrowed a battery-powered record player and we danced and drank *aguardiente* together.

His daughter Natividad had come up from the Caquetá River with her children. Some poor country people had just been shot dead there by the army, falsely denounced, she said, by an envious neighbor as aiding the *guerrilleros*. In another incident, close by, the soldiers shot dead a small Indian girl, a companion of her own children; half the girl's head was blown away by machine-gun bullets, they said.

"The people of the bush came through our place and asked for batteries for their megaphone," said one of the kids about the *guerrilleros* as we sat outside between dances. "They wanted money, and we gave it. They said we needed a road to get to market easier. But we already have a road. Whites came along it and stole our hens."

"The soldiers are killing innocent people. What can we do?" asked his mother.

The young boys were smoking cigarettes. The girls were in flouncy frocks. Young boys asked women to dance. There were but three small records and they were played over and over again as we shuffled and jigged through the night in this broad-beamed house of delights fanned by the cool wind from the river and the forest.

Shortly after midnight I was fixing a pot of coffee over the fire outside when I heard a terrible scream. Santiago's son Antonio had suddenly gone crazy. In the midst of the dancers he had taken a machete and attacked Pablo, a young man contracted two weeks earlier to clean the pastures. Pablo's face was streaming blood from a slash running from eye to mouth. Everyone was motionless, crying, and Antonio himself looked like he was dead, lying on his back on the floor. We staunched the pumping blood and Santiago's wife, Ambrosia, in the flooding of her tears insisted that Santiago cure Antonio and herself as well. Santiago steadied his wailing and began to sing and sweep over Antonio with *ortiga* stinging nettles—to sweep out, as Ambrosia put it, the fury and the anger.

"But," protested Santiago, "how can I cure people when they're drunk?"

He came over to me as if the world had cracked open. For this was a frozen instant of sheer possibility; anything could happen.

"*Yagé* makes the visions," he said in his grief, with unfathomable intensity, "of what is right and wrong. It gives us Indians the *pinta* and it was given by God. It's our study, *es nuestro estudio,*" he repeated as we sat through the chilling night awaiting dawn, in a quiet punctuated by the groaning of the two young men, barely conscious on the floor.

That afternoon the bull died.

When I came back at dusk there were four people out in the mist of the field gathered around Antonio, who was cutting his way into the mass of the bull. They were hungry people from the landless colonists' huts across the river, waiting to hack out steaks of flesh that nobody else would eat because the bull had died of disease.

Antonio came in half an hour later saying he had searched everywhere in the bull's stomach for signs of sorcery but had found nothing.

There Are Things Which Have to Be Cured When the Time Comes . . . or Else: The Butcher Expounds on Sorcery and Drinks *Yagé,* His Sons Tie Up a Young Man from Across the Republic Who Goes Mad with *Yagé,* and José García Returns to Drink *Yagé* with the Indian

Too many cattle of one's own: that was the cause of Rosario's terrible sickness, according to José García, and as her illness worsened, and because she was scornful, if not fearful, of Indian curers, so José García had been noticeably absent from the *yagé* nights over the past two years. I suggested to him to come and join us in taking *yagé* one Sunday in December of 1980, almost exactly a year after Antonio's bull had died.

With us that night was a big placid *campesino* named Eliseo, twenty-eight years old, from the foothills of the Andes in Boyacá on the other side of the republic of Colombia. He was a *blanco,* a white man, who so wanted to become a man of magic that he had traveled this far to learn. I never really understood how this learning was supposed to occur. Sometimes it was said that you could buy this knowledge, while at others it was said to be a vocation of genius beyond purchase. I guess Eliseo was trying to figure this out too.

This was his second time here. The bus fare alone cost him 1,600 pesos. He had come with his cousin, Luciano, who was a few years younger than he. He first heard of Santiago, he told us, from an Indian of the far-off Casanare which flows eventually into the Orinoco and from where that mighty medicine of the *cabalongo* seed can be so easily obtained.

"They get it there out of the trees in sackfuls!" Santiago assured me, and he went on to say that the plains of the Casanare were where the *arch-millionarios* had their stupendously large cattle ranches. "They don't buy cattle by the head out there," he chuckled, "they go up in helicopters and point with their fingers at entire herds!"

There was also a pompous—oh! such a pompous!—middle-aged, garrulous, fat, aggressive white man, a butcher, from one of the little frontier towns of the Putumayo. With him were his two skinny adolescent sons carrying a huge radio. He had a big Stetson hat and a stick with a plaited leather whip of the sort that butchers flaunt to great effect. He had taken *yagé* once before, seven years ago, when nobody would buy meat from his stall in the market. Another butcher had put a *maleficio* on him, he told us in a torrent of words as we gathered on the veranda as night fell, readying ourselves to take *yagé*. These *maleficios* between butchers go on all the time, out of envy, he said.

"That's it! For sure!" emphasized a pregnant woman who owned a small store in a nearby town, "all the time between storeowners." She was here with her husband because they couldn't sell enough to make money. They were suffering a terrible *aburrimiento*—boredom—she said, and an *espiritista* or spirit medium who was helping them gave them something with bones from the cemetery. But things had gotten even worse, and Santiago seemed to think that far from being cured with this, they had been further afflicted with sorcery in the form of *sal*. So they put it back in the cemetery.

The dogs barked as José García came over the hill swinging his flashlight. The butcher started the conversation again, talking of corruption in the local government.

"All Intendentes come here to steal!"

"To steal!" echoed José García. "There's a lot of money in this territory."

"With these mines they've just discovered," noted Santiago, "of copper and platinum."

"Ah! There's so much," said José García, and we were quiet as the dark drew us together. A woman started to talk softly with Santiago, but with desperation, talking of crying. People walked around.

"Here there's no lack of it!" snorted José García, alluding to sorcery. The butcher coughed and spat in agreement. Then he cleared his throat and declaimed in a loud voice to all and sundry.

"I tell you there is a person in the house where I live in Villa Garzón, a señora Inés, the widow of the deceased Gómez. Don't you know her? I've been there five months. This *señora* makes bricks, she makes tiles . . . I'm telling you! She had a mountain of bricks and tiles . . . things to sell. And *nobody* buys even one tile! And *nobody* buys even one brick! Nobody buys anything. Nothing! Nothing!"

"Nothing!" echoed José García.

"And this *señora* has to stop work. There are times when she cries and cries." The butcher paused. We waited.

"And I ask you, what is going on in this house? I ask you! In the name of the blessed Christ that's on the mountain peaks, just today something strange happened to me, very strange. The girl that was there, went yesterday to Umbría to get married. Clearly I couldn't accompany her because I had to work at my stall in Villa Garzón. 'Go with your mother,' I said, 'and tomorrow when the slaughterhouse is closed I'll join you.' But what happened was that there was no marriage! Nothing! She had to come back! And in the early dawn I breakfasted, then went inside and felt funny. An intranquility hardened inside of me, like a thing. But what could there be inside me? I went out and came back in. Nothing. I said to my daughter, 'Little daughter. . . . '" The dogs were barking furiously and his words were lost to us.

". . . Security . . . leaving, and entering. Here! Here!" He thumped the ground with his whip. "And when I closed the door, like a bolt I felt this cold shiver. I thought I would die. Help! For God that is on the mountain peaks get me out of this! I prayed as I staggered against the wall. I was choking to death. Why?"

"When was that?" asked Santiago. "Yesterday?"

"Today. this morning!" The butcher was almost screaming. "And with what force I was held to the wall! My daughter cried, '*Papacito,* what is wrong? Lie down on this bed! What hurt you? What hurt you?' No! Let me cry! Let me cry! And I cried with that strange thing not letting me stop. Unable to stop. 'I feel a terrible *aburrimiento* here in this house, but what can we do?' And that *thing*! I tell you. And that *señora*: how long has it been since she's sold a brick? How she would cry!"

Santiago yelled at one of the young men to make sure there were coals in the fire for burning copal incense.

"Something's got to happen," continued the butcher in a quieter, philosophical, and somewhat sinister tone. "My *señora* lives in Puerto Asís and she said to me, 'Why don't you leave? You can't adjust here!' She visits now and again. The only company I have is my daughter, and she's getting married soon."

José García and Santiago interrupted the ensuing silence to further organize the taking of *yagé*. José García then went back to the butcher's tale with a story of his own concerning an unfortunate brickmaker who turned out to be the victim of sorcery. The woman seated next to him, who sold plantains in the marketplace, started talking about her desperation and boredom, her *aburrimiento*. She couldn't sell plantains. Money left faster than it came. She was sick. Her family was sick. . . .

Santiago laughed. With fearsome gravity the butcher clenched his whip and declared: "There are things that have to be cured when the hour comes, or else. . . ." He said it again slowly.

Breathlessly the plantain seller gave more details to José García, who was asking pointed questions and sighed.

"Two years at your stall and nothing gained!"

"What a thing!" began the butcher, unable to finish.

"*Si! Está salada!*—Yes! It's sorcery!" exclaimed José García excitedly.

We talked some more about the corruption—the *serrucho* or "cross-sawing"—of the government. I quipped: "So there are two problems in the

Putumayo: *serrucho* above and *sal* below—corruption in the governing class, sorcery in the poor class." Everyone laughed. A voice came out of the dark. "*Sal* at the bottom and envy in the middle!" Laughter gushed.

The market woman was excited. She went on with her list of woes, ending with the lament that she couldn't find work.

"That's how it is!" snapped José García with authority. "You can't get anything. You sell, but the money disappears. . . . Ah! *La sal está tremenda*! Sorcery is tremendous!"

Poised on the edge of his seat and still giggling about *serrucho, sal,* and *envidia* in the middle, Santiago poured the *yagé* from its plastic container into a metal bowl resting on a wooden tripod at his knees.

The smell of *yagé* flowed through the dark, and those who had drunk it before shuddered at the memory of its acrid taste—the fecund smell of compressed forest vines, roots, trunks, leaves, thorns, and mosses squelched into millennial mud. Everyone was quiet. The old man called on someone to bring in a brazier, an old sardine can. Yellow granules of copal resin were sprinkled on the coals and clouds of piney fumes like honey were wafted over each of us by the swinging arcs of the assistant's's arm. The old man was half turned away from us in his hammock in the corner. There was a pause for a minute or two. Everything was very still. He bent down from the waist and blew into the *yagé*, just once, paused again, sat quietly, and poured alcohol on his neck, arms, and face. Slowly he rubbed it in.

"Esaís hasn't been for a long time," he said suddenly. Then he picked up a fan of leaves some sixteen inches across, *waira sacha,* wind of the forest, spirit of the forest, *sacha* as forest, as wild, as in *sacha gente,* people of the forest, *aucas,* he said. He poured a little alcohol over the leaves, rubbed them straight on both sides with soft caressing strokes, let fly with one of those rifle-shot clicks of the tongue that cracks the world open, like parting a sun-dried melon, and burst into song, chanting *yagé* sounds, not words, to the rustling beat of the curing fan for some ten minutes.

"Blow that candle out!" he demanded, leaving but one light throwing and retrieving shadows across our faces and Saint Michael's cobwebbed struggle with Satan framed on the wall above our heads. His eye was streaming and he wiped it—the other eye was blind, the eye that Esteban was supposed to have destroyed with *magia* from the highlands two years before. The singing resumed briefly, then he poured out a small gourdful of *yagé,* blessed it with the gesture of the cross, crossed himself, and drank.

He told me that he blows and sings into the *yagé* in order to consecrate it, to purify it "because the *yagé* can come with evil, with spirits of the forest, snakes, frogs, vampires all mixed into the *yagé*. If you drink such *yagé* you see these spirits and have an awful and perhaps dangerous time." But much depended on when and how a question was posed. Years later he said that one consecrates (sanctifies) *yagé* so as to try and ensure that its power is not put to bad ends, "so that Satan gets out of there"; so that the people taking it are not tempted into hurting others with its power: "*Como el yagé es poderoso, entra la tentación.*"

And there was also this question of origin: From where did the power come? *From the shaman* who imparts spirit through blowing and through singing sounds (not words) into *yagé, or from the yagé,* which allows the shaman to see and to sing? No, there was no question of origins here.

Each of the fourteen or so of us in the room was then in turn offered a gourdful of *yagé* about the size of a teacup, and for a few seconds or minutes Santiago sang into each serving. The bitter taste makes you shudder and nauseated even before the medicine trickles into the stomach. We joked a little and lapsed into quiet with the shadows of the solitary flame leaping across the planked walls and into the black hollows of the roof. There was sheet lightning followed by claps of thunder every now and again and the *yagé* made us cold, shivery, and frightened.

I cannot easily speak for others, but after many years and occasions of taking *yagé* myself and talking with others during and after taking it, I do not feel that my experience is unusual or singular, especially with regard to what I would call its *form*—and it is with form or rather the break-up of form that I am chiefly concerned in the evocation of what is important in these *yagé* nights. Yet things are not so simple, and there is this paradox, that in trying to depict the general one has to seize upon the singular, because *yagé* brings out and indeed depends upon intense living at extremity and exploration of the inchoate. There is no "average" *yagé* experience; that's its whole point. Somewhere you have to take the bit between your teeth and depict *yagé* nights in terms of your own experience.

Thoughts become feelings and feelings thoughts, not necessarily in the epiphanal instant conceived by the Romantic conception of the image or the symbol, but in a friction-filled rasping of planes of different types of experience grinding on a sort of no-person's-land where concept and feeling fight it out for priority, leaving a new space where the sensation lives in its glowing self. It is also the case that, associated with this, the world "outside" trembles into life and unison with the world "inside."

I have read that Warao shamans of the Orinoco delta ready themselves for certain types of magic, especially heavy sorcery, by inhaling thick cigar smoke into the spirit-inhabited canyons inside their chest in order to feed and release those spirits, while Yanomamo shamans in southern Venezuela, when they take their hallucinogenic snuff, move into an interior landscape of valleys and mountains forming fantastic worlds that nestle inside the glistening slipping plates of muscle and pillars of bone that become a hallucinatory exoskeleton—telescoping the outside into the inside and the inside into the outside through the portal of the breath and the voice.

But perhaps more important is the stark fact that taking *yagé* is awful: the shaking, the vomiting, the nausea, the shitting, the tension. Yet it is a wondrous thing, awful and unstoppable. From his stay with forest people of the

Vaupés in Colombia in 1939, Irving Goldman concluded (without stating whether or not he had ever taken *yagé*) that "the Cubeo do not take *mihi* [*yagé*] for the pleasure of its hallucinations but for the intensity of the total experience, for the wide range of sensation. I spoke to no one who pretended to enjoy it."[1]

After an hour or so Santiago swung out of his hammock and began vomiting. The sound of his slow gurgling retching filled the room, a waterfall of man expending itself. He wiped his lips clean and beat his chest and legs with *ortiga* nettles. People were stirring in the room. He began to sing, then to retch again, then sing once more. Perhaps he was singing what he heard—what the spirits of *yagé*, the *yagé*-people, were singing. The sounds to me were like those of the forest at night: rasping, croaking frogs in their millions by gurgling streams and slimy, swampy ground. As the waters and the wind rush faster, so did the pace of the song. The curing fan, "wind of the forest," was a blur of rustling motion. That rifle-shot crack of the tongue splintered the quavering air which the raspy voice poured into the cascading shadows. Santiago was curing Don Arcesio's little daughter of the fear, the *susto* she suffered when she got a thorn of a *chonta* palm in her heel. Her parents extracted it all except for the black tip, which receded farther and farther. Two days later her whole leg started to hurt. She became demented, they said, screaming that the spirits of the dead were coming into her body and taking her over. "Evil wind—*mal aires*—spirits of the dead . . ." mumbled Santiago, explaining to me that when a splinter gets into your foot like that in the forest, *mal aires* can enter too. That's why the forest in the Putumayo is dangerous, he said.

She was on a stool in front of him. he was seated on his hammock. He blew a *soplo,* a breath, over her—just he blew into the *yagé* to begin the *yagé* night—and as his song pulsated faster and faster, drawing in succeeding waves of tingling, he swept his curing fan over her chest, legs, and arms, and finally over her face to the crown of her head. He paused to vomit, heaving, rasping, wheezing, and spitting. Somebody unsteadily stumbled to the half-opened door and into the night. The sounds of vomiting came clearly to us. Someone sighed. Someone else giggled. Santiago wiped his face and chortled from deep down in his belly and burst into song. He sang a long time, for maybe ten minutes, then stooped to suck out the evil winds, the spirits of the dead, from her chest, limbs, and head, spitting them out of doors, out into the night, spitting, sucking, and chanting. "Woosh fire, woosh fire . . . wooshh shh shh . . ." it sounded like, getting fainter and fainter until it had become like the tiniest rustle of leaves in another time and place far away in somebody else's dream—only to be swept up mightily by our collective presence, into which, by means of one galvanic crack of the tongue, the song darted like a flame around us all, crackling and purifying.

Our first gourdful was uncooked *yagé* prepared by Don Arcesio and without much kick. "Not enough *chagropanga*," someone said—the leaves of the female companion of *yagé,* said to be essential for visions. The butcher was nervously stomping around in his noisy boots with his cattle whip thwacking his side. Somebody started teasingly to joke about butchers always tricking their customers by selling too much bone and fat and not enough meat, and there was a ripple of mirth. Santiago and José García started teasing each other: "The *Indio* is short and thick; the white man is long and thin." Then José García started talking to the market woman about the sorcery done to his farm at Santa Marta. The words were emphatic; repeated; urgent; superlatives: "all, all . . . nothing, nothing . . . worst, worst. . . ."

Around midnight we drank an older brew, of cooked *yagé.* It was terribly strong and I can't remember much of what happened for a while. then José García was chuckling, "*Serrucho* above, *sal* below." We all chuckled.

"We suffer one and cure the other," I joked.

"If we can," he chuckled again.

Santiago had the butcher take off his shirt and be cured. He spent an hour or so singing over him, sweeping and beating him with nettles, an activity he interrupted many times: to talk softly with the butcher, but with excitement ". . . that's the *envidia* from which you suffer . . ."; to vomit, and to tell us a story about how he couldn't drink alcohol now because of a terrible drinking bout with rum and home-distilled brandy (*chancuco*) forced on him up in the Sibundoy Valley when he went there recently with a couple of friends to drink *borrachera*—datura—to harden themselves. *Yagé* gives far stronger visons and is not crazy-making as *borrachera* (literally, drunk-making plant) inevitably is. Yet *borrachera* does have this role in "hardening"— in firming up one's resistance to sorcery attack, or as they also say here, in becoming *cerrado,* closed.

You could feel every twinge and stab as he described the pains he suffered up there in the valley that night. He then told the butcher that he was in a bad way and needed another cleansing in the morning. With more *yagé,* with visions, sleep, and dream, he might well gain a clearer picture of the butcher's problem and its cure.

The curing fan whooshed down, rustling and crackling the space into a whirling storm of leaves as the chanting churned our tender stomachs and bowels once again. The song's pace changed all the time and in it was the fury and the voyage in the song right there. And then Santiago would stop abruptly, in mid flight, to tell a joke, to tell Luis Antonio to stop the dogs barking, to bring *chondur* to chew while curing, or whatever, and then the tiniest hum might begin, a needle point in the storm of stories and sounds of vomiting and people leaving to shit, and the song darted forth.

The two young men from the other side of the republic, from Boyacá, were lying on a bed of planks. The younger one, Luciano, went crazy, weeping and screaming "*hijeputa, hijeputa. . . .*" He would sing a little too.

It was not hard to imagine what sort of things were passing through him because you yourself felt so crazy too. Then he began to beat his head brutally against the wall, slithering under the bed of planks and, alone in his "cave," as Santiago called it, would wail and bash his head even more forcefully.

Santiago sang over the boy hidden from sight, quivering in his "cave." The song was strong and confident; pleading, enticing, and demanding. The sobbing boy kept on bashing his head against the wall and someone suggested that he be tied up. The butcher's skinny sons had in their fear stayed outside all this night on the veranda, clutching at their mammoth radio. They were experts at tying up squirming, wriggling flesh, especially pigs, because that is an important part of the butchering business. With Santiago's singing fluttering about them and with their father pounding his cattle whip on the

the Butcher

floor as his staff of office, rocking unsteadily on his heels under the broad brim of his hat and behind the beam of his flashlight, supervising and giving instructions, the skinny lads with the stylized ease of experts uncoiled ropes and tied up the boy who had come all the way from Boyacá with his cousin Eliseo to learn magic from the *indio* of the Putumayo.

"Sing *yagé!* Sing *yagé!* Paint *yagé!* Paint *yagé!*" the song resumed, enveloped us, carrying us as we were talking, lying, sleeping, vomiting, shitting, shaking us for hours it seemed.

Then I heard another song. It was José García. he was chanting somewhat like Santiago but with Spanish words and more like a sung Catholic prayer with endless repetition: God . . . the Virgin . . . God . . . the Virgin . . . (no frogs here!). He had taken a curing fan and was curing the market woman and her husband, sweeping out the evil from them, sucking, spitting, singing his song: "Sing *yagé, yagé canta,* paint *yagé, yagé pinta,* good luck, good luck, *suerte, suerte,* heh, heh, heh, blessed God, *Dios Bendita, Espíritu Santo,* ya, heh, heh, help me with the sick, *Gloria del Espíritu Santo. . . .*" He was moving the curing fan fast. The words were tumbling out. Someone was vomiting outside. Santiago was chatting with somebody.

José García's high-pitched voice rose and fell. It was a furious high wail rising to a peak then trailing off: "Sing. Sing. Cure. Cure. *Yagé* sing. *Yagé* paint. Good luck. *Yagé* cure. Heh heh. . . ."

Then came another sound, the raspy baritone of the wind scraping boughs one against the other in the forest, the sound of the river tumbling boulders in the river, sluicing and eddying, the sound of grinning stoic frogs squatting in moolit mud, shaking in their warbling—Santiago had begun to sing too.

The two men were singing with and at one another, with me in between. José García had come across the room to cure me. He was deeply affected by the *yagé.* As I looked up at him towering above me and saw in the moving shadows flung by the candle his deeply etched face with its protruding ears and deep furrows around his mouth, I saw instead another form—a mask, like the great-mouthed, dog-toothed, Indian stone-sculptured heads I think I've seen in the mountains, tomb covers, a week's walk from here at San Augustín.

Seated just behind me was Santiago and I felt I was in a sort of cross-fire. Santiago's singing was beautiful. He slowly sped up to a peak, then suddenly slowed, clicked his tongue, then started again. In the trailing-off, José García adjusted his rhythm so that Santiago's *yagé* sounds and his Spanish praying dove-tailed with each other, through me at their feet amid the flurry of their curing songs and fans in crackling dialogue. I felt that José García had come close to abusing his position, yet what he had done was almost inevitable—curing within the curing session; the consecrated consecrating; the breath and the *yagé;* the sick man himself curing the sick—and he has seized on me as a medium to work on and through. The stony Indian masklike character he appeared in, combined with the singing in duet, seemed to me to make

him into an active echo of Santiago—the "real Indian"—behind me, an echo struggling to approach the Indian but also struggling to be itself.

Santiago was unperturbed, and the two of them kept at it for what seemed a long time.

José García had not taken *yagé* for who knows how many months or even years, and now in one fell swoop he was a *curaca,* a Putumayo Indian shaman, doing and becoming everything.

Later he asked me if in my visions I saw his sick wife Rosario. "How did she look?" he wanted to know. But I had not seen her and he went on to say that only now did he accept that she could die. She was the "queen of my life" he said, "never to die."

Lightning flashed through the open door. Soft rain fell. Now as Santiago's song went faster and faster in the cold early morning of cocks crowing to the echoes of the still-hot memories of crying and laughter of this passing night, the room took on a new feel, as holy as any holy temple but one whose serentity had been achieved by a night-long Dada-like pandemonium of the senses.

In the excretions are visions. The stream of vomit, I had been often told, can become a snake or even a torrent of snakes, moving out from and back into you. In the streaming nasal mucus, in the shitting, in the vomiting, in the laughter as in the tears, there lies a sorcery-centered religious mythology as lived experience, quite opposed to the awesome authority of Christianity in its dominant mode as a state religion of submission.

In this infinitely warmer and funnier Putumayo world of *yagé* nights, there is no way by which shit and holiness can be separated, just as there is no way of separating the whirling confusion of the prolonged nausea from the bawdy jokes and teasing elbowing for room in the *yagé* song's irrestible current, with neither end nor beginning nor climactical catharses but just bits and pieces in a mosaic of interruptedness.

Santiago was now curing Luciano, the young man from Boyacá who had to be tied up by the butcher's sons. He was singing, caressing his body, beating the curing fan, sucking the evil from his body. Here people *externalize* their problems as the creation of the envious Other (whose name is best left unmentioned or left in a film of obscurity) while the whole point of the curing is to go *into* the body, into the head and the chest, into the stomach and the flesh, breaking up the compaction of envy there imploded with the concussion of laughter and the shock of splintering sensation.

Despite its materiality as compacted force within the interstices of the body, the cause will always remain uncertain. Whose envy? Is it sorcery? Why? In this world of epistemic murk whose effect in the body is so brutally felt, the cure also comes forth as something murky and fragmented, splintering, unbalanced, and left-handed. The hands of the curer are powerful and gentle, they wring evil from the body, while the song in its riot of stopping and starting and changes of pace is without destiny or origin, circling that body, rustling and darting, tripping up disorder in its own disorderliness.

TWENTY-SIX
The Whirlpool

Three days after this night with the butcher, with the boy who went crazy, and with José García becoming a *curaca,* Santiago and I were in a bus bouncing along the one road in the territory near the Putumayo River with a gallon of *yagé.* Peasant colonists with tiny clearings in the forest upstream from Puerto Asís at a point called El Remolino—the Whirlpool—had talked him into traveling to their place to heal.

In answer to my questions he was telling me about the Capuchins, about Father Bartolomé who wandered through the forests of the lowlands baptizing *aucas,* wild Indians, with whom he took *yagé.* Santiago had been a servant to Father Fidel Monclar, the head of the Capuchin mission from its inception at the turn of the century, and had had to empty his bedside commode in the mornings.

Now, sixty years later, as that history emerged in stops and starts with the jolting of the bus as it made its way toward the frontier, we were conscious, in so slight a way, of the historical irony of our progress, retracing yet also contradicting, opposing yet also affirming this colonial endowment: the legendary white man, the original colonizer, the holy man, Father Bartolomé, wandering in the dank Putumayo forests baptizing wild Indians and drinking hallucinogens with them, supposedly, while the just-baptized young "wild" Indian, Santiago, destined to become a *yagé* shaman, was pressed into the priests' service in the convent, emptying their commodes. Added to which it was now the Indian, not the priest, who was traveling to the frontier to drink hallucinogens with the poor white colonists there and, if not exactly baptize them, then at least heal and thereby consecrate them.

"Father Monclar was a good man," went on Santiago, "very humble." They had left some twelve years ago, the Capuchins, and while their administrative and spiritual hold over the territory disappeared with them, they undoubtedly left their stamp on the society, a particularly sensitive Church presence made all the more acute by the long shadow cast by the heathen along the frontier. The rubber boom had gone bust by the early 1920s and there was no single crop or product or land-owning class dominating the economy other than the mission. From the late 1950s trucks groaned their way up hairpin bends carrying lumber and plantains and, more recently, cattle. When I first arrived in the early 1970s there was no trace of the cocaine economy. Anyway, that didn't travel on the back of trucks.

"You know how it gets past the police?" an old black man asked me as we waited for a common friend, an Indian herbalist, to prepare some remedy. "They get a dead baby, open up the tummy, take out the tripes, fill it with cocaine, sew it up, and then the baby, held to a woman's breast, passes through as if it was alive." Just a woman feeding her child.

He left it unclear whether the baby was killed or died a natural death—if "natural" is the term applicable where the leading cause of death, infantile gastroenteritis, is something easily reduced with a different political economy.

His story reminded me of other booms I'd heard about, such as the oil boom in Mexico in the 1970s, which, so poor people there told me, required the heads of one hundred children. From the hole in the earth where the drill was boring came a voice demanding them, and eventually the president of the nation agreed to supply them—the sacrifice for the boom. For months then in Guerrero and Morelos parents would not allow their children out of the house as the stories spread of decapitated corpses of children being found. Surely it was a story not just about sacrifice for wealth, but of the sacrifice of the poor and the weak. It made me think not only of the dead baby at the live breast evading the cocaine inspectors, but of Putumayo colonists in general, as illustrated by the life story of Rosario and José García.

It was the Texaco Oil Company that replaced the Capuchin missionaries in the Putumayo. Through its road-building and short-term jobs, Texaco drew a torrent of poor colonists searching for some bit of forest in which to make a farm where they could plant plantains, corn, or rice, raise some pigs and maybe, if lucky, sell it all after a few years. Most arrived with no money and spent their first years as sharecroppers or as field hands to other poor colonists, as independent wage laborers, or any combination of the above.

Many were solitary young men. Some were lost, like the dreamer from Cali who walked into Santiago's one morning searching for curing magic. Others were not quite so lost, but lonely, like Don Juan, a black man from the Pacific coast town of Tumaco. He was hired as a laborer but sat around most of the time nursing a sore foot. One day Santiago said to him, "Sad, no? First thinking about your sweetheart. Second, thinking about being an orphan. Third, worrying about getting work, and fourth about poverty!"

"Preciso!" beamed Don Juan.

Yet sometimes loneliness is sought after. It is good to keep away from other colonists, slipping into the forest like a solitary phantom. That way one avoids problems with people, a man explained to me, and I remember what Manuel Gómez, a firm advocate of such strategic solitude, had told me about those problems.

> About two years ago there was a guy here who had a small farm, but the harvests were poor and hardly anything was produced. His cattle died. In the higher ground there were some strange swamps and holes full of weird worms. Thus they believed that the farm was subject to sorcery. It was cured by a shaman, by Salvador, I think. The guy was sick too. He had no will to work. Each day saw him more and more behind. And he was losing all the money lent him by the Cattlemen's Fund [the *Fondo Ganadero,* set up with World Bank loans]. Each day he was more and more in debt. Thus his enemy had him screwed. Maybe it was Pacho Quintero who cured him. Over in the village of the Ant—*La Hormiga*—there are bad people. So far we are clean. There are fewer colonists here, hence less envy. But as they say, "Small town, big hell."

He was angry at the government and the *gringos* for taking the wealth of the Putumayo and not giving anything back.

> "They are milking and milking the cow. But the cow is dying of hunger. If it weren't for us poor, the rich would die because they need us to work for them. We support the city. But we poor people can't go on like this. We worry all the time. We think all the time about what to do next, how to cope, what to do tomorrow. All that worrying and planning. You can't stop. Not once. All the time. From fear of hunger. From fear of nothing with which to live. . . .

And there were plenty of colonists far poorer than he.

Curing in the Colonist Port

The bus stopped at the end of the road and Santiago and I disembarked into the heat of the great *colono* port of the Putumayo, Puerto Asís, which both of us knew from previous visits: two main streets, one guarded by the army

Puerto Asís.

garrison and stretching into the mountains and cities of the interior; the other running along the port and guarded by the huge church and school built by the Capuchins who founded this port town early in the century; the port itself, a vast sea of mud and brackish water, jostling dugout canoes unloading mountains of plantains and bags of rice and corn up to 150 pounds heaved onto men's backs thence to carts, horses lashed and sworn at, thighs quivering, axles groaning, heaved again onto huge trucks bound for the cities of the interior, hulks of river steamers like papier-mâché castles squatting on their sides on the mud or bobbing out on the water in permanent disrepair; stores full of radio cassette players and television sets, pharmacies bulging with shelf after shelf with every costly useless ointment, capsule, and injectable substance that the fiendish ingenuity of science wedded to transnational drug companies had devised for the ever-complaining, undernourished, parasite-ridden, neocolonial body without decent medical services but always with a few cents to spend on some fancy medicine; traveling salesmen wiping sweat from their eyes, fat *macho* men carrying trim suitcases with electronic calculators together with soap samples or books of lottery tickets; a small hospital that the Indians upriver I knew (probably following the custom of townspeople) called "the slaughterhouse"—and no water for drinking or washing other than the contaminated, child-killing, bowel-infecting slop carried for sale from the muddy river in old oil drums bought from Texaco.

Puerto Asís.

That night we found ourselves in a two-roomed plank house built on stilts out over the mud of the great river. It was the home of a migrant family of Sibundoy Valley Indians, selling herbs and *cacharro*—"little worthless things," mirrors, pictures of the saints, scissors, sulfur, twine, and so forth.

"We are very sick, friend," José Chasoy told Santiago, and he pleaded with us to delay our journey upriver to Remolino so that we could come to this little shop of his by the river to drink *yagé* there and cure it.

Years later Santiago told me they were worried about the competition from a white man from Tolima who had set up a roadside stall opposite their shop. They wanted him *gone*.

We waited for nightfall. Wandering the town we fell in with Don Chepe, one of the upriver peasant-colonists from El Remolino, the Whirlpool, who had been awaiting Santiago. He was very shy, shuffling and scratching the back of his head, and looked at the ground all the time. He invited us to have a beer. Snarling motorbikes made conversation impossible. We met some *colonos,* friends of his who came down from Nariño eleven years ago. A shout rang out. I was hailed by a lanky black man rushing to greet me. It was Gerardo, whom I knew three years before, upriver, when he was working as a sharecropper with Don Salvador, the famous Cofán shaman, and was cooking *yagé* for him.

He was agitated and keeps eyeing Santiago with sidelong glances. After Salvador died two years ago, he said he went to live with another Indian

shaman farther upriver at Umbría: Gerardo, a black man who came to the
Putumayo from the Pacific coast eighteen years ago, becoming a *curaca!* He
talked louder and faster, aware he was attracting curious glances. "The young
of today are no good," he declaimed—meaning that young Indian men were
not becoming shamans because they were too frightened and couldn't or
wouldn't follow the dietary, menstrual, and pregnancy taboos. But Gerardo?

I remembered meeting him in 1977 when he was living at Gratulina's and
Salvador's place. He had come to the Putumayo because the pay was good
for day laborers. Then he and his wife cleared forest off state land by the
river. She died and he got into a fight with her family, so he told me, and
gave up the farm to them, "as they were so many and my family so few."
Since then he had virtually apprenticed himself to Salvador, and was, by his
own account, an accomplished shaman. An unusual story.

He always seemed alone with neither friend nor family, a retiring sort,
and it was when we drank *yagé* upriver in 1977, a half mile or so into the
forest from Salvador's and Gratulina's house by the river, that he took me
by surprise.

The forest there was dense and tall. In a tiny clearing stood a large roof
of palm leaves sheltering hammocks and a small fire. Night fell early where
the trees were so high and you could hear animals—monkeys, someone
said—scuttering in the forest for most of the night, together with hollow
cries and the rasping of frogs vibrating the darkness. Gerardo had been
cooking *yagé* there since the day before. He attended upon Salvador, poured
out the *yagé,* wafted the incense, and was there when needed.

With me was a young black friend from one of the sugar plantation towns
of the Cauca Valley in western Colombia where his parents worked on the
sugarcane plantations as day laborers. His name was José Domingo Murillo
and he drew those strong devils that appear on the cover and title page of
a book I wrote called *The Devil and Commodity Fetishism in South America.*
This was his first time in the Putumayo and he had never drunk *yagé* before
or participated in a *yagé* night. He was seventeen at the time.

"With the second cup," he told me later,

> I saw some figures of seeds with strange colors. Then I saw
> feathers, of a color that I had never seen before. Then some-
> thing like a cloak was passed in front of me with all sorts of
> drawings and paintings. The mantle was passing slowly in front
> of me. After that came more figures, but different and bigger
> and there were things like snakes with all the colors possible
> like brown, clear yellow, green, and black, and then seeds of
> all colors. That went on for a long time until I had to shit.
>
> After that I went to lie down, and once again I began to see
> things . . . animals. First there was a large animal that I didn't
> know. Little by little it changed, into a cayman. It disappeared.

Then a black shape came, catching colors, yellows and greens, and these formed into stripes and then . . . into a huge tiger.

I was scared out of my mind. I was feeling terribly sick. I put my fingers down my throat to vomit, and vomit I did. I took no more *yagé* when Salvador offered it because I was too scared. I stayed awake for hours thinking about that damned tiger.

With the first cup I became drunk and had stomach cramps and saw practically nothing—just some figures, figures I'd never seen before, like the ornaments the Indians dress with, and lots of colors.

When Salvador wiped my head with the curing fan, I felt the inside of my head under the scalp moving as he moved the fan, and it was the same when he wiped down my left arm, like pins and needles moving down my arm and out through my finter tips.

After he cured me I felt tranquil. Comfortable. Then I was able to sleep till the following day when Mateo called me.

Salvador's singing was very soft. Often you could barely hear him, lost in the chatter of the night forest. In the early dawn a strange loud chanting awoke me. It was the black man, Gerardo, singing out his heart, like a Gregorian chant, pacing outside the shelter for what seemed like hours, alone, between the shelter with its sleeping people and the immense wall of the forest so tall you couldn't see the tree tops, walking back and forth, back and forth.

"What were you singing?" I asked him the next day.

"Asking God to give me an idea about how things are," he said, "so I can help my comrades."

Salvador's mother-in-law, who had spent most of her long life with shamans (she had married one and then when he died had moved in with her daughter Gratulina, who had also married one, namely Don Salvador), nodded and agreed later on when we were discussing the matter, that indeed Gerardo was trying to become a shaman. He had a great reputation as a curer of women's diseases when he lived downstream, she noted gravely with a smile in her eyes.

But Gratulina, sitting on the floor with her legs straight out twisting fibers into twine on her thigh, said that Gerardo hadn't a chance of becoming a *curaca* because he couldn't tolerate the amount of *yagé* necessary.

"You have to drink pots to become a *curaca*," she asserted. "That's what Don Salvador did. It's only when you drink pots of *yagé* that you can talk with the animals." She pointed to a five-pint pot. "You have to drink at least two of those. The shaman gives you one. You drink and fall down. You drink the second, and fall. They give you more, until you get up. That's why there are so few *curacas!* Most people are too feeble! "What's more," she added with indifference, "Gerardo can't sing."

. . . she noted gravely with a smile in her eyes.''

That was how I'd got to know Gerardo three years before, and we plied each other with questions about what had happened since then. He was looking for a canoe to take him a full day's journey upstream. Don Flavio, an old white man, something of a shaman himself, very quiet and unassuming, and one of the deceased Salvador's best friends, was sick. Gerardo said he was going to try and cure him. I told him that we were going to take *yagé* in the evening. Once again he eyed Santiago in a manner both arrogant and beseeching.

When we got back to José Chasoy's little shop on stilts over the mud, we found the bar next to it, which shared the same ill-fitted plank wall, belting out loud music on a scratchy jukebox. It was Christmas Eve. Two bored-looking prostitutes were sitting smoking at rickety tables with *colono* men so drunk they could barely leer. Santiago hated the idea of taking *yagé* and curing the shop with so much noise, but José Chasoy and his wife María put a lot of pressure on him. The word had spread that a great curer had come, and other people such as a *compadre* of José Chasoy's and María's had been invited, or invited themselves, as had the three *colonos* from El Remolino and the neighboring shopkeepers Doña Teofila and her aging husband Angel, with his hideous varicose leg ulcers.

Frontiers and especially frontier towns draw a hurly-burly of people from all over, and Don Angel was a case in point. He had been raised on the *llanos,* those massive plains that stretch from the far-off eastern *cordillera* of the Andes to Venezuela. He had spent ten years in Bogotá, capital of the republic, and four in the small city of Ibague in the Magdalena Valley before becoming a peasant-colonist in the Caquetá area. Now, after a long life he was suffering from his wretched ulcers, cardiac insufficiency, and marked edema of the lungs. He and his wife were very taken with Santiago, who took a long hard look at the ulcers, asked the same sort of rapidly fired questions about them as would any well-trained "Western" doctor, and prescribed herbs for topical application.

We started taking *yagé* that night quite late, at around eleven o'clock, when the adjoining bar wheezed to a halt. But there were other bars and brothels going full blast along the street. It was riotously noisy and a long way from the frogs chirruping in the river's rush to which we were accustomed. The *yagé* was strong, from the same brew we had drunk three nights before, and the toilet facilities were miserable—an awful lot of people for a single hole in a plank on a swaying, slippery, three-foot-wide wooden balcony swung out the back high over the mud, with a grunting pig for company.

The *compadre* set the tone for the evening when after only twenty minutes he started retching so horrendously and frighteningly loud that he drowned out the *yagé* singing, filling our ears with thunder, our hearts with pain. It went on for four hours! He sat paralyzed over a bowl in the corner, unable to vomit, pathetically whispering between spasms during all those hours of misery: "My God is great. There is nobody greater than my God. *Mi Dios es harto.* Help me God!"

Santiago spent the whole night curing. Angel was suffering from sorcery. Everyone in the room except the five children seemed to be suffering from sorcery. With the dry retching stabbing to the pit of the soul and the incessant moaning and joking and the power and beauty of the *yagé* chant this rickety house on stilts over the mud-waste became a temple; hell and heaven confused by the shaman's song and the flurry of sorcery.

The tired old man cured the shop and the living quarters—the same space of two rooms and a kitchen. He sprayed special medicines throughout and he danced as he sprayed and he sang as he danced in and out of the rooms, rotating and hopping from one foot to the other, beautiful, poised little flights, little hops, precariously balanced in flight, this seventy-year-old, portly, *yagé*-drunk man.

Then at about three o'clock when the *yagé* song was at its height, there was a loud hammering at the door. It was Gerardo. He wanted to come in and take *yagé*. He was angry. Santiago waivered. I said let him in. Santiago disagreed, emphatically. Gerardo knocked repeatedly, for maybe half an hour as Santiago continued singing.

At seven o'clock in the morning Gerardo reappeared. The door was open. The bar next door started up with a jolly carnival tune. On a stretcher out in the street, the eldest boy of the house was spreading the wares for which the wandering Sibundoy Indian herbalists are famous. There was a smell of chicken stew cooking on a kerosene stove. The baby was crying—and Gerardo was screaming and flailing his arms as he tumbled into the room.

"I am the true shaman, *yo soy taita de verda'*," he screamed, "not the shaman of shit!"

Santiago was lying in his hammock, not having slept a wink last night because of the curing. Gerardo accepted the glass of brandy José Chasoy pressed on him, but continued to be menacing. The carnival music from the bar had stopped and a sprightly tune was blasting through the partition wall. Gerardo was challenging Santiago, whom he wanted to recognize him as a shaman, as an equal or even as superior. He grabbed one of the curing fans and started with his version of a *yagé* chant while beating with the fan and stalking round and round the room. He passed the fan over me as if curing, and followed that with a grotesque retching-out of the evil things he had supposedly sucked from my body. He screamed again and again that he, Gerardo, was the true shaman—"*Yes or no?*" he demanded from all present. He was a strong man acting strange. Beating a furious rhythm with the fan, he chanted and then screamed abuse, allowing no voice other than his and that of the jolly accordians bouncing through from the bar next door.

Santiago muttered something about drunks trying to be the center of attention, and in a moment of quiet started a story about a boring drunk in the town near where he lived. But Gerardo never stopped his ranting. He quieted down a little to adopt a contrite tone, as if praying, and became incoherent. Then he burst into a fury once again.

"I'm a shaman, *soy taita,* I'm a shaman. . . ."

The accordian music from the bar stopped. For once the bar was silent. Birds twittered from a cage. Gerardo was standing over Santiago, who was lying on his back in his hammock slung waist-high above the floor. Gerardo had his fist pulled back ready to strike.

"Stop fucking with me!" burst out Santiago.

"You're a fool! Let's fight," screamed Gerardo. "You're a fool!" A gay waltz started up from the bar.

Santiago was shouting at Gerardo that he didn't know how to behave, that he was drunk, that he didn't know anything. "Hit me! Go ahead! I can't fight," he said.

Gerardo twisted away, stamping. A sentimental love song oozed through the cracks in the wall, getting sadder and sadder.

"I'm the shaman! I'm chief! I'm captain!" yelled Gerardo. He told us how close he was to Salvador before he died—Salvador the esteemed Cofán shaman, Salvador who saved Santiago's life but a few years ago, Salvador from whom Gerardo learned *yagé* and shamanism.

Gerardo wanted Santiago's power while at the same time he wants Santiago to crown him. "It's a terribly envy," Santiago said to me after we left the house, shaking and musing on the swift fall whereby a promising *yagé* apprentice like Gerardo had become an envy-riddled buffoon.

Years later Santiago told me that Gerardo said he couldn't cure properly and that he had done a bad job on the Chasoys' house above the mud at Puerto Asís. "Only a few months back José Chasoy came to see me," he went on, "enormously happy with what I'd done. Now he's got rid of the guy who was in competition with him, selling odds and ends of *cacharro* opposite, and with his profits has built a second story to his house. *Está bien contento!*"

"I'm the shaman, I'm chief, I'm captain . . ." Gerardo had been yelling. But it's obvious that a shaman, although self-made, is not self-named. My thoughts drifted back to the afternoon before the night at the Chasoys when, as we were walking along the street by the river an elderly white man, long established and successful in these Putumayo rivers, hailed us.

"*Cómo está Taita?* How are you father shaman?" he inquired, with neither an introduction nor the regalia of shamanic status to guide him. He said he could speak Inga and hesitantly broke into that tongue, to which Santiago responded, also in Inga.

"What did you say?" I asked later.

"He asked me if there was any gold where I live," said Santiago, "and I asked him if he had any brandy."

Upriver: The Whirlpool

We got a lift on a horse-drawn cart to the river, out of town, where we hoped to find a canoe to take us upstream to El Remolino. It was early afternoon on Christmas Day. It was raining. It was muddy. We were very tired. There was a crude shelter by the bank under which a few people were waiting. Crates of Coca-Cola bottles were stacked on the mud. On the other side of the shelter lying on the mud was a big navy boat—maybe thirty feet long— with the Colombian flag and sheets of dirty plastic drearily flapping on its sides in the rain, oblivious to the *salsa* music pouring from a radio.

A young woman broke away from the group under the shelter, approached Santiago, and asked if he was a curer. He said he did not have time, but took her pulse and said she had *mal aires,* evil winds, and irritation of the kidneys. She should come and visit him at his home. She handed over a young girl.

"This girl too!" she demanded.

"She's the same," Santiago said, "only it's new. Yours is old." And we squelched off in the rain to climb into our canoe. The people from El Remolino had come. The outboard motor burped into life and soon we were skimming over the river.

We clambered out onto more mud on the opposite bank where there was a gravel clearing, four huts, a bulldozer, a dumptruck with its rear end on poles, and a path curling off into the jungle. It was quiet but for some chickens and a soap opera on a radio. Our guide was upset because he'd been counting on this construction gang to provide a lift in a truck for part of the way. But it was Christmas Day, the truck was gone, and we had to walk, Santiago limping slowly because of a badly inflamed foot. We were groggy from not having slept the night before and there was a hallucinogenic fuzz to everything. We passed under giant *ceiba* trees, past great fans of palms and blurring riots of greens.

"It's only ten minutes away," our guide encouraged us.

Close to an hour later we emerged from the forest to arrive at Ana's house where Santiago wanted to stay. It was the loveliest place I had ever seen in all the territory of the Putumayo, perched high on clifflike sandy banks around on oxbow lake formed by the Putumayo River silting up and twisting back on itself, silent, still water alive with fish and birds. Raised four feet high on stilts, Ana's thatch-roofed house was but one large L-shaped room with no wall on the side overlooking the cleared ground of the patio and the lake below. Tiny black flies abounded, biting hard.

She was a soft-spoken Ingano woman, an old friend of Santiago's and delighted to see us. Her little grandson asked me if I was Ana's brother. She lived with her teenage daughter and son, and had a timid white man named Chu Chu all the way from the interior province of Cauca lodging in the house and working for her, clearing land for one hundred pesos a day plus food.

As Santiago sank exhausted into a hammock, she implored him to do his best to cure her wayward son. She was also upset about her daughter, who was fighting with neighbors who were hitting her and stealing from her.

Later Santiago told me that Ana was "family" of his wife. She was born close to the foothill town of Mocoa but was raised right here in the Whirlpool. She was sixty-two years old, born in 1918. The Capuchin, Father Stanislaw, wrote out her baptismal certificate.

People, lots and lots of people, came out of the forest to see Santiago. A cadaverous peasant-colonist man all the way from El Chinche—the Bedbug—came and asked Santiago if he could cure "kidneys." A horse-drawn cart rumbled into the clearing, jam-packed full of raucous *colono* women come to take us away. In their cart they had two very sick women. One, named Doña Pola, was grotesquely misshapen, with matchstick-thin arms and legs protruding not so much from a human body as from a hugely swollen stomach that had virtually become her whole being. She had advanced as-

cites, with pints, if not gallons of fluid in her abdominal cavity, the result, perhaps, of liver failure.

The *colono* woman, including Pola, joked and laughed with Santiago and played at seducing him. More sick people turned up. Santiago was like a magnet. It was not just that people were curious; they wanted and expected help. The *colono* women in the cart put enormous pressure on him to leave Ana's and spend the night with them. But his fatigue dispensed with even the need for excuses. Tomorrow night we would take *yagé,* not now, and people drifted away.

The sun melted into the lake. Fishermen went out. The water reflected stars burning furrows of light into the blackness below us as the fishermen dragged in their nets. They used flashlights and the nets flickered in the orange light. As we dropped off to sleep, Chu Chu, the worker-lodger from Cauca, asked me if I had any of those books on the revolution.

"What revolution?" I ask.

"I don't know," Chu Chu pondered, "the revolution and the oligarchy. . . ." He paused. "There are a lot of revolutionaries where I come from. Lots, with meetings all the time."

"What do they mean by revolution?" I asked

"That things should be for all the people, well done, and in common. They want to change everything at once, because prices are higher than the sky."

We awoke cold and damp, looking into the mist hanging across the lake below. It was trailing all around so you couldn't distinguish water from air. A few tree trunks and strange shapes poked up through the mist. It was still except for bird calls everywhere; hundreds and hundreds of birds.

Ana again implored Santiago to cure her daughter and son. The little black flies were biting. Chu Chu asked Santiago to cure his little son Hugo, all the family he had here in Putumayo. Nobody had a clue as to how old he was, perhaps seven. "Sure to have *espanto*," said Santiago—meaning a form of fright, and he called the little boy over to his hammock and told him to take off his shirt and sit down.

"Why?"

"To cure!"

"What's that?"

Unsure of everything but the strange old man's gentle humor and self-assuredness, the little white boy submitted to the Indian curing him of an illness of which he and his father knew nothing.

That night twenty-seven people showed up. Eleven of them, nearly all women, came to drink *yagé*. There were about ten children, rushing up and down the notched stake that served as a stairway to the house, playing and peeing over the edge. The men who weren't taking *yagé* sat outside on an upturned broken canoe. It was like a party—a carnivalesque encounter of contrasts undoing life so as to engender it; where the lake met the high banks of the forest, where the Indian met the white peasant-colonists, where sickness and sorcery met the decomposing of the world through the strangeness of *yagé*, where the ordinary mediated the extraordinary through purgations, laughter, and storytelling. Every now and again lightning would flash and subside, way off over the top of the forest by the momentarily illuminated mountains. Preparations were slow. People helped Santiago grind up the herbs necessary for the "fresh water," the only liquid you can drink when taking *yagé*. He ground up some *chondur gente,* "people chondur," which he chewed when curing, and got a big stack of lemons in case someone had a really tough time, because lemon and sugar can calm. We remembered the young man from Boyacá who went crazy, banging his head in his "cave."

I was greeted by two women, mother and daughter, colonists from here whom I had met a year before when they carried a sick little boy to Santiago's home far away in the foothills. He was dreadfully swollen and could barely breathe his lungs were so full of water. There was little that Santiago (or I) could do, and he recommended they try the hospital. The child died, his mother told me, as had most of her children. She lived with her mother a few miles down the trail from the lake, raising a little corn and a few *racimos* of plantains. When I visited her broken-backed, earth-floored house she had shining tubes and packets of medicines from the pharmacies of Puerto Asís,

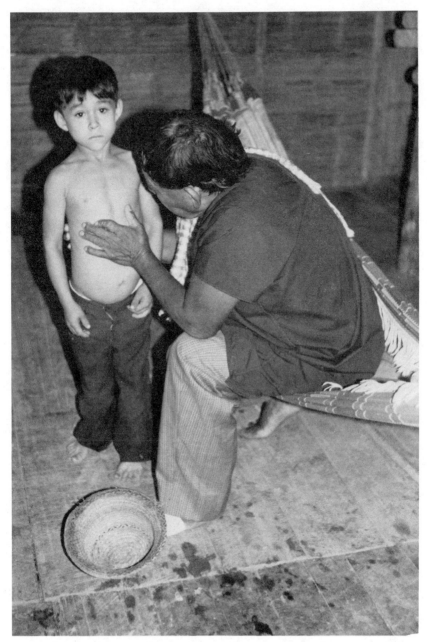

"To cure!" "What's that?"

"The child died, his mother told me, as had most of her children."

pretty well useless stuff, costing her close to 1,500 pesos for what the doctors had diagnosed as a stomach ulcer. As far as I knew Santiago had never charged her a cent—neither for *yagé,* for curing, for herbs, nor for bed and board—although tonight he said he was going to charge everyone 200 pesos for each gourdful of *yagé* they drank and an additional 200 for a curing or *limpieza.*

We waited for the children to quiet down a little and then took our first gourdful. I started to feel awful. Santiago called on Luz, "Light," the buxom, good-natured woman who drove the horse and cart, to bring over her baby, and he began to chant. Dark folds and bright points of fiery color came and receded in the hum threading through the song. Nausea acquired shapes.

A voice stabbed the dark. "What the hell is going on?"

A big man stuck his head over the edge of the floor to peer in at us. He seemed drunk. I suppose we did too. Climbing the notched stake that served as a stairway, with his machete catching his legs, he found a seat next to Santiago, who tried to explain something of *yagé* to him, telling him it was a medicine that allowed you to see what was ailing you and how to cure those causes through friendship rather than through war. But the man wanted to kill. He wanted to drink *yagé* right now to see who had assassinated his father.

"Come back when you're not drunk," suggested Santiago in despair. "If you take *yagé* when you're drunk, you could go crazy!"

"Tomorrow morning I'll be here then," boomed the drunk.

"Come early, around five," said Santiago.

"Can't you give me some to take home? I want to see what happened," pleaded the drunk.

"Sure. But not now."

"But I want to know certain things—how it happened . . . I want to know the truth."

"Surely," a woman's voice joined in.

"With this you can find out all? And who did it and . . . ?" continued the big man.

"Ah, yes!" reassured Santiago.

"Yes, yes," echoed the woman soothingly.

"I want to know who killed my father. None of us at home know who did it!"

"Tomorrow morning. But you mustn't drink any more," advised Santiago, and the big man climbed back down into the night.

One by one the women brought their children to be cured of *espanto* ("fear"). The babies cried. The shaman cried louder still, the song flung hard at the wide night sky and the dark lake below.

"Not *yagé* but *ya sé!*" chuckled Santiago as he cured a baby and talked with its mother—*ya sé* meaning "Now I know," and rhyming with *yagé,* especially the way he deliberately accentuated the words: *ya-gé* like ya-HEH; *ya sé* like ya-SAY.

"That's what they call *yagé* up in Pasto," he continued, recounting his first experiences in that mountain city. He was about fourteen years old and Father Stanislaw (who wrote out Ana's baptismal certificate) needed him and another boy as porters to go up the Andes to Pasto. It must have been around 1926.

> The other boy carried monkeys and I carried birds, four *tentes,* in cages. In those days we had the custom of tying herbs and twine here and here [pointing to his upper arms and legs with quick vague gestures of white movement in the blackness of this veranda-room]. We also wore lots of beads. When we got to Pasto the old people who knew didn't worry us, but the young ones began to tease and insult us.
>
> I lay down in the upper story of the convent but it was full of fleas, so I went down to the main door to the street. No sooner was I standing there than a swarm of kids was upon me. The crowd grew bigger and bigger.
>
> "*Ooh! Eso es indio comegente. Ooh! Esos indios de tierra-dentro. Ooh!* Look at this Indian who eats people. Ooh! That's an Indian from lands far away. Ooh!" Others said "How ugly!" while still others exclaimed, "How beautiful the beads are!"
>
> Because there were so many I stepped back through the doorway into the convent, but with each step back the mass of them grew greater on top of me. "Truly, I need to be careful," I said to myself.

A colonist woman chuckled loudly in the dark. Santiago paused, then went on.

" 'Ooh!' one of them said, pressing close to me, 'these are the Indians that eat people!' "

Another woman tittered, setting off a round of laughter.

"So I said to myself, 'I'm going to catch one of these guys to eat!'" He laughed and laughed. We all did.

> So I caught one of them, opened wide my eyes, bared by gums, and snarled—and they all fled! So fast did they run that they fell over one another and ran on top of the fallen ones, screaming all the way. I jumped back into the convent and ran up to the top of the tower from where I could look down at them far below running crazily to their mothers. They told everyone they'd just escaped from an Indian who was about to eat them. Their mothers gave them a good scolding.
>
> But now in Pasto even people who hardly know me hail me as *compadre,* while the ones who have taken *yagé* call it *ya sé*—"now I know"—and call me Papa Santiago.

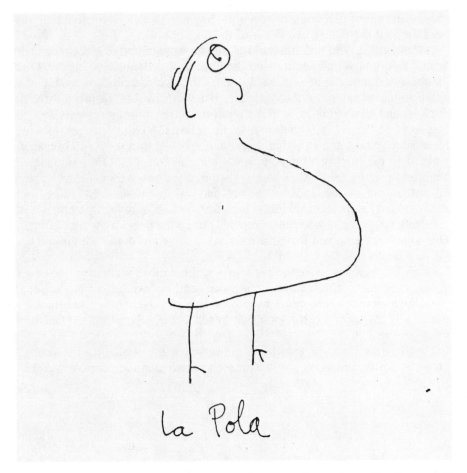

La Pola

He chuckled, boasting: "Now most of Pasto calls me Papa Santiago . . ." and he burst once more into song, curing the tiny bundle of a baby, quiet in front of him on its mother's lap beneath the raspy chanting of the "*indio comegente*, the person-eating Indian," and the wild beat of the curing fan, *waira sacha*, wind of the forest.

There was a sigh. A body fell. We shrieked. Doña Pola had collapsed. She had been standing, supporting her huge tent of a tummy with her sticklike arms and legs, wandering around joking and laughing. But shortly after her second cup of *yagé* she fell as if dead. Only the whites of her eyes could be seen in her ashen face of taut gray skin. "She's not dead," proclaimed Santiago, "just unconscious."

For a few minutes she would recover and moan. Then she would drift back into her other world. We tried to revive her while people laughed crazily, sure she was dying or dead. The only other light was outside on the upturned canoe, an orange flickering between us, huddled over this swollen mass of semilife, and the empty blackness of the lake below.

It was getting cold and misty. Most of the women had shawls over their heads. Every now and again, from the jumble of bodies heaped around the platform, a hooded figure emerged to pass through the candlelight to climb down to the ground, and then another, just as unsteadily, surfaced through the mist and climbed back onto the platform—like *las ánimas perdidas,* the lost souls of Purgatory, wandering wailing ghosts, looking for rest, looking for a place so they can stop thinking and, above all, stop seeing and sensing, wanting to die, to crush the complexity and the fear, to let the brain sleep. But no: down the ladder they went, down into the mist exhaled by the black lake, then back up the ladder of the notched stake, with the mist falling from their hooded heads and shoulders, lost, forever lost, moving into and out of the death space with Doña Pola stretched out on the floor. We were all dying. Only our faces emerged from the mist as we talked of the death around us. We saw death and we wanted it.

Doña Pola moaned. Her sister was watching closely and her look was strange; it was worried, caring, miserable, and malevolent all at the same time, the look of the sorcerer or of somebody worried that others are thinking that she is the sorcerer, the look that in reflecting passes into the cause of what is reflected.

The *yagé* song was everywhere, pulling back the souls into the land of life—the fleshy, sensuous world as it feels, smells, and appears; a world of

Espantos coming up and down through the mist

pure percept, sensate emotion. Then a flood tide of memory pictures surged, swirling in the smoke from the kitchen, coming through the taut strings of the hammock fanned against the running squares of palm thatch.

It was early morning. The babies were snuggled down. Pola was all right, but barely so. Horses were champing and flicking flies with their tails. Mud-spattered women rode in, glued to their horses, with hens and roosters hanging their crimson-gloried feathered heads from the saddle alongside bouncing plastic bottles that would later be filled with kerosene and cooking oil. A garrulous drunk was reeling from person to person, adrift in flowing mustachios and fanned trouser cuffs dragging in the mud. It was Sunday, and the colonists had started early to find a canoe to take them downriver to market at Puerto Asís. They paused to ponder the curious scene of bodies lying in heaps, rising slowly as in the Resurrection—an old Indian man curing a little baby with chanting and chuckling—and they plunged down to the water's edge.

Santiago was paid off, insisted that Doña Pola be brought to his home later, and we made our farewells against a gale of protest at our leaving. The cart lurched. A family of pigs scattered in our path. The smooth hindquarters of the horse swayed by our knees as we rolled along filling our vision with the interiority of moving mountains of delicately veined flesh; the cart seemed not to be going forward but to be suspended in the swaying power of the horse's arse. The trail was moving under us as the night passed from us in a jolting sensateness of sensing pretty well lost to speech.

Curing Secrets

We emerged gingerly from the *yagé* dawn of the Whirlpool and its mist-engulfed house of colonist women nursing their spirit-afflicted babies and their dying companion. As night overtook us Santiago kept wondering about Doña Pola: "Was she dead? Death would put her out of her misery."

When we arrived back home a day later there was a letter for him. Don Eliseo, the pleasant young chubby peasant from Boyacá, whose cousin had gone crazy under the bed, had filled his time waiting by writing a list of what he wanted Don Santiago to teach him. Santiago's daughter read the letter out loud, for her father could barely read.

> Secrets that were forgotten to mention the time before and
> that I want you to teach me. When something is lost so that
> you realize it's missing immediately.
> And to make appear what has been lost. To cure a farm and
> a home suffering from *maleficio* and also to prevent theft, and
> to catch a thief in the act of stealing. And to cure illness if it
> can be cured, of if not, how you can know when a person has
> an animal inside and if they will be able to vomit it out or not.
> To cure sorcery [*daños*] in the throat when one feels bad, and

to make a bad neighbor leave, if possible by them selling their
farm to oneself. To make a person from far away come and appear. To cure leg ulcers. When a person owes you something,
what secret can you use to make sure they pay you back. What
secret ought you to have when the judge or the mayor molests
you with arrest. Secret so that cattle will stay in the enclosed
field or on the savanna. Other secret so that cattle won't stay
in the one spot. And to make cattle gentle so that when they
struggle at the end of a rope they will stop and come without
fighting. Also I need a secret to cure mad people and another
one for epileptic attacks. Secret to have luck in hunting and
fishing and when a shotgun fails to fire or hit the target. How
to cure a dog so that it becomes a good one. Secret so that
cattle will abound and that nobody does sorcery.

Secret to have good luck in commerce. Secret to prepare
love charms. Secret to learn to walk on water. Also when a
man and a woman are not able to marry, secret for them to
separate. When a person forgets you, what remedy can you
use. When the farm or the home has sorcery substance, how
can you find out. When an enemy threatens to kill you or has
put sorcery against you. Power to get rid of whatever. And
when a woman humiliates you or tries to make a fool of you
with sorcery. Secret to become invisible. Remedy so that a
woman need bear no more children. Secret to cure varicose
veins. Secret to know plants. Remedy for sicknesses. Secret
for when one's arms and legs are bitten by sucking witches.
What is the true secret in using the stingray as a weapon.

"He's doubled my work," said Santiago, passing me the letter with a wry
smile.

TWENTY-SEVEN
Montage

Two years later Eliseo was back again, by bus all the way across the country to dip once more into what he saw as the Indian well of magical power. He came with two companions and they stayed one month, working hard on the farm, ready and cheery and with a willing hand, quiet and unobtrusive. He told me he had found *yagé* growing in the forests of the eastern Andes way to the north, in his homeland of Boyacá. I gathered he had quite a following as a healer there. He had put on a lot of weight since we were last together, and I have a vivid memory of him day after day, barefoot, chubby, and agile, leaping behind and in front of the horses laden with sugarcane making their way, floundering and clambering, from the fertile river flats to the tiny *trapiche* for milling the cane beside the house. I used to see him sometimes in the late afternoons on the veranda, absorbed in copying down the medicinal virtues of plants from what Santiago's barely teenaged granddaughter, Delia, had herself copied down from a school textbook on botany.

He found a willing instructor, of sorts, in Santiago's son-in-law, Angel, himself the son of a shaman, Don Apolinar, whose first language was Inga and who had died but two years ago. They had lived far away in the forests of the Caquetá region and Angel seemed to be some sort of beginning shaman himself. But he was also an awful drunk, much to the despair of his poor father and his wife, and was given to vain boasting.

Overwhelming events had thrown Angel into our midst. For a year or so, he told me, the Colombian army had set up a counterguerrilla base near his home. He cured many of the soldiers and got on well with them. He told me they came to him with skin rashes, arthritis, and requests for magic that would stop the captain and the colonel from being so hard on them. For their part, the captain and the colonel came to understand that with *yagé* you could divine what was happening in other places and in the future. With *yagé*, Angel was able to see the captain's wife living in the city of Pereira and, to the captain's surprise, see that she was five months' pregnant. But the captain could not cope with drinking *yagé*. It was too strong, and both he and the colonel asked Angel to drink it to see if they were going to survive the counterguerrilla campaign and where their enemies were hiding. But these last questions Angel could not answer.

Two sets of soldiers came and went from that part of the Caquetá: the ones with epaulettes of the Colombian colors red, blue, and yellow, and those of the counterguerrilla, with green and white. Then came the third set of soldiers, the ones with black epaulettes—black for death, Angel said. They put a helicopter next to his house, blew the roof off and the walls apart. They said he was aiding the *guerrilleros* and they tied his hands tight behind his back and hung him by his wrists for about three hours.

"I'm lucky I can still use my arms and work," he told me, rubbing his shoulders. "People get their arms and shoulders broken that way."

Then he was let down and they stuck the muzzle of a rifle into his mouth. They took him into the forest with his hands tied behind his back and with a gun jabbing him, ordering him to lead them to the enemy. But he knew nothing. "It's worse if you give in and make a false confession that you are an ally of the *guerrilleros*," he explained to me. He pleaded with them to kill him right then and there and cease with the humiliation. But each day they went on again deeper into the forest, a column of some fifty soldiers pushing him in the lead. After eighteen days they untied his hands, now swollen like balloons, and set him free, apparently convinced that he knew nothing important.

"But you'd be better off not going back home to live in the Caquetá," the captain told him, "because the *guerrilleros* will assume you sang and helped us."

"And he's right," said Angel. "They will try and kill me too."

There was little to do but live elsewhere, at least for a while, even though he blustered: "I'm not to be humiliated like that! I'm going to stay in my home! I've done nothing wrong!" Like so many people he had been caught in this struggle in which the vagaries of gossip, envy, and suspicion created

While we were talking, Angel's young son, César, drew these pictures.

realities as confusing as they were cruel and deadly. That was how these country people understood their situation: out of envy someone went to either the army or the *guerrilleros* saying that so-and-so was aiding the enemy—not at all unlike the social circuitry of sorcery.

Angel had been free only two weeks and with gusto joined our farewell for the three men from Boyacá. They were leaving for home in the dawn and this was their night to be cured.

Borbonzay, Santiago's young Indian helper, had gone to the Putumayo river, a day or two's journey away, to get some leaves of *chagropanga*—*yagé's* female companion without which, so it is said, no visions come. In his absence Angel helped out, and as the twelve people, all men, assembled that night to drink *yagé*, he authoritatively explained to a hesitant newcomer what *yagé* could entail: "You take it as a cure, as something to improve your life," he expounded, "and for intelligence—so you can see danger and be more astute. You see beautiful things or horrible things according to the state of your heart. If it's clean, you see beauty. You can see what's happening in Barranquilla, Bogotá, Cartagena, Cali . . . wherever."

Santiago poured out the *yagé* and wiped it clean with the curing fan but did not sing. We all drank and fell into a dreamy doze. About three-quarters of an hour later a tiny hum began. It grew louder to counterpose the wind from the forest and the river's rush. Utterly absorbed and lost in itself, the song went on for a long time. The singer was old and tired. His voice was rough and low. He seemed lost in himself, singing for the sake of singing, the rite singing to itself in complete disregard of our presence or judgments. The room was quiet. People seemed to be asleep. Someone stumbled out and we heard the heart-wrenching retching and vomiting sounds that curl back into your own stomach like the snakes people talk about that come out in your vomit and go back in at the same time—a collective empathizing of nausea, now gathering like a storm. It feels like ants biting one's skin and one's head, now spinning in wave after trembling wave.

"When people are envious of you, then you have an awful time with *yagé*," Santiago said. "Then come the snakes all over your body and your vomit goes back into your mouth as snakes. Frogs, lizards, alligators, wild animals, cockroaches—the ones with big horns—that's what you feel when you are sick. And it smells of shit, too."

We took a second gourdful and the singing started again. Now Santiago had a ring in his hands that Rafael, one of the three men from Boyacá, had given him. He was curing Rafael's ring. The beat was very slow and deliberate with an occasional Spanish word: luck . . . paint *yagé* . . . luck . . . then the gunshot click of the tongue, then singing again. He was wearing Angel's father's necklace, the shamanic necklace of tigers' teeth glinting dully yellow and white, with a large metal crucifix tied to it. Santiago's necklace was stolen or had simply fallen off the roof of the bus bouncing him over the mountain roads to cure the coca growers of Bolívar, Cauca, on the other side of the Andes, where he was also asked to cure the man made crazy by the *duende,* huddled in his rags and long hair in a cave by the river.

Santiago was curing some *chondur* roots, holding the little knobby clumps the size of marbles in his hands together with Rafael's ring and singing over them. He asked me to cut a plastic bag, into which he placed the roots and the ring, and then asked Rafael to come and blow into it. In the jumble of events and objects the song wound its irregular way. Rafael was now sitting on a low stool right in front of him. The curing fan was beating fast, a galloping pulse in the eardrum of the world made suddenly aware of its own life and heart. He was singing into the bag, holding it no more than a hand-breadth from his mouth. He sang into the plastic bag with the knobby little magical roots of peppermint-tasting *chondur* roots and the ring. Then he swept over Rafael's head, singing faster and faster, the rhythm lifting us all, as it were, into the bag with the roots and the ring. Then he stopped abruptly, blew—"whoosh now, whoosh now" into the bag, which he then handed over to Rafael to take away as his talisman on the long trip across the republic the next day.

"Here's the cured stuff," he said, pausing to giggle, "with the love perfume [*quereme*] so you can win the hearts of women," and the giggle burst into a full-blown gale of laughing sweeping us all in its wake. The intense self-absorption of the man in the song in the still-sleeping quiet of the dark room had been cracked open like the husk of a nut, and into this opening we all tumbled, willy-nilly.

Close to midnight he was singing again, curing *yagé* for another round of serving. After a few minutes the singing suddenly stopped. There was ever so faint a sound of music coming through the night from the direction of the town down the valley.

"It's Borbonzay—dancing with the *chagropanga,*" chortled Santiago.

He called on Eliseo, the leader of the three from Boyacá, to bring over his ring too. This whole night, so it seemed, was to generate magical power for these three white men prior to their departure the next day. How many strangers eager for such magic had these Indian shamans thus obliged, giving back in the tangible form of rings and talismans the power that the strangers had given to them?

The curer loomed like a dark rock in the night, massivity compacting around the tiny pin-point of the charm to be cured, singing into its point of power and repose.

Outside soft rain fell and a gasoline lamp on the veranda cast a circle of light into the mist coming off the mountains. The singing also softly covered everything. My thoughts leap-frogged. I saw flowers, a panel on a pink kimono, wet rain on just one shiny blade of grass bending under the weight of a raindrop, a drop on a quivering edge, just this fragment looming, then—as the Indians say, "*otra pinta,* another painting," signifying a sudden swooping change—a curious memory picture of a tiny little corner, again a fragment, of the market in the town where I lived a few months in Australia, an image concentratedly conveying to bursting points of self-destruction the feelings for me of the huge sprawling market as a whole, and then beyond and over that the love and arguments I was embroiled in at that time of my life with my marketing companion at that tiny little corner—that fragment of a life's whole. Then, "another *pinta*," back to the drops of rain on the vibrating edge of a blade of grass with the song gathering us all, people here, people of the troubling past, shiny grass blade bending to the rain . . . the song snapping to a halt like a dry twig snapped into pieces.

"What's this, a sorcery bundle?" Santiago interjected, wiping his one good eye in mock disbelief because Eliseo kept bringing little plastic bags out of the darkness for Santiago to cure. "This one is for my wife," Eliseo gravely declared, pulling at his little bags.

From the hollow of his hammock, Santiago's son-in-law Angel now started to sing too, joining with Santiago to make in that instant of connecting a new tableau with the most beautiful singing I have ever heard, the two together rising and falling through the night sounds, stimulating and soothing turmoil at one and the same time.

Angel was seated on Santiago's chair, beating with the curing fan, while Santiago sat hunched in his hammock peering into his cupped hands holding something precious. Someone was vomiting outside. For a few instants a refrain snaked through the song: "*gente envidiosa, gente envidiosa,* envious people, envious people. . . ." The vomiting got louder. Santiago stopped singing to ask who it was that was suffering so, and gently laughed as did we all.

"Ah! *Así es el yagé;* That's *yagé* for you!" chuckled Santiago and after a short pause went on. "When will it be? One goes from here to there, round and round, trying this, trying that, until the hour comes, the fight with death. When will it come?" he asked thus of Angel, who has just been released from staring death in the face every minute of the day for eighteen days and who, by way of reply, began to hum—a tiny seed of life thrown into the gaping mouth of death-talk that now, humming too, grew into the great beating leaves of the curing fan, *waira sacha,* beating the beat of the galloping wail of the song that is *yagé.*

Now the room, so silent at the beginning of the evening, was buzzing with life. The song stopped and started, stopped and started, as either Angel or Santiago joined in the telling of tales in this carnival of humanity wiping at its tears while snuggling in each other's words, the wittier the saner.

Fundamental to the power of this almost nightlong carnival was montage—immanent and active from the moment the curtain rose, so to speak, an hour after sunset when the old man breathed "whoosh fire" into the *yagé,* cracked his tongue like a gunshot, and began to sing, curing the *yagé* that would cure us all, the old man included. The power of this *yagé* night came only in part from what could be called "mysticism," and that mystery concerned the quite unconscious way in which whites like Eliseo and his two companions from Boyacá attributed magical power to the "Indian." Given this attribution of magical power to tamed savagery, the power of the ritual itself then proceeds to do its work and play through splintering and decomposing structures and cracking open meanings. In this most crucial sense, savagery has not been tamed—and therein lies the magic of colonial healing through the figure of the "Indian." The "mystical insights" given by visions and tumbling fragments of memory pictures oscillating in a polyphonic discursive room full of leaping shadows and sensory pandemonium are not insights granted by depths mysterious and other. Rather, they are made, not granted, in the ability of montage to provoke sudden and infinite connections between dissimilars in an endless or almost endless process of connection-making and connection-breaking.

Montage: alterations, cracks, displacements, and swerves all evening long— the sudden interruptions, always interruptions to what at first appears the order of ritual and then later on takes on little more than an excuse of order, and then dissolves in a battering of wave after wave of interruptedness into illusory order, mocked order, colonial order in the looking glass. Interruptions for shitting, for vomiting, for a cloth to wipe one's face, for going to the kitchen to gather coals for burning copal incense, for getting roots of magical *chondur* from where nobody can remember where they were last put, for whispering a fear, for telling and retelling a joke (especially for that), for stopping the song in mid-flight to yell at the dogs to stop barking . . . and in the cracks and swerves, a universe opens out.

Montage: the manner of the interruptedness; the sudden scene changing which breaks up any attempt at narrative ordering and which trips up sensationalism. Between the swirling uncertainty of nausea and the abrupt certainty of the joke there lies little if any room for either the sensationalistic or the mysterious.

Montage: suddenly altering situations of the group within the room and mood-slides associated with those changing situations, scenes, as it were, from the art of *trompe-l'oeil* passing in a flash from night to day through ages of time from despair to joy and back again without any guarantee of happy endings.

Montage: flashing back and forth from self to group; not simply self-absorption broken up and scrambled by participation in the group or with one or two members of it, but also through such flashing back and forth from self to group and group to self a sort of playground and testing-ground is set up for comparing hallucinations with the social field from which they spring. Hence the very grounds of representation itself are raked over.

Another point: the movements and connections involved here between self and group are *not* susceptible to the *communitas* model that Victor

Turner postulated as a universal or quasi-universal feature of ritual. His basic idea concerning this can be quoted, thus:

> In flow and communities what is sought is unity, not the unity which represents a sum of fractions and is susceptible of division and subtraction, but an indivisible unity, 'white,' 'pure,' 'primary,' 'seamless.' This unity is expressed in such symbols as the basic generative and nurturant fluids semen and milk; and as running water, dawn, light, and whiteness. Homogeneity is sought, instead of heterogeneity [and the participants] are impregnated by unity, as it were, and purified from divisiveness and plurality. The impure and sinful is the sundered, the divided. The pure is the integer, the indivisible.[1]

Impregnating people with unity may fit well with certain fantasies of maleness and fascism. Certainly the *communitas* features of the *yagé* nights are the antithesis of this whiteness, this homogeneity, this soppy primitivism of semen and milk and the unified as the pure. Against that the *yagé* nights pose awkwardness of fit, breaking-up and scrambling, the allegorical rather than the symbolist mode, the predominance of the left hand and of anarchy—as in Artaud's notion of theater of cruelty with its poetic language of the senses, language that breaks open the conventions of language and the signifying function of signs through its chaotic mingling of danger and humor, "liberating signs," Artaud said, in a disorder that brings us ever closer to chaos.[2] It was to what he called "an infinite perspective of conflicts" that this theater of cruelty was directed, and with all the pitfalls and advantages that such a course entailed he drew for inspiration on non-Western theater, a course encouraged by the overwhelming contempt in which he held the bourgeois world so many of whose anthropologists have analyzed ritual as serving to structure and solidify society. Not for them the "infinite perspective of conflicts."

"Collective ritual can be seen as an especially dramatic attempt to bring some particular part of life firmly and definitely into orderly control. It belongs to the structuring side of the cultural/historical process." Thus Sally Falk Moore and Barbara Myerhoff introduce a recent book on ritual and curtly dismiss any notion that what goes on in between the segments of ritual can be as important as "the structuring side" of something so portentous as "the cultural/historical process."[3] By and large anthropology has bound the concept of ritual hand and foot to the imagery of order, to such an extent that order is identified with the sacred itself, thereby casting disorder into the pit of evil—as is so question-beggingly brought out by the citation from Paul Ricoeur with which Bruce Kapferer emblazons the first chapter of his book on exorcizing demons in Sri Lanka: "If evil is coextensive with the origin of things, as primeval chaos and theogonic strife, then the elimination of evil and of the wicked must belong to the creative act as such."[4]

Yagé nights challenge this ritual of explanation of ritual. They make us wonder at the unstated rites of academic text-making, at the means for creating intellectual authority, and, above all, at the conventions of sense-making thereby inscribed through conventions of "ordering" the chaos of that which has to be explained.

And it is precisely at the holy alliance of the orderly with the sacred that Benjamin's Marxist notion of the dialectical image, as developed through Surrealism and more especially his early work on allegory in Baroque drama, comes into play, divesting the totalizing compass of the Romantic concept of the symbol (upon which the aforementioned theories of ritual are based) by the nonwhite, nonhomogeneous, fragmentedness of montage, which on account of its awkwardness of fit, cracks, and violent juxtapositionings can actively embody both a presentation and a counterpresentation of the historical time which through conquest and colonialism matches signs with their meanings.

Montage: the "interior" scenes of dots and dashes of color and of phantasms, coming and going, death scenes, above all fragments of things—shiny blades of grass quivering under the rain, a tiny feathered segment of intricate pattern (the edge of a bird's wing, perhaps?), the quavering *yagé* song butting into the river's rush—all metamorphosing into memory images as the past gains force in its rush into the present "now-time" of the *Jetztzeiten* where time stands still as an image in which past and future converge explosively.

Montage: oscillating in and out of oneself; feeling sensations so intensely that you become the stuff sensed. But then you are standing outside the experience and coldly analyzing it as Bertolt Brecht so wanted from his "alienation effects" in his epic theater. Only here, in the theater of *yagé* nights in the Putumayo foothills, the A-effect, standing outside of one's now defamiliarized experience and analyzing that experience, is inconstant and constantly so, flickering, alternating with absorption in the events and their magic. Perhaps that is the formula for the profoundest possible A-effect, standing within and standing without in quick oscillation. It is not the order of ritual or the equally celebrated mystical "trip" through the more or less harmoniously cadenced zones and stations of cosmology that is of importance here. That cosmology we know well, and it is a fascist fascination too, with the ritual leader, with the harmonics of heroism, with order, with mystical flight, with the organic absorption of the individual into the "tribe" and so forth.

Yet even disorder implies the presence of order, and on the face of things *yagé* nights do have features providing for continuity and in that sense for order too. Chief among these features would be the song and the shaman. But the song resists characterization in these orderly terms. The best we can do is regard it as something like "ordered disorder" and "continuous discontinuity." Its outstanding qualities are its irregularly stopping and start-

ing, its frequent interruptedness, its sudden swerves and changes in pace
and the peculiar way by which it is not only a massively dominating force
but is open to interruption by anyone and anything—including this observation by Artaud in *The First Manifesto for Theater of Cruelty* regarding the
uniquely material side of that theater's language, its humor, to break down,
its poetry to make afresh:

> It extends the voice. It utilizes the vibrations and qualities of
> the voice. It wildly tramples rhythms underfoot [especially
> that]. It pile-drives sounds. It seeks to exalt, to benumb, to
> charm, to arrest the sensibility. It liberates a new lyricism of
> gesture which, by its precipitation or its amplitude in the air,
> ends by surpassing the lyricism of words. It ultimately breaks
> away from the intellectual subjugation of the language, by con-
> veying the sense of a new and deeper intellectuality which
> hides itself beneath the gestures and signs, raised to the dignity
> of particular exorcisms.[5]

As for the shaman, despite his solidity and caring he is also a strategic
zone of vacuity, a palette of imageric possibility. Where he does predominantly swim into focus, however, at least in the eyes of the civilized, is as
the alternating, composite, colonially created image of the wild man, bestial
and superhuman, devil and god—thus reinforcing the montage technique and
in a way its very fount. Just as history creates this fabulous image of the
shaman, so the montaged nature of that image allows history to breathe in
the spaces pried open between signs and meanings.

Furthermore, the decentered character of the shaman as a strategic zone
of vacuity creates havoc with the notion of the hero and of the heroic so
crucial to the tragic form of drama. Brecht's central figures become, notes
Benjamin, like an empty stage on which the contradictions of society are
acted out. The wise man is the perfect empty stage.[6]

Putumayo shamans resist the heroic mold into which current Western
image-making would pour them. Instead, their place is to bide time and
exude bawdy vitality and good sharp sense by striking out in a chaotic zigzag
fashion between laughter and death, constructing and breaking down a dramatic space layered between these two poles. True, there is the cosmic
Christian stage of redemption too. But that cosmos is here not just con-
stricted. It is radically displaced.

The *axis mundi* (of which our cosmologists are so fond) here stretches
not from hell to heaven but oscillates back and forth between laughter and
death in a montage of creation and destruction—figured for the shaman in
the signs of sweet-smelling petals as against the smell of shit, flowers as
against frogs and lizards, birds as against snakes and alligators, clear-head-
edness as against nausea and drunkenness.

As a form of epic theater these *yagé* nights succeed not by suffusing the
participants in unrelieved fantasies. Instead their effect lies in juxtaposing

to a heightened sense of reality, one of fantasy—thereby encouraging among the participants speculation into the whys and the wherefores of representation itself. In a similar vein Stanley Mitchell delineates Benjamin's preoccupation with montage:

> For fruitful antecedents, he looked back beyond German baroque to those forms of drama where the montage principle first made its appearance. He finds it wherever a critical intelligence intervenes to comment upon the representation, in other words where the representation is never complete in itself, but is openly and continually compared with the life represented; where the actors can at any moment stand outside themselves and show themselves to be actors.[7]

The technique of criticism and of discovery imputed here is not bound to an image of truth as something deep and general hidden under layers of superficial and perhaps illusory particulars. Rather, what is at work here is an image of truth as experiment, laden with particularity, now in this guise, now as that one, stalking the stage whose shadowy light conjures only to deconjure. It is this image of truth that flickers through the *yagé* nights of which I write, where it is patently the case that (in Mitchell's words) "the representation is never complete in itself, but is openly and continually compared with the life represented; where the actors can at any moment stand outside themselves and show themselves to be actors." The night-long *yagé* gathering exhibits this as much on the external stage as on what we might call the internal one set by the imagination. To the nights I have described as almost drumming with this alternating beat created by the constant interpolation of the everyday into the fabulous, and the fabulous into the everyday, think back also to the "internal" parallel to this as in José García relating one of his *yagé* visions in which he sees his family and farm being subject to sorcery. In that vision it is clear that the representation of himself in battle with the sorcerer is a representation never complete in itself, but one openly and continuously compared with the life represented, so that by this means the life as much as the representation is not only sensitized by each other's medium, but changed as well.

In this way fate is levered open and it is perhaps possible to overcome misfortune. On the one hand are envy and sorcery, and we are condemned to live out our lives in such a world where inequality breeds more of the same. But on the other hand there are weapons with which that fate can be fought. " 'It can happen this way, but it can also happen quite a different way'—that is the fundamental attitude of one who writes for epic theater," comments Benjamin.[8]

The magic of the Indian—an unconscious colonial creation—can provide the white man such as José García or Eliseo with just this weapon against the fate of inequality and envy. Now, having come from what to many here would seem as far away as Australia, having passed through night after night of taking *yagé,* and equipped with his freshly empowered charms and talismans, he can return home. He may not have got from the Indian all the secrets for which he asked in his letter. In fact he probably has none of them. Nor has the Indian given him magic—magic in the sense of making money magic, winning the lottery magic, making something out of nothing magic, finding gold magic. And there is a lesson in not giving that, for in that direction lies the realm of *magia* and deeply commoditized magic that dances with the magic of money. That is what the charlatans who wander from the Sibundoy Valley are good at. Ask them!

What Eliseo has acquired (and he paid for it), says the Indian curer, who all night long has so laboriously cured his big fleshy body and his plastic bag of rings, is the curing of his cattle and of his hens so that the envy of his neighbors shall not penetrate. Now Eliseo can go home and work hard at being a curer and a farmer and withstand the envy his success will inevitably create—as it did for José García years before.

It is a simple-sounding social function. The magic invested in the Indian by the civilized assuages the envy that comes from inequality among the whites. The shaman's daughter puts it in a slightly different way, that her father tries to make enemies into friends. But how this is done, and how the figure representing inferiority, savagery, and evil, comes to have this power—that is not quite so simple.

To the white man such as Eliseo, the epic theater of the *yagé* night is not merely Indian. It is real. Despite its dazzling array of alienation effects, this theater fails dismally where Brecht would have it most succeed. It is deeply illusionistic and nowhere more so than in the magical power attributed by colonial history to the Indian shaman.

But for the referents of this history and of these practices, namely the Indians who are called upon to provide magical power to blunt the evils of inequality in the rest of society, there *is* doubting about the reality. This uncertainty at what we might call the fount of the system of magical curing has curiously curative effects for us because it cautions against the search for magical power in a unitary being such as the Indian shaman, and instead advises us as to where that power creates itself; namely, in the relation between the shaman and the patient—between the figure who sees but will not talk of what he sees, and the one who talks, often beautifully, but cannot see. It is this that has to be worked through if one is to become a healer.

TWENTY-EIGHT

To Become a Healer

. . . that man of song whom the muse cherished; by her gift he knew the good of life and evil—for she who gave him sweetness made him blind.

Homer, *The Odyssey*

It is an enchanting and empowering notion that, in striking contrast to what we might call the scientific model of healing and sickness on which the university training of doctors is now based, folk healers and shamans embark on their careers as a way of healing themselves. The resolution of their illness is to become a healer, and their pursuit of this calling is a more or less persistent battle with the forces of illness that lie within them as much as in their patients. It is as if serious illness were a sign of powers awakening and unfolding a new path for them to follow. In his essay concerning a Mazatec healer in southern Mexico, Henry Munn sees that the sick man, despondent, unsure of himself, decaying in sadness, and almost willfully entering into the realm of death has only one option if he has but the courage to seize it: to become a healer himself.[1]

The cure is to become a curer. In being healed he is also becoming a healer. In becoming one the option is whether he will succumb to the encroachment of death subsequent to soul loss, or whether he will allow the sickness-causing trauma and the healer's ministrations to reweave the creative forces in his personality and life experience into a force that bestows life upon himself and upon others through that bestowal. In the journey undertaken by the healer and the sick man into an underworld and up into the mountains across the sacred landscape of space and time, it is this option that is being traversed.

The healer relives this journey on the brink of death. Entering into death the question is whether and how there will be a return.

We may think of this space of death as a threshold. It is here that the healer walks. Yet it can be a wide space, wider than the notion of a shadow-line may suggest, and its breadth offers many different positions for advance or retreat. It can be filled with words, just as it can be emptied of them. It may spook us all, the zone into which, willy-nilly, all the stereotypes of "soul-flight" and of "shamanism," that Western projection of a Siberian name, finds life in a language of heroic restraint generally awfully male, poetic, originary, and so on. Yet this death-space may be both tougher and more banal, more upset and upsetting than the discourse of heroic restraint has allowed. There may well be a certain lightness too:

In the dark times
Will there also be singing?
Yes, there will also be singing
About the dark times
[Bertolt Brecht]

It is certainly not necessarily solitary, this death-space, even if it has till now been persistently male. Indeed, it is to a special intertwining of dumbness and insight, of the slow and the swift together, pluralizing the death-space that I must now report on.

There is that sick Indian man, Florencio, who seemed to be saying that he wanted to become a healer and take the bad out of the bodies of the sick. He himself fell sick and entered into what he called the space of death. He approached a limit. He was close to becoming something else in which that limit was inscribed. But he faltered and fell.

Yet, unlike his friend who did not falter and instead journeyed on to become a healer, the person who faltered returned, albeit spinning, to tell us what it was like. In a sense his journey was a failure. But because of that he was here to tell us the tale while the healer was not.

It was said that this healer gives the vision. This was what Florencio said. And that it was the shaman who most truly sees. But it seems that in truly seeing he could not or would not speak of what he sees. Not much, anyway.

That is why the shaman needs the patient, just as the patient, for perhaps more obvious reasons, needs the shaman. The patient who skirts the space of death only to return to us becomes the voice of the shaman.

It is these two poles that stake out the dialogized terrain of the space of death. Between the patient who enters this space and then falters at the final instant of decision, and the healer who has gone on to mesh at their highest intensity the living with the dead, we encounter a special (albeit male) moment in the crafting of what I call implicit social knowledge.

Walking in the Space of Death

In 1976 Florencio was working with a group of people on the bank of the Caquetá River clearing land for the building of a schoolhouse. He got sick and this is what he told me about it three years later.

> The rains attacked me. I was sweating and it gave me a little
> fever. I thought that it would pass, no? Who could divine that
> the fever would attack me so strongly? And after coming home
> I changed my clothes and the fever went on and on. It lasted
> eight days, no longer, and with the fever I was aware of every-
> thing. But after eight days I became unconscious. I knew not
> where I was. Like a madman I wandered, consumed by fever.
> They had to cover me up where I fell, mouth down. Thus after
> eight days I was aware of nothing. I was unconscious; thus. Of
> what people were saying, I remembered nothing. Of the pain of
> the fever, I remembered nothing; only the space of death—
> walking in the space of death.
> Thus; after the noises that spoke, I remained unconscious.
> Now I took account of nothing. Now the world remained be-
> hind. Now the world was removed.
> Well, then I understood. Now the pains were speaking. I
> knew that I would no longer live. Now I was dead. My sight
> had gone. Of the world I knew nothing, nor the sounds of my
> ears. Of speech, nothing. Silence.
> And one knows the space of death. There.
> And this is death—the space that I saw. I was in its center,
> standing. Thus I went to the heights. From the heights a star-
> point seemed my due. I was standing. Then I came down.
> There I was searching for the five continents of the world, to
> remain, to find me a place in the five continents of the world—
> in the space in which I was wandering. But I was not able.
> And then I was presented with the golden rings and shoes of
> gold of the golden child to place my fingers and feet into, no?
> In order to attend the banquet and eat with the Lord.
> *With God?*
> Surely, thus. Death. . . . But in the confusion I fumbled. And
> then I saw a man like a king; like the pope. Little angels came
> to me and passed me by, thus, tiny little ones asking to per-
> fume me. And these angels passed me on to others who re-
> ceived my fingers that didn't fit, just like you say to a person,
> "Please pass!" And the speed with which they wanted to per-
> fume me! They were tiny, no? Angels everywhere. And they
> went past, with such speed, saying, "With this, time passes."
> Umm. . .

Well, this went its way and then the king presented me with
. . . like shotgun cartridges size sixteen, you know, of copper,
that were here once upon a time. This is what he had in his
hands, spraying sparks from each end to all sides. By my name
he said to me: "Florencio. Look! This is the world; that God
has given illness."

Spraying sparks from each point, from here to there, like
fire, let us say. White sparks. This is in the world. God gave
illness—for the white, the black, the Indian—for all it is there.
God gave this. But did God himself give it without remedy?
No! *With* remedy. . . . Umm . . . God gave illness to the world.
God himself created mankind and by the same action gave illness—to everyone.

You talk of the sorcerers that do evil, no? Like the *capach-
eros* [the Indian shaman-sorcerers of the highlands], those
thieves that do evil. No! Not them! The king told me it was not
sorcery but a sickness of the forest or of the river.

And then he said to me: "No! There are remedies, like taking *mejoral* [aspirin] that the herbalists know. First is the person who knows plants for all classes of illness to calm one. The
second type of person has the knowledge of the first and also
the knowledge of the illness that attacks one. He knows more
than the first. The third is the one who knows more than the
first and the second. Umm . . . He knows all classes of illnesses; plants that make you vomit and plants that purge you,
whatever it might be. He knows more. Yes! He! With *him* it is
possible . . . possible to consult. He! Yes! He will cure you. It
will be good. All types of illness, because he knows. He is
competent—the man of *yagé*.

That also passed away. All this I saw. All that was spoken. It
passed away. And I went to the space of the world. In history,
let us say, in the school the teachers make you learn the world
is like an orange—let us put it that way. But don't you know
that it's not round like an orange! No! That could not be. Instead it's like a top, but a little flatter, no? Yet . . . very, very
beautiful. It has the color of the firmament, yet clearer.

Thus, in the space of the world I went to the heights, right
up, and ascended to the very top of the world.

In the world that is there, at the very top, is a huge cross.
To there I went—*compañeros*. And there I stood on my left
foot on a tiny staircase, very finely wrought, seeing the continent of the world . . . like . . . let us say . . . a cup with soapy
water. You blow on it, no? And this bubble floats off, no? To
the heights. It is in the firmament, no? And it touches the
earth nowhere; borne by the airs. Do you believe me in this?
Do you?

And there I knew the world—seeing it spinning, like, let us
say, an orange. And from the space where I was, down below

there was another world. And the heights—infinity! When would it end? Never! Do you believe me?

And then from there I slipped down the steps, like down the fine edge of a palm leaf, and my body became disoriented. And I saw everything spinning. Now I had returned. I could not speak. I was mute. [He laughs, slowly.]

I couldn't speak well. Umm. He had come already—the shaman. They had gone to get Don Santiago. I could hear him slightly. But I couldn't talk well. See! That was what I saw of the space of death, as the fever attacked me.

I think that I was unconscious for two days. Without consciousness; that's how one walks—until death comes, if there is no remedy. Or else there is someone with the capacity to heal. But that's not easy to find; to find a good curer. Thanks to God I didn't believe that someone was attacking me with evil, no? This, one's life, serves for something, no? and if not, the illness that God gives. In this idea I was living.

And if you had thought it was sorcery?

No. It was not sorcery.

God?

Yes. Yes! The humanity. . . . This was something worthwhile, so it seemed to me. For me, no?

And if you had thought it was sorcery you would have less resistance?

Yes! I would not have gained. I would not have won. All would have been lost from the start. This was what God had given me. Nothing more, for the time being.

[Florencio puts out his hands to me.] Don Miguel: Give me your hand, please. This; the death that attacked me. The fever.

Compañeros:

How good that you came back!

Yes. Many thanks. This is the story of the space of death that attacked me; nothing more.

Santiago had been called. He made three attempts to examine Florencio but failed each time. Santiago explained:

With the fourth examination I was able. Yes! He would live! I had sent off for remedies. We were wandering a long way away and when the time came to come here, to Florencio's, I had been drinking liquor and I asked my wife to put the remedies in a bag. But it got lost. When we got to the port of Guzmán, nothing! "Who knows if we'll find him dead or alive" I said. "We have to go. I want to see if he'll live or if he's dead." We arrived. He was still alive but he didn't know me. He was unconscious. Thus I settled down to make an examination, no? But I couldn't. I was unable. The second time, neither. And the third, neither. But on the fourth, I conquered. Yes, it was there. He would live. We prepared uncooked *yagé.*

Florencio added:

> Yes. Those who came to see me here; I was dead. . . . I knew
> nothing. But how was it that this man didn't die who was dead
> for days? To come back again to this world. How is that?
> Never have we seen this? A sick man who is finished—all
> finished—and he came back! How is this? We all witnessed it—
> the friend here who is father to us all. How could it be? Or
> could it be something in our favor—for us to see God, the man
> who came back! . . . And then I remembered the deceased
> *taita* [father, shaman] Salvador.

A year or so before Florencio walked through the space of death, to return,
spinning and mute, barely able to hear Santiago who had come to his side,
Santiago himself was on the point of dying, because, so it was said at the
time, of the sorcery of Esteban, the highland Ingano shaman. The esteemed
Cofán shaman, Salvador, had been called and eventually came with his
family. Florencio was there too, and they took *yagé* together. It was this
that Florencio remembered, suddenly, a year later when he was returning
from the space of death.

> I was at the friend's [Santiago's] place. Salvador was there.
> First the *yagé* that the friend had had no effect. Then Salvador
> said, "Let us begin with this *yagé,* to see if it's stronger, no?"
> Don Apolinar [another shaman, Santiago's daughter's father-in-
> law] was there too, from Yuriaco; he too was sick. The four of
> us took *yagé* that *taita* Salvador brought—the remedy of *yagé.*
> Well! What a *chuma!* We flew like birds. Ah! Santo Dios! . . . I
> was useless. People were entering and leaving, entering and
> leaving. I was lying up against the wall. It seemed as if stones
> were being hurled. Paroom! Paroom! The stones fell. And my
> *compañero* Don Apolinar asked, "What's happening?" Ha!
> Who is making blows with stones against us? Could it be just
> the *chuma* and nothing else? Who knows?" But what was hap-
> pening was that people were grouping there, in this banquet,
> walking backwards and forwards, vomiting, purging, and so
> forth. But I? I was being beautifully drunk. That was the hope
> I had.
> *What do you mean, "That was the hope I had?"*
> Because after my illness I went to Santiago's who took us to
> take *yagé.* I was convalescing from the illness that I had had. I
> hadn't taken *yagé* since I'd been sick. . . . I remembered the
> now deceased Salvador. I remembered the visions I had seen
> then, no? When we had taken *yagé* in Santiago's house.
> Well! Then the *chuma* began. I said, "*Santo Dios,*" to my
> wife I said, "Who knows if I will be able to bear up. I am so
> weak." Well, the *chuma* began. Umm.

And the same that I had seen before—what Salvador had given us four—the *pinta* [vision] of *yagé* was the *very* very same that the deceased Salvador has given me! It was the *pinta* to heal people. It was the *pinta* of *yagé* people [the spirits of *yagé* that have the same appearance as shamans and in a sense are their prototype]; they all had their healing fans, thus. They all had their necklaces of tigers' teeth. Identical, all.

And that's what I had seen the first time taking *yagé* with *taita* Salvador. . . . That's what made me so happy. I remained with my heritage. I saw beautiful things. That is what I saw. Beauty I saw in the *chuma*. And that is certain.

We were taking *yagé* there in Santiago's house with Salvador. I went outside. I had to go to defend myself in order not to collide with another drunken [*yagé*-affected] person that I knew. I seemed to be going, and then this wind roared. It caught me. I almost fell face down. The *chuma* attacked me. And then I was caught at the waist.

Compañeros, how can it be? I neither fell nor got hurt. I was filled with fear. And the friend Salvador said: "Take care! Take care! They are going to let you go. You are going to fall to the ground." Divining—how does *yagé* do it? How does this occur to one? Umm. And *taita* Salvador asked me, "What is this?"

Well, then I *saw*—as the *yagé* healers say. That's how it should be known, no? Strange tales.

Thus, *yagé*. I saw.

Do you remember the time when you took yagé and saw the angels with crystals?

Ah, yes. That was in Puerto Limón [about twenty years ago]. There was a shaman there who was also very good. He told me: "I want to invite you because there is a sick woman who is really very sick and can't come here to my house to be cured. So I have to go there. Let us go together."

"Okay," I said. "Let's go. I am going to accompany you."

Well, I went. With the first cup of *yagé* I became drunk. Really good. Drunk. It passed away. And then the second cup. The shaman said: "Let's take another little one to cure the sick woman." I replied "Yes. Let it be. Let us take another little one."

He cured and he cured, and he drank, and he cured and he cured, with us. I saw it all. In two or three minutes the *chuma* came. With the first one we didn't get drunk, as is correct. And the vision begins.

Three men were seated on a bench, thus. They were all of the same color and height—all the same. You couldn't distinguish one from the other; equal to the smallest detail, in their clothing, in their costume with which the shamans display themselves—competent to take *yagé*. Thus they were seated,

the three men. The *chuma* began to affect me; to make me see.
It passed away. That was what I saw.

And then in three minutes the *chuma* returned, with more
force. A guardian angel entered with an incense burner. What
fragrance? Like those who waft the incense for the saintly
mass onto the priests and onto the altars. The incense was
swirled throughout the room of the houses, no? And how! How
fragrant the incense! How rich! Umm. And then the angel
seemed to turn around and leave. The guardian angel, thus, he
left. Then the *chuma* appeared to leave me, a little.

And in two or three minutes the *chuma* returned but with
more power. Then the angel of the guard, the same first angel
entered. But now he had a very beautiful chalice of pure gold;
very tiny and very beautiful. I was lying down in my hammock, face upwards. And he came up to me to place the heart,
thus, into my chest.

But Sainted God, *compañero!* I almost fell from the hammock in that very instant when the angel placed the heart in
my chest. I almost fell onto the ground. I was hanging there,
from the waist down.

And that could be all that there is to the story—everything
from the beginning, so that nothing is left to one. Nothing!
Compañeros.

Then I remembered and called on the *yagé* people: "Please
save me!" And now I was able once again to lie down properly
in the hammock. Then the curer got up to heal the sick
woman. "Look!" he told me. *"Compadre, compadre,* that's
why I told you that to learn to cure the sick is really a lot of
work for us who have traveled through this career in order to
cure people."

He took up his curing fan and started to heal. Then the
chuma passed away from me, and changed. It changed and
took another form. I felt the body of the sick woman. I was
seeing. I was in another room—the *yagé* making me see. There
I was. The sick woman is there and I am there seeing the sickness and the pain that she had in her head like the bites of the
fangs of scorpions, let us say, that she couldn't tolerate. All
over her head. Thus; me seeing, and pulsing her hand. *Yagé*
was letting me see what healers see!

"*Caramba!*" I thought to myself, "*Caramba!* Thus, drunk.
Like this! I could extract evil too."

Seeing the sick and touching the sick; I myself. The shaman
was healing—seeing all. Then with the curing fan, blowing and
sucking, turning around, gathering the sickness all in one place,
extracting it by mouth and blowing it away so that nothing remains. After that, having touched again, the pain is no longer
felt nor the bites of wasps or anything else in the head. Nothing
is felt. The pulse is normal. All is well. Then one bathes the

head in the fresh water medicine. And with that the healing is
done; all is ready.
   The *chuma* also was done, to that point and no more.
   [Florencio laughs lightly.] Well, take many thanks.

Yagé Is a Great Liar

Florencio was born in 1914 close to the town of Mocoa and his father died
when he was a small boy. His mother remarried a man who was adept at
healing. He was unfriendly to Florencio, who spent much of his early life,
he said, as an orphan. He was interned for three years in a mission school
and at the age of fifteen was appointed to accompany Father Bartolomé on
his apostolic excursion down the Caquetá River to the land of the Huitotos—
to the *auca* Huitotos, as Florence calls them.

He was made sacristan of the small church at Puerto Limón on the banks
of the Caquetá. When war broke out between Colombia and Peru over the
disputed Putumayo border in 1932, he, along with other local Indians, was
pressed into service as a canoe paddler or *boga* transporting cans of gasoline.
The army came and went quickly but their image remained in Florencio's
yagé healing vision of the batallion singing and dancing in golden uniform.

Now and again his stepfather gave him *yagé* to drink, beginning when he
was still a young boy. After the war, when Florencio was about twenty years
old, his stepfather viciously turned on him, saying he was using *yagé* for
sorcery. "This was like torture," Florencio told me, "and I became sicker
and sicker."

In his distress he sought counsel from a shaman living over in Umbría on
the banks of the limpid Guineo River. Hilberio invited him to stay and be
his *yagé* cook. He spoke with Florencio: "Look! My cousin has told me
what you are supposed to be doing. But you aren't making sorcery! Come
and take *yagé* with me. I have land you can work along the Putumayo. Come
here! Let's take *yagé*."

"He liked me a lot," said Florencio, and he told me about *yagé*."

"*Yagé* is a great deceiver," Hilberio said.

> "*Yagé* is not positive. You see a lot of false things. You see
> that so-and-so is doing sorcery, making *capachos* or whatever
> in order to get at you. But quite often it's untrue. The spirits of
> *yagé* can deceive. You see somebody attacking you. But even
> so there's a part of you that doesn't believe what you are
> seeing. You don't know what to believe.

"*Yagé* lies," Florencio told me.

> "*Yagé* makes things visible. You see someone you know doing
> bad to you, no? The *yagé* is making you see this. It gets
> stronger and stronger. Then you start to hate that person, that

friend, and it can even be your own son, mother, or father. . . .
But it's false. You have to keep on taking *yagé,* and then it
comes in another way. You see good things. and they continue.
That's what he explained to me. "No! You are not to blame,"
he said. "If you want to take *yagé,* come with me. Come!
Let's take it together!"

A highland shaman, an Ingano from the town of Santiago in the Sibundoy
Valley, came down the mountain to Puerto Limón. Florencio was in bed,
sick and crying.

> I couldn't tolerate *yagé.* I could take just enough to begin to
> have visions, but I couldn't go on. The curer from Santiago
> said he was really sad for me, that he liked me a lot, and that
> my stepfather could do me no good. I should come to his place
> to get cured. "I have no money," I said. "That doesn't mat-
> ter," he said. "It's not for money. Come! And when you get
> better, you can pay it off by working for me." 'How much will
> it cost?' I asked. "Ten pesos," he said [at that time a day's la-
> bor was worth around twenty cents]. So we went.
> I stayed up there four months fighting the cold. With *bor-*
> *rachera* [the datura shrub, mainstay hallucinogen of Sibundoy
> Valley shamans], if it begins to flower this week, then that's a
> sign that you'll get better. But if it develops yellow leaves that
> fall from the tree, then that's a sign you'll die just as the *bor-*
> *rachera* is dying.
> He told me that when I drank it I would be likely to get up,
> race around screaming, ripping off my clothes, urinating all
> over the place, robbing things—and without me realizing what I
> was doing . . . like in a dream.
> There were two of us patients, me and a porter from Mocoa,
> an Ingano. In almost a quarter of an hour the *chuma* began.
> . . . It's really awful, not like *yagé.* It's as if your clothes come
> off. Your throat becomes dry, dry . . . and then this passes and
> you forget. At around four o'clock in the morning, with the
> other man walking around, I got up and the shaman blessed
> me. Next day we took *yagé.* Two days after that we took *bor-*
> *rachera* again. First I took four pairs of its leaves. The second
> time I took five. Up to ten pairs I took—and at the end the
> flower itself, which is sweet like honey . . . but *strong!* Thus!
> *Boom!* Crash to the floor. Remember nothing. Nothing. Till the
> next day. That's how it went. And in the afternoons we would
> take *yagé.*
> With that I was cured.
> My family had told me that I was doing evil. When I re-
> turned home I took *yagé* with my stepfather, my brother-in-law,
> Hilberio, and three others. That night my brother-in-law got up
> in front of everyone and tried to kill me while we were all

drinking *yagé*. My stepfather stopped accusing me of being a sorcerer. Hilberio explained to me that my stepfather had been believing false visions because all along he had been ensorcelled by someone else and because *yagé* is a great liar.

Yagé is a great liar: yet *yagé* is necessary to gain clear vision. "The very *yagé* makes you see," says Florencio. "It makes knowledge of disease. Without this seeing . . . nothing! We want to cure our family, the people dearest to us. But if we can't see, if the vision of *yagé* doesn't come, how can we cure them? We can't!"

But what is one to do with what is the deepest insight of *yagé*—that its visions may be false?

How Santiago Became a Shaman

Thirty-three years ago, Santiago's newlywed wife was very sick and couldn't walk, She was almost eighteen years old. This was just after she had given birth to a baby girl. Santiago explained:

> Then she began to catch this evil—the sickness with which she couldn't eat, and what little she did eat, did her damage, causing diarrhea. She was a young girl, just married, and never had she suffered thus. This was bad what she had.
>
> A healer told us that she had been *capachado* [ensorcelled by means of a small bundle of hair, fingernails, etc.; the brand-mark of the Ingano shamans of the highlands from the Sibundoy Valley], and that we had to go to a shaman in the highland valley who knew how to cure this. So we went there. But the sickness stayed the same! Finally I ran out of money. What could I do? So I went to my brother Alvaro: "I don't know what to do with this woman of mine; as each day passes she gets sicker and sicker. We have been and tried to exorcise the *capacho,* but the sickness stays the same. I have stopped trying that because you can't see any improvement."
>
> Then my brother said to me: "Just now there has come to the town a Doctor Pardo from Bogotá who is very attentive and is curing very sick people. He has been sent by the government to cure *indios.* Let us go to see what's going on there!"
>
> But what an enormous lot of people there were! Aieee! It was impossible to get in. The doorway was full of people, rich people, whites, with coats and ties. Doctor Pardo was above them, terribly busy, working on the second floor. And we wondered anxiously to ourselves: "How are we going to enter into there?" When suddenly from there someone started making signs. But we didn't know if it was for us. Then the assistants came and opened a way, saying "Make way; make way for

these *indios!*" Slowly but steadily they opened the way. Today
the doctors don't attend the *indios;* they only attend the pretty
young girls. [He laughs.]

"Move over! Here are more people for the doctor! He is
calling them! Enter through here!" They made us enter; all
three. We walked in and they led my wife to a little bed and
made her lie down, naked from shoulders to the waist. Then
the doctor put his hand like this, and with the finger of his
other hand he tapped. He struck and it sounded like a drum.
Tan! Tan! Tan! And when he did the same further down her
chest, the same sound but deeper. Each part of her chest
sounded different when he tapped. Some places sounded
harder, others deeper, but he didn't tell us what she had. He
gave us a remedy, saying "Look! This is so she can resist. She
must take this purgative. But she musn't defecate in dry spots
but in water. Or if not in the water, bury it in the soil so that
nobody walks on it!"

This was anemia. A boy in the town told us what sort of illness anemia was. There are three classes of anemia.

Then what happened was that a huge number of worms
came. She, to see what would happen, defecated there in the
gully where she was going to pick grass for a broom. She
called me: "Look! Come here. Come and See!"

I said to myself, "What could it be? Maybe she has died!"
[He laughs loudly.] So much! What filth this poor woman had
inside her! There was a huge ball of worms; worms everywhere! How was it that she didn't die from this animality?

Thus she was cured. But as we were poor people we had
nothing . . . if we had had a hen we could have taken that. But
we had nothing to give as a gift. And my wife was now very
well and robust. Now she could walk. She felt no pain and had
no attacks, nothing.

Then, look! From that a great anger entered me—*those shamans were thieves! Now I would have to learn to take yagé!*
From that moment I wanted to know how to take *yagé.* They
didn't cure us; they robbed and did not cure! I said to myself,
"*Carajo!* I am capable of taking *yagé* so that I can see if it's
true if the shamans know when one beseeches them." That is
why I started to drink *yagé,* in order to learn that . . . and now
I can do a few things, no? Now I can even cure *gringos,* no?
Don't you agree? [He laughs and laughs.]

From anger. It choked me that the shamans of the highlands
[from the valley of Sibundoy] had laid this trap. I started taking
yagé so that I could learn. That's how it was. . . . I took it
alone with my brother who was still alive in those days. With
him. They killed him later and I remained alone. All alone.
Thus it was. He was a better shaman than I am today. He was

falsely accused of killing a neighbor with sorcery. The neighbor
was killed cross-sawing a log for house building. He was under-
neath. The log fell on top of him. His father-in-law said it was
my brother's doing. They waylaid him in a gulch and came at
him from in front and behind with machetes. They stabbed him
many times in the stomach and in the left side of his chest. My
other brother was frightened and left forever to live down along
the Caquetá River. But I stayed on. "If they're going to kill
you, they will kill you," I said. And I stayed.

People ask me, "How did you learn? With what shaman?"

But no! With a shaman, *no!* I did it *alone.* I myself prepared
yagé and drank it. One or the other happens; you live or you
die.

Others learn from shamans. Yes! But that carries danger too.
He who learns well from a shaman, then the shaman tries to
kill him! . . . That's what happened to my father. That's why
it's better to . . . as the *yagé* itself teaches you, it is better to
take it alone. Then there is no teacher to get envious; nobody
who knows that you are drinking it. Now I have learned
something.

My wife was cured with drugs from the pharmacy. There was
no *capacho!* There was deceit. Thus I began to take *yagé.* It
was no *capacho,* it was microbes! A *capacho* of worms! [He
laughs.] From Sibundoy—pure lies. That's why they are so
wealthy. They exorcise money and the sickness stays the same.

Yet when he began to take *yagé* in order to learn (and he was barely twenty
years old at the time), he saw nothing but snakes and dragons and terrifyingly
ugly women with monkey's tails. He swore to take no more because this
would lead him to death and the inferno. But then the temptation would
seize him once again, and he would drink more, only to have the same awful
visions. "I wanted to know what this was about. But at the start *yagé*
punished me brutally. I thought I would die. I wanted to stop because it was
so ugly. But then I would return and take a little more." This went on for
two years. With those visions he felt death closing in.

I thought that I would no longer live. No longer could I see my
wife, or my family. I was at death's door, dying, and I wanted
my wife's hand so that I could be calmed. Nothing! Nothing!
And then I realized that if I wished to go on, I had to be tough,
I had to be able to take it as it came. And I grew to accept it
and I realized, "Yes! You will have salvation. Yes! You will
have salvation. You will not die!" And then another voice said,
"If you don't take care, if you aren't generous in friendship
and with your family, then there is that world of pure flame and
molten lead. . . ." And I would fall from my hammock. Poom!
Crash to the floor . . . punished!

The Articulation of Implicit Social Knowledge

The contrast between Florencio's and Santiago's accounts is striking and one that is typical, I think, for this reason: that the power of shamanism lies not with the shaman but with the differences created by the coming together of shaman and patient, differences constituting imagery essential to the articulation of what I call implicit social knowledge. Ground in this interplay of Otherness such knowledge brings being and imagining together in a medley of swirling discourses—the shaman's song, the patient's narratives, the bawdiness, the leaden silences, the purging. Florencio says that the curing imagery comes from the shaman, and here we do well to remember the curing vision of the golden battalion of the Colombian army, and the shaman will say it comes from *yagé* itself. I say it comes from the joint construction of the healer and the sick in the semantically generative space of annulment that is the colonial death-space. This is a privileged moment in the casting of the reality of the world, in its making and its unmaking. Here lies power. I am thinking too of the white colonist Manuel Gómez with his *yagé* imagery of the shaman as devil, prelude to his gaining grace.

In his essays on New World shamanism, Claude Lévi-Strauss presents the notion that in their coming together, patient and shaman conduct on behalf of society a joint interrogation of their ideological environment.[2] He states that the experiences of the sick person are the *least* important aspect of this and in his analysis of a Cuna shaman's curing song of Mu-Igala for a woman in obstructed labor, he makes much of the suggestion that shamanism inverts the psychoanalytic technique for achieving abreaction since in shamanism it is not the patient's but the shaman's speech that fills the therapeutic space. The woman lies silent while the shaman's song fills her with imagery ordering the chaos of her being—and as for woman, so for society as a whole with shamanism orchestrating the symphony from chaos to order.

Yet it is clear from the source from which Lévi- Strauss extracts this song that the woman and the rest of society probably do not understand it since it is sung in a special shamanic language, a feature common to shamanism in many societies. The problem then is to see how the notion of a joint interrogation of the ideological environment can be sustained if the parties to this discourse are bound to an unintelligible language. Putumayan healing, as I have learned about it, indicates that such an interpretation of a healing song is little more than a projection into magical ritual of the unstated ritual of academic explanation, turning chaos into order, and that this magic of academe stands opposed, in its upright orderliness, to the type of sympathy necessary to understand that the healing song, magical or not, is but part of a baroque mosaic of discourses woven through stories, jokes, interjections, and hummings taking place not only through and on top of one another during the actual séance but before and after it as well. Moreover, this play cannot be understood without taking into account the patient's partnership in the medley of image-making activities in which the song rests.

It is this coming together in an active grating of intentions and complementary functions of sense and image-making that fascinates me. While Florencio represents his visions to me with the wonder, piety, and delicacy of a gently inquiring mind—"that man of song, whom the muse cherished . . . for she who gave him sweetness made him blind"—Santiago's way is that of a bold, straightforward person, curt and practical. His stated motive for learning the way of a shaman is not the sublime search for truth but anger at having been deceived by shamans. While Florencio suffers in epistemological doubt as to whether *yagé* visions are true or false and constantly hovers on the hermeneutic brink, Santiago jumps into the fray with full force and learns *yagé* on his own so as to deal with deception. It is Florencio, the patient, the afflicted one, and never-to-be but constantly aspiring shaman, who strikes me as the mystic enchanter and sage while Santiago, the shaman proper, busies himself as an artisan facing a down-to-earth problem to be worked at with the diligence of a craft (as opposed to an "art," as the relatively modern distinction in the West would have it). The common notion (in the West, at least) that sees in the wisdom of the poets like Homer the foundations of human society and likewise imagines shamans to be the repositories of this divine and originary wisdom is, in the Putumayo case, curiously confounded. For here it is the patient and not the shaman who sounds the chords of poetic wisdom.

If we turn to the discourses in the shamantic séance itself we see that Santiago's are twofold: the *yagé* sounds that come not from but through him from the *yagé* spirits with whom he is singing and sometimes dancing in his night-long chanting, and counterpoised to this "divine" speech of song in its eddies and whirlings is his gentle mockery, sexual innuendo, and degrading profanities. Between these poles of divine song and laughter there is no trace of the expanding and contracting flower of delicate consciousness that the uncertainties of the space of death cultivate for Florencio.

Santiago learned *yagé* alone, without any shaman-teacher. His father was almost killed while learning *yagé* by the envy of shaman-teachers and Santiago tirelessly reiterates his history, just as others will tell you how dangerous it is to take *yagé* alone without a shaman. Having stepped outside of society, so to speak, avoiding the pitfalls of envy wrought to sharp intensity in the shaman-pupil relationship, Santiago has reentered the social world as the divine trickster of its inevitable envy and in ways both clear and obscure guides the afflicted through its minefields. His navigation of the space of death and his navigation of envy are existentially matched, and his role as a mute visionary and creator of visions for the patients he ministers is steady and sure.

On the other hand, Florencio is more navigated by this space than its navigator. His tenderness as much as his inability to stride through the death-space is expressed in both certainty and doubt with respect to the truth of his visions and this parallels his stance vis-á-vis social relatedness in general and envy in particular. The beauty and wonder with which he renders his vision owe much to this.

But the credibility *and* the impossibility that make the visions what they are, this proper material (as Vico would have it) of the poetics of the imagination, is inevitably a joint construction brought about by the coming together of shaman and patient. The former brings mute certainty, the latter uncertainty but voice, and the credible impossibility is synthesized in this dialogical manner.

Yet both figures, that of the shaman as certainty and that of patient as doubt, only acquire this configuration by their coming together, because both contain within themselves, taken as individuals, the same vexation with regard to the credible impossibilities that course through life's contingencies as much as through the ambiguities of social relations. The creative delicacy of their coming together as patient and shaman lies in the different yet complementary ways this relation allows them to ease or resolve this vexation. Santiago strikes out boldly, grasps the visions and moves into them, singing and dancing, absorbed in his activating the spirits. In being thus absorbed he calls for more. His feathers promote the colors of the birds that are uplifting visions. His jaguar's-teeth necklace promotes the transformation so that one can walk with one's enemies and turn on them as well. Florencio lies still. Now and again he may try to raise himself, to sing and to dance with the vision, but he falls. Each person here provides the other with a special viewpoint and function in the making and always provisional interpretation of society's imaginative infrastructure which is *yagé*'s great gift to the fragmented colonial consciousness.

In modern Western philosophy there is an eminent notion of mind and knowledge that may be invoked here. In Kant's notion of what makes knowledge possible, which begins with the observation that although all our knowledge begins with experience it does not follow that it all arises out of experience, sensory impressions are articulated to the the *aprioris* of knowing through a mechanism he refers to as the "schematism." But while sensory impressions are too concrete, the *aprioris* are too abstract for the process that creates knowledge. In order to cofunction, an intermediary device articulating them is required—the schematism—and this articulator, says Kant, is in many ways dependent upon images.

Kant says that "this schematism of our understanding, in its application to appearances and their mere form, is an art concealed in the depths of the human soul, whose real modes of activity nature is hardly likely ever to allow us to discover, and to have open to our gaze."[3]

It seems to me that the dialogic relationship between healer and patient in the *yagé* night is something like the schematism, that the polyphony therein is the schematism *in vivo*—existing thus neither in the interiority of the mind nor in the hidden and profound depths of the soul. In their coming together, bringing misfortune to a head, healer and patient articulate distinct "moments" of knowing such as the noumenal with the phenomenal and do so in a socially active and reactive process that also connects quite distinct forces of flux and steadiness, humor and despair, uncertainty and certainty.

To this fundamental break with models of knowledge and of knowledge-making that assume the thinker alone with her or his thoughts, or of thought alone with itself, the healer-patient relational model also differs in that included in the "sense data" of raw experience are not merely sensory impressions of light and sound and so forth, but also sensory impressions of social relations in all their moody ambiguity of trust and doubt and in all the multiplicity of their becoming and decaying. By excluding the sensateness of human interrelatedness, the "knowledge" with which traditional Western philosophy from Plato to Kant is concerned cuts itself off from the type of sensory experience and power-riddled knowledge—implicit social knowledge—on which so much of human affairs and intellection rest. Sorcery and (so-called) shamanism, on the other hand, present modes of always locally built experience and image-formation in which such social knowledge is constitutive. In the Putumayo whereof I speak, this power-riddled implicit social knowledge is scored by two forms of looming Otherness, the envious other and the colonial other.

E. E. Evans-Pritchard's famous book on witchcraft and sorcery beliefs among the Azande of central Africa serves to develop further the point I wish to make about implicit social knowledge being sensitive to the uncertainties of self in Otherness, although he was at such pains to render Zande practices intelligible to a Western (upper- and middle-class) readership that he tended to assimilate Zande thought to his readers' understandings of rationality rather than develop the ways by which sorcery beliefs can serve to criticize and enrich those understandings.[4] It is also the case that the easygoing and self-assured tone of the book has ensured totalizing readings that fail to register its problematizing contradictions, patchworked fragmentation, and duplicitous lucidity. Such is the way of the sorcerer, especially the chief sorcerer.

The book has been commonly interpreted as presenting a number of formulas that explain (or purport to explain) sorcery and witchcraft, the most well known of which is the formula "witchcraft explains coincidence." Yet these little security buttons, these handles on the reason of the Other, are but tiny protuberances of rationalized intellection set adrift in the murky sea of a text where the more one reads the less one "understands." Those who follow the text too much in awe of the author would do well to ponder the story recounted near the beginning of the book.

In answer to the question, What is a witch? Evans- Pritchard received many replies, among them that the chief witch beats on his drum to call the other witches. They transport themselves invisibly to the hut of their victim and eviscerate that person. They each place their piece of meat on the edge of the warming cooking pot and each pushes his piece into the pot. The victim sickens or dies. The relatives come armed with evidence from the oracle as to the identity of the witches and ask them to withdraw their evil. But they cannot: they are too far gone and vengeance magic will come and kill them, except for the chief witch. He can calmly blow water on the chicken's wing and evade the vengeance magic because, unbeknownst to the other witches, he did not push his piece of meat into the pot![5] Think about it; what *is* a witch?

Evans-Pritchard stated that (what he called) the mysticism in Zande witchcraft was a response on the part of those afflicted to have a social relational explanation, in terms of envy, for the coincidences that manifested themselves in misfortune. He laid stress on the way in which the belief and the accusation of witchcraft were attempts to understand not what we might call mechanical cause and effect, whose principles, he made a point of saying, were as commonsensical to Azande as to himself, but rather the reasons for such cause and effect to come together in the way that they did at the one time and place. The examples he offered were everyday. A small boy stubs his toe on his way to draw water. The toe fails to heal. Sorcery can explain this unusual (?) occurrence not because Zande fail to understand mechanical causes but because mechanistic causation cannot explain—for Zande or for us—the series of coincidences that misfortune makes one ponder. Why did he stub his toe on this occasion when he had not done so before? Why did the lesion fester? Why did it not respond to treatment? And so forth. By invoking the malevolence of the witch, who stands in a particular social relation to the boy or the boy's household and network of social relations as an envious other, argues Evans-Pritchard, witchcraft explains coincidence (but don't forget the chief witch!). Here then is a model of knowledge that is sensitive, indeed inordinately so, to the sensory impressions of social relations in all their moody ambiguity of trust and doubt.

It is this sort of coincident-sensitive knowledge tracking and backtracking between fate and chance that patients and shamans work with in the Putumayo, too, and it is not only to its reading of social relations into misfortune that should arouse our attention but also the fact that it is coincidence that provides the spark and the raw material, so to speak, with which implicit social knowledge pictures and problematizes the world.

Take the case of Rosario and José García. To assert, following Evans-Pritchard, that sorcery is invoked by them to explain coincidence, is true. But what this illustration also brings out is how stupendously such a formulation flattens our understanding of what their lives are about and what their invocation of sorcery does to what their lives are about. The clarity of the formula is misleading, and powerfully misleading at that. As with the

story of the chief witch, sorcery invokes a mode of explanation that undermines its starting point, while the starting point ineluctably leads to its
undermining. In posing this double-bind as to its own nature, sorcery de-
realizes reality as well.

The formula "sorcery explains coincidence" prevents us from appreci-
ating the extent to which coincidence and sorcery pose questions concerning
one's life's environment, opening out the world as much as closing it in. To
call this, as so many Westerners have, a "closed system" seems woefully
mistaken. It is neither closed nor a system. Think back again to Rosario and
José García. Is there in any sense an "it" anyway? Are we not in the situation
of the Indians scratching their heads as to the meaning and power—above
all the power—of *magia,* Spanish for magic, that colonization lobbed into
their midst? Doubtless this "it" we call magic, calling like calling into an
echoing abyss, existed in third-world countries before European colonization. But equally surely this "it" from that point on contained as a constitutive force the power of colonial differentiation such that magic became a
gathering point for Otherness in a series of racial and class differentiations
embedded in the distinctions made between Church and magic, and science
and magic. Here magic exists not so much as an "it" entity true to itself
but as an imaginary Other to the imagined absoluteness of God and science.

It seems to me that the shamans in the part of the third world of which I
speak are deeply implicated in and constituted by this colonial construction
of determinism's Otherness in which savagery and racism are tightly knotted.
This Otherness is mobilized in creative deployments of improvized building
and rebuilding neocolonial healing ritual wherein fate is wrested from the
hands of God and transcribed into a domain of chance and perhapsness. In
place of the order of God and the steadfastness of his signifiers/signatures
where the divine and the natural fuse, the domain of chance foregrounds
the epistemic murk of sorcery where contradiction and ambiguity in social
relations undermine his steadfastness in a weltering of signs cracking the
divine and the natural apart from one another and into images from which
what Barthes called the third or obtuse meaning erupts into play. "I even
accept for the obtuse meaning the word's pejorative connotation," he wrote,

> the obtuse meaning appears to extend outside culture, knowl-
> edge, information; analytically it has something derisory about
> it: opening out into the infinity of language, it can come
> through as limited in the eyes of analytic reason; it belongs to
> the family of pun, buffoonery, useless expenditure. Indifferent
> to moral or aesthetic categories (the trivial, the futile, the false,
> the pastiche), it is on the side of the carnival.[6]

It is this, so it seems to me, that shaman and patient jointly create in the
space of death.

Yet this very same space can be a source of paralysis enclosing one face to face with the monsters and one's body eviscerated in an ever more fearful mystery. Both sorcery and the Church thrive on this potential that death offers and it is this that is worked with such consummate skill into the culture of terror that sustains military dictatorships and the terror of colonial violence as in the Putumayo rubber boom. In these situations the tenderness inflamed by the death-space becomes the medium for dualizing the world into a mask whose distortions conceal as well as point to a mysterious and terrifying underworld. Here the space of death functions *not* to break up the continuity of time with what Benjamin would have called a messianic cessation of happening, but instead petrifies life in pursuit of an Archimedean point outside of world history whereby its catastrophic power may be narrativized (as with the vision of the colonist Manuel).

On the other hand, as it comes through Florencio, for instance, the space of death created by *yagé* nights can dissolve narrativization with montage. Here death combines with that tradition of the oppressed which, as Benjamin put it in his "Theses on the Philosophy of History," "teaches us that the 'state of emergency' in which we live is not the exception but the rule."[7] In this state wherein the disorder of order rules, death becomes not an underworld but coterminous with life's unstable surfaces and the "historical materialist" (as Benjamin was fond of referring to his brand of Marxist critic) stops telling the sequence of events like the beads of a rosary. This may be launched as an appeal, as with Brecht in the opening chorus of his montaged tragedy, *The Exception and the Rule:*

> We particularly ask you—
> When a thing continually occurs—
> Not on that account to find it natural
> Let nothing be called natural
> In an age of bloody confusion
> Ordered disorder, planned caprice,
> And dehumanized humanity, lest all things
> Be held unalterable![8]

Or it may be that the space of death incorporates the laughter of carnival as oppositional practice. The episode involving that colonized wild man, Santiago, and the policeman from the highland city of Pasto with his tale of horror concerning the wild woman of the swamps, the Turu Mama, illustrates the way in which wildness laughingly scuttles colonial melodrama. This laughter shows us how the combination of wildness and law-and-order writ into the colonized shamanic séance inverts the terror of the mystery of the death-space with its fanatical stress on the mysterious side of the mysterious.

With his *yagé*, the colonially created wild man nourishes this chance against and in combination with the deathly reifications and fear-inspiring mysteries worked into the popular imagination by the official discourse of suffering, order, and redemption, institutionalized by the Church, the state, and the culture of terror. Working with and against the imagery provided by the Church and the conquest, *yagé* nights offer the chance, not to escape sorrow by means of utopic illusions, but rather the chance to combine the anarchy of death with that of carnival, in a process that entertains yet resists the seductive appeal of self-pity and redemption through suffering. It is true that in the Cofán story of the origin of *yagé,* God draws the moral that *yagé* wisdom is dependent on suffering. But it is also true that God himself is here profaned in a left-sided historical process that serves to deny his order. He becomes a character in an epic, not the master of fate.

> With His left hand God plucked a hair from the crown of His head. With His left hand He planted that hair in the rain forest for the Indians only. With His left hand He blessed it. Then the Indians—not God—discovered and realized its miraculous properties and developed the *yagé* rites. Seeing this, God was incredulous, saying that the Indians were lying. He asked for some *yagé* brew, and on drinking began to tremble, vomit, weep, and shit. In the morning he declared that "it is true what these Indians say. The person who takes this suffers. But that person is distinguished. That is how one learns, through suffering."

As with the shaman's visions, we do not know what God saw that revolutionary night in the midst of his suffering, weeping, and shitting. But it is clear that without the Indians he would be less a man and unaware of the powers created by his left hand—the hand of trickery, profanity, and evil, which in the surrealist image evoked by Benjamin against the soul-stirring poetics of facism is the hand that strikes the decisive blows in history with the strength of improvisation.

Unlike that other tree of consciousness which God planted in the Garden of Eden, whose fruit Eve stole at the serpent's bidding so as to open her eyes, the vine of *yagé* brings consciousness to God himself. This eye-opening and bowel-opening consciousness leads not to the Fall and expulsion from paradise whereby humanity is doomed through its original sin to live on cursed ground for the remainder of time, but to a profane illumination that brings the gods to earth. In subjecting them to the powers of their creation, this profanity subjects fate to chance, and determinism to active human agency—as so notably mediated by the shaman and the patient in the jointness of their image-making.

So it has been through the sweep of colonial history in much of Latin America and in the Putumayo today, where the colonizers provided the colonized with the left-handed gift of the image of the wild man—a gift whose powers the colonizers would be blind to, were it not for the reciprocation of the colonized, bringing together in the dialogical imagination of colonization an image that wrests from civilization its demonic power.

TWENTY-NINE
Marlene

My first experience with magical healing was when my landlady in Puerto Tejada, Marlene Jiménez, had a succession of black healers from the Pacific coast come to cure the house we shared. She had been born in Puerto Tejada some time in the 1930s and the little property she inherited from her aunt doubled when her only brother was assassinated during the *Violencia* when imported police and killers shot up supporters of the Liberal Party, the party that had the overwhelming support of people in Puerto Tejada. Wasn't it the Liberals who had freed the slaves? She was not wealthy but by local standards was well off and had spent a year as a student at the national university in Bogotá, unheard of for a woman and exceedingly rare for men from the town at that time. People marveled at her serenity and lucid intelligence. She was a beacon for many and brought good feeling into everyone's life. She was prominent in the only effective organization of political opposition in the town in the 1960s, a locally inspired movement with a populist orientation, and had been jailed on account of it. When I got to know her she would sit in absent-minded nothingness day after day. She spent quite a bit of money trying to cure the house.

Healers came and went unobtrusively with their spells and perfumed liquids. I paid little attention. My mind was absorbed by the study of land tenure records.

Stories were circulating that Guillermo was after her money. There was a lot of malice and envy in those stories, but no doubt he was trying to assert male prerogatives in the shaping of her decisions. He drove a creaking truck that an uncle had helped him buy years before. Now he sat and paced most of the time, an embittered white man in a predominantly black town smoking lots of cigarettes and biting his nails for lack of work. His was a heavy presence, gloomy and tense, and his love for Marlene was heavy too.

It was also rumored, by gesture and intonation rather than in so many words, that his wife who lived on the other side of town was, maybe, trying to get at Marlene, whose burden it now was to live with these misty rumors, fanning the sultry air of the patio, hour after hour, day in and day out, as she and Guillermo stared into space through the latticework of red and orange bougainvillea. Guillermo was impatient and skeptical of these coastal healers paid to cure the house. But he allowed them to bathe his truck in their magic liquids.

One day Marlene's father, Don Chu Chu, arrived from a neighboring village. Unlike Marlene, who was a rather dark mulatta, he was fair-skinned and an odd character indeed. He had lost half a forearm to a machete blow and walked in a funny, jerky way, a bulk of cantankerous asymmetry hauling itself along the hot streets like a lopsided caterpillar, squeezing himself through the innumerable bags of plants and medicines and keys secreted about his person. He did not so much pride himself on being a healer as he loved being one. Although he had little fame and even fewer patients, he spent hours each day making potions with which he filled bottle after bottle in the locked shed behind his house. Last night, he said, he had taken some medicine with an Indian. He had seen angels and gone to heaven.

It was the first time I heard someone talking of *yagé*. Of course at the time I didn't know what on earth he was talking about. Nobody took him seriously except Marlene. She plied him with questions as Guillermo took me aside to say what a charlatan and a dreamer her father was.

I got to know Don Chu Chu better over the next few months, and he told me how he had come to take *yagé*. He lived with a woman on his one-acre farm in the village of Padilla near Puerto Tejada and she made a *maleficio* against him. She used to help him with the harvesting of his few cacao trees and with the chickens, but not with the bottles of remedies. He lent her 8,000 pesos, and rather than pay them back she tried to kill him with sorcery, he said. It was Pedro Tisoy, an Indian, from the town of Santiago, in the Putumayo highlands, who cured him.

She had a witch from the Patia valley prepare this *maleficio*. He was dead now. A black man, he lived in Chu Chu's village at the time and practiced as a herbalist. What they made was a thing with spume of the sea and a

Don Chu Chu.

bearded creature that lives in the sand of the sea, Chu Chu told me, a worm that could be kept in one's home, fed off dried plantain skins.

"I know exactly what she used against me," Chu Chu said, "because another witch from Cartago [at the north of the Cauca valley] told me. He's a *mentalista* and works with plants. That man is a *phenomenon*," he went on. "He's a *mochito* like me; he's got a leg missing. I saw him in the marketplace, making his propaganda, and he called me over. 'You're suffering from a *maleficio!*' he told me. 'You should go to Cartago to get cured,' he said. But it was too far."

It was Pedro Tisoy from the Putumayo highlands who cured him. It took two months and three all-night sessions with *yagé*. They took it out at Chu Chu's farm in Padilla. Pedro Tisoy planted *yagé* there, then left for Panama saying he would be back in twenty years' time.

"He cured my swollen stomach," said Chu Chu, "but not my asthma," and he proceeded to tell me that other people "shoot" against him, meaning attack him with sorcery. "But you can feel it happening," he reassured me, "and can defend yourself by praying these psalms of the Evangelists, especially of San Juan. When you feel desperate, when you can't sleep and things are driving you crazy, light a piece of candle the length of your first finger and pray the Lord's Prayer three times to San Antonio so that you can free yourself from the works of these sorcerers. Put the candle in a bowl surrounded by a little water. The spirits that guard you always need water."

He spent a good deal of time preparing bottles of remedies, using plants that he said came from the far-off Putumayo. When I accompanied him to cure a household suffering from sorcery he chanted like a Putumayo Indian shaman, only he used words instead of sounds, calling on the *caciques* of the Putumayo to come and help.

It reminded me of Sexto up by the lake in the Putumayo mountains, appropriating what he saw as the power of the lowland shamans, not just imitating them but absorbing their power as well. Through the representation came power. And in Chu Chu's case, curing the house, I doubt whether the people of the household had any idea or could even hear the words he was using in his song to those shamans in that imaginary Putumayo land of healers and sorcerers and magical plants.

Chu Chu had never been there outside of his dreams. I don't think he'd traveled more than a few miles from Puerto Tejada and Padilla, and when he heard I was interested in visiting the Putumayo he told me to try and get a *lente,* the quartz crystal that some highland shamans there use for divination. "You'll need a *lente,* a stone of lightning," he told me. "It's a crystal that comes from the sky. They cook it with *yagé* once or twice a year. With the *lente*," Chu Chu continued, "the spirit talks into your ear to tell if it's a cold sickness or a hot one, who did it, and what plants are needed for its cure."

Antonio Benavides in the marketplace had also urged me to procure a *lente*. "You have to have one," he insisted, "with 1,700 lightning flashes of color and seven balls of crystal so that you can diagnose. You have to ask someone to make it for you, someone in . . . the Putumayo, in Tapaje, or in the Guajira [the desert peninsula of salt, coal mines, Indians, powerful women, and contraband, sticking out like a bent finger into the Caribbean]."

"Where's Tapaje?" I asked.

Oh," he replied with a vague gesture, "it's on the other side of the sea. It's an island that belongs to Colombia in the Pacific, an island with an Indian race."

"And when you go to the Putumayo," said Chu Chu, "make sure you get some of that bark they call *kanilón del páramo*." He used it in the bottles of medicines he prepared. "With the right spell it gains money. It would be especially good for you," he told me, "because you wander so carelessly over the country like a half-wit."

"You have to recite prayers when you prepare these remedies," he insisted.

"What ones?" I asked.

"I'll have to look in my book." He picked up a battered Bible, put on some glasses, studied it for a few minutes, couldn't find what he wanted, and started digging under the mattress. There were a lot of loose pages, torn exercise books and books without covers. Loose words and looser pages scattered hither and thither in an eruption of sacred texts and magical spells to settle like leaves in the forest as Chu Chu dug ever more frantically into the mass of magic and sanctity sedimented under his mattress.

"You should get a copy of this," he said as he handed me a copy of *The Saintly Cross of Caravaca*. "The second universal epistle of San Pedro the apostle is excellent for making remedies and also to transport yourself and see long distance," he went on. Advice, recommendations, hermeneusis, textual commentary was pouring out in staccato bursts like water from an old faucet turned on after months of disuse, spluttering into smooth flows amid the shower of jumbled-up texts and pieces of pages. "To get rid of *maleficios* you'll find useful the prayers in this Enchiridiones of Leones Papis." It was a booklet entitled *The Grimorio of the Honorary Pope with a Compendium of the Rarest Secrets*. Rome, 1960. "You'll have to memorize San Juan the apostle. His first epistle. It's very good for curing, for transporting yourself, and seeing long distance. You should learn the second and third epistle too." *Occult Botany, Plants that Kill, The Power of Desire* by W. W. Atkinson and E. E. Beals, *Magnetism, Memory, Infernal Dictionary, Household Medicine*—book after book was heaved out from the cavern of the bed into the feeble light of the windowless room.

"Solomon?" he replied to my question. "Solomon was a great magician born at the beginning of the world."

Chu Chu died when I was away. I stopped by where he'd lived and asked the woman caring for the place what had happened to his books and papers.

"Oh!" she exclaimed as if stung, "I had to get rid of them. I threw them into the river."

A year after Chu Chu had shown me his books, his daughter Marlene had been murdered. Desperate, she had gone to the police to get them to keep Guillermo away. Weeping, Guillermo had sat drinking for days, went to her house and had shot her dead. Then he shot himself, through the ear. They died together. It was just after she had come back from church, it being the anniversary of her mother's death.

Don Chu Chu told me about it in a matter-of-fact way several months later. He said Guillermo smoked too much marijuana. He offered me a drag on a joint he had bought from the police in Santander de Quilichao. They would raid growers and then sell it off illegally. It was a good remedy for asthma Chu Chu told me, breaking into an uncontrollable fit of coughing.

There was a lot to say but nobody did. The enormity. The futility. And here I was in a dark little room on a bright sunny day with Chu Chu wondering what had gone through Marlene's mind and Guillermo's mind in those last few weeks.

Their unquiet spirits return, especially Marlene's, adding with gentle wit her commentary on the histories of good and evil that I had gone on collecting. That's why this is really her book, and Guillermo's—a book of *magia* we might say, with a giggle, if this was being recounted in those distant lowlands of the Putumayo with which Marlene's father, Chu Chu, used to dream and heal.

NOTES

AUTHOR'S NOTE

1. Walter Benjamin, notes in "Konvolut N," translated as "Theoretics of Knowledge; Theory of Progress," *The Philosophical Forum* 15, nos. 1–2 (Fall–Winter 1983–84):8–9.

CHAPTER 1: CULTURE OF TERROR, SPACE OF DEATH

1. Jacobo Timerman, *Prisoner without a Name, Cell without a Number* (New York: Vintage Books, 1982), 164.

2. *New York Times,* 18 February 1985, p. 17. On the *invunche* in mystical authoritarianism in Argentina, see Bruce Chatwin, *In Patagonia* (New York: Summit, 1977), 107–10.

3. Timerman, *Prisoner,* 111.

4. Gerardo Reichel-Dolmatoff, *Amazonian Cosmos: The Sexual and Religious Symbolism of the Tukano Indians* (Chicago: University of Chicago Press, 1971).

5. Antonin Artaud, *The Theater and Its Double,* trans. M. C. Richards (New York: Grove Press, 1958).

6. Miguel Angel Asturias, *El señor presidente,* trans. F. Partridge (New York: Atheneum, 1982), 39.

7. Ibid., 19.

8. Walter Benjamin, "Surrealism: The Last Snapshot of the European Intelligentsia," in the collection *Reflections,* trans. Edmund Jephcott, ed. and intro., Peter Demetz (New York and London: Harcourt, Brace Jovanovitch, 1978), 189–90.

9. Timerman, *Prisoner,* 52.

10. Michel Foucault, "Truth and Power," in *Power/Knowledge: Selected Interviews and Other Writings, 1972–1977* (New York: Pantheon, 1980), 118.

11. Frederick Karl, *Joseph Conrad: The Three Lives* (New York: Farrar, Strauss and Giroux, 1979), 286.

12. Ian Watt, *Conrad in the Nineteenth Century* (Berkeley and Los Angeles: University of California Press, 1979), 161.

13. C.T. Watts, *Joseph Conrad's Letters to Cunninghame Graham* (Cambridge: Cambridge University Press, 1969), 148–52.

14. Brian Inglis, *Roger Casement* (London: Hodder Paperbacks, 1974), 32.

15. Karl, *Joseph Conrad*, 289n.

16. Zdzistaw Najder, *Joseph Conrad: A Chronicle* (New Brunswick: Rutgers University Press, 1983), 414–15.

17. Peter Singleton-Gates and Maurice Girodias, *The Black Diaries: An Account of Roger Casement's Life and Times with a Collection of His Diaries and Public Writings* (New York: Grove Press, 1959), 29.

18. Inglis, *Roger Casement*, 375–76.

19. Roger Sawyer, *Casement: The Flawed Hero* (London, Routledge & Kegan Paul, 1984), 161–63.

20. Joseph Conrad, "Geography and Some Explorers," in *Last Essays*, (Freeport, N.Y.: Books for Libraries Press, 1970), 19.

21. G. Jean-Aubry, *Joseph Conrad: Life and Letters* (Garden City, N.Y., 1927), 1:142.

22. Joseph Conrad, *Heart of Darkness* (Harmondsworth: Penguin, 1973), 10.

23. G. Jean-Aubry, *Joseph Conrad*, 1:143.

24. Karl, *Joseph Conrad*, 289n.

25. Inglis, *Roger Casement*, 46.

26. Ibid., 131.

27. Ibid., 234.

28. Singleton-Gates and Girodias, *The Black Diaries*, 241, 243.

29. Roger Casement, "Correspondence respecting the Treatment of British Colonial Subjects and Native Indians Employed in the Collection of Rubber in the Putumayo District," *House of Commons Sessional Papers*, 14 February 1912 to March 1913, 68:1–165. Hereafter cited as Casement, *Putumayo Report*.

30. Joaquin Rocha, *Memorandum de un viaje* (Bogotá: Editorial El Mercurio, 1905), 125.

31. *House of Commons Sessional Papers*, "Report and Special Report from the Select Committee on Putumayo," 1913, 14:xxxvii. Hereafter cited as *Select Committee*.

32. Ibid.

33. John Hemming, *The Search for El Dorado* (London: Michael Joseph, 1978), 130.

34. Rocha, *Memorandum*, 102.

35. Ibid., 104–5.

36. Ibid., 106–7.

37. Ibid., 108.

38. Walter Hardenburg, *The Putumayo: The Devil's Paradise. Travels in the Peruvian Amazon Region and an Account of the Atrocities Committed upon the Indians Therein* (London: T. Fisher Unwin, 1912), 153–54.

39. Rocha, *Memorandum*, 73.

40. *Select Committee*, no. 11888, 474.

41. Ibid., no. 11890, 474.

42. Ibid., no. 11147, 447.

43. Ibid., no. 11150, 448.

44. Ibid., no. 5921, no. 5923, 226.

45. Hardenburg, *The Putumayo*, 176, 187.

46. Ibid., 175.

47. *Select Committee*, no. 457, 20.

48. Casement, *Putumayo Report,* 10.

49. Carlos A. Valcárcel, *El proceso del Putumayo y sus secretos inauditos* (Lima: Imprenta "Comercial" de Horacio La Rosa, 1915), 31.

50. Ibid., 26.

51. William H. Prescott, *History of the Conquest of Peru* (Philadelphia: David McKay, 1892), 1:448.

52. Hardenburg, *The Putumayo,* 180.

53. Ibid., 182.

54. Singleton-Gates and Girodias, *The Black Diaries,* 206.

55. Hardenburg, *The Putumayo,* 184–85, 213–14.

56. Ibid., 213–14.

57. Ibid., 258.

58. Ibid., 259, 260.

59. Casement, *Putumayo Report,* 35.

60. Hardenburg, *The Putumayo,* 235–36.

61. *Select Committee,* no. 4080, no. 4082, 159.

CHAPTER 2: CASEMENT TO GREY

1. Brian Inglis, *Roger Casement* (London: Hodder Paperbacks, 1974), 190.

2. Ibid., 167.

3. Ibid., 179.

4. Roger Casement, "Correspondence respecting the Treatment of British Colonial Subjects and Native Indians Employed in the Collection of Rubber in the Putumayo District," *House of Commons Sessional Papers,* 14 February 1912 to March 1913, 68:64–66. Hereafter cited as Casement, *Putumayo Report.*

5. Ibid., 39.

6. Ibid., 37.

7. Ibid., 99.

8. Ibid., 39.

9. Ibid., 41.

10. Ibid.

11. Edouard André, "América Equincoccial," in *América pintoresca: descripción de viajes al nuevo continente* (Barcelona: Montaner y Simon, 1884), 759.

12. Miguel Triana, *Por el sur de Colombia: excursión pintorésca y científica al Putumayo* (Bogotá: Biblioteca Popular de Cultura Colombiana, 1950), 351.

13. Casement, *Putumayo Report,* 127–29.

14. Ibid., 14–15.

15. Thomas Whiffen, *The North-West Amazons: Notes of Some Months Spent among Cannibal Tribes* (London: Constable, 1915), 60.

16. Irving Goldman, *The Cubeo: Indians of the Northwest Amazon* (Urbana: University of Illinois Press, 1963), 106–7.

17. Casement, *Putumayo Report,* 56.

18. Ibid., 137–39.

19. Ibid., 138.

20. Ibid., 128.

21. Ibid., 89.

22. Ibid., 90.

23. Ibid., 44.

24. Ibid.

25. Ibid., 99.

26. Ibid., 58.

27. Whiffen, *The North-West Amazons,* 3.

28. See Howard Wolf and Ralph Wolf, *Rubber, a Story of Glory and Greed* (New York: Covici, Friede, 1936), 88; U.S. Consul Charles C. Eberhardt, *Slavery in Peru,* 7 February 1913, report prepared for the U.S. House of Representatives, 62d Cong., 3d Sess., H Doc. 1366, p. 112; Roger Casement, *Select Committee,* xi; Casement, *Putumayo Report,* 33.

29. Casement, *Putumayo Report,* 77.

30. Ibid., 85.

31. Ibid., 120.

32. Ibid., 33.

33. Ibid., 44–45.

34. Ibid., 48.

35. Gaspar de Pinell, *Excursión apostólica por los ríos Putumayo, San Miguel de Sucumbios, Cuyabeno, Caquetá, y Caguán* (Bogotá: Imprenta Nacional, 1929 [also dated 1928]), 230.

CHAPTER 3: THE ECONOMY OF TERROR

1. Enock in Walter Hardenburg, *The Putumayo: The Devil's Paradise* (London: T. Fisher Unwin, 1912), 38.

2. Ibid., 236.

3. Roger Casement, "Correspondence respecting the Treatment of British Colonial Subjects and Native Indians Employed in the Collection of Rubber in the Putumayo District," *House of Commons Sessional Papers,* 14 February to March 1913, 68:66. Hereafter cited as Casement, *Putumayo Report.*

4. Ibid., 92.

5. Ibid., 77.

6. Brian Inglis, *Roger Casement* (London: Hodder Paperbacks, 1974), 131.

7. Bryce in Joseph Froude Woodroffe, *The Rubber Industry of the Amazon* (London: John Bale, 1915), vi.

8. Ibid., vi.

9. Ibid., xii–xiii.

10. Casement, *Putumayo Report,* 62.

11. Ibid., 91.

12. Jules Crévaux, "Exploración del Inzá y del Yapura," pp. 231–64 in *América pintoresca: descripción de viajes al nuevo continente* (Barcelona: Montaner y Simon, 1884), 240.

13. Walter Edmund Roth, "An Introductory Study of the Arts, Crafts, and Customs of the Guiana Indians," pp. 25–745 in *The Thirty-eighth Annual Report of the Bureau of American Ethnology: 1916–1917* (Washington, D.C.: Government Printing Office, 1924), 633.

14. Ibid., 632–33.

15. Ibid., 632.

16. Joaquin Rocha, *Memorandum de un viaje* (Bogotá: Editorial El Mercurio, 1905), 123.

17. Ibid., 60.

18. Charles C. Eberhardt in U.S. Department of State, *Slavery in Peru, Message from the President of the United States, Transmitting Report of the Secretary of State, with Accompanying Papers concerning the Alleged Existence of Slavery in Peru* . . . (Washington, D.C.: Government Printing Office, 1913), 112; see also Charles C. Eberhardt, "Indians of Peru," *Smithsonian Miscellaneous Collections* 52, no. 1921 (1910): 194.

19. Casement, *Putumayo Report*, 138.

20. Ibid., 119.

21. Joseph Froude Woodroffe, *The Upper Reaches of the Amazon* (London: Methuen, 1914), 127.

22. Ibid., 140.

23. Roger Casement, "The Putumayo Indians," *The Contemporary Review 102* (1912): 326.

24. Cristoval de Acuña, *A New Discovery of the Great River of the Amazons* (Madrid: The Royal Press, 1641), trans. and ed. Clements Markham in *Expeditions into the Valley of the Amazons: 1539, 1540, 1639* (London: Hakluyt Society, 1859), 96–98.

25. Samuel Fritz, *Journal of the Travels and Labours of Father Samuel Fritz in the River of the Amazons between 1686 and 1732,* trans. from the Evora MS by the Reverend Dr. George Edmunson (London: Hakluyt Society, 1922), 2d ser., no. 51.

26. Crévaux, "Exploración del Inzá," 262.

27. Thomas Wiffen, *The North-West Amazons: Notes of Some Months Spent Among Cannibal Tribes* (London: Constable, 1915), 69.

28. Ibid., 63.

29. Alfred Simson, *Travels in the Wilds of Ecuador and the Exploration of the Putumayo River* (London: Samson Low, 1886), 209.

30. Ibid., 243–44.

31. Peter Singelton-Gates and Maurice Girodias, *The Black Diaries: An Account of Roger Casement's Life and Times with a Collection of His Diaries and Public Writings* (New York: Grove Press, 1959), 271.

32. *House of Commons Sessional Papers,* "Report and Special Report from the Select Committee on Putumayo," 1913, vol. 14, no. 11148, 447. Hereafter cited as *Select Committee.*

33. Ibid., no. 11150, 447.

34. Casement, *Putumayo Report*, 96.

35. Ibid., 11.

36. Woodroffe, *Upper Reaches*, 90.

37. Ibid., 111–12.

38. Ibid., 141.

39. Michel Foucault, *Discipline and Punish*, trans. Alan Sheridan (New York: Vintage, 1979), 27–28.

40. Rocha, *Memorandum*, 101.

41. Ibid., 102.

42. Casement, *Putumayo Report*, 49.

43. *Select Committee*, nos. 8559–8648, 339–41.

44. Singleton-Gates and Girodias, *The Black Diaries*, 261.

45. *Select Committee*, nos. 2809–2805, 112–13.

46. Alberto Gridilla, *Un año en el Putumayo* (Lima: Colección Descalzos, 1943), 29.

47. Casement, *Putumayo Report,* 50.

48. Hardenburg, *The Putumayo,* 218.

49. Whiffen, *The North-West Amazons,* 257.

50. *Select Committee,* no. 12222, 488.

CHAPTER 4: JUNGLE AND SAVAGERY

1. *House of Commons Sessional Papers,* "Report and Special Report from the Select Committee on Putumayo," 1913, vol. 14, no. 12848, 510. Hereafter cited as *Select Committee.*

2. Ibid., nos. 12881, 12882, 511.

3. Jośe Eustasio Rivera, *La vorágine* (Bogotá: Editorial Pax, 1974), 277, 279; Carlos Fuentes, *La nueva novela hispanoamericana,* (México, D.F.: Editorial Joaquin Mortiz, 1969), 10–11.

4. Joaquin Rocha, *Memorandum de un viaje* (Bogota: Editorial El Mercurio, 1905), 20.

5. Ibid., 29.

6. Ibid., 75–76.

7. Ibid., 127.

8. Thomas Whiffen, *The North-West Amazons: Notes of Some Months Spent among Cannibal Tribes* (London: Constable, 1915), 34–37.

9. Ibid., 14.

10. Ibid., 15.

11. "The Screenplay," in *Burden of Dreams,* ed. Les Blank and James Bogan (Berkeley: North Atlantic Books, 1984), 57.

12. Ibid., 56.

13. Whiffen, *The North-West Amazons,* 37.

14. Roger Casement, "The Putumayo Indians," *The Contemporary Review* 102 (September 1912): 326.

15. Ibid.

16. Joseph Conrad, *Heart of Darkness* (Harmondsworth: Penguin, 1973), 9.

17. Whiffen, *The North-West Amazons,* 188.

18. Gaspar de Pinell, *Excursión apostólica por los ríos Putumayo, San Miguel de Sucumbios, Cuyabueno, Caquetá, y Caguán* (Bogotá: Imprenta Nacional, 1929 [also dated 1928]), 156.

19. Ibid., 249.

20. Ibid., 97.

21. Rocha, *Memorandum,* 118.

22. Francisco Vilanova, "Introducción," in *Indios amazónicos,* Francisco de Igualada, Colección Misiones Capuchinas, vol. 6 (Barcelona: Imprenta Myria, 1948).

23. Walter Hardenburg, *The Putumayo: The Devil's Paradise* (London: T. Fisher Unwin, 1912), 163.

24. Pinell, *Excursión Apostólica,* 196.

25. Roger Casement, "Correspondence respecting the Treatment of British Colonial Subjects and Native Indians Employed in the Collection of Rubber in the Putumayo District," *House of Commons Sessional Papers,* 14 February to March 1913, 68:40. Hereafter cited as Casement, *Putumayo Report.*

26. *Select Committee*, nos. 12941–12959, 513–14.

27. Hardenburg, *The Putumayo*, 38.

28. Casement, *Putumayo Report*, 27–28.

29. Peter Singleton-Gates and Maurice Girodias, *The Black Diaries* (New York: Grove Press, 1959), 249, 251.

30. Casement, "The Putumayo Indians," 324–25.

31. Ibid., 325.

32. Ibid.

33. Ibid., 327.

34. Whiffen, *The North-West Amazons*, 257.

35. Ibid., 118.

36. Ibid., 257.

37. Alfred Simson, *Travels in the Wilds of Ecuador and the Exploration of the Putumayo River* (London: Samson Low, 1886), 233–34.

38. H. Guillaume, *The Amazon Provinces of Peru as a Field for European Emigration* (London: Wyman, 1888), 45–46.

39. Simson, *Travels*, 170.

40. Ibid., 170–71.

41. Ibid., 58–59.

CHAPTER 5: THE IMAGE OF THE AUCA: UR-MYTHOLOGY AND COLONIAL MODERNISM

1. Jonah Raskin, *My Search for B. Traven* (New York: Methuen, 1980), 153.

2. Simson, *Travels in the Wilds of Ecuador and the Exploration of the Putumayo River* (London: Samson Low, 1886), 3–4.

3. Jules Crévaux, "Exploración del Inzá y del Yapura," pp. 231–64 in *America pintoresca: descripcion de viajes al nuevo continente* (Barcelona: Montaner y Simon, 1884), 255–56.

4. Joaquin Rocha, *Memorandum de un viaje* (Bogotá: Editorial El Mercurio, 1905), 164–65.

5. Simson, *Travels in the Wilds*, 58.

6. B. Traven, *March to the Montería* (London: Allison and Busby, 1982), 197.

7. Simson, *Travels in the Wilds*, 166, 168.

8. Roger Casement, "Correspondence respecting the Treatment of British Colonial Subjects and Native Indians Employed in the Collection of Rubber in the Putumayo District," *House of Commons Sessional Papers*, 14 February 1912 to March 1913, 68:45. Hereafter cited as Casement, *Putumayo Report*.

9. *Amazonía* (also titled *Amazonía Colombiana Americanista*), published by CILEAC, Sibundoy, Putumayo, Colombia, 1944, nos. 4–8, p. 35.

10. Casement, *Putumayo Report*, 56.

11. Walter Hardenburg, *The Putumayo: The Devil's Paradise* (London: T. Fisher Unwin, 1912), 226, 246.

12. Brian Inglis, *Roger Casement*, (London: Hodder Paperbacks, 1974), 409.

13. Gaspar de Pinell, *Un viaje por el Putumayo y el Amazonas: ensayo de navegación* (Bogotá, Imprenta Nacional, 1924), 39–40.

14. Casement, *Putumayo Report*, 32.

15. Rocha, *Memorandum*, 124–25.

16. Casement, *Putumayo Report*, 45.

17. Rocha, *Memorandum*, 25.

18. B. Traven, *March to the Monteria* (London: Allison and Busby, 1982), 118.

19. Rocha, *Memorandum,* 126.

20. Casement, *Putumayo Report,* 30.

21. Konrad Theodor Preuss, *Religion und Mythologie der Uitoto* (Göttingen: Vandenhoeck und Ruprecht, 1921), 2 vols.; 1: 143–48; 2: 672–78.

22. Benjamin Ypes and Roberto Pineda Camacho, "La rabia de Yarocamena: etnología histórica de una rebelión indígena en el Amazonas," (Bogotá: mimeograph, October 1984), 3–4; see also B. Ypes, *La estatuaria Murui-Muiname: simbolismo de la gente "Huitoto" de la amazonía colombiana* (Bogotá: Fundación de Investigaciones Arqueologicas Nacionales, Banco de la Republica, 1982), 19–22; Jon Landaburu and Roberto Pineda C. *Tradiciones de la gente del hacha: mitología de los indios andoques del Amazonas* (Bogotá: Instituto Caro y Cuervo and Unesco, 1984).

23. Rocha, *Memorandum,* 110.

24. Gonzalo París Lozano, *Guerrilleros del Tolima* (Bogotá: El Ancora, 1984).

25. Rocha, *Memorandum,* 91–93.

26. Hardenburg, *The Putumayo,* 155.

27. Gaspar de Pinell, *Excursión apostólica por los ríos Putumayo, San Miguel de Sucumbios, Cuyabueno, Caquetá, y Caguán* (Bogotá: Imprenta Nacional, 1929 [also dated 1928]), 93–95, 120.

28. Casement, *Putumayo Report,* 48; Eugenio Robuchon, *En el Putumayo y sus afluentes,* ed. Carlos Rey de Castro (Lima: edición oficial, 1907), 59.

29. Susan Sontag, *On Photography* (New York: Delta, 1973); Michel Foucault, *Madness and Civilization* (New York: Mentor, 1967), 202.

30. Robuchon, *En el Putumayo,* 83.

31. Ibid., 82.

32. Ibid., 67–69.

33. Ibid., xvii.

34. *House of Commons Sessional Papers,* "Report and Special Report from the Select Committee on Putumayo," 1913, 14; no. 13045, 517. Hereafter cited as *Select Committee.*

35. Ibid., nos. 13085–13102, 519–20.

36. Ibid., nos. 13107, 13117, 520–21.

37. Ibid., no. 5300, 202.

38. Rocha, *Memorandum,* 111.

39. Traven, *March to the Monteria,* 43.

40. Rocha, *Memorandum,* 116–17.

41. Rómulo Paredes, "Confidential Report to the Ministry of Foreign Relations, Peru," September 1911, translated in U. S. Department of State, *Slavery in Peru, Message from the President of the United States, Transmitting Report of the Secretary of State, with Accompanying Papers concerning the Alleged Existence of Slavery in Peru* . . . (Washington, D.C.: Government Printing Office, 1913), 146. Paredes's work is magnified in detail in the 400 pages of evidence in Carlos A. Valcárcel, *El proceso del Putumayo y sus secretos inauditos* (Lima: Imprenta "Comercial" de Horacio La Rosa, 1915).

42. Paredes, "Confidential Report," 158.

43. Ibid., 147.

44. Ibid.

45. Preuss, *Religion und Mythologie*, 1: 143–48; Thomas Whiffen, *The North-West Amazons: Notes of Some Months Spent among Cannibal Tribes* (London: Constable, 1915).

46. Whiffen, 204.

47. Ibid., p. 123.

48. Ibid., 204–5.

49. Casement, *Putumayo Report*, 115.

50. Ibid., 118.

51. Ibid., 121–22.

52. Ibid., 103.

53. Ibid., 104.

54. Ibid., 103, 104.

55. Rómulo Paredes in Valcárcel, *El proceso del Putumayo*, 143n.

56. Conversation with William Torres, Departamento de Antropología, Universidad Nacional, Bogotá, Colombia; also see Benjamin Ypes, *La estatuaria Múrui-Muinane: símbolismo de la gente "Huitoto" de la amazonia colombiana* (Bogotá: Fundación de Investigaciones Arqueológicas Nacionales, Banco de la Republica, 1982), 18–22; Ypes and Pineda Camacho, "La rabia de Yarocamena."

CHAPTER 6: THE COLONIAL MIRROR OF PRODUCTION

1. Joseph Conrad, *Heart of Darkness* (Harmondsworth, Middlesex: Penguin, 1973), 8.

2. Bertolt Brecht, "Die Ängste des Regimes," in *Bertolt Brecht: Plays, Poems, and Prose*, ed. John Willett and Ralph Manheim (New York: Methuen, 1976), 296–298. Compare with Aryeh Neier's review in the *New York Review of Books* (10 April 1986, p. 3) of Christopher Dickey's book *With the Contras: A Reporter in the Wilds of Nicaragua* (New York: Simon and Schuster, 1986): "In the early days of the war [between the Reagan-backed *contras* and the Sandinistas], much of the action revolved around a daring *contra* commander known as Suicida . . . an effective leader who accounted for much of the *contra* military punch during 1982 and 1983. Along with some of his ex-*guardia* associates, Suicida also helped to build the *contra* reputation for savagery. Initially directed against the Sandinistas, but then also against each other, that savagery eventually brought down Suicida. He was executed by the *contra* leadership in the fall of 1983. To regulate savagery, but not to stop it, the CIA produced its now infamous manual, 'Psychological Operations in Guerrilla Warfare.' " One of Dickey's *contra* sources says as regards this savagery, "there are people who learn to kill and love it. . . . Here, fiction and reality, they're the same thing." (p. 16).

3. Bertolt Brecht, *"Die Ängste des Regimes,"* 298.

4. Guillaume Apollinaire, "Zone," in *Selected Writings of Guillaume Apollinaire*, translated and with a critical introduction by Roger Shattuck (New York: New Directions, 1971), 117–27.

5. Roberto Pineda Camacho, "El sendero del arco iris: notas sobre el simbolismo de los negocios en una comunidad amazónica," *Revista Colombiana de Antropología* 22 (1979): 29–58.

6. See chap. 5, n. 56.

Chapter 7: A Case of Fortune and Misfortune

1. Alonso de la Peña Montenegro (Obispo del Obispado de San Francisco de Quito), *Itinerario para párocos de indios* (Madrid: Oficina de Padre Marin, 1771: first pub. 1668), 223.
2. Ibid., 185.
3. Ibid., 191.
4. Frank Salomon, "Shamanism and Politics in Late-Colonial Ecuador," *American Ethnologist* 10, no. 3 (1983): 413–28.
5. Hermillio Valdizán and Angel Maldonando, *La medicina popular peruana*, 3 vols. (Lima: Imprenta Torres Aguirre, 1922), 1:18.

Chapter 8: Magical Reality

1. Alejo Carpentier, *El Reino de este mundo* (Argentina: Editorial América Nueva, 1974), 12–14.
2. Ernst Bloch, "Nonsynchronism and the Obligation to Its Dialectics," *New German Critique* 11 (Spring 1977): 22–38. See also in this same issue the commentary by Ansom Rabinbach, "Unclaimed Heritage: Ernst Bloch's *Heritage of Our Times* and the Theory of Facism," 5–21; Susan Buck-Morss, "Benjamin's *Passagenwerk*," *New German Critique* 29 (Spring–Summer 1983): 211–40.
3. Walter Benjamin, "Theses on the Philosophy of History," in *Illuminations*, trans. Harry Zohn, ed. Hannah Arendt (New York: Schocken, 1969), 253.
4. Walter Benjamin, "Paris—Capital of the Nineteenth Century," in *Charles Baudelaire: A Lyric Poet in the Era of High Capitalism*, 155–76 (London: New Left Books, 1973), 159.
5. Susan Buck-Morss, "Walter Benjamin—Revolutionary Writer, Part 1," *New Left Review* 128 (July–August, 1981): 50–75.

Chapter 9: Las Tres Potencias: The Magic of the Races

1. Walter Benjamin, "The Storyteller: Reflections on the Work of Nikolai Leskov," in *Illuminations*, trans. Harry Zohn, ed. Hannah Arendt (New York: Schocken, 1969), 83–110.
2. Chris Gerry and Chris Birkbeck, "The Petty Commodity Producer in Third World Cities: Petit Bourgeois or 'Disguised Proletarian?' " in *The Petite Bourgeoisie: Comparative Studies of the Uneasy Stratum*, ed. Frank Bechhofer and Brian Elliott (London: Macmillan, 1981), 149–50.

Chapter 10: The Wild Woman of the Forest Becomes Our Lady of Remedies

1. Richard Wolin, *Walter Benjamin: An Aesthetic of Redemption* (New York: Columbia University Press, 1982), 49.
2. Walter Benjamin, "Theses on the Philosophy of History," in *Illuminations*, trans. Harry Zohn, ed. Hannah Arendt (New York: Schocken, 1969), 261.
3. Ibid., 262–63.
4. Donald Attwater, *A Dictionary of the Saints* (London: Burns, Oates, 1948).

Chapter 11: Wildness

1. Hugh Honour, *The New Golden Land: Images of America from the Discoveries to the Present Time* (New York: Pantheon, 1975), 53.
2. Richard Comstock, "On Seeing with the Eye of the Native European," *Seeing with a Native Eye*, ed. Walter H. Capps (New York: Harper & Row, 1976), 62.

3. Lewis O. Saum, *The Fur Trader and the Indian* (Seattle and London: University of Washington Press, 1965), xi.

4. John Block Friedman, *The Monstrous Races in Medieval Thought and Art* (Cambridge, Mass., and London: Harvard University Press, 1981), 197.

5. Samuel Morison, *Admiral of the Ocean Sea: A Life of Christopher Columbus* (Boston: Little, Brown, 1942), 1:123.

6. Rudolf Wittkower, "Marvels of the East: A Study in the History of Monsters," *Journal of the Warburg and Cortauld Institute*, 5 (1942): 197.

7. Richard Bernheimer, *Wild Men of the Middle Ages* (Cambridge, Mass.: Harvard University Press, 1952), 21–26.

8. Timothy Husband (with the assistance of Gloria Gilmore-House), *The Wild Man: Medieval Myth and Symbolism* (New York: The Metropolitan Museum of Art, 1980), 51–58.

9. Bronislaw Malinowski, *The Sexual Life of Savages in North Western Melanesia* (New York: Harcourt Brace, 1929), 199.

10. Mary Cathleen Flannery, *Yeats and Magic: The Earlier Works*, Irish Literary Studies 2 (New York: Barnes and Noble, 1977), 129–30.

11. Margaret T. Hodgen, *Early Anthropology in the Sixteenth and Seventeenth Centuries* (Philadelphia: University of Pennsylvania Press, 1964), 133, 279, 412–13.

12. Joseph Conrad, *Heart of Darkness* (Harmondswoth, Middlesex: Penguin Books, 1973), 51.

13. Edmund Burnett Tylor, *Primitive Culture* (New York: Harper, 1958), 1:113.

14. Ibid.

15. Kenneth M. Bilby, "Partisan Spirits: Ritual Interaction and Maroon Identity in Eastern Jamaica," M.A. thesis (unpublished), Wesleyan University, 1979.

16. Fernando Ortiz Fernández, *Hampa afro-cubana: los negros brujos; apuntes para un estudio de etnología criminal, con una carta prólogo de Lombrioso* (Madrid: Editorial América, 1917), 286–88.

17. Alfred Métraux, *Voodoo in Haiti*, trans. Hugo Charteris (New York: Oxford University Press, 1959), 15.

18. Henry Charles Lea, *The Inquisition of the Spanish Dependencies* (New York: Macmillan, 1908), 456.

19. Lea, *The Inquisition*; Manuel Tejado Fernández, *Aspectos de la vida social en Cartagena de Indias durante el seiscientos*, no. 87 (Seville: Escuela de Estudios Hispano-Americanos de Sevilla, 1954); Alonso de Sandoval, *De Instauranda Aethiopium Salute: El mundo de la esclavitud negra en América* (Bogotá: Empresa Nacional de Publicaciones, 1956 [first pub. 1627]); María del Carmen Borrego Pla, *Palenques de negros en Cartagena de Indias a fines del siglo XVII*, no. 216. (Seville: Escuela Estudios Hispano-Americanos de Sevilla, 1973); José Toribio Medina, *La inquisición en Cartagena de Indias* (Bogotá: Carlos Valencia, 1978).

20. José de Acosta, *The Natural and Moral History of the Indies*, trans. E. Grimston (London: Hakluyt Society, 1880), 1:259.

21. Lea, *The Inquisition*, 463–65.

22. Bernheimer, *The Wild Man*, 19–20.

23. Bruce Kapferer, *A Celebration of Demons: Exorcism and the Aesthetics of Healing in Sri Lanka* (Bloomington: Indiana University Press), 1.

24. Bernheimer, *The Wild Man*, 44.

CHAPTER 12: INDIAN FAT

1. Adolph F. Bandelier, *The Islands of Titicaca and Koati* (New York: Hispanic Society of America, 1910), 104.

2. Ibid., 104–6.

3. Ibid., 105.

4. G. M. Wrigley, "The Travelling Doctors of the Andes: The Callahuayas of Bolivia," *The Geographical Review* 4 (July–December 1917): 183.

5. Ibid., 195.

6. Ibid., 192.

7. Clements R. Markham, *Peruvian Bark: A Popular Account of the Introduction of Chinchona Cultivation into British India* (London: J. Murray, 1880), 163.

8. Ibid., 163–64.

9. Johann Jakob von Tschudi, *Travels in Peru during the Years 1838–1842*, trans. T. Ross (New York: Putnam, 1852), 281.

10. Ibid., 327.

11. Garcilaso de la Vega, El Inca, *Royal Commentaries of the Incas*, trans. Harold Livermore (Austin and London: University of Texas Press, 1966 [vol. 1 first published 1609]), 1:438.

12. Ibid., 444.

13. José de Acosta, *The Natural and Moral History of the Indies*, trans. Clements Markham (London: The Hakluyt Society, 1880), 2:530.

14. Wrigley, "The Travelling Doctors of the Andes," 195.

15. Ibid.

16. Robert Hertz, "The Pre-Eminence of the Right Hand: A Study in Religious Polarity," pp. 89–113 in *Death and the Right Hand*, trans. Rodney and Claudia Needham (Aberdeen: Cohen and West, 1960), 96.

17. Georges Bataille, *Visions of Excess: Selected Writings, 1927–1939*, edited and with an introduction by Alan Stoekl (Minneapolis: University of Minnesota Press, 1985), 32–44.

18. Robert Randall, "Qoyllur Rit'i, An Inca Fiesta of the Pleiades: Reflections on Time and Space in the Andean World," *Bulletin de l' Institut Français des Etudes Andines* 11, nos. 1–2 (1982): 37–38.

19. Ibid., 46.

20. Ibid., 52.

21. Ibid., 54.

22. José María Arguedas, *Deep Rivers*, trans. Frances Barraclough (Austin: University of Texas Press, 1978), 159.

23. Frank L. Salomon, "Killing the Yumbo: A Ritual Drama of Northern Quito," in *Cultural Transformations and Ethnicity in Modern Ecuador*, ed. Norman E. Whitten Jr. (Urbana: University of Illinois Press, 1981), 162–208.

24. Ibid., 171.

25. Ibid., 188.

26. Ibid., 163.

27. Walter Benjamin, "Some Motifs in Baudelaire," in *Charles Baudelaire: A Lyric Poet in the Era of High Capitalism* (London: New Left Books, 1973), 131.

28. S. Henry Wassén, "A Medicine-Man's Implements and Plants in A Tiahuanacoid Tomb in Highland Bolivia," *Etnologiska Studier* 32 (1972): 1–196.

29. Frank L. Salomon, "Ethnic Lords of Quito in the Age of the Incas: The Political Economy of North Andean Chiefdoms," unpublished Ph.D. dissertation, Cornell University, 1978, pp. 163–64.

30. Ibid., 195.

31. Bernal Díaz del Castillo, *Historia verdadera de la conquista de la Nueva España* (México, D.F.: Editorial Pórrua, 1969), 51, 100.

32. R. B. Cunninghame Graham, *Hernando de Soto* (London: Heineman, 1912), 42. Cunninghame Graham refers to Antonio de Herrera y Tordesillas, as does Morote Best (see below), *Historia general de los hechos de los castellanos en las islas i tierra firme del mar oceano,* first published in the years 1601–1615 in four volumes.

33. Cristóbal de Molina (de Cuzco), *Relación de las fábulas y ritos de las incas* (Buenos Aires: Editorial Futuro, 1947), 144.

34. Efrain Morote Best, "El degollador (nakaq)," *Tradición: revista peruana de cultura* 11, no. 2, year 2 (September 1951–January 1952): 67–91.

35. Anthony Oliver-Smith, "The *Pishtaco:* Institutionalized Fear in Highland Peru," *Journal of American Folklore* 82, no. 326 (October–December 1969): 363–68.

36. José María Arguedas, "Puquio, una cultura en proceso de cambio. La religión local," in *Formación de una cultura nacional indoamericana* (México DF: Siglo Veintiuno, 1975), 34–79.

CHAPTER 15: THE BOOK OF MAGIA

1. B. Traven, *The Rebellion of the Hanged* (New York: Hill and Wang, 1952), 203–4. This extract comes from Jonah Raskin, *My Search for B. Traven* (New York: Methuen, 1980), 167.

2. Jean Langdon, "The Siona Medical System: Beliefs and Behaviour," unpublished Ph.D. dissertation, Tulane University, 148.

3. Marcelino de Castellví, cited in Fancisco de Igualada, *Indios amazónicas,* (Barcelona: Imprenta Myria, 1948), 206–8.

4. Damián de Odena, "Presentación," in Jacinto María de Quito, *Historia de la fundación del pueblo de San Francisco en el valle del Sibundoy* (Sibundoy, Putumayo: CILEAC), v.

CHAPTER 16: FILTH AND THE MAGIC OF THE MODERN

1. Walter Benjamin, "Paris—Capital of the Nineteenth Century," pp. 155–76 in his book *Charles Baudelaire: A Lyric Poet in the Era of High Capitalism* (London: New Left Books, 1973), 159. For an extraordinarily stimulating commentary on this text, utilizing previously unpublished notes by Benjamin that went into his *Passagen-Werk* (now published, in German, in 1982), see Susan Buck-Morss, "Benjamin's Passagen-Werk: Redeeming Mass Culture for the Revolution," *New German Critique* 29 (Spring–Summer 1983), 211–40.

CHAPTER 18: ON THE INDIAN'S BACK

1. The illustration here is entitled "The Ascent of Agony" and comes from *Le Tour du Monde: Nouveau Journal des Voyages* ("illustré par nos plus célèbres artistes") 38 (1879): 363, attributed to the artist Maillard (who was equally adept at illustrating scenes from Africa ("the mysterious continent"), Oceania, Russia, or Siam as he was at those of Colombia. In fact it was not always easy to distinguish between the societies and places depicted because of the rather uniform manner of

representing third-world exotica. This particular engraving, "The Ascent of Agony" (named after the local name of that trail), was made from a sketch drawn in 1876 by the French explorer Edouard André, depicting his ascent from Barbacoas, Colombia, roughly the same latitude as Mocoa but on the other (Pacific Ocean) side of the *cordillera*.

2. Gwynn Williams, "The Concept of 'Egemonia' in the Thought of Antonio Gramsci: Some Notes of Interpretation," *Journal of the History of Ideas* 21 (1960): 586–99; Michel Foucault, "Truth and Power," in *Power/Knowledge: Selected Interviews and Other Writings, 1972–1977,* ed. Colin Gordon (New York: Pantheon, 1980), 118.

3. Raymond Williams, *Marxism and Literature* (Oxford: Oxford University Press, 1977), 121–35; see also his *Politics and Letters: Interviews with New Left Review* (London: New Left Books, 1979), 156–61.

4. Ernest J. Becker, *A Contribution to the Comparative Study of the Medieval Visions of Heaven and Hell with Special Reference to the Middle English Versions* (Baltimore: John Murphy, 1899), 4.

5. J. H. Parry, *The Discovery of South America* (London: Paul Elek, 1979), 223.

6. Ibid., 231–32.

7. Ibid., 232.

8. Ibid., 232–33.

9. Ibid., 233.

10. Joaquín Tamayo, "Don Gonzalo Ximénez de Quesada," *Boletín de historia y antiquedades* [Bogotá] 25, nos. 285–86 (1938): 468–69.

11. Ibid., 470–71.

12. Tamayo, 475.

13. John Hemming, *The Search for El Dorado* (London: Michael Joseph, 1978), 128–32.

14. Alexander von Humboldt, *Views of Nature; or Contemplations on the Sublime Phenomena of Creation; with Scientific Illustrations* (London: Henry G. Bohn, 1850), 398.

15. Hermann Trimborn, *Señorio y barbarie en el valle del Cauca* (Madrid: Instituto Gonzalo Fernández de Oviedo, 1949).

16. Robert Cooper West, *Colonial Placer Mining in Western Colombia* (Baton Rouge: Louisiana State University Press, 1952), 126.

17. Ibid., 127.

18. Sergio Arboleda, *La republica en américa española* (Bogotá: Biblioteca Banco Popular, 1972), 328.

19. Charles Empson, *Narratives of South America; Illustrating Manners, Customs, and Scenery; Containing Also Numerous Facts in Natural History Collected During a Four Years Residence in Tropical Regions* (London: W. Edwards, 1836), 45–52.

20. Charles Stuart Cochrane, *Journal of a Residence and Travels in Colombia During the Years of 1823 and 1824* (London: Colburn, 1825), 2:81–84.

21. John Potter Hamilton, *Travels through the Interior Provinces of Colombia* (London: J. Murray, 1827), 1:73–74.

22. Ibid., 2:210.

23. Cochrane, *Journal* 2:356.

24. Isaac Holton, *New Granada: Twenty Months in the Andes* (New York: Harper, 1857), 365.

25. Ibid., 84–85.

26. Cochrane, *Journal* 2:402.

27. Ibid., 2:414–15.

28. Holton, *New Granada,* 292.

29. Arthur Clifford Veatch, *Quito to Bogota* (New York: George H. Doran, 1917), 202, 204.

30. Manuel Alvis, "The Indians of Andaqui, New Granada: Notes of a Traveller," published by José María Vergara y Vergara and Evaristo Delgado, Popayán, 1855, *American Ethnological Society* 1 (1860–61): 53.

31. Ibid., 63.

32. Ibid., 61.

33. Edouard André, "América Equinoccial," pp. 477–859 in *América pintoresca; descripción de viajes al nuevo continente* (Barcelona: Montaner y Simon, 1884), 754–62.

34. Benigno de Canet de Mar, *Relaciónes interesantes y datos hístoricos sobre las misiones católicas del Caquetá y Putumayo desde el año 1632 hasta el presente* (Bogotá: Imprenta Nacional, 1924), 276.

35. Ibid., 118–19; also Gaspar de Pinell, *Excursión apostólica por los ríos Putumayo, San Miguel de Sucumbios, Cuyabeno, Caquetá, y Caguán* (Bogotá: Imprenta Nacional, 1928 [also dated 1929]), 304–9.

36. *Misiones Católicas de Putumayo: documentos oficiales relativos a esta comisaría,* Edición Oficial Ilustrada (Bogotá: Imprenta Nacional, 1913), end plates.

37. Las misiones en Colombia, *Obra de los misioneros capuchinos de la delegación apostólica del gobierno y de la junta arquidiocesana nacional en el Caquetá y Putumayo* (Bogotá: Imprenta de la Cruzada, 1912), 23.

38. Ibid., 111.

39. Ibid., 116–17.

40. Ibid., 117.

41. Damián de Odena (director de CILEAC y del Párroco de San Francisco), "Presentación," in Jacinto María de Quito, *Historia de la fundación del pueblo de San Francisco en el valle del Sibundoy* (Sibundoy, Putumayo, Colombia: CILEAC, 1952), vi.

42. Las misiones en Colombia, 119.

43. Ibid., 120.

44. Ibid., 121.

45. *Misiones Católicas,* end plates.

46. Las misiones en Colombia, 121.

47. Leonidas Medina (bishop of Pasto), *Conferencia sobre las misiones del Caquetá y Putumayo dictada en la Basilica de de Bogotá el 12 de octubre de 1914* (Bogotá: Imprenta de San Bernardo—atrio de la catedral, 1914).

48. Victor Daniel Bonilla, *Servants of God or Masters of Men? The Story of a Capuchin Mission in Amazonia* (Harmondsworth: Penguin, 1972), 92.

49. Benigno de Canet de Mar, *Relaciónes interesantes,* 52.

50. CILEAC (Centro de Investigaciones Linguísticas y Etnográficas de la Amazonía Colombiana), *Amazonía colombiana américanista* 1, nos. 2 and 3 (1940):29.

51. Jean Langdon, "The Siona Medical System: Beliefs and Behavior," (unpublished Ph.D. dissertation, Tulane University, 1974), 169–87.

52. Francisco de Igualada, *Indios amazónicos* (Barcelona: Imprenta Myria, 1948), 202.

53. Bertolt Brecht, "Theatre for Pleasure or Theatre for Instruction," *Brecht on Theatre: The Development of an Aesthetic,* John Willett ed. and trans. (New York: Hill and Wang, 1964), 70.

54. Alejo Carpentier, *The Lost Steps* (first published in Spanish in 1953), Harriet de Onis (New York: Knopf, 1974), 184.

55. Hans Richter, *Dada: Art and Anti-Art* (London: Thames and Hudson, 1965), 41.

56. Miguel Triana, *Por el sur de Colombia: excursión pintoresca y científica al Putumayo,* Prologo de Santiago Pérez Triana (Bogotá: Biblioteca Popular de Cultura Colombiana, 1950).

57. Ibid., Prólogo, 22.

58. Ibid., 355–56.

59. Ibid., 337–39.

CHAPTER 24: HISTORY AS SORCERY

1. Roland Barthes, "The Third Meaning," in *Image, Music, Text,* trans. Stephen Heath (New York: Hill and Wang, 1977), 54–55.

2. Walter Benjamin, "Theses on the Philosophy of History," in *Illuminations,* trans. Harry Zohn, ed. Hannah Arendt (New York: Schocken, 1969), 253–64.

3. Silvia Bovenschen, "The Contemporary Witch, the Historical Witch and the Witch Myth: The Witch Subject of the Appropriation of Nature and Object of the Domination of Nature," *New German Critique* 15 (Fall 1978): 83–119.

4. Benjamin, "Theses," 254.

5. Ibid., 255.

6. Walter Benjamin, "One Way Street," in *Reflections,* ed. and intro. Peter Demetz, trans. E. Jephcott (New York and London: Harcourt Brace Jovanovich, 1978), 63.

7. F. Gary Smith, "The Images of Philosophy: Editor's Introduction," *The Philosophical Forum* 15 (Fall–Winter 1983–84):iii.

8. From "Konvolut N" of the *Passagen-Werk,* here entitled "Theoretics of Knowledge," Theory of Progress," *The Philosophical Forum* 15 (Fall–Winter 1983–84):21.

9. T. W. Adorno, "Benjamins Einbahnstrasse," in *Über Walter Benjamin* (Frankfurt am Main: Suhrkamp Verlag, 1970), 53, cited in Richard Wolin, *Walter Benjamin: An Aesthetic of Redemption* (New York: Columbia University Press, 1982), 125.

10. Stanley Mitchell, introduction in Walter Benjamin, *Understanding Brecht,* trans. Anna Bostock (London: New Left Books, 1973), xii.

11. Benjamin, "Theoretics of Knowledge, Theory of Progress," 6.

12. Benjamin, "One Way Street," 61.

13. Benjamin, "Theses," 255.

14. Haydée Seijas, "The Medical System of the Sibundoy Indians of Colombia," unpublished Ph.D. dissertation, Tulane University, 1969, p. 124.

15. Ibid., 178.

16. Ibid., 179.

17. Robert Hertz, "The Collective Representations of Death," in *Death and the Right Hand,* trans. Rodney Needham and Claudia Needham (Aberdeen: Cohen and West, 1960), 78.

18. Ibid., 86.

19. Seijas, "The Medical System," 122.

20. Gonzalo Fernández de Oviedo y Valdés, *Historia general y natural de las indias,* Biblioteca de Autores Españoles, 5 vols. (Madrid: Ediciones Atlas, 1959), vol. 1, book 5, chap. 1, pp. 112–13.

21. Alonso de la Peña Montenegro (Obispo del Obispado de San Francisco de Quito), *Itinerario para párocos de indios* (Madrid: Oficina de Padre Marin, 1771 [first pub. 1668]), 185. On shaman-led uprisings in the montaña region during the sixteenth century see José Rumazo González, *La región amazónica del Ecuador en el siglo XVI* (Seville: Escuela de Estudios Hispano-Americanos de Sevilla, 1946).

22. Peña Montenegro, *Itinerario,* 171.

23. Ibid., 191.

24. Milciades Chaves, "Mitica de los Siona del Alto Putumayo," in *Miscellanea Paul Rivet,* ed. Santiago Genoves (México, D.F., 1958), 131–32.

25. Gaspar de Pinell, *Excursión apostólica por los ríos Putumayo, San Miguel de Sucumbios, Cuyabeno, Caquetá y Caguán* (Bogotá: Imprenta Nacional, 1928 [also dated 1929], 7.

26. Ibid., 101–2.

27. Ibid., 291.

28. Ibid.

29. Ibid., 93–95, 104, 120.

30. Ibid., 94.

31. Ibid.

32. Ibid., 95.

33. Benigno de Canet de Mar, *Relaciones interesantes y datos históricos sobre las misiones católicas del Caquetá y Putumayo desde el ano 1632 hasta el presente* (Bogotá: Imprenta Nacional, 1924), 32–33.

34. Gaspar de Pinell, *Excursión apostólica,* 95.

35. Claude Lévi-Strauss, "The Effectiveness of Symbols," in *Structural Anthropology,* trans. Claire Jacobson and Brooke Grundfest Schoepf, (Garden City, N.Y.: Doubleday, 1967), 181–201.

36. Roland Barthes, "The Third Meaning," 54–55.

CHAPTER 25: ENVY AND IMPLICIT SOCIAL KNOWLEDGE

1. Irving Goldman, *The Cubeo: Indians of the Northwest Amazon* (Urbana: University of Illinois Press, 1963), 211.

CHAPTER 27: MONTAGE

1. Victor Turner and Edith Turner, *Image and Pilgrimage in Christian Culture: Anthropological Perspectives* (New York: Columbia University Press, 1978), 254–55.

2. Antonin Artaud, *The Theater and Its Double,* trans. Mary C. Richards (New York: Grove Press, 1959), 61.

3. Sally Falk Moore and Barabara Myerhoff, eds., *Secular Ritual* (Amsterdam: Van Gorcum, Assen, 1977), 3–24.

4. Bruce Kapferer, *A Celebration of Demons: Exorcism and the Aesthetics of Healing in Sri Lanka* (Bloomington: Indiana University Press, 1983), 1.

5. Artaud, *The Theater and its Double,* 91.

6. Walter Benjamin, *Understanding Brecht,* London: New Left Books, 1973), 8.

7. Stanley Mitchell, "Introduction," in Walter Benjamin, *Understanding Brecht,* xiii.

8. Benjamin, *Understanding Brecht,* 8. Compare with Raymond Williams contrasting the indicative to the subjunctive mode of dramatic presentation; the subjunctive being the experimental "as if" and "could perhaps be" mood that he discerns in Brecht's intention; Raymond Williams, *Politics and Letters: Interviews with New Left Review* (London: New Left Books, 1979), 218; and also his *Modern Tragedy* (Stanford: Stanford University Press, 1966), 190–204.

CHAPTER 28: TO BECOME A HEALER

1. Henry Munn, "The Mushrooms of Language," in Michael Harner, ed., *Hallucinogens and Shamanism* (London, Oxford, New York: Oxford University Press, 1973), 86–122.

2. Claude Lévi-Strauss, "The Sorcerer and His Magic" and "The Effectiveness of Symbols," in *Structural Anthropology* (Garden City, N.Y.: Doubleday, 1967), 161–201.

3. Immanuel Kant, *Critique of Pure Reason,* trans. Norman Kemp Smith (New York: St. Martin's Press, 1965), 183.

4. E. E. Evans-Pritchard, *Witchcraft, Oracles and Magic among the Azande* (Oxford: The Clarendon Press, 1937); see esp. 63–117.

5. Ibid., 35–36. Clifford Geertz has recently published a brilliant and entertaining article in which he pursues a point related to this. Geertz puts forward the idea that the clarity of Evans-Pritchard's realism is every bit as dependent upon the construction of a tone or mood as it is on conceptual argumentation, and, equally if not more importantly, that the clarity of this sort of realism is highly duplicitous in its attempt to conceal the fact that ethnography cannot exist outside writing, outside of representation. Style is not mere adornment; style is the substance. Geertz makes the necessary political observation that one effect of this clarity of style is not merely to simplify contradictory realities but "to demonstrate that the established frames of social perception, those upon which we ourselves instinctively rely, are fully adequate to whatever oddities the transparencies may turn out to picture." Professor Geertz seems to me less sound, however, where he writes that Evans-Pritchard's "colonial mentality" is not of importance to us today: "Let he [*sic*] who writes free of his time's imaginings cast the first stone." This sociologism not only performs what Evans-Pritchard is accused of—namely simplifying through duplicitous clarity—but totally ignores that there was in England from the time of Evans-Pritchard's childhood, and certainly at the time of the writing of the Azande book on magic, a vigorous anti-imperialist movement, especially among writers and intellectuals. Think of Leonard Wolf and George Orwell, for instance, or of the "Africanists" like Edmund Morel and Conrad himself. Were these people free of their time's imaginings? See Clifford Geertz, "Slide Show: Evans-Pritchard's African Transparencies," *Raritan* 3, no. 2 (Fall 1983):62–80.

6. Roland Barthes, "The Third Meaning," in *Image, Music, Text,* trans. Stephen Heath (New York: Hill and Wang, 1977), 54–55.

7. Walter Benjamin, "Theses on the Philosophy of History," in *Illuminations,* trans. Harry Zohn, edited by Hannah Arendt (New York: Schocken, 1969), 257.

8. Bertolt Brecht, *The Exception and the Rule,* trans. Eric Bentley in *The Jewish Wife and Other Short Plays* (New York, Grove Press, 1965), 111.

BIBLIOGRAPHY

Acosta, José de. *The Natural and Moral History of the Indies.* [First published 1588.] Reprinted from the English edition, 1604. Translated by Edward Grimston. Edited by C. R. Markham. 2 vols. London: Hakluyt Society, 1880.

Acuña, Cristóval de. *A New Discovery of the Great River of the Amazons.* [First published Madrid, 1641.] Translated and edited by Clements Markham in *Expeditions into the Valley of the Amazons: 1539, 1540, 1639.* London: Hakluyt Society, 1859.

Alvis, Manuel. "The Indians of Andaqui, New Granada." [Notes of a Traveler; published by José María Vergara y Vergara and Evaristo Delgado, Popayán, 1855.] *Journal of the American Ethnological Society* 1 (1860–61):53–72.

André, Edouard. "América Equinoccial." In *América pintoresca: descripción de viajes al nuevo continente.* pp. 477–859. Barcelona: Montaner y Simon, 1884.

Arboledo, Sergio. *La republica en américa española.* Bogotá: Biblioteca Banco Popular, 1972.

Arguedas, José María. "Puquio, una cultura en proceso de cambio. La religión local." In *Formación de una cultura nacional indoamericana,* pp. 34–79. México, D. F.: Siglo Veintiuno, 1975.

——. *Deep Rivers.* Translated by Frances Barraclough. Austin: University of Texas Press, 1978.

Artaud, Antonin. *The Theater and Its Double.* Translated by M. C. Richards. New York: Grove Press, 1958.

Asturias, Miguel Angel. *El señor presidente.* Translated by F. Partridge. New York: Atheneum, 1982.

Attwater, Donald. *A Dictionary of the Saints.* 2d ed. London: Burns, Oates, etc., 1948.

Ball, Hugo. *Flight out of Time.* Edited and with an introduction by John Elderfield. Translated by Ann Raimes. New York: Viking Press, 1974.

Bandelier, Adolph F. *The Islands of Titicaca and Koati.* New York: Hispanic Society of America, 1910.

Barthes, Roland. "The Third Meaning: Research Notes on Some Eisenstein Stills." In *Image, Music, Text,* translated by Stephen Heath, pp. 52–68. New York: Hill and Wang, 1977.

Bataille, Georges. *Visions of Excess: Selected Writings, 1927–1939.* Edited and with an introduction by Allan Stoekl. Minneapolis: University of Minnesota Press, 1985.

Becker, Ernest J. *A Contribution to the Comparative Study of the Medieval Visions of Heaven and Hell with Special Reference to the Middle English Versions.* Baltimore: John Murphy, 1899.

Benjamin, Walter. "The Storyteller: Reflections on the Work of Nikolai Leskov" and "Thesis on the Philosophy of History." In *Illuminations,* edited by Hannah Ardent. Translated by Harry Zohn, pp. 83–100 and 253–64. New York: Schocken, 1969.

———. "One Way Street." In *One Way Street and Other Writings,* translated by Edward Jephcott and K. Shorter, pp. 45–106. London: New Left Books, 1979.

———. *Understanding Brecht.* Translated by Anna Bostock. London: New Left Books, 1973.

———. "Surrealism: The Last Snapshot of the European Intelligentsia." In *Reflections,* edited by Peter Demetz. Translated by Edmund Jephcott, pp. 177–92. New York and London: Harcourt Brace Jovanovitch, 1979.

Bernheimer, Richard. *Wild Men of the Middle Ages.* Cambridge, Mass.: Harvard University Press, 1952.

Bilby, Kenneth M. "Partisan Spirits: Ritual Interaction and Maroon Identity in Eastern Jamica." M.A. thesis (unpublished), Wesleyan University, 1979.

Brecht, Bertolt. "Theatre for Pleasure or Theatre for Instruction." In *Brecht on Theatre: The Development of an Aesthetic,* edited and translated by John Willett, pp. 69–76. New York: Hill and Wang, 1964.

Bonilla, Victor Daniel. *Servants of God or Masters of Men? The Story of a Capuchin Mission in Amazonia.* Harmondsworth: Penguin, 1972.

Borrego Pla, María del Carmen. *Palenques de negros en Cartagena de Indias a fines del siglo XVII.* No. 216. Seville: Escuela de Estudios Hispano-Americanos de Sevilla, 1973.

Bovenschen, Silvia. "The Contemporary Witch, the Historical Witch and the Witch Myth: The Witch Subject of the Appropriation of Nature and Object of the Domination of Nature." *New German Critique* 15 (1978):83–119.

Buck-Morss, Susan. "Benjamin's Passagenwerk." *New German Critique* 29 (Spring–Summer 1983): 211–40.

———. "Walter Benjamin—Revolutionary Writer, Part 1." *New Left Review* 128 (July–August 1981): 50–75.

Burroughs, William, and Allen Ginsberg. *The Yage Letters.* San Francisco: City Lights Books, 1963.

Camacho, Roberto Pineda. "El sendero del arco iris: notas sobre el simbólismo de los negocios en una comunidad amazónica." *Revista Colombiana de Antropología* 22 (1979):29–58.

Canet de Mar, Benigno de. *Relaciones interesantes y datos históricos sobre las misiones católicas del Caquetá y Putumayo desde el año 1632 hasta el presente.* Bogotá: Imprenta Nacional, 1924.

Carpentier, Alejo. *The Lost Steps.* Translated by Harriet de Onis. New York: Knopf, 1974.

Casement, Roger. "The Putumayo Indians." *The Contemporary Review* 102 (1912):317–28.

————."Correspondence Respecting the Subjects and Native Indians Employed in the Collection of Rubber in the Putumayo Districts." *House of Commons Sessional Papers* 68 (14 February 1912–March 1913): 1–65.

Chatwin, Bruce. *In Patagonia*. New York: Summit, 1977.

Chaves, Milciades. "Mitica de los Siona del Alto Putumayo. In *Miscellanea Paul Rivet*, edited by Santiago Genoves. Universidad Nacional Autónoma de México, 2:121–51.

CILEAC [Centro de Investigaciones Lingüísticas y Etnográficas de la Amazonía Colombiana. Bogotá and Sibundoy, Putumayo, Colombia]. *Amazonia Colombiana Americanista* 1, nos. 2, 3 (1940).

————. *Amazonía Colombiana Americanista*, nos. 4–8 (1944).

Cochrane, Charles Stuart. *Journal of a Residence and Travels in Colombia during the Years of 1823 and 1824*. 2 vols. London: Colburn, 1825.

Colombia, República de. *Misiones Católicas de Putumayo: documentos oficiales relativos a este comisaría*. Edición Oficial Ilustrada. Bogotá: Imprenta Nacional, 1913.

Comstock, Richard. "On Seeing with the Eye of the Native European." In *Seeing with a Native Eye*, edited by Walter H. Capps. New York: Harper and Row, 1976.

Conrad, Joseph. "Geography and Some Explorers." In *Last Essays*. Freeport, N.Y.: Books for Libraries Press, 1970.

————. *Heart of Darkness*. Harmondsworth: Penguin, 1973.

Crévaux, Jules. "Exploración del Inzá y del Yapura." In *América pintoresca: descripción de viajes al nuevo continente*, pp. 231–64. Barcelona: Montaner y Simon, 1884.

Díaz Del Castillo, Bernal. *Historia verdadera de la conquista de la Nueva España*. México, D. F.: Editorial Porrua, 1969.

Eberhardt, Charles C. "Indians of Peru." *Smithsonian Miscellaneous Collections* 52 (1910):181–94.

Empson, Charles. *Narratives of South America: Illustrating Manners, Customs, and Scenery; Containing also Numerous Facts in Natural History Collected during a Four Years Residence in Tropical Regions*. London: W. Edwards, 1836.

Evans-Pritchard, E. E. *Witchcraft, Oracles and Magic Among the Azande*. Oxford: Clarendon Press, 1937.

Fernández, Fernando Ortiz. *Hampa afro-cubana: los negros brujos; apuntes para un estudio de etnología criminal, con una carta prólogo de Lombrioso*. Madrid: Editorial América, 1917(?).

Flannery, Mary Cathleen. *Yeats and Magic: The Earlier Works*. Irish Literary Studies 2. New York: Barnes and Noble, 1977.

Foucault, Michel. *Madness and Civilization*. New York: Mentor, 1967.

————. *Discipline and Punish*. Translated by Alan Sheridan. New York: Vintage, 1979.

————. "Truth and Power." In *Power/Knowledge: Selected Interviews and Other Writings, 1972–1977*, edited by Colin Gordon. New York: Pantheon, 1980.

Friedman, John Block. *The Monstrous Races in Medieval Thought and Art*. Cambridge, Mass.: Harvard University Press, 1981.

Fritz, Samuel. *Journal of the Travels and Labours of Father Samuel Fritz in the River of the Amazons between 1686 and 1723*. Translated from the Evora MS by the Reverend Dr. George Edumundson, 2d ser., no. 51. London: Hakluyt Society, 1922.

Fuentes, Carlos. *La nueva novela hispanoamericana*. México, D. F.: Editorial Joaquin Mortiz, 1969.

Geertz, Clifford. "Slide Show: Evans-Pritchard's African Transparencies." *Raritan* 3, no. 2 (Fall 1983):62–80.

Gerry, Chris, and Chris Birkbeck. "The Petty Commodity Producer in Third World Cities: Petit Bourgeois or 'Disguised' Proletarian?" In *The Petit Bourgeoisie: Comparative Studies of the Uneasy Stratum,* edited by Frank Bechhofer and Brian Elliott, pp. 121–54, London: Macmillan, 1981.

Goldman, Irving. *The Cubeo: Indians of the Northwest Amazon*. Urbana: University of Illinois Press, 1963.

Graham, Robert Bontine Cunninghame. *Hernando de Soto*. London: Heineman, 1912.

Gridilla, Alberto. *Un año en el Putumayo*. Lima: Colección Descalzos, 1943.

Guillaume, H. *The Amazon Provinces of Peru as a Field for European Emigration*. London: Wyman, 1888.

Hamilton, John Potter. *Travels through the Interior Provinces of Colombia*. 2 vols. London: J. Murray, 1827.

Hardenburg, Walter E. *The Putumayo: The Devil's Paradise. Travels in the Peruvian Amazon Region and an Account of the Atrocities Committed upon the Indians Therein*. London: T. Fisher Unwin, 1912.

Hemming, John. *The Search for El Dorado*. London: Michael Joseph, 1978.

Hertz, Robert. "The Pre-Eminence of the Right Hand: A Study in Religious Polarity." In *Death and the Right Hand*. Translated by Rodney and Claudia Needham. Aberdeen: Cohen and West, 1960.

Herzog, Werner. "The Screenplay." In *Burden of Dreams,* edited by Les Blank and James Bogan, pp. 19–66. Berkeley: North Atlantic Books, 1984.

Hodgen, Margaret T. *Early Anthropology in the Sixteenth and Seventeenth Centuries*. Philadelphia: University of Pennsylvania Press, 1964.

Holton, Issac. *New Granada: Twenty Months in the Andes*. New York: Harper, 1857.

Honour, Hugh. *The New Golden Land: Images of America from the Discoveries to the Present Time*. New York: Pantheon, 1975.

House of Commons Sessional Papers, vol. 14. "Report and Special Report from the Select Committee on Putumayo, together with the Proceedings of the Committee, Minutes of Evidence, and Appendices. Session 10 March 1913–15 August 1913." London: His Majesty's Stationery Office, 1913.

Humboldt, Alexander von. *Views of Nature: or Contemplations on the Sublime Phenomena of Creation; with Scientific Illustrations*. Translated by E. C. Otte and H. G. Bohn. London: Henry G. Bohn, 1850.

Husband, Timothy (with the assistance of Gloria Gilmore-House). *The Wild Man: Medieval Myth and Symbolism*. New York: The Metropolitan Museum of Art, 1980.

Igualada, Francisco de. *Indios amazónicos*. Barcelona: Imprenta Myria, 1948.

Inglis, Brian. *Roger Casement*. London: Hodder Paperbacks, 1974.

Jean-Aubrey, G. *Joseph Conrad: Life and Letters*. 2 vols. Garden City, N.Y.: 1927.

Kapferer, Bruce. *A Celebration of Demons: Exorcism and the Aesthetics of Healing in Sri Lanka*. Bloomington: Indiana University Press, 1983.

Karl, Frederick R. *Joseph Conrad: The Three Lives*. New York: Farrar, Strauss and Giroux, 1979.

Landaburu, Jon, and Roberto Pineda Camacho. *Tradiciones de la gente del hacha: mitología de los indios andoques del Amazonas*. Bogotá: Instituto Caro u Cuervo, y Unesco, 1984.

Langdon, Jean. "The Siona Medical System: Beliefs and Behavior." Ph.D. dissertation (unpublished). Tulane University, 1974.

———. "Yagé among the Siona: Cultural Patterns in Visions." In *Shamans, Spirits, and Stars,* ed. David Bowman and Ronald Schwarz, pp. 63–80. The Hague: Mouton, 1979.

Langdon, Jean, and Robert Maclennan. "Conceptos etiológicos de los Sibundoy y de la medicina occidental." Mimeo. ICMR. Cali., 1973.

Lea, Henry Charles. *The Inquisition in the Spanish Dependencies.* New York: Macmillan, 1908.

Lévi-Strauss, Claude. "The Sorcerer and His Magic" and "The Effectiveness of Symbols." In *Structural Anthropology,* pp. 161–80 and 181–201. Garden City, N.Y.: Doubleday, 1967.

Llanos Vargas, Hector, and Roberto Pineda Camacho. *Etnohistoria del Gran Caquetá.* Bógotá: Banco de la Republica, 1982.

López, Narvaez, Carlos. *Putumayo 1933: Diario de guerra.* Bogotá: Ediciones Espiral, 1951.

Malinowski, Bronislaw. *The Sexual Life of Savages in North Eastern Melanesia.* New York: Harcourt Brace, 1929.

Markham, Clements R. *Peruvian Bark: A Popular Account of the Introduction of Chinchona Cultivation into British India.* London: J. Murray, 1880.

Medina, José Toribio. *La inquisición en Cartagena de Indias.* Bogotá: Carlos Valencia, 1978.

Medina, Leonidas (bishop of Pasto). *Conferencia sobre las misiones del Caquetá y Putumayo dictada en la Basilica de Bogotá el 12 de octubre de 1914.* Bogotá: Imprenta de San Bernardo—atrio de la catedral, 1914.

Métraux, Alfred. *Voodoo in Haiti.* Translated by Hugo Charteris. New York: Oxford University Press, 1959.

Misiones en Colombia, Las. *Obra de los misioneros Capuchinos de la delegación apóstolica del gobierno y de la junta arquideocesana nacional en el Caquetá y Putumayo.* Bogotá: Imprenta de la Cruzada, 1912.

Mitchell, Stanley. Introduction to Walter Benjamin, *Understanding Brecht.* Translated by Anna Bostock, vii–xix. London: New Left Books, 1973.

Molina (de Cuzco), Cristóbal de. *Relación de las fabulas y ritos de las incas.* Buenos Aires: Editorial Futuro, 1947.

Moore, Sally Falk, and Barbara Myerhoff, eds. *Secular Ritual.* Amsterdam: Van Gorcum, Assen, 1977.

Morison, Samuel. *Admiral of the Ocean Sea: A Life of Christopher Columbus.* 2 vols. Boston: Little, Brown, 1942.

Morote, Best, Efraín. "El degollador (nakaq)." *Tradición: Revista peruana de cultura,* año 2, 4 (1952):67–91.

Najder, Zdzistaw. *Joseph Conrad: A Chronicle.* New Brunswick: Rutgers University Press, 1983.

Odena, Damien de. "Presentación." In *Historia de la fundación del pueblo de San Francisco en el valle del Sibundoy,* edited by Jacinto María de Quito. Sibundoy, Putumayo, Colombia: CILEAC, 1952.

Oliver-Smith, Anthony. "The Pishtaco: Institutionalized Fear in Highland Peru." *Journal of American Folklore,* 82:363–68.

Oviedo y Valdés, Gonzalo Fernández de. *Historia general y natural de las Indias*. 5 vols. Biblioteca de Autores Españoles. Madrid: Ediciones Atlas, 1959.

Paredes, Rómulo. "Confidential Report to the Ministry of Foreign Relations, Peru." Pages 144–72 in *Slavery in Peru . . .* , 62d Congress, U. S. House of Representatives, document no. 1366, 7 February 1913. Washington, D.C.: Government Printing Office, 1913.

Paris, Lozano, Gonzalo. *Guerrilleros del Tolima*. Bogotá: El Ancora, 1984.

Parry, J. H. *The Discovery of South America*. London: Paul Elek, 1979.

Peña Montenegro, Alonso de la. *Itinerario para párrocos de indios*. [First published in 1668.] Madrid: Oficina de Padre Marin, 1771.

Pinell, Gaspar de. *Excursión apostólica por los ríos Putumayo, San Miguel de Sucumbios, Cuyabeno, Caquetá, y Caguán*. Bogotá: Imprenta Nacional, 1929 [also dated 1928].

———. *Un viaje por el Putumayo y el Amazonas: ensayo de navegación*. Bogotá: Imprenta Nacional, 1924.

Prescott, William Hickling. *History of the Conquest of Peru, with a Preliminary View of the Civilization of the Incas*. 2 vols. Philadelphia: David McKay, 1892.

Preuss, Konrad Theodor. *Religion und Mythologie der Uitoto*. 2 vols. Göttingen: Vandenhoeck und Ruprecht, 1921.

Quito, Jacinto María de. *Historia de la fundación del pueblo de San Francisco en el Valle de Sibundoy*. Sibundoy: CILEAC, 1952.

Randall, Robert. "Qoyllur Rit'i, an Inca Fiesta of the Pleiades: Reflections on Time and Space in the Andean World." *Bulletin de l'Institut Français d'Etudes Andines* 11 (1982):37–81.

Raskin, Jonah. *My Search for B. Traven*. New York: Methuen, 1980.

Reichel-Dolmatoff, Gerardo. *Amazonian Cosmos: The Sexual and Religious Symbolism of the Tukano Indians*. Chicago: University of Chicago Press, 1971.

Rey de Castro, Carlos. *Los pobladores del Putumayo*. Barcelona: Imp. Vda de Luis Tasso, 1914.

Richter, Hans. *Dada: Art and Anti-Art*. London: Thames and Hudson, 1965.

Rivera, José Eustasio. *La vorágine*. Bogotá: Editorial Pax, 1974.

Robinson, Scott. "Towards an Understanding of Kofan Shamanism." Latin American Studies Program Dissertation Series, Cornell University, 1979.

Rocha, Joaquin. *Memorandum de un viaje*. Bogotá: Editorial El Mercurio, 1905.

Roth, Walter Edmund. "An Introductory Study of the Arts, Crafts, and Customs of the Guiana Indians." In *The Thirty-Eighth Annual Report of the Bureau of American Ethnology: 1916–1917*, 25–745. Washington, D.C.: Government Printing Office.

Rumazo González, José. *La región amazónica en el siglo XVI*. No. 19. Seville: Escuela de Estudios Hispano-Americanos de Sevilla, 1946.

Salomon, Frank L. "Ethnic Lords of Quito in the Age of the Incas: The Political Economy of North Andean Chiefdoms." Unpublished Ph.D. dissertation, Cornell University, 1978.

———. "Killing the Yumbo: A Ritual Drama of Northern Quito." In *Cultural Transformations and Ethnicity in Modern Ecuador*, edited by Norman E. Whitten, Jr. Urbana: University of Illinois Press, 1981.

Sandoval, Alonso de. *De Instauranda Aethiopium Salute: El mundo de la esclavitud negra en América*. 1627. Bogotá: Empresa Nacional de Publicaciones, 1956.

Saum, Lewis O. *The Fur Trader and the Indian.* Seattle and London: University of Washington Press, 1965.

Sawyer, Roger. *Casement: The Flawed Hero.* London: Routledge and Kegan Paul, 1984.

Seijas, Haydée. "The Medical System of the Sibundoy Indians of Colombia." Unpublished Ph.D. dissertation, Tulane University, 1969.

Select Committee on Putumayo. *See* House of Commons Sessional Papers, vol. 14.

Simson, Alfred. *Travels in the Wilds of Ecuador and the Exploration of the Putumayo River.* London: Samson Low, 1886.

Singleton-Gates, Peter, and Maurice Girodias. *The Black Diaries: An Account of Roger Casement's Life and Times with a Collection of his Diaries and Public Writings.* New York: Grove Press, 1959.

Tamayo, Joaquín. "Don Gonzalo Ximénez de Quesada." *Boletín de historia y antiquedades* 25, nos. 285–86 (1938):458–76.

Tejado, Fernández, Manuel. *Aspectos de la vida social en Cartagena de Indias durante el seiscientos.* No. 87. Seville: Escuela de Estudios Hispano-Americanos de Sevilla, 1954.

Timerman, Jacobo. *Prisoner without a Name, Cell without a Number.* New York: Vintage Books, 1982.

Le Tour du Monde: Nouveau Journal des Voyages 38. Paris: Librairie Hachette, 1879.

Traven, B. *March to the Monteria.* London: Allison and Busby, 1982.

Triana, Miguel. *Por el sur de Colombia: excursión pintoresca y científica al Putumayo.* Prólogo de Santiago Pérez Triana. Bogotá: Biblioteca Popular de Cultura Colombiana, 1950.

Trimborn, Hermann. *Señorio y barbarie en el valle del Cauca.* Madrid: Instituto Gonzalo Fernández de Oviedo, 1949.

Tschudi, Johann Jakob von. *Travels in Peru During the Years 1838–1842.* Translated by T. Ross. New York: Putnam, 1852.

Turner, Victor, and Edith Turner. *Image and Pilgrimage in Christian Culture: Anthropological Perspectives.* New York: Columbia University Press, 1978.

Tylor, Edmund Burnett. *Primitive Culture.* 2 vols. New York: Harper, 1958.

Valcárcel, Carlos A. *El proceso del Putumayo y sus secretos inauditos.* Lima: Imprenta "Comercial" de Horacia La Rosa, 1915.

Veatch, Arthur Clifford. *Quito to Bogotá.* New York: George H. Doran, 1917.

Vega, Garcilaso de la. *Royal Commentaries of the Incas.* 2 vols. Translated by Harold Livermore. Austin and London: University of Texas Press, 1966.

Vilanova, Francisco. "Introdución." In *Indios amazónicos,* Francisco de Igualada, Colección Misiones Capuchinas, vol. 6. Barcelona: Imprenta Myria, 1948.

Wassén, S. Henry. "A Medicine-Man's Implements and Plants in a Tiahuanacoid Tomb in Highland Bolivia."*Etnologiska Studier* 32 (1972).

Watt, Ian. *Conrad in the Nineteenth Century.* Berkeley and Los Angeles: University of California Press, 1979.

Watts, C. T. *Joseph Conrad's Letters to Cunninghame Graham.* Cambridge: University of Cambridge Press, 1969.

West, Robert Cooper. *Colonial Placer Mining in Western Colombia.* Baton Rouge: Louisiana State University Press, 1952.

Whiffen, Thomas (Captain, 14th Hussars). *The North-West Amazons: Notes of Some Months Spent among Cannibal Tribes*. London: Constable, 1915.

Whitten, Norman, Jr. *Sacha Runa: Ethnicity and Adaptation of Ecuadorian Jungle Quichua*. Urbana: University of Illinois Press, 1976.

———. *Sicuanga Runa: The Other Side of Development in Amazonian Ecuador*. Urbana and Chicago: University of Illinois Press, 1985.

Williams, Gwynn. "The Concept of 'Egemonia' in the Thought of Antonio Gramsci: Some Notes of Interpretation." *Journal of the History of Ideas* 1 (1961):586–99.

Williams, Raymond. *Marxism and Literature*. Oxford: Oxford University Press, 1977.

———. *Politics and Letters: Interviews with New Left Review*. London: New Left Books, 1979.

Wittkower, Rudolf. "Marvels of the East: A Study in the History of Monsters. *Journal of the Warburg and Cortauld Institute* 5 (1942):159–97.

Wolf, Howard, and Ralph Wolf. *Rubber, a Story of Glory and Greed*. New York: Covici, Friede, 1936.

Wolin, Richard. *Walter Benjamin: An Aesthetic of Redemption*. New York: Columbia University Press, 1982.

Woodroffe, Joseph Froude. *The Rubber Industry of the Amazon*. London: John Bale, 1915.

———. *The Upper Reaches of the Amazon*. London: Methuen, 1914.

Ypes, Benjamin. *La estatuaria Murui-Muiname: simbolismo de la gente "Huitoto" de la amazonía colombiana*. Bogotá: Fundación de Investigaciones Arqueológicas Nacionales, Banco de la Republica, 1982.

Ypes, Benjamin, and Roberto Pineda Camacho. "La rabia de Yarocamena: etnología histórica de una rebelión indígena en el Amazonas. Bogotá: mimeograph, 1984.

Wrigley, G. M. "The Travelling Doctors of the Andes: The Callahuayas of Bolivia." *The Geographical Review* 4 (1917):183–99.

INDEX